The Young

JEFFERSON

1743 - 1789

Books by Claude G. Bowers

BEVERIDGE AND THE PROGRESSIVE ERA

THE TRAGIC ERA

JEFFERSON AND HAMILTON

THE PARTY BATTLES OF THE
JACKSON PERIOD

JEFFERSON IN POWER

THE SPANISH ADVENTURES OF
WASHINGTON IRVING

THE YOUNG JEFFERSON

The Young
JEFFERSON
1743 - 1789

by Claude G. Bowers

ILLUSTRATED

HOUGHTON MIFFLIN COMPANY, BOSTON
The Riverside Press Cambridge

TO THE HONORABLE

HARRY B. HAWES

TO WHOSE GENIUS FOR FRIENDSHIP

THE AUTHOR HAS BEEN INDEBTED

FOR MANY YEARS

The Riverside Press
CAMBRIDGE · MASSACHUSETTS
PRINTED IN THE U.S.A.

PREFACE

IN *Jefferson and Hamilton* I showed Jefferson in his great struggle to place the indelible imprint of democracy on American institutions under the Constitution; and in *Jefferson in Power* I followed his efforts to consolidate the victory which 'definitively determined that ours should be a democratic republic.'

But everything that enters into the political philosophy of Jefferson had been thought out, formulated, and clearly and concisely expressed before the establishment of the Republic under the Constitution. The social and political theories that have come to be synonymous with what we call 'Americanism' had been set forth by Jefferson before the inauguration of Washington; and in such completeness by no other man of the period of the Revolution. Here, then, we have the nation in the making; and I hope a textbook of Americanism. That is what Lincoln had in mind when he said that 'the principles of Jefferson are the definitions and the axioms of a free society.'

The American patriots of the Revolution were not inspired by a common motive. Some went to war on grievances of taxation; some on accumulated prejudices against misrule; some with little thought other than a change in the governmental régime; and some with the idea of securing for the Americans the advantages of British institutions. But, once the Revolution was forced on the Americans, Jefferson saw an opportunity for the creation of a new, distinctly American system for the better protection of the rights and liberties of all the people. Very few of the leaders of the Revolution thought in terms of democracy; and Jefferson easily was the foremost of the few.

Too little significance has been attached by historians to Jefferson's iconoclastic reforms in Virginia which demolished the sustaining pillars of feudalism, and gave humanity one of the noblest documents ever penned by man, his Statute of Virginia for Religious Freedom. During his three years in the legislature, from 1776 to 1779, Jefferson was working feverishly and effectively in the laboratory of democracy. Before his blows fell primogeniture and entail, the combination of Church and State, the trenches of religious intolerance; and it was then that he outlined and proposed his revolutionary system of education conforming to his conception of a democratic society. Years were to elapse before the adoption of his plan, but in the end the public-school system of the nation, crowned with State Universities, would be patterned on the model that so shocked his contemporaries. In his activities of these three years we have Jefferson's political philosophy complete. He was dealing with one State, but consciously he was proposing a model for a Nation. I have therefore shown him in the midst of his bitter battles of these three epochal years.

This period of his career before the adoption of the Constitution should impress the reader with his almost uncanny prescience and vision. Before the Constitution was framed, he was interesting himself deeply in a Panama canal. His view of the proper relation of the colonies to the British Empire, as set forth in his *Summary View,* foreshadows the British Commonwealth of Nations which Britain was to accept more than a century and a half later. More than any other American of his time, he foresaw the westward sweep of the nation to the Pacific sea, and, before the establishment of the Republic, he was ready to fight for the right of navigation on the Mississippi.

But no one can read this story without marveling at the Providence which guided us to independence and nationhood and to dignity and stability as a nation. Nothing stands out more dramatically than the revelation from the record that nothing less than the persistently applied lash of a mad monarch, supported by a weak Ministry and a subservient Parliament representing but a meager proportion of the English people, could have driven the Americans to take up arms. The First Continental Congress we shall find overwhelmingly against independence; and this was true of the Second until a few weeks before the Declaration. It was only when George III contemptuously spurned the last obsequious petition for redress of grievances and denounced the Americans as rebels to be put down by force that the conservatives, who clung with an almost pathetic devotion to the connection, conceded the necessity of a separation.

This book will show that there was nothing unreasonable in the demands of the colonies, and nothing incomprehensible to anyone with even a rudimentary knowledge of English institutions and rights. Against the appeals and protests of the American leaders, I have set the vehement denunciations of the American policy of the British Government by Chatham, Burke, and Shelburne; the voices and the accent are different, but the sentiments and arguments of these British statesmen were but echoes of those of the Americans. Up to the hour Washington unsheathed his sword, the Americans fought as Britons, and for no more than the rights, the liberties, and the constitutional guarantees of British subjects.

More marvelous, as is here indicated, the triumph of the Revolution. Soldiers laid down their arms to tend their fields; soldiers within sight of Yorktown mutinied in Pennsylvania, Connecticut, and New York; soldiers deserted in moments of crisis; there was a dearth of arms at critical moments; treasuries were empty; crop failures contributed to the distress; disloyalty was rife in commercial centers; and Washington won by masterful retreats.

And still more marvelous, as the reader will conclude, that, with independence won after seven years of struggle, interest had so diminished that only after weeks of importunate appeals could enough States be assembled in Congress to ratify the peace treaty Britain had signed.

Then, with the treaty ratified at last, we shall here find the States under the Articles of Confederation drifting indifferently and with little sense of responsibility toward utter demoralization and disgrace. From his legation on the Champs Elysées in Paris, Jefferson was to see this with a clearer vision than most of his contemporaries. Debts were left unpaid and debtors who had fought with Washington sat on the doorstep of the legation with duns; the credit of the nation declined; Vergennes complained that arrangements with the Americans could not be counted on; the enthusiasm that flamed after Yorktown in the liberal circles of the Old World rapidly turned to cynicism and skepticism; and Jefferson and Adams saved the nation's credit and honor by risking themselves without authorization in the negotiation of a loan.

I have gone more fully than has been customary into Jefferson's five years of diplomatic life in Paris because he played a leading part in the determination of the fundamentals of our foreign policy. But aside from this, it has seemed worth while to observe the processes of his mind as he followed with fascination the developing drama of the French Revolution; and especially worth while to destroy the malicious myth, born of partisan hate a few years later, that he was a member of the Jacobin Club and a friend and associate of the bloodiest figures of the Terror. This can best be done by showing him among the political leaders who actually were his friends, some of the noblest figures among the reformers of France; by listening in on his conferences with these men and hearing his advice; by reading his own contribution to the Revolution in the Charter of Rights he would have offered and have the King proffer to the people. The truth, as here appears, is that he doubted the preparation of the French people for a Republic, while hoping for radical reforms within the framework of the monarchy that would have converted a tyrannical autocracy into a democratic state.

And it is during this period of his life that it is possible to present the Jefferson of flesh and blood, the human being, for he is more intimately revealed during these younger years before he was so completely absorbed in political controversies. To most Americans, including historians, he has been a symbol, a flag, a steel engraving, a philosopher in an ivory tower, or, more often, a cunning politician spinning his web of intrigue in dark corners. I have tried here to rescue a very human being from the wilderness of myth and fable.

The Jefferson practicing on his violin for hours before breakfast, or seated beside a punchbowl by candlelight raving with boyish enthusiasm over the poems of Ossian, or bending over his drafting board giving form to architectural dreams of beauty in blueprints; Jefferson the gentle and considerate host conducting guests over the grounds of Monticello, planning gardens, planting shrubs, supervising his broad acres, and entertaining with courtly courtesy, with music and meals, the German and British officers who surrendered with Burgoyne — this Jefferson is too little known.

Even less known the Jefferson who frequented the salons of Paris, who tramped the Bois with Madame de Corny, and rambled with Maria Cosway through the groves of Saint-Germain; who thrilled to the beauty of English gardens and fought a duel with Buffon with bones; who haunted the bookstalls of Paris and peered into the kettles of the peasants and tested the softness of their beds; who walked the woods of Fontainebleau with a serving woman to learn about French poverty from her — this very human Jefferson has been largely hidden behind a popular conception of a cold and calculating political strategist and master of men. There was a reason why those who knew him best loved him most.

Had Jefferson died before Washington's inauguration he would still be one of America's few immortals, as I hope this volume will clearly show.

Claude G. Bowers

CONTENTS

III . *Young-Men-in-a-Hurry* 56

IV. *Penman of the Revolution*   83

Jefferson plans to speak for all colonies — To express views on relation of
Parliament and King to colonies — A deeper basis than the usual — Real-
ized views anathema to appeasers — 'No halfway house' — America's relation to Britain that of Hanover — Only Wythe agrees — Jefferson pre-
pares instructions for Virginia's representation in Continental Congress —
Hot July work — Jefferson starts to Convention under blistering sun — At-
tacked by dysentery — Turns back — Sends copies to Henry and Peyton
Randolph — Randolph lays document on table — A unique document —
Denies right of Parliament to tax colonies — Goes back to Saxon precedent
— Randolph reads paper to a gathering — Many parts praised — All impressed — Too strong for Convention, but its publication determined on —
Summary View — It declares right of migration and establishment of new
society — As the Saxons did in England — Similarity in two migrations —
No assistance from England until colonies firmly established — Assistance
waited on commercial advantages — Colonists continued old laws — And
the Union — Under common ruler as link to empire — Jefferson anticipates
Commonwealth of Nations — Tyranny of the Stuarts, who parcel out American land not theirs — No King dared so much in England — Listeners

CONTENTS

IX. *Happy Days at Monticello*

XIV. *Jefferson in Paris*

XIX. *America Calls Him Home*   499

ILLUSTRATIONS

(Between pages 288 and 289)

The Young

JEFFERSON

1743 - 1789

CHAPTER

I

YOUTH IN VIRGINIA

I

THE VIRGINIA of the eighteenth century, into which Thomas Jefferson was born, was by long odds the most important and extensive of all the American colonies. It embraced in its possessions the present States of West Virginia, Kentucky, Ohio, Illinois, Indiana, Michigan, and Wisconsin. It was an empire.

Within the confines of the present State, it differed greatly from the Virginia of the preceding century. This had been brought about largely through an event in 1619, when a Dutch privateer sailed up the James River and disembarked its cargo of twenty slaves from Africa. In those days the Dutch, having thoroughly fortified themselves on the African coast, had a monopoly of the lucrative slave trade and rigidly excluded other nations from the traffic in human flesh; and while the arrival of the twenty blacks created a demand for slave labor, the monopoly of the Dutch made it impossible to satisfy the demand. Even after six years the record shows no more than twenty-two slaves in the colony, and while the increase in the number of slaves was noticeable during the next half-century, there were still too few to make any notable alteration in the economic life of the people.[1]

The difficulty in getting slaves forced the colonists to look elsewhere for labor for the fields, and alluring promises of opportunity and a new life made an appeal to the large and chronically poor element in England. But even here there were difficulties because

[1] Wertenbaker, *The Planters of Colonial Virginia*, 31.

1

of the high cost of transportation. The traveler, content with the most miserable and crowded quarters, could not cross the sea for less than six pounds sterling, and this was utterly prohibitive to most.

Thus were the planters driven to the indenture plan. They were prepared to advance the passage money on the condition, rigidly laid down, that the indentured worker would be the property of his benefactor until he had worked out in full the cost of his transportation. No disgrace, however, attached to the indentured worker, for public opinion did not consider him in any sense in servitude, but as one engaged in a purely business transaction in which he voluntarily exchanged his labor for the price of passage.[2]

Years later, it became fashionable to describe these indentured servants as of the criminal or degenerate class, since some of them had served terms in prison, but the 'crimes' for which these had been incarcerated were mostly of a political nature. In truth, the greater part of those who had been in prison were of the hardiest and soundest of the British nation, since their crime had consisted in rebellion against the tyranny of the Government of their time. If impoverished in purse, they were not in principle, and if not ennobled by blood, they were among the noblest of Englishmen who courageously had stood for their rights and liberty.

So vital to the economic necessities of the colony had these men become that the Government actually pledged itself to the bestowal of fifty acres on any person who would pay the passage money for a worker. This meant that anyone bringing over a hundred workers would be put in possession of five thousand acres of good land. This worked like magic. Here was a new road to a landed estate. The same Government pledge was made to any worker able to pay his own fare, and, in his case, an additional fifty acres were given for his wife and for each of his children.[3]

Contrary to the popular understanding that it was the cavaliers who peopled the early colony, it appears that very few scions of the great old English families went to Virginia. Few were of the historic houses, and these few were not among those who were to attain to wealth and distinction. They who were to become the aristocracy of Virginia in both wealth and intellect came mostly from the merchant class of England.[4]

[2] *Ibid.*, 32.   [3] *Ibid.*, 35.   [4] *Ibid.*, 27, 28.

Because of the difficulty of manning the large estates during the greater part of the seventeenth century, most of the people owned small farms. It was only toward the end of this century that a few wealthy men, in possession of slaves, had large estates. Then it was that William Byrd boasted of his 179,440 acres, and Robert Carter, of Nomini Hall, of his sixty thousand. But at this time most of the wealthier class along the rivers owned from four to six thousand acres. The Virginia of that period was largely one of small farms on which their owners did their full share of work; and even that greater part of the plantations had but a few hundred, ranging from one to five hundred.[5] Even in the early days of the eighteenth century, the rent roll of Governor Nicholson reveals that the vast majority of the farms were small.[6]

It is significant of the enterprising character of the indentured servants that in many instances they bought small farms after working out their passage money. The interest many of them had taken in politics, which had led them into rebellion and prison in England, persisted; and not a few, in the first half of the seventeenth century, found their way into the House of Burgesses.[7] In those days this legislative assembly was the stronghold of the yeomen, the small farmers, and they determined the course of history. Members of the developing aristocracy in the Burgesses legislated with the interest of the yeomanry in mind.

Thus, the Virginia of the greater part of the seventeenth century was a land of small planters. The mansion houses had not yet appeared except in rare instances. The average plantation house was a wooden structure of one story, small, but convenient and comfortable. It had large airy rooms, and the table of the yeomanry was abundant. No attempt was made to beautify the surroundings, which were usually very plain, if not ugly. The yards were without fences. In most cases, a few forest trees remained on the grounds. Near-by was always the garden for vegetables, and sometimes, though not often, flowers.[8]

Then Slavery intervened to change everything. The poor whites began their exodus to the North, where their muscles were soon cultivating the fields and turning the wheels of industry. The day of the indentured worker was gone. With the solving of the labor

[5] *Ibid.*, 46.   [6] *Ibid.*, 183-247.   [7] *Ibid.*, 75.   [8] *Ibid.*, 105.

problem through slavery, the great plantations appeared, with their own weavers, tan houses, brick factories, and shoemakers. Every effort to encourage the building of cities had failed, since the people thought in terms of the English upper class and considered landed estates the sure indication of a gentleman. This absence of cities and the difficulty of locomotion because of the bad roads forced the planters to depend upon themselves and to manufacture their necessities on their own grounds. They felt no need for cities of commerce, since those on the rivers loaded their produce for the English markets on their own lands and unloaded there their purchases.

The social cleavage became more pronounced. The landless poor were now pariahs, and, tragically enough, the small farmers, the yeomanry, found themselves fighting for existence with their backs to the wall. Unable to compete with the great plantations manned by slaves, many turned their backs on Virginia and migrated to Pennsylvania, the Jerseys, and Delaware, to enrich the citizenry of those colonies. While the small farmer was generally unable to compete with the slave-operated plantations of thousands of acres, some were able to survive for a time through the production of a higher grade of tobacco than could be produced by the unskilled negroes fresh from Africa. Some of these were able to buy a few slaves and hold on, but gradually the prestige of the old yeomanry passed into history.

Yeomanry made the seventeenth century; Slavery, the eighteenth.

Thus, the golden age of the slave-owners was in the century of Jefferson's birth and early manhood. Then it was that the beautiful and imposing mansions with the pillared porticoes dominated the plantations of thousands of acres; that the gardens were planted; that fine furniture was installed; that imported silver service shimmered on the dining-tables; that paintings adorned the walls; that books filled the libraries and choice wines the cellars. Then began the building of the brick mansions, the interiors beautiful and elegant. The prevailing taste was for silver — candlesticks, snuffers, decanters, snuffboxes, basins, goblets, pitchers, and spoons; and the host, serving his guest with punch from a silver bowl, dished it out with silver ladles into silver cups.[9] The masters of the mansions

[9] *Ibid.*

cantered over the countryside on the best-blooded horses, and the ladies rode forth in costly and elegant berlins and coaches, the body highly varnished, the inside lined with the finest colored cloth and trimmed with laces, with polished plate windows and mahogany shutters. The body was carved with scrolls, and on the door panels were painted Prince of Wales ruffs and crests.[10] Every gentleman of pretensions had his chariot drawn by four horses and sometimes six, always attended by slaves in livery, trained to a dignified demeanor.[11]

The work of the slaves was not confined to the field alone, for the greater plantations were industrial centers, and skilled mechanics worked in copper, blacksmith shops were constantly busy, tanners, carpenters, shoemakers, and distillers made the plantations hum with life. Though skilled white mechanics were the original industrial workers, the slaves, soon trained, took over later.

Then it was that Aristocracy took to the saddle, booted and spurred. And the gallant yeomanry went into political eclipse, though still fighting.

The gay blades of the aristocracy, fond of display, lived robustiously beyond their means, protected by the law of entail from utter ruin. They followed the chase like the English squires they imitated, entertained with reckless prodigality, their tables groaning and their cellars bursting. They loved the music of the cracking whips as they drove their coaches and six. They gambled gamely, bet on races and cockfights, flirted and fought, and drank as deeply as the gayest dogs at Brooks's in London.

Burk, the Virginia historian, himself of the eighteenth century, gives us a glimpse of the life of the rich planters:

> The character of the people for hospitality and expense was now decided, and the wealth of the landed proprietors, particularly on the banks of the rivers, enabled them to indulge their passions even to profusion and excess. Drinking parties were fashionable in which the strongest head or stomach gained the victory. The moments that could be spared from the bottle were devoted to cards. Cockfighting was also fashionable.[12]

10 *Ibid.*
11 Wertenbaker, *Patrician and Plebeian in Virginia,* 122-123.
12 Burk, *History of Virginia,* III, 102.

An English traveler of the time has drawn an almost incredible picture of the life of a gentleman of fortune. He rose at nine, walked to the stables before breakfast consisting of tea or coffee, bread and butter, and very thin slices of hung beef. He then stretched out on a pallet on the floor in the coolest room, in his shirt and trousers only, with a negro at his head and at his feet to 'fan him and keep off the flies.' Between twelve and one, he took a draught of bombo or toddy, 'a liquor composed of water, sugar, rum, and nutmegs.' Between two and three, he dined on ham and greens or cabbage. At dinner, he drank cider, toddy, punch, port, claret, and madeira. After dinner he again sought his pallet with the negroes to shoo off the flies and fan him and 'continued to drink toddy all the afternoon.' Between nine and ten, he had his supper of milk and fruit or wine. Thus ended the day.

That this was true of some we have no doubt, but the traveler could not have gathered his impressions on the plantations of the Byrds, the George Masons, the Lees, and Washington, for it was among the rich planters that were found, later, the deeply read and astute statesmen of the Revolution.[13]

Perhaps a more accurate and general picture is that drawn by a German traveler. He was impressed by the mediocrity of the mansion house and the great number of surrounding outhouses and cabins, and with the negligence of their upkeep, strangely contrasting with the ladies of the house, 'generally clothed and adorned with great fastidiousness.' No matter how little the probability of encountering strangers or even neighbors, they 'could not resist the propensity to make themselves fine.' No matter how crude the cabins and the grounds, he found he could usually count on meeting ladies 'dressed tastefully in silk and decked with plumes.'[14] Along the rivers he found the homes luxurious. 'The rich Virginians, who have their luxury and love of display,' he writes, 'have for many years been of evil repute among their more frugal neighbors of the North, prefer generally to live in the country, and, according to the circumstances and opportunities, spare nothing in rendering their houses agreeable, both outside and in.'[15]

These aristocrats at heart were mostly Tories, and, despite their

[13] Smythe, *A Tour in the United States*, 41-43.
[14] Schoepf, *Travels in the Confederation*, II, 33.   [15] *Ibid.*, II, 44.

levity and insobriety, were devoted to the Established Church which was rapidly losing caste with the mass of the people. The members of the clergy, drawing their money from the taxation of the people, were lax in the performance of their duties and more concerned with what they could get than with what they could give. They made but little effort to educate their flocks. In the first quarter of the eighteenth century, when the Bishop of London inquired of the Virginia clergymen concerning schools and culture, only three of the whole Dominion were able to report any schools at all. One proudly replied that he had a parish library, consisting of the Book of Homilies, 'The Whole Duty of Man,' and Singing Psalms. A quarter of a century later, a few schools had been established and some of the clergy were taking boarders.

Among the old yeomanry the Established Church had lost prestige, and many of these were of the dissenters, despite the savage laws of intolerance still on the statute books.

Thus, there were distinctly two Virginias. The aristocracy, as differentiated from the merely rich planters described by the English traveler, was well educated both by books and travel, highly intelligent and of polished manners, warmly hospitable to the stranger, and thoroughly devoted to King and Church. And notwithstanding the plight of the yeomanry, few white men had left the Tidewater country, which embraced the whole of the coast and the marshy lowlands, where were to be found the great plantations with their thousands of acres and their hundreds of slaves. This, then, was the stronghold of the aristocracy. Between Tidewater and the mountains lay the Piedmont country, and soon the more enterprising were pouring into this region. But among these pioneers to face the wilderness were scarcely any of the families of the aristocracy. Living lavishly, they felt secure against the penalty for extravagance because of the convenient law of entail. Having abundant leisure for reading and meditation, this element had produced a large number of men of great political wisdom and capacity, but the dominion of the mind was passing to the men of the Piedmont.

In none of the other American colonies was the cleavage between the classes so pronounced. The upper class, the aristocracy, we have described. In the second class, consisting of perhaps half the colony, the hospitality to the stranger was in evidence to the full extent of its limitations, but its members were rude, unpolished, sometimes quarrelsome, and had something of the haughtiness to be found among those who feel on the defensive. These were attached to sport, to gambling and cockfighting. Among them were some richer than some of the aristocracy, but where the latter had culture and family tradition, these had sprung literally from the soil.[16] But the old yeomanry was intelligent, industrious, belligerently independent, and instinctively democratic.

Jefferson's own view of the social cleavage was set forth in a letter to William Wirt:

> To state the difference between the classes of society and the lines of demarcation which separated them would be difficult. The law, you know, admitted none except as to the twelve Councillors. Yet, in a country isolated from the European world, insulated from its sister colonies, with whom there was scarcely any intercourse, little visited by foreigners, and having little matter to act upon within itself, certain families had risen to splendor by wealth and the preservation of it from generation to generation under the law of entails; some had produced a series of men of talents; families in general had remained stationary on the grounds of their forefathers, for there was no emigration to the westward in those days. . . . In such a state of things, scarcely admitting any change in station, society would settle itself down into several strata, segregated by no marked lines, but shading off imperceptibly from top to bottom, nothing disturbing the order of their repose. There were, then, aristocrats, half-breeds, pretenders, a solid independent yeomanry, looking askance at those above, yet not venturing to jostle them, and last and lowest, a seculum of human beings called overseers, the most abject, degraded, and unprincipled race, always cap in hand to the Dons who employed them, and furnishing material for the exercise of their pride, insolence, and spirit of domination.[17]

This was the Virginia into which Thomas Jefferson was born.

II

He was less concerned with his ancestry than some of his biographers. Just when the first of the name reached America is

[16] Smythe, *A Tour in the United States,* 67.
[17] Ford, *Writings of Thomas Jefferson,* IX, 473.

not known. There was one of the name at a time long before the first positively known to be an ancestor. He himself said in his *Autobiography* that 'the tradition of my father's family was that their ancestors came to this country from Wales and from near the mountain of Snowdon, the highest in Great Britain.'[18] He notes that in reading a law case in Wales he had found his family name and also that he had noticed a Jefferson among the secretaries of the Virginia Company. That he did not attach too much importance to such matters may be deduced from the fact that he apparently made no serious effort to trace his ancestry beyond his grandfather, 'who lived at a place in Chesterfield called Osbornes and owned the land afterwards the glebe of the parish.' The Jefferson of Osbornes had three sons. One of these died young; another settled on the waters of the Roanoke and left many descendants, and the third was Peter, born in 1707. At the age of thirty-two, this man without family prestige or social pretensions married Jane, the daughter of Isham Randolph, and thus a Jefferson became identified with one of the leading and most aristocratic families in Virginia, whose forebears had been squires in Northumberland and Warwickshire in England, and who had been allied with the powerful Scottish clan of the Earls of Murray. The Randolphs boasted that in the golden literary age of Elizabeth they produced the poet, Thomas, who was a close friend and drinking companion of rare Ben Jonson. He was a great-uncle of the William Randolph who migrated to the Old Dominion in 1660.

Thus, while Jefferson's father was of the sturdy yeomanry, rather than of the aristocracy and the best, the Randolph family easily ranked among the first families. In his *Autobiography*, Jefferson dryly observes that his mother's family traced its ancestry back to England and Scotland, and he adds: 'to which let everyone ascribe the faith and merit he chooses.'[19] He consequently had in his veins the best of the blood of the liberty-loving yeomanry and of the aristocracy, and, within bounds, he was unfaithful to neither. He was to carry on his father's love of liberty and human rights in his political philosophy and career, and in his personal living to continue the Randolph partiality for the refinements of life.

It is not of record that Peter received any formal education worth

[18] *Autobiography*, 10.   [19] *Ibid.*

mentioning, but, as his son writes, 'being of a strong mind, sound judgment, and eager after information, he read much, and so improved himself that he was selected, along with Joshua Fry, a professor of mathematics at William and Mary, to continue the boundary line between Virginia and North Carolina.' Also, with Fry, he is credited with having made the first map of Virginia.[20]

Thoroughly authenticated tradition has it that Peter was a man of tremendous physical strength, and that he had been known to stand between two hogsheads of tobacco, each weighing a thousand pounds, and to head them both at once — a feat beyond the strength of any two normally strong workmen. On another occasion, when he had ordered three able-bodied slaves to pull down a shed with a rope and they had made three futile attempts, he ordered them aside, wrapped the rope about himself, and pulled it over in an instant. He was a terror to the surveying parties that accompanied him because he knew no fatigue, and could live on the raw flesh of game and sleep with ease in a hollow tree while wild beasts roamed the woods.[21]

These stories, living in tradition, of his enormous strength, his passion for improvement, and his popularity among the hardy people of the frontier are strikingly similar to the pictures painted of the Lincoln of the Salem days. In every sense he may be described as a lusty pioneer; for when he settled where he did he had been preceded by but three or four white men.

He loved the outdoor life. He was an expert in the saddle and in the hunting field. He was a tireless swimmer. His work as surveyor gave him an abundance of exercise, and such were the demands upon his services that he prospered. His first ambition was to acquire some land, for in the Virginia of those days this was essential to either social or political standing. He was soon in possession of a thousand acres at the eastern opening of the mountain group through which flowed the waters of the Rivanna. He was soon on terms of intimate friendship with William Randolph, a young aristocrat, who owned twenty-four hundred acres adjoining the land of Peter. Soon thereafter we find Randolph transferring two hundred acres of his land to Jefferson, and thereon hangs a story typical of the times. The documentary evidence proves that no

[20] *Ibid.*   [21] Randall, *The Life of Jefferson*, I, 13.

money was exchanged in the transaction, but that the land was given in consideration of 'Henry Weatherbourne's biggest bowl of arrack punch.' On his death, Peter was in possession of several thousand acres.

The possession of land and his marriage to the daughter of the Randolphs of Dungeness clearly fixed Peter's status as among the first people of the community. On the land acquired in return for the bowl of punch, he built a plain frame house and called it 'Shadwell,' after the parish in London where his wife's mother was born during her parents' sojourn in England. The house was placed on a slight rise of the ground in a clearing, surrounded with trees of the forest. While not a pretentious dwelling, it was not in any sense a frontiersman's cabin, and, after the fashion described by the German traveler, it was but one of many buildings on the place. Four miles away was the village of Charlottesville, and a mile and a half distant, across the fields, was the mountain on which the son of Peter was to build a classic mansion he would call 'Monticello,' to which pilgrimages would continuously be made almost two centuries later by devotees of liberty and democracy.

The professional skill, the physical strength, the commanding stature, the sound judgment, the keen intelligence, and the integrity of Peter Jefferson made him a natural leader for the people of his community. He was the county surveyor. He was a justice of the peace. He was a member of the House of Burgesses. As county colonel, he was responsible for the preservation of order on the Indian frontier. He kept the peace by making friends and playing fair with the red men, and frequently these natives of the forest enjoyed the generous hospitality of his home.

It was in the modest frame house called 'Shadwell' that Thomas Jefferson was born on April 13, 1743.

III

But his early childhood was not to be spent at Shadwell. When Colonel Randolph, the wealthy and aristocratic owner of the fine estate of Tuckahoe on the James River, a few miles from Richmond, died, he expressed the wish that Peter Jefferson should become the guardian of his son, Thomas Mann Randolph, and supervise the estate. Nothing could more convincingly prove the high reputation of Peter as a man. The distance made it difficult for the supervisor to give the meticulous care to the estate which he thought necessary; and thus it came about that, at the age of two, Thomas Jefferson, in arms, carried on a pillow by a slave on horseback, made the journey to Tuckahoe where he was to remain mostly for seven years. This was Jefferson's earliest memory of his childhood.[22] It was at Tuckahoe that Thomas had his first schooling. The father, self-taught, felt the loss of a systematic education, and he was determined that his son should have the advantages he had missed.

Thus, he was entered in an English school at five, and at nine he was sent to a Latin school, where he remained until his father's death. His first teacher was a Scotch clergyman named Douglas, who taught him the rudiments of Greek, Latin, and French. Later, Jefferson was to remember him as 'a superficial Latinist, less instructed in Greek,' who, 'with the rudiments of these languages, taught me French.' After his father's death in Thomas's fourteenth year, the boy attended for two years the school of the Reverend Doctor Maury, reputed to have been a classical scholar. The son of the schoolmaster is authority for the report that Thomas was both diligent and proficient in his studies. Even so, he seems to have had a tendency he was to overcome later to put off the mastering of lessons, and when the situation became serious he sought an excuse for a holiday. Too shy to request it himself, he sometimes persuaded other boys to make the application. This granted, he would go into retirement until he was word-perfect on all the neglected work and then triumphantly rejoin the class.[23]

But this schooling does not embrace the whole of his education in these earlier years. He found much to amuse him in the small but select library of his father, whose well-worn Shakespeare and Bible were open to him, along with the works of Swift, Addison, and Steele. In poring over the pages of the last three we may be sure he got his fine sensitivity to a graceful prose style.

But Peter Jefferson's idea of the proper training for a boy was not confined to books and classrooms. He himself had wrung his degree from the University of Nature. And he saw to it that his

[22] Randolph, *Domestic Life of Thomas Jefferson*, I, 11.
[23] Tucker, *Life of Thomas Jefferson*, I, 27.

son should know and appreciate the lore and delights of the forest, the mental exhilaration of the naturalist familiar with plant and animal life. Many were the days young Jefferson stalked or rode through the Southwest Mountains in hot pursuit of game, or sat on the banks of streams, an expert with the rod. And he came to know the forest as few men did, the names of all the various birds and their qualities and habits. In the enumeration he then made appear scores that Catesby had not discovered. Even the insect life of the fields and forests was an open book to him.

It was in these boyhood days that he became the great friend and champion of the red men. The Indian chiefs, going frequently to Williamsburg before the Revolution, usually made a stop at Shadwell to visit Tom's father, and Thomas came to know them personally. Years later, in a letter to John Adams, he was to recall the famous Indian chieftain, Ontassete, the great warrior and orator of the Cherokees, who, in his frequent visits to the colonial capital, never failed to stop at Shadwell. Young Tom, happening to be in his camp the night before the chief departed for England, heard his moving farewell speech to his people. 'The moon was in full splendor,' he wrote, 'and to her he seemed to address himself in his prayers for his own safety on the voyage, and for the welfare of his own people during his absence. His sounding voice, distinct articulation, animated action, and the solemn silence of his people at their several fires, filled me with awe and veneration, although I did not understand a word he uttered.' Later, as we shall see, when the chief's people were threatened with extermination, Jefferson, his memory of that moonlight night fresh, did more than any other public man to save them.

Meanwhile, young Tom made good progress under the tutelage of James Maury in his studies. Always he was to remember this Whig clergyman of Huguenot ancestry, who had come to Virginia to tutor the Monroe family. He liked the teacher all the more because of his broad and liberal views. His home was but fourteen miles from Shadwell, and Jefferson lived with him, paying for his board and tuition the then princely sum of twenty pounds a year.

Two years had passed with Maury when Jefferson, spending the night at Peter Randolph's and discussing his schooling, was advised that the time had come for him to enter college. The advice of

Randolph coincided with Jefferson's desire. In a letter to his guardian he set forth his reasons:

> In the first place, as long as I stay at the mountain, the loss of one fourth of my time is inevitable by companies coming here and detaining me from school. And likewise, my absence will, in a measure, put a stop to so much company, and by that means lessen the expense of the estate in housekeeping. And so, on the other hand, by going to college, I shall get a more universal acquaintance which may hereafter be serviceable to me; and I suppose I can pursue my studies in the Greek and Latin as well there as here, and likewise learn something of the Mathematics.

The father had died three years before, and the son was taking his responsibilities as the head of the family seriously. He was but sixteen years old when he turned toward Williamsburg, the seat of William and Mary.

At this time he could not have been described as a handsome lad. He was tall, thin, rawboned. His hair was red, his face freckled, and his features pointed. But he possessed charm because of the unusual intelligence shining in his face, the benevolence of his expression, the fluency of his conversation, and the humor and pleasantry that brightened it. If his angular height made him a bit awkward, he was none the less a favorite with the girls.

The sixteen-year-old youth was bubbling with enthusiasm and eagerness when he paused on his way to Williamsburg to spend a few days in Hanover County as the guest of Colonel Dandridge. There he lingered, riding, walking, dancing, flirting — and he was fond of all four diversions. One day during his sojourn, a strange young man, a bit uncouth both in dress and speech — for he spoke the language of the yeomanry — appeared upon the scene, as he frequently did, from his home not far distant. He was eight years older than Jefferson, and at this moment the future appeared to hold but little promise for him. He had tried merchandising, but a little while before Jefferson met him his business had failed from mismanagement and neglect. The younger boys and girls at Dandridge's found him immensely entertaining because of his boisterous, carefree ways, and his contagious gaiety. He danced and played the fiddle with an air, and Jefferson, who liked fiddling and dancing, was literally entranced. This was Patrick Henry, his name then unknown to fame. Very soon he would have a meteoric rise, and write his name with his marvelous eloquence into American history. That Henry was likewise attracted by the auburn-haired youth at the awkward age, we may assume, since, throughout Jefferson's college days and during the period of his legal studies, Henry frequently was to be his guest in Williamsburg.

The road to Williamsburg was better than most because well beaten by the travel to the capital, but an English traveler at the time found 'the whole land . . . one continuous immense forest, intercepted by openings where the trees had been cut down, and the land cultivated.' He observed that the 'plantations are generally from one to four miles distant from each other, having a dwelling-house in the middle, with kitchens and outhouses all detached.' [24] At this time Williamsburg was described by him as having 'one handsome street in it, just a mile in length, where the view is terminated by a commanding object each way; the Capitol, an elegant brick building in which the Assembly, or Senate, and courts of justice are held, at one end of the street; and the College of William and Mary, an old monastic building, at the other end. About the center, on the north side, a little distance retired from the street, stood the Palace, the residence of the Governor, a large, commodious, and handsome building.' [25] The College building had been designed by Sir Christopher Wren. Jefferson was to haunt the Capitol, to work at the College, and to frequent the Palace as a favorite of the Royal Governor.

The colonial capital was little more than a village, with about two hundred houses 'of wood chiefly, painted white,' [26] and the population rose and fell according to whether the legislature was in session or in recess, since numerous landed gentlemen maintained quarters there for occupancy during the session only. A German traveler found that 'the houses stand at convenient distances apart, have a good exterior, and, on account of the general white paint, have a neat look.' [27] The streets were all unpaved, sandy and dusty, and the stranger found it 'very disagreeable to walk in, especially

[24] Smythe, A Tour in the United States, 15-16.   [25] Ibid., 17-18.
[26] Ibid., 19.   [27] Schoepf, Travels in the Confederation, II, 78.

in summer, when the rays of the sun are intensely hot, and not a little increased by the reflection of the white sand, wherein every step is almost above the shoe, and where there is no shade or shelter to walk under unless you carry an umbrella.'[28]

But small though the town was, there were few larger cities that offered more gaiety, dissipation, high life, and fashion during the season. During the sessions of the legislature, the rich planters with their wives and daughters flocked to the town, and here the most clever men of a brilliant age foregathered. At such times it may be safely said that neither in New York nor Philadelphia could so many men of genius and great political capacity be found at a given time. The aristocracy of the Tidewater liked to think that going to Williamsburg was like going to court in London, and, indeed, the Palace of the Royal Governor was far gayer at this time than the court at Saint James's or Windsor. The matrons, with their lively daughters in their richest gowns, were beaued about by gentlemen with manners as courtly as those of courtiers. Madame Finette's emporium then did a flourishing business with rich silks, velvets, laces, and ribbons spread out on the counter for the temptation of the ladies. It was no ordinary village in which men advertised the loss of 'an elegant toothpick case, lately imported from Paris, with a smelling bottle and gold stopper at one end,' with the offer of a reward.[29]

If the homes were not pretentious, they were noted for their taste, hospitality, and profusion. The sandy streets usually were thronged with animated groups of belles and beaux. Coaches with six horses, bearing ladies in rich brocades, fluttering with feathers and laces, and gentlemen in velvet with ruffles, rumbled over the unpaved road. Twice a year, in the spring and fall, the town was crowded for the races, and the betting was fantastic, for the gambling vice was fashionable, and men and college youths would hazard their all at cards or dice or at the cockpit with a bravado that was to reduce some of the ancient families to the verge of ruin. The track near the west end of the town offered an excellent course. The purses were raised by subscription and went to the horse that won two four-mile heats out of three. There were often matches and sweepstakes for considerable sums. An English observer was sure that the horses 'were such as to make no despicable figure at Newmarket' and that 'their speed, bottom, or blood [was not] inferior to their appearance.'[30]

We may be sure that Jefferson, who loved horses, was always among the spectators during the racing weeks.

Less than a decade before Jefferson's arrival, a theater had been built on Waller Street, and occasionally, particularly in season, ladies and gentlemen of this village Vanity Fair were regaled by companies from England in Shakespearean tragedies and comedies; and better still, for most, with the thoroughly *risqué* but brilliant comedies of Congreve, so much admired by the good Queen Mary of sainted memory. A Virginia historian has thought it a 'curious age when young ladies, who would have thought it highly improper to have gone out after dark with a young man without papa or mamma, attended the plays written by Wycherley and Congreve.'[31] Companies of players from New York appeared often, and the Hallams came from London.[32] Young Jefferson's account book assures us that he was rather constant in his attendance.

The giddy social life centered in the Palace of the Governor, by odds the most pretentious and stately house in town. Brilliant receptions and balls, at which ladies and gentlemen appeared in court costumes, set the pace. The favorite promenade was along the Duke of Gloucester Street, a hundred feet wide. The Raleigh Tavern rocked with activity and rang with festivity, for here lived distinguished lawyers attending court or the legislature, and the solons of the Dominion, and here at the bar the wisest of men drank with the abandon of the times, and here, in the Apollo Room, destined to a conspicuous place in Revolutionary history, the younger people, including Jefferson, weaved in the dance. On the occasion of the balls at the Raleigh, chariots and coaches with pawing horses and servants in livery congested the street, the rooms blazed with light, and from a balcony musicians with flutes, fifes, and fiddles furnished the music, while the rooms rang with laughter. Here for some years the susceptible Jefferson often danced in the quadrilles and minuets and the Virginia reel.

[30] Smythe, *A Tour in the United States*, 21-22.
[31] Lyon Tyler, *Williamsburg, the Old Colonial Capital*, 228.   [32] *Ibid*.

That the Raleigh Tavern was an excellent hostelry we may gather from the confession of a super-critical English traveler that he 'dined very agreeably at the Raleigh,'[33] and his German contemporary, while finding the black cooks, butlers, chambermaids, 'made their bows with much dignity and modesty,' found it 'very dear entertainment.'[34]

Thus, the stranger, meandering about the little capital and college town, would have found it picturesque and colorful enough, with the politicians in velvet coats, those of the frontier in coonskin caps, with judges trailing scarlet robes, and students and pretty flirtatious young ladies in gay garments.

V

The College of William and Mary, of ancient origin, was built of brick after Sir Christopher Wren's design for the Chelsea Hospital. This was the main building, constructed in 1694. At one side stood the President's House built in 1732, and on the other side was Brafferton Building, dating from 1723. The College was the training ground of some of the greatest of the men who made the Revolution, its honor roll exceeding that of Harvard; for here within its halls had studied Jefferson, Wythe, Monroe, and John Marshall. For some reason celibacy was preferred for the professors, who lived in the College a really monastic life, and at the College, too, lived a large portion of the students. Jefferson lived within the grounds save for a little time when he appears to have had quarters on Gloucester Street. Just what course of study he favored is not positively known. But here it was that he sowed some wild oats, studied with assiduity, and finished in two years. Young and attractive, the tall country squire with land and money was at a susceptible age. The gaiety and recklessness about him appear to have led him into some excesses during the first years, without interfering seriously with his studies. The student body was composed in large part of rowdy youths on pleasure bent, and Jefferson was swept along with the current.

These college days were well worth while had they done nothing

[33] Smythe, *A Tour in the United States,* 16.
[34] Schoepf, *Travels in the Confederation,* II, 81.

more than bring him under the influence of Doctor William Small, professor of mathematics, who was much more than a professor of mathematics. He was a thinker and philosopher. This Scot was one of the three men who had a profound influence in the molding of Jefferson's character and career. Long afterward the student paid tribute to the Scotch professor, who soon returned to Scotland to become a friend of Darwin:

A man profound in most of the useful branches of science [Jefferson wrote], with a happy talent of communication, correct and gentlemanly manners, and an enlarged and liberal mind. He, most happily for me, soon became attached to me, and made me his daily companion when not engaged in the school; and from his conversation I got my first views of the expanse of science and of the system of things in which we are placed. Fortunately, the philosophical chair became vacant soon after my arrival at college and he was appointed to fill it; and was the first who gave in that college regular lectures in Ethics, Rhetoric, and Belles-Lettres. He returned to Europe in 1762, having previously filled up the measure of his goodness to me by procuring for me, from his most intimate friend, George Wythe, a reception as a student of law under his direction, and introduced me to the acquaintance of the familiar table of Governor Fauquier, the ablest man who had ever filled that office. With him, and at his table, Doctor Small, and Mr. Wythe, and myself formed a *partie carrée,* and to the habitual conversations on these occasions I owe much instruction. Mr. Wythe continued to be my familiar and beloved mentor in youth and my most affectionate friend through life.[35]

Nothing could more conclusively prove that in early youth Jefferson possessed most extraordinary qualities. A boy of sixteen to eighteen accepted as the familiar friend and daily associate of three great minds — a learned Scotch professor, a great lawyer and jurist renowned in his generation, and one of the most brilliant and charming royal governors ever sent to Virginia — could not have been an ordinary youth. The three men offered him the three things his nature craved. In Small he found the philosopher, in Wythe, the lawyer and the lawgiver, in Fauquier the elegant and accomplished man of the great world. He profited from all the contacts.

[35] *Autobiography,* 2, 3.

Throughout his college days this precocious youth was to be a favorite at the Palace. Fauquier had one vice among all his various virtues — a propensity and passion for cards and gambling. Tradition has it that in a single night in London, in an all-night gambling bout with Anson on his return from his voyages, he lost the whole of his patrimony; and that the victor, impressed by the gay and gallant manner in which his victim had accepted defeat, was said to have procured him his post in Virginia. However that may be, experience taught him nothing, and to the end of his days he remained a gambler. Burk, the Virginia historian, concludes that to him was due the introduction of reckless gambling among the landed aristocracy of Virginia; and that in visiting the plantations of the wealthy during the recesses of the Assembly, he carried his contagion.[36]

Fauquier's father had been a director of the Bank of England. He himself had been a director of the South Sea Company. He was also a member of the Royal Academy, and he had written an excellent book on public finances which had run through three editions. But because he was an admirer of the writings of the orator and statesman, Bolingbroke, and because he was partial to Shaftesbury, some biographers have concluded that he was a freethinker and had influenced the views of his young friend. We know, of course, that Jefferson read and admired the style of Bolingbroke, and he would have done so had he never met Fauquier, since the orator's works were on the shelves of most of the private libraries of Virginia.

On the whole, however, none named Fauquier but to praise him. A brilliant conversationalist, an accomplished musician, an exquisite courtier in his manners, though with generous and liberal views, perhaps tinctured with the mild cynicism of the man of the world, suggesting now and then a figure from the period of the Restoration, he was enormously popular among Virginians. Burk says that he 'left an impression of taste, refinement, and erudition on the character of the colony' and certainly on that of the red-headed youth whom he made a companion.[37]

Fauquier was an elderly man at the time of his association with the student, his rubicund face betraying his taste for rich foods and

[36] Burk, *History of Virginia*, III, 333.   [37] *Ibid.*

indicated no prejudice against the bottle. He was to Williamsburg what Richard Brinsley Sheridan was to London.

It was at his table, with the professor of philosophy and the learned judge and lawyer, that this boy of seventeen participated in conversations that inevitably ranged over a vast field — philosophy, politics, travel, poetry, drama, architecture, art, and science. Years later, in conversation with Girardin, another historian of Virginia, Jefferson, recalling the dinner-table conversations at the Palace, said, 'I have heard more good sense, more rational and philosophical conversation [there], than in all my life beside. They were truly Attic societies.' [38]

The gay Fauquier, who hid his disillusionment behind the mask of merriment, was also a lover of music, described by Jefferson as 'a good performer'; and he gathered about him three or four amateurs, including young Jefferson, who, we may be sure, performed upon the fiddle. Once a week they staged a concert in the drawing-room for their own delectation. Here, in the light from the globe lamps that ornamented the salon, with the portraits of the King and Queen looking down from the wall, the future author of the Declaration of Independence could have been seen many times playing with the Royal Governor. Sometimes in the Palace he played cards with his host, and usually lost, and sometimes, when the hour was late, he probably stayed the night there in a silk-curtained bed, lighted by candles in their candlesticks of silver.

VI

However, it would be a mistake to assume, from his intimacy with the mature minds of his three great friends, that young Jefferson superciliously stood aloof from his college mates and entered not at all into their boyish pranks. At one time he shared a room in a house with John Tyler, afterward distinguished in public life and on the bench and as the father of a future President, and with Frank Willis, of Gloucester County. Young Tyler was studious and in search of an education, like Jefferson, but it appears that young Willis was more of a rowdy. The latter kept his horse in the cellar. Something of a wag, given to youthful dissipations, he spent

[38] Girardin, *History of Virginia.*

his evenings in the pursuit of pleasure while his two friends remained at home bent above the books and papers on the table; and it is recorded that not infrequently on his late return from his nightly revels he was wont to tease his more studious companions by upsetting the table at which they were studying and running away with the books.[39]

With Tyler, Jefferson shared a love of the violin, and, in practicing together, he was sure that, had he had the bow arm of his friend, he 'would yield the palm to no man living in excellence of performance,' but he was young and optimistic.[40]

With all his extraordinary advantages, Jefferson was not of easy conscience when, at the close of the first year, he reviewed his conduct. As we have seen, the society of Williamsburg was gay to the point of dissipation; and the sporting crowd, playing the races recklessly, squandering its money at the card-table, or consuming its time in chase of the fox, made some impression at first on the callow youth from Shadwell. We know that he plunged into this life of dissipation, and in later years often marveled that he had emerged unscathed.

> I was often thrown into the society of horse racers, card players, fox hunters, scientific and professional men; and many a time I have asked myself, in the enthusiastic moment of the death of the fox, the victory of a favorite horse, the issue of a question eloquently argued at the bar or in the great council of the nation, 'Well, which of these kinds of reputation should I prefer? That of a horse jockey? or a fox hunter? an orator? or the honest advocate of my country's rights?' In a moment of temptation or difficulty, I would ask myself, 'What would Dr. Small, Mr. Wythe, do in this situation?'

But, examining his accounts of his first year at college, and noting such heavy items charged to fancy dress and fine horses and entertainment, he was stricken with remorse. He then wrote his guardian, admitting the college bills to have been excessive, and proposing that the whole of these expenditures be charged to his separate share of the property. The wise guardian replied that, since he had sown his wild oats in such a comparatively harmless way, 'the estate can well afford to pay the bill.'

[39] Lyon Tyler, *Letters and Times of the Tylers*, I, 54-55.   [40] *Ibid.*

VII

The vacations at Shadwell reflected Jefferson's remorse over the squandering of time and money during the first year. He now applied himself fully fifteen hours a day. It was usually two o'clock in the morning when he snuffed his candle, and with the first pale rays of dawn he was out of bed and ready to resume his studies. He watched the clock, placed on the mantel near his bed, and as soon as it was light enough to distinguish the hands, he rose. Even his meager exercise and recreation were not unassociated with his future plans.

In the evening, after the setting of the sun, he would go to the Rivanna River where a small canoe was kept ready for his use, and he would paddle across the stream. Thence he plodded along over the fields, through the woods, to the summit of his favorite mountain, where, even then, he was planning the building of Monticello.[41]

During his second year in college, he put behind him the temptations that had betrayed him in the first. He gave up his horse, and fox-hunting went with it. It is said that for the first time he abandoned his loved fiddle, though this seems incredible. Certain it is that he studied fifteen hours a day, as during his vacation at Shadwell. Not content, now, merely with his textbooks prescribed by the College, he began the collection of the library that was to be consumed in the burning of his home. The greater part of this extra-curricular reading was in the field of history and philosophy. His boyish poring over the crystalline pages of Swift, Addison, and Steele had set for him a high standard as to style. Only now and then did he read fiction, but his favorite novelists, as they have come down to us, indicate that he ignored few worthy of serious attention at the time. Like any Englishman of his day, he read Fielding, Smollett, and Sterne, and, outside the English, *Gil Blas* and Cervantes. Thus he chose wisely and was well advised. In the long conversations around Fauquier's dining-table he had a liberal training in the choice of books. Though he was never to find his favorite reading in fiction, and probably never reread a novel with the exception of Cervantes' masterpiece, he was urging the reading of

[41] Randolph, *Domestic Life of Jefferson*, 31, 32.

fiction on Robert Skipwith three years after leaving college, on the ground that 'everything is useful which contributes to fix in the mind principles and practices of virtue'; that 'we neither know nor care whether Laurence Sterne really went to France, whether he was there accosted by a Franciscan . . . or whether the whole be fiction'; and that *King Lear* presents a more 'lively and lasting sense of filial duty' than 'all the dry volumes of ethics and divinity that ever were written.' Thus we may be sure that fiction entered into his college reading. In the more serious branches of literature, he thought more highly of the Greeks than of the Romans, found Demosthenes much greater as an orator than Cicero, but thought Cicero a greater philosopher than Socrates or Epictetus. He eagerly thumbed the pages of Thucydides and Tacitus, and while disappointed at first with Plutarch, came to like him, too. Among the English historians he was pleased with the style, but disgusted with the principles, of Hume. Among the ancient classics he favored Homer, Horace, and the Greek dramatists. He admired Virgil, but Petrarch wearied him. He knew, in his youth, Shakespeare, Milton, Dryden, and Pope, and he read Dante and Molière.

Applying himself meticulously to his prescribed studies, mastering his Greek and Latin, and acquiring an excellent speaking and reading knowledge of French, browsing among his newly acquired books in general literature, he scarcely took time for the physical exercise to which he had been accustomed. But the reduction of his exercise was compensated by its strenuosity. Toward evening, the tall, lanky, red-headed youth might have been seen running swiftly from his quarters into the country, running a mile and back at a rapid pace without pausing. He still presented a lively face to his friends, and in company appeared the soul of levity, but even his companions knew he had grown serious underneath, and his friend Page marveled at the ease with which he could pass from light-hearted entertainment to concentration on his studies.

VIII

In the last year of his college life, Jefferson did find time for a mild romance which has been taken much too seriously by some biographers. That he was a prime favorite among the charming belles in and about Williamsburg we may assume from the record, and he was no stranger to the ballrooms and the flowering grounds of the country seats near-by. Here was a youth possessed of landed estates, and with ability enough beyond the ordinary to cause Fauquier, Doctor Small, and Wythe to take him into their inner circle of familiar friends and make him an intimate of the Palace, and he appealed to the young women by his appearance and manner. Physically he was now impressive and distinguished. He had sprung up to his more than six feet in height when scarcely more than a boy. Slender and erect as a mountain pine, his fair complexion and his thick reddish hair of a silky texture would have made him conspicuous in any assembly had there been nothing else to recommend him to the favors of the fair ones. But even in college he had a kindly, benevolent expression that invited confidence. In his long straight nose and strong chin they found strength, and in the sensitivity of his mouth they could imagine an affectionate disposition. And his hazel-blue eyes were eloquently expressive.

But his appeal was not confined to his physical attractions. He was playful, bubbling over with fun, vivacious and spirited in manner, and he whose talk could entertain the brilliant and worldly Fauquier was unequaled among the eligible beaux as a conversationalist. And though he instinctively bore himself with a courtly dignity, no one could unbend more gracefully in society, and his ability as a dancer was not lost on the young ladies. In the dances of the Apollo Room of the Raleigh, in the promenades in the sands of the Duke of Gloucester Street, in the Williamsburg homes of the landed aristocracy, and under the blossoming apple trees of the near-by plantations he was a familiar figure.

Among the young women he had many friends, but one appears to have made a stronger appeal than the others. Rebecca Burwell, who figures in his early boyish correspondence as 'Belinda,' seems to have been not indifferent to his interest and admiration. But there is nothing to indicate the grand passion that some biographers have discovered. The lady, then seventeen, was pretty and charming, graceful and elegant, with rosy cheeks, bright blue eyes, and golden hair, and with a proper social background. Tradition has it that she was quite a grown-up lady, and powdered her hair with the best of them. Though Jefferson was plainly interested in an adolescent way, he was not so impetuous in the midst of his studies as to think of early matrimony; and the lady, following the fashion, evidently had no thought of an indefinite postponement which might leave her a spinster. We have an illumination of Jefferson's 'passion' in a letter to his friend Page, written a few weeks after finishing his college course, in which reference is made to 'Belinda' and to other young women friends. The letter is interesting, too, as an illustration of his conception of a fashionable young man's epistolary style. It was written from Fairfield:

This very day, to others the greatest day of mirth and jollity [Christmas], sees me overwhelmed with more and greater misfortunes than have befallen a descendant of Adam for these thousand years past, I am sure; and, perhaps, after excepting Job, since the creation of the world. I think his misfortunes were somewhat greater than mine, for, although we may be pretty nearly on a level in other respects, yet I thank God that I have the advantage of brother Job in this, that Satan has not yet put forth his hand to load me with bodily afflictions. You must know, dear Page, that I am now in a house surrounded by enemies who take counsel against my very soul; and when I lay me down to rest, they say among themselves, 'Come, let us destroy him.' I am sure that if there is such a thing as the Devil in this world, he must have been here last night, and have had some hand in contriving what happened to me. Do you think the cursed rats (at his instigation, I suppose) did not eat up my pocket book within a foot of my head? And not content with plenty for the present, they carried away my jemmy-worked silk garters and half a dozen new minuets I had just got to serve as a provision for the winter.

But, in addition, the tragedies of the night irreverently touched with sacrilegious hands the romance with Belinda. A soaking rain had fallen during the night and Jefferson found his watch 'all afloat in water let in at a leak in the roof.' The watch was precious, since it contained a picture of Belinda, and in trying to get it out to dry it, it was destroyed. 'Although it may be defaced,' he wrote, 'there is so lovely an image imprinted on my mind that I shall think of her too often, I fear, for my peace of mind; and too often, I am sure, to get through old Coke this winter; for God knows I have not seen him since I packed him up in my trunk at Williamsburg. Well,

Page, I do wish the devil had old Coke, for I am sure I never was so tired of an old dull scoundrel in my life.'

Then the writer turned to college memories of the young women. Would Page remember him 'affectionately to all the young ladies of [his] acquaintance, particularly Miss Burwell and Miss Potter, and tell them that though the heavy earthly part of [him] is absent, the better half of [him], [his] soul, is ever with them.' And would Page tell Alice Corbin that he believed the rats 'knew I was to win a pair of garters from her,' else they would not have been so cruel. And then again — Belinda. 'I would fain ask the favor of Miss Rebecca Burwell to get me another watch paper of her own cutting, which I would esteem much more, though it were a plain round one, than the nicest in the world cut by other hands.' Would she think it 'presumptuous' after he had 'permitted the other to be spoiled'? If Page thought he could excuse him to her, he would be glad if he would ask her.

And what had he done to offend Miss Sukey Potter? 'What it is, I do not know; but this I know, that I never was guilty of the least disrespect to her in my life, either by word or deed.' He was afraid that when next they met she would repay 'an imaginary affront with a real one.' But Page was to tell her to save herself the trouble 'for nothing that she may say or do shall ever lessen her in my esteem.' [42]

There is little here to indicate a grand passion. One gathers that he was not so much enchanted with a girl as with girls. About the same time he was writing his college friend, William Fleming, in ecstatic mood of Jenny Taliaferro. He could 'view the beauties of this world with the most philosophical indifference,' he had been 'vastly pleased with her playing on the spinette and singing, but could not help calling to mind those sublime verses of the Cumberland genius —

'Oh I was charmed to see
Orpheus' music all in thee.'

And would Fleming tell Patsy Dandridge 'God bless her'? The young man did not like the 'ups and downs of a country life,' be-

[42] Washington, *Writings of Thomas Jefferson*, I, 181.

cause 'today you are frolicking with a fine girl, and tomorrow you are moping by yourself.'

Thus, with his wining, dining, dancing, fox-hunting, cockfighting, reading, writing, and conversing with Wythe and Small, the college days of Jefferson were not entirely free from the entanglements of Cupid.

With college now behind him, Jefferson turned seriously to the study of the law. As we have seen, before Doctor Small returned to Scotland he had urged Wythe to undertake the legal training of the young companion of them both. Wythe had readily agreed, and for five years we shall find Jefferson seriously pursuing his legal studies while delving deep into history, political science, and philosophy.

CHAPTER

II

LAW, POLITICS, AND LOVE

I

WHEN JEFFERSON entered the chambers of George Wythe
as a student, the latter was, concededly, one of the ablest
men his profession had produced in Virginia or in any other colony.
He was more than a great lawyer, he was a great man; and he
was more than a great man, he was a genius. When Jefferson came
under his tutelage, he had one of the three most opulent and largest
practices in the Dominion. It was truly said of him that 'in the
solid learning of the law he stood, with the exception of Thomson
Mason, almost alone.'[1] Though an impressive and convincing
speaker, his arguments were always prepared with great care, and
Jefferson once said that 'in pleading he never indulged himself
with a useless or a declamatory word.' His mind was too methodi-
cal, his thoughts too carefully meditated, to make him so facile as
some of his contemporaries in rough-and-tumble, extemporaneous
debate, but in the give-and-take of battle his wit stood him in good
stead. His greatest rival was Edmund Pendleton, and in a case in
which both had an assistant the latter asked a continuance because
of the absence of his own. Lord Dunmore, who, to the credit of
Wythe, hated him, said, 'Go on, Mr. Pendleton, for you will be a
match for both of them.' 'Yes,' replied Wythe, bowing, 'with your
lordship's assistance.'[2]

He had absorbed and made his own the very whole of Coke and

[1] Grigsby, *The Virginia Convention of 1776,* 120.
[2] Lyon Tyler, *George Wythe,* 74.

Locke. Though he had neglected the classics in his youth, his close association with those who had not and the richness and beauty of their conversation determined him in maturity to master Greek and Latin, and in a short time this was reflected in his own literary style. So much did he come to love the classics in Latin and Greek that when he was on the bench he opened a class in Williamsburg for their study, along with English prose and poetry, and he accepted no compensation for his teaching.[3] He knew, too, as familiar friends the great literary figures of the Elizabethan and Cromwellian periods.

The very fact that Wythe thought of law in its fundamentals gave his mind the cast of a statesman. He had habitually discussed natural philosophy with Fauquier, a man of learning, and in their erudite conversations about the dinner-table no topics appeared more frequently than the laws of nations and the natural rights of man.[4] He had strong principles and convictions, and these were on the side of liberality. He was a tenacious supporter of popular rights when it was not yet fashionable, and he stood four-square for religious liberty and toleration when such a stand invited enmity. Never in his life was he to hesitate to sacrifice personal popularity in support of ideals, no matter what the loss in money.

In the House of Burgesses, which he had entered four years before Jefferson became his student, he had been among the most audacious in defending colonial rights, which he insisted were guaranteed to every citizen of the British Empire. But he was not a firebrand. His mind was too legalistic and too conservative. Thus, when Henry presented his Stamp-Tax resolution, he opposed it on the ground that the petitions of the year before had not yet been answered; and when the fiery orator hurled his flaming sentence about Caesar having his Brutus, he was one of the two or three who shouted 'Treason.' But later, when his student, Jefferson, wrote his *Summary View,* Wythe among the leading members of the bar put upon it the stamp of his approval; and in Congress no one was to give to Jefferson's Declaration of Independence more ardent support.

As we have seen, Jefferson did not enter his chambers as a stranger, since the college boy had been one of the charmed circle

[3] *Ibid.,* 70.   [4] *Ibid.*

of Fauquier. Master and student had intimate contacts of the mind. They had numerous mental qualities in common. Like Jefferson, Wythe maintained the utmost reserve about his religious views, believing these to be between himself and his Maker, but that he subscribed to the religion of Jesus Christ there can be no doubt. Jefferson, in later life, was to say of him that 'that religion must be good which could produce a life of such exemplary virtue.'[5]

In appearance, Wythe was impressive, his form slender but erect and vigorous, his forehead overhanging with a magnificent sweep, and his dark gray eyes glowed with feeling and intelligence. His finely chiseled lips, his Roman nose, and his broad, strong chin suggested the natural leader.

Many students of the law profited by his teaching, and some were to be among the greatest lawyers and statesmen of the early Republic. John Marshall, the future Chief Justice; Littleton Tazewell, the brilliant lawyer and Senator; and Henry Clay sat at his feet. It is significant that among all these his favorite student was, not Marshall, but Jefferson, to whom, on his death, he bequeathed his library.

And Jefferson had set a high standard for himself. It was at a time when one could enter the practice of the law on a flimsy fundamental base: Patrick Henry studied three months in a cursory fashion; Jefferson was to subject himself to the most intensive and extensive study for five years.

That George Wythe tremendously affected Jefferson's life there can be no doubt.

II

Even in his youth, Jefferson had a contempt for superficiality, and his study of the law, along with his reading and thinking on the science of government and political philosophy, was not to be perfunctory. He was in no hurry. He did not spend his entire time during the five years of onerous research in the chambers of Wythe in Williamsburg, but, wherever he was, whether at his home or elsewhere, he pursued his studies meticulously. Soon after he began the practice of law he prepared an outline of study for a student

[5] Grigsby, *The Virginia Convention of 1776,* 120-24.

of the law which unquestionably was based on the method he himself had followed. This plan called for early rising in the morning and a course of reading until eight o'clock. During these trying early hours he advised reading on Agriculture, Chemistry, Anatomy, Zoology, Botany, Ethics, and Natural Religion. He recommended Tull and Arthur Young for Agriculture; Locke, Stewart, Condorcet, Cicero, Seneca, and Hutchinson for Ethics; the Bible, the sermons of Sterne, and Priestley's *History of the Corruptions of Christianity* for Religion; and Vattel for Natural Law.

Thus he clearly believed of the lawyer, what Cicero believed of the orator, that he should know something of everything.

From eight to twelve he suggested solid reading of the law. Citing a number of lawbooks, he proposed a method for assimilation:

> In reading the reporters, enter in a commonplace book every case of value, condensed into the narrowest possible compass which will admit of presenting distinctly the principle of the case. This operation is doubly useful, insomuch as it obliges the student to seek out the pith of the case, and habituates him to a condensation of thought and to an acquisition of the most valuable of all the talents, that of never using two words when one will do.

In his own *Commonplace Book* we have abundant evidence that he himself followed this method.

From twelve to one he assigned the student to the reading of Politics. Here, again, he recommended Locke, who unquestionably had a determining influence on Jefferson's thinking. But he also suggests Sidney's *Discourses Concerning Government*, Priestley's *First Principles of Government*, Montesquieu, Hatsell's *Precedents of the House of Commons*, and *Select Parliamentary Debates*, in England and Ireland.

During the afternoon he proposed the reading of History, particularly the Greek and Roman historians, and Gibbon's *Decline and Fall of the Roman Empire*.

And between sunset and bedtime he would have the student devote his reading to literature, criticism, rhetoric, and oratory.

It was during his days under the watchful eye of Wythe that Jefferson began keeping his own *Commonplace Book* in which he followed his own suggestions. Written in a small hand, concisely but clearly and fully, are his notes and observations covering his studies in law and politics. For years these were thought, even by Jefferson, to have been consumed in the fire that burned Shadwell to the ground, but later they were found, and today they may be consulted in the Congressional Library, or in the valuable compilation prepared by Doctor Chinard and published by Johns Hopkins. That he began making his notations while a student of the law is shown in a letter to Doctor Thomas Cooper, written five years after he had retired from the Presidency of the Republic:

> When I was a student of the law . . . after getting through Coke-Littleton, whose matters cannot be abridged, I was in the habit of abridging and commonplacing what I read, meriting it, and of sometimes mixing my own reflections on the subject. . . . They were written at a time of life when I was bold in the pursuit of knowledge, never fearing to follow truth and reason to whatever results they led, and bearding every authority which stood in their way.

These notes reveal an astonishing range of reading, which, contrary to the favorite fallacy of anti-Jeffersonian historians, do not indicate that either Rousseau or Voltaire made more than a mild impression on his mind. They show that during his formative years he was imbibing his philosophy and ideas largely from British founts, with John Locke and Lord Kames, the Scotch philosopher, in the lead. He clearly was impressed with Sir John Dalrymple's *Essay Toward a General History of Feudal Property in Great Britain.* Here undoubtedly, as in a lesser degree in Locke, we may find the genesis of his future attack on primogeniture and entail. From Pelloutier he gleaned his justification for his instinctive passion for natural rights and his belief in the right of colonies to rule themselves; from Stanyan and his *History of Greece* he got his justification of popular sovereignty. Though many quotations in his *Commonplace Book* are from Montesquieu, of an uncertain date, it appears that, while at first impressed with the *Esprit des Lois,* he afterward became a severe critic.[6] While Voltaire appears in the voluminous notes, Doctor Chinard observes that he clearly did not 'make any lasting impression upon his mind.'[7]

[6] See Chinard, *Commonplace Book,* 31-38.   [7] *Ibid.,* 48.

A general survey of Jefferson's reading as revealed in the *Commonplace Book* would be beyond the scope of this work. It is important to our purpose in that it so plainly shows that, during his formative years while a student of the law, Jefferson subjected himself to an exhaustive course of reading, not only in the law, but upon the science of government, and that he drew very deeply upon the philosophers.

III

His studies were not confined to the chambers of Wythe, since wherever he was, and most of all at home, he literally lived with his books, draining them to the dregs, and fixing them permanently in his thinking by his concise abbreviation of that part of their contents that interested him. Nor did he always study alone. From early years his most intimate and cherished friend was Dabney Carr, with whom he attended William and Mary. Carr's all too brief career was prematurely ended at a time when he held forth the most brilliant promise, and, though but thirty, was considered as the most probable rival of Patrick Henry in forensic eloquence. William Wirt, the biographer of Henry, has described him at the time as of dignified person and engaging manners, with all the attributes of an accomplished gentleman. He had a thoroughly trained and disciplined mind with 'conceptions quick, and clear and strong,' with a great capacity for cogent reasoning, and endowed with an imagination that gave beauty to his style of speaking. His feelings were acute, his speaking voice 'finely toned.'

The training and disciplining of his mind may easily have been due in part to his intimacy with his friend, Jefferson. While students of the law, as before during college days, the two friends both extraordinary, were wont to take their books to the hillside of Monticello, where, under a favorite oak that spread its branches to furnish shade, the two young men stretched out upon the grass with their studies, reading aloud, discussing the contents of the tomes, talking about government, politics, philosophy, and literature. It was a beautiful relationship which was soon afterward to be strengthened by the marriage of Carr to his friend's sister, Martha.

A few years later, in a letter to a friend, Jefferson described Carr

with that peculiar felicity which was his. At this time Carr was his
brother-in-law:

> This friend of ours, Page, in a very small house, with a table, a
> half-dozen chairs, and one or two servants, is the happiest man in
> the universe. Every incident of life he so takes as to render it a
> source of pleasure. With as much benevolence as the heart of a man
> will hold, but with an utter neglect of the costly apparatus of life,
> he exhibits to the world a new phenomenon in philosophy — a
> Samian sage in the tub of a cynic.[8]

In visualizing the Jefferson of these student days, he cannot be
disassociated from his bosom companion, Carr, as they tramp across
the fields and up the hill, with books under their arms, happy, carefree, and in animated conversation, seeking the favorite tree under
which, from a lofty height, they could look out on the world in the
effort to unravel its mysteries and meaning.

IV

It was the year after leaving college that Jefferson witnessed the
first oratorical triumph of Patrick Henry, with whom he was then
on such terms of intimacy as to justify the latter in staying with
him when in Williamsburg on his occasional visits to the capital.
He appreciated Henry's unconventional conversation, his mimicry,
his genius, but his mind did not click with Henry's as it did with
Carr's. The great orator was not a bookish man or a scholar. But
in 1763, Jefferson's admiration flamed for the strange, almost uncouth
figure who appeared occasionally in his quarters.

The clergy of the Established Church received their pay in
tobacco, and, a few years before, the Virginia Assembly passed the
Two Penny Act providing that the salaries thenceforth should be
paid in money calculated on the basis of the unquestionably low
rate of twopence per pound of tobacco. The clergy seethed with
indignation, the Bishop of London fulminated against the blas-
phemy, and the Privy Council of George III declared the clergy entitled to pay in tobacco, at its market price in money. In 1763, a
parson of Hanover brought suit to recover his salary of sixteen thous-
and pounds of tobacco; and when the court ruled that he could

8 Washington, *Writings of Jefferson*, I, 193-95.

recover, but that the amount would be determined by a jury, Patrick Henry was engaged to make the appeal to the jury against the granting of the sixteen thousand pounds.

Jefferson was in Williamsburg at the time. Feeling ran high. There was bitter resentment against both royalty and the clergy. And Henry's bitter, brilliant, biting excoriation of the clergy, which had collected their tobacco but neglected their duties, literally drove them in a panic from the courtroom where they had gathered with the thought of intimidating him by their presence. The orator was at his revolutionary best, declaring that the King had forfeited the right to obedience from his subjects by supporting the claims of the parsons against the people and in arbitrarily setting aside the act of the legislators. The courtroom roared its approval. It was a drama. The clergyman was given the smallest possible verdict, and Henry was carried from the courtroom on the shoulders of the people.

V

But that year Jefferson's delving into dusty tomes of law and politics had not obliterated from his consciousness the charms of Williamsburg and its feminine allure. Writing in January from his home in the country, one concludes from his letter that he was not finding life all cakes and ale. 'We rise in the morning that we may eat breakfast, dinner, and supper, and go to bed again that we may get up the next morning and do the same; so that you never see two peas more alike than our yesterdays and todays,' he wrote. And then, too, all was not well with Belinda. 'How did Nancy look at you when you danced with her at Southall's?' he asks. And 'how does R. B. do? Had I better stay here and do nothing, or go down and do less? . . . Inclination tells me to go, receive my sentence, and be no longer in suspense; but Reason says, if you go, and your attempt proves unsuccessful, you will be ten times more wretched than ever.'

But even here one is left in doubt whether his depression is due entirely to the pouting of Belinda, for he appears to have been deprived of his favorite solace of the printed page by overstrain on his eyes. 'In my last letter, I told you of the losses I had sustained, he wrote. 'In the present, I may mention one more, which is the loss of the whites of my eyes, in the room of which I have got reds, which gives me an exquisite pain.' He had been unable to read anything for days, 'and God knows,' he adds, 'when I shall be able to do it.'

Without the solace of his books the young man's fancy seemed a-wandering. Perhaps he would go to Petersburg 'if the actors go there in May.' And maybe he would go to Europe, visit England, Holland, Spain, France, and Italy, where — happy thought — he could 'buy a good fiddle.' Would Page go along? It would take two or three years, 'and if we could not be cured of love in that time, I think the devil would be in it.'[9]

Thus the summer of 1763 found Jefferson in a strange state of mind and a bit more unsettled than he had ever been before or was ever to be again. He had, somehow, convinced himself that the trip to Europe was not a figment of the fancy, and when Page suggested that he 'lay siege in form' to the lady of his aspiration, he replied that, in view of the contemplated journey, which would require two or three years, 'to begin an affair of that kind and carry it on so long a time in form is by no means a proper plan.' And then — more earnestly — 'No, Page, whatever assurances I may give her in private of my esteem for her, and whatever assurances I may ask in return from her, depend upon it — they must be kept in private.' He agreed that it was not fair to treat with a ward without obtaining the approbation of her guardian, but he could 'not remain in suspense so long a time.' Then, too, were he to meet with disappointment, 'the sooner I know it, the more of life I shall have to wear it off.' Certain it was that were Belinda to refuse him, he would never propose to another.[10]

Young Jefferson in his callow youth was seemingly impervious to the impertinence of expecting a Virginia belle, who in those days expected to be married at eighteen or to be doomed to spinsterhood, to wait two or three years for the convenience of an absent lover. Of course he did 'not know how she would like it' and he was afraid 'not much.' And when, one evening in Williamsburg, he was dancing with Belinda in the Apollo Room and had 'planned to say a great deal,' he was, alas, able to say but little, 'a few broken sen-

[9] *Ibid.*, I, 184-85.   [10] *Ibid.*, I, 186-88.

tences, uttered in great disorder, and interrupted with pauses of uncommon length.' He could not understand his 'strange confusion.' [11] But a little later, when he was capable of coherent speech, he explained the necessity for his journey and the long delay entailed and the reasons — 'which appeared to have given that satisfaction I would have wished.' [12] From which we may assume that the young lady smiled and turned to other and more immediate prospects, for within a few weeks she had engaged herself to another.

Too much has been made of Jefferson's anguish of spirit at that early age. In love, at least, he was a mere child, and one gathers from the correspondence that he was more in love with the idea of love than with any object of it, and that he enjoyed phrasing his emotional reactions in the literary form of the novels he had read.

VI

Meanwhile, he was attending court regularly as a part of his training, and thinking some of building his own lodgings in Williamsburg 'to prevent the inconvenience of moving my lodgings in the future.' It would be a small house which, he promised Page, would have room for him, 'unless Belinda should think proper to favor us with her company . . . in which case I will enlarge the plan as she pleases.' [13]

In the meantime, the stupidity of the British Ministry was sowing the seeds of revolution in America. The Ministry of Grenville determined to impose a stamp tax on business transactions in the colonies, on wills, mortgages, contracts, newspapers, of from three-pence to ten pounds. The revenue thus derived was to be used in the maintenance of the British troops.

Instantly the colonies were in a tumult of vehement protest. They did not want or require a garrison of British troops among them. They thought they themselves had fought against the red men and the French. They resented the assumption that the English could thus deprive the local legislatures of sources of revenue. The protest against taxation without representation shook the continent.

[11] *Ibid.*, I, 188-89.   [12] *Ibid.*, I, 189-90.   [13] *Ibid.*, I, 186-88.

And the tragedy was that the Stamp Tax Act had passed in London without attracting the attention of the English people. Indeed, when it was up for repeal a little later, Arthur Lee, then in London, heard members of Parliament commenting that, while members of the House on its passage, they had paid no attention to it when it was read and had voted blindly on it as a ministerial measure. The English had their excitement closer home, for they were in the midst of the battle over John Wilkes, and it was not until their American correspondents wrote that they learned that a grave constitutional issue had been raised by their blind votes.

But in Virginia, the authors of the stamp tax had their apologists, a militant minority priding itself in the name of 'friends of Government,' who were more concerned at this juncture in moderating the zeal and thwarting the plans of the younger patriots. When it appeared that no vigorous protest would be made in the Virginia Assembly, one of the members resigned his seat to bring in Patrick Henry because of his audacity, his tempestuous eloquence, his fighting spirit.[14] Realizing the purpose, the 'friends of Government,' composed mostly of the rich landowners, thought to reduce his efforts to absurdity by turning ridicule upon him. He was of the yeomanry, uncouth in manner and conscious of his defects, and the tittering that surrounded him momentarily made him ill at ease. Arrayed against him with bitterness were the old leaders, men of great ability, who, until now, had easily dominated the House — Peyton Randolph, Richard Bland, Pendleton, and Wythe. The dress of Henry was certainly not that of a courtier and his figure was scarcely that of a graceful gallant of the court, while the 'friends of Government' appeared in their most exquisite bib and tucker to set off as conspicuously as possible the rusticity of the upstart who dared to challenge the power of the Government in London.[15]

Though not a member, young Jefferson, whose keen penetration had reached beyond the raiment of the rustic to the heart and soul of the fervent patriot and to his genius, was in Williamsburg and keenly interested in the event.

Undaunted by the tittering and the scowls of the 'friends of Government,' Henry, 'alone, unadvised, and unassisted,' hurriedly wrote

[14] Burk, *History of Virginia*, III, 299.   [15] *Ibid.*, III, 305.

'on the blank leaf of an old lawbook' (Henry's notation on the back of the original resolutions) his resolutions. These resolutions are essential parts of the history of the Revolution:

> Resolved, that the first adventurers and settlers on this, his Majesty's colony and dominion, brought with them and transmitted to their posterity, and all other his Majesty's subjects, since inhabiting in this, his Majesty's said colony, all the privileges, franchises, and immunities that have at any time been held, enjoyed, and possessed by the people of Great Britain.

> Resolved, that by two Royal charters granted by King James I, the colonists aforesaid are declared entitled to all the privileges, liberties, and immunities of citizens and natural born subjects, to all intents and purposes as if they had been abiding and born within the realm of England.

> Resolved, that the taxation of the people by themselves, or by persons chosen by themselves to represent them, who can only know what taxes the people are able to bear, and the easiest mode of raising them, and are equally affected by such taxes themselves, is the distinguishing characteristic of British freedom without which the ancient Constitution cannot subsist.

> Resolved, that his Majesty's liege people of this most ancient colony have uninterruptedly enjoyed the rights, and being thus governed by their own Assembly in the article of their taxes and internal police, and that the same hath never been forfeited, or any other way given up, but hath been constantly recognized by the King and people of Great Britain.

> Resolved, therefore, that the general assembly of this colony have the sole right and power to lay taxes and impositions upon the inhabitants of this colony; and that every attempt to vest such power in any person or persons whatsoever, other than the general assembly aforesaid, has a manifest tendency to destroy British as well as American freedom.

Young Jefferson was standing in the doorway of the House during the ensuing debate, and thus heard what he described as 'the sublime eloquence of Henry.' It was distinctly as a partisan that he listened to one of the most moving pieces of eloquence ever uttered anywhere. It was when the Speaker, a 'friend of Government,' objected strongly to the stout style of the resolutions that Henry was amazed and aroused to fever heat. That Jefferson in the doorway shared his friend's amazement we may be sure. 'I was then a student and stood at the door of communication between the house and the lobby during the whole debate and vote,' he wrote later. He thought the debate on the last and strongest of the resolutions, which passed by only one vote, 'bloody.' His other more legalistic friend and mentor, Wythe, shared the misgivings of the Speaker. And when the orator reached his climax with 'Caesar had his Brutus, Charles I his Cromwell, and George III may profit by their example,' one of the two or three men who shouted 'Treason' was Wythe, in whose chambers Jefferson was then a student. Years later, in his *Autobiography*, Jefferson wrote that he had 'heard the splendid display of Mr. Henry's talents as a popular orator — great indeed,' and 'such as he had never heard from any other man,' since Henry 'spoke as Homer wrote.' [16]

And Jefferson, standing in the door after the division, heard Peyton Randolph, as he excitedly rushed by him into the lobby, saying, 'By God, I would give five hundred guineas for a single vote,' since, with the tie thus created, the 'friend of Government' in the chair would have defeated the resolutions. And the next morning, after Henry had left town, Jefferson saw Peter Randolph, then of the Council, and also 'friend of Government,' thumbing over the volumes of journals to find a precedent for expunging a vote of the House. 'I stood by him at the end of the table,' wrote Jefferson, 'looking on as he turned over the leaves.' And when the House convened, some of the timid members who had voted for the resolutions, becoming alarmed by their temerity, were prepared to backtrack. Henry, who had hurried back, bitterly denounced the trick and called on all who favored the resolutions to secede from the House. The 'friends of Government' now took alarm, and nothing happened.

Jefferson learned much that day of the spirit of the old leadership of the legislature, and he was to carry that knowledge with him into the House a few years later when he became a member. It is a pity that no Boswell was near to overhear the conversation that night between Jefferson and the mentor he so much admired.

[16] *Autobiography*, 4.

VII

Jefferson was not to make his journey to Europe for some years, and, in the meanwhile, Belinda was lost to another without appearing to have left any ineradicable grief upon him. He was dividing his time between the courts and Wythe's chambers in Williamsburg and his home at Shadwell, where he spent his vacations, continuing his studies there with interludes of tramps or rides over the countryside and to the top of his favorite mountain. He also found time for his fiddle.

By the time he had attained his majority, he had an assured position. He was the sole owner of a fine estate, and, as one of the lords of the manor, he was made a squire and a justice of the peace. His neighbors already thought of him as one of their future representatives in the legislature. On his twenty-first birthday he planted an avenue of locust trees at Shadwell. It was in these days that he was sorely stricken by the death of his favorite sister, Jane, whose mind clicked with his and whose spirit was in accord with his. The two had shared their innermost thoughts with one another and her loss was irreparable. Many years after his death a member of the family, rummaging among his papers, found an epitaph in Latin:

> Ah, Johanna, puellarum optima,
> Ah, aevi virentis flore praerepta,
> Sit tibi terra laevis;
> Longe, longeque valeto.

In his twenty-third year, and near the completion of his legal studies, Jefferson made his first journey beyond the boundaries of Virginia. Unlike others of his class and financial status, he was to be purely a product of the Old Dominion. Others studied abroad and made their continental tour after the prescribed fashion of the English, and others prepared for the bar by enrolling in the Temple in London. Jefferson's Temple was the office of Wythe; and his continental tour was a journey that took him to Annapolis, Philadelphia, and New York. No young blade of the Middle Ages, faring forth through primeval forests and along bandit-infested highways, could have had more misadventures than the young Virginian in the first stages of his journey. On the first day his horse took fright and ran away, imperiling his life, and then repeated the performance. The following day he rode drearily for two hours in a deluge of rain, unable to find a single house for shelter. On crossing an unfamiliar ford on the third day, the water was so deep it covered the cushion on which he sat, and one wheel mounted a rock as high as the axle, and, as he wrote to Page, 'rendered it necessary for me to exercise all my skill in the doctrine of gravity in order to prevent the center of gravity from being left unsupported.'

He stopped at the homes of friends en route, and at one of these he lingered for three days, since he found Sukey Potter there, but at length he reached Annapolis. He thought the Maryland capital 'extremely beautiful and very commodious for trade,' and noted that the houses were better than those of Williamsburg, but the gardens not so fine. He visited the Assembly, which amused him because of the utter lack of order and the picturesque costume of the Speaker. It was here the news reached him that the stamp tax had been repealed, and with the young men of the town he joined in the jubilation, which was to be found a bit premature.

Then on to Philadelphia, which was to furnish the setting for the most dramatic and immortal performance of his life but a few years later. But that which interested him most was the Philosophical Society and the work of the scientists. The doctors had just begun to inoculate for smallpox, and Jefferson, with the avid curiosity that always possessed him regarding the onward march of science, sought Doctor John Morgan, of the University of Pennsylvania, to whom he had a letter of introduction, to submit himself to the operation. It was on this visit that he made the acquaintance of the celebrated Doctor Shippen and a lifelong friendship was begun.

In New York he lived under the same roof with Elbridge Gerry, a young man of unusual promise and with a social background similar to his own. The house was in what is now the financial district near the Battery. Partial to dinners, dances, and the theater as he was, we can imagine the entertainment that he found. The friendship with Gerry was to continue uninterrupted for many years and to play an important part in the later political life and fortune of the young traveler.

The next year, in 1767, sponsored by no less a man than George

Wythe, Jefferson was admitted to the bar. He had devoted five years of intensive research and grueling labor to his preparation, delving deep, not only into the statutes, but into the fundamental principles and theories of the law, and few Americans of his time could have entered the practice so thoroughly equipped. The notations in his *Commonplace Book* denote the wide range of his legal studies, but quite as valuable to Jefferson must have been the long intimate conversations with Wythe.

He settled down seriously to the practice of his profession, maintaining chambers in Williamsburg.

The next two years found him preoccupied with his practice and his private affairs. That he was not unmindful of the political developments which were rushing the colonies toward a crisis, we must assume from his character; but, for the moment, the seething excitement over the Stamp Act had subsided; and, looking back at a later period, he was to conclude that during the two years following, the people seemed to have fallen 'into a state of insensibility and inaction.' While still living at Shadwell, in the house of his birth, Jefferson was planning and building the house on his favorite mountain he was to call 'Monticello.' Even while a student of law, he was leveling the hilltop. Having architectural ideas of his own, he prepared the plans for the mansion in detail, determined to make it a house of his heart's desire. In time, he succeeded in making it a poem in brick and mortar.

As it turned out, he had begun his building none too soon. In the spring of 1770, during his absence, his birthplace and home, where he lived with his mother and sisters, was burned to the ground. By this time he had accumulated a library, large and important for the time, and this was utterly wiped out, together with his papers.

He hurried to Shadwell, in despair over the loss of his books and papers, and one of the slaves ran to meet him with a beaming, satisfied face and the exclamation, 'Oh, my young master, they [the books] was burned up, but we done save your fiddle.' [17]

Jefferson had one pavilion of his house on the mountain available for quarters, and into this he moved. One room had to suffice as bedroom, study, sitting-room, and kitchen for a time. The loss of

[17] Randolph, *Domestic Life of Jefferson*.

the books was a blow, and, in a letter to Page, he lamented his fate:

> My late loss may, perhaps, have reached you by this time. I mean the loss of my mother's house by fire, and in it of every paper I had in the world and almost every book. On a reasonable estimate I calculate the cost of the books burned to have been 200 pounds sterling. Would to God it had been the money, then it never would have cost me a sigh. To make the loss more sensible, it fell principally on my books of common law, of which I have but one left, at that time lent out. Of papers, too, of every kind I am utterly destitute. All of these, whether public or private, of business or amusement, have perished in the flames. I had made some progress in preparing for the succeeding General Court; and having, as was my custom, thrown my thoughts into the form of notes, I troubled my head no more with them. These are gone, and, like the baseless fabric of a vision, leave not a trace behind.[18]

However, he turned at once to the restoration of a library. From Skipwith in London he received a catalogue, and within two years after the fire he could boast a library of twelve hundred and fifty volumes in his home — no mean acquisition for the time and place.

But even his loss failed to disturb his serenity or to change his playful disposition. In a letter to Page, with whom he occasionally visited at his home at 'Rosewell,' chiding him for his lack of punctuality in correspondence, his cavalier attitude toward attractive women looms large. If Page felt too dull to write, why not delegate the task to Mrs. Page? 'Methinks I should with wonderful pleasure open and peruse a letter written by so fair, and, what is better, so friendly hands,' he wrote. 'I reflect often with pleasure on the philosophical evenings at Rosewell in my last visit there. I was always fond of philosophy, even in its drier forms, but from a ruby lip it comes with charms irresistible. Such a feast of sentiment must exhilarate and lengthen life, at least as much as the feast of the sensualist shortens it.' In truth, were Page to assemble the company of previous visits, and give him three days' notice, he would 'certainly repair to [his] place as a member of it.' Indeed, he would be happier were he nearer Rosewell and Severn Hills, but he supposed the gods were 'apprehensive that if we were placed together, we should pull down the moon, or play some such devilish pranks with their works.' [19]

That at this age Jefferson was exceedingly susceptible to the charms of beautiful women there can be no doubt. It was about this time, in his twenty-fifth year, that he became infatuated with the young wife of an absent friend of the neighborhood and made advances that were repelled. Almost forty years later, when he was President and the victim of scurrility, a bitter enemy prevailed upon the husband to make specific charges which make sorry reading in history. The lady was a woman of charm and beauty, vivacious, and perhaps unconsciously seductive, and probably, without considering the consequences, not a little flirtatious. At any rate, the youth made love to the lady and was rebuffed. This is probably the whole of the story. But eager to give the Federalist scavengers a full measure, running over, even to the discomfiture of his wife, the husband charged that a year later, when it appears he had not scrupled to conduct his wife on a visit to the home of the gay seducer, Jefferson had 'renewed his caresses' and slipped into her gown sleeve cup a paper pleading the innocence of adultery. And not content with this, the outraged husband charged that on another occasion the wicked youth had stolen into his room where the lady was undressing or in bed. Even so, this did not dissuade him from inviting the dangerous young man to spend the night at his house, where he made another assault upon the lady's virtue.

When this amazing indictment was made public, and it was written for that purpose in a period of incredibly bitter and unscrupulous political struggle, Jefferson made no reply in public. But for the sake of the record he wrote a personal letter to two members of his Cabinet (Levi Lincoln and Robert Smith). 'I plead guilty to one of the charges,' he wrote, 'that when young and single I offered love to a handsome lady. I acknowledge its incorrectness. It is the only one founded in truth in all their allegations against me.' [20] That this youth of twenty-five, susceptible to women, was not 'pure as light and stainless as a star,' we would prefer to believe. But the rash and persistent pursuit after the rebuff is not in character.

[19] *Ibid.*
[20] Marie Kimball, *Jefferson*, 142-46.

It was not long after this incident that the young squire of Monticello was attracted to another lady with more serious intent. Belinda was gone, probably unmourned, and the married charmer was an unpleasant memory, when a young widow appeared in Jefferson's path.

A few years before, this young daughter of John Wayles, described by Jefferson as a lawyer with a large practice because of his 'great industry, punctuality, and practical readiness,' and as 'a most agreeable companion, full of pleasantry and good humor and welcomed in every society,' had been left a widow at twenty-three.[21] Her husband, Bathurst Skelton, had died soon after her marriage, leaving no issue. She was living with her father on his fine estate, 'The Forest,' in Charles City County. Thither numerous young gentlemen, not unmindful of the fact that in addition to the attraction of the widow was the wealth of the father, beat a pathway, and among these was Jefferson. Frequently he found his way to 'The Forest,' and while appreciating the genial companionship of the father, it was clear that it was the company of the daughter he sought. She was beautiful, a little above medium height, and 'with a lithe and exquisitely formed figure, with a graceful and queenlike carriage.'[22] But she possessed other qualities that appealed as much to the young suitor from Monticello. She was better educated than the average Virginia belle of the day and her mind was superior. She read more widely than most and could discuss books with intelligence and discrimination. From her father she had inherited a capacity for business, and he entrusted her with the keeping of the accounts of the plantations. Thus, she was well qualified as a helpmate on a large estate. But nothing appealed more to Jefferson than her love of music and her accomplishments as a musician. When he appeared at 'The Forest,' he played the fiddle to her singing, and often they sang together. This gave Jefferson such an advantage over his two principal rivals that they finally abandoned the field in despair. There was a tradition in the family that the two rivals happened to call at 'The Forest' at the same time and met in the hall leading to the drawing-room. From within they heard Jefferson playing and Martha singing. They looked at each other in

21 *Autobiography*, 4.
22 Randolph, *Domestic Life of Jefferson*, 44.

consternation, accepted their fate, and, taking their hats, departed, leaving Jefferson in undisputed possession of the field.[23]

Jefferson and Martha were married on New Year's Day in 1772 at 'The Forest' when she was twenty-three and he six years her senior. After the festivities they began their drive of many miles to Monticello, which was scarcely ready for the reception of a bride. It was the dead of winter and very cold. The snow was falling when they started and the roads were bad at best. As their carriage rumbled over the intermediate miles, the snow increased alarmingly in depth. The carriage made hard going, and at length the young couple abandoned the vehicle, mounted the horses, and pressed on. They paused for a brief rest at 'Blenheim,' where only an overseer was in charge, and then, with courage renewed, they dared the mountain track at sunset. They were still eight miles from Monticello, and the snow was from eighteen to twenty-four inches deep. When, late at night, they reached the unfinished house upon the hill, they found the servants in bed and the fires all out. Without awakening the servants and in the spirit of a lark, they took up their quarters merrily in a room of a finished pavilion. Rummaging among the books on a shelf, they found a bottle of wine to warm the blood after the chill of the journey. Drinking the wine, their spirits rose, and soon the deserted hilltop reverberated with the joyous singing of the lovers.[24]

A little later, Martha's father died, and the portion of his estate that fell to Martha doubled the holdings of Jefferson. His own reference to the fact is the only justification I can find for the conclusion of some biographers that the marriage was a 'marriage of convenience.' The wooing had not been perfunctory nor cold, and the profound love that marked their married life makes more than questionable any such conclusion.

VIII

But, if Jefferson had gained a devoted friend, he was soon to lose one. Dabney Carr, married now to Jefferson's sister, Martha, died after a brief illness. We have seen these two friends in the exchange of boyish confidences and ambitions, tramping the fields to the

[23] *Ibid.*   [24] *Ibid.*

great oak tree on the slopes of the mountain crowned by Monticello, to stretch upon the grass with their reading and discussions. Their relations were those of Damon and Pythias. Their love was real. They had become so delighted with their favorite oak that in boyhood they had promised one another that the first to die should be buried beneath it. Some years had passed. Carr's genius as a political thinker and his gifts as an orator had blossomed. He had entered the House of Burgesses with Jefferson, and just a little while before he had made his début on a notable occasion through the contriving of Jefferson, and his brilliant eloquence had convinced those who heard him that Henry would have to look to his laurels as a speaker. Jefferson, later, was to recall that début:

> I well remember [he wrote] the pleasure expressed in the countenance and conversation of the members generally on the début of Mr. Carr, and the hopes they conceived as well from his talents as his patriotism it manifested. . . . His character was of a high order. A spotless integrity, sound judgment, handsome imagination enriched by education and reading, quick and clear in his conceptions, of correct and ready elocution, impressing every hearer with the sincerity of the heart from which it flowed. His firmness was inflexible in what he thought was right; but when no moral principle stood in the way, never had man more of the milk of human kindness, of indulgence, of softness, of pleasantry of conversation and conduct.

He died suddenly during Jefferson's absence and was buried at Shadwell. On Jefferson's return he had the body disinterred and laid to rest under the favorite oak on the slope of Monticello, in accordance with the boyish pledge. Later, Jefferson, his wife, and immediate family were to be buried in the same ground.

The widow of Carr and his six children were taken into Jefferson's household at Monticello, and he was to give his personal supervision to the education of the children.

IX

Meanwhile, Jefferson had been elected by his county to the House of Burgesses, but, in the organization of this narrative, it is best, perhaps, to begin with the chronicle of his political career after the conclusion of his activities at the bar, since he was to abandon the practice for politics and public service.

His laborious preparation for the bar was to bear rich fruit and to have an early blossoming. Immediately he entered upon a large, and, for those days, a lucrative practice. He maintained chambers at Williamsburg and commuted back and forth whenever possible to Monticello, besides riding the circuit of neighboring counties. Too much has been made of the fact that a weakness of the voice, an incurable shyness, and an utter distaste for self-dramatization deprived him of the laurels of a fine forensic orator. Brilliant though he was as a conversationalist, he was too self-conscious to display his talents on a stage. Few could have written a more eloquent oration, but it has been assumed from many of his biographers that few could have done less justice to it in delivery. But it must not be taken for granted from this that he was not strong and impressive in arguments before a court. No less an authority than Edmund Randolph in his history of Virginia gives us an entirely different picture:

> Indefatigable and methodical, Jefferson spoke with ease, perspicacity, and elegance. Without being an overwhelming orator, he was an impressive speaker who fixed the attention. In two signal arguments before the General Court in which Mr. Henry and himself were coadjutors, each characterized himself. Mr. Jefferson drew copiously from the depths of the law, Mr. Henry from the recesses of the human heart.[25]

From which we may conclude that before the Supreme Court of our own times, Mr. Henry's method would have been more annoying than convincing, and Mr. Jefferson's more impressive and effective.

The conclusion of some biographers that he despised oratory is just as confusing. We have seen that he considered its study one of the essentials. His enthusiasm for Henry's eloquence was freely expressed, and his delight over the forensic triumph of Dabney Carr was manifest. It is true that he had little regard for the purely rhetorical or florid discourses of his day, since he insisted on concise and cogent reasoning, simplicity and directness; and throughout his life the loquacity and superficiality, the pose and pretense of mediocrity, repelled him. In some parliamentary bodies he resented the

25 Randolph MSS.

consumption of time by pompous poseurs who had no real contribution to make to the debate. His own self-training in condensation made him impatient with superficial speakers, having more heat than light, who meandered over the field aimlessly and at interminable length without terminal facilities and without adding anything in reasoning to the subject under discussion. But he had a deep respect for real eloquence, and, if he did not figure at the bar as a great advocate, it was due to his temperamental and physical disqualifications and his knowledge of his own limitations.

He became, therefore, and remained, what may now be described as a great legal counselor and office lawyer. Williamsburg was not a great metropolis, but in the first year of his practice he recorded in his register sixty-eight cases. Thereafter, until the Revolution ended his legal career, the register shows at least a hundred cases a year. In 1771, he had four hundred and thirty cases, and it appears in the biographies of the leading Virginia lawyers of the time that only George Wythe, Pendleton, and Henry, all his seniors, had larger practices; and not only were these older men, but the last two appeared in many cases calling for dramatic appeals. Henry had a much larger criminal practice, but Jefferson figured in more civil suits. He brought to every case an erudition in the law equaled probably by none but Wythe. Though many of his cases were of the routine sort, involving estates and money, and while he gave to every case the fullness of his equipment, he was occasionally fortunate enough to have a case involving the fundamentals, and these called forth his utmost endeavors.

During his period at the bar he was a working lawyer, devoting himself assiduously to his clients. In view of his interest in the fundamentals and the principles of the law, he must have been irked at times with the usual sordid matters that demanded his attention — quarrels over the building of fences, the trespassing of stock, the defense or challenging of wills, the administration of estates, with occasional cases of assault and battery. These also constituted much of the routine practice of his three rivals. If he was not spectacular in passionate and persuasive appeals to prejudices and emotions, he was ideally equipped for the presentation, to the judges of the General Court, of facts and the legal principles applying to them. He had all the qualifications to have become a distinguished jurist had fortune taken him to the bench instead of into the field of practical politics.

Two of his cases have an abiding interest, and happily he has himself given us the substance of his arguments in his *Reports of Cases Determined in the General Court of Virginia,* published after his death. The most significant of the two cases, that of Howell *vs.* Netherland, was argued by Jefferson in his twenty-seventh year, and called forth opinions, humanitarian and political, with which few Virginians of his day could have had much sympathy. The facts follow:

> In 1705, sixty-five years before, a white woman gave birth to a mulatto by a negro. The law of the time sentenced her to service or slavery until she reached her thirty-first year. During the years of her servitude, she gave birth to a daughter, and in time the daughter gave birth to a son. This son was sold into slavery by the slave-owner to whom the grandmother was bound and the new owner claimed his service until his thirty-first year. There was no questioning of the legality of the proceeding in the case of the grandmother. Jefferson admitted that the Act of 1705 doomed the first mulatto to slavery, and that another Act in 1723 extended the sentence to her children, but in the absence of further legislation he insisted that there was no law which reached to the grandson. 'It remains for some future legislature, if any shall be found wicked enough, to extend [slavery] to the grandchildren and other issue more remote,' he said.

But we are interested primarily in the argument, reflecting as it does Jefferson's deeply rooted political opinions of human rights, with which the country was soon to be familiar. I suppose, he said, it will not be pretended that the mother, being a servant, the child would be a servant also under the law of nature, without any particular provision of the act. Under the law of nature, all men are born free; everyone comes into the world with a right to his own person, which includes the liberty of moving and using it at his own will. This is what is called personal liberty, and is given him by the author of nature, because necessary for his own sustenance. Therefore, he audaciously declared, the reducing of the mother to servitude was a violation of the law of nature. Could the law, then, prescribe a continuance of the violation to her issue, and that, too, without end? Because, he said, if it extends to any, it must be to every degree of descendants.

Though he cited classic authority to support his argument, the court was shocked and thoroughly impatient. 'The law of nature'? 'All men are born free'? 'Personal liberty'? Dangerous and subversive doctrine, thought the court, and when Wythe, employed on the other side, rose to reply, he was motioned to his seat and judgment instantly was rendered for his client. Jefferson's client, the boy, went into slavery.[26]

The other case involved the jurisdiction of the courts in ecclesiastical matters. A clergyman named Lunan, in the upper parish of the county of Nansemond, had become a sore trial to the church wardens and vestrymen of the parish, and they appealed to the General Court, as a court of ecclesiastical jurisdiction, for his removal and punishment. It appears they charged he was 'of evil fame and profligate manners'; that he was given to drunkenness and was often so drunk in church that he was unable to perform his priestly functions; that he frequently appeared in church in apparel fantastic and unbecoming a minister; that he disturbed the peace, and quarreled and fought and used profane language. Other charges were even more indecent. Jefferson appeared for the wardens and vestrymen. Lunan pleaded to the jurisdiction of the court and the issue was made.

In his argument, Jefferson's deep delving into ecclesiastical history stood him in good stead, for he was able to cite historical precedents as far back as 854, and was able to convince the court that it 'possessed ecclesiastical jurisdiction, and that, as an ecclesiastical court, it might proceed to censure the defendant if there should be just cause.' The court agreed and Jefferson won his case at the age of twenty-eight.

The young lawyer's keen interest in the relation of Church and State, which was soon to enter into his battle for reforms, was clearly aroused by the case, for in an appendix to his *Reports* he makes the observation that the English judges had a 'pious disposition ... to connive at the frauds of the clergy.'[27]

At the time Jefferson disposed of his practice and retired, his in-

26 Jefferson's *Reports*; Marie Kimball, *Jefferson*, 93-95.   27 *Ibid.*

come from the law alone amounted to about three thousand dollars, which was large in the period and place. Like most of his Virginia contemporaries, he appeared occasionally without fee; and the lawyers were amazingly modest in the fixing of their fees, as Jefferson's record shows. That many clients were careless about the paying of fees at all is indicated by a notice published in the *Virginia Gazette,* and signed by Pendleton, John Randolph, Henry, and Jefferson, that after October 10, they would 'not give an opinion in any case stated to us but on payment of the whole fee, nor prosecute nor defend any suit or motion unless the tax and one-half of the fee be previously advanced, excepting those cases only when we choose to act gratis.' In justification of their action, they set forth that 'the fees allowed by law, if regularly paid, would barely compensate our incessant labors, reimburse our expenses and the losses incurred by the neglect of our private affairs.' [28]

The facts that Jefferson appeared regularly with the greatest lawyers in the colony, was busily engaged, and numbered among his clients such important personages as Lord Fairfax, William Byrd, Benjamin Harrison, and Richard Henry Lee attest his distinguished success in the practice of his profession.

X

At this time the combined income of his practice and from his farms was opulent enough, but he made no pretensions, continuing with his two horses and a phaeton instead of the coach and six that the grandees favored. He found infinite pleasure in planning improvements at Monticello, and this was to continue his favorite diversion for many years. He took his duties as the master of a large plantation seriously, teaching the slaves various trades useful on the estate. He was bent on making his plantation as self-contained as possible. Astride his blooded horse, he daily visited every nook and corner of his domain. The early hours of the afternoon, when at home, invariably found him on horseback, and he was then a daring equestrian. Until he had passed middle age he never drew rein because of broken ground or minor obstacles, and he would urge his horse into the Rivanna River when it was in flood

[28] *Virginia Gazette,* May 20, 1773.

and turbulent. Nothing pleased him more than to coax his favorite mounts into doing stunts for the delectation and delight of admiring neighbors and to the consternation of his family.

These were the halcyon days of his life. He had built, or was still building, the house of his heart's desire. At the age of twenty-six he was the master of his destiny, the proprietor of broad acres, related to the best families in Virginia, and admired and appreciated by all his neighbors as a brilliant and sound adviser on public affairs. Still a British subject, he had been honored by the Royal Government, when Governor Botetourt had made him 'Chief Commander of His Majesty's Horse and Foot' in his county of Albemarle. His college of William and Mary had honored him with the appointment of surveyor of his county. And his people had chosen him as their spokesman in the House of Burgesses.

Such was the background of a youth of twenty-six when he entered the Assembly and plunged as a patriot into the midst of the struggle for the conservation and vindication of the rights of the Americans under the British Constitution.

YOUNG-MEN-IN-A-HURRY

I

ONE DAY in 1769, all sorts and conditions of men — planters, farmers, frontiersmen — might have been seen wending their way hilariously to Shadwell near Charlottesville, and even more noisily wending their way back again, for they had been welcomed by the master of the house with an abundance of heady punch and the hearty handshake of an aspiring young politician. Young Jefferson, aged twenty-six, was a candidate for the House of Burgesses, and, after the generous fashion of the Virginians, he was holding open house. No one of his neighbors but knew his mettle and his caliber, for the young squire's studious habits and professional ability had been impressed upon them. Similar scenes might have been witnessed all over the Old Dominion, for Washington, Henry, and Pendleton were likewise smiling on the sovereign people. Jefferson's election was a foregone conclusion.

Thus it was that, in May, when the countryside was fragrant with flowers and foliage, Jefferson rode over the dusty road to Williamsburg for the meeting of the legislature. It was like going to a second home, and he knew what to expect. The Raleigh Tavern would be seething with solons and their wives and daughters, and noisy with the clicking of glasses and loud laughter. The houses, closed during the recess of the legislature, would be thrown open to air and sunshine for the welcoming back of the pretty girls and anxious, designing matrons of the wealthier planters, and soon the Apollo Room would reel with the dance. In the unpaved street, belles and beaux would resume their everlasting promenade, drawing back on the approach of pretentious coaches to spare their clothing from the dust and sand. Perhaps a traveling company of players would regale the sojourners of the village capital with good or indifferent presentations of the dramas of Shakespeare, Congreve, and lesser men. There would be parties in the freshly opened houses of the town and in the mansion houses of the near-by plantations, and on their spacious grounds with their flowering trees; there would be racing and cockfighting, and the *Virginia Gazette* would give fair warning. In this cavalcade of men and women in pursuit of pleasure would move not a few men destined to immortality in the making of a nation.

But Fauquier, the friend of the young lawmaker, who had contributed to his polishing, would no longer be in the Governor's Palace to delight him with dinner-table conversation. He had passed from the scene and was sleeping now beneath the stone flooring of Burton parish church. A little while before, a successor had arrived with much éclat, entering the capital in a coach of state drawn by eight milk-white horses and to the merry cracking of whips. It was thus that he appeared for the opening of the session. It was an imitation of the opening of Parliament in London by the King. The state coach had been presented him by George III, or by the King's brother, for the purpose. And the ceremonious opening of the legislative session was patterned as closely as possible after that at Saint Stephen's. Strangely enough, this display of elegance and opulence, intended to delight the people, had a reverse effect. Suspicious now, after the stamp tax and the Townshend duties, they interpreted the display as an attempt to overawe them into submission to the will of London.[1]

Lord Botetourt, the new Royal Governor, had come with the best intentions in the world and with a view to conciliation. He was to live within the colony at the capital, as one of the people. He had decent instincts and his feelings were friendly. No ruler was ever more easily accessible to the people. He saw and gave cordial greeting to everyone who called, even though many were moved solely by curiosity.[2] And toward Lord Botetourt, personally, the people warmed in appreciation of his qualities.

The prancing white horses drew the ornate coach to the legislative

[1] Burk, *History of Virginia,* III, 342.   [2] *Ibid.,* III, 362.

hall, the Governor was received with the ceremony that the King exacted at Saint Stephen's, and he delivered his speech 'from the throne.' It was a conciliatory address of polite inanities. But, after the fashion of Saint Stephen's, it called for a reply, for 'a most humble, dutiful address,' and the twenty-six-year-old gentleman from Albemarle was designated by his colleagues to prepare it. Nothing is indicated here beyond a disposition to encourage the green member of whose precocious talents most had heard.

And here the sensitive author was to suffer a humiliation. Nothing could have been more dutiful or humble than Jefferson's address. Botetourt was warmly thanked for his 'very affectionate speech,' and something was injected about the people's devotion to 'His Majesty's sacred person.' Yes, and in all matters relating to the welfare of the British Empire, His Excellency might be assured that they would be approached with a full realization 'that her interests and ours are inseparably the same.' The most case-hardened Tory might well have been content with the obsequiousness of the wording, but flattery could not be too fulsome for a creature of the King, and Jefferson suffered the mortification of having his address pronounced unsatisfactory. Never again was the embarrassed author to parrot the language of a courtier.

During his first term he had another rebuff when he failed in his effort to get legal permission for slave-owners to emancipate their slaves if they wished. Throughout his life we shall find him always opposed to slavery and making numerous attempts to pave the way to its extermination; and it is significant that one of his first moves in the legislature was in this direction. Unfairly, perhaps, he ascribed his failure to the reactionary spirit of the Royal Government. 'Indeed, during the regal government, nothing liberal could expect success,' he wrote, later, in his *Autobiography*. 'Our minds were circumscribed within narrow limits by an habitual belief that it was our duty to be subordinate to the mother country in all matters of government, to direct all our labors to subservience to her interests, and even to observe a bigoted intolerance for all religions but hers.' [3]

Within a few days he was to have ample opportunity to demonstrate his repudiation of that course.

[3] *Autobiography*, 3.

II

The sweetening effect of the repeal of the Stamp Act speedily soured and turned to bitter resentment when Parliament passed the Townshend Act, which again imposed taxation on the colonies without their representation in the process. Even the debate on the repeal of the stamp tax disclosed a grim determination on the part of the die-hards to hold on to the right of Parliament to levy taxes on the colonies, with or without their consent. The superb eloquence of Chatham, rejoicing that Americans resisted, since 'three million people, so dead to all feelings of liberty as voluntarily to submit to be slaves, would be fit instruments to make slaves of all the rest of us,' had no effect. The Government, leading a majority, predicated its proposal for repeal on the sordid ground that it had turned out to be 'bad for business,' and that the British merchants wished it repealed. Chatham thundered that it should be repealed 'absolutely, totally and immediately,' since it was un-English, unconstitutional, and contrary to a thousand years of English history, but to no avail. The most significant feature of the debate, and the most disturbing to the colonies, was that so many of the governmental advocates of repeal made emphatic their insistence on the right of Parliament to force taxes on the colonies without their voice being heard in the halls of Saint Stephen's. This stupid, stubborn statesmanship, without vision or imagination, was driving under the lash the most conservative Americans, attached to the connection with the Empire, into the ranks of the radicals. The moderate Washington at this time was writing Mason of Gunston Hall that 'our lordly masters in Great Britain will be satisfied with nothing less than the deprivation of American freedom,' and that steps should be taken 'to avert the stroke and maintain the liberty which we have derived from our ancestors.' Armed revolution? This moderate friend of the connection thought that 'no man should scruple or hesitate a moment to use arms in defense of so valuable a blessing,' but he would use them as a 'last resort.' [4]

It could not, therefore, be wholly unexpected when, in the next session of the Parliament, Charles Townshend made his fatal blunder. He is known to the American people largely because of

[4] Rowland, *Life of George Mason,* I, 139.

this stupid act of his. His brilliancy is beyond all question, but his weaknesses were known to his English contemporaries. One of these, Tobias Smollett, the novelist, who observed him in the flesh, has described him in *Humphrey Clinker* with such perfect fidelity that the appraisement of all historians might have been based on the estimate of this clever man of literature:

> He certainly knows more than all the Ministry and all the Opposition, if their heads were laid together, and talks like an angel on a vast variety of subjects. He would really be a great man if he had any consistency or stability of character. Then, it must be owned, he wants courage, otherwise he would never allow himself to be cowed by the great political bully, for whose understanding he has justly a very great contempt. . . . Besides this defect, Charles has another which he is at no little pains to hide. There is no faith to be given to his assertions, and no trust to be put in his promises. However, to give the devil his due, he is very good-natured; and even friendly, when close urged in the way of solicitation. As for principles, that's out of the question. In a word, he is a wit and an orator, extremely entertaining, and he shines very often at the expense of even those ministers to whom he is a retainer. . . . His vanity runs away with his discretion.

Aside from the assumption that he knew more than all the opposition, including Burke and Chatham, this portrait harmonizes with that of history. He stands high on the not inconsequential roll of the most brilliant failures in English history.

The Townshend Act levied taxes on the colonies, insisting on the right, and providing for the quartering of unwanted and unneeded soldiers on the colonists, to be paid for from the revenue thus raised, according to the militant element. Taxes were levied on numerous articles, including glass, white and red lead, tea and paper imported by Americans.

In addition, as though bent on prodding the Americans to revolution, a law was proposed providing that Americans charged with certain offenses, mostly political, should not be tried by their own countrymen, but should be sent three thousand miles to England for their trial. This act broke in with a jar on the rejoicing over the repeal of the stamp tax.

So it was that, after the gay and gaudy ceremonial attending the formal opening of the Assembly, the members awaited some word from Lord Botetourt as to the disposition of the Government toward matters in controversy.

When not one word was uttered, the members turned with zest to the consideration of a circular appeal from the militant patriots of Massachusetts, who had been thoroughly aroused by the crusading of Samuel Adams, requesting the sister colonies to join with her in organizing a fighting resistance to the new duties.

Within three days four resolutions were offered and passed, denouncing taxation without representation and the despotic proposal to send Americans charged with political offenses to London for trial, and consenting to the co-operation of the colonies for the redress of grievances. An address to the King asking for this intervention was promised.

Apparently it did not occur to these loyal men that it was the King himself, and not the English people, who was responsible for the grievances complained of. Not a few of the ablest men in Parliament, under the leadership of Chatham and Burke, fought the imposition tooth and nail. The mass of the English people not only were in complete ignorance of what was transpiring, but had they known they would have been utterly without power to alter the policy of the Ministry. Their voice in the government of England at that time was feeble.

An English historian has written that at this time seven hundred voters elected fifty-six members of the House of Commons, while eleven thousand voters elected but two hundred and fifty-four. Land and possessions counted for more than men. The beautiful but scantily populated shires of Cornwall sent as many representatives to the Commons as London; while important industrial towns, such as Manchester, had no more representation in Parliament than Virginia or Massachusetts.

In many sections, notably in Scotland, elections were a mockery. The King and his clique, the landed gentry, manipulated these with the recklessness of political racketeers, completely without scruple. And just as the people were victims of a system, even the Ministers of the King were scarcely more than vassals. 'George III dragged his ministers along the path of coercion, not to please the people, but to please himself,' says an English writer.[5]

5 Hirst, *Life and Letters of Thomas Jefferson*, 36.

Thus, the threat to ask for the intervention of the King must have brought a cynical smile to the pale lips of Botetourt. He, too, was the victim of a system, though he was growing restive under the yoke. But he had a duty to perform. He was merely the servant of the King, as subservient as the valet or the groom.

III

On receiving an intimation that such resolutions had been prepared, Botetourt was making an effort to get a copy, when the members, fearing a dissolution before the resolutions could be passed, assembled instantly on the ringing of the bell, and rushed them through and on the record. At noon on the following day the Governor summoned the Speaker to his presence and dissolved the Assembly.

The stage-setting of the Revolution now shifts. Driven from their legislative halls, twenty-eight of the more than one hundred members filed the next day into the Apollo Room of the Raleigh, the scene of so much dancing and flirting. The militants were still in a minority. Eight years before, Richard Henry Lee had written his brother in London that not more than one-third of the members were democrats.[6] But among the twenty-eight were four men of heroic stature destined to immortality in the making of the nation — George Washington, Thomas Jefferson, Patrick Henry, and Richard Henry Lee. The last three, especially, were chafing under the restraining hand of the old and more conservative leaders of the oligarchy of the aristocracy.

Here, in the small room of a country tavern, they formed the Non-Importation Association and pledged its members against the purchase of British merchandise so long as the Townshend Act remained among the statutes. They agreed to buy no articles taxed for revenue except paper which was indispensable. They would keep their sheep for the wool and have it spun and woven at home, rather than buy English cloth.

Having thus perfected an organization of open resistance, the members returned to their constituents to be triumphantly re-elected. The Revolution was on the march.

[6] *Memoirs of the Life of Richard Henry Lee*, I, 20.

Jefferson was now launched upon his revolutionary career. If the pledges given were redeemed, it would be a blow to British trade. No more carriages, furniture or tables, chairs or mirrors, no more pewter, jewelry, gold or silverware, no more laces, millinery or ribbons, no more linen, calico, or cotton goods, no more stockings, boots or shoes, no more fabrics or spices from India — no more of these from English merchants.

The court in London smiled over this 'childish gesture,' but Botetourt was not so optimistic. He knew the caliber of the patriots.

IV

And he knew them to be practical men.

Instantly, therefore, in all the counties, beginning in the Tidewater region of the wealthy planters, committees were organized to supervise and rigidly enforce the non-importation pledge. Men of stature and local prestige formed the personnel of these committees, and they took their duties in grim earnest. Many of the small merchants resented this extra-legal interference with their profits, but drastic action forced most of them into line. The patriots dispensed at this stage with drawing-room amenities in dealing with men who would subordinate patriotism to profit.

Every county was divided into small districts with a subcommittee charged with the most meticulous investigations into violations of the agreement. Soon a perfect system of espionage covered the colony. And the power of these committees was unlimited. They walked into the stores of the merchants and forced them to show their books, and woe to the wite thus betrayed by his ledger. When merchants took advantage of the scarcity to increase prices, they were taken roughly in hand. When charges were brought against alleged violators of the agreement, they were summoned summarily before the committee to exonerate themselves or stand condemned. If guilty and contrite, they were given one more opportunity to make good; if belligerent, they were denounced and advertised as enemies of their country; and few dared popular contempt by trading with a merchant thus proclaimed.

Rigid and uncompromising as the committees were, there was no violence and no injustice. It was an orderly revolution, directed in each county by men of character and substance, and many, falsely accused, were speedily exonerated. The guilty suffered. It was in these days that the die-hard Tories began their exodus from the colony. Never, perhaps, in any revolutionary movement was such order maintained and such judicial fairness exercised by men who had no limitations on their power.

Young Jefferson, foremost among the younger men in the creation of these committees, played his part in their enforcement in his own county of Albemarle.[7]

V

The light laughter of London over the comic antics of the rustics of the colonies in the boycotting of British goods was silenced suddenly when it was found that the English manufacturers and merchants were nine hundred thousand pounds worse off in trade. And Botetourt was sympathetic toward the Virginians. He had come with an honest desire to effect a reconciliation, even before he met them and found grotesque the preconceived notions of their character, capacity, and culture. When, courageously, he had made known to London the reactions of these people to the arbitrary acts that had harassed them, the Ministry had led him to believe that it proposed to change its policy in the interest of conciliation. Happy in this promise, he again summoned the Assembly.

We are now approaching the climactic period in Virginia history and in the career of Jefferson. If he had not won the laurels of eloquence in his brief time in the Assembly, the oldest and wisest of the statesmen had been deeply impressed with the breadth and depth of his erudition, the soundness of his judgment, the clarity of his opinions, the intensity of his political convictions, and the value of his counsels. It was no mean achievement to have made that reputation in the House of Burgesses of that time.

For this Assembly, if not housed in marble halls, challenged in dignity and worth any other in the world, not excepting the Parliament of England. The utmost decorum was exacted of its members. No one could absent himself without leave, except in the case of sickness. When the Speaker rose to put a question, no one could

[7] Eckenrode, *The Revolution in Virginia,* 96-122.

engage in conversation on the floor, stand up, walk in or out or across the room, or read a book. On any question in which any member was personally and immediately involved, he was forbidden to cast a vote. No one was permitted to enter the council chamber before the Speaker, and when the members went through the halls to attend the Governor, the passages were cleared of visitors. No member could use indecent or disrespectful language in the presence of the Speaker, and, not without justification in those robustious days, there was a rigid rule forbidding the chewing of tobacco.[8] It was a decorous and serious Assembly.

And such an Assembly! Seldom in history, never in American history, have more men of distinguished merit gathered for the making of the laws. A stranger, standing in the entrance and surveying the scene, could not have formed the most remote idea of their true greatness. He would have been impressed by their dignified demeanor, the keen intelligence stamped upon their countenances, and the courtly manner of most, but no more. A native cicerone, by pointing out the celebrities, might convince him that he was in the presence of a goodly company, though some, destined to live into future centuries, were then little more than local figures.

Thus, the native might call the stranger's attention to a stiff and stately figure whose manner and movements denoted a consciousness of superiority and power, and inform him that this was George Washington, a planter of Mount Vernon, who had fought in the Indian and foreign wars with more than ordinary skill. But there was nothing dramatic in his bearing, and he was mostly silent, but attentive.

But the rather awkward figure, so clearly indifferent to dress, and, at first glance, insignificant in appearance, was not unknown to fame, and the stranger's interest might kindle at the mention of the name of Patrick Henry, whose torrential eloquence already had gone over the continent like an electric current. No doubt, the native, pointing out the celebrities, would be an admirer, and would tell how the great George Mason once declared that had Henry lived 'in Rome at the time of the first Punic War, when the Roman people had arrived at their meridian glory, his talent would have

[8] Hilldrup, *Life and Times of Edmund Pendleton,* 81.

put him at the head of the glorious commonwealth.' Perhaps he would relate some current stories of the orator's simplicity and indifference to fashion — how once he had displayed a coat the worse for wear with the remark: 'Here is a coat good enough for me; yet I must get a new one to please the eyes of other people.'[9] The stranger might, if sensitive to atmosphere, detect, among the older and more staid and conventional, a certain aloofness toward the firebrand.

Perhaps the traveler, observing a tall, powerfully built man who seemed so much at home in the Assembly, and so much admired and trusted by his colleagues, would inquire his identity. 'Ah,' the native would explain, 'that is Peyton Randolph,' and then launch into a panegyric on his virtues and career. A generation before, at the age of twenty-five, he had served as Attorney General, and he was not new to the Assembly, where he surpassed all others as a parliamentarian. Not in eloquence, but by the sheer weight of his reasoning, did he impress his views. Distinguished as a lawyer, trusted as a statesman, conservative in his tendencies, but patriotic to the core, he, more than any other, seemed to hold the confidence of his associates.[10]

'And the slender man standing so erect, with the magnificent sweep of forehead, the penetrating gray eyes, the Roman nose, and the prominent adamantine chin?' inquires the stranger. 'That,' replies the native proudly, 'that is George Wythe, learned in the law, leader of the bar, courageous and independent in his public conduct, and stout defender of colonial rights within the framework of the Empire, proud of the English connection, but militant in his demand that British citizenship, even in America, should carry British rights.'

'And the handsome man with whom he is talking?' asks the visitor, indicating a man six feet in height, with a lithe, graceful form, luxuriant hair, alert blue eyes, with the suave courtly manner of a gentleman. With a smile the native would reply that this was Edmund Pendleton, one of Wythe's two rivals for the leadership

---

[9] Grigsby, *The Virginia Convention of 1776*, 152-53.
[10] Wirt, *Sketches of the Life and Character of Patrick Henry*, 45; Grigsby *The Virginia Convention of 1776*, 61.

of the bar, a great advocate with a richly stored and disciplined mind, and with a silvery voice that charmed like the song of a nightingale. A patriot, too, though he had frowned on Patrick Henry's outburst on the stamp tax, for he believed in moving slowly in the legalistic groove and conciliating the mother country by patience. And what dexterity in parliamentary debate! Count on him to find the crack in his opponent's armor. To which the native would add that he was the champion and spokesman of the old aristocratic oligarchy of the Tidewater and the James, himself the owner of ten thousand acres and many slaves. All agreed that he was a patriot, held in check by that dread of change inherent in the legalistic mind.[11]

And now, his eyes roaming over the Assembly, the stranger's notice falls on an old man, seemingly bent with age, his complexion that of parchment, his blue eyes dimmed with time and usage, and clearly almost blind, to whom all men showed deference. That, explains the native, is Richard Bland, and, despite his frailty, only fifty-eight. But his had been a laborious life devoted to his country. 'Old Antiquarian,' they called him, because he was an encyclopedia of history. In some respects his fame just then surpassed that of any of his contemporaries of Virginia, since, but two years before, his pamphlet, *An Inquiry into the Rights of the British Colonies,* the earliest written exposition of the American position, had made a stir that had reached across the sea; and before that, his controversy with the clergy over the reduction of their salaries had brought forth two pamphlets, *A Letter to the Clergy of Virginia* and *The Colonel Dismounted,* that had won the acclaim of the patriots. At this moment he was easily their foremost champion of the pen. The scion of an old family, educated at William and Mary, he had entered the Assembly more than a quarter of a century before, and had notably identified himself with the struggle for colonial rights. But he, too, was of the old oligarchy, devoted to the connection with the mother country, and still wedded to the hope that American rights could be won by argument. Like Pendleton and Wythe, he frowned impatiently on the impetuosity of

[11] Grigsby, *The Virginia Convention of 1776,* 46-55; Wirt, *Sketches of Henry,* 40-41; Hilldrup, *Life of Pendleton,* 11.

the young-men-in-a-hurry, one of whom very soon would supplant him as the literary draftsman of the Revolution.[12]

The traveler's eye now falls on a tall man with delicate features and slightly bald, listening deferentially to Bland. 'That,' explains the native, 'is Robert Carter Nicholas,' another of the little coterie of conservatives who had dominated the Assembly. He describes him as an able lawyer and financier, one of the mouthpieces of the old aristocracy, and, if not an eloquent speaker, a strong and resourceful debater. Something would be told of his aggressive championship of the Established Church, of his defending salaries of the clergy as he would the Ark of the Covenant, and of his denouncing the suggestion of a separation of Church and State as sacrilege: a very religious man as well as a churchman, austere but benevolent, implacably honest, and capable of sacrificing pecuniary interests to public service. But, like the other appeasers, he was willing to suffer much and long in the hope of softening the heart of the King and his ministers.[13]

And now a Falstaffian figure, fantastically overfed and fat, but with his not unattractive face beaming with the humor of one whose inner man is completely satisfied, joins Bland and Nicholas and our visitor lifts his eyebrows in mute interrogation. 'Ah,' says the native with a smile, 'that is Ben Harrison,' of one of the oldest families, a fluent and rapid if not brilliant speaker, and equally capable with both voice and pen, a veteran and skilled parliamentarian, a good politician, respected for his common sense, his courage, and his love of the Old Dominion and its rights under the British tradition. Even-tempered, frank and open, cheerful and amusing, he invariably had his joke and laugh under the gravest circumstances. No one was more intimately identified with the old leadership of the Assembly, or more responsive to the will of the Tidewater aristocracy; and, like the others, he made his thrust at the policies of the British Ministry only after a deep and dutiful obeisance to the King.[14]

The stranger's gaze shifts now to a splendid patrician, with head

[12] Grigsby, The Virginia Convention of 1776, 57-60; Dictionary of American Biography, II, 354.

[13] Grigsby, The Virginia Convention of 1776, 91-93; Randolph MSS.; Tyler, Letters and Times of the Tylers, I, 57.

[14] Grigsby, The Virginia Convention of 1776, 95-97.

and features that might have been copied from a Roman coin, of commanding stature, a slender figure, with reddish hair on a shapely head held 'persuasively and gracefully forward,' now gesticulating with noticeable grace with a crippled hand bound with a black silk handkerchief. 'That,' says the native proudly, 'is the Cicero of the House,' Richard Henry Lee. For seven years, it would be explained, he knew the moors of Yorkshire, England, in his boyhood when attending school, and, but for his father's death, he would have followed his brother to his law studies in the Temple. Born at the ancestral seat of Stratford, he was now living modestly on his estate at Chantilly on the Potomac, but his mind was less on planting than on politics. In his fourteen years in the Assembly, where he had been a parliamentary strategist without a peer, a silver-tongued orator of the classic mold, graceful, argumentative, and persuasive, his deep melodious voice was sometimes described as 'the canorous voice of Cicero.' Some critics, the stranger learns, thought him 'too smooth and sweet,' with a style that 'flowed on like a quiet and placid river without a ripple,' the very antithesis of Henry. Though most of his speeches were carefully prepared, he was the Prince Rupert in extemporaneous debate. And on the topic of colonial rights, this scion of the highest aristocracy was shocking others of his class by frankly avowing admiration and sympathy for Sam Adams in Boston and his revolutionary followers of the streets. Educated in England, he had no reverence for the King; cradled in the aristocracy, he had turned away from the aristocrats of the Tidewater and the James to hail with enthusiasm the tumultuous defiance of the Massachusetts mobs. About him the more ardent younger members flocked as to a standard.[15]

Even now the stranger observes him listening, his haggard face aglow, to a young man of six feet and more, most personable, with an imposing presence and grace of bearing, and with suavity and courtliness in his manner; and even in the color of his hair, in the blue of his eyes, and the benevolence of his expression, one sensed in him a kindred spirit of the older man to whom he was talking. The stranger comments on these points of similarity.

'That,' says the native, 'is young Thomas Jefferson of Monticello,

15 Grigsby, *The Virginia Convention of 1776*, 131-41; Wirt, *Sketches of Henry*, 49; Hendrick, *The Lees of Virginia*, 85-100.

a young man of great learning and high promise. He shares Lee's views on the futility of the hope of exacting colonial rights through humble petitions to the throne.'

Such were some of the more conspicuous figures on the floor when Botetourt called the Assembly into session once again.

VI

And the Virginians, all patriots, but with clashing views on policy and strategy, had come to the parting of the ways.

The old group, almost oligarchic in character, representing the planters of the Tidewater who had so long dominated the legislature and the politics of Virginia, was under the clever and powerful leadership of Edmund Pendleton, Benjamin Harrison, Robert Carter Nicholas, and Richard Bland. There was not one among these who was not thoroughly devoted to the interests of the colony; not one who did not bitterly resent the crass encroachments on colonial rights by the Parliament, acting under the whip and spur of a mad monarch; not one who did not know, and say with force, that the obnoxious laws were written in flagrant violation of the spirit and tradition of the British law. But in all their policies of opposition, they refused to face the fact that, in the last analysis, it might be necessary to break the connection with the British Empire. They yielded to none in their denunciation of the offensive acts of Parliament, but, oblivious to the fact that these were actually the acts of the monarch, they clung with a pathetic and inexplicable persistence to the fantastic hope that the parliamentarians might be checked through the intercession of the very king who gave them orders. They thought of themselves as Englishmen living across the sea and entitled to all the rights and guarantees the Constitution threw around the British citizen at home. And they concentrated their fight on purely legal grounds. They would make a lawsuit out of a controversy which involved elementary political rights and submit their cause to the decision of a prejudiced judge and a packed jury.

With the raw-meat polemics of Samuel Adams and the revolutionists of Massachusetts they had no sympathy at first. Adams had no reverence for the King; they did. He felt no sentimental attachment to the connection; they did. He impetuously brushed aside the legalistic twaddle of the lawyers to make his fight on political principles; and they frowned on such temerity. He appealed to the masses, which, with the Tidewater aristocracy, was proof of his vulgarity. Harrison was to find him offensive because he was not the possessor of broad acres or at least of houses and lots, and even to this day some writers would discredit him as a patriot because he was a failure as a money-grubber.

And the old oligarchy had been shocked, sincerely shocked, by the bold anathemas of Patrick Henry. To these staid citizens the unfashionable orator of the forest, the spokesman of the yeomen and with the yeoman's rustic pronunciation, was an irresponsible firebrand with whom they would have no truck. They were willing enough to argue, and with great skill, about the constitutionality of the stamp tax — but why drag in the King?

But there were other members, mostly younger men, who viewed the ultra-conservatism of the graybeards with distaste and complete disapproval. Behind these, and almost unsuspected by the aristocracy of the Tidewater, was a great and rapidly growing element of the Piedmont and the mountains, which was essentially, inherently democratic; men with no real affection for the England they had never seen and would never see. To them, the Virginia countryside and the forests was their home — none other.

For some years the strength and confidence of this element had been increasing, and more and more of the radical group in the Assembly were numbered among the 'forward men.' And these had, for leaders, two aristocrats, who were men of learning, distinguished at the bar, but not slaves to legalistic inhibitions — young Thomas Jefferson and Richard Henry Lee. The latter had concluded that the marked indifference of the English Parliament to the interests of the colonies had divorced the Americans from their allegiance and reduced them to a state of nature. And young Jefferson, who so laboriously had delved into all the highways and obscure byways of political history and philosophy, had reached about the same conclusion. Patrick Henry, another of the group, had found his mind in harmony with theirs, more through instinct than reasoning. And the youthful Dabney Carr, the most intimate friend and now the brother-in-law of Jefferson, had read his way to

the same conclusions under the great oak on the slopes of Monticello. And there was another among the leaders of the 'forward
men'—Francis Lightfoot Lee, educated in the leisurely bu
thorough school of the great plantations where men had time to
soak themselves in erudition and season themselves by sober think
ing. He had wit and ineffable charm in conversation and wa
known as the 'Atticus of the House.'

These 'forward men' instinctively drew together more and more
discussing events in the seclusion of rooms at the Raleigh Taverr
and perfecting programs that were carefully planted and passed in
the Assembly before the graybeards realized that there was an or
ganized opposition to their policies of procrastination and appeal.

That young Jefferson, soon to demonstrate his unique genius for
leadership and management, played a conspicuous part in the dis
cussions and the planning there can be no doubt.

And now the hour was approaching for action.

VII

When Botetourt summoned the Assembly he really believed the
reports from London that the Government had changed its policy
toward the colonies and that the repeal of the Townshend Act
would be the signal for a general reconciliation. But, alas, he was
to be deceived. It was not the taxes that had enraged the colonies,
but the assumption that the Parliament could tax the colonies at all,
without their representation and consent. But when the Parliament
met, with the East India Company suffering heavy losses because
of the tax on tea and begging for its repeal, and with his own judgment urging to that course, Lord North found a sullen, stubborn,
and stupid King standing like Gibraltar in his path.

Thus it was that all the taxes of the Townshend Act were repealed
except that on tea, which was retained and proclaimed as a defiant
declaration to the obstreperous Americans that Parliament had, and
would exercise, the right to tax them without representation or
consent. There appears no doubt that North, who was not a stupid
man, and personally a very charming one, literally begged the
monarch to relent, but without effect. Finally, North, who always
preferred to follow the line of least resistance, acquiesced; and,

ronically enough, so strong was the sentiment favoring the repeal of the tea tax that, when the calling of the roll disclosed a tie, he was forced to cast the deciding vote for the tax he himself thought stupid.

VIII

The fight on the tea tax was now on in earnest.

From the wrath of the colonies came a more rebellious spirit. In the fervor, nay fever, of resentment, colonists all over the land voluntarily carried their tea to public bonfires. Then for a period there was a pause. Thinking it over, many concluded that with all the other Townshend taxes eliminated, the tax on tea might not be so bad.

But again Fate played havoc with the English connection. Resentment became intensified after the Tea Act of 1773, with its threat of similar monopolies over other commodities.

Tea-ladened ships for America were hurried forward to Boston, New York, Philadelphia, and Charleston. This was a flaunting of the ministerial victory, and the indignation of the more ardent spirits among the colonists rose again. The tea, unloaded at the wharves in Charleston, was purposely consigned to damp vaults and ruined. When the tea ship reached New York, Nature intervened, and a stiff gale drove the vessel out to sea again. And when a sister ship arrived in the river at Philadelphia, the captain could not proceed because no man dared affront the people of the city by giving any assistance in bringing the vessel into port. Citizens assembled, and summoned Captain Ayres to warn him that an attempt to land his cargo would be met by stout resistance and that blood might flow. He was treated with courtesy and invited to determine from his own observations the temper of the town. He was soon convinced of the inadvisability of making the attempt. The people, in common fairness, provisioned his ship for the homeward journey, and it sailed away with the tea.

Writing the Earl of Dartmouth, Joseph Reed described with accuracy the general reaction of all the colonies:

> Your lordship will judge from these facts how general and unanimous the opinion is that no article subject to duty for the

purpose of raising revenue ought to be received in America. An further attempt to enforce this act, I am humbly of opinion, mus end in blood. We are sensible of our inability to contend with th mother country by force, but we are hastening fast to despera resolutions, and unless internal peace is speedily settled, our mos wise and sensible citizens dread the anarchy and confusion tha must follow. This city has been distinguished by its peaceful an regular demeanor, nor has it departed from it on the present occa sion, as there have been no mobs, no insults to individuals, n injury to private property; but the frequent appeals to the peopl must in time occasion a change, and we every day perceive it mor and more difficult to repress the rising spirit of the people.

And the less sedate action of the Boston 'mobs'?

The destruction of the tea in Boston has occasioned much specu lation in this city, and there is some difference of opinion, but i general their conduct is approved as proceeding from necessity.[16]

It was in Boston that the protest was dramatized, when the peopl in a fever, under the inspiration of Samuel Adams and his militant had proceeded to the wharf and had dumped the first shipload o tea into the harbor. The story of this episode, one of the classics o American history, is too well known to require repetition here.

IX

Thus, when the resentment of the retention of the tea tax in th repeal of the other taxes in the Townshend Act was dying dowr the arrival of the three tea ships fanned the smouldering ember into lurid flame again. Even then, after the first excitement, th colonists might easily have subsided into lethargy again but for th action of the King and his doubting but spineless Ministers.

When, at the instance of the King, the Government proposed i Parliament the closing of the port of Boston in retaliation for th dumping of the tea, along with the suppression of town meeting so intimately identified with the normal life of Massachusetts, an when Americans charged with crime were ordered to England o Nova Scotia for trial, George III and the indolent and complacen

16 Reed, *The Life and Correspondence of Joseph Reed*, I, 54-55.

orth cut the connection between the Empire and America as
efinitely as though they had used a knife.

Not a few of the more enlightened English statesmen saw it, and
ain Chatham, with Edmund Burke and Shelburne, made elo-
uent protests that fell on ears of stone. When four regiments of
oops were ordered to Boston and vicinity, the limit of patience
d been reached.

But most of the statesmen who thought at all about the American
tuation remained utterly blind. When a wellwisher sent a warning
the Earl of Dartmouth from Philadelphia, the latter replied hotly,
flecting the spirit of the dominant clique about the court. The
ople of America, particularly those of Boston, had committed
eason, he said.

> Upon the principle of every government on earth [his lordship
> argued], the Mother Country, unwilling to proceed to extremities,
> passes laws, indisputably within its power, for the punishment of
> the most flagrant offenders, for the reformation of abuses, and for
> the prevention of like extremities in the future. The question, then,
> is whether these laws are to be submitted to. If the people of
> America say 'no,' they say in effect that they will no longer be part
> of the British Empire; they change the whole ground of the con-
> troversy — they no longer contend that Parliament has not the
> right to enact a particular provision — they say that it has no right
> to consider them at all within its jurisdiction.[17]

Thus, long before many or most of the colonists were prepared to
onsider their protest and opposition as calling for a complete
paration from the Empire, the King and his court party were
sisting on that interpretation of their acts.

George III had burned his bridges.

X

When the Boston Port Bill was enacted, Lord Botetourt no longer
as suffering from the necessity of rebuking people with whom he
ncerely sympathized. With the discovery that he had been de-
ived as to the conciliatory disposition of the Ministry in London,

[17] *Ibid.*, I, 73.

he was both humiliated and indignant. Utterly disgusted by th
dissimulation of the Government, he had asked to be relieved of h
post, but before his release could come, he was dead. His delica
constitution and his worries, together with the ravages of an acu
disease, put a period to his honorable life. He was genuine
mourned by the Virginians as 'a man possessed of every public ar
private virtue which can adorn human nature.' [18]

While Jefferson did not enjoy the intimate social relations wit
Lord Botetourt that had made him a frequenter of the Palace i
the days of his predecessor, he respected him as an honest man
right impulses, more sinned against than sinning. And we have
way of knowing what Botetourt thought of the young squire
Monticello as a politician and legislator.

Less happy was the selection of Lord Dunmore as Botetourt
successor. Though descended in the female line from the roy
house of Stuart, he appears to have had many of the vices wit
none of the graceful virtues of these ancestors. While his few d
fenders among his friends insist upon his culture, it was the com
mon observation of most that his manners were coarse and his i
tellect mediocre.[19] Edmund Randolph, who knew him, has d
scribed him as 'as low in stature as in morals,' and his feelings
'coarse and depraved.' He was convinced that his lordship 'ge
erally preferred the crooked path,' not possessing 'the genius to pe
ceive, nor the temper to seek, the plain and direct way.'[20] His r
lations with young Jefferson must have been most formal ar
remote, though, in planning for an extension at William and Mar
we know that his lordship requested the master of Monticello
submit plans which may be seen today at the Huntington Librar

Enjoying life in New York where he was serving as Royal Go
ernor, he had incurred the displeasure of the proud Virginians b
delaying his departure from the fleshpots of that city. When final
he appeared, accompanied by Captain Foy, a military officer of co
siderable reputation, in the rôle of secretary, it was generally bruite
abroad that Foy's functions were more military than secretarial, an
that his presence boded no good. The fact that he was loaded dow
with unaccustomed sinecures deepened the mystery and distrus

[18] Burk, *History of Virginia*, III, 361.   [19] Tyler, *Williamsburg*, 55.
[20] *Virginia Magazine*, 43, 137-38.

nd when, soon after his arrival, Dunmore made an inexplicable
urney into the settlements about Pittsburgh, it was whispered
oout that his mission was to stir up a boundary dispute between
ennsylvania and Virginia to keep the Virginians occupied.

However, the arrival of Lady Dunmore, with a numerous family,
romised for a brief moment to blot out the unpleasant impression
reated by her spouse. She was accorded all the courtesies that a
enerous hospitality could conceive. But there was a fly in the social
intment, too; for aristocratic court rules as to precedence were
rawn up under the special direction of the herald. These, when
ublished shortly after the Assembly met, caused some annoyance.[21]

Some smiled, some shrugged, but this inconsequential action was
s the buzzing of a fly to the roaring of a lion when the news of the
oston Port Bill fell on the members of the Assembly with the
esounding noise of a bursting shell. Lady Dunmore did all she
ould with pageantry to divert the attention of the patriots. On
ne birthday of Queen Charlotte she gave an elegant ball at the
alace to which all the aristocracy was invited, and in a graceful
ttempt to cultivate the people, her youngest daughter, on the
fternoon before the evening ball, was christened 'Virginia.' The
irginians accepted the compliment with cordiality and attended
he ball and smiled upon the hostess, but they did not change their
olitics.[22]

XI

It was even before this that the younger and more militant mem-
ers had determined to grasp the leadership from the old conserva-
ives who had dominated so long. One day young Jefferson sat
lown with the two Lees, Patrick Henry, and Dabney Carr, behind
losed doors in a room at the Raleigh Tavern, without consulting
he Pendletons and the Blands, to determine their course of action.
The thought that accompanied them into the conference room has
een indicated by Jefferson: 'We were all sensitive that the most
rgent of all measures was that of coming to an understanding
vith all the other colonies, to consider the British claims as a com-

21 Burk, History of Virginia, III, 375-76.
22 Rowland, Life of Mason, I, 184.

mon cause to all, and to produce a unity of action.'[23] Lee had con sulted Samuel Adams on such a course. 'Do you not think, sir, that the first essential step for our Assembly to take will be an invitatio to a general congress as speedily as the nature of the thing wi admit, in order that our plan may be unanimous and therefor effectual?' he wrote. 'It will be exceedingly agreeable to me to know your sentiments fully on this.'[24] The reply of Adams may well b imagined. It was the thought of the Virginia militants that ther should be a committee of correspondence in each colony for th purpose of constant intercommunication. And it was thought tha this should lead to the calling of a continental congress, with eac colony represented, to take charge of the measures to be adopted i common.[25]

There are plausible reasons to assume that no one of the men i the Raleigh Tavern that day had thought this out more thoroughl than Jefferson, who had a genius for practical politics. In Massa chusetts, Samuel Adams had created a committee of correspondenc for the Old Bay State and he had favored a continental committee but nothing had come of it. That Richard Henry Lee, who s greatly admired the firebrand of Boston, was in complete accord there is abundant evidence to show. But the fact that the men be hind the closed doors of the tavern urged on Jefferson the reporting of the proposed resolutions to the Assembly implied, in accordanc with custom, that he had drawn the resolutions. The designatio could not have fallen to Jefferson because of his powers as an orator for these were negligible.

But Jefferson had other plans. He knew and appreciated Dabne Carr, who, until then, had been given no opportunity to impress hi ability on his colleagues. Jefferson, who knew his natural capacit as a speaker, had absolute faith that, given the opportunity, Car would forge ahead. He, therefore, urged that the reporting of th resolutions be entrusted to his friend.[26]

Thus, the history-making resolutions were pressed upon th Assembly by Carr in a speech so brilliant that from that hour on until his untimely death he was considered a rival of Henry i forensic eloquence.

[23] Autobiography, 5.   [24] Lee, Memoir of Richard Henry Lee, I, 112.
[25] Autobiography, 5.   [26] Ibid.

The Assembly adopted the resolutions; Dunmore went through the routine motion of dissolving the body; and the five 'forward men' and all who supported the resolutions went back to their constituents for a vote of confidence, which was speedily forthcoming.

America was now working in unison through correspondence.

The actual leadership of the Assembly had definitively passed from the Pendletons, Nicholases, Harrisons, to young Jefferson, the Lees, and Patrick Henry.

But it was the closing of the port of Boston that was to bring the colonies together in the flesh.

On learning of the drastic action of the British Ministry, the younger militants, consulting among themselves again behind closed doors at the Raleigh Tavern, agreed upon a course of action and then notified the unhorsed leaders. Thus it was that on a warm day in May, the new leaders met in a private room at the Raleigh and agreed that the challenge of the King had to be accepted.

Uncomfortably conscious of a certain lethargy in the public, they deliberated on some dramatic gesture that would reach the hearths of the people and appeal to their imagination. Here was a problem for a political psychologist, and none greater than Jefferson has ever appeared on the American scene. What would be more impressive as a protest than a day of fasting and prayer? A full generation had passed in Virginia since last the people had called on Heaven during the distresses of the war of 1755. A day of fasting and prayer in 1774 would attract and arouse public sentiment by its solemnity. It was young Jefferson who proposed the plan.[27] And thus it was that Jefferson and his little coterie bent above a volume of Rushworth, who had preserved the revolutionary precedents and forms of the Puritans; and thus it was, as Jefferson relates, that they cooked up' a resolution, somewhat modernizing the phrasing, for appointing the first of June, on which day the operation of the port bill was to commence, for a day of fasting.[28]

In determining who should present the resolution, this group of practical politicians and political psychologists, Jefferson foremost of them, realized the weakness of having the presentation made by anyone not generally known as a religious character. And who better than Robert Carter Nicholas of the relegated Old Guard?

[27] Conway, *Omitted Chapters of History*, 15.   [28] *Autobiography*, 6-7.

His was 'a grave and religious character,' and the words of the resolution would fall naturally from him. His was a voice that woul
not clash with the phrases. And then, too, the 'forward men,' wit
young Jefferson now definitely in the lead, were clever enough t
appreciate the justice and to realize the importance of making th
unhorsed leaders of the past, whose patriotism was unquestioned
members of their team. So Nicholas was approached, and thoug
his group had been deposed from the leadership in initiative, h
was a lover of his country. And thus, in May, the Assembly hear
these words:

> This House, being deeply impressed with apprehension of th
> great dangers to be derived to British America from the hostil
> invasion of the city of Boston in our sister colony of Massachusett
> Bay, whose commerce and harbor are, on the first day of June nex
> to be stopped by an armed force, deem it highly necessary that th
> said first day of June next be set aside by the members of thi
> House, as a day of fasting, humiliation, and prayer, devoted t
> implore the Divine interposition for averting the heavy calamit
> which threatens destruction to our civil rights; and that the mind
> of His Majesty and his Parliament may be inspired from above wit
> wisdom, moderation, and justice, to remove from the loyal peopl
> of America all cause of danger from a continued pursuit of meas
> ures pregnant with their ruin.

It was, therefore, ordered that the members should assemble i
their places at ten o'clock in the morning of June 1 'to proceed wit
the Speaker and the mace to the church in this city'; and that th
Reverend Mr. Price should 'read the prayers and preach a sermo
suitable to the occasion.'

The resolution was passed; and the next day Dunmore dissolve
the House for having published an order 'conceived in such term
as reflect highly on His Majesty and the Parliament of Grea
Britain.'

Whatever may have been the misgivings of such as Pendleto
and the Old Guard, the 'forward men' could have asked nothing
better. In high spirits they met at the Raleigh and issued a state
ment to the people. Having been denied the right to advise th
people in their legislative capacity by their dissolution, they wer

reduced to the 'hard necessity' of addressing them by another method on measures 'to secure our dear rights and liberty from destruction by the heavy hand of power.' Not only had the colony's respectful appeals to the King been disregarded, 'but a determined system is formed and pressed for reducing the inhabitants of British America to slavery, by subjecting them to the payment of taxes without the consent of the people.' The outrageous closing of the port of Boston was 'a most dangerous attempt to destroy the constitutional liberty and rights of British America.'

And then followed a ringing Jeffersonian sentence that was vital:

> An attack made on one of our sister colonies to compel submission to arbitrary taxes is an attack made on all British America and threatens ruin to the rights of all, unless the united wisdom of the whole is applied.

This was followed with another recommendation of the greatest historical significance — that the Committee of Correspondence, which Jefferson's little group had created and of which he was a member, should immediately communicate to the committees of all the other colonies on the expedience 'of appointing deputies from the several colonies . . . to meet in general Congress at such place annually as shall be thought most convenient; there to deliberate on those measures which the united interests of America may, from time to time, require.'

The Jefferson group had not miscalculated the effect of the day of fasting and prayer. Jefferson records that 'the people met generally with anxiety and alarm in their countenances, and the effect of the day throughout the whole colony was like a shock of electricity, arousing every man and placing him erect and solidly on his center.' [29]

Pressing the anticipated advantage, the leaders of the Raleigh Tavern conference recommended that each of the counties of Virginia hold meetings and elect delegates to meet in Williamsburg on August 1, to consider the state of the colony, and to elect the representatives of Virginia to the First Continental Congress.

The people of Albemarle, Jefferson's county, met in July for the purpose, and Jefferson wrote the resolution, which act is important

[29] *Autobiography,* 7.

in the tracing of his influence in the directing of the revolutionary stream:

> Resolved, that the inhabitants of the several States of British America are subject to the laws which they adopted at their first settlement and by such others as have been since made by their respective legislatures, duly constituted and appointed with their own consent; that no other legislature whatever can lightly exercise authority over them; that these privileges they hold as the common rights of mankind, confirmed by the political constitutions they have respectively assumed, and also by the several charters of compact from the Crown.

No other meetings in Virginia went so far or struck so deep — including those in which Washington and Patrick Henry participated.

It was inevitable that Jefferson's county should elect its most famous son, young Jefferson, to represent it at the Williamsburg Convention. This, as we shall see, was to pave the way to the preparation of one of the most brilliant and celebrated literary contributions to the Revolution, which was to make the young man of Monticello known to the entire American continent and to the highest political circles in London.

PENMAN OF THE REVOLUTION

I

JEFFERSON, having been chosen to speak for Albemarle in the Convention, determined to speak for Virginia and all the colonies as well. He had his decided views about the relations of King and Parliament to the colonies, which no one had expressed; and, in the interval of waiting for the meeting at Williamsburg, he bent over his desk at Monticello putting his iconoclastic views on paper. It was his intention to submit them as instructions to the representatives of Virginia to be sent to the Continental Congress. He had read and thought deeply on government, on the history and ways of colonies, on their relations to the mother country, on the setup of the British Empire, and on the lessons he had learned by his reading and thinking.

His thinking differed from that of others, in that, while others were pressing the almost stereotyped arguments of the hour, his mind was going back into the far centuries for precedents and suggestions to sustain his own conclusions. And in so doing he found himself out of harmony, not only with the conciliators who would cling to the connection with the Empire at any cost, but also with many of his own group, who, as he wrote later, 'Stopped at the halfway house . . . admitted that England had a right to regulate American commerce and to lay duties upon it for the purposes of regulation but not of raising revenue.' This did not conform with his opinion, resting on his reading far into the past. For the concessions his friends made to empire, he could find 'no foundation in compact, in any acknowledged principles of colonization, nor in reason, expatriation being a natural right, and acted on as such by all nations.'[1]

He had reached the conclusion, startling enough to the conservatives, that the proper relation of Great Britain to the colonies was none other than that of Hanover to England, though he admitted that the only one among his intimates who could see with him, eye to eye, on this was George Wythe.[2]

There on the hilltop, then, in the mansion designed by him on which he was still at work, he sat down in the heat of July to the expression of his thoughts. These he would take to Williamsburg and urge upon the Convention for the guidance of the Virginia delegates in the Congress. Perhaps he would fight for them and then abide by the result. It was during this period, when he was working on his famous paper and meditating on his course, that an unusual and uncanny event momentarily disturbed his serenity. Early one afternoon the mountain quivered and the house was shaken by an earthquake which repeated itself on the following day, to the terror of the servants; and a little later a younger sister died.

It was late in July when his phaeton rolled down the hill at Monticello and turned toward Williamsburg, a hundred and fifty miles away, along a road none too good and now oppressive with the heat. A blistering sun poured down its enervating rays upon him, and the red dust of the dirt road raised by his horses' feet enveloped and stifled him, and on the way he was attacked by dysentery. Finding it impossible to proceed, he abandoned the journey, but he sent two copies of his proposed instructions on ahead, one to Patrick Henry and the other to Peyton Randolph. It may be doubted if the orator, not fond of reading or of application, so much as gave a glance at the copy, and certainly he did nothing about it. Peyton Randolph, however, laid it on the table for the perusal of the members of the Convention.

It was a unique document, in some respects as important as the Declaration of Independence was to be, and more expressive, in detail, of Jefferson's line of thinking. The most famous document previously produced in support of the cause of the colonies had conceded that, because of the migration of the colonists, Parliament

[1] *Autobiography*, 8.   [2] *Ibid.*

had a right to levy taxes upon them. Such had been the admission of John Dickinson in his celebrated *Letters of a Pennsylvania Farmer,* and of John Delaney in his equally acclaimed pamphlet, which had called forth the comment of Lord Chatham that it was a veritable textbook of American rights.

But Jefferson thought otherwise. He was thinking in terms of the Saxon migration to England, over a thousand years before, and of the relations of England to Scotland after James ascended the throne and before the Act of Union. Here was something for the delegates, thinking solely in terms of the eighteenth century, to turn over in their minds.

It may be assumed that some of the delegates took the trouble seriously to examine the document on their table. That it was found by the more timid too robust and sweeping must also be assumed from the fact that this, the most famous and important document submitted to the Convention, was not even published in the record.

That it made a deep impression on Peyton Randolph is evident in the fact that one day he invited a large company of the leaders to his house to listen to the reading of the views of a young man scarcely thirty-one. It was remembered later by Edmund Randolph, who was present, that many parts of the paper were highly praised, but that other parts were questioned as to the wisdom of their promulgation. But he recalled 'the applause bestowed on most of them,' and that, while 'the old required time for consideration before they could tread this lofty ground,' the 'young ascended with Mr. Jefferson to the source of these rights.' After all, the document was raw meat. It was highly iconoclastic, and the leaders agreed that it was then too advanced for the times. One thing it did disclose to all — that young Jefferson was doing his own thinking, and some planning out of the beaten path.[3] And some were sufficiently impressed, when Jefferson's instructions were put aside for others more bromidic and conventional, to subscribe for the publication of the paper as a pamphlet. In the preface the editors placed their estimate upon it:

> In it the sources of our unhappy differences are traced with such
> faithful accuracy, and the opinions entertained by every free

[3] Edmund Randolph MSS.

American expressed with such manly firmness, that it must be pleasing to the present, and may be helpful for the future, ages. It will evince to the world the moderation of our late convention who have only touched with tenderness many of the claims insisted on in this pamphlet, though every heart acknowledges their justice.

Thus it was that a company of men, distinguished lawyers, jurists, patriots, and statesmen, assembled in the parlor of Peyton Randolph's house with its columned portico and two wings, while the host slowly read the *Summary View of the Rights of British America.*

No doubt all acquiesced in the opening paragraph referring to the 'unwarranted encroachments and usurpations attempted to be made by the legislature of one part of the Empire upon the rights which God and the laws have given equally and independently to all.'

But some must have batted their eyes a bit when, immediately following, came the assertion that their ancestors, before their migration to America, 'possessed the right, which Nature has given to all men, of departing from the country in which chance, not choice, had placed them, and of going in quest of new habitations, and of establishing new societies, under such laws and regulations as to them shall seem most likely to promote public happiness.'

If this interested, the next sentence probably startled them, when Jefferson declared that 'their Saxon ancestors had, under this universal law, in like manner left their native wilds and woods in the North of Europe, had possessed themselves of the isle of Britain . . . and had established there that system which has so long been the glory and protection of that country.'

If this unexpected evocation of the remote past astonished the little audience was more startled with what followed. 'Nor was there ever any claim of superiority or dependence asserted over them by that mother country from which they had migrated.' And suppose such claim had been made? the author asked. 'It is believed that His Majesty's subjects in Great Britain would have had too firm a feeling of the rights derived to them from their ancestors to bow down the sovereignty of their State before such visionary pretensions.'

After all, Jefferson continued, was there any difference between the Saxon migration and that of the Americans? 'America was conquered, and her settlements made and firmly established at the expense of individuals, and not of the British public. Their own blood was spilt in acquiring lands for their settlement, their own fortunes expended in making that settlement effectual. For themselves they fought, for themselves they conquered, and for themselves alone they have a right to hold.' Indeed, until they were firmly established, 'no shilling was ever issued from the public treasures of His Majesty, or his ancestors, for their assistance.'

And why and whence the change? Only when they had become commercially valuable had Great Britain lent them assistance, and only then for her own selfish interests. And no appreciation of that assistance? By all means, yes, but that debt is paid 'by giving such exclusive privileges in trade as may be advantageous to them, and at the same time not too much restrictions to themselves.'

The settlements made, continued Jefferson, the emigrants adopted the system of laws under which they previously had lived, continued their union with the mother country 'under a common sovereign who was thereby made the central link connecting the several parts of the Empire thus newly multiplied.'

It was not to their discredit that the men at Randolph's, listening to these then novel views, could not foresee the far-off day when England would place a similar interpretation on the Empire in the Commonwealth of Nations, and on the monarch as the connecting link.

And then, Randolph read on, came the Stuarts — 'a family . . . whose treasonable crimes against their people' was to call forth the 'sacred and sovereign rights of punishment.' It was under the Stuarts that the land in America, 'acquired by the lives, the labors, and the fortunes of individual adventurers . . . was several times parcelled out and distributed among the favorites and followers' of the monarchs. But nothing of that sort had any king dared attempt in England.

And had England the right to regulate the commerce of the colonies?

Jefferson's answer to this question must have fallen like an exploding shell among the gentlemen assembled under Randolph's roof. Most of the patriot pamphleteers, while protesting against taxation without representation, had conceded the right of Parliament to regulate the commerce of the colonies. The restrictions on the markets of the colonists, the denial of their right to trade where most to their advantage, said the author, could not be justified.

And why?

Because of the misuse made of the pretended right.

Thus, the American had been forbidden 'to make a hat for himself of the fur he had taken from his own soil — an instance of despotism to which no parallel can be produced in the most arbitrary ages of British history.'

The iron Americans produced they were forbidden to manufacture, and it had to be sent to England and the finished product shipped back at great expense 'for the purpose of supporting, not men, but machines in Great Britain.'

American lands were made liable for British debts, while British landowners could not be touched by creditors.

And then — the clap of thunder that may well have brought shivers to the more conservative and timid — the primary crime was this — that 'the British Parliament has no right to exercise authority over us.'

If the conservatives in the company were a little depressed by now, they must have recovered confidence when the author reached the reign of George III. 'Scarcely have our minds been able to emerge from the astonishment into which one stroke of parliamentary thunder has involved us,' he said, 'before another, more heavy and more alarming, is fallen on us.'

And what the significance?

'Single acts of tyranny may be ascribed to the accidental opinion of a day, but a series of oppressions, pursued unalterably through every change of Ministers, too plainly prove a deliberate, systematic plan for reducing us to slavery.'

Yes, so far had the pretensions of Parliament now gone that legislatures of the colonies were regularly dissolved by the act of London. And why? Whence the right? 'Shall these governments be dissolved, their property annihilated, and their people reduced to a state of nature at the imperious breath of a body of men whom they never saw, in whom they have not confided, and over whom they have no power of punishment or removal?'

And who were these members of Parliament? One hundred and sixty thousand men in England elect the Parliament. Could any reason be advanced why these should give law to four million Americans? If this be true, then four million men would be the slaves of 'one hundred and sixty thousand tyrants.'

Then, too, the infamy of the Boston Port Bill — whence did it come?

A tax on tea had been levied over the protest of the Americans. The East India Company, 'which has never sent a pound of tea to America on their own account,' step forth as the asserters of parliamentary right to force numerous shiploads of tea upon her. Most of the captains of these vessels 'wisely attended to admonition and returned with their cargoes.' In Boston alone did the master flatly refuse — whether from obstinacy or instructions 'let them say who know.' An exasperated group of people threw the tea into the harbor. Now, said Jefferson, these men were amenable to the law and were subject to punishment. But that was not enough. Massachusetts had stoutly resisted ministerial and parliamentary oppression. The entire people should be punished — and thus the measure closing the port of Boston. Yes, 'men who had spent their lives in extending the British commerce; who had invested in that place the wealth their honest endeavors had merited, found themselves and their families thrown at once on the world for sustenance by its charities. Not the hundredth part of the inhabitants of that town had been concerned in the act complained of; yet all were involved in one indiscriminate ruin by an executive power unheard of till then — that of a British Parliament. A property of the value of many millions of money was sacrificed to revenge, not repay, the loss of a few thousands.'

All this the gentlemen at Randolph's could understand and applaud.

But hard on this came something even more severe. In the tumult of the town a man was murdered, and the murderer was, if the Royal Governor agreed, to be 'tried in the Court of King's Bench, in the island of Great Britain, by a jury of Middlesex.' Witnesses were to be forced to England. True, their actual expenses would be paid, 'but who was to feed the wife and children whom he leaves behind and who had no other subsistance but his daily labor?'

And — Randolph read on — the wretched criminal, 'stripped of his privilege of trial by peers of his own vicinage, removed from the place where alone full evidence could be obtained, without money, without counsel, without friends, without exculpatory proof, is tried before judges predetermined to condemn.' Ah, 'the cowards who would suffer a countryman to be torn from the bowels of their society, in order to be offered a sacrifice to Parliamentary tyranny, would merit that everlasting infamy now fixed on the authors of the act.'

II

We may assume that those assembled in Randolph's house were moved by this arraignment. But Jefferson was not through, for he passed immediately to a denunciation of the acts of the King in vetoing laws of the colonial legislatures. Did he exercise that right in England? True, he there possessed the power, but His Majesty and his ancestors, 'conscious of the impropriety of opposing their single opinion to the united wisdom of the two houses of Parliament,' had 'modestly declined the exercise of his power in England. Not so in America.' Nay, 'for the most trifling reasons, and sometimes for no conceivable reason at all, His Majesty had rejected laws of the most salutary tendency.'

This led inevitably to a subject on which young Jefferson felt strongly, and with which he was to concern himself throughout this earlier period of his life — the slave system he sought throughout his life to limit or end. And on this the men at Randolph's listened to one of the most severe of his denunciations:

> The abolition of domestic slavery is the great object of desire of those colonies where it was, unhappily, introduced in their infant state. But previous to the enfranchisement of the slaves we have, it is necessary to exclude all further importations from Africa. Yet our repeated attempts to effect this by prohibitions, and by imposing taxes which amount to a prohibition, have been hitherto defeated by His Majesty's negative; thus preferring the advantages of a few British corsairs to the lasting interest of the American States, and to the rights of human nature, deeply wounded by this infamous practice.

This, he concluded, was 'a shameful abuse of power.'

Nor was that all, he said. The King had vetoed all measures for the carving of new counties in Virginia, 'unless the new county will consent to have no representatives in the Assembly.' Since the lands of the colony extend hundreds of miles to the westward, 'was it possible that His Majesty could have bestowed a single thought on the situation of those people, who, in order to obtain justice for injuries, must, by the laws of that colony, attend their county court at such a distance, with all their witnesses monthly till their litigation is determined?'

What, then, the object of the veto?

Was it 'meant to confine the legislative body to their present members that they may be the cheaper bargain whenever they shall become worth a purchase'?

And more abuses — the repeated dissolution of the legislative bodies of the colonies. Why, in the reign of Richard II, the Judges of Westminster Hall 'had suffered death as traitors because they had advised the King . . . that he might dissolve the Parliament at any time.' And, since the adoption of the British Constitution, no monarch had dared assume the right. 'But how different their language and their practice here! To declare . . . the known rights of their country, to oppose the usurpation of every foreign judicature, to disregard the imperious mandate of a minister or governor, have been the avowed causes for dissolving houses of representatives in America.'

Worse still — having dissolved one legislature, George III had refused to call another — a violation of natural laws. 'From the nature of things, every society must, at all times, possess within itself the sovereign powers of legislation,' for 'the feelings of human nature revolt against the supposition of a State so situated as that it may not, in any emergency, provide against dangers which perhaps threaten immediate ruin.' And so, 'when the privilege is denied, the people act together beyond the written law and according to the law of nature' — as they have been acting in Virginia. Were not the 'dangers conspicuous with which this practice is replete'?

III

At this juncture we may be sure that many of the gentlemen shifted uneasily in their chairs when they heard the young statesman's observations on the feudal tenures in the land. Here they heard a bold denial of the monarch's property in the soil. And here, again, he went back a thousand years to the practice of their Saxon ancestors; and again to English history:

> In the early stages of the Saxon settlement, feudal holdings were certainly altogether unknown [said Jefferson], and very few, if any, had been introduced at the time of the Norman Conquest. Our Saxon ancestors held their lands, as they did their personal property, in absolute dominion, disencumbered by any superior, answering nearly to the nature of those possessions which the feudalists term allodial. William the Conqueror introduced the feudal system, parceling out the land of those who fell at Hastings to his followers, and subject to feudal duties. Out of this ultimately grew the theory that all the lands in England were held mediately or immediately by the Crown.

But — 'America was not conquered by William the Norman, or its lands surrendered to him or to his successors.' However, the early settlers were 'laborers, not lawyers,' and, accordingly, these took grants of their own land from the King. This was not so intolerable so long as the Crown continued to grant for small sums and for reasonable rents, and there was 'no inducement to arrest the error.' But now that His Majesty had doubled the terms of purchase, 'by which means the acquisition of lands being rendered difficult, the population of our country is likely to be checked.'

And what should be done about it?

> It is time for us to lay this matter before His Majesty and to declare that he has no right to grant lands of himself. From the nature and purpose of civil institutions, all the lands within the limits, which any particular body has circumscribed around itself, are assumed by that society, and subject to their allotment.

Thus was Jefferson the reformer superimposing himself on Jefferson the revolutionist.

IV

The small audience at Randolph's, a little dazed perhaps by the iconoclastic nature of the paper they were hearing read, next listened to a stout denial of the King's right 'to send large bodies of armed forces, not made up of the people here, nor raised by the authority of our laws,' for, 'did His Majesty possess such a right . . . it might swallow up all our rights whenever he should think proper.' He, thought Jefferson, had 'no right to land a single armed man upon our shores.' Would the people of England permit the King to introduce a foreign army in their midst? When in war, George II wished to bring in Hanoverian troops for the defense of England, he applied to Parliament for permission. How different in America! Not only was George III unloading armed men upon American shores over the protest of the Americans, but he was subjecting the civil to the military authorities.

Such, thought Jefferson, were the grievances of Virginia and her sister colonies.

He then, having set them forth, entered upon a direct appeal to George III:

> Open your breast, Sire, to liberal and expanded thought. Let not the name of George III be a blot on the page of history. You are surrounded by British counsellors, but remember that they are parties. You have no Minister for American Affairs, because you have none taken from among us, nor amenable to the laws on which they are to give you advice. It behooves you, therefore, to think and act for your people. The great principles of right and wrong are legible to every reader; to pursue them requires not the aid of many counsellors.

> [Yes] the whole art of government consists in the art of being honest. Only aim to do your duty, and mankind will give you credit where you fail. Stop sacrificing the rights and interests of one part of the Empire to the inordinate desires of another, and deal out equal and impartial right. This, Sire, is the advice of your great American Council, on the observance of which depend your felicity and future fame.

> [Independence?] The Americans wish for the preservation of harmony between America and the Empire. It is neither our wish nor our interest to separate from her. We are willing, on our part, to sacrifice everything which reason can ask, for the restoration of that tranquillity for which we all wish. On their part, let them be ready to establish union on a generous plan. Let them ask their terms, but let them be just. [And remember, that] the God who

gave us life, gave us liberty at the same time; the hand of force
may destroy, but cannot disjoin them.

Thus, young Jefferson spoke across three thousand miles of water
to the King, and spoke with his own voice, out of his own mind,
and in the language of liberty which the friends of freedom in
England should have understood. It was the language of Hampden
and Sidney, not unknown on the glowing pages of English history.
And it was understood and applauded by some of the choicest
spirits then on the English scene.

V

The reading was finished. It is not surprising that not a few of
the delegates in Williamsburg shied away from a statement so
robust. Not a few of the more conservative unquestionably felt that
Jefferson had delved too deep and required too much. But there
were others who realized that here was a document that deserved
to live in the literature of free men; and thus it came about that,
through a subscription, the pamphlet was published in Philadelphia
and ran through numerous editions. It was read with admiration
by most of the delegates in the First Continental Congress, sitting
in the city of its publication, who realized that a new giant had
appeared on the horizon. They discussed it at the mess at the City
Tavern and in the rooms of men like Samuel Adams. They would
not overlook him later. He was now a national figure.

And the pamphlet was printed likewise in England. When
copies reached London, the gallant and brilliant Opposition to
ministerial madness seized upon it as a powerful presentation that
could be used effectively in the mother country. The greatest of
their political philosophers and most eloquent of their writers was
Edmund Burke, whose parliamentary speeches on 'American Taxation' and 'Conciliation with America' warmly espoused the
colonial cause. He went over the work of Jefferson, making a few
alterations to meet the English situation. No copy seems extant,
which is a pity, since it would be interesting to know which parts
were thought unpalatable to the English taste of the time. In his
Autobiography, Jefferson tells us merely that 'it found its way to
England, was taken up by the Opposition, interpolated a little by

Mr. Burke so as to make it answer Opposition purposes, and in that form ran rapidly through several editions.'[4]

The pamphlet established the author as a leader of the first order in America, and made his name known to the most liberal circles in England; but the appeal to the King to open his breast 'to liberal and expanded thought' thoroughly enraged him and his blind and complacent advisers, and soon the agent of the Burgesses in London was sending Peyton Randolph excerpts from a bill of attainder containing a list of proscriptions in which the name of Jefferson is found. The increasing seriousness of the crisis, however, prompted caution, and the measure did not reach a vote.

But the name of Jefferson was known at Windsor, and he had been found an eligible candidate for the Tower in London.

VI

Detained in the meanwhile at Monticello, Jefferson was by no means inactive, for neighbors constantly found their way to his hilltop to confer on the enforcement of the Non-Importation Act and to discuss problems of defense with the young member of the Committee on Public Safety for Albemarle. While riding over his plantation supervising and organizing the work, planning for and adding new features to the mansion which tangibly expressed his love of beauty, working or directing in his gardens with his Italian gardener and improving his grounds, he was never happier than when at Monticello with the wife to whom he was devoted and the small children he adored. But all this was now subordinate to the call of public duty.

Thus, when in the spring of 1775 a convention was called at Richmond, he drove thither as a delegate. The town was but a hamlet, the facilities for even a small colonial convention were inadequate, and the delegates and spectators had to pack themselves into the little church of Saint John, a small wooden structure of no architectural distinction, but destined to become doubly sacred because of the events in that second Virginia Convention.

The cleavage between the ultra-conservatives and the more fiery and militant could no longer be concealed; and while the latter

[4] *Autobiography*, 9.

filed into the little church determined to force action, the former were equally insistent that nothing drastic be undertaken.

In Massachusetts, the patriots were preparing to meet General Gage in battle, but the war had not yet begun, and the appeasers could see no reason why it should begin. The boycott, they thought, would bring the British Government to terms. The sympathies of the English people, they contended, had turned to the colonies — which was not entirely true. The industrialists and merchants of England were feeling the pinch of the boycott and were putting pressure to bear on Parliament. And in Parliament, America had friends working for justice, who should not be embarrassed in their constitutional fight. It was the ancient plea for procrastination — 'Don't rock the boat.'

Such were the views of Bland, Pendleton, Harrison, and Nicholas, veteran patriots, no doubt, and all honorable men. But they were optimistic beyond all reason. The English manufacturers and merchants were restive, but ineffectual; the mass of people were in complete ignorance of the colonial struggle three thousand miles away, and scarcely gave a thought to the colonies. Everything rested with a mad monarch and a Parliament that need concern itself only with one hundred and sixty thousand electors out of the millions on the island. And while some of the noblest and most commanding men in Parliament were brilliantly championing the colonial cause, their voices were those of men crying in the wilderness, and with no answer but a cry.

Even so, the leaders of the old aristocratic oligarchy in Virginia were prone to pursue a bromidic course of pious hope, clinging to measures and resolutions that meant no more than words uttered in a void. They were preparing to express 'an ardent hope' for 'the speedy return of those halcyon days when we lived, a free and happy people.' This resolution was read in the little church packed with delegates and such spectators as could find standing-room.

Scarcely had the resolution been read when one of the delegates sprang to his feet, his face aflame, and with a voice that rang out like a bugle call, Patrick Henry, the incorrigible patriot, demanded a truce to words — and action — immediate action — the immediate organization of a militia and the immediate perfecting of plans for the defense of the colony.

No one can stand, as thousands do, in the little church of Saint John even to this day without feeling the throb of Henry's immortal oration, one of the most stirring of all time. 'Peace! peace!' came the voice of scorn, 'when there is no peace!' The time had come to fight. With Americans of other colonies in the field, 'why stand we here idle?' he demanded. 'Is life so dear or peace so sweet as to be purchased at the price of chains and slavery?' No, 'we must fight.' 'I know not what course others may take, but as for me, give me liberty or give me death.'

The orator sank into his seat. An awesome silence brooded on the room. No one but knew he had listened to the most eloquent and moving speech ever heard on American soil, in no wise inferior to the clarion call of Demosthenes. All else was anticlimax. True, the conservatives sought to offset the effect with pleas for patience, but some of these supported Henry.

It was inevitable that young Jefferson should give his voice and vote for action. Eloquent beyond other men with the pen, eloquent in conversation, his weak voice and distaste for dramatization put such oratory as he had just heard beyond his reach, but those packed in Saint John's that day heard him 'arguing closely, profoundly and warmly' in support of Henry's position.[5] And one there was, arrayed among the delegates with Henry, who probably found more solid substance and reason in the calm argument of Jefferson than in the flaming speech of the greater orator — George Washington. For he, too, had come to the conclusion that the colony must at least be prepared to fight.

It is significant of the strength of those men, willing at almost any cost to avoid the issue of separation, that the Henry resolution carried by a majority of only five out of the hundred and twenty-five votes cast.

But victory had perched on the banner of the 'forward men.'

Soon thereafter, the committee named to draw up plans for a militia and for defense sat down to their historic task. Strange that no artist has ever visualized that significant scene. For there sat Washington, Jefferson, Richard Henry Lee, and Patrick Henry, who had prevailed; and there, too, equally zealous now that the die was cast, sat Pendleton, Harrison, and Nicholas.

[5] Edmund Randolph MSS.

Virginia now, as never before, was on the march.

Meanwhile, Lord Dunmore, living an increasingly lonely life in the Governor's Palace in Williamsburg, was realizing more and more that he was much too light to withstand the impact of angry public sentiment. He was dropping hints that he had reason to believe that he would soon receive a conciliatory proposition from Lord North, and that he would summon the House of Burgesses to pass upon it.

This meant that Peyton Randolph, the Speaker of the Virginia Assembly, would have to leave his post in the Continental Congress, since his presence in Williamsburg would be imperatively required. The Virginians turned to the brilliant young author of the *Summary View* as worthy to fill Randolph's seat in Philadelphia. But when the Burgesses were summoned to consider the proposition of Lord North, Randolph, who had hurried back to Williamsburg, insisted that Jefferson delay his journey to Philadelphia long enough to hear Lord North's proposition and to prepare Virginia's answer. When Johann David Schoepf was traveling in Virginia in this period, he observed in his book of travels some pride in the people for the political writers, but that, 'on inquiring, I could hear only of a Mr. Jefferson.'[6] Nothing could more conclusively show Jefferson's pre-eminence at this time, and he was but thirty-two.

Here we may leave Jefferson in Williamsburg waiting for the proposition of Lord North.

VII

While waiting for Lord North's proposition, it is illuminating to take a backward glance into the immediate past to get the background necessary to an understanding. In the generations that have intervened since America broke her connection with the British Empire, public taste in the United States has quite properly come to frown on the once popular sport of 'twisting the lion's tail.' This is as it should be, since in two world wars the Americans and the British have fought side by side in a common cause; but this can be carried to extremes, and some historians, to prove their immunity from bestial prejudice and vulgar passion, are prone to treat the

[6] Schoepf, *Travels in the Confederation,* II, 62.

American Revolution almost apologetically, and to write with scant respect of some of the American leaders in that transcendent event. This is not so much bad taste as bad patriotism, and is not justified by the facts. History is presumed to be an honest record of what actually took place. Sometimes this is sad, indeed, but the historian cannot change the fact, and any attempt to do so is a degradation of history. The honest historian must write down what he finds.

We have but recently come from the house of Peyton Randolph, where we have heard the reading of Jefferson's *Summary View*, a fierce indictment of the American policy of a monarch, abnormal and to become insane, and an ill-informed or complacent Parliament. Should that be blotted from the record of the fight for liberty?

Then what shall we do with the equally fierce denunciations of that policy that fell like molten fire from the eloquent lips of Chatham in the House of Lords?

And what with the majestic speech of Edmund Burke on 'Conciliation with America' which has been read for generations in the high schools of the United States? Shall we exclude it from the libraries and the schools and blot it from the record?

Shall only the tame, sophisticated speeches of Lord North and the tirades of Townshend remain as a record of what the controversy was about?

I have tried to show that the more militant and advanced of the American leaders, like Jefferson and Washington, considered themselves citizens of the British Empire, demanding the guarantees of the British Constitution, the protection of the British law, and as fighting anew, on American soil, the battles for liberty and inherent rights which have given a glow to the brightest pages of British history.

Now, if the American revolutionary leaders were mere ranting demagogues, we shall find a striking similarity between the sentiments expressed in the *Summary View* of Jefferson and those proclaimed in the British Parliament at the time by Chatham, Burke, and Shelburne. While waiting for Lord North's proposition to be presented to the Virginia Assembly, then, let us pay a brief visit to the Parliament in London and hear the echo of the American contention in the voices of Burke and Chatham.

VIII

In February, 1775, after Lord Dartmouth, Secretary of State for the Colonies, laid before the House of Lords numerous papers concerning American affairs, the famous Lord Chatham, then old at sixty-seven, and infirm, rose from a sick bed to propose the immediate withdrawal of British troops from Boston and to give his blessing to the American contention.

He rose in an intense silence, for there was something to inspire awe in the manner of this venerable figure, who had been so brilliantly identified with the most inspiring incidents of imperial history. He rose to speak for the American colonies, but as an Englishman speaking for the Empire. Those who heard him were impressed by his great animation and with the feeling that he seemed 'inspired.' The dignity of this old man with fierce eagle eyes was almost an affront to the ministerial benches on which no man was free.

'I will knock at the door of this sleeping and confounded Ministry and will arouse them to a sense of their danger,' he began. Its 'violent acts and declarations have disseminated confusion throughout your empire.' Its conduct in Boston had inflicted 'intolerable wrongs.' Its 'indiscriminate, unmerciful proscription of the innocent with the guilty, unheard and untried,' was indefensible. It had aroused the 'just indignation of an injured and insulted people.'

But did the Americans owe obedience?

Yes, 'to a limited extent'— obedience to 'our ordinances of trade and navigation,' but 'the sacredness of their property must remain inviolable'; and taxed though it should be, taxed 'by their own consent, given in their provincial assemblies.'

And now, since conciliation is required by public policy, the time had come 'to review and repeal, if it should be found necessary, as I affirm it will, those violent acts and declarations which have disseminated confusion throughout the empire.'

But the colonies had resisted?

Why, 'resistance to your acts was necessary, as it was just; and your vain declarations of the omnipotence of Parliament and your imperious doctrines of the necessity of submission will be found equally impotent to convince or to enslave your fellow subjects in

America who feel that tyranny, whether ambitioned by an individual part of the legislature or the bodies who compose it, is equally intolerable to British interests.'

What then?

Why, drop the idea of 'dictating reconciliation,' remove at once 'the obnoxious cause of the disturbances, abandon the idea that you can crush a brave, generous, and united people with arms in their hands and courage in their hearts — three millions of men, the genuine descendants of a valiant and pious ancestry driven to those deserts by the narrow maxims of a superstitious tyranny.'

And these people not to be heard? as the Ministry insisted.

'They have been condemned unheard. . . . The indiscriminate hand of vengeance has lumped together innocent and guilty, with all the formalities of hostility has blocked up the town [Boston] and reduced to beggary and famine thirty thousand inhabitants.'

Crush such a people?

'You might destroy their towns and cut them off from the superfluities, perhaps the conveniences of life,' but they would 'despise your power, and would not lament their loss while they have — what, my lords? — their woods and liberty.'

And was it possible Ministers were surprised at American opposition to arbitrary methods of taxation?

Why, it was obvious from the nature of things and of mankind; and above all from the Whiggish spirit flourishing in that country. *The spirit which now resists your taxation in America is the same which formerly opposed loans, benevolences, and ship money in England;* the same spirit which called all England on its legs, and, by the Bill of Rights, vindicated the British Constitution; the same spirit which established the great fundamental, essential maxim of our liberties, *that no subject of England shall be taxed but by his consent.* [Yes, England] superintends and controls their trade and navigation, but she taxes herself.

And then, as the figure of the revered statesman seemed to expand, its stature lengthen, came these words that were heard in substance from the Americans:

Let this distinction, then, remain forever ascertained; taxation is theirs; commercial regulation is ours. As an American, I would recognize to England her supreme right of regulating commerce and navigation; as an Englishman by birth and principles, I recognize to the Americans their supreme inalienable right to their property; a right which they are justified in the defense of, to the last extremity. To maintain this principle is the common cause of the Whigs on the other side of the Atlantic, and on this. 'Tis liberty to liberty engaged, and they will defend themselves, their families, and their country. In this great cause they are immovably allied; it is the alliance of God and Nature — immutable, eternal — fixed as the firmament of heaven.

Referring then to the American leaders in the Continental Congress, the Parliament of England heard from the lips of Chatham, the superior of them all, that 'for solidity of reasoning, force, or sagacity, and wisdom of conclusion, no nation or body of men can stand in preference to the general Congress in Philadelphia.'

And then, the conclusion: 'Every motive, therefore, of justice and of policy, of dignity and of prudence, urges you to allay the ferment in America by a removal of your troops from Boston, by a repeal of your acts of Parliament, and by a demonstration of amicable disposition toward your colonies.' Unless the Ministers so agree, Chatham would 'not affirm that they will make the crown not worth the wearing,' but he would say 'that the King is betrayed' and the 'kingdom undone.'

So spoke the foremost man in England in the language used by the Jeffersons in America; and we cannot dismiss the language of the Americans as demagogic without a simultaneous denunciation of Chatham as a demagogue — and that he was not.

The result? The resolutions of Chatham were voted down by the peers of England. That was in early February.

IX

In March, in the House of Commons, Edmund Burke introduced his resolutions for conciliation with America, supporting them in a superb oration which probably is the greatest masterpiece of his genius. To attempt to sketch this great speech, which ranks with the greatest orations of all time, would be an impertinence. He proposed to remove the disease of colonial unrest by a removal of the cause. He asked from the Commons a frank admission that the

colonies were denied 'the liberty and privileges' of representation in
'the high court of Parliament'; that it be conceded that, in the absence of representation by men familiar with conditions, onerous
burdens had been placed upon them, and 'in a manner prejudicial
to the commonwealth, quietness, rest, and peace of the subjects';
that, because distance made almost prohibitive a representation in
Parliament, the colonies be conceded the privilege of taxing themselves in their own assemblies; that experience had shown this best,
both for the colonies and for harmony within the Empire. He denounced the act ordering Americans to England for trial as a 'justly
obnoxious act,' and asked for its repeal.

It was while the Burke resolutions still were pending that Lord
North, to the disgust of many of the blind followers of reaction,
and to the equal disgust of the friends of liberty, presented his own
'conciliatory proposition.' To this Burke turned toward the close
of his great oration, and pronounced it a 'ransom by auction . . . a
thing new, unheard-of, supported by no experience, justified by no
analogy, without example of our ancestors or root in the Constitution . . . neither regular parliamentary taxation nor colony grant.'

And how 'conciliatory'?

'They complain that they are taxed without their consent; you
answer that you will fix the sum at which they shall be taxed.'
Would all the colonies accept? Assuredly not. Was not the purpose,
then, more 'designed to breaking the union of the colonies than for
establishing a revenue'?

This, it may be noted, is the interpretation Jefferson was to put
upon it.

The resolutions of Burke went to a vote and went down with
but seventy-five supporting them and two hundred and seventy
opposing.

Thus we have the background to Lord North's propositions of
'conciliation,' to reply to which Peyton Randolph was holding young
Jefferson in Williamsburg.

X

Peyton Randolph wanted a robust reply to North which he dared
not hope to get were it prepared by Pendleton or any of the other

conciliators and appeasers. He knew where Jefferson stood. Long an admirer of the young man's mind, the *Summary View* had convinced him that no pen in America was more effective. And no one ever had to inquire, when liberty and human rights and the rights of the colonies were concerned, where Jefferson would be found.

Like all the others, Jefferson had followed the proceedings in Parliament. His opinion of Burke's proposal is not so clear, but he had found, in the proposition of Lord Chatham, a promise for the settlement of all differences within the Empire. At least it offered a basis for serious negotiations. He wrote his old friend, Doctor Small, then in Scotland:

> When I saw Lord Chatham's bill, I entertained high hopes that a reconciliation could have been brought about. The differences between his terms and those offered by our Congress might have been accommodated if entered on by both parties with a disposition to accommodate. But the dignity of Parliament, it seems, can brook no opposition to its power. Strange that a set of men who have made sale of their virtue to the Minister, should yet talk of retaining dignity.

It is not without interest that more than a century later, Lord Rosebery, a brilliant British statesman, himself an ardent champion of the Empire, should have shared Jefferson's opinion that an accommodation might have been found under the enlightened leadership of Chatham.[7]

But Lord North proposed to exempt from taxation by act of Parliament any colony which, on its own volition, would tax itself for imperial defense and make such provision for the salaries of judges and governors as would meet with the approval of Parliament. Parliament was arbitrarily to determine how much each colony should raise, and it would still retain the power to veto. The method of taxation was changed, but nothing more.

And so it came to pass that the veterans of the Burgesses stood aside and assigned to young Jefferson, just thirty-two, the privilege of making the reply to the Prime Minister of England. This reply was so completely to satisfy the Continental Congress, which

[7] Crewe, *Lord Rosebery.*

Chatham had pronounced the equal in capacity of any in the world, that, a little later, with North's proposition before it, along with Jefferson's reply for the Virginians, it assigned to him the task of speaking for that body. The two replies, quite similar, of course, may be treated here as one.

Both were stiff but dignified rejections. Jefferson found the proposition 'unreasonable and insidious; unreasonable, because, if we declare that we accede to it, we declare without reservation we will purchase the favor of Parliament, not knowing, at the same time, at what price they will please to estimate their favor.'

And 'insidious,' because of the reasons pointed out by Burke — that their probable purpose was to disunite the colonies on the supposition that some would accept and others not. Never, said Jefferson, would Virginia desert a single sister colony.

And why, he asked, should Parliament ask for a perpetual revenue? Why should it be compelled by English public opinion to vote revenue from year to year, while demanding a perpetual revenue from the colonies? Was not the primary demand of the colonies for equality of treatment under English laws and traditions?

And how came these proposals? At the point of the bayonet, and with hostile alien troops upon our shores. Would England accept treaties 'from any power on earth when borne on the point of the bayonet by military plenipotentiaries'?

And by what right had Parliament to fix the amount that the colonies should contribute? Had they not always contributed to imperial defense with a lavish hand?

Thus far, Jefferson had gone along with Burke and Chatham, but now he reached a parting of the ways. What, he asked, had been offered as to the rectification of the laws of trade which arbitrarily determine where and how the colonies should sell their produce, when, under existing laws, they dare not sell that which England did not buy? 'If we are to contribute equally with all other parts of the Empire, let us equally with them enjoy free commerce with the whole world.'

And, he continued, 'by what right did Parliament propose to meddle' with our provisions for the support of civil government, or our administration of justice? The colonists had made the provisions that pleased themselves; they did not propose to be burdened with oppressive taxes to secure sinecures for the idle or wicked, under color of providing for a civil list. 'While Parliament pursues their plan of civil government within their own jurisdiction, we hope, also, to pursue ours, without molestation.'

And why had Lord North so completely ignored so many of the grievances of the colonies?

He proposed no renunciation of the right to tax.

He proposed no repeal of acts for restraining the trade and altering the form of government of the Eastern colonies.

He did not hint at abandoning the protested 'right' to transfer Americans for trial before Middlesex juries.

He did not abandon the right to quarter soldiers on the colonies in days of peace and without the consent of the colonies.

He did not renounce the pretension that his ministers and governors could dissolve the colonial legislatures at their will.

And then the close:

The proposition seems also calculated to lull into fatal security our well-affected fellow subjects on the other side of the water till time shall be given for the operation of those arms which a British Minister pronounced would instantaneously reduce the 'cowardly' sons of America to unreserved submission. But when the world reflects how inadequate to justice are the vaunted terms; when it attends to the rapid and bold succession of injuries, which, during the course of eleven years, have been aimed at these colonies; when it reviews the pacific and respectful expostulations which during the whole time have been the sole arms we opposed to them; when it observes that our complaints were either not heard at all, or were answered with new and accumulated injuries; when it recollects that the Minister, himself, declared on an early occasion that he would 'never treat with America till he had brought her to his feet,' and that an avowed partisan of Ministry has, more lately, denounced against America the dreadful sentence, 'Delenda est Carthago,' and that this was done in the presence of the British senate, and, being unreproved by them, must be taken to be their sentiments; when it considers that the great armaments with which they have invaded us, and the circumstances of cruelty with which they have commenced and prosecuted hostilities; when these things, we say, are laid together, and attentively considered, can the world be deceived into an opinion that we are unreasonable, or can it hesitate to believe with us that nothing but our own exertions may defeat the ministerial sentence of death or submission?

Such was young Jefferson's answer to Lord North, which both the Virginia Assembly and the Continental Congress accepted as their own.

Jefferson was now released to proceed to Philadelphia.

XI

Meanwhile, before he left, there was drama in Virginia. When Henry's resolution providing a militia for defense was passed, and Washington, Jefferson, and others formulated plans, Lord Dunmore conceived the unhappy thought of having the powder in the magazine in Williamsburg put beyond the reach of the Virginians. One night he landed a squad of marines from a British warship in the James, who marched to Williamsburg in the darkness and seized the powder by stealth and bore it away.

Instantly, the Virginians were aroused. In various centers they rushed to arms, prepared to march upon the capital and the blundering Governor. The conservatives or appeasers urged the rebels to disperse, and in some communities they harkened to the voice of the old leaders. But the men from Hanover, under the command of Patrick Henry, scorned the voice of conservatism and marched on. Henry hurried his men along the road to Williamsburg intent on dealing summarily with Dunmore. The Governor now took alarm, and when Henry's men were within sixteen miles of the capital, Dunmore sent an emissary to meet them with the offer of more money than the powder was worth. Then, only, did Henry turn back.

And then, one night, while Jefferson was still in Virginia, some young men entered the old magazine to seize some arms and were wounded by a spring gun set on the orders of Dunmore. The town roared and trembled with indignation, threats, and curses, and furious eyes were turned toward the Palace of the cowering Governor who stood not on the order of his going but hurried away post-haste to the refuge of a British man-of-war. Thus the last of Virginia's Royal Governors passed ingloriously from the scene forever. Before his departure he had converted the Palace, which

had resounded with mirth and music in the halcyon days of
Fauquier, into a fortress, with arms in readiness to repel any
possible attack.[8]

With the flight of Dunmore, the Assembly adjourned. Before
leaving, Richard Henry Lee lingered for a moment on the familiar
portico of the Capitol and on one of the white pillars smilingly
scratched these words:

> When shall we three meet again?
> In thunder, lightning, or in rain.
> When the hurly-burly's done,
> When the battle's lost and won.

It was after these manifestations of determination that Jefferson,
seated in a phaeton, with two spare horses, drove toward Philadelphia, where greater triumphs, both for himself and his country,
awaited him. He was now a national figure, his name known in
parliamentary circles in London, and he was not yet thirty-three.

[8] Tyler, *Williamsburg*, 217.

FIGHTING IN THE
CONTINENTAL CONGRESS

I

TO UNDERSTAND the atmosphere of the Second Continental Congress when Jefferson was foremost, it is necessary to review the tone, tendencies, and alignments of the First.

The convocation of a congress of all the colonies was hailed with enthusiasm by the people. In the letters of New England delegates describing their triumphant journey to Philadelphia, one still feels the thrill and throb of it. Armed guards met them in one community and passed them on to guards in the next, and thus they drove between grim patriots with fixed bayonets. In New York City, it seemed to Silas Deane that 'well-nigh every open carriage in the city and thousands on foot, trudging and sweating through the dirt,' gave welcome. He found 'the doors, the windows, the stoops, the roofs loaded with all ranks, ages and sexes.' Near the town the populace had unhitched the horses of the delegates' carriages to drag them through the cheering throng. At the lodgings of each of the delegates in New York was stationed a guard of grenadiers in blue and scarlet uniforms. So accustomed did the delegates become to the popular adulation that a number of them, arriving at Stamford, Connecticut, and finding a goodly company assembled at a house for dinner, 'stumped in' and seated themselves without ceremony at the table, and it was not until after they had finished that they discovered they had taken possession of a wedding feast.[1] With bands playing, people cheering, the gaily uniformed

[1] Deane, *Correspondence*, 222-23.

grenadiers marching with fixed bayonets, the New England leaders were escorted to the ferry, and three miles from Newark a troop of horse and a company of grenadiers became their escort through New Jersey.[2]

Thus they proceeded on their historic journey, and within six miles of Philadelphia 'two hundred of the principal gentlemen, with their swords drawn,' joined the procession. The procession that moved into the city had half the men on horseback in the van, followed by ten more with drawn swords, and then the carriage of Adams and Hancock, with other equestrians in the rear. Thus did they enter the new capital, with the bells ringing and the narrow streets seething with excited men and women.[3] On entering the town, 'dusty, dirty, and fatigued,' John Adams records that they were taken to Smith's Tavern, 'the most genteel one in America,' where, after some conversation, 'a curtain was drawn, and in the other half of the chamber a supper appeared as elegant as ever was laid upon a table.'[4]

Followed then an orgy of calling and returning calls, and invitations to the aristocratic houses poured in on the more conspicuous and promising members. John Dickinson, of Philadelphia, destined to play a dramatic part in the first two Congresses as spokesman of the aristocratic and proprietary interests, appeared at Adams's door in a carriage drawn by four horses and with much cracking of the whip.[5] The conversations were political and interminable. Delegates, visiting their colleagues in their lodgings, lingered far into the night, and at Smith's 'genteel' tavern glasses clicked, tongues clacked, toasts passed almost every evening. The coffee-houses did a thriving business. Even the staid and serious John Adams rather proudly boasted of going to a man's store, where he 'drank punch and ate dried smoked sprats with him,' and tarried until eleven at night drinking toasts. Meanwhile, Richard Henry Lee and Ben Harrison, of Virginia, had been regaled with Burgundy at Dickinson's, and when Adams saw them they were 'very high.'[6] Every man was proud he was a member of the Congress, and, after dinner at Mifflin's, when the guests had retired to the tavern, the corpulent

---

[2] *Ibid.*, 227-29.   [3] *Ibid.*
[4] Burnett, *Letters of Members of the Continental Congress*, I, 1.
[5] *Ibid.*   [6] *Ibid.*, I, 2.

Harrison was declaring that he would have walked to Philadelphia had it been necessary, and Bland, who looked older than he was and was not sweet on independence, announced that on such an occasion he would have 'gone to Jerico.'[7] When, at a dinner given by the Pennsylvania House of Representatives, a sentiment was offered: 'May the sword of the parent never be stained with the blood of her children,' Adams heard someone say, 'This is not a toast; it is a prayer.'[8]

That it was a goodly company that composed the Congress we must assume, since the censorious John Adams wrote a friend that 'Congress is such an assembly as never before came together on a sudden in any part of the world. Here are fortunes, abilities, learning, eloquence, astuteness equal to any I have ever met in my life. Here is a diversity of religions, educations, manners, interests such as it would seem impossible to unite in one plan of conduct. Every question is discussed with moderation, an acuteness and minuteness equal to that of Queen Elizabeth's Privy Council.' But, he added a bit sourly, to give it the Adams touch, 'this occasions infinite delays.'[9]

But the social lobby began working early upon the members, for the aristocratic houses were the homes of rigid conservatives, bent on keeping the Congress out of mischief. The atmosphere of these merchants' mansions was not congenial to the taste of the real revolutionists like Sam Adams and Richard Henry Lee. The former, one of the older members, spent most of his spare time in his room, writing letters to his henchmen in Boston and girding his loins for the struggle he knew to be inevitable. Throughout, this stalwart was to be the center and soul of the movement for independence. He had concentrated so exclusively on public affairs that he had been reduced to something near poverty; and he was so indifferent to his appearance that only through the stealth of his family and friends had a new suit been forced upon him for his journey to Philadelphia.[10] His arch-enemy, Joseph Galloway, who led the forces absolutely hostile to independence, described him as a man who 'eats little, drinks little, sleeps little, thinks much, and is most decisive and indefatigable in the pursuit of his objects.' Day

---

[7] Ibid.   [8] Ibid., I, 79.   [9] Ibid., I, 60.
[10] Wells, Life and Speeches of Samuel Adams, II, 208.

and night, when released from the sessions, he sat at his desk in his simple quarters, writing, writing, writing, and organizing, not only the masses of the people of Boston, but of Philadelphia, where it was not fashionable to have truck with common folk.[11] Realizing instantly that nothing decisive could be expected from the politicians in Congress, Adams began systematically to build fires behind them.

Especially true was this in Pennsylvania, which was governed under a charter granted William Penn by Charles II, and the Proprietary Government, supported by the aristocracy, was conducted arbitrarily and in utter disregard of the interests of the colony. The Penn family, in possession of 55,252 square miles of land, or 35,361,300 acres, took full advantage of the charter to serve their most sordid selfish interests. They made themselves immune from taxation on their millions of rich acres; their treatment of the Indians was atrocious; and the white settlers, who fell victims to the red man's natural resentment in consequence, were left with scant protection. Settlers in the colony were given no consideration by the Government dominated from England by the Penns, who were primarily concerned with profits for the family, frowned on any expenditures for the benefit of the public, since that reduced the golden flow of cash into the family money chest.

As so often is the case with wealth and power, the family easily surrounded itself with many of the ablest men in the colony for the protection of its greed; and because they represented prestige and fortune, the society of the community was subservient to its will. With independence the charter would go; the domination of the Penns would end; the mass of the people would have a voice in the determination of their destiny; and thus it was that, during the First Congress, it was subtly influenced and guided by the drawing-rooms and the counting-rooms of the friends, employees, and beneficiaries of the proprietary interests.

II

Of the Philadelphia enemies of independence, John Dickinson and Joseph Galloway, both members of the Congress, were of the most imposing stature. We shall present a miniature of the former

11 *Ibid.*, II, 230.

a little later when he assumes the leadership of the forces opposed
to separation from the Empire. The latter's congressional career
ended with the First Congress in which he was powerful.

A contemporary had no doubt that in going to Congress 'his
design undoubtedly was to impede if he could not divert the current
of affairs.' [12] Born to wealth, intellectually superior and thoroughly
trained, Galloway had easily won a commanding position as a
pleader at the bar, and his marriage into one of the richest families
had not tended to make him more democratic. He possessed ability
of a high order. He was familiar with the classics, with history and
with the political philosophy of the seventeenth and eighteenth
centuries. He was vice-president of the American Philosophical
Society, which Jefferson admired. During his twenty years in the
Pennsylvania Assembly he had been a faithful and efficient servant
of the aristocratic merchant class. Cold, austere, haughty, contemptuous of the common people, he owed his repeated elections,
not to his personal popularity, but wholly to the powerful political
machine of the Quakers. This, too, had elevated him to the Speaker-
ship of the Assembly which he held for seven years until the eve
of the Revolution. Throughout the First Congress, he worked unceasingly and with consummate ability to hold back the flood with
which the Adamses and Lees threatened to sweep away the connection with the Empire.

His task was all the easier at this time because few among the
patriots were thinking in terms of absolute independence. Only
a small coterie, under the leadership of Samuel Adams, Richard
Henry Lee, and Patrick Henry, had any purpose other than to
force a stubborn King and a pliant Parliament to rectify the
wrongs and establish the rights of the colonies on a firm foundation. John Jay and the New York delegates were firm supporters
of the Empire, and in the Virginia delegation, Ben Harrison, an
enemy of Lee, symbolized the same conservative opposition that
he had in the Virginia Assembly. Silas Deane wrote his wife that
Harrison was 'an uncommonly large man' who was 'rather rough
in his address and speech'; [13] and John Adams thought him an
'indolent, luxurious, heavy gentleman of no use in Congress or
committee, but a great embarrassment to both.' [14]

[12] Graydon, *Memoirs,* 117.   [13] Burnett, *Letters,* I, 28.   [14] *Ibid.,* I, 32.

However, Harrison was more in accord with the majority in the First Congress than Adams. And it must be noted that the greatest personage on the Virginia delegation was in accord with Harrison — a very silent man described by Deane as 'nearly as tall as Colonel Fitch and almost as hard of countenance, yet with a very young look and an easy soldier-like air and gesture.'[15] This was Washington, and at this time nothing was more remote from his thought or wish than independence. It is improbable that he had ever approved wholeheartedly the impetuous methods of Patrick Henry, who had momentarily raised the tone and spirit of the Congress with an opening speech of fiery defiance.

This orator's contempt for the appeasers knew no bounds. One night, during a talk-fest with John Adams, he expressed a 'horrid opinion' of Galloway and Jay, whose position he thought 'would ruin the cause of America.' He writhed under the torture of not having 'the liberty to describe them in their true colors.'[16]

More in accord with Adams and Henry was Benjamin Franklin, one of the minority on the Pennsylvania delegation, constant in attendance, attentive, 'composed and grave,' who was wise enough to bide his time and do his work quietly behind the scenes. John Adams had found that 'he does not hesitate at our boldest measures, but rather seems to think us too irresolute and backward . . . a good and great man.'[17]

III

Within a month after the Congress convened, John Adams, noting the ultra-conservative and conciliatory spirit of his colleagues, realized that those among them who secretly hoped for offensive measures were doomed to disappointment. 'I have had opportunity, both public and private,' he wrote, 'to learn with certainty the decisive sentiments of the delegates. . . . They will not at this session vote to raise money or men or arms or ammunition. Their opinions are fixed against hostilities and rupture, except they should become absolutely necessary.'[18]

Galloway saw the delegates divided into two coteries, one wishing to demand American rights, petition for the remedy of wrongs, and avoid all sorts of sedition or violence; the other aiming at inde-

[15] *Ibid.*, I, 28.   [16] *Ibid.*, I, 71.   [17] *Ibid.*, I, 174.   [18] *Ibid.*, I, 65.

pendence. The first he describes as 'men of property,' which, in the eyes of Galloway, made them superior; the second, he was sure, were 'Congregational and Presbyterian republicans, or men of bankrupt fortunes, overwhelmed in debt to the British merchants.' [19]

During the first part of the session, the Galloways were in the ascendant and played the fiddle of conciliation to which the others danced. Even so, Galloway had received some snubs that left him wondering. As Speaker of the Assembly, he had offered the State House for the sessions, and when the city placed Carpenter's Hall at the disposal of the delegates, he took the proffer as a challenge. But one day the delegates met at the tavern and walked in a body to Carpenter's Hall, and, finding it to their liking, accepted it, to the chagrin of Galloway.[20] But more pointed was the snub he received when the delegates elected as Secretary of the Congress, without his approval, a Philadelphian anathema to him. Charles Thomson had been summoned to Carpenter's Hall and informed that 'Congress desires the favor of you, Sir, to take their minutes.' Thus early were the Adamses, Franklins, and Lees getting in their work. Writing Franklin's bastard son, then Governor of New Jersey, who, like himself, was to prove a traitor to America, Galloway expressed astonishment that Thomson had been elected unanimously, and explained that the New Yorkers and himself, finding themselves in a minority, thought it unwise to make a fight. 'Both of these measures'—the choice of Carpenter's Hall and the election of Thomson—'were privately settled by an interest made out of doors,' he wrote. The sharpness of the rebuke to Galloway and his group in Pennsylvania lay in the fact that they, with the aid of the proprietary machine, had prevented Thomson's election to Congress.[21] He was an enemy of the Penns, an ardent champion of stern measures, and, worst of all according to Galloway, an organizer of the people. 'Charles Thomson is the Sam Adams of Philadelphia, the life of the cause of liberty, they say,' wrote John Adams to his wife.[22]

The strategy of Galloway was to dampen the spirits of the more ardent patriots by subterfuges or procrastinations. He proposed sending commissioners to London, as did the colonies of Rome, Greece, and Macedonia. If their proposals did not meet with ap-

[19] *Ibid.*, I, 55.   [20] *Ibid.*, I, 4, 7.   [21] *Ibid.*, I, 9.   [22] *Ibid.*, I, 1.

proval, they could remain in London to advise the colonies. This would postpone any decisive action for many months. Later, he proposed a Constitution for the Empire, utterly impossible, as he must have known, at that time.[23] He, and those working with him, planned to wear out the patience of the delegates and tire them with interminable talk. Every memorial address or petition was made the subject of discussions until John Adams, in disgust, wrote in his *Diary* that 'these great wits, these subtle critics, these refined geniuses, these learned lawyers, these wise statesmen are so fond of showing their parts and powers as to make their consultations very tedious.'[24]

Another part of the Galloway strategy was to divide the patriots. In the naming of two vitally important committees, one to organize the purchase of arms and ammunition and the other to explore the possibilities of a foreign alliance, the committees were packed with the friends of the King. Some were the most extreme Tories. Among the Virginians, only Harrison, notoriously opposed then to independence, was included. The members were largely from New York and Pennsylvania whose delegates were appeasers. In the appointment of committees before this, all sections of opinion had been included.

A few days later, John Jay insinuated himself into the lodgings of John Adams to explain his exclusion. In a play to his well-known vanity, Adams was told that he was one of the foremost men in the country, but that his relations with Samuel Adams and Richard Henry Lee had operated against him. But young Jay did not know Adams. The old patriot flamed. Of course, he said, he had been astonished that no Massachusetts man had been put on either committee. It was a trick that had been arranged 'out of doors.' True, he was attached to Samuel Adams and Lee, and why not? They were 'able men, inflexible in the cause of their country.' And then, in frigid accents, he added that he would not cool in his friendship for such men 'for the sake of any distinction that Congress can bestow.' To which he added something uglier — that the purpose of the committees was well known and that the choice was dictated by 'commercial projects and private speculations.'

The attempt to divide the militants had failed.

[23] *Ibid.*, I, 6.   [24] *Ibid.*, I, 81.

IV

But Galloway and the conservatives, bent on the connection with the Empire at any cost, were fighting against a current growing stronger because of the insane stupidities of the court in London. There was little they could say for conciliation when the erroneous word reached Philadelphia that Boston had been bombarded. The streets rumbled and growled their resentment and muffled bells tolled, while every countenance bore 'unfeigned marks of sorrow.' The excitement and disgust of the streets penetrated and affected even the usual complacency of the Congress.[25] Then Paul Revere, one of Samuel Adams's 'vulgar men,' rode into Philadelphia with the resolutions of Suffolk County, Massachusetts, and they were 'read with great applause' in Carpenter's Hall, where resolutions pledging sympathy and support were passed.[26]

This shocked Galloway and his followers, who feared that such stout defiance might interfere with their plans of bringing a gentle persuasion on the King through dutiful, if not obsequious, petitions. One of the appeasers (Ross, of Pennsylvania) actually offered a motion threatening that, if Massachusetts persisted in her method of resistance by force, she would be left to her own resources. Galloway sprang to his feet to second the motion. Even though this motion failed, the greater part of the Congress clung with a pathetic faith to the hope that George III would soften his resentment and grant its humble petitions.

Thus it came to pass that another petition to the King was planned, and it fell to John Dickinson to prepare it. In the selection of the writer, the First Congress gave unmistakable proof of its repugnance to independence. The petition was the persuasive plea of a child to a parent, predicated on the false assumption that the King's Ministers were persecuting his people without his knowledge or approval. Never was a monarch to read a petition indicative of more loyalty and devotion to his person. It made a vigorous and manly protest against the violation of the rights of the Americans, but closed with the amusing thought that 'the language of free men cannot be displeasing to Your Majesty.' Nothing, of course, was to come of it.

[25] *Ibid.*, I, 11, 19.   [26] *Ibid.*, I, 37.

This was the most celebrated paper of that Congress and little was achieved. Even so, the members managed to live hectic lives. 'My time is totally filled from the moment I get out of bed until I return to it,' wrote John Adams. 'Visits, ceremonies, company, business, newspapers, pamphlets, etc.'[27] The congressmen met at nine and sat until three daily, 'by which time,' wrote Adams, 'we are unable to do anything but eat and drink the rest of the day.'[28] This note recurs constantly in his correspondence. 'Tedious indeed is our business — slow as snails. We sit only before dinner. We dine at four o'clock. We are crowded with levees in the evening.'[29] After debating 'the most obtuse mysteries of state until three in the afternoon,' the members adjourned to 'dine with some of the nobles of Pennsylvania . . . and feast upon a thousand delicacies, and sit drinking Madeira and Burgundy till six or seven.'[30]

Later, the sessions extended beyond the dinner hour, for one delegate wrote that if the sessions ended at three instead of five he might 'bear it tolerably well,'[31] and Deane protested that 'eleven hours sitting is too much for my constitution.'[32] But these prolonged sittings came later in the second session. The members fared much better in the first, when so few thought seriously of independence that Samuel Adams and his militant group from Massachusetts were forewarned by their Philadelphia friends that open talk of independence would destroy their influence. These, with the Lees, continued to work toward their determined end, but under cover. Samuel Adams realized that there were many 'prejudices' to be overcome before progress would be possible. On the eve of their adjournment, Washington sought John Adams and Richard Henry Lee at their lodgings to ask their assurance that their policy did not have independence as its aim. The assurance was given.

But there was one member who could not, and would not, have given that pledge. Samuel Adams was not seen so frequently eating the 'thousand delicacies' and drinking the rare wines of the 'nobles of Pennsylvania,' for he had other things in view. He sat in his lodgings and wrote incessantly — letters to the Bostonians, to his henchmen, letters to the press signed by some Roman name, and he wrote pamphlets; and, if he conversed less than others with the

27 *Ibid.*, I, 31.   28 *Ibid.*, I, 34.   29 *Ibid.*, I, 47.   30 *Ibid.*, I, 60.
31 Reed, *Life of Joseph Reed,* I, 98.   32 *Ibid.*, I, 130.

'nobles,' he talked infinitely more with 'people of no importance' in the Philadelphia which had not yet effectively rebelled against the domination of the proprietary machine. He was planning his appeal to the people behind the backs of the politicians.

V

One month before the Congress met again, the British army had gone into action against the colonies at Lexington and Concord, where the 'embattled farmers fired the shot heard round the world.' Soon thereafter the patriots fought and died at Bunker Hill. The story of these clashes electrified the country, giving pause to the pacifists and arousing the fighting spirit of the patriots. Even so, when the Congress met, the conciliators, still in control, were more grimly opposed to independence than before. The American blood shed at Lexington, Concord, and Bunker Hill had not shaken their confidence in the loving kindness of the King. But the 'forward men' no longer dissimulated their desires. Samuel Adams was now openly demanding a definitive breaking of the connection with the Empire. John Adams, who had once cherished the hope of a rectification of colonial wrongs within the framework of the union, had now abandoned all hope of conciliation. Richard Henry Lee, of course, was vigorously insisting on a manly declaration of absolute independence and an appeal to arms. Wythe, whose shout of 'Treason' had broken in on the flood of Patrick Henry's burning eloquence, had now taken his stand against the supine and futile policy of sending abject petitions to a monarch indifferent to colonial rights.

And moving quietly, with a cold dignity, among the delegates was Washington, whose silence was less noticeable than the military uniform in which he now appeared upon the floor. It was more eloquent than words.

And at this time the delegates familiar with the *Summary View* were awaiting the appearance of Jefferson with curiosity and respect. He had not arrived for the opening sessions, having been detained in Virginia to prepare the Reply to North. Word had percolated into Philadelphia that he had written that, as well.

But all the Virginians had not been affected by the 'shot heard round the world.' Harrison and Carter Braxton, representing a caste in retreat, were as bitterly opposed to separation as ever — Braxton especially. He hated republicanism, despised democracy, and loathed the thought of political power in Virginia passing from the aristocrats of the Tidewater and the James to the smaller farmers of the new settlements.

In the first months of the Second Congress, the enemies of independence remained in the majority, despite a few losses from their camp. But the fight now was in the open. No more dissimulation, no more working under cover for the militants.

VI

Meanwhile, Joseph Galloway had retired to write his *Candid Examination of the Mutual Claims of Great Britain and the Colonies,* on the thesis that, with unlimited patience, all grievances would ultimately be redressed without recourse to revolution. But Philadelphia had changed, and with 'people of no importance' now articulate in the streets, he had left the city for the greater security of the country. Soon he would have to escape again — to the protection of the British army, and, as an underling of Lord Howe, when Philadelphia fell to the redcoats, he would act as civil administrator and superintendent of police. And a third time he would be in flight when Washington recaptured the city, but this time he would escape to England to continue his fight against his countrymen, to furnish evidence against them, and to be crushed by the event at Yorktown. His property would be confiscated and he reduced to the status of a miserable pensioner of a contemptuous court. His petition for permission to return to Philadelphia would be scornfully denied, and he would die in England and there be buried, unwept, unhonored, and unsung. Such was the end of the man who, more than any other, dominated the First Continental Congress.[33]

However, his retirement had not weakened the force of the Pennsylvania delegation as a spearhead in the fight against independence. Most of the delegates were the hand-picked favorites of the proprietary machine and reactionary in the extreme. Benjamin

[33] *Dictionary of American Biography,* VII, 116-17.

Franklin was an exception, as before. Most of the others were primarily champions of the Penns against the people. And among these was one of commanding ability, who, from this time until the fight was lost, would lead with brilliance and finesse the fight against independence.

VII

John Dickinson was in his forty-third year. At this time John Adams wrote of him that 'he is a shadow; tall but slender as a reed; one would think at first sight that he could not live a month; yet upon a more attentive inspection [he] looks as if the springs of life were strong enough to last many years.' Less prejudiced observers found him to have a fine presence and a handsome countenance illuminated by the glow of his keen intelligence. In speech, he was fluent and persuasive, if not inspiring and eloquent, and the sweetness of his tone and the pleasant modulation of his voice made an agreeable impression. Nature intended him for the senate and the courts, not for great popular assemblies.[34] Deborah Logan, who knew him well, found his conversation fascinating, and thought his mind 'a rich casket of all the various knowledge which history contains, for he had read the most and brought his judgment to bear upon his reading the best of any person I ever knew.' [35] His manner, ordinarily, was mild and amiable, and all his instincts, in private intercourse as well as in politics, tended toward the conciliatory and deferential. His sincerity and good intentions were so manifest that most of those who differed with him held him in affection. He was always frank and honest in the expression of his opinions.

Dickinson's family had migrated in the previous century from England where they had been middle-class landowners and city merchants. In childhood he studied at home under an Irish tutor who instilled in him a love of the classics which may account for the clarity, strength, and dignity of his style. Maturing early, he began the study of law in Philadelphia in his eighteenth year, but later he went to London, where, in the Middle Temple, he studied for four years. That he found time for gossip in the coffee-houses

[34] Stillé, *Life and Times of John Dickinson*, 37.   [35] *Ibid.*, 334.

and for an occasional debate in the Commons, we may assume; that he delved deep into history and political philosophy is seen in his own literary labors. It is significant that, unlike Jefferson, he was not an admirer of John Locke. Certain it is, that when he returned to Philadelphia he was a Constitutional Whig of the English pattern, whose ideas of political opposition were based on English traditions and English law. It was this conviction, formed in the Middle Temple, that all political wrongs could be righted through legal methods, that determined his course up to the Declaration of Independence. He despised and dreaded the demagogue, and he had an aristocratic contempt for appeals to the mass mind. To him the town meetings of Massachusetts were little more than mobs.

His consistent support of the Proprietary Government of Pennsylvania, however, was not purchased, for he held no office of its bestowal, and he owed no obligations to the Penns. He realized their sordid selfishness, their cruel indifference, their lack of vision, their prostitution of everything to profits, and, in his long-drawn battle with Franklin, who opposed them, he conceded the weakness of their system. He justified his championship of their cause on the ground that, because of certain privileges guaranteed by their charter, the colony was better served than it would be if governed by the Ministers in London and completely at the mercy of the King. That the alignment of the aristocracy of the 'Pennsylvania nobles' with the Penns had some effect upon his attitude is more than probable.

He had opposed the Stamp Act as heartily as any patriot, but when, at a meeting of the Philadelphia bar, it was proposed that the lawyers should transact their business without buying stamps, he was sincerely shocked. 'Revolutionary!' he complained, and certainly, he said, such disregard of the law was unbecoming the dignity of the bar.[36]

And yet no man rendered greater service to American liberty than John Dickinson, in the writing of the famous letters of the 'Pennsylvania Farmer,' published over a period of time in the *Pennsylvania Chronicle*, setting forth the cause of the colonies against the extraordinary measures of the Ministry. Brilliant, crystal-clear in reasoning, striking in phrasing, they were statesmanlike in tone,

[36] *Ibid.*, 74.

and might have been written by a Burke or Bolingbroke, with no personal interest in America. They dressed the arguments of the colonies in the garb of legality, free from the passionate declamation and denunciation of the times. With a serenity of treatment indicative of complete confidence in his cause, Dickinson defined the law, evoked the traditions of British liberty, and with a quiet force he crucified the Ministry that had trampled upon the law, denied their rights to British freemen, and threatened to alienate the affections of the colonies.

But, unlike Jefferson, Lee, and Adams, he did not deny the right of the Parliament to levy taxes on them without their representation or consent. He merely showed that it had never been done before.

The spirit of these papers is reflected in a brief extract:

> The cause of Liberty is a cause of too much dignity to be sullied by turbulence and tumult. It ought to be maintained in a manner suitable to her nature. Those who engage in it should breathe a sedate, yet fervent spirit, animating them to actions of prudence, justice, modesty, bravery, humanity, magnanimity. If at length it becomes undoubted that an inveterate resolution is formed to annihilate the liberties of the governed, English history affords frequent examples of resistance by force. What particular circumstances will, in any future case, justify such resistance cannot be ascertained until they happen. Perhaps it may be allowable to say generally that it can never be justified until the people are fully convinced that any further submission would be destructive of their happiness.

As the author of these letters, the fame of Dickinson spread throughout the colonies and reached England, where Chatham paid tribute to the genius of the writer. They remain classics in the literary history of the Revolution. Dickinson was the hope and the darling of the Tory drawing-rooms, but the brilliance and charm of the man, differing perhaps in pace with the 'forward men,' drew them to him in social intercourse.

VIII

And the social lobby never was employed more consciously to influence history than in the Philadelphia of that time.

Nothing could have been more delightful than a summer afternoon at 'Fairhill,' the country home of Dickinson, built after the plan of 'Dolobran,' an ancient seat in Wales, set in a lovely countryside, with the country houses of others of the aristocracy not remote. The courts and gardens, with the gravel walks after the English fashion, and the primeval trees, gave it an air of elegance and ease. In the garden, apart from the house, stood a low building with several rooms that contained the extensive library of the owner; and there, through the ivy-covered windows, came the hum of the bees of the neighboring hives. The mansion itself, constructed of material brought from England, when built, was thought the most beautiful in the colony.

Here the most aristocratic society of Philadelphia, mostly devoted to the interests of the Penns, and a few inclined to independence from the mother country, wined, dined, talked, and walked the garden paths. These grounds had been reserved for the socially élite. But during the fight in Congress the gates were unlatched to lesser people who had votes, and these frequently were found at Dickinson's table drinking his choice wines. That Jefferson visited 'Fairhill' and rummaged among the books there can be no doubt. Both he and the host were masters of the pen in political polemics, and each had a reputation that reached to England. But Adams and the more advanced of the revolutionists found the atmosphere uncongenial.[37]

The social lobby played a conspicuous part in the strategy of those who stood steadfast against a definite break with England, and 'Fairhill' was its happy hunting-ground.

However, Dickinson and his followers were not staking everything on a reed so puny. It served with puny men, but there were others; and to make sure of these, Dickinson and his aids were urging loyalist legislatures in the various colonies to instruct their delegates against independence. Their efforts bore fruit. But Samuel Adams and the Lees were writing popular leaders in the colonies to bring the pressure of an aroused people to bear upon the legislatures.

As is usually the case, the real drama was in the wings.

[37] *Ibid.*, 311-15.

IX

Though the session opened May 10, 1775, Jefferson did not reach Philadelphia until June 21, having been ten days upon the road. Not only had he been held in Williamsburg for an important service, but Jefferson, who enormously admired and trusted George Mason, made an earnest effort to have him chosen in his stead. In conversation with Philip Mazzei, he had said of Mason that 'he is one of those strong, very rare intellects which are created only by a special effort of nature, like that of Dante, a Machiavelli, a Galileo, a Newton, a Franklin, a Turgot, a Helvetius.' [38] Writing at the time, Mason said that 'a strong party was formed at the head of which were Colonel Henry, Mr. Jefferson, and Colonel Carrington, for sending me to Congress at all events.' [39] It is worthy of note that Jefferson was singularly free from personal ambition.

The journey in the phaeton, with the two spare horses, had not been an easy one, and, having lost his bearings between Fredericksburg and the Potomac, and again between Wilmington and Philadelphia, he had been forced to engage guides.

Though a new man, and one of the youngest in the body, his reputation as the author of the *Summary View* and of Virginia's Reply to Lord North, had preceded him and assured him a warm welcome among the militants. From the moment of his appearance there was a general disposition to make use of his pen. Almost immediately he was placed upon a committee to frame a declaration of the causes for taking up arms. Seated beside him was Governor Livingston, who proposed at once that young Jefferson should draft it.

'We are as yet but new acquaintances, sir,' said the astonished Jefferson. 'Why are you so in earnest for me doing it?'

'Because I have been informed you drew the address to the people of Great Britain, a production certainly worthy of the finest pen in America,' was the reply.

Jefferson, no doubt embarrassed, suggested that Livingston might have been misinformed. Nevertheless, he drew that draft. And, quite inevitably, Dickinson found it much too heady for his taste and calculated to interfere with his attempts at reconciliation. He

[38] Mazzei, *Memoirs*, 205.   [39] Henry, *Life of Patrick Henry*, I, 315.

found some of the raw-meat facts offensive. But, as Jefferson was afterward to explain, 'he was an honest man, and so able a one, that he was greatly indulged even by those who did not feel his scruples.' Thus, he was asked 'to take the paper and put it into a form he could approve.' Whether he actually wrote the new draft as is generally agreed, or it was written by John Jay as others say, does not matter since it is certain that the two conferred and quite as certain that the new draft was less a modification than an entirely new creation. Jefferson himself said that only the last four and a half paragraphs of his draft were retained.[40] This was approved by Congress. Incidentally, the part retained from Jefferson's draft was the most spirited part of the whole:

> Lest this declaration should disquiet the minds of our friends and fellow subjects in any part of the empire, we assure them that we mean not to dissolve that union which has so long and so happily subsisted between us, and which we sincerely wish to see restored. Necessity has not yet driven us into that desperate measure, or induced us to excite any other nation to war against them. We have not raised armies with ambitious designs of separating from Great Britain and establishing independent states. We fight not for glory nor for conquest. We exhibit to mankind the remarkable spectacle of a people attacked by unprovoked enemies, without any imputation or even suspicion of offense. They boast of their privileges and civilization, and yet proffer no milder conditions than servitude or death.
>
> In our native land, in defense of the freedom that is our birthright and which we ever enjoyed till the late violation of it; for the protection of our property, acquired by the honest industry of our forefathers and ourselves; against violence actually offered, we have taken up arms. We shall lay them down when hostilities shall cease on the part of the aggressors and all danger of their being renewed shall be removed, and not before.
>
> With a humble confidence in the mercies of the supreme and impartial Judge and Ruler of the Universe, we most devoutly implore His Divine goodness to protect us happily through this great conflict, to dispose our adversaries to reconciliation on reasonable terms, and thereby to relieve the empire from the calamities of civil war.[41]

[40] *Autobiography*, 11.　　[41] *Journal of Congress*, II, 153.

Meanwhile, Jefferson found himself on numerous committees, and entrusted very frequently with the writing of reports. Other events momentarily overshadowed these. It was in June, 1775, that Major Skene arrived in America bearing a commission as Governor of Ticonderoga, but with 'unlimited orders to draw on the Treasury for any sums necessary to bribe and buy members of Congress.' [42] It was whispered in the coffee-shops of Philadelphia that his slush fund had not found some members of the New York legislature indifferent to its charms. Made a prisoner on his parole, he soon passes from the picture. More significant was the day the delegates in Congress turned to the strong, silent man in uniform and unanimously called George Washington to the supreme command of the Continental Army. 'This appointment will have a great effect in securing the union of these colonies,' wrote John Adams to his wife.[43]

Immediately afterward, Washington rode out of the city on the country road toward Boston, accompanied a part of the way by the Massachusetts delegation on horseback, and by 'a large troop of light horse in their uniforms; many officers of militia in theirs; a band playing music.' [44]

Thus, grim events were closing in rapidly on the appeasers. The conciliatory proposals of Lord North reached Congress for consideration in July. Fearing the tone and temper of the reply if entrusted to the suave pen of Dickinson and his group, Peyton Randolph, in appointing Jefferson, Franklin, and John Adams to frame the answer, asked Jefferson again to undertake the task. It was a preference not likely to be resented by Franklin or Adams, since they and all other members of the Congress had read Jefferson's Reply on behalf of Virginia. He wrote the answer — following the line of the Virginia document.

X

June passed drearily. Sweltering in the heat, the congressmen were discussing the feasibility of moving to Connecticut. Washing-

[42] Burnett, *Letters of Members of Continental Congress*, Dyer to Trumbull, 116; Virginia delegates to unknown, I, 124.
[43] Adams, *Letters to His Wife*, I, 130.   [44] *Ibid.*, I, 142.

ton was now at the head of an army in the field. George III was sending out feelers on the possibility of engaging mercenary soldiers to meet him. Bitterness was intensifying, the mass of the people were awakening and rumbling. The talk of independence was increasing throughout the country, and here and there a congressman was shying away from the doubtful banner of Dickinson, to join the more positive forces of the 'forward men.' Washington no longer hoped for conciliation. And the ingratiating, personally popular Dickinson was pleading less convincingly now, with Washington at the head of his soldiers, that nothing rash be done until another pleading petition, duly humble, could be laid at the feet of the King.

Strangely enough, even at this late day, after Washington had actually unsheathed his sword, the majority in Congress agreed with Dickinson that another obsequious petition should be sent to the monarch. The delegation from Massachusetts, Hancock excepted, frothed with fury and disgust as Dickinson sat down to its preparation. 'This measure of imbecility will find many admirers among the ladies and fine gentlemen,' wrote John Adams, 'but it will not be to my taste. Pettiness, juvenilities, and much less puerilities become not a great assembly like this, the representative of a great people.'

That it was to be all this, and more, may be assumed from Dickinson's letter to Arthur Lee in London. 'Our rights have been already stated,' he wrote, 'our claims made . . . War is actually begun and we are carrying it on vigorously. If Administration is desirous to stop the effusion of British blood, the opportunity is now offered to them *by an unexceptionable Petition praying for an accommodation*. If they reject this application with contempt, the more humble it is, the more such treatment will confirm the minds of our countrymen to endure all the misfortunes that may attend the contest.'[45]

This, however, reveals a Dickinson passionately devoted to the connection, passionately opposed to an arbitrament by the sword, but now prepared, if necessary, to take his stand with his people and fight. Many others in Congress and out, who have escaped the lash of history, were convinced of the wisdom of this last

[45] Burnett, *Letters*, I, 157.

appeal, to the end that posterity might know where the responsibility rested. Charles Thomson, political enemy of Dickinson in Philadelphia, thought the final attempt necessary, 'else it would have been impossible to convince the bulk of the people of Pennsylvania that an humble petition, drawn up without those clauses against which the Ministry and Parliament had taken exception in the former petition, would not have met with a favorable reception and produced the desired effect.' [46]

Even so, the debate was bitter. Most of the militants knew that nothing but contemptuous indifference would follow, and they thought the majority of the people shared their skepticism. But the New England delegates, particularly those from Massachusetts, were beside themselves with fury, and fighting words were uttered in the debate. So biting was the wit and sarcasm of the clever Irishman, Sullivan, of New Hampshire, that Dickinson, losing his head, as his biographer admits, infuriated by the ridicule of the Irish wasp, rushed into the yard, where he found John Adams cooling himself. Dickinson's usually serene face was suffused with anger, and he rushed on Adams in a frenzy. 'What is the reason, Mr. Adams, that you New England men oppose our measures of reconciliation?' he spluttered. 'There, now, is Sullivan, in a long harangue, following you in a determined opposition to our Petition to the King. Look ye — if you don't concur with us in our pacific system, a number of us will break off from you in New England and we will carry on our opposition in our own way.' Adams, astonished at the rudeness of the usually suave, soft-spoken lawyer, replied coldly. It was the last time the two were to speak.

XI

Had this encounter not ended the intercourse of the two men, an incident at this time would have put a termination to their relations. A few days later, the British had intercepted letters from members of Congress en route to Boston. One was from Adams to James Warren; the other from Ben Harrison to Washington. In his letter Adams had referred to 'a certain great Fortune and piddling genius whose fame has been trumpeted so loudly' who had

[46] Stillé, *Life of Dickinson,* 158.

'given a silly cast to our whole doings.' And he had added: 'We are between Hawk and Buzzard.' [47] This was to have a political effect, but it was the letter of Harrison that gave the greatest glee to the British and the Tories. He had complained bitterly of the New England men, but the British had added a story of a meeting with the pretty daughter of his washwoman. The Tory press was to give scant notice to the denunciation of the New Englanders and to concentrate on the flirtation with the girl.

As I was in the pleasing task of writing to you, a little noise occasioned me to turn my head around and who should appear but pretty little Kate, the washerwoman's Daughter over the way, clean, trim and rosy as the morning. I snatched the golden glorious Opportunity, and but for that cursed Antidote to Love, Sukey, I had fitted her for my General against his return. We were obliged to part, but not until we had contrived to meet again; if she keeps the appointment I shall relish a week's longer stay. I give you now and then some of these adventures to amuse you and unbend your mind from the cares of War. [48]

The forgery is clearly shown by the original in the Public Records Office in London and in the transcript of the letter in the Library of Congress. But Draper, of the *Massachusetts Gazette*, a fierce Tory and partisan of the British army in Boston, was to use it to picture the American-patriot leaders as a lecherous brood bent on the seduction of washerwomen's pretty daughters. The campaign of scurrility reached even to the London press and the *London Gazetteer* carried some sharp comments from a correspondent who called himself 'A Boston Saint.' [49]

The moral and unctuous Mr. Benj. Harrison exhibits to us a picture of American hypocrisy . . . ; for while he and his rebel brethren of the Congress are incessantly clamoring . . . he is at the same time debauching all the pretty girls in his neighborhood on purpose to raise a squadron of whores to keep his old General warm during the winter quarters. . . . It has become fashionable in America for the Saints to have their procurers and their Delilahs.

[47] Adams, *Letters*, I, 176.   [48] *Massachusetts Gazette*, August 17, 1775.
[49] *London Gazetteer*, September 20, 1775, quoted in *Massachusetts Gazette*, February 22, 1776.

Whilst the General is fighting the Lord's battles in Massachusetts, his procurer, the holy Mr. Benj. Harrison, is fitting pretty little Kate, his washerwoman's daughter, for the Lord's General. Even Hancock, who presides over and directs the collective wisdom and virtue of all America, travels with a vestal in his train. He himself can never fit her for the General, though pious Benjamin, the procurer-general to the Congress, may.

Nevertheless, the delegates in Philadelphia must have chuckled over the forgery and we may be sure that the corpulent Harrison chuckled with them and drowned his embarrassment in Burgundy.

The Tory press made the most of the intercepted letters in an effort to drive a wedge between the patriots. Adams never again was to pace the gravel walks of 'Fairhill.' Two months after Draper's paper published the letters, Adams passed Dickinson on Chestnut Street 'near enough to have touched elbows,' and, as Dickinson passed 'without moving his hat or head or hand,' Adams 'bowed and pulled off [his] hat.' The Philadelphian 'passed haughtily by,' and Adams confided to his *Diary* that 'in the future [he] would pass him in the same way.'[50]

But the appeasers were still predominant in Congress, and the Petition, in all conscience obsequious enough, was approved. Dickinson controlled the delegations from New York, New Jersey, Pennsylvania, Delaware, and Maryland; and North Carolina, South Carolina, and Georgia were standing stoutly against independence.

XII

When, that same month, Peyton Randolph choked to death at a country place near Philadelphia, and John Hancock succeeded him as President of the Congress, it was not a triumph for independence, despite the popular impression gleaned from history. He had been sent to Congress as a man of wealth to counteract the charge that only the ragtag and bobtail were affiliated with the patriots' cause. Of a mercurial temperament, inordinately vain, and eager for association with the rich and fashionable, he had actually, at one time, created consternation among the patriots of Boston by deciding to

[50] Stillé, *Life of Dickinson*, 158; Adams, *Diary*, I, 198.

join the Tory Club; but through pressure, he was finally dissuaded. The early days of his presidency of the Congress found him acting on strictly republican principles, but very soon he was drawn, like the moth to the flame, to the aristocracy of the New York delegation and became more intimately allied with the appeasers than with the militants. Susceptible to the flattery of wealth, he was ripe for the picking by the social lobby.[51]

July fell from the calendar — and August and September — and in October, 1775, word arrived from England that George III not only had contemptuously refused to read the humble petition, but in Parliament had denounced the Americans as rebels to be put down by force. Two months before, he had written North that he was 'unalterably determined at every hazard and at every risk of every consequence to compel the colonies to absolute submission,' since 'it would be better totally to abandon them than to admit a single shadow of their doctrines.' In his speech from the throne, he had declared his determination 'to put a speedy end to these disorders by the most decisive measures.' This was much too strong for members of the Parliament, and, in the Lords, Lord Mansfield, usually found aligned with the forces of reaction, made his protest, supported by Lord Camden, the Bishop of Peterborough, the Earl of Shelburne, and the Dukes of Richmond, Manchester, and Grafton. In the Commons, Burke, Charles James Fox, Barré, and John Wilkes took up the cudgels for the Americans. The debate was acrimonious. When the Duke of Richmond said the Americans were but 'resisting acts of the most unexampled cruelty and oppression,' he was loudly called to order. The Duke of Denbigh hysterically exclaimed that there was 'little difference between the traitor and he who openly or privately abets treason'; to which Richmond contemptuously replied, referring to Denbigh's evident condition, that 'the noise your lordships have heard has reached below the bar and must convince you that the noble earl has been heard there.'

Meanwhile, the King was scouring the petty German courts for mercenaries for his army, kidnapping men by the press gangs in London, and releasing criminals from prison on their agreement to

[51] Wells, *Life of Samuel Adams,* II, 382-83; *Boston Independent Chronicle,* February 21, 1789.

fight the Americans. Holland had refused to release a Scotch brigade in its service, and Russia had coldly declined to lend twenty thousand of her army.

Washington, with his troops, wrote Reed in Philadelphia that he had 'never entertained an idea of an accommodation since I heard of the measures which were adopted in consequence of the Bunker Hill fight,' and that 'the King's speech has confirmed the sentiments upon the news of that affair.' He was tired of delays. He would give an answer short and clear — 'that if nothing else would satisfy a tyrant and his diabolical ministry, we were determined to shake off all connections with a state so unjust and so unnatural.' [52]

Yet, when the news reached Philadelphia, the appeasers were less concerned over the contemptuous refusal to read their dutiful petition than over the King's declaration that the Americans were rebels, bent on independence. This threw some of them into a fever of repentance. The effect on the advanced patriots was the opposite. Samuel Adams read the King's speech and exploded. 'The tyrant!' he exclaimed. 'His speech breathes the most malevolent spirit, and determines my opinion of its author as a man of wicked heart. I have heard that he is his own minister; why, then, should we cast the odium of distressing mankind upon his minions?' [53] Joined now by Wythe, the friend of Jefferson, he intensified his fight for a declaration of absolute independence.

But from the Pennsylvania delegation came a contrite wail — from Wilson of the proprietary group. Rushing into Carpenter's Hall with the King's speech in his hand, he hysterically shouted that 'the true state of feeling here has been misrepresented in England.' He demanded, not a declaration of independence, but the most solemn declaration that the Americans had no thought of setting up an independent nation. This, in January, 1776, was carried by a large majority, and John Hancock voted for the declaration.[54]

For a moment even the stout heart of Samuel Adams sickened — but for a moment only.

[52] Reed, *Life of Joseph Reed*, I, 157-60.
[53] Wells, *Life of Samuel Adams*, II, 353.
[54] *Ibid.*, II, 373-74.

XIII

Then, in January, 1776, a genius of the pen entered the arena. Tom Paine produced a dynamic pamphlet, *Common Sense*. Soon more than a hundred thousand copies were passing from hand to hand in town and countryside. Brilliant and vigorous, it presented the case of the colonies with a refreshing candor, free from cant and cowardice, and the effect on public sentiment was magical. It was worth many divisions in the field. The 'people of no importance,' lounging in front of the country stores, read it with a thrill, and Washington and Jefferson with admiration and gratitude. Coming at a time when it was clear that nothing decisive could be done until the people were put upon the march to hammer authoritatively upon the doors of semi-Tory legislatures, it was a Godsend. In the fight of the 'forward men' against the proprietary reactionaries of Pennsylvania, it rendered yeoman service.

But these reactionaries were not easily put down. Under the cloak of a religious purpose, some of the Quakers of Pennsylvania, supporting the Penn interests, met with co-religionists from the Jerseys in convention in Philadelphia to issue an address 'to the people in general.' The purpose was purely political. 'The benefits, advantages, and favors,' it said, 'we have experienced by our dependence on, and connection with the Kings and government under which we have enjoyed this happy state, appear to demand from us the greatest circumspection, care, and constant endeavors to guard against any attempt to alter or subvert that dependence and connection.' It could scarcely have gone further to bolster up the selfish proprietary régime, then under a heavy fire.

To Samuel Adams this was as a bugle call to a war-horse. Rushing to his desk, his pen spluttered over the paper in the writing of his *Address to the People of Pennsylvania*:

> Shame on the men who court exemption from present troubles and expense at the price of their posterity's liberty [he wrote]. The honest party in England cannot wish for the reconciliation proposed. It is as unsafe for them as for us, and they thoroughly apprehend it. What check have they now upon the crown, and what shadow of control can they pretend, when the crown can command fifteen to twenty million a year which they have nothing

to say to? . . . Now we are called a pack of villainous rebels, who, like the St. Vincent's Indians, can expect nothing more than a pardon for their lives, and the sovereign favor respecting freedom and property to be at the King's favor. God Almighty grant that I may be numbered with the dead before that day dawns on North America.[55]

And to bear out Adams's opinion of the feelings of the liberals of England, within two months an English pamphleteer had published his *Observations on the Nature of Civil Liberty, the Principles of Government and the Justice and Policy of the War with America,* vigorously defending the contentions of the colonists. So strikingly similar were the arguments advanced to those of Jefferson's *Summary View* that it is a fair surmise that Richard Price, the author, was familiar with the pamphlet of the Virginian.

> From the nature and principles of civil liberty [it said] . . . it is an immediate and necessary inference that no one community can have any power over the property or legislation of another community that is not incorporated with it by a just and adequate representation. Then only . . . is a State free when it is governed by its own will. But the country which is subject to the legislation of another country, in which it has no voice, and over which it has no control, cannot be said to be governed by its own will. Such a country, therefore, is in a state of slavery. And it is deserved to be particularly considered that such slavery is worse on several accounts, than any slavery of private men to one another, or of kingdoms to despots within themselves.

And quite as striking:

> The truth is that a common relation to one supreme executive head; an exchange of kind offices; ties of interest and affection, and compacts are sufficient to give the British Empire all the unity that is necessary. But if not — if in order to preserve its unity, one half of it must be enslaved to the other half, let it, in the name of God, lack unity.

This English version of Jefferson's *Summary View* had a wide and instant popularity, and within a short time it had run through eight editions; the author was in constant demand for public appearances and speeches; and on March 14, 1776, there was an

55 Wells, *Life of Samuel Adams,* II, 362.

impressive ceremony in the Guild Hall in London, when the Lord Mayor presented to the champion of the American contention the resolutions granting him the Freedom of the City in a gold box. Nothing could more conclusively prove that America had militant friends in England than the declaration of the resolutions that the pamphlet set forth 'those sure principles upon which alone the supreme legislative authority of Great Britain over her Colonies can be justly or beneficially maintained.'

Thus spoke the city government of the greatest commercial center of the British Empire. The fame of the pamphlet spread to America, and two years later Richard Price was invited to the colonies by the American Congress to assist in the financial administration of the States.

But it made no impression on the colonial Tories and the fight went on.

XIV

However, progress was being made among the people, and in late May, Virginia instructed her delegates in Congress to press for independence.

Jefferson had returned to Virginia in December, 1775, and he did not rejoin his colleagues until early in May. Unfriendly critics have condemned his absence without inquiring into his activities during this period.

It was not a period of relaxation and indifference. The frail health of his wife, who had been unable to accompany him to Philadelphia, was primarily responsible for his return to Virginia. Unsatisfactory letters from home had given him the impression that she was seriously ill. His venerable mother was in her final illness, and died in March. As an active member of the Committee of Safety in his county, to which he had been elected at the head of the list, he had much to do. He went about collecting money from his friends for the sufferers in Boston, and he organized a supply of powder for the use of the Virginia soldiers. He was detained at home, however, six weeks after he had planned to return to Philadelphia by an illness — 'a malady of which Gilmer can inform you,' he wrote Thomas Nelson.[56] That he was intimately identified with

[56] Ford, *Writings of Jefferson*, II, 2-4.

the activities of his friends, culminating in the Virginia resolutions declaring the colonies free and independent States, there can be no doubt. Throughout his life, when Congress was hostile and had reached a stalemate, it was his policy to go back to the people.

For a month after his return, he was sporadic in his attendance at Carpenter's Hall, since he spent much time bending over his desk in the preparation of a paper that is sacred to Americans. Meanwhile, he had served on committees engaged on matters of comparative unimportance. Writing the report on the treacherous action of a British captain at the Cedars, in violation of the terms on which an inferior force of Continentals had capitulated, it is indicative of the persistent opposition to independence that Jefferson's words, 'States of America,' were hastily changed to 'Colonies of America' by the conservatives still in control.[57] For while public opinion, in so far as it was reflected in public meetings, was closing in on the foes of independence, they were fighting on.

And Jefferson and Lee had their opponents on the Virginia delegation. Carter Braxton, contemptuous of democracy and enamored of the trappings of monarchy, was writing in April that the colonies were too defenseless for a declaration of independence, and it would be stupid to defy England on the mere hope of an alliance with France. True, he said, the New Englanders want 'separation,' but they 'enjoy a government purely democratical, the Nature and Principles of which, both civil and religious, are so totally incompatible with Monarchy that they have ever lived in a restless state under it.'[58] And Ben Harrison shared Braxton's views. But Jefferson, who had just returned from Virginia, knew that Braxton and Harrison were moving against the current.

Under the leadership of Dickinson, Pennsylvania threatened the most serious obstacle. 'You ask why we hesitate in Congress,' wrote Richard Henry Lee. 'I'll tell you, my friend, because we are heavily clogged with instructions from these shameful Proprietary people.' Having long foreseen this, Samuel Adams, using the methods he had successfully employed in Boston, was putting the common people on the march within the shadow of Carpenter's Hall. All the social prestige and political power of the proprietary interests was being used under the direction of a majority of the Pennsylvania

[57] *Ibid.*, II, 30-39.   [58] Burnett, *Letters*, I, 420.

delegation against the slightest inclination toward independence. Franklin, who had often fought the machine, was in opposition, but, in the critical months of May and June, he was nursing his gout at home. That he was not too ill to whisper suggestions to the runners stirring up the mass of the people, we may be sure. But the situation was confused. A few weeks earlier, the delegate, Edward Tilghman, was writing his father of the fight in Pennsylvania. Colonel McKean, of the delegation, was 'one of the violents,' but he was a 'true Presbyterian,' which apparently explained it. Franklin had 'hurt himself much' with the appeasers, and 'reigns only with the Presbyterian interests.' These were in the minority, but they were 'indefatigable and try all schemes in all shapes' and 'act in concert.' [59]

Everything now depended on Pennsylvania, since it was the sustaining pillar of all the opposition to independence. Its Assembly, machine-picked, and machine-run, had refused in April, 1776, to rescind its instructions against separation. But Washington was now at the head of the army, fighting was in progress, the King had denounced the Americans as 'rebels' and was scouring the slums for gunmen to turn against them. Tom Paine's *Common Sense* was being read, Samuel Adams's *Address to the People of Pennsylvania* was being pondered, and Adams's propagandists and organizers were seeking the 'people of no importance' in Philadelphia highways and byways. Soon Dickinson would be protesting bitterly against the pressure of public opinion beyond the walls of Carpenter's Hall. [60]

And with the machine-run Pennsylvania Assembly growing apprehensive because of the rumble and roar in the streets near the State House, it began to hedge and concentrate on the preservation of the Proprietary Charter. Independence might be possible, provided it did not mean the deprivation of the special privileges of the Penn family. Unhappily for them, the people outside had found their tongues. Mass meetings roared their robustious protests against the Assembly, demanding its dissolution and the establishment of an independent State Government in accordance with a law passed by Congress. Even the military forces of the colony joined in the demand.

[59] Stillé, *Life of Dickinson,* 174.   [60] *Ibid.,* 194.

But the instructions stood — stood until word came that Virginia in convention had instructed its congressional delegation to propose a declaration of independence. Then only did the Proprietary Assembly agree to new instructions that went no further than an authorization to its delegates to confer with those of other colonies.

But the proprietary interests had lost their battle.

And at this stage young Jefferson stepped from the wings to the center of the stage. It was his immortal hour.

CHAPTER

VI

JEFFERSON'S IMMORTAL HOUR

I

ON HIS RETURN to Philadelphia in May, 1776, Jefferson wrote Thomas Nelson that he was 'at present in our old lodgings' at the Randolph house, but he thought, 'as the excessive heats of the city are coming on fast,' he would seek rooms on the outskirts where he 'could have the benefit of freely circulating air.' This project evidently was abandoned, for on May 23 he moved to quarters in the new brick house of a young German bricklayer named Graaf, on the south side of Market Street, between Seventh and Eighth. He was to recall much later that, 'if not the only house on that part of the street . . . there were few others near it.' There, on the second floor, he had two rooms, a parlor, which served also as a study, and a bedroom. For these accommodations he paid thirty-five shillings a week, and, as before, he took his meals at the City Tavern, where he shared a table with some colleagues. This house, in whose parlor the leading men of the Revolution met to devise plans, and in which the most sacred document in American history was written, continued to stand, utterly neglected, its significance overlooked until 1883, when it was advertised for sale. No one appears to have thought of buying it by popular subscription for preservation as a national shrine. One man with historical imagination witnessed its demolition with sorrow and disgust.

Early on the morning of Wednesday, February 28, 1883, there was snow on the ground, I was riding down Market Street in a streetcar. We halted on the opposite side of Seventh and Market and I happened to look up at a dormer window on the Jefferson house . . . when I saw a man come out of the window with an iron bar in his hand. Presently another came out, and, after a bit, a dozen or more men, similarly armed, were on the roof of the historic house. I saw a huge Celt, at the word of command, thrust his crowbar under the shingles of the roof and the destruction of one of the most historic buildings on the globe began.[1]

That which piqued his curiosity most was the fact that no relic-hunters were about.[2]

II

The Virginia Assembly, which hastened the end in the congressional struggle, was brilliant. Some of the great figures of the Old Dominion were absent. Washington was with the army. Jefferson and Lee were in Congress, but Pendleton presided, Patrick Henry poured forth his exciting eloquence, and Jefferson's friend, Nelson, offered the resolutions instructing the colony's delegates in Congress to move at once for independence, a confederation of the colonies, and a foreign alliance. The instructions were hurried to Philadelphia. Lee hastened to comply.

The resolutions were presented on June 7. For two days, on Saturday and Monday, the debate continued under high pressure. When Lee offered his resolutions, six of the colonies were under instructions against a declaration of independence — Pennsylvania, New York, New Jersey, Delaware, Maryland, and South Carolina. And Dickinson, keyed to the highest pitch of grim determination, stepped forward to lead the opposition. Wilson, of Pennsylvania, Robert Livingston, of New York, and Edward Rutledge, of South Carolina, supported him. And bearing the brunt of the battle for the resolutions were three giants of debate — John Adams, Richard Henry Lee, and George Wythe.

History is the poorer because none of the speeches were reported or preserved. No better report exists than a fragmentary sketch of Jefferson's in his *Autobiography*, written much later, but doubtless

[1] Donaldson, *The House in Which Thomas Jefferson Wrote the Declaration of Independence,* 78-79.
[2] *Ibid.,* 80.

from notes taken at the time. With consummate skill, pressing every possible point, seeking to prejudice the delegates against the voice of the streets, and all with a lawyer's art, Dickinson based his opposition on the argument that the time was not opportune. It was a desperate man's plea for procrastination. The voice of the people had not yet been clearly heard — wait. Some of the colonies, though not yet ripe, were 'fast ripening' — so why not wait? Other colonies had instructed their delegations against independence and their delegates could not bind their people, and some colonies might withdraw their delegations and abandon the union. Then, too, the colonies were not yet prepared to meet the onslaught of British military power. Wait — wait until an alliance could be made with some important European power. What! break with England without first having the assurance of a friend? And who the friend — France? Spain? More likely they would 'form a connection with the British court.' Weeks, months, must intervene before we could know the result of an appeal for aid to the court at Versailles — so wait. So ran the argument — as Jefferson remembered it, and as Dickinson afterward described it — based on the idea that the time had not yet arrived, pleading for postponement.

Adams, Lee, and Wythe argued that the debate was closed when Washington took the field, when American blood was shed, when the mad monarch denounced the colonists as rebels and scoured the world for mercenary troops to shoot them down. Would France or any other power form an alliance with a people who lacked the courage to declare their independence? The hour had struck.

At the close of the debate on June 10 action was postponed until July 1. Elbridge Gerry wrote that this was 'to give the Assemblies of the Middle colonies an opportunity to take off their restrictions and let their delegates unite on the measure.' [3] Jefferson explains that the debate had disclosed that some of the colonies had 'not yet matured for falling off the parent stem,' but were rapidly maturing, and that time was allowed for the fall. To hurry the event before unanimity was reached would be unwise, when in a little while the colonies would present a solid front.

[3] Burnett, Letters, I, 484.

III

Then followed three weeks of hectic struggle — weeks of canvassing, intriguing, caucusing, persuading. Among the delegates leading for independence there was a concentration on Dickinson to overcome his fears and scruples. Such was his reputation and his character that, though he led the opposition and loomed mountainhigh among his co-workers in that cause, he retained the respect of his antagonists. But it is significant of the popular hatred of the Proprietary Government in Pennsylvania that, despite his personal popularity within the walls of Carpenter's Hall, he was thoroughly hated in the streets. The autocratic domination of Pennsylvania had ended.[4]

With the tide now running strongly toward independence, there was little the opposition could do to hold it back. It had done its best before, in having the loyalist legislatures instruct their delegates against separation, though the militants had been putting the people on the march against these colonial assemblies. Dickinson could urge these assemblies to stand fast by their instructions, but the militants could urge them to rescind with the power of the people hammering on their doors.

Soon Edward Rutledge was hysterically summoning John Jay back from New York to help in holding the line. The Carolinian knew how useful Jay's presence was in New York, but it had become 'absolutely necessary' for him to be in Philadelphia, where the 'exertions of the honest and sensible part of the members' were required.[5]

Meanwhile, the two Adamses, Franklin, Lee, and Jefferson were pressing the advantage an aroused public sentiment had given, working on individual members, meeting in caucuses as Samuel Adams had arranged in Boston. For consummate skill in political organization and management no one could remotely approach Jefferson and Samuel Adams. When these men met, programs were devised and each man was assigned his separate task. The three weeks' battle was largely behind the scenes.

With public sentiment rising, the delegates from New York and New Hampshire, previously pledged against independence, were

[4] Stillé, *Life of Dickinson*, 191.   [5] Burnett, *Letters*, I, 517.

asking for fresh instructions. The popular feeling was sweeping in an irresistible wave over the aristocracies of Pennsylvania, Maryland, and Delaware. In New Jersey the people rose, spewed forth the bastard son of Franklin from the gubernatorial chair, and sent fresh delegates pledged to independence. Colony after colony fell into line and step — all but New York. 'There is not any doubt of any colony on the continent except New York and Maryland, and they will not impede us for a moment,' Gerry wrote James Warren [6] six days before the ballot.

On July 1, when the debate was resumed, the resolutions of Lee carried, with Pennsylvania and South Carolina voting against them, Delaware dividing, and New York mute. The next day Pennsylvania, Delaware, and South Carolina lined up with the rest, and a little later the New York Convention acquiesced.

But John Dickinson persisted in his opposition to the bitter end, and refused to vote. However — and this is illuminative of his character — within a week, when Congress sent a military force to New York to meet the threat of General Howe, the brigade that marched from Philadelphia followed the sword of Dickinson. When his country spoke, he responded.[7] But when actually in camp he was deprived of his seat in Congress, he wrote with feeling that, 'while I was exposing my person to every hazard and lodging every night within half a mile of the enemy, the members of the Convention in Pennsylvania, resting in quiet safety, unanimously voted me unworthy of my seat.' [8] This humiliation softened the heart of even John Adams. Writing his wife, he said that 'Dickinson, and others, all fallen like grass before the sickle, notwithstanding all their advantages in point of fortune, family and abilities'; but, he added, 'I am inclined . . . to wish that these gentlemen may be restored at a fresh election, because, although mistaken on some points, they are good characters and their great wealth and numerous connections will contribute to strengthen America, and cement her union.' [9]

During this period, and previously, Dickinson was thoroughly imbued with faith in the aristocratic concept of society. He feared, if he did not despise, the people. But his association with Jefferson

[6] *Ibid.*, I, 508.   [7] Stillé, *Life of Dickinson*, 201.
[8] *Ibid.*, 206.   [9] Adams, *Letters to His Wife*, I, 135.

in those days resulted in a sincere mutual attachment; and, a little later, after the adoption of the Constitution, he became an anti-Federalist and a warm supporter of Jefferson's principles and policies. This conversion meant a sweeping repudiation of all the principles that had formed the basis of his earlier political career. An intimate correspondence with Jefferson was maintained, and when he died, Jefferson wrote that 'a more estimable man or truer patriot could not have left us,' and that 'his name will be consecrated in history as one of the great worthies of our Revolution.' They differed in method and in timing, but the author of the *Farmer's Letters*, like the author of *Common Sense*, remained, with Jefferson, a patriot of the first order to the end.

IV

When on June 10, the debate on the Lee resolutions was recessed for three weeks, it was agreed that a committee should be named to prepare, in the event of a successful issue, a Declaration of Independence. This committee was elected, and while John Adams and Franklin, along with Roger Sherman and Robert Livingston, were chosen, the highest vote cast for any of the five went to young Jefferson.

Since there has been much idle speculation as to why Jefferson was chosen, it may not be without interest. It unquestionably was out of the ordinary that the author of the resolutions calling for a Declaration was not elected as one of the five. There certainly was an intrigue to keep Richard Henry Lee off the committee. We have observed that Lee's advanced views and close association with Samuel Adams and the militants of Massachusetts had not endeared him to the reactionaries and appeasers of his own colony. It was no secret that Harrison and Braxton, primarily representing the aristocracy of the Tidewater, hated Lee as a renegade to his class, and the faction with them sought to defeat him with Ben Harrison. But just as Lee was obnoxious to the appeasers, Harrison was repugnant to the more militant patriots; and, reading between the lines of the numerous conflicting explanations of what took place, it is reasonable to assume, as has been said, that Jefferson was selected as a compromise. Certain it is that the friends of Lee supported Jefferson; and the fact that he received more votes than Adams or Franklin indicates that numerous others, not entangled in the feud, voted for him because they felt that he belonged on the committee. Though he certainly was as militant as Lee, he had been less aggressive in method. Where Lee carried his political disagreements as far as personal animosity, Jefferson could disagree politically and remain on friendly social terms. Lee carried the proverbial chip upon his shoulder, and Jefferson, unyielding in his principles, bore the olive branch.

During his year in Congress, Jefferson had been absent four months, and in later years Adams could not recall that he had ever spoken in debate. 'In fact,' he wrote, 'during the time I sat with him, I never heard him utter three sentences together.' This, of course, refers to public sittings in Carpenter's Hall, and not to the very important caucuses, where, as in private conversation, he was a fluent talker.[10] But Adams adds that Jefferson had 'the reputation of a masterly pen . . . had been chosen a delegate in Virginia in consequence of a very handsome public paper . . . which had given him the character of a fine writer.'[11] And, as Adams goes on, he was made chairman of the committee 'because he had the most votes, and he had most votes because we united on him to the exclusion of Richard Henry Lee in order to keep out Harrison.'

All five members of the committee had attained distinction on solid grounds. Franklin was one of the most commanding figures of his time, and his name was known in the chancelleries of Europe. Adams was one of the two most famous patriots in Massachusetts, whose reputation as a political thinker and speaker had long since attracted the attention of ministerial and parliamentary circles in London. Roger Sherman was the most distinguished patriot in Connecticut, with years of notable public service behind him. And Robert Livingston, while comparatively new in public station, was destined to a brilliant career, and, as Chancellor of New York, to administer the oath to George Washington on assuming the Presidency of the Republic. He alone was younger than Jefferson — by three years. Adams was forty-one, Sherman was fifty-five, Franklin was seventy, and Jefferson was thirty-three.

When these five men met, probably in a committee room in Car-

[10] Adams, *Works*, II, 510.   [11] *Ibid.*

penter's Hall, Jefferson was immediately made chairman. About the conference table in Carpenter's Hall, and probably in the parlor of Jefferson's quarters with the bricklayer, there were discussions of the general nature of the Declaration. Then, apparently as one man, they turned to Jefferson to write it. The author of the *Summary View*, who had been held in Williamsburg to frame the Reply to Lord North, who was chosen to write the Reply for Congress, who had been put upon the committee to draw the paper on taking up arms within five days of his appearance in Carpenter's Hall, and then asked to write it, had no equal as a writer among his colleagues. Jefferson, in his *Autobiography*, merely says that 'the committee for drawing up the Declaration of Independence desired me to do it.'[12] Adams, in his *Autobiography*, records that, after several discussions and an agreement on the general tenor of the document, the committee appointed him and Jefferson 'to draw them up in form and clothe them in proper dress.' This inclusion of Adams is not borne out by any other source. It certainly was not the recollection of Jefferson, who, in a letter to Madison, denied that there was a subcommittee of two.[13] It does not really matter.

However, Adams insists in his *Autobiography* that Jefferson requested him, as his sole associate on the subcommittee, to 'take them [the minutes] to my lodgings and make the draught.' He claims that he had declined, and given Jefferson several reasons: first, that Jefferson was a Virginian and he a Massachusetts man; second, that Jefferson was a Southerner and he a Northerner; third, that he had become obnoxious to the conciliators by his early and constant zeal, and that this would subject anything he wrote to an unfriendly scrutiny; and lastly, that there was one reason, which was enough, that he had 'a great opinion of the elegance of [Jefferson's] pen and none at all of [his] own.' He says that he insisted that no hesitation should be made on Jefferson's part, who thereupon took the minutes and 'in a day or two produced to me his draught.'[14]

That Adams's recollection may have been at fault, we must assume from the fact that in a letter to Timothy Pickering he gave a slightly different version. Still insisting on the subcommittee of

[12] *Autobiography*, 18.   [13] Burnett, *Letters*, I, 514-16.
[14] Adams, *Works*, II, 510.

two, he gives what purports to have been the actual conversation between Jefferson and himself. Jefferson, he says, asked him to prepare the draft.

'I will not,' Adams replied.

'You should do it,' said Jefferson.

'Oh, no.'

'Why will you not?' asked Jefferson.

'I will not.'

'Why?' pressed Jefferson.

'Reasons enough,' said Adams.

'What can be your reasons?'

'Reason, first, you are a Virginian and a Virginian ought to appear at the head of this business. Reason second, I am obnoxious, suspected and unpopular. You are very much otherwise. Reason third, you can write ten times better than I can.'

'Well,' said Jefferson, 'if you are decided, I will do as well as I can.'

'Very well,' said Adams, 'when you have drawn it up we will have a meeting.' [15]

V

However this may be, Jefferson prepared the draft. According to Adams's recollection it was submitted to him and he was 'delighted with its high tone and the flights of oratory with which it abounded, especially that concerning negro slavery, and which [he] knew his Southern brethren in Congress would never suffer to pass. [He] certainly never would oppose.' But Adams, the critic, found other expressions he would 'not have inserted,' particularly that which called the King a tyrant, 'which he thought too personal.' [16]

According to Jefferson's recollection, in his letter to Madison, the original draft was submitted to but two members of the committee at first — to Adams and Franklin. [17] Adams did not recollect that either Franklin or Sherman offered a single criticism.

It is true that Jefferson did not sit down at his desk with any friendly feeling for the King. Some years later, in a letter to M. Soules, who had submitted to Jefferson his history of the trouble

[15] Burnett, *Letters,* I, 514-16, notes.   [16] *Ibid.*   [17] *Ibid.*

between the Americans and England for criticism, he placed the responsibility for the obnoxious measures that precipitated the Revolution squarely on the shoulders of the King alone:

> The Tory education of the King was the first preparation for that change in the British Government which that party never ceased to wish. This naturally assured Tory administration during his life. At the moment he came to the throne, and cleared his hands of his enemies by the peace of Paris, the assumptions of unwarranted right over America commenced; they were so signal, and followed one another so close as to prove they were part of a system, either to reduce it under absolute subjection and thereby make it an instrument for attempts on Britain itself, or to sever it from Britain so that it might not be a weight in the Whig scale. This latter alternative, however, was not considered as the one which would take place. They knew so little of America that they thought it unable to encounter the little finger of Great Britain.[18]

To the distress of some of his colleagues, this feeling on the part of Jefferson impelled him to describe George III as a tyrant.

Delighted as Adams was with the 'high tone and flights of oratory,' this mercurial statesman, the victim throughout his life of his irascibility, later was to write slightingly to Pickering that there was not a new thought in the document and that every idea in it had been found in a revolutionary pamphlet by James Otis, written some years before. Commenting on this criticism, made during the writer's bitter feud with Jefferson and persisted in years later, the author of the Declaration wrote Madison that it was quite possible, though to that day he had never seen the pamphlet of Otis. 'Whether I had gathered my ideas from reading or reflection, I do not know,' he wrote. 'I know only that I turned to neither book nor pamphlet while writing it. I did not consider it as any part of my charge to invent new ideas altogether, and to offer no sentiment that had never been expressed before.' And to this, with characteristic fairness, he added: 'This, however, I will say for Mr. Adams, that he supported the Declaration with zeal and ability, fighting fearlessly for every word of it.'

Thus we see Jefferson at his desk in the sultry heat of a mid-June day, without a book or pamphlet within reach, writing rapidly on

[18] Ford, *Writings of Jefferson*, IV, 307.

paper made in Holland. He had absorbed the literature and philosophy of liberty from early youth and made it part of his own thinking. That Locke and the philosophers, whose pages he had pondered and whose sentiments he had copied into his *Commonplace Book*, entered into the Declaration there can be no doubt.

Having completed the first draft in two days, as Adams remembered, he submitted it first to Adams and then to Franklin, who had been confined to his room with the gout. The record shows that this draft received fifteen alterations, mostly in phrasing and in the choice of words. Most of these appear to have been made by Jefferson himself. Adams made a few, and Franklin fewer. The committee as a whole acquiesced in the document with its alterations, and it was laid upon the table in Carpenter's Hall on June 28, four days before the adoption of the resolutions of Lee. With Dickinson and his cohorts perusing it in the meanwhile with critical eyes, it is not difficult to imagine the suffering of the too sensitive author. It was during these days that he acquired a straw hat for ten shillings, bought a map and spurs, and paid his wine merchant and his hairdresser. He was not moping in his room.

VI

With the adoption of the Lee resolutions, Congress turned at once to the consideration of the Declaration. The debate continued through part of the second, the whole of the third, and until the evening of the fourth of July.

There sat Jefferson in silence, in evident distress over the criticism of the style and substance, and cringing over the emasculation of parts to which he attached importance.

The document can be divided into two parts: the Preamble, the most immortal part of it, setting forth the then revolutionary philosophy of democracy; and the body of the Declaration, containing the stinging indictment of the misgovernment of America by the King. The body is interesting now only as a history of far-off unhappy events having no connection with the present; but the Preamble must remain as the most concise and happy expression of the fundamentals of Americanism so long as America retains its freedom and its pride.

Again history is the poorer because, in the debate behind closed doors, no record was made of the speeches. We only know that, with Jefferson sitting in embarrassed silence, John Adams was constantly on his feet, fighting with all his fine capacity for every line of the document as it came from the pen of the author. Jefferson was to remember him then as 'the Colossus of the debate,' and all the future years of political controversy and animosity were not to dim his gratitude and admiration for John Adams. Even when, later, Adams was to turn against him in stubborn opposition, Jefferson was to retain a real affection for the man, who, though often difficult, was genuine and honest.

Seated beside young Jefferson during the ordeal was the venerable and wise Franklin, whose skin was not so tender to attacks. Noting the writhing of his young friend under the rude and sometimes crude criticisms, he sought to relieve the tension and soften the blows by saying he had made it a rule never to prepare papers to be passed on by a public assembly, and by telling an amusing story.

In the midst of the jarring noises of the debate, the wise old philosopher was talking in an undertone to Jefferson.

'When I was a journeyman printer,' he was saying, 'one of my companions, an apprenticed hatter, having served out his time, was about to open shop for himself. His first concern was to have a handsome signboard with a proper inscription. He composed it in these words: "John Thompson, Hatter, makes and sells hats for ready money," with a figure of a hat subjoined. But he thought he would submit it to his friends for their amendments. The first he showed it to thought the word "hatter" tautologous, because followed by the words "makes hats," which show he was a hatter. It was struck out. The next observed that the word "makes" might as well be omitted, because his customers would not care who made the hats. If good and to their mind, they would buy by whomsoever made. He struck it out. A third said he thought the words "for ready money" were useless, as it was not the custom of the place to sell on credit. Everyone who purchased expected to pay. They were parted with, and the inscription now stood, "John Thompson sells hats." "Sells hats," says his next friend, "why, nobody would expect you to give them away. What, then, is the use of that word?" It was stricken out, and "hats" followed it, the rather as there was one painted on the board. So the inscription was reduced ultimately to "John Thompson," with the figure of a hat subjoined.'

With the critics finding fault with this and that and Adams stoutly defending every word, with the delegates stewing in the sultry heat of Carpenter's Hall, with the horseflies from a neighboring stable annoying them no end as they slapped their stockinged legs, the wise and experienced Franklin sat whispering to Jefferson the amusing story of the hat merchant's sign. The suffering and harassed author did not find the story amusing at the moment. It failed to salve his wounds that hot day in Philadelphia. But he was to recall it with amusement in later life.

VII

It does not appear that the Preamble was attacked, which is surprising in view of the bitter hostility to democracy on the part of so many members of the Congress. To Jefferson, inwardly writhing in his seat, uncomfortable in the heat and with the horseflies subjecting his legs to torture, the sections entirely stricken out galled him most.

Hating slavery as an institution detrimental to the interest of the slave-owners, economically as well as morally, and resenting the action of the King in setting aside the attempts of the Virginia legislature to end the traffic in human flesh, he had submitted his draft to the committee of five with the following declaration:

He [the King] has incited treasonable insurrections of our fellow citizens, with the allurements of forfeiture and confiscation of our property. He has waged cruel war against human nature itself, violating its most sacred rights of life and liberty in the persons of a distant people who never offended him, captivating and carrying them into slavery in another hemisphere, or to incur miserable death in their transportation thither. This piratical warfare, the opprobrium of infidel powers, is the warfare of the Christian King of Great Britain. Determined to keep open a market where men should be bought and sold, he has prostituted his negative by suppressing every legislative attempt to prohibit or restrain this execrable commerce. And to add to this assemblage of horrors of distinguished dye, he is now inciting those very people to rise in arms among us, and to purchase that liberty of which he had deprived them, by murdering the people on whom he had obtruded them; thus paying off former crimes committed against the liberties of our people, with crimes which he urges them to commit against the lives of another.

Adams had foreseen the inevitability of opposition to this clause from some of the congressmen of slave-owning States other than Virginia. Despite Adams's ardent defense of the passage, it was voted out. When, later, this was charged exclusively to Georgia and South Carolina, Jefferson wrote in protest that 'our northern brethren also, I believe, felt a little tender under these censures; for though their people had few slaves themselves, yet they had been pretty considerable carriers of them to others.' [19]

And tender, as some still were, about the sensitive feelings of George III, the passage beginning with 'a prince, whose character is thus marked in every act which may define a tyrant, is unfit to be the ruler of a people,' was emasculated by the elimination of these words:

> Future ages will scarcely believe that the hardiness of one man adventured, within the short compass of twelve years only, to lay a foundation so broad and so undisguised for tyranny over a people, fostered and fixed in principles of freedom.

More significant, and, to Jefferson, disgusting, was the striking-out of the passage in which he denied the right of the British Parliament to dominate and dictate to the colonies. This was the assertion that the American settlements had been built up 'unassisted by the wealth and strength of Great Britain,' and that, 'in constituting, indeed, our several forms of government, we have adopted one common king, thereby laying a foundation for perpetual league and amity with them; but that submission to their Parliament was no part of our constitution, nor ever in idea, if history may be credited.'

That we had racial groups, even in the America of those days, in whom the politicians were interested in anticipation of favors to come, may be gathered from the fate of another passage: 'At this very time, they [the English people] are permitting their Chief

[19] *Autobiography,* 19.

Magistrate to send over, not only soldiers of our common blood, but Scotch and foreign mercenaries, to invade and deluge us in blood.' The fear that the Scotch settlers, who were really among the best, might resent the reference, resulted in the hasty elimination of this sentence. Since neither they nor the people of Scotland nor the Scotch soldiers could have been held responsible for the action of the King, this sensitivity might have been a little strained.

Thus, the proceedings in the oven-like confinement of Carpenter's Hall, with the droning voices of the speakers, the hum of conversation, and the buzz and bites of the horseflies from the neighboring stable.

Toward evening on the fourth of July the discussion petered out. Jefferson was always to think that the invasion of the horseflies through the open windows contributed somewhat to the termination of the debate, for Carpenter's Hall had been converted into a chamber of torture.

The vote was taken; the Declaration, thus amended, was adopted.

Immediately afterward, Jefferson sat in his lodgings on Market Street at his desk, making copies of the Declaration and indicating the changes that had been made by Congress. These were for his friends, George Wythe, Page, Richard Henry Lee, Pendleton, and Mazzei, the Italian. Those made for Wythe, Page, and Pendleton, with the accompanying letter of observations, have been lost. Mazzei gave his copy to the Countess of Tessé in France, of whom Jefferson was to see much later, but this has disappeared. But Lee presented his copy to the Philadelphia Philosophical Society, and this has been preserved.

However much the admirers of Lee in after years may have resented the substitution of Jefferson for Lee in the writing of the Declaration, the incident cast not even a shadow on the intimate friendly relations of the two men. In his letter to Lee, the author of the Declaration showed no bitterness over the alterations. 'I inclose a copy of the Declaration of Independence, as agreed to by the House, and also as originally framed; you will judge whether it is the better or the worse for the critics.' [20] John Adams thought it worse. 'Congress cut off about a quarter of it, as I expected they would,' he wrote Pickering, 'but they obliterated some of the best

[20] Ford, *Writings of Jefferson*, II, 59.

of it.' He had often wondered why the original draft had not been published, but he supposed it was due to 'the vehement philippic against negro slavery.' [21]

Richard Henry Lee, having read the original draft sent him by Jefferson, clearly shared Adams's view that the critics had wrought no improvement. 'I wish sincerely, as well for the honor of Congress, as for that of the States, that the Ms. had not been mangled as it is,' he wrote Jefferson. 'However, the Thing in its nature is so good that no cookery can spoil the dish for the palates of freemen.'

Certainly it does not matter now. Even as it finally appeared, it takes its place with the Magna Charta as one of the greatest documents in the history of Anglo-American freedom.

VIII

As Jefferson sat and writhed inwardly over the observations of the critics in the debate, he was not easy in his mind for other reasons also. He was puzzled and annoyed by the news of the elections of delegates to the next Congress in Virginia. If he found any satisfaction in the defeat of Braxton and Harrison for re-election, he gives no sign in a letter to a Virginia friend. But the fact that he himself was 'next to the lag' alarmed him. The defeat of Braxton and Harrison might be explained by their stout opposition to the 'forward men' in Virginia, but Jefferson had been among the foremost of these. 'It is a painful situation to be three hundred miles from one's country, and therefore open to secret assassination without any possibility of defense,' he wrote William Fleming. 'I am willing to hope nothing of this kind has been done in my case, and yet I cannot be easy.' And then he added, proudly and defiantly: 'If any doubt has arisen as to me, my country will have my political creed in the form of a Declaration which I was lately directed to draw. This will give decisive proof that my own sentiment concurred with the vote they instructed me to give.' [22]

Whether Jefferson 'ran next to the lag' because of machinations against him or merely because of his absence is not important. It was not the seat he craved, but the good opinion of the people, for he was already occupying himself with the coming session of the

[21] Burnett, *Letters*, I, 514, note.   [22] Ford, *Writings of Jefferson*, II, 39.

Virginia Assembly in which he hoped to play a conspicuous part and force some drastic democratic reforms.

He was worried, too, because of his prolonged absence from an ailing wife. 'I wish I could be better satisfied on the point of Patty's recovery,' he wrote Francis Eppes eleven days after the adoption of the Declaration. 'I had not heard from her at all for the two posts before, and no letter from herself now.' [23] That month he was writing Edmund Randolph that his domestic affairs rendered it imperative to solicit the substitution of some other delegate in his stead. He would not urge it, were it not 'unavoidable.' He would continue until the end of the session, and then return to Monticello.[24]

He was also gravely concerned over the reforms in Virginia, and three days after the adoption of the Declaration, he was writing Wythe that the judiciary would demand attention among the reforms contemplated in the coming legislative session. He urged that the judiciary be kept entirely apart from the executive and legislative departments. 'The dignity and stability of government,' he wrote, ' . . . the morals of the people, and every blessing of society depend so much upon an upright and skillful administration of justice.' The judges, he thought, should always 'be men of learning and experience in the laws, of exemplary morals, great patience, calmness and attention; their minds should not be distracted with jarring interests; they should not be dependent on any man or set of men.'

The day he wrote, his colleagues, if not Jefferson himself, were a bit disturbed by 'jarring interests,' for a paper had been privately laid upon the table in Carpenter's Hall reminiscent of the Gunpowder Plot of the British Parliament. The members were therein warned of a plan for their destruction and advised to take care of themselves. Some, however, not easily excited, had a sense of humor. 'Some were for examining the cellars under the room where we sit,' wrote Joseph Hewes. 'I was against it, and urged that we ought to treat such information with contempt and not show any marks of fear or jealousy. I told some of them that I would almost as soon be blown up as to discover to the world that I had thought myself in danger. No notice has been taken, which I think is right.' [25] If

[23] *Ibid.*, II, 62.   [24] *Ibid.*, II, 61.
[25] Burnett, *Letters*, II, 5.

any notice was taken by Jefferson, it does not appear in his correspondence.

IX

Whatever enemies the members may have had, their friends appeared in force two days later, when, from a platform in the State House yard, the Declaration of Independence was read to a cheering throng of three thousand people, while a military battalion paraded on the Common and salutes were fired 'notwithstanding the scarcity of powder.' All day and most of the night the bells in all the church steeples pealed forth merrily, and, as John Adams wrote happily, 'even the chimers chimed in.'[26] That morning the entire Declaration had been published in the *Pennsylvania Gazette*.[27]

Within a few days, Jefferson's document was read at the head of each brigade of the Continental Army in and near New York City amidst 'demonstrations of joy,' and that evening the plain people sallied forth to tear the statue of George III from its pedestal and break it into pieces. The lead was to be used in the molding of bullets for Washington's men.[28] And a week later, when the Declaration was posted in front of the Court House in New York City, a demonstrative throng tore down His Majesty's coat of arms and 'burnt it in the presence of the spectators.'[29] Similar scenes were witnessed in Boston.

Just before the tumultuous rejoicing in New York, one of the delegates of that State in Congress sent his resignation to the New York Convention as a protest against the Declaration of Independence. This was Joseph Alsop, a merchant and importer. It was all against his 'judgment and inclination,' and, he might well have added as a major explanation, that it was against his immediate business interest. His patriotism was a bit 'distracted.' Now that 'the door of conciliation' had been closed, he was 'obliged' to resign.[30] The Convention voted 'cheerfully and unanimously' to accept the resignation, with some severe and cutting reflections on his conduct. These were sent to Congress, where the reflections on

---

[26] *Ibid.*, II, 7.   [27] July 16, 1776.
[28] *Pennsylvania Gazette*, July 17, 1776.
[29] *Ibid.*, July 24, 1776.   [30] Burnett, *Letters*, II, 13.

a colleague were heard with the utmost complacency. A New Hampshire delegate wrote that he 'believed [Alsop's] boarding with our friend Wharton had been no advantage to him,' and that 'possibly he was obliged to resign his seat as a previous condition to his taking full possession of the lady' — a mysterious reference.[31] Even so, he was soon honored with the governorship of New York, which he held until 1780, with the support of the Tory element among the merchants and financiers.

But John Dickinson, who had refused to sign the Declaration, aligned himself with his countrymen; and Samuel Adams found that the Declaration had 'given vigor to the spirits of the people.'[32]

X

During the remainder of the session, Jefferson was overburdened with committee work and in the preparing of reports. He served on a committee of three to draw up rules and regulations for the Congress, and six days after the adoption of the Declaration the report was ready. Partly because rough notes in Jefferson's handwriting exist, and partly because the rules are so similar to those written for the Virginia Assembly by Pendleton, it is a reasonable conclusion that the report was largely the work of the Virginian. 'No person to read printed papers,' 'no person to walk while question putting,' 'every person to sit when not speaking,' 'no member to be absent without leave of House' — borrowed almost verbatim from the rules with which Jefferson was familiar in Williamsburg.[33]

Thus, during the remainder of the session until the first of August, Jefferson, instead of resting on his laurels, was a working member. He was following the military developments with the keenest interest, particularly the growth of Washington's army and the designs of the British on New York.[34] Like Washington, he was thinking, not as a Virginian only, but as an American engaged in a common cause with all the colonies. We shall find him thinking thus five years later, when, as Governor of Virginia, faithful to the policy of Washington, this trend of thought was to arouse the ire of a few of the Virginians. Learning that three thousand pounds of

31 Joseph Bartlett to John Langdon, *ibid.,* II, 39.   32 *Ibid.,* II, 11.
33 Ford, *Writings of Jefferson,* II, 60.   34 Letter to Eppes, *ibid.,* II, 62.

lead imported into Virginia had been landed at Fredericksburg, he wrote Governor Henry urging that it be sent at once for the use of the army in the Jerseys, since 'the flying camp forming in the Jerseys in the face of a powerful enemy are likely to be in distress for this article.' He thought Virginia would be 'wanting in the public cause, which includes that of our own country,' if she hesitated. Even this supply would be wholly inadequate, he wrote, since 'the army in Canada and the army in New York will want much lead, and there seems to be no certain source of supply unless the mine in Virginia can be rendered such.' He urged, therefore, that Henry send all the lead that could be spared at Williamsburg, 'and moreover thirteen to twenty tons to be brought here immediately from the mine.' He took the liberty of recommending 'the lead mines as an object of vast importance.' They could not be worked to too great an extent. 'Considered as, perhaps, the sole means of supporting the American cause, they are inestimable,' he concluded.[35]

Thus had he adopted all the colonies as his country.

He was following the military moves anxiously, and in late July he was distressed by the slow recruiting for Washington's army and that of Mercer in the Jerseys. But for this, he thought, something might have been undertaken on Staten Island, but the British were there now, ten thousand strong. The army at Ticonderoga was 'getting out of the smallpox,' and, with a hundred and fifty carpenters ordered there, he hoped they would 'outbuild the enemy so as to keep our force on the lake superior to theirs.' Eager as he was to leave for home because of the disturbing reports on his wife's health, he could not leave his post.[36]

Three days later, he was even more anxious. Everyone was depressed by the ill results in Canada. He could not understand the retreat from Crown Point, which he had thought should be 'a certain stand,' and the retreat thence to Ticonderoga seemed 'against everything which wears the shape of reason.' And Washington's army had been exaggerated. He had but thirteen thousand men. Why, he asked, should not Virginia send men to Washington, and at once? 'I hope that country is perfectly safe now,' he wrote Francis Eppes, 'and if it is, it seems hardly right that she should not

---

[35] *Ibid.*, II, 66-67.
[36] Letter to Page, *ibid.*, II, 69-72.

contribute a man to an army of forty thousand, and an army, too, on which was to depend the decision of all our rights.' [37]

Here again, the voice of the robust nationalist.

A few days later, he was more infuriated by the slow recruiting of Washington's army. He had heard that the General then had but seventeen thousand men 'of whom four thousand are sick and three thousand at our posts in Long Island.' He wrote indignantly that 'every influence in Congress has been exerted in vain to double the General's force, but it was impossible to prevail on the people to leave their harvests.' Now that the harvests were in, recruits were appearing, but they could not reach Washington's army in time to save New York. And the Virginia Council actually complaining of the calling away of two of its battalions? Is it reasonable? he asked.

> They have no British enemy and if human reason is of any use to conjecture future events they will not have one. The Indian enemy is not to be opposed by their regular battalions. Other colonies of not half their military strength have put twenty battalions in the field. Think of these things and endeavor to reconcile them not only to this, but to yield greater assistance to the common cause, if wanted. I wish every battalion we have was in New York.[38]

Again the voice of the nationalist.

In August, Jefferson, Franklin, and Adams, the three most commanding figures in the Congress, composing a special committee, deliberated on a plan for crippling the British forces by drawing off the German soldiers. They proposed to Congress the granting of a thousand acres of unappropriated land to colonels, eight hundred acres to lieutenant-colonels, six hundred acres to majors, four hundred acres to captains, two hundred acres to ensigns, and one hundred acres to every non-commissioned officer, on condition that they sheathe their swords and settle in the country. The resolutions thus offered were promptly adopted.[39]

Torn cruelly by conflicting claims upon his presence, Jefferson was still in Philadelphia the last of August when word reached Con-

[37] *Ibid.*, II, 72-73.
[38] Letter probably to John Taylor of Caroline, *ibid.*, II, 78-83.
[39] *Ibid.*, II, 89.

gress from Washington that he had refused Lord Drummond a pass through the colonies on a mission of proposing peace. This reflected the hope that, through the support of appeasers and Tories, an inconclusive peace might receive some consideration. Thoroughly aroused by the threat, Jefferson supported a resolution, unanimously adopted, declaring against peace discussions or negotiations, 'which do not, as a preliminary, acknowledge these States to be sovereign and independent.' [40]

However, in August, Jefferson and his colleagues could rejoice in Washington's victory on March 17, in Boston. It was decided to strike a gold medal in commemoration. Designs were suggested by both Jefferson and Franklin. The latter proposed Moses lifting up his wand and dividing the Red Sea and Pharaoh in his chariot overwhelmed by the waters, with the motto, 'Rebellion to tyrants is obedience to God.' Jefferson suggested the children of Israel in the wilderness led by a cloud by day and a pillar of fire by night, and, on the opposite side, Hengist and Horsa, the Saxon chiefs, 'from whom we claim the honor of being descended and whose political principles and form of government we have assumed.' Again we note Jefferson's insistence on the Saxon ancestry, and its implications.[41]

Thus, after the completion of his great work, Jefferson was constant in attendance at Carpenter's Hall through July and August, serving on committees, writing reports, following eagerly the movement of armies and the recruiting, and insisting that Virginia furnish lead for the armies of the North. He was already thinking of the united colonies as one nation with one destiny, frowning on sectionalism and local selfishness and jealousies.

He was one of the earliest of the nationalists.

XI

Throughout these hectic days in Philadelphia, Jefferson had been deeply concerned over the organization of the new State Government in Virginia and the new constitution in process of incubation. Here was a task to his liking; and his thinking from his student days had brought certain convictions for which he would have

[40] Ibid., II, 90.   [41] Ibid., II, 50.

liked to battle. It was not merely a new constitution under a republic that he envisioned, but a thoroughly democratic constitution. To him, the breaking with the past effected by the separation offered an opportunity to advance the frontiers of democracy. Eagerly, he wrote his friend, Thomas Nelson, to keep him intimately supplied with 'convention intelligence,' and he suggested that he and some of the other delegates be recalled to Virginia to participate. 'It is a work of the most interesting nature,' he wrote, 'and such as every individual would wish to have his voice in. It is the whole object of the present controversy; for should a bad government be instituted for us [in Virginia] in future, it had been as well to have accepted at first the bad one offered to us from beyond the water without the risk and expense of contest.'

Thus, it is clear that Jefferson was one of the comparatively few with whom the Revolution was to mean something infinitely more important than a change in government — it was to mean a change in systems.

But Virginia did not take the hint, and Jefferson sat on in Philadelphia. The old oligarchic group was clearly not eager to invite a militant democrat into its councils. But Jefferson was not idle as to the constitution in the making at home. First, he stoutly challenged the right of the convention to frame a constitution. He felt strongly that the Virginia Convention, elected to wage war, should not undertake the making of a constitution without a direct mandate from the people. In a large measure, he was responsible for the resolution of the Continental Congress recommending that 'a full and free representation of the people' in such a convention should be assured by the election of delegates for that specific purpose. When, however, his recommendation was ignored, and it was evident that a convention, not elected on the issue of a constitution, would undertake the task, Jefferson, always a realist, sat down to the preparation of a fundamental law he thought would tend to the happiness of the people. When not in his seat at Carpenter's Hall in these sultry days, he could have been found bending over his desk in the parlor of the Graaf house on Market Street.

He called his paper 'A Bill for the remodeling of the form of Government and for establishing the fundamental principles thereof in the future.' But, still firm in his conviction that no body, not

lected for the specific purpose, had a right to frame a constitution,
he stipulated that, should his model be accepted, it should be 'referred . . . to the people, to be assembled in their respective counties;
and that the suffrage of two-thirds of the counties should be requisite to establish it.'

The Jefferson paper struck the revolutionary note in the beginning
by deposing George Guelf, King of Great Britain, from the chief
magistracy of the American colonies. By his 'detestable and insup-
portable tyranny in putting his negative on laws the most wholesome . . . by answering our repeated petitions for redress with a
repetition of injuries . . . by abandoning the helm of government
and declaring us out of his allegiance and protection,' he had forfeited the kingly office and has rendered it 'necessary for the preservation of the people that he should be immediately deposed.'

In Jefferson's draft for a constitution, he provided for the separation and independence of the executive, legislative, and judicial
branches. The House of Representatives was to consist of not less
than one hundred and fifty members and not more than three
hundred, and any elector was qualified. Every four hundred citizens
was entitled to elect one member, and every citizen of full age who
owned twenty-five acres in the county, or one-fourth of an acre in
town, who had paid rates and taxes, was qualified as an elector. The
Senate, consisting of between fifteen and fifty members, would be
elected by the House of Representatives, and one-third should be re-
elected every three years. The judges of the highest courts should
have a right to sit and speak in the Senate, but not to vote. The
money bills were to originate solely in the House, elected by the
direct vote of the people.

Capital punishment and torture were abolished, except in cases of
murder and military offenses. An 'Administrator' was to be elected
annually to head the Government; but he was denied the power to
veto money bills, to dissolve the Assembly, to declare war, pardon
crimes, or confer dignities. Assisting him in an advisory capacity
there was to be a Privy Council, as before, but its members were to
be elected by the House. The judges were to be appointed by the
Administrator, with the advice and consent of the Council. In the
courts, juries were to pass on evidence and trials were to be in open
court. Every citizen, unpossessed of land, should be given fifty

acres, but the land thus appropriated had to be purchased from the Indians.

Thus, Jefferson's model foreshadowed his reform fights within few months in the Virginia legislature. The laws of descent were to be gavelkind, with women having equal rights with men.

No human being, entering the State thereafter, should be held in slavery 'under any pretext whatever.'

The people were to have complete freedom of religion.

There were to be no standing armies in time of peace.

There was to be absolute freedom of the press.

No salaries were to be paid to congressmen, members of the legislature, judges or privy councilors, but a reasonable sum for subsistence would be allowed.

And just as Jefferson contended that the constitution, to be binding, should be accepted by the people at the polls, so he provided that no single clause should be stricken out until voted out by the people in elections.

The kernel of the whole plan is in the fact that power is confined exclusively to the body elected directly by the people.

This interesting document was worked out on the desk in the parlor at Graaf's on which, between May and the middle of June in 1776, Jefferson had written the Declaration of Independence.

Denied the privilege of returning to Virginia personally to participate in the Convention, he sent his paper to Edmund Pendleton, its President, for submission to that body. He sent it, as he says, 'or the mere possibility that it might suggest something worth incorporation into that before the Convention.'

XII

Meanwhile, absent himself, Jefferson had urged Edmund Randolph to oppose a permanent constitution until the people should have an opportunity to elect delegates for the special purpose of framing a fundamental law.[42] But the young man, finding himself surrounded by much older men of wide reputation who had scant sympathy with such democratic notions, could not muster the courage to act.

[42] Edmund Randolph MSS.

Whether Pendleton, who, though a friend of Jefferson, was an ultra-conservative, could have been counted upon to urge the consideration of the model sent under any circumstances, we may well doubt. But it so happened, as he wrote Jefferson, that the document reached him on the day on which the Committee of the Whole had reported the plan the delegates had agreed upon. Thus, he had a good excuse for not pressing for the consideration of quite a different document. He wrote Jefferson that the matter had 'been so long in hand and disputed inch by inch, and the subject of so much alteration and debate, that [the delegates] were worried by the contentions it had produced and could not, from mere lassitude, have been induced to open the instrument again.' However, he said, they were so 'pleased' with Jefferson's preamble that they had 'adopted it in the House by way of an amendment.'

XIII

At the time, and ever afterward, Jefferson insisted that the Virginia Convention did not have the power to adopt a permanent constitution, since the decision to separate from the British Empire had not been reached when the delegates were elected, and when no one thought of creating an entirely new State Government. In addition, he thoroughly disapproved of the constitution thus framed, and he was never to cease his efforts to amend it in conformity with his more liberal and democratic ideas. He frowned on the franchise provisions, clearly adopted to protect the political and economic interests of the old aristocracy. He strongly resented the all too plain and purposeful discrimination against the western counties, to the end that the big planters and the Tidewater representatives might continue their advantage in the legislature.

His disappointment over the constitution convinced him that his mission was in Virginia. He promptly resigned his seat in Congress to accept election to the legislature, where he planned to launch his great and historic battle for the notable democratic reforms which are as intimately identified with his fame as the Declaration.

The legislature was to meet in October, but it was not until the first of September that he packed his belongings, including the

desk he had designed, and started on the long journey to Monti
cello, where he arrived on the ninth. He was to have eighteen days
for meditation and preparation on his hilltop. He reached Williams
burg on October 1 with a program that was dynamic and revolu
tionary. He had left Virginia a champion of independence; and
now, that assured, he returned with the determination to battle the
reactionaries in favor of drastic liberal reforms and the more democratic way of life.

CHAPTER

VII

JEFFERSON WIELDS AN AXE

I

AT THE AGE of thirty-three, distinguished achievements stood to the credit of young Jefferson, and had death claimed him at that early age, he would remain one of the greatest figures in American history. His *Summary View* had presented the case for the Americans with such clarity and persuasiveness that it had repercussions within the shadow of Saint James's Palace. He had been chosen among all the brilliant men in Congress to frame the Reply to the propositions of Lord North. He had just written the Declaration of Independence. And now, while almost all the others were concerned with the immediate problems of the hour, his active mind was formulating plans to make the Revolution mean something more than a change in the personnel of government. No American of his time compared with him in vision, and his philosophic mind penetrated to a change in systems that would mean, not only political amelioration, but an alteration in the social system. And he knew his goal. He knew where he was going, and he was on his way.

He had awaited his release from Congress with impatience, and, having made his immortal contribution there, he sprang eagerly into his phaeton and turned his horses on the road to Virginia. He looked forward with keenest anticipation to his return to the familiar haunts of sandy Williamsburg.

The position he had attained at thirty-three was illuminated, a few years later, when Washington, distressed by the procrastination of Congress, cried out, 'Where is Jefferson?'—and anti-Jefferson historians have seized upon that cry to point an accusing finger at Jefferson as a deserter from a post of patriotic duty. They fail to notice that, by lingering in Congress, he could have spared himself the most arduous labors of his life and a malice that was to pursue him for more than a century. They close their eyes to the fact that never in his long career was he to render more vital service to democracy than during the three years he proposed, championed and sacrificed for the reforms that undermined the deep foundation of an incipient aristocracy of privileges and laid the foundation of democratic institutions. For the most part, biographers have touched with timid fingers this most significant period of his career.

The men of the Revolution may be divided into three categories. First, those who most reluctantly agreed to the separation from Britain because of the arrogant pretensions of King and Parliament in the matter of taxation and gave no serious thought to what was to come afterward. Then, there was a much larger element to whom the Revolution was to mean little more than an exchange of rulers. No thought of real social or political reforms disturbed the serenity of this group. The social structure was to remain as before.

The old aristocracy was to retain its privileges and continue its domination of Church and State. The mansion in Williamsburg would be occupied by a governor chosen by the colony and not one sent by the King—and that was all.

And to young Jefferson, that was nothing.

Easily could he have been reconciled to monarchical rule but for its stout resistance to social and political reforms on which he had meditated from the days when he and Dabney Carr sat beneath the oak on the hillside at Monticello and let their minds rove free.

He had turned against the monarchy because it persistently vetoed every attempt to end the importation of slaves—and he was opposed to slavery.

And because he opposed the creation or the maintenance of a privileged aristocracy in the land through the laws of primogeniture and entail—and he was a convinced democrat, opposed to privilege.

And because it imposed a church establishment, representing a minority of the people, upon the colony and forced dissenters to support an institution with which they had no sympathy — and he believed in religious freedom and the separation of Church and State.

And because it was indifferent to popular education, which he thought essential to a free society.

His mind was occupied with his reforms as his carriage jolted through the dust and over the ruts to Williamsburg — reforms that were the fruit of intensive reading and reflection. He knew precisely what he intended to urge upon the legislature.

This program, already framed, was one of democracy and humanity.

We have seen that he had frankly frowned on the constitution but recently imposed in Virginia and had questioned the authority of the body that framed it without a direct mandate from the people or its authority to impose it without submitting it to the ratification of the people.

And then, too, he found too little of the democratic trend of the people reflected in the framing of that document. He knew his Virginia, and his Virginians, and he knew that the constitution was the work of the old ruling oligarchy. Nor was he alone in this belief. Richard Henry Lee, similarly convinced, had written to John Adams before the Convention met that 'there is, amongst most of our opulent families, a strong bias to aristocracy,' and that even a republican form of government had 'many and powerful enemies.'

It was at this time that a pamphlet appeared in Philadelphia advising as to the character of the constitution to be adopted in Virginia. The author hid under the *nom de plume* of 'A Native,' but his reasoning and conclusions accurately reflected the well-known views of Carter Braxton, one of the spokesmen of the ruling planter class of the Tidewater and a member of the Convention. Lee thought 'the whole performance an affront and disgrace to the country.' [1]

'The people!' exclaimed the author with a grimace. There was no public virtue in the mass. Virtue was monopolized by the aristocracy. Democracy? It was 'inimical to elegance and refinement, to manufactures, art, and science, and to the accumulation of wealth' — with emphasis, we have no doubt, on the 'accumulation of wealth'

[1] Henry, *Life of Patrick Henry*, I, 412-13.

through privilege. His ideal government? A house of representatives, elected for three years by some of the people, would elect a senate which would serve for life, and the laws would be interpreted by judges appointed by the governor for life.[2]

The 'Native,' or Braxton, undoubtedly was an extremist, but the aristocracy and the old social régime was powerfully represented among Jefferson's associates in the legislature he was entering. They would dominate all the crucial committees, and numbered among them would be some of the most brilliant minds in Virginia.

It was to be the younger, comparatively unknown men from the more democratic region of the Piedmont and the mountains that would rally around Jefferson in his fights to advance the frontiers of democracy during his three epochal years in the Assembly.

On October 27, 1776, he drove down the Monticello hill toward Williamsburg, eager as a racer waiting for the signal.

We must bear in mind that the primary thought of young Jefferson during these three legislative years was concentrated consciously on undermining or destroying the whole superstructure of an artificially built and legally maintained aristocracy. A more zealous iconoclast never swung a hammer.

II

But scarcely had Jefferson reached Williamsburg when a messenger arrived, bearing a letter from the President of the Continental Congress offering him the appointment as Commissioner to France. He was clearly reluctant to refuse, but there were reasons why he could not accept. Even so, he held the messenger for three days before writing his declination.

It would argue great insensibility in me could I receive with indifference so confidential an appointment from your body [he wrote Hancock]. My thanks are a poor return for the partiality they have been pleased to entertain for me. No cares for my own person, nor yet for my private affairs would have induced one moment's hesitation to accept the charge. But circumstances very peculiar to the situation of my family, such as neither permit me to leave nor to carry it, compel me to ask leave to decline a service so honorable and at the same time so important to the American cause.[3]

[2] *Ibid.*, I, 421.   [3] Ford, *Writings of Jefferson*, II, 91.

His decision was dictated by his inability to leave an ailing wife, and no doubt, in part, to his indisposition to abandon the fight he had planned in the legislature.

Within four days after taking his seat, he had exploded a bomb among his more complacent colleagues by introducing his bill providing that tenants in tail should hold their lands in fee simple. This, in his opinion, would 'strike at the very root of feudalism in Virginia.' During his studies, while preparing for the bar, he had concluded it easy to prove that 'our lands were allodial possessions'; that the feudalistic land system was primarily intended to serve the purpose of a military establishment; and that it had, long since, become 'an engine of immense oppression.' It was feudalism, and feudalism could not be reconciled with either liberty or democracy.

With the introduction of this measure for the abolishment of entail, young Jefferson boldly struck a deadly blow at the old aristocracy, and what made his action the more reprehensible to his caste was that he had struck it from their own side of the barricade. He had 'turned upon his own class.'

In the earliest days of the colonies, when lands could be had for little or nothing and the more obsequious of the courtiers could receive vast grants from the Crown, enormous estates were created; and the owners, bent on the establishment of a great and powerful family and the perpetuation of their estates in the family, resorted to the English system of entail and primogeniture. This made it possible for the most dissolute and improvident son to hold on to his broad acres under the protection of the law, regardless of debts, indolence, or slovenly mismanagement. Thus was created a class immune from payment of the penalty for improvidence and dissipation.

All this was provided by the English law, but to the embryo aristocracy in Virginia this was not enough, since in England the practice of docking estates was permissible; the Virginians prohibited it by law in the Old Dominion.

Thus, the system created was nothing less than the perpetuation of wealth in a few privileged families and the artificial creation of an aristocracy based entirely on land and money. These families, therefore, without fear of the future, could, and did, live in luxury; and, because of their wealth, they had been accorded a certain

primacy in the determination of the policies of government. It i
significant enough that it was from this element that the King ha
drawn his counselors of the Royal Governor.

That this explains the motive behind Jefferson's determinatio
to strike down entail is made crystal clear in his own language.

> In the earliest times of the colonies [he wrote], when lands wer
> to be obtained for little or nothing, some provident individuals ob
> tained large grants; and desirous of founding great families fo
> themselves, settled them on their descendants in fee tail. The trans
> mission of this property from generation to generation in the sam
> name raised up a distinct class of families, who, being privileged b
> law in the perpetuation of their wealth, were thus formed into
> Patrician order, distinguished by the splendor and luxury of thei
> establishments.

To a convinced democrat like Jefferson, determined that the new
order should rest on a democratic basis, privilege was abhorrent
And so, to quote further, 'to annul this privilege, and, instead of a
aristocracy of wealth, of more harm and danger than benefit to
society,' he proposed to substitute 'an aristocracy of virtue and talen
which Nature has wisely provided for the direction of the interest o
society, and scattered with equal hand through all its conditions.
This, he declared, was 'essential to a well-ordered republic.' [4]

It is significant of young Jefferson's genius in leadership in the
championing of democratic principles that he was thinking clearly
and with concentration of a new deal in the social setup, far in advance of any other leaders of the Revolution. And he was thinking
constructively. But three months had intervened since the American
people had declared their independence in the sacred document
young Jefferson had written. The minds of most of the patriots
did not go beyond the immediate military and political problems,
while that of Jefferson was intensively occupied with a post-war
system from the very beginning of the revolutionary struggle.

III

Nothing could have been more startling to the representatives of
the old oligarchy. None but could have known that this single

[4] *Autobiography,* 36-37.

measure, if enacted, would mean a social as well as a political revolution and put a termination to the political domination of the aristocracy, since this would strip them of the special legal privileges which guarded their possessions.

And no one of them was more startled or distressed than Edmund Pendleton, whose brilliant legal mind and parliamentary cleverness were always at the command of the landed oligarchy. Patriot though he was, virtuous and well-meaning, he had the lawyer's reverence for precedent and fear of change. Thus, he stepped forward in full armor to give battle, and the other defenders of the ancient system rallied to his support. But sentiment was now running strong with Jefferson. The younger and comparatively obscure members of the western country, the Piedmont and the mountains and the then frontier, gathered about him with ardor. And in view of the iconoclastic nature of the measure, the marvel is that the struggle should have lasted but eleven days.

One glance at the field, and Pendleton, a veteran of many battlefields, realized that he was outnumbered and impotent, and could not hope to swerve the Assembly by any line of reasoning nor successfully appeal to a nonexistent devotion to tradition. He fell back on his cleverness in parliamentary maneuvering, simulated a disposition to capitulation, and sought to save the day by a suave offer to write the terms of the surrender.

Never was he more dangerous than when in this almost sweet mood of conciliation. Jefferson was to pronounce him 'the ablest man in debate [he] had ever met,' and to describe him as 'never vanquished; for if he lost the main battle, he returned upon you and regained so much of it as to make it a draw, by dexterous maneuvers, skirmishes in detail, and the recovering of small advantages, which, while singly unimportant, were important all together.' The persistency of his fight exhausted patience. And to add to his strength, despite his passion for tradition and for the ancient system, he was respected for his impeccable integrity and loved for his amiable qualities that never soured in the bitterness of battle.

Thus, realizing his inability to prevent the passage of the measure, he took his last stand on a sophistry and with an amendment. Was not Jefferson an avowed champion of personal liberty? he asked. How, then, could he oppose the granting of permission to the owners of entailed estates to decide for themselves whether the would hold their lands entailed or by fee simple? And he offered his amendment giving them liberty of choice.

This sophistry, while transparent, has been used throughout American history when privilege has been threatened, and appeal have been made to the 'robust individualism' of 'Jeffersonian democracy.' This amendment meant granting to the defeated part the fruits of victory, since it was fighting the abolishing of entail

But the legislators were not confused and the amendment was promptly voted down after a contest of but eleven days; and thus a change amounting to a social revolution had been wrought The backbone of the ruling feudalistic aristocracy had been broken.[5]

IV

Jefferson now turned to his long-cherished plan of putting an end to the importation of slaves into Virginia. Nothing had so embittered him against the conduct of the King as his constant overriding of the repeated efforts of the Virginia legislature to stop this vicious traffic in human flesh. We have seen that in the Declaration of Independence, as he submitted it to Congress, he had included a fierce arraignment of the monarch for his interference and that it was stricken out on the objections of some slave-owning States. It is not surprising, therefore, that one of Jefferson's first acts was the introduction of a bill ending the importation of slaves.

We must not conclude, however, that the ending of the importation of slaves went as far as Jefferson, who wished the extermination of slavery, would have desired. On the death of his father, he had come into possession of thirty slaves, and in the succeeding years the number had augmented. The economic system of the State was based on slavery, and, while he would have gladly joined all others in the freeing and colonization of the slaves, he alone could not do so and compete with slave labor. Such action, on his part alone, would have been Quixotic and destructive of his own economic life. Throughout his life he was never to conceal his attitude toward slavery, and he was never to miss an opportunity to attempt the writing of his conviction into law.

[5] *Autobiography*, 36; Tucker, *Life of Jefferson*, I, 22.

Meanwhile, on his own plantation he sought to make the system as humane and just as possible. He was loved by his slaves, and he was invariably kind to them. He saw to it personally that they were not overworked. He detested flogging, and gave instructions to his supervisors that, in the case of a consistently obstreperous and ungovernable slave, he should be sold rather than lashed.

And now, when he put his hand to the task of breaking down the old ruling, feudalistic aristocracy, the emancipation of the slaves gave him much concern. He actually prepared a bill looking to emancipation. It provided that all negroes, born after a stipulated date, should be free.

Submitting it to his colleagues among the revisers of the laws, he found them all agreed that such a measure would fail of passage and that the attempt might create a bitterness that would militate against the other reforms attainable and accomplish nothing. In old age, he recalled his efforts and his hopes, describing what actually was done:

> The bill on slavery was a digest of the existing laws, without any intimation of a plan for a future and general emancipation. It was thought better that this should be kept back and attempted only by amendment, whenever the bill should be brought on. The principle of the amendment, however, we were agreed on — that is to say, the freedom of all born after a certain day, and deportation at a certain age. But it was found that the public mind would not bear the proposition, nor will it bear it even to this day. Yet the time is not distant when it must bear and adopt it, or worse will follow.

To which he added:

> Nothing is more certainly written in the book of fate than that these people are to be free.[6]

In his *Notes on Virginia*, in his *Autobiography*, in his voluminous correspondence, he leaves no possible doubt of his abhorrence of slavery, and, a little later, we shall find him again attempting in his Ordinance of the Northwest Territory to strike a blow at human bondage.

However, sentiment supported the suppression of the importation of slaves, and Jefferson's bill was passed without opposition.

[6] *Autobiography,* 48-49.

V

In the first days of the session Jefferson gave his attention to the reorganization and reformation of the courts. With the advent of the Revolution, all courts of justice had been closed, and Jefferson the lawyer, with a keen realization of the relation of the courts to society, naturally took the lead in their re-establishment. But his plans contemplated not only their re-establishment, but their reform — and here he was to encounter a stubborn opposition.

His first measure, presented in the very beginning, provided for the reopening of the courts. Two weeks later, he presented measures for the establishment of a Court of Appeals, a High Court of Chancery, a General Court, and Courts of Assizes.

The first bill passed promptly; but the forces of reaction succeeded in postponing a vote on the others for almost two years, and it was not until 1778 that the Jefferson bills for the creation of other courts came up for action. This was after the more liberal element had grown stronger.

Even so, as late as 1778, a determined effort was made to postpone action until after the termination of the session, which meant defeat. Again the forces in opposition were led by the suave and resourceful Pendleton.

Thoroughly angered by the tactics of his opponents and firmly convinced that the members of the legislature held views they dared not admit to their constituents, Jefferson broke all precedents. He demanded a public roll-call and a public vote!

It was a typical Jeffersonian appeal over the heads of men in office to the people who put them there. And the ultra-conservatives thought the maneuver in bad taste — an appeal to the 'mob'; the mob being the people. It aroused the ire of those who preferred, from motives of self-preservation, to conceal their attitude from the constituents they misrepresented. Now Jefferson relentlessly had turned the searchlight upon them, and when the roll was called on the General Court bill and the Courts of Assizes, the measure passed, with Pendleton recorded in the same column with Jefferson.

But the real battle was reserved for Jefferson's bill creating a Court of Chancery. This stipulated that on all matters of fact, a jury should pass upon the facts. 'Revolutionary!' cried his opponents. 'Shocking!' complained the conservatives. And again, under the cunning leadership of Pendleton, the conservatives marshaled their full strength for the contest.

Realizing, again, that there was little hope of victory without resorting to the strategy of which he was a master, the astute Pendleton moved smilingly into action. With the greatest suavity he proposed an amendment, the significance of which the average layman among the legislators did not grasp. This provided that a litigant could have a jury pass upon the facts *if he cared to make a demand upon the court.*

There was no lawyer but understood that, if this amendment were adopted, it would defeat the purpose of the bill; since no lawyer or litigant would dare offend the judge by making the demand. But to the layman the amendment was both reasonable and harmless, and it carried.

In old age Jefferson was to write that 'the consequence has been that, as no suitor will say to his judge, "Sir, I distrust you, give me a jury," juries are rarely, I might say, perhaps, never, seen in that court.'[7]

However, despite some emasculating amendments to his bills, it may be truly said that, in the first legislature after the Declaration of Independence, the judicial system of Virginia was set up under the supervising leadership of young Jefferson.

VI

One day Jefferson introduced his bill for a general revision of the laws, to bring them into harmony with the new form of government and for such modifications and reforms as might be deemed desirable. Out of this seemingly routine proceeding, some of the most important reform measures of Jefferson's career were to come.

The resolution passed. A committee of revisers, composed of great minds, was named. On the committee were Jefferson, George Wythe, and Edmund Pendleton, successful lawyers; George Mason, the statesman and publicist; and Francis Lightfoot Lee. The task to which they were assigned was of vast magnitude and first importance.

[7] *Ibid.*, 37.

This committee was named on November 6. Thirty-eight days later, Jefferson was at Monticello during the week for the Christmas holidays, before driving to Fredericksburg where the members had agreed to meet.

Few up until then had given any serious consideration to the work, but young Jefferson, who never acted on unpremeditated impulse or lightly, had very definite notions about what he wished to do. 'When I left Congress in 1776,' he wrote later, 'it was in the persuasion that our whole code must be reviewed, adapted to our republican form of government, and, now that we had no negatives of Councils, Governors, and Kings to restrain us from doing right, that it should be corrected in all its parts with a single eye to reason and the good of those for whose government it was framed.'

It was with this single object that he entered the conference at Fredericksburg. But scarcely had the revisers seated themselves about the table when a controversy arose as to what should be undertaken. Pendleton and Lee, strangely enough, proposed to abolish the entire system of laws under which Virginia so long had lived and to substitute a new and complete Institute. It may well be doubted if even Pendleton realized the enormity of the task he was proposing and his position seemed out of character. Opposing this ambitious plan, as impractical and unwise, Jefferson suggested instead the preservation of the general system with such modifications as the new situation might demand.

At first blush, this would seem a reversal of the traditional positions of Jefferson and Pendleton. The former was the 'radical,' the 'iconoclast,' popularly supposed to be in favor of the uprooting of all things ancient and a complete breaking with the past; and the latter was presumed to be an ultra-conservative, prone to hold tenaciously to tradition. But, aside from the enormity and extreme difficulty of the plan proposed by Pendleton, Jefferson was persuaded that in the creation of the committee the legislators had nothing of the sort in view. He, who had proposed the revision, certainly had not. He urged that the legislature 'had been in the habit of revising, from time to time, the laws of the colony, permitting the expired and repealing the obsolete, amending only those retained, and probably meant that we should do the same, only including the British statutes as well as our own.'

But Pendleton had more ambitious plans, having in mind an entirely new Institute, with Justinian, Bracton, and Blackstone in mind as models. But, protested the astonished Jefferson, the task would be arduous. It would call for the most intensive and extensive research that might properly require years. And even when completed and reduced to writing, he urged, 'every word of that text, from the imperfections of human language and its incompetence to express distinctly every shade of ideas, would become a subject of question and chicanery until settled by repeated adjudications, and this would involve us for ages in litigation and render property uncertain, until, like the statutes of old, every word had been tried and settled by numerous decisions, and by new volumes of reports and commentaries.'[8]

Without reflecting on the good faith of Pendleton, the issue was one between the lawgiver and the practicing lawyer; between one who wanted the utmost simplification of the laws for the better understanding of the layman and one who thrived professionally on litigation. Pendleton's was primarily the legal mind; and Jefferson's the mind of a statesman.

It is not surprising that aligned with Jefferson in his interpretation of the legislature's intent was George Wythe, one of the greatest of the lawyers, and also one of the soundest of the jurists and statesmen. The deciding vote fell to George Mason, and the sound statesmanship of the master of Gunston Hall threw him into the company of Jefferson and Wythe.

Thus, it was agreed that there should be no completely new Institute, but a revision and simplification of the old statutes.

This decision made, the next step was the division of the labor among the five members. It was at this moment that both Mason and Lee asked to be relieved, on the ground that they were not lawyers — something the legislature had overlooked. Their excuses were accepted, and thus all the actual work fell upon the three remaining members, who divided the task among them.

It was agreed that Jefferson should deal with the common law and statutes to the fourth year of James I, when Virginians were granted their separate legislature, and that Wythe should carry on with the British statutes where Jefferson left off and continue through to the

[8] *Ibid.*, 42-43.

time of the revisers. The laws of Virginia were to be handled by Pendleton.

On receiving his assignment, Jefferson excused himself from the legislature for a brief retirement at Monticello to prepare for his grueling task. He had determined on style and method. He would not change the diction of the ancient statutes, because they 'had been so fully explained and defined by numerous adjudications as scarcely ever now to procure a question in our courts'; but he would eliminate all verbosity and tautologies, 'their evolution of a case within a case, and parenthesis within parenthesis, and their multiplied efforts at certainty by "saids" and "aforesaids," by "ors" and "ands."'

This work was to extend over a period of more than two years, and it was not until June, 1779, that the fruit of this labor was presented to the Assembly in the form of bills.

When each of the three revisers had completed his task, a meeting was called at Williamsburg for February, 1779, before the presentation of the revisions, for the purpose of a critical examination. Pendleton, who was soon called home from the meeting, authorized Jefferson and Wythe to make unanimous any decision reached. The various revisions were scrutinized with meticulous care, sentence by sentence. To their dismay, the two revisers found that their absent associate had failed to conform with the general plan agreed upon. Instead of seeking a clarification and simplification of the language of the old statutes, he had done no more than copy the exact phrasing, merely eliminating the parts no longer applicable to the changed conditions.

Since both Jefferson and Wythe had conformed, it was necessary to uniformity that Pendleton's revisions should be made similar in style. There was nothing to be done but to rewrite Pendleton's revision of the Virginia laws, and the two revisers bent to the task, with the greater portion of the labor falling on Jefferson.

By arduous labor and severe condensation and elimination, the three men had been able to include all the British statutes from Magna Charta down, with all the enactments of Virginia from the first legislature in the fourth year of James I, to one hundred and twenty-six bills that could be printed in a folio of but ninety pages.

Jefferson himself took a modest view of the general work of the revisers. 'The only merit of this work,' he said, 'is that it may remove from our bookshelves about twenty folio volumes of our statutes, retaining all the parts of them which either their own merit or the established system of our laws required.'[9]

This was much too modest, for among the bills Jefferson submitted were some that not only served to better the social system, but contributed to the ultimate success of his democratic crusade.

VII

Thus, in the division of the labor, the law of descent came within his province. On this he held views, not only iconoclastic, but well-nigh revolutionary.

He had forced through the abolishment of entail. This had dealt a deadly blow at the old feudalistic segment of society. He had reserved until now another blow, for there still was a remnant of the feudalistic system that had to go. He had determined to abolish, as well, the sanction of primogeniture, through which real estate descended to the eldest sons, to the neglect of the other sons and daughters. Thus, vast landed estates of thousands of acres could not be broken up by natural process, but would be held intact by one of a family. He proposed simply that the head of the family should have the right to distribute his real estate, like his personal property, among his children. He saw no reason why the elder son, merely because of his earlier birth and without reference to his character or qualifications, should be so signally preferred over the younger children who might easily be more worthy; and, as the father of daughters to whom he was devoted and with a deep respect for the intelligence of women, he could see no justice in the practical disinheritance of women.

Having determined a plan in his own mind, he summoned his associate revisers to determine by discussion the guiding principles in the drafting of the bill.

Jefferson could not have been surprised when Pendleton again made a stubborn stand against this new attack upon the old system of building up a few great and powerful families to the detriment of the common good. In Wythe, the liberal, Jefferson found a

9 Ford, *Writings of Jefferson*, II, 195.

faithful supporter. Pendleton argued and pleaded; but finding himself defeated in the discussion about the revisers' table, he again had recourse to his favorite method of the flank attack. If he could not kill, he might maim the plan of Jefferson.

'Why not, then,' said Pendleton, 'give a double portion to the eldest son?'

Jefferson was both amazed and amused by this evocation of the old Hebrew principle.

'If the eldest son could eat twice as much and do double work,' he replied with jocularity, 'it might be natural evidence of his right to a double portion; but, being on a par in his powers and wants with his brothers and sisters, he should be on a par also in the partition of the patrimony.' [10]

Such was the opinion of Wythe as well, and this time Pendleton failed in his purpose.

Thus had young Jefferson knocked down two of the principal props of the old artificial, legally privileged aristocracy — primogeniture and entail; and thus had he leveled the road in Virginia for the onward march of democracy.

VIII

He was especially thinking of democracy when he turned to well-matured plans for popular education for the masses and a more intensive training for prospective leaders of the people than was then available. He could not reconcile illiteracy and ignorance with the processes of democratic institutions — and on these he was determined. His whole faith in popular government was conditioned on reasonable knowledge in the people governed. He knew that, without freedom of speech and the liberty of the press, democracy would become anaemic and die literally of starvation. Give the people the facts, he often said, and they will decide rightly. But he also knew that a certain background of knowledge, if only on the elementals, would then be necessary to a reasoned appraisement of the facts.

Experience has shewn [he wrote] that, even under the best forms, those entrusted with power have, in time and by slow operations,

[10] *Autobiography,* 43.

perverted it into tyranny; and it is believed that the most effectual means of preventing this would be to illuminate, as far as practical, the minds of the people at large, and more especially to give them knowledge of those facts which history exhibiteth. [He thought that] people will be happiest whose laws are best and are best administered, and that laws will be wisely formed and honestly administered in proportion as those who form and administer them are wise and honest; whence it becomes expedient for promoting the public happiness that those persons, whom Nature hath endowed with genius and virtue, should be rendered, by liberal education, worthy to receive, and able to guard, the sacred deposit of the rights and liberties of their fellow citizens, and that they should be called to that charge without regard to wealth, birth, or other accidental condition or circumstance.

Here again, we have Jefferson's respect for the aristocracy of intellect and virtue, and his indifference to the aristocracy of wealth; again his democratic thesis.

Refusing to accept the theory that the capacity to govern is confined to the wealthy, able to educate themselves, he continued:

The indigence of the greater number disabling them from so educating at their own expense those of their children whom Nature hath fitly formed and disposed to become instruments for the public, it is better that such should be sought for, and educated at the common expense of all, than that the happiness of all should be confided to the weak or wicked.

To appreciate the revolutionary nature of such thinking at the time, it must be borne in mind that the State of Virginia had made absolutely no provision for elementary schools for the education of the masses. The old clergy of the Established Church had furnished some elementary training to the children of the more prosperous, but even this, in most instances, was slovenly. The State, as such, had recognized no obligation to the people in the field of education. The old landed aristocracy, resting so largely on primogeniture and entail, had scant sympathy with the idea of developing the thinking capacity of the masses. 'Coddle the workers and you will spoil them' was heard then, as now, among the reactionaries, with no real democratic bias. And then, too, public education would mean taxation which would touch the purses of the wealthy.

Happily, three of the men who sat in conference on this subject were men of vision and apprehension, and all agreed on the necessity for popular education for the masses and a more specialized training for the superior minds than was then offered in Virginia.

This subject fell more within the province of Pendleton's labors, but Jefferson so clearly surpassed the others in his delvings into educational systems that it was agreed that the drawing of the bills should be assigned to him. No more congenial task could have been entrusted to him.

In the preamble to his educational bills he set forth the conviction that free government depends on knowledge and on its dissemination among the masses of the people. This was startling, radical, revolutionary, and, strangely enough, not a few thought dangerous.

In his plan for primary or elementary schools, he proposed the division of each county into hundreds or wards. Three aldermen were to be elected who should proceed to the division of each county into districts, each including enough children for a school. Under the supervision of the aldermen, schoolhouses should be erected at public expense.

In the elementary schools should be taught reading, writing, and arithmetic, which was inevitable; but Jefferson, thinking always in terms of popular government, proposed that the reading should be so selected as to familiarize the students with Grecian, Roman, English, and American history. The clear purpose was to furnish the citizen of tomorrow with background information on fundamental principles of government, with which to test contemporary politics.

For every ten schools an overseer was to be appointed, who would choose the teachers, make periodic visits to the schools, and personally examine the students.

During the first three years tuition was to be furnished free, and thereafter a small tuition was to be charged, on the theory that those sufficiently fired with a desire for knowledge would find a way to meet the cost; and the others, not interested, would drop out.

IX

In the case of the grammar schools, Jefferson divided the State into sections with certain specified counties in each section, and in one of these, in the most central and convenient spot, a grammar school was to be established. The building was to be of brick or stone and to be located in the center of a hundred-acre lot. It was to consist of a large schoolroom, a dining-hall, four rooms for master and ushers, and ten or twelve lodging-rooms for students living on the premises. A steward was to have charge of the procuring of provisions for the table, fuel for heating, servants for the cooking, cleaning, waiting, washing, and mending.

In these schools were to be taught Latin, Greek, English grammar, geography, and the higher mathematics.

While in these schools there was to be a small tuition, provision was made that, among the poor who could ill afford the cost, free tuition should be given one of the best of the students from each county in the district. And from each grammar-school district one of the most promising of the students was to be granted lodging and tuition free at William and Mary College for three years.

X

This brought him up to his alma mater, William and Mary. Its course of studies and its spirit had not favorably impressed him during his own student days. Because of the original royal charter, the college contributions to the Commonwealth had not been commensurate with the expense, and, under the royal domination, the necessary amendments to the charter had been impossible.

Now all was changed. The College was now the property and the obligation of the State. Jefferson proposed to reorganize and strengthen its course of studies and its professional staff, and to convert it into a University, with special emphasis on the higher sciences. The University was to be governed by five visitors, appointed by the legislature. It was to be converted into a State University in the modern sense.

Thus, here again, Jefferson was thinking far in advance of his time.

His plan provided for the suspension of the course in theology, and for eight departments, including Ethics, Fine Arts, Municipal and Common Law, Equity, Commercial, Marine, and Ecclesiastical Law, Economics, dealing with politics and commerce, Mathematics, Natural Philosophy, and Ancient and Modern Languages.

Not content with these drastic reforms and improvements, he capped his plan by the introduction of a bill for the support and radical extension of a State Library, with an annual appropriation of two thousand pounds to be expended in the purchase of books under the supervision of men 'of learning and of attention to literary matters.'

Such was young Jefferson's comprehensive scheme for the revolutionizing of education in Virginia. Thus, as early as 1777, he had raised the framework of the educational system of today, on the same principles and motivated by the same purpose.

Simple and reasonable as it appears today, it literally aroused the wrath of a large part of the well-to-do citizenry of the Commonwealth of his time. It was 'revolutionary.' It was 'radical.' It was a threat to the social order. It was chimerical and fantastic. It was the work of a dangerous visionary. And, besides, it would increase taxes — and that, perhaps, was the one sincere objection of most.

It is not surprising that these Jeffersonian educational measures, designed to give democracy a chance, fell like a wet blanket on the legislators. They refused even to consider them seriously. So deep-rooted was this antipathy to popular education that it was not until 1796, eight years after the establishment of the Republic under the Constitution, that a vote could be had on even the Elementary School Bill, and even then an amendment was tacked on making it optional with each county to act upon it or to ignore it.

Years later, Jefferson was convinced that the placing of the cost on the people in proportion to their capacity to pay, thus making wealth assist in the education of the poor, was responsible for the unpopularity and defeat of his measures. The amendment killed the Elementary School Bill in 1796, because, as Jefferson wrote later, 'the Justices, being generally of the more wealthy class, were unwilling to incur the burden, and I believe it was not suffered to commence in a single county.'

Years more were to intervene before Virginia, one of the richest States in the Union, would have a public school system or a university worthy of the name, but young Jefferson had placed his vision on a hill toward which the people groped in time.

It is amazing that so little significance has been attached by most historians and biographers to these educational measures, since they were so far in advance of the times. An eminent Frenchman, educator and historian, has concluded that the system adopted in France, years later, was probably inspired in part by the views of Jefferson, set forth in his *Notes on Virginia,*[11] and he concludes that 'one may state here, without any fear of contradiction, that no system so complete, so logically constructed, and so well articulated has ever been proposed in any country of the world.'[12]

XI

When, in the revision, the subject of crimes and punishment fell to Jefferson, he could undertake the task with an enlightened interest. Even in his student days, he had read and thought much upon the subject and had reached conclusions in advance of his time in the United States. He had been influenced to some extent in his thinking by Montesquieu, but, admittedly, more by Beccaria, the Italian publicist, who, in turn, had been inspired by the *Spirit of the Laws.*

Thirteen years before Jefferson undertook his reforms on crimes and punishment, Beccaria had published his then famous work, and, nine years before, it had been translated into English. Jefferson, deeply impressed, had pored over the Italian edition before the translation, since his lengthy quotations from the work, covering eighteen closely written pages of his *Commonplace Book,* are in Italian.[13] Both in his *Autobiography* and in his notations in his bills an acknowledgement is made to the Italian humanist, who had declared that experience had proved both the unrighteousness and the inefficiency of the death penalty. Jefferson realized that public opinion in Virginia would not consent to the entire abolishment of the penalty of death. In the conference of the revisers, before Jefferson settled down to his task, there was a general agreement that the death penalty should be confined to treason and murder.[14] 'Beccaria and other writers on crime and punishment had convinced the reasonable world of the unrighteousness and inefficiency of the punishment of crimes by death,' he wrote, much later, 'and hard labor on roads, canals, and other public works had been sug-

[11] Chinard, *Jefferson,* 98.   [12] *Ibid.*
[13] *Commonplace Book,* 298-316.   [14] *Autobiography,* 43.

gested as a proper substitute. The revisers had adopted these opinions, but the general idea of the country had not yet advanced to that point.'[15]

Having prepared his bill, Jefferson submitted it to the critical examination of George Wythe.

> I . . . enclose it to you with the request that you will be so good as scrupulously to examine and correct it. In its style I have aimed at accuracy, brevity, and simplicity, preserving, however, the very words of the established law wherever their meaning had been sanctioned by judicial decisions or rendered technical by usage.

Here again he returned to his favorite grievance against the phrasing of the laws.

> The same matter, if couched in the modern statutory language, with all its tautologies, redundancies, and circumlocutions, would have spread itself over many pages and been unintelligible to those whom it most concerns. Indeed, I wished to exhibit a sample of reformation of the barbarous style into which modern statutes have degenerated from their ancient simplicity.

And then, with a note of apology, followed a reference to one savage feature that was not abolished:

> I have strictly observed the scale of punishments settled by the committee without being entirely satisfied with it. The *Lex Talionis* . . . will be revolting to the humanized feelings of modern times. An eye for an eye and a hand for a hand will exhibit spectacles in execution whose moral effect would be questionable.

Thus, Jefferson makes it clear enough that, while bound by the decision of the revisers in the inclusion of this barbarous feature, he had opposed it in committee.

XII

The spirit animating Jefferson in dealing with crimes and punishment, set forth in the preamble of the bills, indicates how far in advance of his time was his thinking outside the sphere of politics:

> Whereas it frequently happens that wicked and dissolute men, resigning themselves to the domination of inordinate passions,

[15] *Ibid.*, 46.

commit violations on the lives, liberties and property of others; and the secure enjoyment of these having induced men to enter society, government would be defective in its principal purpose were it not to restrain such criminal acts by inflicting due punishments on those who perpetrate them; but it appears at the same time equally deducible from the purposes of society that a member thereof committing an inferior injury does not wholly forfeit the protection of his fellow citizens, but, after suffering a punishment in proportion to his offense, is entitled to their protection from all greater pain, so that it becomes a duty of the legislature to arrange in a proper scale the crimes which it may be necessary for them to repress, and to adjust thereto a corresponding gradation of punishments.

And whereas the reformation of offenders is not affected at all by capital punishments, which exterminate instead of reforming, and should be the last melancholy recourse against those whose existence is become inconsistent with the safety of their fellow citizens; which also weakens the State by cutting off so many, who, if reformed, might be restored sound members of society, who even under a course of correction might be rendered useful in various labors for the public, and would be a living and long-continued spectacle to deter others from committing the like offenses.

And forasmuch as the experience of all ages and countries hath shown that cruel and sanguinary laws defeat their own purpose, by engaging the benevolence of mankind to withhold prosecutions, to smother testimony or to listen to it with bias; and by producing, in many instances, a total dispensation and immunity under the names of pardon and privilege of clergy; when, if the punishment were only proportioned to the injury, men would feel it their inclination, as well as their duty, to see the laws observed; and the power of dispensation, so dangerous and mischievous, which produces crimes by holding up a hope of impunity, might totally be abolished, so that men while contemplating to perpetrate a crime would see their punishment ensuing as necessary as effect follows cause; for rendering crimes and punishments therefore more proportionate to each other.[16]

But the reforms proposed by Jefferson seemed to many, if not most, of his generation as a straining of sentimentality. They met with vigorous opposition; and when, through the stubborn efforts

[16] Ford, *Writings of Jefferson*, II.

of Madison, they were brought to a vote as late as 1783, they were defeated by one vote in the House of Delegates. However, for some years these bills were brought forward from time to time and passed.

In time, Jefferson began to doubt the wisdom of using convicts for public work on roads and canals. He had keenly followed the experiment in Pennsylvania and noted its failure. The fact that convicts were made a humiliating public spectacle, with their shaven heads and mean clothing, convinced him that the result was a certain 'prostration of character and abandonment of self-respect,' and 'instead of reforming, plunged them into the most desperate and hardened depravity of morals and character.' [17] He was persuaded that the prison system would be better. And thus it came to pass that this plan was adopted in Virginia, and while he was in Paris, he was asked to submit architectural plans for the prison. The prison he planned, soon erected in Richmond, was a model of its time, and was to be one of the monuments of his labors for the reform of the laws on crimes and punishment. [18]

XIII

Thus, along with his occasional defeats or setbacks, Jefferson won many notable victories. None of these was a greater vindication than the passage of his bill acknowledging the right of expatriation.

Under the British law anyone born in Britain could not renounce his allegiance and assume the citizenship of another country. In his *Summary View*, Jefferson had stoutly challenged and repudiated this doctrine. Indeed, he based the right of the colonies on the doctrine of expatriation, insisting that it was a natural right. He could find no justification for the claim that the exercise of such a right worked an injury on the country left, since, in the nature of things, most men live, work, and die in the country of their nativity. But where economic conditions persuade them that they can better their situation by migration, or where the spirit or institutions of another country offer them greater peace of mind, he thought them entitled to serve their individual interest.

He hoped for immigrants for the development of the vast national

[17] *Autobiography*, 46.   [18] *Ibid.*

domain, with millions of acres untouched by axe or plow, but indiscriminate immigration held dangers that did not escape him. He envisioned immigrants settling on the land, redeeming the wilderness, contributing to the national economy, and fraternizing in spirit with the natives. He feared mass migration of men born under systems opposed to ours, settling in colonies, and keeping to themselves. These views he set forth in his *Notes on Virginia,* and, strangely enough, the reasons given are almost identical with those put forth by Macaulay, the English historian, in his much-quoted letter to Jefferson's biographer,[19] as making inevitable the ultimate overthrow of the American system.

Every species of government has its specific principles [wrote Jefferson]. Ours perhaps are more peculiar than those of any other in the universe. It is a composition of the first principles of the English Constitution, with others derived from natural right and natural reason. To these, nothing could be more opposed than the maxims of absolute monarchies. Yet from such we are to expect the greater number of immigrants. They will bring with them the principles of the government they leave, imbibed in their early youth, or, if able to throw them off, it will be in exchange for an unbounded licentiousness, passing, as is usual, from one extreme to another. It would be a miracle were they to stop at the point of temperate liberty. These principles, with their language, they will transmit to their children. In proportion to their numbers, they will share with us the legislation. They will infuse it onto their spirit, warp and bias its direction, and render it a heterogeneous, incoherent, distracted mass.[20]

Happily, Jefferson's worst fears have not been realized. It is remarkable that he did not foresee the certainty that vast numbers of immigrants would be drawn to America by the American principles of government, that the oppressed of tyranny would come for freedom and appreciate it more. Perhaps he had a premonition of the distant day when supremely selfish major industries, interested more in private profit than in public good, would maintain agencies in Europe to mobilize small armies of cheap laborers and send them to America to live together, untouched by the influence of amalgamation, to be voted at the polls for a consideration, and with no

[19] Randall, *Life of Jefferson.*   [20] *Notes on Virginia,* 90.

other thought than of returning in time to the land of their nativity

But Jefferson had no prejudices against foreigners, as such. He did have against foreign ideologies and influence. When a foreigner of his own volition and for the betterment of his condition, desired to come with intent to stay and merge his life and future with America, he would bid him welcome. 'If they come by themselves they are entitled to all the rights of citizenship,' he wrote, 'but I doubt the expediency of inviting them by extraordinary encouragement.'

Holding these views, young Jefferson introduced his Naturalization Bill, providing for admission to citizenship after two years residence and a declaration in court of a determination to live within the State and to respect its institutions. In the light of after events, this seems more than generous, but in the last days of the eighteenth century few could have foreseen what the future would bring forth.

We must now turn to one of the greatest reforms young Jefferson ever wrought, after the bitterest battle he ever fought, to make America a land of religious liberty and toleration.

HIS BATTLE FOR
RELIGIOUS FREEDOM

I

IN THE INTEREST of continuity we have disregarded chronology in dealing with young Jefferson's reforms during the three epochal years in the legislature, concluding it best to follow the struggle over each measure from beginning to end. We shall now follow him through the most bitter fight he was ever to encounter — his fight for the complete separation of Church and State, for absolute religious freedom on American soil, and for the snuffing of the sinister flame of religious intolerance. This was to culminate in his Statute of Virginia for Religious Freedom which he was to rank on a level with the Declaration of Independence.

The first settlers in Virginia brought to the new land no political or religious grievance. They did not migrate to escape a political system or a religious establishment. They actually sought a re-creation of the England they had left, with the same social system and distinctions, and the same Church. Coming on the heels of the complete triumph over the dissenting religions or sects, they soon enacted laws of intolerance aimed at the suppression of the dissenters.

Thus came the Dale Code, the first in Virginia. It was both brutal and bloody. He who blasphemed suffered a thrust of the bodkin through his tongue. He who failed once in the observance of the Sabbath was tortured with the whip. He who uttered doubts about the Trinity suffered death. A fanatic Governor, in 1617, ordered that everyone should go to church on Sundays and holidays 'or lye Neck and Heels that night and be a slave to the colony the following week; for the second offense should be a slave for a month; and for the third, a year and a day.' [1]

Indeed, anyone looking in upon the activities of the first Virginia Assembly might well have thought it was an ecclesiastical congress, since laws bearing on religion vastly predominated over all others.[2]

Making rapid progress in religious tyranny, it was but a few years until all dissenting religions were proscribed. The slightest modifications of the old forms were prohibited. A fine of fifty pounds was inflicted for a failure to appear at church or for offending God by traveling on Sunday.[3] And in every parish, regardless of their belief, the people were forced to build a parsonage for the minister of the State Church and to grant him two hundred acres of glebe land.

By the middle of the seventeenth century, the character of the Church oligarchy had been fixed, not to be altered until the Revolution through the efforts of Jefferson. Absolutely autocratic power in all parochial matters had been granted to the vestries; and the vestries, once named, were self-perpetuating, and no one dared question their complete control.

The inevitable result was that the powerful possessors of entailed estates, the leading men of the parish, dominated the Church; and, since these were more concerned with the domination of the State, lay politics largely determined the policy of the vestries. It was as true then as now that many who cared nothing for religion, as such, used it as an instrument to serve political and economic ends. Doctor Eckenrode, in his comprehensive study, describes this control of 'a local oligarchy of hardfisted and often ignorant squires who were interested in keeping expenses down.' [4]

Because the pay was poor, the ministers frequently were utterly unfit, both intellectually and spiritually, for their functions. They were noted for their slovenliness in religion and the looseness of their private living. The small ruling group that used politics in determining the policies of the Church used the Church in determining the policies of the Government — the invariable result of the combination of Church and State.[5]

[1] Eckenrode, *Separation of Church and State*, 6.   [2] *Ibid.*
[3] *Ibid.*   [4] *Ibid.*, 14.   [5] *Ibid.*

While, during that period, the Church in Virginia was nebulously included in the Diocese of London and under the direction of the Bishop of London, the latter accepted the responsibilities in the Pickwickian sense, and no bishop was forthcoming. There is an interesting record to the effect that, for a moment, serious consideration was given to sending as bishop the matchless satirist and literary genius, Jonathan Swift.[6] What a loss to historic literature the failure of this project!

It was inevitable that this self-perpetuating oligarchy of the Church should fall foul of public opinion, and one of the first acts of Bacon in his rebellion was to abolish the system and provide for the election of vestrymen every three years. But with the crushing of the rebellion, the next Assembly restored the old system under which Virginia lived until the fight of Jefferson.

II

Thus, for more than a century the Anglicans exercised complete sway over religion, and then the dissenters began to challenge their autocratic and despotic power. In 1642, a number of Puritans, who had migrated to Virginia, began to draw large and curious crowds by their fervent preaching. The oligarchy frowned. The Assembly acted. The Puritans were driven from the colony, along with all others not subservient to the Church of England.[7]

A little later, the Quakers fell under the frown of the country squires, who, fantastically enough, had made themselves the custodians of the souls of men, and these were expelled. A fine of one hundred dollars was laid on the captain of a vessel who dared give transportation to this pernicious sect. Should one of these return to the colony after expulsion, he was subjected to imprisonment for the first and second offenses and the death penalty followed the third.[8] In the hot hunt of the dissenters, it was declared a crime for them to hold religious services even in their homes, or to distribute books or tracts in support of the tenets of their faith.[9]

---

[6] *Ibid.*, 15.   [7] *Ibid.*, 9.
[8] *Notes on Virginia*, 166; Eckenrode, *Separation of Church and State*, 12.
[9] *Notes on Virginia*, 167.

Then, in 1683, the Scotch-Irish Presbyterians appeared upon the
scene to test the resources of the guardians of the Church monopoly
They brought with them all the fighting qualities of the Irish and
the tenacity of the Scotch. Unlike the early English settlers, these
came from a religious motive. Wishing freedom for their faith
they had obtained permission to settle in the valley of Virgini
with the promise to hold the western frontiers against the in
cursions of the red men. They asked but little in return — 'that they
should be allowed the liberty of their consciences and in wor-
shiping God in any way agreeable to the principles of their education.' They conceded the supremacy of the King, but they insisted
on the right to a free Church. Their training and their tempera
ment, however, made them natural enemies of arbitrary governmen
in either Church or State, and the very organization of their Church
was democratic. Men of both brain and brawn, they were not easily
intimidated or awed by authority; and these qualities caused no
little concern among the landowning aristocracy of the Tidewater
The fear was not misplaced, for these were to be the backbone of
the democratic movement and to become the stalwarts among the
supporters of Jefferson in his fight for democracy.

At first, they forced some slight concessions in a bromidic Toleration Act. But it was enough to make the aristocratic squires
squirm in their chairs before their hearths. 'Church and State had
been closely ruled by the upper class of planters,' says Doctor
Eckenrode. 'The setting-up of a rival sect in the colony, with a form
of government responsible to popular wishes, broke in upon the
autocracy of the old régime. The crust of privilege was broken
and democratic ideas in religion and politics spread and strengthened.' [10]

If the none too pious country squires who ruled the Church
through their self-perpetuating vestries found the prudent Presbyterians annoying, it was the crusading fervor of the Methodists and
Baptists that reawakened the persecuting wrath of the old régime
and its political allies. The religious revival that had swept over
England, due in large measure to these two sects, aroused the ire
and awakened the disgust of the clergy of the Established Church,
who found religious enthusiasm in bad taste. The State Church

[10] Eckenrode, *Separation of Church and State,* 34.

clergy attended their land, collected their tithes, taught a very little, and once a week delivered a prosy sermon to a drowsy congregation — but why become emotional over religion? 'Hypocritical fools!' they shouted. It was fantastic and ridiculous to take religion too seriously. And many of the clergy of the Established Church did not. Their enthusiasm was largely reserved for the landed aristocracy with whom they were in alliance, and their duty was to preach the sanctity of privilege and the damnation of the democrats.

It naturally followed that, among the mass of the people, the clergy inspired no reverence and scant respect. Their permanent source of fixed revenue many thought out of proportion to their services, and they had 'insensibly lapsed into listless indolence which is the usual result of ease and wealth.' [11] The politicians, controlling the vestries and buttressing the privileges of the aristocracy, cared nothing about the intellectual shortcomings or the moral lapses of the clergy, so long as it could be summoned at will to the support of the political oligarchy of the established order.

But the itinerant preachers of the Methodists and Baptists, roving the countryside and preaching with the fervor of a faith, had become a menace. Something had to be done, not so much for the protection of the Anglican Church as for the preservation of the established social and political systems.

And so the persecution of the Baptists began.

The Presbyterians, more legalistic, and carefully skirting the edge of the bromidic Toleration Act, which was within itself an act of persecution, managed to escape; but the Baptists, haranguing the people in town and country, disdained discretion, and denounced the establishment and the intolerant laws.

Soon they were being pounced upon and beaten. Even preaching in the private homes of members of the sect was pronounced a disturbance of the peace. Preachers were dragged from the midst of their flock and thrown like common felons into the filthy jails of the period. The arrest of the Baptists, the storm troops of democracy in Virginia, became the favorite outdoor sport. A brilliant youth, home in Virginia from Princeton University, witnessed this crude persecution with dismay and disgust. He wrote a friend:

11 Girardin, *History of Virginia*, 181.

I want again to breathe your free air. I expect it will mend my constitution and confirm my principles. I have, indeed, as good an atmosphere at home as the climate will allow, but have nothing to brag of as to the state and liberty of my country. Poverty and luxury prevail among all sorts; pride, ignorance, and knavery among the priesthood; and vice and wickedness among the laity. This is bad enough; but it is not the worst I have to tell you. That diabolical, hell-conceived principle of persecution rages among some; and, to their eternal infamy, the clergy can furnish their quota of imps for such purposes. . . . There are, at this time, in the adjacent county, not less than five or six well-meaning men in close jail for publishing their religious sentiments, which, in the main, are very orthodox. I have neither patience to hear, talk, or think of anything relative to this matter; for I have squabbled and scolded, abused and ridiculed so long about it to little purpose that I am without common patience. So I must beg you to pity me, and pray for liberty of conscience to all.[12]

The author was James Madison, who was to play a conspicuous and important part in the fight Jefferson was launching.

Four years before the Revolution, Jefferson witnessed some of these turbulent scenes. And now the Baptists of Lunenburg County were hotly protesting in petitions to the legislature. They were 'restricted in the exercise of their religion.' Their preachers were imprisoned under fantastic pretenses. Their ministers were attacked and mauled in the streets by screaming, spitting mobs. Certain it is that in some counties the sheriffs specialized in the arrest of Baptists as 'public nuisances,' because of meetings at night, which were forbidden; and in the open air, where 'proper order could not be maintained.' That outdoor assemblies in the dark offered opportunities for vice among those drawn by curiosity alone is more than probable. But the greatest fault was found with the Baptists for receiving slaves at the Lord's Supper, which was thought repugnant to the religion of Jesus Christ.

Nor was this baiting of the Baptists confined to the mobs alone. The politicians, fighting for the preservation of the privileges of the ruling oligarchy, participated with gusto, and even the pious and brilliant Pendleton, who comes down to us in the odor of sanctity, and who was to lead the opposition to Jefferson in his battle

[12] Rives, *Life and Times of James Madison*, I.

for the separation of Church and State, availed himself of his opportunity, as a magistrate in Caroline County, to cast six Baptist ministers into jail for preaching without a license and 'disturbing the peace.'

There is little doubt that the ruling members of the oligarchy of Church and State had been disturbed.

Because of this act of Pendleton's there may be seen today in Bowling Green, the county seat of Caroline County, a monument bearing the names of the preachers who had fallen foul of the official frown of Edmund Pendleton.[13]

For four years now petitions had poured in sporadically on the Assembly praying for relief from religious persecution and intolerance. Young Jefferson had found them interesting. But his concept of the relations of Church and State had preceded these events. He had thought deeply on the subject and read extensively, and when the Assembly opened, he was ready for battle.

III

He had begun his preparation long before. In his *Commonplace Book* he had copied the opinions of Montesquieu on religion and the civil law,[14] and he had studied Locke's system of Christianity.

Just before entering on his crusade at Williamsburg, he had made many notes setting forth the views of thinkers on the nature of God. He had reached his own conclusions, and among these, on the system of State religion, he had written:

> Another plea for Episcopal Government in Religion in England is its similarity to the political Government of a King. This, then, with us, is a plea for government by a presbytery which resembles republican government.

And again:

> The clergy have ever seen this. The bishops were always the tools of the Crown.

Concerning the legitimate powers of the Church, he had written that they 'are exhortations, admonitions, and advice, and ultimately

[13] Hilldrup, *Life of Pendleton*, 91-92.
[14] *Commonplace Book*, 291-92.

expulsion or excommunication,' which he considered 'the utmost limit of power.' And on toleration: 'No church is bound by the duty of toleration to retain within her bosom obstinate offenders against her laws.' But, he added, 'we have no right to prejudice another in his civil enjoyment because he is of another church.'

And on State control:

> Each church being free, no one can have jurisdiction over another one, not even when the civil magistrate joins it. It neither acquires the right of the sword by the magistrate's coming to it, nor does it lose the right of instruction or excommunication by his going from it.

No, no, run the notes, the State has no jurisdiction over the conscience of the subject, nor the right to intervene between that conscience and his God.

> No one complains to his neighbor for ill management of his affairs, for an error in sowing his land, or marrying his daughter, or consuming his substance in taverns, pulling down buildings, etc.; in all these he has his liberty; but if he does not frequent the church, or there conform to ceremonies, there is an immediate uproar. [And yet] the care of every man's soul belongs to himself. But what if he neglected the care of it? Well, what if he neglects the care of his health or estate, which more nearly relates to the State? Will the magistrate make a law that we shall not be poor or sick? Laws provide against injury from others, but not from ourselves. God Himself will not save men against their wills. I cannot give up my guidance to the magistrate because he knows no more the way to heaven than I do and is less concerned to direct me right than I am to go right.

But, asks Jefferson, is this persecution because religion is due to love? 'When I find them persecute their nearest acquaintance for gross vices, I shall believe it may proceed from love.'

No, continue the notes, the State has no business meddling with the religion of the subject. The Commonwealth is 'a society of men constituted for protecting their civil interests.' And what are these? 'Life, health, liberty, and property.' Beyond this, the magistrate, the State, dare not go. For whence does the magistrate derive his power? From the people. Did the people entrust him with the 'care of souls'? No, 'no man has power to let another prescribe his faith. No man can conform his faith to the dictates of another. The life and essence of religion consist in the internal persuasion of belief of the mind. External forms of religion, when against our belief, are hypocrisy and impiety.'

These notes, written on the eve of his departure for Williamsburg, were unquestionably the chart by which he would be guided in the fight he was about to make. Here we have the processes of his mind. That he wrote them down to clarify, in his own mind, the arguments he would use on his colleagues is almost certain. The points here made are unquestionably those he urged in his innumerable conferences of persuasion in the rooms in the Raleigh. We have none of his speeches in the Assembly, and no stenographer took down the proceedings of the conference rooms. But with these notes in mind it is easy to imagine the conversations of Jefferson in persuading others to the separation of Church and State, and finally to the immortal Ordinance of Religious Freedom.[15]

IV

The dusty little capital of Williamsburg again buzzed with activity. The town houses of the Tidewater aristocracy were reopened, the women looking forward eagerly to the famous balls at the Raleigh, which was crowded with legislators. The one long street was thronged with promenaders every day. In the sadly dismantled Palace, where young Jefferson had acquired polish from contact with a Royal Governor, sat Patrick Henry. Over the Assembly presided the able and austere lawyer and statesman, Edmund Pendleton, who had sent the Baptist ministers to jail. In the legislative chamber it was not difficult to surmise the varying attitudes of members toward any attempt to disturb the social status through any reforms involving the combination of Church and State, for even the untrained eye could not but note the difference in dress and bearing of the supporters of the oligarchy and the men of the Piedmont.

The gavel of Pendleton called the Assembly to order on October 7, 1776. Three months before, young Jefferson had written and signed the Declaration of Independence. And four days later, he

15 For notes see Ford, *Writings of Jefferson*, II, 92-105.

was appointed to the Committee on Religion. On this committee were found representatives of most of the different religious sects, but the stern, determined defenders of the Establishment were in a comfortable majority. In other words, the committee had been packed. Jefferson was to lead a fighting minority in that quarter.

As though the naming of the committee was the signal, petitions began to pour in upon the legislators protesting against the discrimination suffered by the dissenters. The first of these, from Prince Edward County, struck with the force of a sledgehammer, and instantly awakened the passions that were to flame fiercely, and then fitfully, to the end.

> Raise religious as well as civil liberty to the zenith of glory and make Virginia an asylum for free inquiry, knowledge, and the virtuous of all denominations [it said]. Justice to ourselves, and to our posterity, as well as regard for the honor of the Commonwealth, makes it our indispensable duty in particular to entreat that without delay you would pull down all church establishments, abolish every tax upon conscience and private judgment . . . and define accurately between civil and ecclesiastical authority.[16]

Followed then a veritable flood of petitions in a similar vein — petitions from the county of Albemarle, the home of Jefferson, from Buckingham, Richmond, and Culpeper. One demanded that religious 'as well as every other yoke may be broken, that the oppressed may go free, so that every Religious denomination, being on a level, animosities may cease.' [17]

And how act otherwise, demanded the Presbyterians of Hanover, if any respect is to be paid to the spirit of the Revolution? This petition carried an argument. With the frontier counties, numbering one-fifth of the State and with very few Episcopalians, the inhabitants were compelled to contribute to the purchase of glebes and the support of a Church in whose tenets they did not believe. Could anything be more unjust? And, materially, the Establishment retarded the development of the Commonwealth; since, because of laws for the support of the State Church, many skilled

[16] Eckenrode, *Separation of Church and State*, 46.
[17] *Ibid.*, 47.

mechanics and artisans, who otherwise would have located in Virginia, had preferred the greater freedom of some Northern States. And why, demanded the irate Hanoverian dissenters, should the Church have temporal power? Did not Christ renounce temporal power in Rome in the establishment of Christianity? Would not religion flourish best without the meddling of the politicians?

The apprehension of the old landed aristocracy, devoted to the existing social system, grew in proportion as these petitions, passionately demanding radical action, poured in. Something had to be done to stem the flood. It was then that the legislators were stirred and startled when the Methodists, of all people, presented a petition actually opposing the disestablishment and praying that everything possible be done to strengthen it. Pendleton and Nicholas smiled and were encouraged. Perhaps they knew how it had come about. 'Divide and rule.' The dissenters' solid front was broken; but just how, and why, history does not say.

More natural was the consternation of the Established Church clergy, and one day they laid their memorial before the legislature. Did they not have 'a lifelong contract with the State'? Was this not a contract on which rested the 'sanctity of all private property'? Had they not actual 'vested right in a State-paid salary for life'? Had they not spent their money educating themselves on this assumption? Here we see the handwriting of the politicians, less interested in religion than in property that might fall foul of change. And, concluded the memorial, would not a separation of Church and State be a blow at the Christian religion?

And who but the clergy, they continued, could prevent confusion among the ignorant by passing authoritatively on disputed doctrine? Was it not proper that there should be an Established Church clergy to pass definitively on the propriety of the tenets of the Presbyterians, the Methodists, the Baptists, and the Catholics? Who was to tell the people what to think? Besides, they concluded lamely, the majority of Virginians wished the Establishment maintained — which was not true.

The issue was drawn, clear-cut.

The antagonists were passionately in earnest.

The fight was on.

V

In this fight Jefferson was a host within himself. With his profundity of knowledge, his genius in the persuasion of men, and in the organizing and subtle directing of forces, he had no equal among his colleagues. His forte was in the conference, his eloquence in conversation. In the rooms of the Raleigh, in the sandy streets where men stopped to gossip, and in the homes of his aristocratic friends, we can hear him urging the arguments of his preparatory notes.

It was at this juncture that two powerful and faithful allies stepped to the fore. George Mason, of Gunston Hall, one of the greatest and freest minds Virginia has produced, and James Madison, fresh from his studies, and now enlisted for life under the Jeffersonian banner, entered the lists to do battle with intolerance. Young Madison then was a pale, frail young man with the student's pallor on his cheeks. Like Jefferson, he made no pretense to emotional oratory, but in argument of the sounder sort, backed by notable erudition, he had few equals in his time. If Mason was more prone than Jefferson to compromise, more considerate of the traditional feelings of his friends, he was solid as Gibraltar on the main issue. In his declaration on religion in the Virginia Bill of Rights he had made an enormous contribution to the victory ultimately to be won. Had he not declared

> That religion, or the duty which we owe to our Creator and the manner of discharging it, can be directed only by reason and conviction, not by force or violence; and therefore all men are equally entitled to the free exercise of religion, according to the dictates of conscience, unpunished and unrestrained by the magistrates, unless, under color of religion, any man disturb the peace and happiness or the safety of society.

The dissenters were already pointing to this declaration, then adopted, and demanding that the laws be made to conform with the principle there set forth.

In opposition stood the greater part of the spokesmen of the old aristocracy of Church and State. Edmund Pendleton and Robert Carter Nicholas were to bear the brunt of the battle. Both were men of the highest character and the greatest capacity, but both were zealous, almost fanatical champions of the Establishment; the latter because of the deepest religious convictions, and the former moved, not a little, by his ultra-conservative dread of change. Both deservedly enjoyed the respect of all the members of the Assembly, both were resourceful in argument, and the suave Pendleton was, as we have seen, a master strategist, noted for the subtle manner through which, by flanking movements and the appearance of surrender, he so often turned defeat to victory. Jefferson was to declare him the most dangerous opponent he ever was to meet.

With the issue drawn, with the leaders at the head of their columns, the atmosphere was tense with feeling, and passions were never at such white heat as when questions of religion were involved.

VI

The first struggle continued for three months, while petitions poured in on both sides, pamphlets and press articles peppered the legislators, men argued heatedly in the sandy street and in the homes, and the leaders conferred, planned their strategy, and fought from behind the closed doors of the Raleigh.

On November 6, the petitions had been referred from the Committee on Religion to the Committee of the Whole House. Thus, the packed committee was unable to smother the proposed reforms in a pigeonhole. On the floor there was a struggle in debate, resulting in the adoption of resolutions that went far toward the realization of Jefferson's purpose.

These declared that every statute rendering 'criminal, opinions in religion, forbearing to repair to church, or the exercising any mode of worship whatever, or which prescribes punishments for the same, ought to be declared henceforth of no validity or force.'

They conceded that the objections of dissenters to being taxed for the support of a church or religious society to which their conscience did not conform were reasonable.

They agreed that public assemblies for divine worship should be regulated, but that all acts providing for the support of the clergy through taxation should be repealed 'after securing to the present incumbents all arrears in salary, and to the vestries a power of levying for the performance of their contracts.'

But they provided that all glebe lands, churches, chapels, and plate should be confirmed in the Church for all time, and that all arrears of money or tobacco should be paid.

This was a long step in the direction of Jefferson's goal, but Pendleton and Nicholas had forced some compromises. A committee, consisting of Jefferson, Mason, Madison, Henry, Tazewell, and Robert Carter Nicholas, was then named to draw a bill in conformity with the resolutions. Again the result was a compromise. A large concession to religious liberty was made, but there remained a connection between Church and State.

The bill repealed all laws making criminal religious opinions and the failure to attend church. It exempted all dissenters from the payment of taxes for the support of the Established Church, while granting the vestries the power to assess all salaries and arrears of salaries on dissenters up to January 1, 1777. And it reserved the glebes, churches, chapels and property in them, together with arrears in money and tobacco, for the use of the Established Church and its ministers.

But most significant and vital of all, it suspended the levy for the support of the clergy of the Established Church until the end of the next session of the Assembly in the summer of 1777.

This avowedly was done because, by the exemption of dissenters, it placed a burden upon the members of the State Church in some parishes that would have been unbearable. The way was left open for voluntary contributions, and the champions of the Church hoped that the suspension would not be continued after the summer session of 1777.[18]

Nevertheless, as events speedily were to prove, there no longer was a combination of Church and State. With much more than half the people released from the support of a State religion, an attempt to force the entire burden of maintenance on the Anglicans would have driven many into the ranks of the dissenters. Never again was a tax for religious purposes to be levied in Virginia. The future battles were to determine the relation of the State to religion in general.

Pleased with the progress made, Jefferson was far from counting this a decisive victory. By hard fighting, he had gained ground, but he was far from his goal. Little had been accomplished, it

[18] *Ibid.*, 51-52.

seemed, but the release of the dissenters from the support of a State Church. He did not like the regulation of religious assemblies by the State. He foresaw a bitter battle in the plan of his opponents for a general assessment to be applied to the maintenance of the ministers of the various denominations. He stoutly maintained his thesis that a man's religion is personal and not political, and that each denomination should maintain itself through voluntary contributions. He abhorred the idea of State interference in any form.

VII

But the May session brought keen disappointment to the champions of the Establishment. Their attempt to prevent the continuance of the suspension of the payment of salaries to the clergy of the State Church was stubbornly opposed and frustrated.

Abandoning this attempt, they now began to concentrate their efforts to force a general assessment, and here they hoped, not without reason, to win over some of the dissenters. But the Presbyterians of Hanover went forth to meet the threat. In a remonstrance to the Assembly, they declared a general assessment 'contrary to our principles' and 'subversive of religious liberty.'[19]

And when, in the autumn of 1777, the legislators continued the suspension of salaries, the bitterness among the champions of the Establishment intensified. Feverishly, the faithful were encouraged to petition and remonstrate. The irate churchmen of Caroline County, in demanding the assessment, declared that trickery had been used in forcing the original suspension of salaries. 'The undue means taken to overthrow the Establishment by imposing upon the credulity of the vulgar and engaging infants to sign petitions handed down by dissenters,' should be rebuked.

But the lines of the Jeffersonians did not waver; the assessment was not broached; the suspension of the salaries was continued.

Even so, it was not until the session of 1779 that the Jeffersonians were prepared for a decisive engagement. The spirit of the Revolution had spread. While the Establishment practically was ended, the old hated vestries, self-perpetuated and dominated by politics, remained, and the rising democratic tide was beating angrily against

[19] *Ibid.*, 54.

them. In some parishes the old obnoxious vestrymen had died, some had moved away, some had abandoned the struggle, but Government officials continued in the performance of their functions. Impatient petitioners were now demanding the abolishment of the vestries, and those of Northumberland were urging as a reason that they were not elected by the people. Democracy was encroaching on the Church. This infuriated and alarmed the old reactionaries. And the fight on the glebes began.

Bowing to the storm, the legislators named a committee to deal with the vestries, and Jefferson was made chairman. Instantly he responded with a bill providing for the election by the people of a new order of poor officers, unassociated with religion. Before this revolutionary move, the legislators paused. Action was deferred. The opposition rallied and stiffened.[20]

But it was only a pause; and the self-perpetuating vestries of the ruling squires, serving political ends, and often wearing the livery of the Court of Heaven to serve the Devil in, were finished. And soon the glebes were gone.

The opposition, thoroughly alarmed by now, rallied for a desperate fight to force a general assessment, and their prospects brightened. Jefferson no longer was in the Assembly personally to direct and manage. He had been transferred to the Palace of the Governor; and to make matters worse for the reformers, Pendleton and Nicholas had now been joined by the powerful Mason and the fiery Patrick Henry, who alone challenged the popularity of Jefferson among the masses.

The acquisition of Henry, who henceforth will be found consistently with the conservatives who so recently had thought him vulgar, was of immeasurable value to the aristocracy. The mass of the people had no confidence in the democracy of the old leaders of the oligarchy of Church and State, but the great orator had cast his spell upon them. Jefferson, removed from the actual arena, could direct, only from behind the scenes, the maneuvering of his young disciple, Madison. Pitted against Henry, he was at a great disadvantage. In erudition, in philosophic vision, in logic, Madison was vastly the superior of his gifted antagonist, but, to the mass, the flame of Henry's genius and eloquence blinded them to the

[20] *Ibid.*, 56.

perfect reasoning of the younger man. The older man was glorified by his early revolutionary fervor, and few foresaw the luminous future of the young man fresh from Princeton.

The fight was prolonged, but Madison, representing Jefferson, persisted, and in the end, but not until 1785, the general assessment was definitively defeated.

VIII

Then, when early in the spring of 1779 the legislature ordered the framing of a bill for religious freedom, the supreme hour for Jefferson struck. It was toward this end that his entire pressure had been applied. Unhappily, when the hour struck he had been removed from the legislative chamber; but from the Palace of the Governor he gave to Madison, his flagbearer, the Ordinance of Religious Freedom he had framed out of his own vast reading and meditation. This he was to place alongside the Declaration of Independence as his supreme contribution to American civilization.

Incredible as it seems today, the presentation of this Ordinance created a furor. Churchmen, really devout, but also politicians with more pious pose than piety, fumed with rage. Some pretended to be horrified by the sacrilege. It was yet too early to ascribe the Ordinance to the 'bloody monsters of the French Terror,' but it was agreed in a great company that it clearly was the emanation of the anti-Christ. So noisy was the protest that the legislature hesitated and postponed its consideration.

Removed from personal leadership on the floor, Jefferson, behind the scenes, threw himself with all his fervor into the fight, and in the autumn session of 1779 his Ordinance was introduced again. From the savage caves of intolerance and religious hates bitter remonstrances poured in upon the legislature. The infuriates of Essex County declared a bill for religious freedom was an attack on the Christian religion! [21] The legislative opposition closed ranks for a last desperate stand, and in that session the Ordinance for Religious Freedom could not even reach a third reading.

Encouraged by their success, the strategists of the opposition now made the mistake of taking the offensive. They introduced a bill

21 *Ibid.*, 57.

declaring 'the Christian Religion shall in all times coming be deemed and held to be the established religion of the commonwealth.' If a State Church could not be revived, a State Religion would serve the purpose of intolerance.

This was a direct challenge to Jefferson's whole philosophy, which rested on the conviction that the State has no business meddling with religion. Because of the very audacity of this move, the liberals now rallied and prevented the measure from reaching its third reading. And George Mason introduced his bill, which definitively ended the paying of the salaries of clergymen out of the State taxation of the people.

But the Ordinance of Religious Freedom made no progress. The fight was to continue through the two years of its author's gubernatorial service and through the period of his retirement, and through his congressional service at Annapolis into the years, when, three thousand miles across the sea, he followed the struggle with unabated interest. Incredible as it seems, it was not until the legislative session of 1785, six years after its original introduction, that the Assembly was prepared to act on one of the noblest documents in American history.

IX

The Ordinance of Religious Freedom proposed by Jefferson in 1779 was both an argument and a bill. It asserted:

That the opinions and belief of men depend, not on their own will, but follow involuntarily the evidence proposed to their minds:

That Almighty God hath created the mind free, and manifested His supreme will that free it shall remain, by making it altogether insusceptible to restraint:

That all attempts to influence it by temporal punishments, or burdens, or by civil incapacitations, tend only to beget habits of hypocrisy and meanness, and are a departure from the plan of the holy author of our religion, who, being lord of both body and mind, yet chose not to propagate it by coercion on either, as was in His Almighty power to do, but to exalt it by the influence of reason alone:

That the impious presumption of legislatures and rulers, civil as well as ecclesiastical, who, being themselves fallible and uninspired men, have assumed domination over the faith of others, setting up their own opinions and modes of thinking as the only true and infallible, and as such endeavoring to impose them on others, hath established and maintained false religions over the greater part of the world and through all time:

That to compel man to furnish contributions of money for the propagation of opinions which he disbelieves and abhors is sinful and tyrannical:

That even the forcing him to support this or that teacher of his own religious persuasion is depriving him of the comfortable liberty of giving his contributions to the particular pastor whose morals he would make his pattern, and whose powers he feels most persuasive to righteousness; and in withdrawing from the ministry those temporal rewards, which, proceeding from an approbation of their personal conduct, are an additional incitement to earnest and unremitting labors for the instruction of mankind:

That our civil rights have no dependence on our religious opinions, any more than our opinions in physics or geometry; and therefore, the proscribing any citizen as unworthy of the public confidence by laying upon him an incapacity of being called to office of trust or emolument, unless he professes or renounces this or that religious opinion, is depriving him injudiciously of those privileges and advantages to which, in common with his fellow citizens, he has a natural right:

That it tends also to corrupt the principles of that very religion it is meant to encourage by bribing with a monopoly of worldly honors and emoluments those who will externally confess and conform to it:

That though these are criminals who do not withstand such temptation, yet neither are those innocent who lay the bait in their way:

That the opinions of men are not the object of civil government, nor under its jurisdiction:

That to suffer the civil magistrate to intrude his powers into the field of opinion and to restrain the profession or propaganda on supposition of their ill tendency is a dangerous fallacy, which at once destroys all religious liberty, because he, of course, being judge of the tendency, will make his opinion the rule of judgment, and approve or condemn the sentiments of others only as they shall square with or differ from his own:

That it is time enough for the rightful purpose of civil government for its officers to interfere when principles break out into overt acts against peace and good order; and finally, that Truth is great and will prevail if left to herself:

That she is the proper and sufficient antagonist to error, and has nothing to fear from the conflict unless, by human interposition, disarmed of her natural weapons, free argument and debate; errors ceasing to be dangerous when it is permitted freely to circulate them.

Such, the argument.

And now, the law:

We, the General Assembly of Virginia, do enact that no man shall be compelled to frequent or support any religious worship, place of ministry whatsoever, nor shall be enforced, restrained, molested or burdened in his body or goods, nor shall otherwise suffer on account of his religious opinions or beliefs; but that all men shall be free to profess, and by argument maintain their opinions in matters of religion, and that the same shall in no wise diminish, enlarge or affect their civil character.

Conscious of the fact that at intervals the spirit of fanaticism emerges from its caves, and that future generations of legislators would have the legal right to emasculate or repeal this Ordinance, Jefferson had added that 'the rights hereby asserted are of the natural rights of mankind, and if any act shall be hereafter passed to repeal the present, or to narrow its operations, such act will be an infringement of natural right.' [22]

Such the argument and the law.

We are now ready for the battle.

X

A futile and ill-timed attempt to levy a general assessment and to incorporate the Episcopal Church helped pave the way for the final favorable consideration of the Ordinance of Religious Freedom. The liberal spirit, born of the Revolution, had spread enormously since the introduction of Jefferson's Ordinance in 1779. No longer were the stout champions of the combination of Church and State able to pack the committees or to dominate the Assembly. The rule of the Tidewater aristocracy was in decline, and the ro-

[22] Ford, *Writings of Jefferson*, II, 237-39.

bustious men of the Piedmont and the Blue Ridge were in the ascendant. That year, Ben Harrison, so long the ardent, trusted champion of the old oligarchy, actually failed of re-election by his neighbors in the county of Charles City, and he moved with his family to Surrey County, where he possessed no property, to be elected there, only to have his election challenged by the Committee on Privileges and Elections, and to win his seat by a meager majority of the whole House.[23] And, though unquestionably a patriot, he was elected Speaker by a margin of but five votes.

Despairing of holding the people bound to the religious system they championed, Pendleton and Nicholas now went into a huddle on strategy. Thus they planned to emasculate, weaken, or utterly destroy the Ordinance by amendments. Pendleton, so masterful and resourceful in the art of injecting a word or phrase that might escape detection and yet completely change the character of a measure, took charge. What could be more inoffensive to the sponsors of the Ordinance than his amendment recommending 'Christian' forbearance, love, and charity? But Madison caught the significance at a glance and the amendment was promptly voted down.

Another amendment speedily was forthcoming, with a reference to 'Jesus Christ, the holy author of our religion'; but since the very purpose of the Ordinance was to protect the religious freedom of not only Christians of all denominations, but also of Jews, Mohammedans, or infidels, it also was defeated.[24]

Unable to defeat the Ordinance through amendments, the opposition now fought desperately to postpone the vote, but out of the ninety-four votes cast, it was unable to muster more than twenty-four.

The struggle now shifted to the Senate, which pounced upon the Ordinance with more amendments calculated to emasculate and deform. It was proposed to strike out the preamble or argument and to substitute the Mason Bill of Rights in the Constitution of Virginia, but the majority would not have it.

When the attempt to strike out the first full page and twenty lines of the second failed, the Senate asked for a conference. Madison,

[23] Hunt, *Writings of James Madison,* Madison to Jefferson, II, 215.
[24] *Autobiography,* 45.

fighting for Jefferson's Ordinance, thought the objections of the Senate 'frivolous indeed.' But to give proof of an accommodating disposition, the House sent back to the Senate the preamble with a few minor changes in phraseology; the Senate added a few more, and when Madison concluded that 'they did not affect the substance, though they somewhat defaced the composition,' he agreed, rather than assume further risks in the dangerous tailend of the session.[25]

Thus, in 1786, ten years after he had written the Declaration of Independence, Jefferson's Ordinance of Religious Freedom became the law of the land and its influence spread throughout the nation. Jefferson, in Paris, rejoiced over the belated triumph and had copies printed which he distributed among his colleagues of the diplomatic corps for transmission to their countries, and he sent a copy to Mirabeau. The fame of the Ordinance spread throughout the world.[26]

In the twilight of his days, Jefferson, recalling the seven years' struggle for the separation of Church and State and for an Ordinance of Religious Freedom, was to record it as the most bitter and stubborn he had ever known. In some of the New England States, where religious sects had a strangle-hold on civil government and the clergy preached vicious political sermons, the story was spread that Jefferson was an infidel, with no regard for any religious faith, and this was to invite their pulpit denunciations when, some years later, he was fighting the national battle which conclusively determined that the American Republic should be democratic.[27]

XI

Washington's exclamation, 'Where is Jefferson?' which implied a compliment to his congressional service, had been sufficiently answered during the three years in the Virginia legislature. The answer was written indelibly in the statutes. No American leader of his time was making a contribution to the molding of the system which has come to be known as 'the American system' that re-

[25] Hunt, *Writings of Madison,* II, 216.
[26] Eckenrode, *Separation of Church and State,* 114-16.
[27] Bowers, *Jefferson and Hamilton.*

motely approached that of Jefferson during these two fruitful years.

It appears, however, from the journal of the Assembly that, during these legislative sessions, Jefferson shared the disposition of many of his colleagues sometimes to seek fresh air and recreation outside the hall. Time and again the Speaker was forced to order the sergeant at arms to take into custody specified members and bring them to the House; and Jefferson was not infrequently among them. It is amusing to note that while on May 28, 1778, a committee was named 'to enforce the attendance of the members of the Assembly,' with Jefferson on the committee, he does not appear to have taken it too seriously. Thus, a little later it was ordered 'that the Sergeant of Arms attending this House take into custody Thomas Jefferson' and some others.[28] Soon afterward we note that 'Mr. Thomas Jefferson, one of the members from the county of Albemarle, attended in the custody of the Sergeant of Arms.'[29] Less than a month later: 'Ordered that the Sergeant of Arms take into his custody the following members of the House, to wit: Thomas Jefferson . . .'[30] And two days later the Journal announced that Jefferson had returned, paid his fine and been 'discharged from custody.'[31]

Despite these lapses, no period of his career so clarifies in action his philosophy and his concept of a good society, and at no time does the wisdom of his leadership shine so luminously. The weakness of the average revolutionist is that his genius lies so predominantly on the side of tearing down and is so weak in constructive building on the ruins. They destroy, but they do not create. In Jefferson we have the rare revolutionist who would destroy only that he might build from blueprints drawn before the demolition, and who, in the very midst of the demolition of the old, was already wisely building for the future generations.

In these three years he had achieved some results that entered into the making of 'the American system,' and some that greatly advanced the frontiers of democracy.

Successfully, he had fought his battle for the separation of Church and State.

He had written the immortal Ordinance of Religious Freedom

[28] *Journal*, October 7, 1778. [29] *Ibid.*, November 30, 1778.
[30] *Ibid.*, December 12, 1778. [31] *Ibid.*, December 14, 1778.

that protected all men in their civil rights against religious intolerance and persecution.

In the abolishment of entail he had struck a deadly blow at the artificially maintained aristocracy, dependent on governmental protection and privilege, and thus definitively put Virginia in the vanguard of the onward march of American democracy.

In the abolishing of primogeniture he had completed what he had begun in the elimination of entail, and in the process had, incidentally, given a new dignity to womanhood.

He had made it clear that democracy and popular government cannot thrive in ignorance, that popular education cannot be neglected in a free society, and he had proposed a popular educational system which, up until that time, had never been approached in any country in the world.

Putting aside his arduous labors in the revision of the laws, these measures, together with his authorship of the *Summary View*, his Reply to North, his Declaration of Independence, would have assured him immortality in American history had he died at the age of thirty-six.

But because of his battle for democracy and religious freedom during these three years, he never again was to enjoy in Virginia the universal popularity he had known before.

He had incurred the abiding hostility of the stricken aristocracy, whose privileges he had taken away that democracy might have an open road; and the reactionaries of Virginia were to hate him for a generation.

He had called down upon his head the maledictions of the clergy and the political allies of the Establishment in the separation of Church and State, and throughout the remainder of his life political preachers were to denounce him from the pulpit as an enemy of Christianity.

These hatreds, that even affect some in the writing of history to this day, were born at this time.

Here we may pause in the story of his political activities to visit the Monticello he so loved and to see the private person in the serenity of his hilltop before he enters on his arduous duties as Governor of Virginia.

CHAPTER

IX

HAPPY DAYS AT MONTICELLO

I

IT WAS ABOUT THIS TIME that the Marquis de Chastellux, under the guidance of a native and in search of the home of the young philosopher whose fame had already reached France, emerged at length from the woods within sight of Monticello and dismissed his guide. His impressions have been preserved in the interesting book in which he recorded them:

On the summit (of one of the mountains) we discovered the house of Mr. Jefferson, which stands pre-eminent in those retirements. It was himself who built it, and preferred this situation; for although he possessed considerable property in the neighborhood, there was nothing to prevent him from fixing his residence wherever he thought proper. But it was a debt Nature owed to the philosopher, and a man of taste, that in his own possession he should find a spot where he might best study and enjoy her. He called his home Monticello (Italian, Little Mountain), a very modest title, for it is situated on a very lofty one, but which announces the owner's attachment to the language of Italy; and, above all, to the fine arts, of which that country was the cradle, and is still the asylum. As I had no further necessity for a guide, I separated from the Irishman; and after ascending by a tolerably commodious road for more than half an hour, we arrived at Monticello.

This house, of which Mr. Jefferson was the architect, and often one of the workmen, is rather elegant, and in the Italian taste, though not without fault. It consists of one large pavilion, the entrance to which is by the porticoes, ornamented with pillars. The ground floor consists of a very large, lofty salon, which is to be decorated entirely in the antique style; above it is a library of the same form; two small wings, with only a ground floor and attic story joined to this pavilion, and communicate with the kitchen, offices, etc., which form a kind of basement story, over which runs a terrace.

The Marquis explains that his detailed description has for its object to show the difference between this and other houses of the country, since he could 'safely aver that Mr. Jefferson is the first American who has consulted the fine arts to know how he should shelter himself from the weather.' [1]

If the building the Marquis found 'not without fault,' it was very far from completion. Jefferson actually had dwelt for nine years at Monticello at the time he was summoned to Williamsburg to assume the then dangerous duties of a republican governor. During his boyhood at Shadwell, he had cast longing eyes on the mountain, and even then he had determined that on reaching his majority he would there build himself a home after his heart's desire. In youth, he had wandered with his gun over the thickly timbered mountain, entranced with the varying views of the panorama spread before him, differing in the shifting lights. Always an individualist, never afraid of innovation, and unimpressed by precedent, he was almost unique among his Virginia contemporaries in selecting a mountain-top for a home. The tendency was to prefer the valleys. And, in keeping with his innovation in choosing a mountain-top, he had in mind another of greater significance, in the architectural planning of the house. At that time and in the past, there was little disposition among the Virginians to give heed to the possibilities of architecture in their building. Most of the dwellings were of frame, and few of even the larger ones made any pretension to architectural charm or beauty. Houses were constructed to afford a comfortable protection from the weather, and with no thought of the aesthetic. It was, therefore, almost revolutionary for Jefferson to approach the building of Monticello in the spirit of the artist.

The origin of his passionate love of architecture is not clearly revealed. Certainly there was nothing in the region with which he

[1] Chastellux, *Voyages dans l'Amérique.*

was familiar to arouse his interest, and, since his imagination had been stirred even during his college days at Williamsburg, it is a safe surmise that he owed the development of this side of his character to his intimacy and conversations with Fauquier, the accomplished Royal Governor, and with Professor Small, the Scot. No doubt one or the other brought to his attention the works of Andrea Palladio, the leader of the Italian classical architecture of the fifteenth century, with whose plates he was familiar. In the plans young Jefferson drew for his house on the mountain-top, and in the many other plans he was to draw for numerous other houses on the request of friends, the influence of Palladio is clearly reflected. In the Massachusetts Historical Society library one may examine almost three hundred of these drawings of the unprofessional architect, which have commanded the admiration of the critics of our time. No less an authority than Fiske Kimball has said of them that 'his architectural draughtsmanship, as illustrated in the earlier elevation of Monticello, is beyond comparison with the crudeness of the published drawings of other native designers of the time, and remained unrivaled till the advent of Thornton and the first well-trained architects from abroad, during the last years of the eighteenth century.'

We are indebted to this famous critic for the monumental book, with illustrations, on Jefferson the architect, which, published privately and too expensive for general sale, is to be found in certain libraries in the United States and abroad.

In later life, as we shall see, the master of Monticello was to draw the plans for the State Capitol in Richmond and for the University of Virginia; and it is significant of his genius that when, a generation ago, Stanford White, the brilliant architect, was engaged to draw the plans for the restoration of the Rotunda, the library of that institution, he asked for time to study the architectural scheme of Jefferson, on the ground that it would be a profanation to strike a discordant note in the plans of the statesman.

Thus, in these comparatively serene years with which we are concerned, the carroty-headed young man, already distinguished internationally in political polemics and at the bar, might often have been seen bending over his drafting-board, giving happy rein to his imagination and his love of beauty in brick and stone. Because his gift was well known to his friends, he was frequently importuned to draw the plans for houses they were building, and a number of the charming mansions to be seen today in the neighborhood came from his blueprints.

In advanced years he worked lovingly over plans for Monroe's beautiful house in Loudoun County, Virginia; and long before, when Monroe was very limited in his means, it was Jefferson who planned the house of 'Ashlawn,' near Monticello, and nothing could be more interesting than the ingenuity with which he made the most of the financial limitations of his disciple. It is probable that he found a request of older and seasoned statesmen to frame a state paper less pleasing to his soul than an invitation from his friends to exercise his talent at the drafting-board.

II

It was in 1767 that he began to move toward the realization of his dream of a mansion on the top of the little mountain. It was no mean undertaking. The mountain, rising five hundred feet, was literally covered from base to crest with a thick first growth of timber. There was not an open spot for the building of the smallest hut without the felling of trees and the leveling of the ground. A bridle-path was shaped at this time into a rather rough and steep road leading to the top, where a small clearing had been made and an equally rough shelter house erected.

The next year, young Jefferson turned grimly to his task of leveling the mountain-top when he contracted with a 'Mr. Moore' to 'level 250 square feet of the top of the mountain at the N.E. end by Christmas, for which I am to give him 180 bushels of wheat and 24 bushels of corn.' The site thus described is the site of the present mansion of Monticello.[2] And while there is no further record, it is evident that this was speedily followed by the leveling of the entire plateau of one hundred and twenty thousand square feet, six hundred by two hundred feet, since, within a year, one building had been raised somewhat south of the part leveled by Moore. This building, at the southeast corner of the open square on the mountain-top, a little, one-story brick structure of one room, and standing

[2] Wilstach, *Jefferson and Monticello*, 21-22.

today, was unquestionably part of Jefferson's well-matured plan for the mansion.[3]

The mansion, as it stood at Jefferson's death and as preserved today, covered twenty-five years in the building, since he was constantly making improvements. That the mansion was not ready for occupancy when the burning of Shadwell drove him to the mountain is certain, and in 1773 he was contracting for the manufacture of one hundred thousand bricks; and in the following year we find him ordering from London 'fourteen pairs of sash windows to be sent, ready made and glazed, with a small parcel of spare glass to mend breaks.'[4]

Four years later, if the main building was not entirely habitable, it was sufficiently advanced to be occupied, not only by Jefferson and his wife, but also by the widow of Carr and her six children; and he was keeping open house for his friends with the generous hospitality of his class and time.

Pressed by his political duties and activities as he was at this period, he was giving every moment he could spare to the realization of his ideal of an estate. It was not enough that only the house should be beautiful, since his fastidious taste demanded that the surroundings should harmonize. Along with his passion for architecture went a kindred taste for landscape gardening, and he was his own landscape gardener as he was his own architect. He alone had to plan the grove and terrace. He alone had to lay out the gardens and the walks and to design the drive. His eyes alone determined where the flower beds should be and where the vegetable garden would be least in evidence. He personally selected the trees that were to be planted and he indicated the spots. The vines, the shrubs, the bulbs, the roots, were of his choice alone, and he alone placed them. There was not to be a spot on the mountain-top that would not bear the imprint of his taste. While he engaged an Italian landscape gardener for a time, that worthy soon found that his sole function was to follow the instructions of his employer. Fired with the enthusiasm of the artist, Jefferson consecrated all his leisure to the beautification of the mountain.

Nor was it enough for him to have a park. It had to be made animate with animal life; and soon twenty or thirty deer were

3 *Ibid.*   4 *Ibid.*, 38.

grazing within a few rods of the mansion. These became so attached to him under his care that at this time they were prone to follow him about, and he repaid their faith by feeding them Indian corn from his hand. His frequent visitors were invariably taken to the park to see these animals 'walk, run and bound.'[5]

III

Essentially, instinctively a builder, he continued for years lavishing money on tools for the shops erected on the grounds, on new scientific instruments that fascinated him, on new agricultural and industrial machinery that delighted him, and on new inventions. Even at this early day, he had a machine for the spinning and weaving of cloth. He had his own plant for the making of brick. He carefully taught his slaves brickmaking, and something more than crude carpentering, how to make nails, to set a window or a door, and how to lay floors in patterns. Nothing excited him more than the discovery of a slave who showed some aptitude for mechanics, and he gave him every encouragement and opportunity for the development of his talent.

Throughout these early years, he was also a successful farmer. He owned five thousand acres at Monticello and four thousand acres at Poplar Forest, and, more than his neighbors, he resembled in his methods the scientific farmer of many years later. Every day found him astride his horse cantering over the estate, watching the work and supervising his supervisors. The cultivated acres at Monticello were given largely to the growing of wheat, those at Poplar Forest to wheat and tobacco, though he also grew a great deal of corn. In his vegetable garden he was always experimenting with something new to the region, and his garden book reveals the probable influence of Philip Mazzei, the Italian who lived for some time as a neighbor on the small property of Colle, since he experimented with Italian specialties, including — God save the mark! — garlic.

From his earliest boyhood he was fond of horses, and on his farms he kept a number of brood mares of excellent pedigree. His riding-horses had to be of the best stock to be found in the Old

[5] Chastellux, *Voyages dans l'Amérique*.

Dominion. He was insistent always that his grooms keep these animals in the pink of condition. In his more dandified youth the groom had reason to tremble when he saw his master passing a white handkerchief over the horse's flank and finding it soiled. A reproachful glance from his cold eyes and the groom hurried the animal back to the stable without a word.

The fact that in these earlier years his farming brought him an average profit of two thousand dollars is evidence enough that he was a practical farmer. Out of the proceeds of his tobacco crop, largely sent to London, he bought his books, his better clothing, his European wines, his furniture and musical instruments.

Some time before the Revolution, he, with some others, conceived the idea of growing grapes on a large scale for winemaking, and it was in furtherance of this plan that Philip Mazzei and a group of Italian *vignerons* were brought from Tuscany and the estate of Colle was purchased in the neighborhood of Monticello. Vineyards of Italian grapes were bravely planted on the hillside, but nothing worth while came of it; and when, a little later, Colle was rented to Baron de Riedesel, one of the Saratoga prisoners of war, the latter's horses 'finished the vines in a week.' That ended the attempt to grow Italian grapes on a Virginia hillside; but several of the Tuscans found employment at Monticello, and they appear to have attended the native vines with such success that Jefferson was able to send his friends at Williamsburg some wine from his own vintage. Even so, his own epicurean taste in table wines was such that he stocked his cellar with the juice of France.

Thus he found time, despite his constant building, reading, writing, to raise wheat, corn, tobacco, blooded horses, to experiment with exotic vegetables and with winemaking, and to conduct his farm on a practical business basis.

IV

It was at this period that Jefferson became a close friend of the Philip Mazzei, whose indiscretion, years later, was to cause him some annoyance. The master of Monticello was thirty-two years old when the Florentine, with his wife and stepdaughter, arrived on the hilltop. Early on the morning following his arrival, when the rest of the household was still asleep, Jefferson took him for 'a walk in the neighborhood,' which led them to the 'home of a poor man who owned a cabin and about four hundred acres of land' which bordered on Monticello. The man was eager to sell, and Mazzei concluded that the cabin was large enough for the Tuscan *vigneron* he had brought with him. The place was purchased, and thus Mazzei became a neighbor and a friend.[6] The Florentine was astonished to find that Jefferson 'understood the Tuscan language very well, though he had 'never heard it spoken before.' The Italian laborers were delighted — so much so that Mazzei was 'touched.' Liking the Tuscan hunting-coat, Jefferson adopted it and the neighbors imitated his example, to the joy of the Italian tailor Mazzei had brought with him with the understanding that he alone should profit from any work not done for the tiny Italian colony.[7] While the house at Colle was being prepared, the Florentine lived at Monticello with his wife and her daughter, and while the Jeffersons became fond of the stepdaughter, Jefferson was soon to find that the mother showed 'traces of vanity and pride.' Quite soon she was to become a thorn in the side of Mazzei and a provocation to Jefferson, who sympathized deeply with his friend. One day he described her to Mazzei as a 'bitch,'[8] and later, in Paris, hearing more of her meanness, he had reiterated 'she is really a great bitch.'[9] Even so, the master of the mansion thoroughly enjoyed the companionship of the Florentine, following his advice in experimenting with Italian vegetables and vines, while restraining his temper and dissimulating his dislike of the vain and proud lady who was constantly running in and out of Monticello. The daughter, as much a victim as Mazzei, however, found her way to the heart of both the Jeffersons, and when the family finally left, she wept on leaving Colle, but 'she cried even more when [she] left Jefferson's home.'[10]

Soon, as we shall see, some German prisoners of war will take possession of Colle and there will be another foreign lady who will make quite a different impression.

[6] Mazzei, *Memoirs,* 192.
[7] *Ibid.,* 193.
[8] *Ibid.,* 284.
[9] *Ibid.,* 293.
[10] *Ibid.,* 227.

V

The combination of the artistic with the practical temperament is rare. In the midst of his experimenting with new machinery and inventions and in his supervising of the sowing and the reaping, we have seen young Jefferson zealously working out his architectural ideals.

In those days also, before the Revolution and during its progress, he had other artistic interests. He was a lover of music. In the year previous to his election as Governor and at a time when he was feverishly pushing his reforms, he wrote an illuminating letter to a friend in Europe:

> If there is a gratification which I envy any people it is, to your country, its music. This is the favorite passion of my soul, and fortune has cast my lot in a country where it is in a state of deplorable barbarism. From the line of life in which we conjecture you to be, I have for some time lost the hope of seeing you here. Should the event prove so, I shall ask your assistance in procuring a substitute who may be proficient in singing, etc., on the harpsichord. I shall be contented to receive such a one two or three years hence, when it is hoped he may come safely and find here a greater plenty of those useful things which commerce alone can furnish. The bounds of an American fortune will not admit the indulgence of a domestic band of musicians, yet I have thought that a passion for music might be reconciled with that economy which we are obliged to observe.[11]

Jefferson's favorite instrument being the violin, he might have been heard, during these comparatively serene days at Monticello, practicing two and three hours a day. We have seen him, as a red-headed boy, one of the little group of music-lovers in his college days that gathered periodically in the Governor's Palace, to play with Fauquier. In those happy days at Williamsburg, he often played duets with another student, destined to be the father of President Tyler. He often played with his wife, who, according to legend, he won in a brisk competition because of his prowess with the fiddle. Even on his journeys in those days he was wont to carry his fiddle along, and in the early morning, before his host had arisen,

11 Randolph, *Domestic Life of Jefferson*, 54.

the soft notes of his loved instrument might have been heard from the guest-room. It was this mutual passion for music, more than anything else, that made him and his wife so congenial. Martha Wayles Jefferson performed on the harpsichord, and we have the record of one ordered for her from England with the proceeds of her husband's tobacco sale.

About this time, Alberti, the Italian, appeared in America with a band of musicians, and he remained for some years. He had been engaged to instruct Mrs. Jefferson, and a friendship developed between him and Jefferson, who employed him to assist him in his struggle with the violin. For many months, Alberti made frequent visits to Monticello for the purpose, and, whatever may have been the aptitude of his distinguished pupil, he could have asked for none more zealous and appreciative.

In the early days of their association, before their divergent political views brought a cleavage between them, Jefferson shared his enthusiasm with Patrick Henry, who likewise was clever with the fiddle. They differed, however, in their tastes. The orator's preference was for the lively airs popular in the rustic dances of the early day; Jefferson was content with nothing less than the classic music of the operas.

But among public men devoted to the fiddle, Jefferson's favorite partner in the playing of duets was John Randolph, a distinguished lawyer of the time, who had served as Attorney General under Lord Dunmore. Though satisfied with his comparative skill, Jefferson made no secret of his envy of Randolph because of his possession of a very fine instrument. And out of this longing for the Randolph fiddle came, perhaps, the most amazing bargain he ever struck. It was agreed that should Jefferson outlive Randolph, he was to have the fiddle for three hundred dollars. And Jefferson's part of the agreement was even more amazing, in view of his passion for books: since, if Randolph outlived Jefferson, he was to have books from the latter's library to the value of four thousand dollars. The bargain struck, Jefferson, in dead earnest, insisted that the agreement should be put in strictly legal form, and this was done. Several people of historical significance signed their names in attestation, including Patrick Henry and George Wythe. The document was proved before the clerk of the court and spread upon the records.

This was the John Randolph who, in loyalty to the King, turned
from his own country to England in the early days of the Revolution. But despite his hurry in taking his departure, he remembered
the bargain made with Jefferson and the latter's warm desire for the
fiddle. Possibly thinking that he might not care to recall old memories in his exile, but probably because he felt he could use the money
to greater advantage, he offered now to sell the fiddle to his friend
for sixty-five dollars. And so it came to pass that, in the Monticello
of those days of the Revolution, the fiddle of Randolph was often
heard. The latter's exile in poverty was not happy. At the seat of
Lord Dunmore in Scotland, he was taken in and welcomed, but he
died in a few years with the prayer that his body should be taken
back to his Virginia home.

VI

The period verging on his gubernatorial trials and tribulations was,
in many respects, to be the happiest Jefferson was to know at Monticello for many years. The mansion was not finished to his satisfaction, nor was it to be so for years to come, but it was now a home.
He had taken under his protection the six children of Dabney Carr,
to whom he became a father; and these, with his daughter, Martha,
now toddling about, contributed to the merriment of the household.

The routine of life at this time did not greatly vary. Each day
found the tall, eager, red-headed master looking in upon the progress of his mechanics, visiting all parts of the estate to observe the
work in the fields, practicing conscientiously on his fiddle before
breakfast, poring over his treasured volumes in his library, bending
over his desk writing voluminous observations on his reading, writing letters to friends and public men. Though an omnivorous
reader, he was in no sense a bookworm, for he favored his love of
the outdoors and of physical exercise. He eagerly followed the
budding and the unfolding of the flowers in his garden, visited
the deer in the park, never forgetting to take a pocketful of corn,
inspected his stables and kept his grooms alert. Almost every day,
weather permitting, he mounted his horse promptly at one o'clock
for a two-hour canter over the broad acres.

And Martha, the young wife, had her routine, too, since, under the
training of her very practical father, she had become a mistress of

accounts, and she assumed the management of the household. Since it does not appear that a portrait of her was ever painted, we are dependent solely on the descriptions of her contemporaries, who all agree upon her beauty and great charm. She was above the average in height for a woman, her figure was lithe and exquisitely molded and she moved with a queenly grace. Visitors were impressed by her amiability, hospitality, charm, and accomplishments. While Jefferson was occupied with his inspection of the sowing, the reaping, and the building, she was busy in the management of the domestic household and in keeping the account books. During the ten years of her life with Jefferson, she was to bear six children, of whom three were to die in infancy. In childbearing and in the performance of her self-imposed duties, her married life was largely one of confinement to her home. She had neither time nor strength for the frivolities of Williamsburg, nor had she the slightest desire to visit the stately homes of Philadelphia and its environs when her husband was in Congress. Childbearing, and at such short intervals together with the misfortune of losing three of her children, had made inroads on her delicate constitution. But her spirits were high and her amiability was never affected. When Jefferson had finished his work and she her own, she could find time daily to sit down at the harpsichord he had ordered from London, and the red-headed mate would take up his fiddle, as in the old days of the wooing. They were to remain lovers to the end.

It was a happy household.

Even at this early period, Jefferson had begun to keep open house. Guests poured in and out constantly and without ceremony or notice, and the hospitality was all that could be expected of a prosperous Virginia squire. His boyhood love of hunting persisted, as he was as fond of following the fox to the music of baying hounds as any squire in England. His love of horses drew him occasionally from home to attend the races, then popular in Virginia.

VII

A short time before Jefferson took residence in the Governor's Palace in Williamsburg, Monticello was enlivened by a strange company. For fifty years all sorts and conditions of men were to

nd their way up the mountain road to the mansion, but never was
he hilltop to see another such group. Because this was unique, and
ecause their generous reception and entertainment throw a white
ight on the character of Jefferson, more than a reference to these
fficers of the enemy in the Revolutionary struggle is necessary.

Early in 1779, the four thousand German and British prisoners
aken at the surrender of Burgoyne at Saratoga were ordered from
3oston to the neighborhood of Charlottesville, to remove them
rom the immediate scene of military operations. The march in the
lead of a bitterly harsh winter over roads almost impassable was
chieved, but on their arrival at the camp assigned them, five miles
rom Charlottesville, it was found that, because of the dearth of
aborers, the barracks were unfinished, and there was also a shortage
f bread. The speed with which all this was remedied through the
ndustry and ingenuity of the prisoners themselves won Jefferson's
dmiration. The barracks were completed and the private soldiers
et themselves to the task of making the surroundings not only
omfortable, but pleasing to the eye. The ground was cleared and
hen divided into small lots which were neatly enclosed and cul-
ivated.[12] The officers rented houses and small farms in the imme-
liate neighborhood, bought sheep and cows, and settled down seri-
usly to farming, to the delight of the master of Monticello. They
nade necessary repairs to the rented houses at their own expense,
ought furniture to make them agreeable, and with remarkable
generosity paid rent for a year in advance.

The transformation made in the camp, where the private soldiers
first lived in blockhouses without windows or doors, was magical.[13]

Then the silly rumor spread that the presence of so many prisoners
hreatened the community with a food famine. A petition was sent
to Governor Patrick Henry, asking for the removal of at least a
portion. By their own cultivation the prisoners themselves were
producing much of the food they required, and they had all they
could ask but money, which the outspoken wife of one of the
Brunswick officers thought the British were slow in furnishing.
But since Henry usually found it disagreeable to refuse a popular
demand, there was every probability of his acquiescence.

[12] Girardin, *History of Virginia,* 325.
[13] Riedesel, *Letters and Memoirs,* 215.

No one knew this better than Jefferson. He therefore sat down at his desk to write an equally energetic protest. Nothing he ever did is more illuminative of his humanitarian instincts and his rule of discriminating between men, as human beings, and as political agents:

> Their health is also of importance [he wrote Henry]. I would not endeavor to show that their lives are valuable to us, because it would suppose a possibility that humanity was kicked out of doors in America, and interest only attended to. . . . But is an enemy so execrable that, though in captivity, his wishes and comforts are to be disregarded and even crossed? I think not. It is for the benefit of mankind to mitigate the horrors of war as much as possible. The practice, therefore, of modern nations of treating captive prisoners with politeness and generosity is not only delightful in contemplation, but really interesting to all the world — friends, foes, and neutrals.

And what, he asked, were the facts pertaining to these prisoners? 'After considerable hardship' the officers had rented houses 'at such exorbitant rates as were sufficient to tempt independent owners to go out of them and shift as they could.' They had made repairs at their own expense. One officer had taken a place for two years, paying in advance, and, to accommodate his family, had erected additional buildings. The officers had bought grain and other provisions and purchased cows and sheep and settled down to actual serious farming. The private soldiers had 'laid off hundreds of gardens, each enclosed in its separating paling.' General Riedesel alone had bought two hundred pounds of garden seed for the Germans. In addition to the barracks built for them, the private soldiers had built more, and in their gardens they could raise almost enough vegetables for their subsistence.

> Having thus found the art of rendering captivity comfortable and carried it into execution at their own expense and labor, their spirit sustained by the prospect of gratifications rising before their eyes, does not every sentiment of humanity revolt against the proposition of stripping them of all this and removing them into new situations where, from the advanced season of the year, no preparations can be made for carrying themselves comfortably through the heats of summer?

So ran the protest.

But more: These men had been marched seven hundred miles to Virginia, and what would be the interpretation of an order to move on again?

> Indifferent nations will charge this either to ignorance or to whim and caprice; the parties interested, to cruelty [wrote Jefferson]. They now view the proposition in that light, and it is said there is a general and firm persuasion among them that they were marched from Boston with no other purpose than to harass and destroy them with eternal marches.

And more:

> The separation of these troops would be a breach of public faith. What would it mean? The health of the troops neglected, their wishes crossed, and their comforts torn from them, the character of whim or caprice, or, what is worse, cruelty, fixed on us as a nation, and to crown the whole, our own people disgusted with such proceedings.[14]

The protest had its effect and the prisoners remained.

This spirited and humane action of Jefferson, known to the German and British officers and men, made an indelible impression. Here was the arch-revolutionist, author of the *Summary View* and the Declaration of Independence, bespeaking humanity for the enemy in the midst of a bloody struggle. Even Major-General Phillips, usually prone to insolence in his communications with Americans, though otherwise amiable enough, was deeply moved, and wrote Jefferson an expression of his gratitude. 'The great cause which divides our countries is not to be decided by individual animosities,' Jefferson replied. Brigadier-General Specht, Baron de Geismer, Baron de Unger, and others wrote glowingly in their appreciation. The news of Jefferson's fight for a just treatment of the prisoners found its way to Europe in the letters of the prisoners, which were published in some instances in the German papers.

VIII

But Jefferson did not limit his generosity to this letter of protest. He personally treated the prisoners with marked civility and wel-

14 Ford, *Writings of Jefferson*, II, 167-80.

comed them to the hospitality of Monticello. His discovery tha
among the officers were some who shared his love of music espe
cially delighted him. Thereafter, it was not unusual to find Germa
and English officers gathered together at Jefferson's house for a
afternoon or evening of musical entertainment, with each con
tributing his share. Certain it is that Jefferson often played violi
duets with Bibby, the aide-de-camp of Frazier, who had fallen a
Saratoga. In young Baron de Unger he found a congenial com
panion, since this accomplished officer shared his literary an
scientific tastes, and the lively conversation of the two bound then
with the bonds of a sincere friendship. In Baron de Geismer, h
discovered another lover of music, capable of making his contribu
tion to the unconventional musicales; and ten years later, as we sha
see, he was to encounter the Baron quite by accident in a Germa
town where he was stationed with his regiment, and to receive
warm welcome from the erstwhile prisoner and his comrades, wh
had often heard from him the story of Jefferson's hospitality an
kindness. Baron de Geismer shared Jefferson's partiality for th
violin on which the German played with skill and feeling. O
these musical occasions the Baroness de Riedesel, who had a pleasin
voice, often sang Italian airs to de Geismer's accompaniment.

Soon the prisoners felt free to appear without ceremony at Monti
cello, with the certainty of a cordial welcome. The library of thei
host was at their disposition, his scientific apparatus and his musica
instruments were theirs to use. Mrs. Jefferson joined heartily i
these unique entertainments. And very often the German officer
enjoyed the generous bounty of their table.

In the beginning, these foreigners, accustomed to the stiff for
mality and protocol of courts and in the houses of the nobility, wer
not a little puzzled by Jefferson's utter disregard of precedence a
prescribed by protocol. But they soon found something to commen
in their host's placing of a minor officer on a level with a genera
at the table; or, at any rate, they accepted it as part of the eccen
tricity of a well-meaning person. So Monticello at this time becam
a green spot in the desert, and the Jeffersons, while amazing them
were nevertheless loved.

IX

But no one amused Jefferson so much as the Baroness de Riedesel. Colle, the small estate a short distance from the eastern base of Monticello, where Philip Mazzei, his provocative wife, and attractive stepdaughter had been living, was turned over to Baron General de Riedesel and his daring wife and children. The Baroness was long to remain a favorite subject of conversation among the neighbors of the statesman. Daring and unconventional, entirely natural, she was to appear at frequent intervals on Jefferson's hilltop, unannounced. Her own story of her adventures among the 'quaint' Americans of the Revolutionary period has happily been recorded in her published letters.

The Baron was the commander of the Brunswick troops his King had kindly sold into the service of George III, when it was found impossible to get enough recruits in England. Soon after he had sailed for America, the Baroness, who was ardently devoted to him and unable to bear the separation, determined to join him despite the serious handicap of children who would have to be taken along. It meant the harshest of hardships in travel by land and sea and submitting herself to the inconveniences and dangers incidental to following the fortunes of an army. Discouraged by her friends, she nevertheless fared forth on her long journey, pausing for a time in London where she was presented to the Queen by Lady Georgia Germain, and found 'the saloon . . . very ugly and the furniture old-fashioned.' On inquiring as to the procedure in her presentation to the King, she was told that it was the monarch's custom to greet the English marchionesses with a kiss, but that she would be expected only to stand quietly in her place. When, to her astonishment, the King gave her a kiss, she 'could not help blushing'; and, turning to her sponsor, she cried out triumphantly that she had 'been naturalized by a kiss.' The fact that both King and Queen showed her marked attention is significant of the importance George III attached to his mercenary troops in the American Revolution.[15]

The daring Baroness reached America in time to make contact with bloody battles and to suffer the hardships of frequent movements of the army. When at one time the presence of herself and

15 Baroness Riedesel, *Letters*, 90-91.

children with her husband's army put them in peril and the Baron proposed sending her for protection to the American camp, she indignantly refused. 'Nothing could be more painful to me,' she said, 'than to live on good terms with those with whom [her husband] was fighting.' [16] But she was to find the Americans confusing and inexplicable. When, after the surrender at Saratoga, she was told to follow her husband and she drove in her calash through the American camp, she was astonished that 'nobody looked at us with disrespect, but, on the contrary, greeted us, and seemed affected by the sight of a captive mother with three children.' And when at the American camp she was greeted with exquisite courtesy by General Schuyler, the father-in-law of Alexander Hamilton, she was really touched.[17]

But when the prisoners were sent to Boston, her fighting spirit against the Americans flamed. The people there she found 'outrageously patriotic,' and 'among them many wicked people, and the persons of my own sex the worst,' since they gazed at the Baroness 'with indignation and spit when [she] passed near them.' [18] A lady of spirit was the Baroness, and she took her revenge on the birthday of her husband when she gave a ball to which the German and British officers among the prisoners were invited. With the yard and garden illuminated and with eighty people sitting down to supper, when the health of George III was drunk, she was sure that 'never was "God Save the King" sung with more enthusiasm.' That, then, for the wicked women of Boston that 'spit when they passed near her'! She was sure the prisoners were 'proud to have the courage to display such sentiments in the midst of our enemies.' [19]

Then came the order to move to Virginia. In an 'elegant English coach' the Baroness set forth with the army over the all but impassable winter roads, and sometimes the soldiers had to lift her coach from the mire. On reaching Virginia, Jefferson's small estate at Colle was placed at the disposal of the Baron, who 'had a large house built . . . with a spacious saloon in the center, and with two rooms on each side which cost one hundred guineas, and was quite elegant.' [20] He ordered seed and took to serious farming, and the

16 *Ibid.*, 182.   17 *Ibid.*, 188.   18 *Ibid.*, 196.
19 *Ibid.*, 199.   20 *Ibid.*, 215.

Baroness was soon to boast in her letters home that she had 'turkeys
weighing fifty pounds.'

X

And so it came to pass that Jefferson had a neighbor who made
free use of his hospitality. The Baroness made such an impression
on her neighbors that for a full generation they were to gossip about
her with zest. It was rather novel and a bit shocking to the Virginians of that day to encounter, in the woods, a lady in breeches,
astride a horse like a man, confronting the staring eyes of the natives
with a haughty complacency. A woman of Amazonian proportions,
though handsome despite her weight, she commanded admiration
and respect. Perhaps her popularity sprang in part from her perfect
naturalness and the unrestrained frankness with which she expressed her contempt for republican institutions. Having settled
down for a while at Colle, it did not occur to her that she could not
claim the rights of a free neighbor whenever she was in need of
anything for her house, garden, or table. Whenever she wanted information or advice, she mounted her horse, astride, and cantered
through the woods to Monticello. Soon the sight of the Baroness on
her horse climbing the hill to the mansion attracted no more attention than a house servant walking across the lawn.

The establishment at Colle was not in keeping with the style of
living to which she was accustomed. She lived, too, 'in constant
apprehension of rattlesnakes.' She suffered from the heat, and when
she left doors and windows open in the night, bats would wing
their way in to flutter about her bed in the dark. In the absence of
enough chairs, she had recourse to 'round blocks of timber' that
served as substitutes. This had an advantage in that a table could
be improvised by laying planks across the blocks.[21]

She came to like her neighbors in a condescending way, especially the poorer farmers, whom she described as 'peasants.' She has
described a scene with one of these which throws some light on her
character. One day, when Geismer was playing the violin and she
was singing some Italian airs, a 'peasant,' from whom some futile
efforts had been made to purchase butter, appeared upon the scene.

[21] Ibid., 217.

Fond of music, as all his countrymen are [she wrote], he listened eagerly; when I had finished my song he desired me to sing some more. I asked him, in jest, what he would give me for doing so 'for it cannot be expected,' said I, 'that I should sing without being paid for it.' 'Two pounds of butter,' he immediately rejoined. The joke amused me. When I had finished, the rustic cried out, 'Play again, but something livelier.' He must have been pleased with my performance, for he came the next day with his wife, and, giving me four or five pounds of excellent butter, begged me to sing. I thus gained his good will, and no longer was in want of many things, which, for a long time, I had been unable to procure. The most amusing part of the story is that he actually believed that I expected to be paid for the pleasure I afforded him, and wondered that I insisted on paying him for the butter.[22]

XI

Such was the Baroness Riedesel, who was to afford no little entertainment to Jefferson during these halcyon days at Monticello. She had no earthly use for anything that Jefferson represented and made no secret of her antipathy, but Jefferson found her most diverting. She was welcomed because of her humor and warm heartedness, and especially, we may be sure, for her Italian songs. We can imagine her sitting on the lawn with Jefferson and his family and friends, for Madison met her there, talking volubly and in downright honesty of sentiment, regardless of the political proclivities of her audience. But she was a clean enemy and not a spy and Jefferson could appreciate this type.

When she found anything at Monticello that she needed at College she borrowed without blushing. What were neighbors for? And, indeed, we may gather from the record that blushing was reserved largely for her audience, since tradition has it that she loved and told with zest a *risqué* story and stood not on the order of the telling. There was clearly something of the barrack-room about her, and the notation of the editor of her letters that portions had been expunged because too *risqué* leaves us in no doubt. Her conversation, we are led to believe, had many of the scarlet patches of a heroine of the Congreve comedies, and smacked not a little of

[22] *Ibid.*, 219.

Fielding and Smollett.[23] But, to do her justice, it appears that some of her alleged vulgarity of expression was quite unconscious, since, like the lady in *The Rivals,* she made many amusing blunders through her unfamiliarity with the English language. Many years after she had returned to Germany, Madison, who knew her at Monticello, was wont to keep a dinner-table in roars of laughter by recalling her mistakes.

That she was an inveterate gossip is generally agreed among those who knew her in her Virginia days. But if she made acidic observations on the neighbors, she did not spare herself. General Loos, of the Hessian troops, who had known her in the first flush of youth, exclaimed, on meeting her: 'Ha, ha, what have you done with your elegant figure, your brilliant complexion, and your pretty taper white hands? They are gone.' She advised him not to mention to a lady her lost beauty, 'since many would not be as indifferent as I am.' [24]

On hot days she found the refreshing breezes of Jefferson's mountain-top pleasant and his dinner-table to her taste, and the host was amply repaid for his hospitality with her rollicking barrack-room humor, her spicy gossip, her malicious caricatures of his neighbors, but most of all by her singing of her favorite Italian songs.

It was while living in Virginia that she gave birth to another daughter, though she had made no secret of her determination to have a son. Writing from Richmond to the Baron, who had sent him notice in a letter expressing his gratitude for the spirit in which he had sought to lighten the burdens of captivity, Jefferson said: 'I sincerely condole with Madame de Riedesel on the birth of a daughter, but receive great pleasure from the information of her recovery, as every circumstance of felicity to her, yourself and family is interesting to us. The little attentions you are pleased to magnify so much never deserved a mention or a thought. My mortification was that the peculiar situation in which we were put it out of our power to render your stay more comfortable.'

This extended story of the Riedesels and the German and British prisoners is justified, I hope, because these contributed not a little to the home pleasures of Jefferson just before he became Governor, but mostly because it throws a clear light on the humanitarian

[23] *Ibid.*, 133.   [24] *Ibid.*, 240.

impulses and the unusual toleration of his nature. In these latter days, when some nations make a virtue in war of bestial treatment, persecution, and even torture and assassination of captured enemies, it is refreshing to one's faith in humanity that a patriot as militant as Jefferson was able to treat prisoners, not only with decency, but with hospitality. A little later, we shall find in his attitude toward Hamilton, the British officer taken prisoner at Vincennes, that he could be as severe and unrelenting in treatment of prisoners as circumstances might require. But Hamilton was not a gentleman, and the officers near Charlottesville were of a different kind.

XII

These years before his election as Governor were probably the happiest Jefferson was to know at Monticello. There was to be a short interval between his retirement from the gubernatorial office and his brief congressional career and long diplomatic service when he would be able to live the quiet life of a country gentleman at home, but this was to be far from happy or serene because of his wife's illness and death. With the exception of the three years from 1794 to 1797, until his retirement from public life in 1809, he was to be able to make but few visits to the spot dearer to him than any other. Nothing would have pleased him more than the privilege of living quietly at Monticello, in the midst of his family and friends, tending his fields, superintending his improvements on the house, looking after his flowers and vegetables, feeding from his hand the deer in the park, riding over his estate daily on one of his thoroughbreds, reading and writing in his library, amusing himself with his violin, and conversing on the lawn in the warm weather with congenial spirits like Madison and Monroe. But this was not to be. When he assumed the duties of the governorship at the most desperate period for Virginia throughout the war, he entered upon a new phase of his career. No longer would he move to the general applause, for henceforth envy and malice were to attack his almost every act and follow him throughout the remainder of his life.

We must now leave the rural charms of the mansion on the hilltop and follow him through the most trying period of his career.

CHAPTER

X

GOVERNOR OF VIRGINIA

I

A S THE EXPIRATION of Patrick Henry's term as Governor approached and his retirement was foreseen, the Virginians, thinking in terms of conservatism and liberalism, prepared for the contest over the succession. So conclusively had Jefferson impressed his personality and political philosophy upon the Commonwealth through his sponsorship of the Virginia reforms that his popularity surpassed that of Henry and his leadership of the liberal and progressive forces was beyond all cavil. Among the supporters of these reforms, there appears to have been no thought of anyone but Jefferson.

The old reactionary aristocracy, patriotic, but wedded to the old social order of pre-Revolutionary days, was not prepared to surrender without a fight, and it finally rallied around John Page in the gubernatorial contest.

It so happened that between Jefferson and Page had existed a warm friendship from college days and a mutual appreciation which had suffered nothing because of the divergence of their views. Never, perhaps, has any commonwealth been so abundantly blessed with men of genius or extraordinary ability as was the Virginia of those days; and, while maintaining their opposing opinions on the fundamentals of government and the structure of society, they were much too big to permit political differences to poison their personal and social relations.

Neither Jefferson nor Page actively participated in the contest.

239

The campaign was waged by their respective friends and partisans, who threw themselves into the fight with fervor. It was really a struggle between the new and the old orders, a battle of principles, not personalities. On the first ballot Jefferson received fifty-five votes, Page thirty-eight, and Thomas Nelson thirty-two, but on the second ballot Jefferson received sixty-one votes and was declared elected.

When Page immediately sent his congratulations, Jefferson replied with feeling, clearly grateful for the opportunity of reiterating the assurance of his warm personal regards and affection.

> It has given me much pain that the zeal of our respective friends should ever have placed you and me in the situation of competitors [he wrote]. I was comforted, however, by the reflection that it was their competition, not ours, and that the difference of the numbers which decided between us was too insignificant to give you a pain, or me a pleasure, had our dispositions toward each other been such as to admit these sensations. I know you too well to need an apology for anything you do, and hope you will forever be assured of this: and, as to the construction of the world, they would only have added one to the many sins for which they are to go to the devil. As this is the first, I hope it will be the last, instance of ceremony between us. A desire to see my family, which is in Charles City, carries me thither tomorrow, and I shall not return until Monday. Mrs. Jefferson, I believe, will not come shortly to town. When she does, however, she has too much value for Mrs. Page not to consider her acquaintance as a principal among those circumstances which are to reconcile her to her situation. . . . Be pleased to present my compliments to Mrs. Page, and add this to the assurances I have given you that I am, dear Page, your affectionate friend.[1]

The personal relations of Jefferson and Page were to remain close and affectionate throughout their lives.

In a brief address to the General Assembly, expressive of his appreciation, young Jefferson pledged his utmost to realize the expectations of his friends.

> In a virtuous and free state, no rewards can be so pleasing to sensible minds as those which include the approbation of our

[1] Ford, *Writings of Jefferson*, II, 187.

fellow citizens. My great pain is lest my poor endeavors shall fall short of the kind expectations of my country. [But, he continued], so far as impartiality, assiduous attention and sincere affection to the great American cause shall enable me to fulfill the duties of my appointment, so far, I may, with confidence, undertake; for all beyond, I must rely on the wise counsel of the General Assembly and of those whom they have appointed to those duties.[2]

Among the letters of congratulation that poured in upon him, none could have been more illuminative of his character than that which he received from his tenant of Colle, the captive officer in command of the Brunswick troops in Burgoyne's army, who, as we have just seen, had so frequently been a guest at Monticello with his amusing wife. Jefferson thought that 'condolences would be better suited for the occasion, not only on account of the labors of the office and its withdrawing me from retirement, but also the loss of the agreeable society I have left, of which Madame de Riedesel and yourself were an important part.'[3]

Thus it came to pass that Jefferson, as master, moved into the Palace in Williamsburg, where, as a youth in college, he so often had gathered about the board of the charming and accomplished Fauquier, the Royal Governor, with the little group of choice spirits, and, with them, had made one of the amateur orchestra. The few intervening years had brought many changes. The courtly Governor was now sleeping beneath the stones of the Williamsburg Bruton Church, and a new spirit permeated the society of the town. The interior of the Palace was by no means the same. The portraits of the King and Queen no longer looked down on the guests in the drawing-room. After the frightened Dunmore had converted the Palace into a fortress, it was never again to possess its earlier charm.

And now Virginia was at war.

And because she was at war, Williamsburg was less attractive as a capital. Not only was it too open to attack, but too remote from the center of the State, and Jefferson was persuaded that a more comfortable climate and a more desirable situation could be found. He had urged a change, and presented a bill providing for it as early as 1776. He foresaw that in war the old capital with its

[2] *Ibid.*, II, 186.   [3] *Ibid.*, II, 247.

magazines and stores was too exposed to the enemy, but he was quite as much motivated by the feeling that it was now too remote from the center of population. In the many years since it had been established as the capital, there had been a notable shift in population across the mountains and there were other citizens to be considered. That Richmond would be more convenient to Monticello could hardly have entered into his conclusion.

But more than half of his gubernatorial service would be over before the capital was removed to Richmond. In those days it was a mere scraggly village, and some years would elapse before an adequate mansion for the Governor would be constructed, and the Capitol in which the Assembly would function would be a makeshift until long after Jefferson's tenure had expired. He would be thousands of miles across the sea, in Paris, when his architectural talents would be requisitioned by the Assembly and he would be bending above his desk in the Legation on the Champs Elysées drawing plans for the capitol that was finally built.

II

In normal days of serenity, Jefferson would have found his post to his liking. Nothing would have pleased him more than the congenial task of aiding in the realization of the reforms he had sponsored in the legislature and written into law. The development of the schools and the improvement of the University, the amelioration of the means of transportation and travel through the bridging of streams and the building of roads, would have appealed to his taste. But he entered upon his duties in the darkest hours Virginia was to know throughout the Revolution. The ancient Commonwealth and the South had, until about this time, been happily free from the molestation of the enemy. The British and their mercenary troops had been busy in the northern colonies. And in that region, State after State had been overrun by the superior British forces, and Washington, with an untrained army, inadequately manned and with inadequate supplies, had saved the Revolution more than once through the masterful strategy of his retreats. It was not until the closing days of Henry's administration that Virginia was given a taste of actual war upon her own soil. It was then that the British swept into the State, seized Fort Nelson near Norfolk, demolished the naval stores at Gosport, gave Suffolk to the flames, and created confusion before the militia could be assembled to meet them. Thereafter there was to be no time until the final victory at York-town when Virginia would not be in peril. That the easy success of this foray into the ancient Dominion in Henry's time determined the British to turn their attention to Virginia, there can be no doubt.

When Jefferson took the helm there was a general discontent among the patriots throughout the entire country. Within a few months Madison would be writing pessimistically to Jefferson from Congress that the military situation was critical. 'Our army threatened with an immediate alternative of disbanding or living on free quarters . . . the public treasury empty . . . public credit exhausted . . . the people complaining of extortion' — so ran the narrative. Washington was complaining 'that a failure of bread has already commenced in the army' and that meat could be had 'only for a short season.' [4]

And then, too, Madison found an entire change in the situation of the Continental Congress. He wrote Jefferson that 'whilst they exercised the indefinite power of emitting money on the credit of their constituents they had the whole wealth and resources of the continent within their command and could go on with their affairs independently and as they pleased'; but that now they were 'as much dependent on the States as the King of England is on Parliament.' They no longer were in position to 'enlist, pay or feed a single soldier, nor execute any other purpose than as the means are first put into their hands.' Indeed, 'unless the Legislatures are sufficiently attentive to this change of circumstances and act in conformity to it, everything must necessarily go wrong or rather must come to a total stop.' [5]

Even before hearing from Madison, Jefferson, within a few days after entering upon his duties, was writing that, with peace and independence within the grasp of the colonies, Congress was failing in its functions. He had heard that its hesitations and vacillations had so disgusted the French Minister that he was on the point of returning to France. This, thought Jefferson, would be the most 'dreadful calamity.' It had been suggested that the Committees of

[4] Burnett, *Letters*, V, 97.   [5] *Ibid.*, V. 128.

Correspondence be revived, but others, thinking this too slow a process for the emergency, favored sending a congressional committee to the Minister to reassure him, and to canvass the colonies for some assurance of united action.[6]

Then, too, on taking office, Jefferson had found that the finances of the Commonwealth were in a confused and lamentable condition. He had hoped for some relief through the opening of the land office and the sale of British property. He pinned some hope on the amendment of the tax laws, which he favored. He wrote a friend that 'these measures, I hope, will put our finances into a better way and enable us to co-operate with our sister States in reducing the enormous sums of money in circulation.' Any other remedy, he thought, would be 'nonsensical quackery.'[7]

No one, certainly, had a keener appreciation of the evil effect on the patriots' cause of the serious depreciation of money. 'It is a cruel thought,' he wrote Richard Henry Lee, 'that, when we find ourselves standing on the firmest ground in every respect, the cursed art of our secret enemies, combining with other causes, should effect, by depreciating our money, what the open arms of a powerful enemy could not; that, notwithstanding its increased amount, there will still be a greater depreciation than ever.' He could see little hope but in peace 'or a plentiful loan of hard money.'[8]

But the money problem was to persist throughout the war and throughout the continent until the adoption of the Constitution some years later.

III

It was just before his accession to office that George Rogers Clark, in a forced march in the western wilderness which challenges comparison with the most grueling and heroic in the annals of military achievements, had attacked the British garrison at Vincennes, Indiana; and soon after his accession, some of the redcoat prisoners reached Chesterfield in Virginia. We have noted the courtly hospitality and kindness shown by Jefferson to the prisoners at Charlottesville. This is evidence enough to prove his humanitarian

[6] Letter to William Fleming; Ford, *Writings of Jefferson*, II, 188.
[7] *Ibid.*   [8] *Ibid.*, II, 192.

attitude toward prisoners of war. We are now to observe that no one could be more rigid and uncompromising toward a type of prisoner not represented among those who played, sang, and dined at Monticello.

Indisputable evidence had reached Jefferson and the Council that three of the captives of Vincennes, including Governor Hamilton, had been guilty of such barbarous practices, in conjunction with the Indians, that he ordered them sent to Williamsburg. Within a week after taking office, Jefferson had explained the special treatment planned for Hamilton in a letter to Theodorick Bland:

> The indiscriminate murder of women and children, with the horrid circumstances of barbarity practiced by the savage Indians, was the particular task of Governor Hamilton's employment, and if anything could have aggravated the acceptance of such an office and made him personally answerable in a high degree, it was that eager spirit with which he is said to have executed it ... which ... seems to have shown that his feelings and disposition were in unison with his employment.

There would be an investigation, he wrote, and the punishment measured out to Hamilton would be commensurate with his crime.[9] As a result of the investigation, the Council, with Jefferson's hearty approval, sentenced Hamilton to solitary confinement in chains.

Hamilton reached Williamsburg, 'wet, jaded, dispirited,' wondering what form the judicial inquiry would take. By the time he and his captors reached the Governor's Palace, his 'escort of curious persons had become numerous.' There he sat haughtily on his horse at the door of the Palace, 'expecting the civilities naturally to be looked for from the Man in first place in the Province.' After half an hour he flung himself 'from his horse, fatigued and mortified to be left a Spectacle to a gazing Crowd.' But a little later he was 'relieved from the painful state of uncertainty by the appearance of the Officer,' and conducted 'to the common prison, distant a small mile,' with the crowd 'increasing every step.' Reaching his destination, he was received by the jailer, 'a Character, however, beneath other people's notice.'[10]

9 Ibid., II, 191.
10 Hamilton's Journal, quoted in A Brief and True Report for the Traveller Concerning Williamsburg, 103-04.

Jefferson, whose sense of humanity and decency had been outraged by Hamilton's conduct, had refused to see him. He was 'received by the jailer.'

It is important to note that, on learning of the crimes of Hamilton and the sentence, Washington wrote Jefferson that he had 'no doubt of the propriety of the proceedings against Governor Hamilton, Dejean, and Lamothe,' since 'their cruelty to our unhappy people who have fallen into their hands, and the measures they have pursued to excite the savages to acts of the most wanton barbarity, discriminate them from common prisoners, and most fully authorize the treatment decreed in their case.' [11]

Instantly, General Phillips of the British Army demanded that Hamilton be released from confinement, on the ground that, having capitulated at Vincennes, he could not, under the laws of war, be subjected to such indignity. Jefferson immediately sent Washington a copy of the order of the Council, together with the Phillips letter, and a letter of his own. In his letter he said he understood that prisoners of war, whether by capitulation or otherwise, were subject to the same treatment unless special stipulations were written into the terms of capitulation. There was nothing in the terms of capitulation for the protection of the man who had set savages with tomahawks upon American women and children. In no book in his possession or in his knowledge could he find in any single line anything to justify the stand of Phillips. However, he might be ignorant of such matters and he would be the last man in the world to violate a contract. 'If you shall be of opinion that the bare existence of a capitulation in the case of Governor Hamilton privileges him from confinement, though there be no article to that effect in the capitulation, justice shall most assuredly be done him,' he wrote Washington. 'There is no other person whose decision will so authoritatively decide this point in the public mind, and none with which I am disposed so implicitly to comply.' [12]

In the meantime, while awaiting Washington's reply, Sir Guy Carleton, the Governor of Canada, had written demanding the reason for the drastic sentence of Hamilton, and Jefferson had replied with dynamic vigor. It had been given, he wrote, on the prin-

[11] Fitzpatrick, *Writings of Washington,* XV, 401.
[12] Ford, *Writings of Jefferson,* II, 246.

ciple of national retaliation. And then, with all the force of which his pen was capable, he drew an indictment of the treatment of American prisoners by the British under Hamilton:

To state to you the particular facts of British cruelty to American prisoners would be to give a melancholy history from the capture of Colo. Ethan Allen at the beginning of the war to the present day, a history I would avoid, as equally disagreeable to you and to me. I, with pleasure, do you the justice to say that I believe these facts to be very many unknown to you, as Canada has been the only scene of your service in America, and in that quarter we have reason to believe that Sir Guy Carleton and the three officers commanding there, have treated our prisoners (since the instance of Colo. Allen) with considerable lenity.

But how different elsewhere!

I will only observe to you, Sir, that the confinement and treatment of our officers, soldiers and seamen, have been so rigorous and cruel that a very large portion of those captured in the course of the war and carried to Philadelphia while in possession of the British army, and to New York, have perished miserably from that cause alone.

Were not soldiers confined in jails like common malefactors and seamen to prison ships of the most loathsome character? Who, then, began the policy of rigor? Not the Americans. The first instance of such rigor on the part of the Americans was in the case of Hamilton. And why? Because of his conduct at Detroit — the use of savages in indiscriminate attacks on men, women, and children.

No distinction can be made between a principal and an ally [he wrote]. He who employs another to do a deed makes the deed his own. If he calls in the hand of the assassin and murderer, himself becomes the assassin and murderer. . . . Governor Hamilton undertakes to be the conductor of the war. . . . He associates small parties of the whites under his immediate command with large parties of the savages, and sends them to act — not against our forts, our armies in the field, but the farming settlements of our frontiers. Governor Hamilton himself is the butcherer of men, women, and children.

Had not Hamilton in a proclamation invited American officers and men to join the British army? And had he not distributed these proclamations through the agency of the savages? And in every house they had visited on this mission had they not murdered or carried away the family? Had not some of the proclamations been 'found sticking on the breasts of the persons murdered, and one under the hand and seal of Governor Hamilton come into our hands'? Had not 'other papers of Hamilton come to our hands, containing instructions to officers going out with scalping parties of Indians and whites,' proved the case against him?

In the light of the facts, of which Carleton evidently was ignorant when he wrote his letter, Jefferson hoped that he would understand that the treatment accorded Hamilton was inspired by a desire to 'stop the effusion of inoffending blood of women and children.'[13]

IV

About this time, Loring, the British Commissary of Prisoners, wrote Washington on the treatment of Hamilton and threatened to retaliate on all American prisoners. Washington, perhaps a bit disturbed, wrote Jefferson of the threat, but went no further than to say that 'your Excellency will be able to Judge how far it may be expedient to relax in the present treatment of Mr. Hamilton.'[14] And Jefferson did not budge.

Almost a month elapsed before Washington advised the removal of the irons and a parole was offered under certain conditions. But when Hamilton refused the stipulation that the prisoners should refrain from propaganda against the American cause, Jefferson wrote Washington that he had returned the prisoner to his confinement and that he would positively remain there until he pledged himself and his companions to be 'inoffensive by word as well as deed.'[15]

Thoroughly aroused by the arrogance of Hamilton, Jefferson followed, the next day, with another letter to Washington:

It is impossible they can be serious in attempting to bully us in this manner. We have too many of their subjects in our power and

[13] *Ibid.*, II, 248.
[14] Fitzpatrick, *Writings of Washington*, XVI, 272.
[15] Ford, *Writings of Jefferson*, II, 258.

too much iron to clothe them with and I will add, too much resolution to avail ourselves of both, to fear their pretended retaliation.

Washington instantly acquiesced in the remanding of Hamilton. 'The measure of the Council in remanding Govr. Hamilton and his companions back to confinement, on their refusal to sign the parole tendered them, is perfectly agreeable to the practice of the enemy,' he wrote. But he was clearly becoming concerned, and he hoped there would be 'no necessity for a competition in cruelty with the enemy.' He was hopeful that they had learned their lesson on the treatment of prisoners, and since Sir Henry Clinton had taken command, their policy had been 'more within the line of humanity, and, in general, very different from that . . . experienced under his predecessors.' [16]

Even so, when an exchange of prisoners was in process, and word arrived that no Virginians would be exchanged until Hamilton was free, Jefferson had 'stopped our flag, which was just hoisting anchor with a load of privates for New York.' [17]

Outraged by the atrocities of Hamilton, Jefferson wrote Washington again, requesting that he be kept informed of the treatment of American prisoners, with the warning that for every instance of mistreatment there would be retaliation in Virginia.[18] And when a paroled American prisoner wrote Jefferson that American prisoners suffered as a result of the retention of Hamilton, Jefferson hotly replied that the treatment of Hamilton was based on three authenticated charges—his 'cruel treatment of our captive citizens,' his 'barbarous species of warfare on our western frontier,' and for 'particular acts of barbarity of which he himself was personally guilty' —any one of which charges richly justified the measures taken in his case.[19]

Four months later, he wrote Washington that some of Hamilton's companions were on parole, but that the Governor and four others, being 'still obstinate,' were yet in close confinement.[20] He was in no contrite mood. It was almost a year later that Washington wrote that when forty British prisoners exchanged reached New York, he did not observe Hamilton on the list. Since his case

16 Fitzpatrick, *Writings of Washington*, XVII, 166.
17 Ford, *Writings of Jefferson*, II, 250.
18 *Ibid.*, II, 260. 19 *Ibid.*, II, 261. 20 *Ibid.*, II, 279.

would, no doubt, be the subject of discussion in the negotiations of exchange, he would be 'embarrassed' if he did not know 'on what footing to place him.' [21]

The embarrassment of Washington effected what the storming of the enemy had been unable to effect; and thus, after many months in captivity, in confinement for weeks in chains, Hamilton was finally exchanged for a lieutenant-colonel.

Thus Jefferson, who had won the heart of the British and German prisoners near Charlottesville by his kindness and hospitality, had known how to deal with a different type of prisoner, responsible for the murder of women and children on the western frontier.

V

And he was intensely concerned with that frontier.

Unlike some of his contemporaries in Virginia, Jefferson knew that his jurisdiction and responsibilities were not limited to what is now the confines of the Commonwealth. He was keenly conscious always of his duty to the rich empire that now embraces the States of Ohio, Indiana, Illinois, Michigan, and Wisconsin, and nothing was nearer to his heart than the recovery of Detroit.

Thus, one of his first acts on taking office was to authorize an expedition under the command of George Rogers Clark against the British at that point. That valiant warrior asked nothing better, but he was disappointed with the number of men he had been able to muster at Vincennes, and the plan was momentarily postponed.

But by February, 1780, the prospects had brightened. Jefferson informed Washington that Clark had been instructed to use his own judgment as between employing his forces against Detroit and chastising the Indian tribes nearer by, who were causing trouble. He thought it probable Clark would prefer Detroit. He had heard that a Colonel Broadhead was contemplating an expedition against Detroit, and he was fearful of some confusion in the plans. He could vouch for his old Virginia friend, Clark. Indeed, 'the enterprising and energetic genius of Clark' was not unknown to Washington. But Jefferson knew nothing of the capabilities of Broadhead. However, if Washington felt that Broadhead was the better

[21] Fitzpatrick, *Writings of Washington,* XIX, 500.

man for the attack on Detroit, Clark would be diverted to other objects.[22]

That was in February. In late December, when the conditions were grave in the Old Dominion, Jefferson wrote Washington again that conditions in the West had so changed as no longer to leave it optional to move against Detroit. 'From intelligence received, we have reason to suspect that a confederacy of British and Indians, to the amount of 2000 men, is formed for the purpose of spreading destruction and dismay through the whole extent of our frontier in the ensuing spring,' he wrote. He was not unmindful of the grave danger in the South, where the greater part of the Virginia militia would have to be employed. But, because of this very danger in the South, there was need for a diversion for the enemy on the frontier. With the force already under Clark's command and with a draft of the militia beyond the Alleghenies and some of the extreme northern counties, the gallant Clark was convinced that he could reduce Detroit. Jefferson had therefore authorized the attempt.[23]

In his letter to Washington he asked that certain stores and equipment at Fort Pitt should be turned over to the expedition. That Washington found nothing chimerical in the project we must assume from his reply to Jefferson. He had 'ever been of opinion that the reduction of the post of Detroit would be the only certain means of giving peace and security to the whole Western Frontier,' and he had constantly 'kept his eye upon that object.' He had been deterred from action in that direction by 'the reduced state of our Continental Force' and by 'the low tide of our funds.' But he thought it would be a 'most happy circumstance' if Virginia, with the aid of Continental stores, could accomplish it. He would give orders to Colonel Broadhead, in command at Fort Pitt, to turn over to Clark the articles Jefferson had stipulated, in so far as possible.[24]

Five days after writing Washington, Jefferson sent his instructions to Clark. The expedition was to be timed between the spring and the breaking-up of the ice on the Wabash, so Clark could transport his troops by water. Instructions had been sent that Clark be furnished '1000 of rifle powder from New London and 1500 pounds

22 Ford, *Writings of Jefferson*, II, 298.
23 *Ibid.*, II, 375.   24 Fitzpatrick, *Writings of Washington*, XXI, 23.

of lead from the lead mines of Montgomery Court House . . . 300 pack mules with pack saddles, etc., 40 bell tents, 40 common tents, chest of medicine, some summer clothing, etc.' An agent had been sent to Philadelphia to purchase four tons of cannon powder. Washington had been asked to lend from Continental stores at Pittsburgh four cannon, six-pounders mounted on field carriages, a mortar with shells, two howitzer grapeshot, one thousand spades, two hundred pickaxes, five hundred axes, a travel forge, carpenters' tools, boats for transportation. Another agent had been sent to Fort Pitt to purchase two hundred thousand rations of beef and flour, and to arrange for one hundred light barges for the movement of the men.

Washington had warned Jefferson that if the six-pounder cannon were intended by Clark for the reduction of works of any strength, he would be disappointed, since his own experience had shown that 'they are not equal to battering a common Log Block house at the shortest range.'[25]

VI

Then followed Jefferson's instructions to Clark, worked out, no doubt, in conjunction with his military advisers. He was to proceed down the Ohio and up the Wabash unless he found another route better, and to construct forts en route to provide for the safety of his men in case of a reverse. Should he succeed in reaching Detroit, and the prospect of acquiring Lake Erie seem fair, he was to pursue that object. His expedition was to end when he had accomplished both objects or had found that either or both were impossible.

In the event he took Detroit, he was to promise protection to persons and property of the Americans and French, or to any others taking the oath of fidelity to the Commonwealth. He was to permit them to continue under their own laws. He was to use either fear or friendship in dealing with the red men, according to their mood.[26]

Such was the plan thought out by Jefferson in conjunction with his military advisers, at a moment when Virginia was in imminent danger of invasion. Later, he was to be criticized because at such a time he had actually been giving serious thought to the protection and retention of the Northwest Territory, out of which so many of the richest States in the Union were to be carved. It is not surprising that the average man in the street or in the corn row, utterly ignorant of the significance of this timbered empire, should have been puzzled and even a bit resentful at the time, but it is amazing to find that here and there some historians are prone to ridicule Jefferson's plan at the period — which had the complete sanction of Washington.

But there were many in what is now Virginia and along the James who thought solely of this Commonwealth and the protection of their property from the rough treatment of the invader, to the exclusion of the general, or what may be called the national, cause. This was quite as true among many public men and politicians. These would have retained, in what is now Virginia, the regulars and the militia raised in that State and sent to Washington in the North and to Greene in the South. And these would have abandoned the Northwest Territory, to the end that all resources of the Commonwealth might be kept within its borders.

But Washington and Jefferson even then had vision that was national. And thus, Washington, knowing full well that his calls for men and guns and food from his own State weakened it for the moment in its defense, insisted that these be assigned to the common cause elsewhere. And Jefferson, who, from his youth, had envisioned a nation reaching far into the then Western wilderness, could not look with the indifference of the shortsighted on the importance of holding on to the Northwest Territory.

But the plan formulated was not to be put to the test in precisely the manner he had expected. Where he had planned to give the British on the frontier too much to do to send assistance to the British armies operating in the South, the British had perfected plans for a big offensive to retake the lost territory in Illinois, and the falls of the Ohio, and Pittsburgh. Jefferson had exerted himself to strengthen the forces of his friend, George Rogers Clark, and if this could not be applied to the taking of Detroit, it could be used effectively in meeting this offensive of the British. Had the British succeeded in their plans, the end of the war would have found the British in possession of the entire region west of the Alleghenies to the Mississippi.

Thus, Clark was forced to postpone his plan — and Jefferson's — to take Detroit, and to hold, as hold he did, the territory then in possession of the Americans through his genius and exertions.

VII

Meanwhile, from the moment he took office Jefferson was struggling with accumulating difficulties. The territory under his jurisdiction surpassed in magnitude that of almost all the other governors combined. The Northwest Territory was in his keeping; and in this vast domain white Americans were settled and were battling with the British and the savages. Then, too, he had inherited a grave financial problem which would be humanly impossible to solve until long after the final victory, when the new nation, with virile powers, would be created in the Constitutional Convention.

And then, to deepen the shadows that glowered upon him, a blight fell upon the crops in the autumn of 1779. Constantly, Virginia was being called upon for food and soldiers for the armies of the North and South, and the failure of the crops with the consequential distress was not to reduce the importunate demands upon the Commonwealth. Jefferson described the effect of the crop failure in a letter to John Jay, then President of the Continental Congress: 'The various calamities which during the present year have befallen our crops of wheat have reduced us to so very low as to leave us little more than the seed for the ensuing year, were it to be solely applied to that purpose.' Thus, he wrote, Virginia was unable to furnish the necessary supplies of flour for the Continental troops.

Such was the gravity of the food problem, thus created, that Jefferson issued a proclamation in November, 1779, placing an embargo on provisions such as beef, bacon, wheat, Indian corn, peas, 'or other grain or flour or meal made of the same.' [27] Not only was the embargo based on the necessities of Virginia, but on the certainty that much of it that might be sent elsewhere would probably go to the feeding of the armed forces of the enemy. [28]

Now, nothing is clearer in the policy of Washington than this — that the prospective needs of Virginia had to be subordinated to the

[27] *Ibid.*, II, 257.   [28] *Ibid.*, II, 281.

imperative necessities of the main armies, whether in the North or south of the Old Dominion; and that the best-trained troops in the Virginia line should be sent to support these armies and not kept at home in idleness waiting for a raid that might never eventuate. Constantly, therefore, Virginia was being importuned for soldiers, for food, for money, for armament, and to Jefferson the policy of the great Commander was as a pillar of cloud by day and of fire by night. Throughout these darkest of years, Washington and Jefferson were steadfast nationalists, thinking in terms of the whole. And despite the empty treasury and the alarming depreciation of the currency, when Jefferson's salary of forty-five hundred pounds was not sufficient to meet the food demands of the Palace and his household, and when, as has been calculated, his salary in his second year was not enough to have bought a saddle, it is of record that in his first year in office he had more than met the heavy demands on Virginia for money.[29]

VIII

Meanwhile, Jefferson was in comparative ignorance of what was preparing south of Virginia because of what he afterward described as the 'lamentably defective' intelligence. We may well wonder why the trained military men, on whom depended the defense of the Commonwealth, had so signally failed to provide for this necessity. Jefferson knew, in June, that Charleston had been in the hands of the enemy for a month, but he had no inkling of British movements, though rumor bruited it abroad that they were marching northward toward Virginia. He took upon himself the duty that really devolved upon the commanders. He wrote Washington that to remedy this evil, he was establishing a line of expresses to the neighborhood of the British army in the Carolinas, which, he believed, would convey information one hundred and twenty miles in twenty-four hours. He hoped something could be arranged to Washington's headquarters. 'Perfect and speedy information of what is passing in the South might put it in your power to frame your measures by theirs,' he wrote. He knew that North Carolina was 'without arms,' and while they did not abound in Virginia, arms would have been sent but for the impossibility of 'moving a

[29] *Ibid.*, II, 282.

single musket from this State to theirs.' However, a Virginia army was preparing to march to the succor of the Carolinas.[30]

Thus, at this time Jefferson was busy organizing an intelligence service that should have been the duty of the military authorities. Some time before he had established a line of communications between Richmond and Fort Henry; and now, at the request of Congress, he was extending it to Philadelphia.

To the neighborhood of the British army in Carolina, he had sent a young man with whom his political career was to be intimately identified — Colonel James Monroe. The younger man, even then, found in Jefferson the god of his idolatry. About this time he had written his idol:

> Had I not formed a connection with you I should most certainly have retired from society. . . . In this situation you became acquainted with me and undertook the direction of my studies and believed in me. I feel that whatever I am at present in ye opinion of others, or whatever I may be in the future, has greatly arisen from your friendship.[31]

Monroe fully justified Jefferson's faith in him. Soon he was informing Jefferson of the embarkation at Charleston of the British under General Clinton, presumably for Virginia.[32]

Thus, establishing lines of communication, recruiting soldiers with difficulty, and unable to see how he was to arm as many as three thousand, hampered as to money because of the inability of the Virginians to sell their tobacco,[33] and with the troops and officers 'in the utmost distress for clothing,'[34] Jefferson was struggling against desperate odds all through the year 1780.

IX

Nothing daunted, though pitifully handicapped, Jefferson threw himself with feverish fervor into an attempt to repair the damage done at Camden. He wrote Washington of the disaster, sending him extracts from the letters he had received from Generals Gates and Stevens and Governor Nash of North Carolina. He was drumming up new recruits, but despaired of getting them to the field of

[30] *Ibid.*, II, 308.   [31] Hamilton, *Writings of Monroe*, I, 8-11.
[32] *Ibid.*, I, 3-6.   [33] Ford, *Writings of Jefferson*, II, 319.   [34] *Ibid.*

action within six weeks. Three hundred and fifty regulars from Chesterfield were on the march, fifty more would follow on the morrow, perhaps two hundred more as cleared from hospitals. But, alas, while he could find men, he could find nothing with which to arm them. Though Virginia under him had been lavish in supplying the armies of the North and to the South, his insistent calls on Congress for arms had availed him nothing as yet. 'Almost the whole small arms seem to have been lost in the late rout,' he wrote Washington. 'There are on their way southward three thousand stand of arms sent by Congress and we have still a few remaining in our magazine. I have written [Congress] to send us immediate supplies.' [35]

He turned from the signing of this letter to write General Stevens, in command of the Virginians, consoling him on the late misfortune when his untried troops broke and ran before the approaching bayonets, but subordinating laments to future preparations. Two thousand men had been called out to his command from the middle and the northern counties, beyond the adjoining Blue Ridge, and Jefferson understood that 'the spirit of raising volunteers is springing up,' though he did not know. Meantime, he would 'exert every nerve to assist [Stevens] in every way in our power, being as we are without money in ye treasury.' [36]

And to Congress he wrote again, demanding arms without delay. 'The men proposed for the field will be unarmed unless it is within your power to furnish arms,' he wrote. 'Should any disaster like the late one befall that army which is collecting, and which will be much weaker in regulars . . . the consequences will be really tremendous if we are found without arms.' With arms, there would be 'no danger in the end.' Losses, in the meantime, would be great, distresses cruel, but 'there can be no doubt of the ultimate recovery of the country.' But the new army of militia were strangers to actual conflict, and 'habit alone will enable them to view this with familiarity, to face it without dismay.' [37]

Meanwhile, in spite of all that was being done, Gates was requisitioning more supplies from Virginia, and in a letter to Congress Jefferson wrote bluntly. Tents? Impossible! 'We cannot produce a single one, because the stuff is not in our country and we have no

[35] Ibid., II, 331.   [36] Ibid., II, 333.   [37] Ibid., II, 334.

money to procure them elsewhere, our treasury being entirely exhausted.' Sugar and coffee? None to be had. The other articles he would send.[38]

And, to deepen the shadows, disloyalty was emerging from hidden places — disloyalty to Washington in Montgomery, Henry, Washington, and Bedford counties, where, Jefferson reported to Congress, 'many hundreds have actually enlisted to serve his Britannic Majesty, and taken the oath of allegiance to him.'[39]

To Washington he wrote again that seven thousand soldiers had been ordered from Virginia to the South, but that no more than fifty-five hundred could be positively counted upon. 'But we have arms for three thousand only,' and unless arms were sent speedily by Congress it would be necessary 'to countermand a proper number of these troops.'[40]

When Virginia troops reached Gates at Hillsborough, he complained bitterly that they had arrived 'without clothes, tents or arms.' He wanted no more sent unless fully equipped. 'This would put an end to marching a single man there,' Jefferson wrote Congress. 'They are clothed as militia. Few of them carry blankets. Nor shall we be able to furnish tents or arms for more than half of them.' However, they would be sent on in the hope that Congress would send the arms long prayed for. Virginia had been generous to a fault in furnishing money for the defense of other colonies, in furnishing thousands of their very best soldiers, in furnishing food, in furnishing arms, and now that Virginia was threatened, why were not arms sent promptly?

This policy, let it be reiterated, of supplying the Continental Army even at the risk of Virginia, was the positive policy of Washington, and Jefferson stood four-square behind the Commander. He believed in Washington.

X

And just then the British fleet sailed into the harbor of Portsmouth and the redcoats disembarked. Eight hundred light horse landed there, and at Newport a thousand more.

This called for the supremacy of the military. Jefferson called to

[38] *Ibid.*, II, 336.   [39] *Ibid.*, II, 341.   [40] *Ibid.*, II, 343.

the command General Muhlenberg, whom Washington had entrusted with the military defense of Virginia, General Weeden of the line, and Generals Nelson and Stevens of the militia.

From this hour on, Jefferson worked in the closest co-operation with these generals, supporting their efforts in every way within his power and interfering with their plans in nothing. Every human effort possible was made to collect an adequate body of men to oppose the enemy, and a portion of the soldiers intended for Gates were diverted to this end.

It is significant of Jefferson's loyalty to the cause in general that, even at this critical juncture, he did not abandon Gates. 'We shall not by any means consider his reinforcement as no longer interesting, but clearly see the necessity of supporting him with our utmost abilities,' he wrote Congress.

But, again, the hideous lack of arms, the failure of Congress to respond to the necessity, made an adequate defense impossible.[41] To Gates, Jefferson wrote of the invasion with the assurance that no calls would be made for men in the Virginia counties closest to him, and these might continue his reinforcement.[42]

XI

The presence of British troops on Virginia soil confronted Jefferson with two new problems. On the frontier, an insurrection burst, but it was speedily suppressed. Even so, Jefferson was fearful lest the presence of the redcoats give courage to the Tories in Virginia, who had been lying low.

And now, too, he was confronted with the necessity of removing the Saratoga prisoners from their quarters near Charlottesville. Should the British break through that far, the prisoners would be released to reinforce the invading army, and the danger of escape to the enemy lines was obvious. Instantly Jefferson acted. Orders were issued for their removal and for guarding and subsisting them upon the way.[43] The difficulty of getting wagons necessitated the removal in two batches. The British first, because of the 'danger of desertions to the enemy and of correspondence with the disaffected in our southern counties.' Jefferson found little disposition among

41 *Ibid.*, II, 351.   42 *Ibid.*, II, 352.   43 To Congress, *ibid.*, II, 355.

the Germans to join the British. Soon the redcoat prisoners were over the Blue Ridge.

Among the Brunswickians, as we have seen, were numerous charming and keenly intelligent men and women, who often had enjoyed the hospitality of Monticello, and among these none had been more welcome than Lieutenant Baron John Louis de Unger, who dabbled in philosophy. It was at this time that the Baron wrote Jefferson an expression of his gratitude, and the latter found time to reply in a courtly letter:

> When the course of events shall have removed you to distant scenes of action where laurels not tarnished by the blood of my country may be gathered, I shall urge sincere prayers for your attaining every honor and preferment that may gladden the heart of a soldier. On the other hand, should your fondness for philosophy resume its merited ascendancy, is it impossible to hope that this unexplored country may tempt your residence by holding out materials wherewith to build a fame founded on the happiness and not the calamities of human nature? Be this as it may, whether philosopher or soldier, I wish you many felicitations.[44]

The invasion under Leslie was to be a mere incident. Jefferson had assumed, along with his military advisers, that he had landed with the expectation of a conjunction with the forces of Cornwallis, but at this moment, Cornwallis was retreating in the South and not advancing toward Virginia. The invaders were not a little puzzled by the lack of information. Then, one day a British spy, making his way to Carolina, was captured. He was observed removing something from his pocket and putting it in his mouth. When recovered, it proved to be a letter from Leslie to Cornwallis, written on silk paper rolled up in a clothbeater's skin. Jefferson was no end intrigued by this device and wrote Washington the details. It verified the theory of the intended meeting of the two British forces. Leslie wanted instructions, since Cornwallis was not in sight.

The end came speedily thereafter, when, failing to hear from Cornwallis, Leslie and the invaders took ship and sailed away. But there no longer could be any doubt of an organized plan for the invasion of Virginia.

[44] Ford, *Writings of Jefferson*, II, 373.

INVASION; AND DICTATORSHIP

I

THE INVASION of Leslie was to prove but a curtain-raiser for what was to follow.

General Muhlenberg, sent by Washington to take command of the defense of Virginia, had left, and General Steuben, the stout-hearted Prussian martinet, sent by Washington to take over, had arrived. The Prussian, with his own ideas of discipline, was to find the Virginians a little difficult to understand or appreciate. He had not been reared in an atmosphere of democracy where every citizen carried his sovereignty under his hat, and he was to suffer, in amazement, from the then American idea of an army; was to suffer what Washington and Jefferson had suffered, not without understanding. Many soldiers were willing to fight in an undisciplined manner, but they could see no reason why it should interfere with their accustomed tilling of the soil.

Early in December, 1780, Washington informed Jefferson that a British expedition was in preparation for some place, unknown, in the South. Some swivel-chair military critics have thought that, on this vague report from Washington, Jefferson instantly should have mobilized an army, equipped them without guns, and sent them — where? There was no information that the expedition in process of preparation was anywhere near readiness; and if there was, no way of knowing its intended destination; and no special reason for believing it was going to Virginia or to the Carolinas, where the British were then operating. One thing is certain — Washington was insisting that the militia should be sent out of Virginia to the aid of General Greene. However, the idea of calling all the militia into the field as a precautionary measure did occur to Jefferson and the military advisers about him, in whose judgment Washington himself had confidence. But they all realized that, should the expedition fail to sail, or should it sail for some destination other than Virginia, it would have meant a heavy demand upon an empty treasury and intense dissatisfaction among the soldiers hurried from their homes into dismal camps. We need not argue the pros and cons of this attitude — it is enough that this was the attitude of a goodly portion of the men who fought in the war of the Revolution.

Then, too, the average American of that time had no conception of the operations of a professional army. Thousands, who would gladly have responded to meet an immediate recognized emergency, would very bitterly have resented being taken from the comfortable glow of their firesides and kept in camps, inactive. Desertions, as all history records, were a commonplace. It was not in the least extraordinary for men in the army lightly to drift away and find their way back home. Washington was to complain bitterly of this throughout the war. A standing army of militia was impractical at that stage of our national existence.

Thus, the unanimous opinion of the Council, called to take preliminary steps, was to await the determination of the destination of the British expedition. Food was scarce because of the failure of the crops, money was almost nonexistent, and the army was pitifully inadequately equipped because Virginia had stripped herself to serve the Continental Army and the forces in Carolina, in accordance with the wish of Washington. Plans, therefore, were perfected, but they were held in abeyance pending more definite information.

But the British expedition had clearly been ready when Washington thought it still in process of preparation, for early on the morning of the last day of the year 1780, General Nelson received a letter from a citizen, informing him that, on the morning of the preceding day, twenty-seven sail of vessels had entered the capes. The writer had no notion whether they were friends or foes. The French fleet had been eagerly awaited. Nelson immediately informed Jefferson, and he at once sent General Nelson to the lower country with full power to act, to call on the militia of that section, and to take whatever additional steps the situation might demand.

However, it was not until the second day of January that it was definitely ascertained that the new arrivals were enemies and not friends. By that time they had advanced up the James River as far as Marrasqueak Bay. The day before it was positively known that the fleet bore enemies, Jefferson had summoned Benjamin Harrison, Speaker of the House of Delegates, and requested him to inform that body before it rose, in the event it had any advice to offer.

The same day he notified the House, Jefferson wrote General Nelson, sending him a commission, and informing him that orders had gone forth for the mobilization of half of the militia of the counties closest to the enemy, and of one-fourth from more distant counties. It was the intention to call forty-six hundred militiamen into the field.[1]

And in another letter to Nelson, written the same day, Jefferson invited his counsel in the determination of the force to be collected.[2] And that same day Jefferson wrote the county lieutenants of twenty-one counties, ordering them to assemble their companies. The men were to find their way individually to the meeting-place by the speediest means possible. 'That there may not be an instant's delay, let them come in detached parties as they can be collected,' he wrote. 'Every man who has arms, bring them.' He added that the good of the service required that the field officers should be experienced, but that this was not to be interpreted as a reflection on the officers of the militia.[3]

At the same time, the county lieutenants of four other counties, near Richmond, were instructed to assemble their men and 'repair immediately to Richmond, armed with good rifles and accoutrements suitable, as far as they have them.' If the men had no rifles, they should bring muskets and join the battalion of musketry.[4]

On the evening of the third day of January, Jefferson learned, by letter, that the enemy had anchored a little below Jamestown on the preceding evening. On the morning of the fourth, he instructed the county lieutenants of Henrico, Hanover, Goochland, Powhatan, and Chesterfield counties that, since the indications pointed to an

[1] Ford, *Writings of Jefferson*, II, 395.
[2] *Ibid.*, II, 397.   [3] *Ibid.*, II, 394.   [4] *Ibid.*, II, 398.

attack on Petersburg or Richmond, they were to 'send every man of [their] county able to bear arms to rendezvous at Westham,' without waiting to be formed into companies. Lest the Saratoga prisoners avail themselves of the confusion to join the enemy, it was at this juncture that Jefferson instructed Colonel Richard Meade to move them across the Blue Ridge without waiting for their baggage.[5]

And that same day he appointed Colonel Meade to superintend the officers of the Commissary and Quartermaster's Department, since they had necessarily been invested with great powers that might conceivably be abused. This was done on the suggestion of General Steuben, who had urged the selection of 'some gentleman of distinguished character and abilities.'[6]

On the evening of that hectic day, Jefferson was advised that the enemy fleet had anchored at Kennon's, and he summoned the militia of the adjoining counties. At five that evening the enemy stopped at the historic seat of the Byrds at Westover on the James, where it appears they made free of the comforts of that elegant old mansion.

Late in the evening, Jefferson took to saddle and rode to Westham, personally to direct the loading and transporting of the war material and to order that the work be continued without ceasing throughout the night. That night he lodged at Tuckahoe, the home of his earliest childhood.

Early the next morning he sent his family to Fine Creek; and then, mounting his horse, he galloped at full speed to Westham again, himself to see to the removal of the arms and ammunition. Having satisfied himself here, he again mounted and spurred his horse on to Manchester, where he could get a view of the enemy. He had been incessantly in the saddle, riding at full speed, and on this journey his horse collapsed under him from exhaustion. He borrowed another and galloped on to Chetwood's, which had been indicated by General Steuben as his headquarters. But Steuben was not to be found. Jefferson was informed that he probably had gone to Colonel Henry's, and Jefferson rode there, without finding him.

Meanwhile, the British force was moving rapidly, and, before the militia in sufficient numbers could be assembled, the redcoats, under the command of the traitor, Benedict Arnold, rushed upon

[5] *Ibid.*, II, 399. [6] *Ibid.*, II, 400.

Richmond about noon on the fifth. Without pausing for even a contemptuous glance at the then scraggly new capital, they swept on to the foundry which they put to the torch, along with the magazines. Then on to Westham.

Night found the redcoats again at Richmond, and Arnold sent to Jefferson the demand that he compound his property. This demand was dismissed with a shrug. And on the morning of the sixth, the invaders were giving houses and stores to the flames, until they finally retired to Four Mile Creek.

In the meanwhile, astride his horse, Jefferson was galloping back to Westham to salvage whatever might have escaped destruction by axe or flame. Thence he spurred his horse on to Manchester, where he lodged.

Arnold and his men were then encamped at Westover and Berkeley, the birthplace of William Henry Harrison. It was from his lodgings at Manchester that Jefferson wrote to Steuben of his unsuccessful attempt to get in touch with him for two days, though they had been 'riding over the same ground.' He had heard that the General was at Ampthill, and, though worn by so many hours in the saddle, he had been on the point of mounting again to pursue the search when he was told that in reality Steuben was at Osborne. 'Having rode thirty miles through the rain,' he added, 'I have not resolution enough to undertake to go on to Osborne this evening.' [7]

The next morning found Jefferson again at Richmond. It was then that he set down the numerical strength of the defenders. Gibson had a thousand men, Steuben eight hundred, Davis two hundred, and Nelson two hundred and fifty — two thousand and fifty in all.

This ended the humiliating raid of Benedict Arnold, the traitor; for, two days later, this miserable man embarked his men and horses and dropped down the river. The material loss was inconsequential, but the humiliation was all the greater because Arnold, the renegade, had led the pack. Jefferson ascribed his success in the raid to the complete lack of information which delayed action for two days. With two days' grace, he thought a sufficient force could have been mustered to meet the invaders.[8] To that, and to the fact that both

[7] *Ibid.*, II, 403.
[8] To Governor Nash, *ibid.*, II, 422.

wind and tide so favored the enemy that 'they almost brought news themselves of their movements.'

II

There then followed an interlude of inactivity during which Jefferson was asked to pass on the propriety of Americans importuning the invader for the restoration of stolen property. It was disgusting to him that Americans should lower themselves to begging favors of the foe. He could find nothing inspiring in the spectacle of Americans negotiating individually with the enemy. He made it clear that he was 'not fond of encouraging an intercourse with the enemy for the recovery of property.' However, he wrote, if Arnold chose to discriminate between different species of property, offering to restore some and not others, Jefferson was willing that the victims of the pillage should avail themselves of such discrimination. 'But,' he added sharply, 'no distinction of person must be admitted,' since 'the moment it is proposed that the same species of property shall be restored to one which is refused to another, let every application to him for restitution be prohibited.' And then, more sharply still, he added: 'The principles by which these discriminations would be governed are too obvious, and they are the reverse of what we should approve.' [9]

A large number of horses that had been stolen by the invader had been left at Westover, and it was Jefferson's plan to hold them there until they could be restored to their owners. When he was informed that they had been 'plundered and carried off' by a body of American soldiers, he wrote indignantly to General Nelson: 'These men, being under your command, I beg you to take the most coercive measures for compelling a restitution, and letting them know that the most rigorous and exemplary punishment will be inflicted on every man who shall be known to have one of them and not deliver it up.' [10]

All thieves looked alike to him.

III

With the greater part of Virginia's best-trained regulars in the North, with others in the South, with a tragic lack of arms because

[9] To Colonel John Nichols, *ibid.*, II, 409.　　　[10] *Ibid.*, II, 410.

the Old Dominion had stripped herself to serve the Continental Army, the incredible happened — Congress chose this moment to make new demands on Virginia!

When she was asked to furnish one-half the food supplies for the feeding of prisoners in Maryland, Jefferson's indignation flamed. He sent a sizzling reply to Congress. Was it possible Congress did not even know that at that hour the enemy was concentrating its fury on Virginia? That redcoat reinforcements were on the way? That to meet these, a proportionately large army would have to be assembled and fed? Since it was known that the British were sending reinforcements from the South, was it not time for sending a portion of the American army from the North? 'Instead of sending aid of any kind to the Northward,' he wrote, 'it seems but too certain that unless very timely and substantial assistance is received from thence, our enemies are yet far short of the ultimate term of their successes.' [11]

But, unhappily, the clouds were dark in the North as well. Madison was writing Jefferson of a 'general mutiny of the Pennsylvania line stationed near Morristown,' when officers were killed by the men. They mutinied because they wanted to go home on the expiration of their term of enlistment, regardless of the effect on the cause, and because they were without clothing or sufficient food, and had not received their pay.[12]

And scarcely had this mutiny of the Pennsylvania line been settled when Madison again wrote Jefferson of 'great discontent prevailing in New York among the German troops for causes similar to those which produced the eruption of the Pennsylvania line.' [13] And there was similar trouble in Connecticut.

Meanwhile, with a real crisis for Virginia looming large, Jefferson was clamoring to Congress for arms, above all for arms, but also for reinforcements from the regulars or trained troops in the North, but with no response. Even Washington promised no succor in reply to Jefferson's appeal. He thought it probable that Virginia would suffer even greater hardships.

But [he said], as the evils you have to apprehend from these predatory incursions are not to be compared to the injury to the

11 *Ibid.*, II, 413.   12 Burnett, *Letters,* V, 524.   13 *Ibid.*, V, 543.

common cause and with the danger to your State in particular, from the conquest of those States southward of you. I am persuaded the attention to your immediate safety will not divert you from the measures intended to reinforce the Southern army and put it in condition to stop the progress of the enemy in that quarter. The late accession of force makes them very formidable in Carolina, too formidable to be resisted without powerful succors from Virginia.[14]

Thus, even at this critical juncture in Virginia, Washington was insisting that Jefferson continue to send soldiers away from the Old Dominion to the Carolinas.

Jefferson, of course, knew that Cornwallis was planning to join the invaders in Virginia and that everything depended upon Greene's capacity to hold him back. Soon thereafter, Greene, for whose army Virginia had made heavy sacrifices in men and material, would turn his back on the Old Dominion to march south, and Cornwallis, with nothing to interfere, would hurry north.

Meanwhile, Jefferson was concerned about the movements of Arnold's and Phillips's men. Feeling that 'want of intelligence might eventually prove fatal,' he carefully organized an express, to be stationed at various points, so that no one rider would be more than fifteen miles distant in the relay.[15]

And still keenly conscious that the situation was supremely critical and that arms and aid were imperative, Jefferson hurried Benjamin Harrison, then Speaker of the House, posthaste to Philadelphia in the hope that this agreeable emissary, eating and drinking with the congressmen at the tavern, might be able to make an impression by the robust vigor with which he was capable of hammering home the facts. Help actually was then promised, but it was to be delayed for many critical weeks.[16] Madison, on the Virginia delegation in Congress, was doing all he could, but the results were meager.

14 Fitzpatrick, *Writings of Washington*, XXI, 191.
15 To General Nelson; Ford, *Writings of Jefferson*, II, 416.
16 Burnett, *Letters*, V, 577.

IV

Even while struggling with seemingly unsolvable problems, Jefferson had one dominant obsession in those days. He could not forget nor forgive the invasion of the traitor, Arnold, of whom he could not think without hate and revulsion. He was possessed by a passionate determination ˙to effect his capture and summary execution.

Writing George Rogers Clark at the time, he said that during the Arnold raids the culprit might easily have been captured by a man or men of resolution. It was not then too late, though now it would be more difficult and require more finesse. It is illuminating to note here, as on so many occasions throughout his life, that Jefferson pinned his faith on the hardy pioneers of the frontier, such as the men who marched with Clark on the epochal advance to the capture of Vincennes.

Wanting 'men of resolution,' his mind now instinctively turned to Clark. And thus we see him one day, at his desk in Richmond, pouring forth from his pen his plans and hopes to the superb soldier in whom he had such confidence. 'Having peculiar confidence in the men of the western side of the mountains,' he wrote, 'I meant as soon as they shall come down to get the enterprise proposed to a chosen number of them, such whose courage and fidelity would be above doubt.' Would not Clark himself make the choice of men? He knew them personally, and his discretion was perfect. Would he not 'pick from among them characters in such number as [he] may think best . . . to bring off this greatest of all traitors'?

Jefferson did not know 'whether this would be best effected by their going in as friends and awaiting their opportunity, or otherwise.' Clark would know best. But the smaller the number, the better, 'so that they be sufficient to manage him.'

These men, he thought, would certainly be entitled to a suitable reward and he suggested five thousand guineas. Should the capture be made, the men were to be given enough military aid to cover their escape. He, therefore, enclosed an order from General Steuben, authorizing Clark to dispose of any force necessary to cover the enterprise and to secure the retreat of the party.

Soon, a man named Newton was making his way through the wilderness, carrying Jefferson's letter to Clark. This man, otherwise unknown to fame, was instructed to furnish the party chosen for the dramatic enterprise with men as guides who could be completely trusted. Of course, Jefferson wrote Clark, it would be unnecessary to admonish them 'how necessary profound secrecy is in this business, even if it is not undertaken.' [17]

This project, which might have been taken from a page of Dumas dealing with the robustious days of Louis XIII, was very close to Jefferson's heart, but just why nothing came of it the record does not reveal. It is probable that, before arrangements could be made, the traitor had shaken the red dust of Virginia from his feet. He was able to reach his English friends and safety across the sea, where he was to be treated with a deserved contempt.

V

Throughout February, 1781, Jefferson was anxiously following, as well as communications would permit, the course of the struggle between General Greene and Cornwallis in the Carolinas. But he found time to issue a proclamation addressed to the numerous mercenary soldiers in the British army, supplied by foreign princes 'who were in the habit of selling the blood of their people for money.' He called their attention to the advantages of residence in America and to the action of Congress in offering fifty acres of unappropriated land to any one of them wishing to try his fortune in the new country. To this offer of Congress, for which he was largely responsible, he now added a pledge in behalf of Virginia of a grant of 'two cows and exemption from all taxation during the war.' [18]

But of more concern to Jefferson were the fortunes of the fight in the Carolinas. He had heard that reinforcements had been hurried to Cornwallis,[19] and that the British general, infuriated by his losses at Cowpens and Georgetown, had burnt his own wagons to facilitate his march toward the Virginia line. Greene, with inferior numbers, was unable to prevent the advance. It was Jeffer-

---

[17] Ford, *Writings of Jefferson*, II, 441-43.
[18] *Ibid.*, II, 445.   [19] To Congress, *ibid.*, II, 447.

son's firm conviction that Greene could prevent a large-scale invasion of Virginia by the British. He, therefore, ordered the county lieutenants near the Carolina line to collect all available militia, to arm them, and hurry them to the support of Greene. In a letter to the latter he impressed upon him the heavy responsibility he bore and urged him to his utmost efforts.[20] To Washington he wrote that Cornwallis, near the Moravian towns, was moving rapidly in the hope of forcing battle on Greene with his inferior forces.[21] To General Gates he wrote that Greene had two thousand regulars and no militia, while Cornwallis had three thousand, and Arnold, awaiting Cornwallis at Portsmouth, had fifteen hundred more — forty-five hundred against two thousand. For that reason, Jefferson was ordering a thousand militiamen from Virginia to assist Greene in holding the British beyond the boundary of the State.

But even with men, the American cause would suffer unless Congress furnished arms. Harrison, he wrote, had been sent to Philadelphia to insist on action there. 'If they would repay us the arms we have lent them, we should give the enemy trouble,' he said.[22] Always arms and supplies! To Steuben he wrote that the militia in service near Williamsburg were suffering physically from the lack of shoes and were indulging in mutinous murmuring.[23] A few days later he was informing the House of Delegates that, in a number of counties, members of the militia were refusing to enter the field, and that others, in the army, were deserting and carrying their arms from camp. And this in the most critical days!

With the invasion of Cornwallis now almost certain, Jefferson, mindful always of Washington's point of view, was still sending Virginia militia into Carolina to the aid of Greene, and there was much grumbling among many Virginians then, as there has been since by anti-Jeffersonian historians, who carefully conceal the fact that Jefferson's action was inspired by loyalty to Washington's plan. And yet Jefferson shared the thought of many Virginians that, at this critical moment, the presence of Washington in his own State at the head of the army would work a miracle. He wrote as much to Washington, who replied that, because of the arrangements 'concerted between the French commanders and [himself],' this

---

20 *Ibid.*, II, 451. 21 *Ibid.*, II, 457.
22 *Ibid.*, II, 457. 23 *Ibid.*, II, 466.

was then impossible. He hoped that the threat to New York would tend to reduce the British to the necessity of recalling part of their force from the South to support New York. Indeed, he wrote, 'the prospect of giving relief to the Southern States by an operation in this quarter' had been the principal motive for the plans against New York.[24] And this was enough for Jefferson. He never questioned the strategy of the great Commander. Thinking the capture of New York of paramount importance and lamenting the raids of Arnold and the threat of Cornwallis, Washington persisted in his policy of insisting that his own State send troops elsewhere for the common cause and in the interest of the general plan.

Washington was convinced that one of the objects of Arnold's raid was to discourage Virginia from sending the needed reinforcements to the southern army in Carolina. Writing in this vein to Steuben, to whom he had entrusted the military defense of Virginia, he urged that everything possible be done 'to make the defense of the State as little as possible interfere with an object of so much more importance.'

And yet, while standing four-square with Washington and squarely on his policy, Jefferson kept on impressing on the Commander and Congress the desperate need of arms. The imminence of the invasion in force by Cornwallis was too obvious, and it was just as clear that without arms for the militia it could not be repulsed. Thus, at this time Jefferson was pressing Congress constantly for arms, or at least to send back some of the arms so generously sent by Virginia to the North in compliance with the wish of Washington.

And there was no response.

Convinced, as events proved, that the British were planning to make their supreme effort to conquer Virginia, which had been so troublesome with its men, its arms, its money and supplies, Jefferson was also urging that the regulars, seasoned soldiers of the Continental Army, be sent. But through these days of gravest apprehension, with leaden skies above, nothing happened. Then Lafayette appeared upon the Virginia stage with regulars, but with an insignificant number.

With the situation grave and Congress doing nothing, the usually

24 Fitzpatrick, *Writings of Washington*, XXII, 189.

serene, soft-spoken Madison made his motion in Congress in mid-April that Washington be instructed to 'send as effectual a force to the southward as may be necessary.' Another of the Virginia delegation in Philadelphia observed that since Virginia had done more than her part in the war, and certainly more during the Jefferson régime, and had 'afforded succor to the Southern States at her own expense,' a little reciprocity might be in order.

It was at this juncture that Samuel Adams, the robust patriot and stout man of Boston, declared his willingness that the whole of Washington's army should be sent to Virginia and the South, leaving the less threatened Northern States to the defense of the militia.[25]

The arrival at length of Lafayette with a small force had scarcely relieved the situation. It was almost impossible to secure enough boats for the landing of his men and cannon.[26] A month later, because of the pressure of the Virginia delegation in Congress, hope of help from the North was held forth, but there was to be no realization of the promise. The Virginia delegation informed Jefferson that 'a large Detachment of the Pennsylvania line was at length in motion toward Virginia,'[27] but alas, the promise was but wishful thinking; and days later the delegation had to write that the progress of even starting them on the march was leisurely, but that some militia might be sent from Maryland.[28]

But arms — where were the arms?

The Virginia delegates had found some rampart arms in Philadelphia, and had concluded that, by altering them a little and fixing bayonets on them, they might be used. They appealed to some Virginia merchants in Philadelphia to purchase these arms from the Continentals and send them to the Old Dominion for a price that would give the merchants a reasonable profit on their patriotism, but the proposition of the merchants called for profit far more than reasonable. It was 'business as usual,' and let the old home take care of herself. When this plan failed, the delegation secured an order on the Board of War for the immediate shipment of two thousand stands of arms.[29]

25 Burnett, *Letters*, VI, 62.
26 Jefferson to Lafayette; Ford, *Writings of Jefferson*, II, 496.
27 Burnett, *Letters*, VI, 110.   28 *Ibid.*, VI, 110.   29 *Ibid.*, VI, 69.

VI

But, unhappily for the patriots, Cornwallis showed no disposition to accommodate his movements to their leisurely deliberations. Leaving Greene to his own devices in Carolina, he was pushing his men by forced marches along the coast into Virginia. The militia in this region was with Greene, in accordance with the wishes of Washington, and so he passed on, unopposed, to Petersburg, where he joined forces with the traitor, Arnold.

Thus, with a superior force and under a clever commander, the British were ready for a lightning blow that would bludgeon the Old Dominion to her knees. Hurrying on, Cornwallis crossed the James at Westover, where more reinforcements, under Leslie, awaited him. He was moving on toward Richmond, where Lafayette, with a pitifully inadequate force, had arrived a little before. The gallant Frenchman knew better than to accept the gage of battle, and he made a truly masterly retreat. So masterly as to annoy Cornwallis, who had a profound contempt for 'the boy,' as he called him.

Meanwhile, Jefferson had summoned the legislature in Richmond for March 1; but a few days later, with Cornwallis sweeping on, it adjourned to meet at Charlottesville, without accomplishing anything worthy of mention.

At this time Cornwallis ordered Simcoe to the south to destroy arms and stores. At the point where the Rivanna River meets the James, Baron Steuben, with but five hundred men, stood guard over the war material. He had taken the precaution to move the stores across the river. Reaching the opposite bank under cover of the night, Simcoe built many fires to create the impression that the entire British army was assembled there waiting for the dawn to pounce upon and annihilate the puny American force. The ruse succeeded, and Steuben beat a hasty retreat, leaving the stores to be destroyed at leisure on the morrow.

At the same time, Tarleton and his cavalry were galloping toward Charlottesville under instructions to capture Thomas Jefferson and the members of the legislature. But for a three-hour pause at Louisa Court House to seize a few notables and burn a number of wagons carrying clothing to Greene's army, he might have succeeded in his mission. Fortunately, a patriot named Jouett, stopping at the Cuckoo Tavern in Louisa, mounted a fast horse and rode furiously toward Monticello to give the alarm. The night before Jefferson had had, as guests, Ben Harrison, John Tyler, Patrick Henry, and some others, and a little before daybreak the next morning the clatter of horses' feet on the road up the mountain awakened the leaders; and Virginia's Paul Revere dashed up the hill with his warning of the near approach of Tarleton's cavalry.

Not succumbing to a stampede, the leaders lingered long enough to enjoy a Virginia breakfast, and a little later they made their way down the hill to Charlottesville, where the two houses met and hastily adjourned to meet again at Staunton.

Tarleton's men galloped into Charlottesville just as the Assembly was dispersing. They took a few members, but the greater part escaped. The fiery and tempestuous General Edward Stevens, one of the most important, simulating a plain farmer, was ignored, and he made his escape.

As Henry, Tyler, and Harrison made their way along the road toward Staunton, they met numerous country people, two and three sometimes on a horse, riding to the defense of the town, for the news of Tarleton's approach had spread quickly over the countryside. Late in the day, fatigued and eager for food and drink, they drew their horses up to the door of a small hut in the gorge of the hills and asked for refreshments. A rugged woman asked who they were; and when they replied that they were members of the legislature who had been forced to flee before Tarleton's cavalry, the old woman's eyes flashed with contempt. 'Ride on, ye cowardly knaves,' she said. 'Here have my husband and sons just gone to Charlottesville to fight for ye, and you running away with all your might. Clear out — ye shall have nothing here.'

'But,' said Patrick Henry, in tones of expostulation, 'we were all obliged to fly. It would not do for the legislature to be broken up by the enemy. Here is Mr. Speaker Harrison; you do not think he would have fled had it not been necessary.'

'I always thought a good deal of Mr. Harrison until now,' said the woman, 'but he'd no business to run away from the enemy' — and she was on the point of shutting the door in their faces.

'Wait a moment, my good woman,' said Henry, 'you would

hardly believe Mr. Tyler or Colonel Christian would take to flight if there was not good cause for so doing.'

'No, I wouldn't.'

'But Mr. Tyler and Colonel Christian are here,' said Henry.

'They here? Well, I never would have thought it,' she said, weakening a bit.

Then her fighting mood returned.

'No matter,' she went on, 'we love those gentlemen and I didn't suppose they ever would run from the British, but since they have, they shall have nothing to eat in my house. You can ride on.'

Tyler then tried his hand.

'What would you say, my good woman, if I were to tell you that Patrick Henry fled with the rest of us?'

'Patrick Henry? I would tell you there was not a word of truth in it. Patrick Henry would never do such a cowardly thing,' she said, bristling.

'But this is Mr. Henry,' said Tyler, pointing to him.

The old woman pulled nervously at her apron, looking her amazement.

'Well, then,' she said, 'if that is Patrick Henry, it must be all right. Come in and ye shall have the best I have in the house.' [30]

The 'flight' of the legislators was justified by every rule of common sense, but we shall find that when Jefferson 'fled,' when utterly alone before the dash on Monticello by Tarleton's cavalry, he, too, was to be ridiculed for 'cowardice' all the rest of his days by the poisonous partisan propagandists.

VII

Just before reaching Charlottesville, Tarleton had sent Captain McLeod on ahead with orders to capture Jefferson without fail.

After a serene breakfast with his guests, Jefferson had sent his family in a carriage to Enniscorthy, the seat of Colonel Coles, some fourteen miles away. He then gave instructions that all possible speed be made by his blacksmith in shoeing his horse, which was to be sent to the gate opening on the road that led to the Coles plantation. Then, telescope in hand, Jefferson walked up Carter's Mountain, whence, with the aid of his instrument, he could get a

[30] Tyler, *Life and Times of the Tylers*, I, 81.

perfect view of the town. He found the town drowsing in the sun with no unusual activity, and he concluded he had been the victim of a false alarm. He started walking slowly back toward the house. Then he noticed that, in kneeling to level his telescope, he had dropped his sword. On returning to recover it, he again leveled the telescope on the town and he found the streets swarming now with the dragoons of Tarleton. He then hastened to the gate where his horse awaited him, mounted, and rode away to join his family at the Coles plantation. Ten minutes later, Captain McLeod's men entered the grounds of Monticello. Jefferson, single-handed, had not remained to fight them, as the old woman and some historians would have had him.

To the lasting honor of Tarleton, he had admonished his agent scrupulously to observe the usages of civilized warfare, and during his eighteen hours at Monticello Jefferson's property was neither damaged nor treated with indignity and his books and papers were unmolested. When McLeod entered the grounds, two faithful slaves, Martin and Caesar, were hurriedly hiding plate in a dark hole under the front portico. Martin instantly dropped the plank in place, leaving the unfortunate Caesar in the dark and stuffy cavity, and there the loyal fellow remained in absolute silence for almost the entire day without food, water, or light.

It was while Martin was showing McLeod over the house that the soldierly chivalry of the latter was most conspicuously shown. When the slave opened the door to Jefferson's study, the redcoated captain stood in the doorway a moment surveying the room; and then, without so much as crossing the threshold, he locked the door and gave Martin the key. Had Tarleton and McLeod heard of the hospitality to the captive British officers among the Saratoga prisoners?

Caesar, who lived to a ripe old age, amused Jefferson's family and friends for many years with his dramatic recital of the happenings of the eighteen hours, not without much embroidering of the tale. McLeod's men helped themselves to some of the choice wines in the cellar, but everything else was left untouched, and the only wine molested was that which they drank in moderation like gentlemen.[31]

31 Girardin, *History of Virginia*, 501.

But Jefferson's 'cowardly flight' was seized upon by those whose enmity he had incurred by his reforms, and it seems the women, like the old woman of the hut in the gorge, were by far the worst. They apparently could not understand why their leaders did not prefer capture to flight. One lady, whose father had been among the members of the Government in flight and could find nothing amusing in the escape of her father, was immensely and rather contemptuously amused by the flight of others. Describing the precipitate flight of one man of a boastful nature, she wrote that this was 'not more laughable than the accounts we have of our illustrious Governor Jefferson who, they say, took neither rest nor food for man or horse till he reached Carter's Mountain.' She used initials instead of names, but the recipient of the letter could have had no doubt of the identities.[32] By the criterion of these ladies, Washington was an arrant coward throughout the greater part of the Revolution when he led his army in 'flight' to prevent its capture or an engagement against vastly superior forces. It does not appear, however, that Jefferson was greatly annoyed by the silly gossip of his enemies or their circulation later of the story, much embroidered. He dismissed the story in a few words:

> Would it be believed, if it were not known, that this flight from a troop of horse whose whole legion, too, was within supporting distance, has been the subject with party writers of volumes of reproach on me, serious or sarcastic? That it has been sung in verse and said in humble prose, that forgetting the noble example of the hero of La Mancha and his windmills, I declined a combat singly against a troop, in which victory would have been so glorious? Forgetting themselves, at the same time, that I was not provided with the enchanted arms of the Knight, nor even with his helmet of Mambrino. These closet heroes, forsooth, would have disdained the shelter of a wood, even singly and unarmed, against a legion of armed enemies.

VIII

The honorable conduct of Tarleton brings out in darker colors the conduct of Lord Cornwallis, who stationed himself on Jeffer-

[32] *Atlantic Monthly*, XXXIV, 538; Beveridge, *John Marshall*, I, 144.

son's property and in his house at Elk Hill, opposite Elk Island, and where, in the language of an English historian, he 'plundered and pilfered like a bandit.'[33] He had entered Virginia with a bad reputation in that respect, since Washington had warned Jefferson in advance in reporting on the British commander's conduct in Carolina. 'He seems determined to try what severity will do,' he wrote. 'I hope that sooner or later he will be stopped in his career and that the rigorous policy he is pursuing will contribute to this.'[34] Certainly he and his men stole the plate of Jefferson, and from many other houses he took the silver that afterward adorned his lordship's table.

A realist himself, Jefferson did not complain because his cattle, sheep, and hogs were killed for the feeding of his lordship's soldiers, or because his horses were taken for the British army, but so insensate was Cornwallis's hate for the author of the *Summary View* and the Declaration of Independence that he stooped to the cutting of the throats of the young colts, too young for service. From the house he occupied he could survey the scene all over the plantation, and he witnessed the destruction of the corn and tobacco crops, the burning of all the barns and all the fences. Jefferson could have forgiven his lordship's pilfering of thirty slaves had the captor set them free, but he records in a letter, written in Paris seven years later, that Cornwallis consigned them 'to inevitable death from the smallpox and putrid fever then raging in his camp.'[35]

> When I say Ld. Cornwallis did all this [he wrote], I do not mean that he carried about the torch in his own hands, but that it was all done under his eye, the situation of the house in which he was, commanding a view of every part of the plantation, so that he must have seen every fire. I relate these things of my own knowledge in a great degree, as I was on the ground soon after he left. . . . Wherever he went, the dwelling houses were plundered of everything that could be carried off. Lord Cornwallis's character in England would forbid the belief that he shared in the plunder, but that his table was served with the plate thus pillaged from private houses can be proven by hundreds of eye witnesses.[36]

[33] Hirst, *Life of Jefferson*, 170.
[34] Fitzpatrick, *Writings of Washington*, XX, 147.
[35] To Dr. Gordon, Ford, *Writings of Jefferson*, V, 36.   [36] *Ibid.*

That his brutal treatment of the slaves most embittered Jefferson, who was a gentle and much-loved master, is evident in this letter:

> From an estimate I made at the time, I suppose the State of Virginia lost under Ld. Cornwallis's hands that year about 30,000 slaves, and that of these about 27,000 died of the smallpox and camp fever, and the rest were partly sent to the West Indies and exchanged for rum, sugar, coffee and fruit, and partly sent to New York.[37]

At the time of this invasion and these raids, no help, aside from the entirely inadequate aid of Lafayette and his meager force, had been sent to Jefferson, who so lavishly had sent aid to both the armies of the North and South. At this very time, the darkest, the Virginia delegates in Congress were writing him that, despite their utmost endeavors, they had just succeeded in putting the soldiers of the Pennsylvania line on the march. They had also urged Washington to take personal command in Virginia, and were sure he would 'do all in his power.' [38]

Soon thereafter, Washington and his army would be in Virginia to confront Cornwallis, the French fleet would be in close co-operation, and the war would end at Yorktown, but by then Jefferson would have been out of office several months.

IX

It was in these days, when the shadows rested deepest on the hills and valleys of Virginia, that Jefferson was shocked on learning of a movement to set up a dictatorship with absolute autocratic power over property and human life. It was not the first time the idea had been broached. As early as December, 1776, when the clouds hung low over the national cause, when Washington had lost Long Island and his army was in full retreat before greatly superior forces in New Jersey, the faith and courage of some of the Virginia legislators failed, and they fell back on the last recourse of the timid — the creation of a dictatorship.

There can be no possible doubt that the sponsors had Patrick Henry in mind. His personal popularity at the time was great, though he had clearly demonstrated his utter incapacity in military

[37] *Ibid.*   [38] Burnett, *Letters*, VI, 110.

matters. The fact that in future years the biographer of Henry was unable to find among the legislators, then surviving, any who would admit having been implicated in the plan is not conclusive as to the fact. In more serene times it is not in human nature that any man would care to admit his panic in darker days and his willingness to abandon free institutions for a dictator.[39] Jefferson, who carefully exonerated of unpatriotic motives all who looked with favor on the plot, was to write with intense feeling of the incident almost immediately after the second attempt to set up a dictatorship. Tradition has it that, at the time of the first attempt, Colonel Archibald Cary, Speaker of the Senate, encountering Colonel Syme, the half-brother of Henry, in the lobby of the Senate, turned upon him fiercely: 'I am told that your brother [sic] wishes to be a dictator,' he said. 'Tell him from me that the day of his appointment will be the day of his death, for he shall feel my dagger in his heart before the sunset of that day.'[40] The story is in character with the intrepid and passionate temperament of Cary.

In the last dark days of Jefferson's régime, the project was revived; and, writing within two years of the event in his *Notes on Virginia,* Jefferson says that 'it wanted a few votes only of being passed.'

It is impossible to believe that, writing within two years and during the lifetime of all who could have been implicated, Jefferson would have dared make the charge had there been a scintilla of doubt. The *Notes* were published within five years, and it is not in evidence that the charge was challenged in the days of the author's contemporaries.

Nor could Jefferson have written with such vehemence and passion about a figment of the fancy. There would have been no occasion for it. And in these days when Nazi, Fascist, and Falangist dictators have wrought ruin everywhere with their savage and ruthless crusades of unprecedented brutality for the extermination of personal liberty and democracy, it is worth while to record anew, for every generation, Jefferson's observations on the system proposed:

> One who entered into this contest from a pure love of liberty and a sense of injured rights, who determined to make every sacrifice,

39 Wirt, *Sketches of Henry,* 204.   40 *Ibid.*

to meet every danger for the re-establishment of those rights on a firm basis, who did not mean to expend his love and substance for the wretched purpose of changing this master for that, but to place the powers of governing him in a plurality of hands of his own choice, so that the corrupt will of no one man might in future oppress him, must stand dumbfounded and dismayed when he is told that a considerable portion of that plurality had meditated the surrender of them into a single hand; and, in lieu of a limited monarchy, to deliver him over to a despotic one. How must we find his efforts and sacrifices abused and baffled if he may still, by a single vote, be laid prostrate at the feet of one man.

In God's name, from whence have they derived this power [he continued]? Is it from your ancient laws? None such can be produced.

Is it from any principle in our new Constitution, expressed or implied? Every lineament of that, expressed or implied, is in full opposition to it. . . . It provides a republican organization, proscribes under the name of prerogatives the exercise of all powers undefined by the laws. . . .

Or was this proposition moved on a supposed right, in the movers, of abandoning their posts in a moment of distress? The same laws forbid the abandonment of that post even on ordinary occasions; and much more a transfer of their powers into other hands and other forms without consulting the people. They never admit the idea that these, like sheep and cattle, may be driven from hand to hand without an appeal to their own will.

Was it from the necessity of the case? Necessities which dissolve a government do not convey its authority to an oligarchy or a monarchy. They throw back into the hands of the people the powers they had delegated and leave them, as individuals, to shift for themselves. A leader may offer, but not impose himself, nor be imposed by them. Much less can their necks be submitted to his sword, their breath to be taken at his will or caprice.

Referring, then, to the fact that the long series of military disasters in Rhode Island, Pennsylvania, New York, and New Jersey had brought no suggestion of the abandonment of free government for the tyranny of a dictatorship, Jefferson went on, with intense feeling:

In this State alone did there exist so little virtue that fear was to be fixed in the hearts of the people, and to become the motive of their exertions, the principle of their governing? The very thought alone was treason against the people; was treason against mankind in general, as riveting forever the chains which bow down their necks, by giving to their oppressors a proof, which they would have trumpeted throughout the universe, of the imbecility of republican governments in times of pressing danger. . . .

And how arrogant the expectations of the sponsors of a dictatorship!

Those who assume the right of giving away the reins of government in any case must be sure that the herd whom they hand on to the rods and hatchet of the dictator will lay their heads on the block when he shall nod to them. . . . What a cruel moment was this for creating such an embarrassment, for putting to the proof the attachment of our countrymen to republican government.

And whence, he asked, the inspiration of the outrageous plan?

Those who meant well, of the advocates of this measure — and most of them meant well, for I know them personally and had been their fellow laborer in the common cause, and had often proved the purity of their principles — had been seduced in their judgment by the example of an ancient republic, whose constitution and circumstances were fundamentally different. They had sought this precedent in the history of Rome, where alone it was to be found, and where at length, too, it proved fatal. They had taken it from a republic rent by the most bitter factions and tumults where the government was of a heavy-handed unfeeling aristocracy, over a people ferocious and rendered desperate by poverty and wretchedness. . . . Their constitution, therefore, allowed a temporary tyrant to be erected under the name of dictator; and that temporary tyrant, after a few examples, became perpetual.[41]

Nothing that Jefferson has passed down to his countrymen and the friends of liberty everywhere is of more priceless value than these observations, and nothing more vividly sets forth the political principles and philosophy that guided his life.

X

The movement for a dictatorship was abandoned. Since there is nothing in the published proceedings of the legislature to indicate

[41] *Notes on Virginia*, 131-34.

that the motion actually was made, it is reasonable to assume, as has happened in innumerable cases, that, for the sake of precaution, there had been a careful counting of noses before the formal presentation of the motion; and on the discovery that it would fail by a few votes, it was not submitted.

Bitterly opposed to any dictatorship, Jefferson was convinced that, since the problems of the gubernatorial office were then exclusively military, it would have a reassuring effect upon the people were a military man in office. He had given all possible co-operation to Muhlenberg and Steuben and to his local military officers, as they themselves attest, but he himself was not military-minded. Thus, putting aside the importunities of his friends, he announced his retirement at the end of his second term, after the failure of the dictatorship was certain, and it was on his suggestion that General Nelson was chosen.

In a letter to Washington, begging him to return to Virginia and assume personal command of the defending forces, Jefferson had announced his determination to retire. In replying, Washington had explained the reason for his delay in responding to the appeals that reached him from his own State. And in this letter taking leave of Jefferson in his official capacity, the great Commander left no doubt to historians of his estimate of Jefferson's services and his loyalty to him:

Give me leave, before I take leave of your Excellency in your public capacity to Express the obligations I am under for the readiness and zeal with which you have always forwarded and supported every measure which I have had occasion to recommend through you, and to assure you that I shall esteem myself honored by a continuation of your friendship and correspondence shou'd your Country permit you to remain in the private walk of life.[42]

XI

But Jefferson's complete co-operation in every detail with Washington's plan as Commander of all the Revolutionary forces had impelled many personal enemies, and others, stricken with panic, to turn upon him with abuse. He had raised money in Virginia to be

[42] Fitzpatrick, *Writings of Washington,* XX, 190.

sent elsewhere for the common cause — as Washington insisted. He had parted with the Virginia regulars that they might battle under Washington in the defense of other colonies — as Washington wished. In days of imminent danger, he had raised militia and hurried them to the succor of Gates and Greene in the Carolinas — because Washington so desired. He had sent Virginia's military stores both North and South — because Washington thought it best.

But when the invasion came, and Virginia suffered from the lack of men, arms, money, and provisions, some turned upon him with abuse.

Thus it came about that the overemphasized motion of inquiry in the legislature was proposed. Every man who had lost a cow or pig through the invaders was prone to hold Jefferson personally responsible. And everyone in Virginia, who hated him for the enlightened reforms he so brilliantly had sponsored a little while before, saw an opportunity to vent their hate. And every ambitious politician who resented his popularity joined the pack. And so loud was the barking of the pack when it thought it had him down that a few well-meaning and honest men were impressed. Thus it was that some personal enemies and shyster politicians took advantage of the youth and inexperience of George Nicholas, a member of the House from Jefferson's own county, to have him submit some questions and to propose an inquiry. That no one took them seriously, as some anti-Jeffersonian historians have taken them a century and a half later, is proved by the event.

None of these historians have undertaken to explain why at this very moment the 'discredited' Jefferson was asked by his countrymen to go to Europe on a vitally important diplomatic mission. He instantly rejected the application with the explanation that he would remain in Virginia and have it out with his critics, man to man.

When the legislature met in December, he was there of his own volition. It was his enemies, and not he, who were embarrassed. They were quite eager to forget the motion of inquiry — but Jefferson was not. He rose in his place and announced that he was there to meet the charges, to face his accusers, and to give his answers.

Intimidated by his mere presence, these accusers stood mute.

No one rose.

No one uttered a word.

And then Jefferson made it plain that he insisted on the inquiry. And since no one had the courage even to read the charges, he himself read them as a reminder of what they had proposed. One by one he read them and gave his unanswerable reply.

When he had concluded, he stood in silence for some response from those who had fathered the motion against him. And Nicholas himself sat immovable in his chair. His critics had no stomach for a fight. Silent and apparently ashamed, no one spoke. No one asked a single question.

And the only thing done by the legislature in this much-flaunted 'impeachment' was the immediate unanimous passing, in both houses, of a motion expressing the gratitude of the Commonwealth for the services Jefferson had rendered.

That all this cut to the heart the too sensitive Jefferson there can be no doubt. But he was to be fair to those who had hurt him most. In commenting on the incident of the inquiry later, he described young Nicholas as 'then a very young man, but always a very honest one,' who had been prompted by more cowardly and mature persons in the background to sponsor the charges. It is not remarkable that soon afterward, the young man who was 'always a very honest one' most conspicuously, of his own free will, retracted everything and made reparations like the gentleman he was. Thereafter, he was one of Jefferson's most faithful friends and followers.

XII

Jefferson's term had expired in the midst of the most serious invasion of the war, which he had foreseen and foretold to Washington. Soon thereafter the entire complexion of things changed in Virginia, but through no action of his successor, as a distinguished English historian appears to have thought. The French arrived in force. The French fleet drew up in the Virginia waters. And Washington himself, with his army, bearing arms that had been sent from Virginia to the North and with Virginia regulars who had been sent to the assistance of other States, marched into the State. We have seen that Jefferson had urged him to do so just before his retirement, and Washington, while realizing the need, had written him the reason he could not do so at the moment. Now the reason had passed — and Jefferson's successor had nothing to do with it. The great Commander returned. The French landed and put themselves in battle formation. And at Yorktown, a short time after Jefferson's term expired, Cornwallis handed his sword to Washington and the independence of America was achieved.

But Henry Lee, a disappointed and sour man, and certainly no friend of Jefferson's, attacked him in his *Memoirs* along the lines indicated, though he himself was not in Virginia at the time and was not familiar with the circumstances there. Years later, when Lee's son was preparing a second edition of his father's *Memoirs,* he wrote Jefferson, who replied that were his father living then he undoubtedly would revise that portion of his *Memoirs.*

'He was then, I believe, in South Carolina, too distant from the scene of these transactions to relate them of his own knowledge, or even to sift them from the chaff of the rumors then afloat,' he wrote. He suggested that if Lee would visit him at Monticello, where all the papers and the letters of Washington, Gates, Greene, and Steuben were kept, they would be put unreservedly at his service.

Nothing in his life reflects so luminously the loyalty and sense of honor which were Jefferson's as his refusal to pass responsibility to any other men. He might have produced the letters of Washington to prove that it was his policy — and a wise one in the long run — to denude the State of men and arms to serve the broader interest, but he remained silent about the letters. He might easily have complained that, after he had made every exertion to send men and arms, ultimately needed for the defense of Virginia, to the aid of Greene in the Carolinas, to the end that he might hold back the invasion, the General left Virginia to her fate to occupy himself and his men in the retaking of the Carolinas — but here, again, not one word of reproach. He might have put responsibility on Steuben, to whom Washington so largely had entrusted the defense, or on Nelson, whom he had placed in command with full powers, but evidently this did not occur to him.

But his resentment of the gross unfairness of the attacks remained, and when even some historians began to point to the capture of the utterly indefensible village of Richmond as an unbearable humiliation reflecting on Jefferson, he wrote, in the latter days of his life:

> Which of our capitals during the war was not in possession of the same enemy, not merely by surprise and for a day only, but permanently? That of Georgia? Of South Carolina? North Carolina? Pennsylvania? New York? Connecticut? Rhode Island? Massachusetts?

History answers.

Under the circumstances it is surprising that the great English historian, Trevelyan, in his otherwise fair history of the Revolution should have accepted the flimsy opinions of Lee, a personal enemy who was remote from the scene, and have attacked Jefferson and praised Nelson his successor, as though the event at Yorktown had any connection with any activities of the latter.

It is not remarkable, therefore, that, after his sweeping vindication by the legislature, Jefferson should have carried some disgust with public life into his retirement at Monticello.

THOMAS JEFFERSON
From the painting by Mather Brown

GOVERNOR FRANCIS FAUQUIER

GEORGE WYTHE

MAIN BUILDING
WILLIAM AND MARY COLLEGE

HOUSE OF BURGESSES
(*Restored*)

RALEIGH TAVERN, WILLIAMSBURG

RICHARD HENRY LEE

PATRICK HENRY

EDMUND PENDLETON

BENJAMIN HARRISON

GOVERNOR'S PALACE, WILLIAMSBURG
(*Restored*)

JOHN DICKINSON

for abolishing our most valuable Laws

for taking away our charters & altering fundamentally the forms of our governments

for suspending our own legislatures & declaring themselves invested with power to legislate for us in all cases whatsoever

he has abdicated government here, [withdrawing his governors & declaring us out of his allegiance & protection]

he has plundered our seas, ravaged our coasts burnt our towns & destroyed the lives of our people:

he is at this time transporting large armies of foreign mercenaries to compleat the works of death, desolation & tyranny already begun with circumstances of cruelty & perfidy unworthy the head of a civilized nation

he has endeavored to bring on the inhabitants of our frontiers the merciless Indian savages, whose known rule of warfare is an undistinguished destruction of all ages, sexes, & conditions [of existence]

[he has incited treasonable insurrections of our fellow-citizens with the allurements of forfeiture & confiscation of our property.

he has waged cruel war against human nature itself, violating it's most sacred rights of life & liberty in the persons of a distant people who never offended him, captivating & carrying them into slavery in another hemisphere, or to incur miserable death in their transportation thither. this piratical warfare, the opprobrium of infidel powers, is the warfare of the Christian king of Great Britain. determined to keep open a market where MEN should be bought & sold he has prostituted his negative for suppressing every legislative attempt to prohibit or to restrain this execrable commerce: and that this assemblage of horrors might want no fact of distinguished die, he is now exciting those very people to rise in arms among us, and to purchase that liberty of which he has deprived them, by murdering the people upon whom he also obtruded them: thus paying off former crimes committed against the liberties of one people, with crimes which he urges them to commit against the lives of another]

in every stage of these oppressions we have petitioned for redress in the most humble terms: our repeated petitions have been answered only by repeated injuries. a prince whose character is thus marked by every act which may define a tyrant, is unfit to be the ruler of a [free] people [who mean to be free.] future ages will scarce believe that the hardiness of one man, adventured within the short compass of twelve years only, to build a foundation so broad & undisguised, for tyranny over a people fostered & fixed in principles of freedom]

FACSIMILE OF JEFFERSON'S FIRST DRAFT OF THE DEC-
LARATION OF INDEPENDENCE CONTAINING HIS STATE-
MENT ON SLAVERY

SHIPPEN HOUSE, PHILADELPHIA

CARPENTERS' HALL, PHILADELPHIA

COMTE DE VERGENNES

THOMAS JEFFERSON
By Jean-Antoine Houdon

MARIA COSWAY

MONTICELLO

SHADOWS ON AN IVORY TOWER

I

JEFFERSON was now able to realize his cherished desire for retirement at Monticello, but the serenity of spirit to which he had looked forward was to be denied him. His musical, philosophical, and conversational friends among the Saratoga prisoners, with whose merry company he had been wont to regale himself two years before, were no longer among his neighbors, for he had sent them posthaste across the Blue Ridge. He was growing more and more apprehensive about the health of his wife. And very soon after his return to his loved hilltop, when engaged in his favorite recreation astride his horse, he was violently thrown, and so serious were his injuries that he was confined to the house for several weeks. His account book of this period shows that for two calls from his physician he had paid six hundred pounds — so low had American money fallen!

But it was not in his nature to remain idle. A congenial task suggested itself. Some time before, the Marquis de Marbois, of the French Legation, who, years later, was to be intimately associated with Jefferson's negotiations for the purchase of Louisiana,[1] had appealed to him for information regarding Virginia. The Frenchman had submitted many questions pertaining to the ancient Dominion, and Jefferson, with characteristic thoroughness and with no thought that his answers would ever be seen by any eye other than that of the Marquis, worked zealously and enthusiastically on

[1] See author's *Jefferson in Power.*

the manuscript which ultimately was to appear under the title of *Notes on Virginia*.[2] There is nothing to indicate that Jefferson, who found so much solace in his library, entertained any aspirations to literary fame. His work as a writer had been confined to political polemics.

But when the request of the Marquis reached him, it found him not unprepared. For years, with his passion for facts and his love of the Old Dominion, he had written down, from time to time, rough notes concerning his native State — notes covering every imaginable subject, botanical, historical, geological, geographic, political, and everything concerning animal life and birds, flowers, and plants. The request of Marbois, coming at a moment of enforced idleness, offered the opportunity to assemble these voluminous jottings and whip them into literary shape. Thus, owing to an accident and his consequent confinement to the house, the notes were to be put into literary form and finally, though quite by chance, were to be published as a book.

This work is of interest to the student of Jefferson, not only because it was his first and only essay in authorship, but because it reveals so much of the man himself, his interests and his opinions at this period. So unique and valuable was it at the time that it attracted wide attention and some controversy. But for the fact that a pirated edition, with an unsatisfactory translation, was about to be published in Paris, it is probable that it never would have reached the general public. In self-defense, the author was forced to print an authorized edition some years later. And, after a century and a half, it remains a work worth while. It is of importance to our purpose because, primarily, nothing is to be found in his fragmentary *Autobiography* that throws such an intimate light on his tastes, curiosities, and political and social opinions. Aside from the innumerable interesting facts assembled, the work had a number of purple patches worthy of the author of the *Summary View* and the Declaration of Independence. That these were written consciously with a view to literary distinction is entirely improbable. He wrote of things that interested him deeply and from his heart, and with no thought of the art of expression.

Among these purple patches must be mentioned his eloquent in-

[2] Letter to Madison; Ford, *Writings of Jefferson,* IV, 46-47.

lictment of a dictatorial form of government, quoted in the previous
hapter, his vivid descriptions of Virginia scenery, his observations
·n slavery, his reflections on the life and character of the Indians,
nd his salvaging from obscurity of the moving eloquence of
Logan, the Indian chief.

In his preface, written some years later, he tells us that the book
vas written in the year 1781, 'somewhat corrected and enlarged in
he winter of 1782, in answer to questions proposed to the author
·y a foreigner of distinction, then residing amongst us.' The sub-
.eads of the manuscript give an idea of the magnitude of his un-
.ertaking. They refer to boundaries, rivers, seaports, mountains,
nd cascades, to minerals, vegetables, and animal products, to cli-
nate and the nature of the population, to the military power of the
borigines, to counties and towns, to the constitution and the laws,
ɔ colleges, buildings, and roads, to the proceedings of the Tories,
ɔ religion and manners, to manufactures and commerce, to weights,
neasures, and moneys, to public revenues and expenses, to histories,
nemorials, and State papers.

None of these subjects are treated lightly or superficially. The
.etails of the information given astound the reader, and all the
nore because the facts were gleaned from his notes alone.

Thus, in describing the Ohio River, the Mississippi and the Mis-
ouri, he records the length of each, the tributaries that feed them,
heir navigability, the fish in their waters, and the game that
bounded on their banks. To him, the Ohio, which he had never
·een but of which he had read everything available, was 'the most
·eautiful river on earth, its currents gentle, waters clear, and bosom
mooth . . . unbroken by rocks or rapids, a single instance alone
xcepted.'[3]

While the author is at his best in the more eloquent passages
lealing with his political philosophy, he is lively enough in his
lescriptions of scenery with which his own eye was familiar. An idea
·f his style may be gathered from one or two citations. Often men-
ioned, but seldom quoted, is his description of the passage of the
'otomac River through the Blue Ridge Mountains:

> The passage of the Potomac through the Blue Ridge is perhaps
> one of the most stupendous scenes in nature. You stand on a very

[3] *Notes on Virginia*, 8.

high point of land. On your right comes up the Shenandoah, having ranged along the foot of the mountain a hundred miles to seek a vent. On your left approaches the Potomac, in quest of passage, also. In the moment of their juncture, they rush together against the mountain, rend it asunder, and pass off to the sea. The first glance of this scene hurries our senses into the opinion that has been created in time, that the mountains were formed first, that the rivers began to flow afterwards; that in this place particularly they have been dammed up by the Blue Ridge Mountains, and have formed an ocean that filled the whole valley; that, continuing to rise, they have at length broken over in this spot, and have torn the mountain down from its summit to its base. The pile of rocks on each hand, but particularly on the Shenandoah, the evident marks of their disruption and evulsion from their beds by the most powerful agents of nature, corroborates the impression. But the distant finishing which nature has given to the picture is of a very different character. It is a true contrast to the foreground. It is as placid and delightful as that is wild and tremendous. For the mountains being cloven asunder, she presents to your eye through the cleft a small patch of smooth blue horizon at an infinite distance in the plain country, inviting you, as it were, from the riot and tumult roaring around, to pass through the breach and participate in the calm below. Here, the eye ultimately composes itself; and that way, too, the road happens actually to lead. You pass the Potomac above the junction, pass along its side along the base of the mountain for three miles, its terrible precipices hanging in fragments over you, and, within about twenty miles, reach Fredericktown and the fine country around.

This scene is worth a voyage across the Atlantic. Yet here, as in the neighborhood of the Natural Bridge, are people who have passed their lives within half a dozen miles, and have never been to survey these monuments of a war between rivers and mountains, which must have shaken the earth itself to its center.[4]

From youth, Jefferson had found nothing more fascinating than the famous Natural Bridge, to which, throughout his life, he was accustomed to conduct visitors to Monticello. Inevitably it found place in his chronicle:

Though the sides of this bridge are provided in some parts with a parapet of fixed rocks, yet few men have resolution to walk

4 *Ibid.*, 17-18.

them, and look over into the abyss. You involuntarily fall onto your hands and feet, creep to the parapet and peep over. Looking down from this height about a minute gave me a violent headache. If the view from the top be painful and intolerable, that from below is delightful in an equal extreme. It is impossible for the emotions, rising from the sublime, to be felt beyond what they are here; so beautiful an arch, so elevated, so light, and springing, as it were, up to heaven — the rapture of the spectator is really indescribable.[5]

II

In none of Jefferson's writings do his admiration and sympathy for the Indians appear so convincingly. His interest had been keen from his childhood, when the red men's chiefs frequently paused for refreshments at his father's house. He made a study of their vocabularies, their customs, their character, their history and origin.

In the *Notes,* he presents an interesting theory as to their derivation. He was sure that even in ancient times, with their imperfect navigation, it had been possible and practical for Americans to have communicated with the Old World by water. 'In going from Norway to Iceland, from Iceland to Greenland, from Greenland to Labrador, the first traject is the widest,' he wrote, 'and this having been practiced from earliest times of which we have any account . . . it is not difficult to suppose that the subsequent trajects may have been sometimes passed.' Then, too, 'the late discoveries of Captain Cook, coasting from Kamchatka to California,' had shown that the continents of Asia and America, if separated at all, had been by a narrow strait. 'So that from this side, also, inhabitants may have passed into America,' he concluded, 'and the resemblance between the Indians of America and the eastern inhabitants of Asia would induce us to conjecture that the former are the descendants of the latter, or the latter of the former.' How unfortunate, he thought, that the vocabularies of some of the Indian tribes had been permitted to become extinct. 'Had these been collected and preserved, it might have been possible for scholars to have gotten a very good idea of the derivatives of this part of the human race.'[6]

More amusing is the polemic vigor with which the author rushes to his attack on de Buffon, the famous French naturalist, whose

[5] *Ibid.,* 21-23.   [6] *Ibid.,* 103-04.

world reputation at that time has suffered somewhat in the intervening years. The naturalist, who had never seen the American
red man, had made much of his theory that the Indians were less
ardent and more impotent with their females than the whites.

> I am able to say in contradiction of this representation [countered
> Jefferson] that he is neither more defective in ardor, nor more im-
> potent with his female than the white, reduced to the same diet and
> exercise; that he is brave when an enterprise depends on bravery,
> education with him making the point of honor consist in the de-
> struction of an enemy by stratagems, and in the preservation of his
> own person free from injury; or, perhaps, this is nature, while it is
> education which teaches us to honor force more than finesse. [At
> any rate, Jefferson declared], he will defend himself against a host
> of enemies, always choosing to be killed rather than surrender,
> though it be to the whites who he knows will treat him well; that
> in other situations also he meets death with more deliberation, and
> endures torture with a firmness unknown almost to religious en-
> thusiasm with us; that he is affectionate to his children, careful
> of them and indulgent in the extreme; that his affections compre-
> hend his other connections, weakening, as with us, from circle to
> circle as they recede from the center; that his friendships are strong
> and faithful to the uttermost extremity; that his sensibility is keen,
> even the warriors weeping most bitterly on the loss of their children,
> though in general they endeavor to appear superior to human
> events; that his vivacity and activity of mind is equal to ours on
> the same situation — hence his eagerness for hunting and for
> games of chance.[7]

Inspired by his enthusiasm for the red man, he hurries on to a
description of their oratory, citing the pathetic protest of Logan, the
red chief, whose family had been wantonly exterminated by the
white man's cruelty:

> I may challenge the whole orations of Demosthenes and Cicero
> . . . to produce a single passage superior to the speech of Logan, the
> Mingo chief, to Lord Dunmore, then Governor of the State. And
> as testimony of their talents I beg leave to introduce it, first stating
> the incidents necessary to understand it.
>
> In the spring of the year 1774, a robbery was committed by some
> Indians on certain land adventurers on the river Ohio. The whites,

[7] *Ibid.*, 61.

in that quarter, according to their custom, undertook to punish this outrage in a summary way. Captain Michael Cresap, and a certain Daniel Greenhouse, leading on these parties, surprised, at different times, traveling and hunting parties of the Indians having their women and children with them, and murdered many. Among these unfortunates were the family of Logan, a chief celebrated in peace and war, and long distinguished as a friend of the whites. This unworthy return provoked his vengeance. He accordingly signalized himself in the war which ensued. In the autumn of the same year, a decisive battle was fought at the mouth of the Great Kanhaway, between the collected forces of the Shawnees, Mingoes, and Delawares, and a detachment of the Virginia militia. The Indians were defeated, and sued for peace. Logan, however, disdained to be among the suppliants. But lest the value of a treaty from which so distinguished a chief absented himself should be disturbed, he sent by a messenger the following speech to Lord Dunmore:

'I appeal to any white man to say if ever he entered Logan's cabin hungry, and he gave him not meat; if ever he came cold and naked, and he clothed him not. During the course of the last long and bloody war, Logan remained idle in his cabin, an advocate for peace. Such was my love for the whites that my countrymen pointed as they passed and said: "Logan is the friend of the white man."

'I have even thought to have lived with you, but for the injuries of one man, Colonel Cresap, who, the last spring, in cold blood, and unprovoked, murdered all the relations of Logan, not even sparing my women and children. There lives not a drop of my blood in the veins of any living creature. This called on me for revenge. I have sought it; I have killed many; I have fully glutted my vengeance. For my country I rejoice at the beams of peace. But do not harbor a thought that mine is the joy of fear. Logan never felt fear. He will not turn on his heel to save his life. Who is there to mourn for Logan? — no one.' [8]

Fifteen years after Jefferson wrote the shameful story of the murder of Logan's children, and eleven years after the publication of the *Notes*, he was ferociously assailed in the scurrilous columns of *Porcupine's Gazette* by Luther Martin, demanding the author's authority, in behalf of 'two amiable daughters' of Cresap. This

[8] *Ibid.*, 65-66.

was in the midst of the most bitter political struggle America has known, and Martin was a virulent Federalist enemy of Jefferson. Since the letter clearly was written for political purposes and not out of tenderness for the 'amiable daughters,' Jefferson ignored it, and Martin wrote a second letter more abusive than the first, which was also ignored.[9] But later, on the publication of a new edition of the *Notes,* under Jefferson's own supervision, many pages of the appendix were devoted to the printing of affidavits and letters of eye-witnesses to the murder of the Logan children.

III

Nor was this the only instance in the *Notes* in which the author was to find himself involved in controversy. We have seen him, with lance fixed, rushing upon the then sacred de Buffon in defense of the red man. He was probably one of the very few Americans entirely familiar with the works of the French naturalist, whom he admired, because, as he wrote, 'I think him the best informed of any naturalist who has ever written.' Notwithstanding his admiration, he not only challenged de Buffon's ideas about the red men, but other *ex-cathedra* statements as well.

The Frenchman had written that in the case of animals known to both the Old World and the New, they were smaller in the New. He attempted to explain this on the theory that the heat in America is less intense than in Europe, and that more water was spread over the American continent and less drained off by the hand of man; and he asserted that heat is conducive to the production of large animals, and water is adverse.

To this Jefferson replies:

> I will not meet this hypothesis on the first doubtful ground, whether the climate of America is comparatively more humid . . . because we are not furnished with observations sufficient to decide this question. . . . The hypothesis, after this supposition, proceeds to another — that moisture is unfriendly to animal growth. The truth of this is inscrutable to us by reasoning, *a priori*. Nature has hidden from us her *modus agendi*. Our only appeal on such questions is to experience; and I think that experience is against the

[9] See author's *Jefferson and Hamilton,* 352.

supposition. It is by the assistance of heat and moisture that vegetables are elaborated from the elements of earth, air, water, and
fire. We accordingly see the more humid climates produce the
greater quantity of vegetables. Vegetables are mediately and immediately the food of every animal; and in proportion to the quantity of food, we see the animals not only multiplied in their numbers, but improved in their bulk as far as the laws of their nature
will admit.

To bear out this reasoned statement, Jefferson then submits a
long table of animals common to both continents, setting forth their
weight in contradiction to the fanciful assertions of de Buffon. The
author was to carry this controversy with the French savant, then
the fashion of the salons of Paris, to great lengths, basing his arguments on science, common sense, and observation; and a little later,
when he was Minister in France, we-shall find Jefferson confronting
the French naturalist with positive proof of the incorrectness of his
theories. Commenting on his table of animals and their weights,
he points out that the tables showed eighteen quadrupeds peculiar to
Europe and seventy-four peculiar to America, and that the first of
the seventy-four American animals weighed more than the whole
column of the European.[10]

The controversy thus early begun with de Buffon carried no
animosity, since Jefferson, in keeping with the fashion of the time,
placed a very high estimate on his genius as a naturalist.

But he was less tolerant with Abbé Raynal, another Frenchman,
who was prone to belittle the Americans. Was it not true, asked
the Abbé with a sneer, that America had not produced a poet or
a great name in science or mathematics?

> When we shall have existed as a people as long as the Greeks
> did before they produced a Homer, the Romans a Virgil, the French
> a Racine or Voltaire, the English a Shakespeare or Milton, should
> this reproach be still true, we will inquire from what unfriendly
> cause it has proceeded [replied Jefferson]. . . . In war we have pro-
> duced a Washington whose memory will be adored while liberty
> shall have votaries, whose name will triumph over time, and will
> in future ages assume its just station among the most celebrated
> worthies of the world, when that wretched philosophy shall be

10 *Ibid.*, 56.

forgotten which would have arraigned him among the degenerate of nature. In physics, we have produced a Franklin, than whom no one of the present age has made more important discoveries, or has enriched philosophy with more, or more ingenious solutions of the phenomena of nature. We had supposed Mr. Rittenhouse second to no astronomer living; and in genius he must be the first, because he is self-taught. He has not, indeed, made a world; but he has, in imitation, approached nearer its Maker than any man who has lived from the creation to this day. As in philosophy and war, we might show that America, though but a child of yesterday, has already given hopeful proof of genius, as well of the nobler kinds which arouse the best feelings of man, which call him into action, which substantiate his freedom, and conduct him to happiness. . . . We therefore suppose that this reproach is unjust as it is unkind; and that of the geniuses that adorn the present age, America contributes her full share.[11]

To the names of Washington, Franklin, and Rittenhouse, another writer might have added the name of the close friend of the three, inferior in genius to none — the name of the author of the *Notes,* the philosopher of democracy that was to permeate a large section of Europe, pre-eminent among all the democratic thinkers of his age.

IV

No student of the *Notes* can fail to be impressed with the author's very conclusively set forth repugnance to the institution of slavery. Writing as he was for the eyes of a foreigner, it is not unnatural that he should have sought to palliate the evil. He certainly, and with justification, placed on England her full share of responsibility in the establishment and continuance of the slave system of labor. He notes that at one time, under the Royal Government, a law had been enacted by the Virginia legislature which all but put a period to the importation of slaves, but under a previous King this law was repealed — a repeal that 'met a joyful sanction from the then sovereign.' Never afterward, under the Royal Government, had it been possible to re-enact the law, though the attempt was made in almost every session of the legislature.

11 *Ibid.,* 67-69.

But, he adds, 'in the very first session under the republican government, the Assembly passed a law for the perpetual prohibition of the importation of slaves.' And this, he thought, would 'in some measure stop the increase of this great political and moral evil, while the minds of our citizens may be ripening for the complete emancipation of human nature.' [12]

Returning to slavery later in his book, Jefferson declared the system destructive, not only of the morals of the people, but of their industry. 'For in a warm climate,' he wrote, 'no one will labor for himself who can make another labor for him.' So true this is, he added, that of the proprietors of slaves 'a very small proportion, indeed, are ever seen to labor.' And then he concluded with the most fervent declaration against the slave system that was ever to emanate from him:

> And can the liberties of a nation be thought secure when we have removed their only firm basis, a conviction in the minds of the people that these liberties are of the gift of God? That they are not to be violated but with his wrath? Indeed I tremble for my country when I reflect that God is just; that his justice cannot sleep forever; that considering numbers, nature, and natural means only, a revolution of the wheels of fortune, an exchange of situation, is among possible events; and that it may become probable by supernatural interference.

Even as he wrote, he might, from his windows, have seen slaves toiling and many singing about Monticello, all of them devoted to the master who felt for them and yet did not set them free. Jefferson was a practical man, not a mere theorist as his political critics would have us think, and he knew that nothing could be achieved by the freeing of a few slaves who were treated as human beings by humane masters. He looked forward to the day of emancipation by consent:

> I think a change already perceptible since the origin of the present Revolution. The spirit of the master is abating, that of the slave rising from the dust, his condition mollifying, the way, I hope, preparing under the auspices of heaven for a total emanci-

[12] *Ibid.*, 93.

pation, and that this is disposed in the order of events to be with
the consent of the masters rather than by their extirpation.[13]

V

It is not surprising that into the *Notes* he wrote anew his view
on the relation of religion to the State, reiterating the opinions long
expressed, and formulated into a series of reforms in the legislature
His hostility to the combination of Church and State did not mean
a prejudice against either Catholicism or Protestantism. Indeed, his
fight in Virginia was to break the strangle-hold of the Church of
England on the liberties of the conscience. In the *Notes* he painted
a picture of the situation in Virginia which drove him into the
battle for religious liberty and toleration. He painted the picture in
heavy colors:

> The first settlers in this country were emigrants from England
> of the English Church, just at a point of time when it was flushed
> with complete victory over the religions of other persuasions. Pos
> sessed, as they became, of the powers of making, administering
> and executing the laws, they showed equal intolerance in this
> country with the Presbyterian brethren who had emigrated to the
> northern government. The poor Quakers were flying from perse
> cution in England. They cast their eyes on these new countries a
> asylums of civil and religious freedom; but they found them fre
> only for the reigning sect. Several acts of the Virginia Assembly in
> 1659, 1662, and 1693 had made it penal in parents to refuse to have
> their children baptized; had prohibited as unlawful the assembly
> ing of Quakers; had made it penal for any master of a vessel to
> bring a Quaker into the State; had ordered those already here, and
> such as should come thereafter, to be imprisoned until they should
> abjure the country; provided a milder punishment for their first
> and second return, but death for their third; had inhibited all per
> sons from suffering their meetings in or near their houses, enter
> taining them individually, or disposing of books which supported
> their tenets.

Such, indeed, was the law of religious intolerance, which, if not
rigidly enforced, had not, until a recent day, been repealed. Nor did
Jefferson give credit for the non-enforcement of these cruel law
to a spirit of toleration.

[13] *Ibid.*, 169-71.

'If no executions took place here,' he wrote, 'as did in New England, it was not owing to the moderation of the Church or the
spirit of the legislature, as may be inferred from the law itself; but
to historical circumstances which have not been handed down to
us.'

These circumstances, as he described them, were, that while the
Anglicans remained in full possession of the country for a century,
the 'other opinions began to creep in,' and the governmental support
of the Established Church had 'begotten an equal degree of indolence in its clergy,' and 'two thirds of the people had become
dissenters at the commencement of the present Revolution.' The
laws remained, barbarous as they were, but the Anglicans had taken
on moderation and the dissenters 'had risen to a degree of determination which commanded respect.'

Thence Jefferson, the author, went on to state his own opinion of
religious bigotry and persecution in a paragraph which stands among
the finest ever traced by his pen:

> The rights of conscience we never submitted, we could not sub-
> mit. We are answerable for them to our God. The legitimate
> powers of government extend to such acts only as are injurious to
> others. But it does me no injury for my neighbor to say there are
> twenty gods or no God. It neither picks my pocket nor breaks
> my leg. If it be said his testimony in a court of justice cannot be
> relied on, reject it then, and be the stigma upon him. Constraint
> may make him worse by making him a hypocrite, but it will never
> make him a truer man. It may fix him obstinately in his errors, but
> will not cure them. Reason and free inquiry are the only effectual
> agents against error. It is error alone which needs the support of
> government. Truth can stand by itself.[14]

VI

Since nothing impressed Jefferson as more important in the
amelioration of the condition of man or in the preservation of his
rights and liberty than an enlightened citizenry, it was inevitable
that in his *Notes*, written for a foreigner, he should have set forth
in detail the educational system he had proposed for Virginia. But
more important, in the illumination of his political philosophy, are

[14] *Ibid.*, 166-67.

his comments on the necessity for popular education among a democratic people:

> History, by apprising them of the past, will enable them to judge of the future. It will avail them of the experience of other nations and other times; it will qualify them as judges of the actions and designs of men; it will enable them to know ambition under every disguise it may assume; and, knowing it, to defeat its views. In every government on earth is some trace of human weakness, some germ of corruption and degeneracy which cunning will discover and wickedness insensibly open, cultivate, and improve. Every government degenerates when trusted to the rulers of the people alone. The people themselves, therefore, are its own safe depositaries. And to render even them safe, their minds must be improved to a certain degree.

VII

In his discussions of international relationships, commerce, and war, it must be borne in mind that he was writing for the latter days of the eighteenth century, and some of his observations, while true then, are not so true now that modern invention has wiped out distance. He shared all civilized men's hatred of war, but he was not so unmindful of human weaknesses as to cherish the belief that his country would escape it altogether. Even so, he said, 'it should be our endeavor to cultivate the peace and friendship of every nation, even of that which has injured us most, when we shall have carried our point against her.' In the cultivation of civilized relationships he proposed that we should 'throw open the doors of commerce, and knock off all its shackles, giving perfect freedom to all persons for the vent of whatever they may choose to bring into our ports, and asking the same of theirs.'

No one has stated the case against war more persuasively than the author of the *Notes* when he says:

> Never was so much false arithmetic employed on any subject as that which has been employed to persuade nations that it is to their interest to go to war. Were the money which it has cost, to gain, at the close of a long war, a little town, a little territory, the right to cut wood here, or to catch fish there, expended in improving what

they already possess, in making roads, opening rivers, building ports, improving the arts, and finding employment for their idle poor, it would render them much stronger, much wealthier and happier.

Consequently, he could see little need for a land army of any size in America, since it would be worthless for offense, so far removed from a probable foe; and, because of our isolation, it seemed little likely to him that we should have much occasion to use it for defense. Our troubles, he thought, would come on the ocean, because on that element our vessels would come into closer contact with possible rivals and foes. To abandon the ocean, however, would be repugnant to the American people, who were wedded to commerce. 'The habits of our citizens attach them to commerce,' he wrote. 'They will exercise it for themselves. Wars, then, must sometimes be our lot, and all the wise can do will be to avoid that half of them which would be produced by our own follies and our own acts of injustice; to make for the other half, the best preparations we can.' [15]

Thus early, Jefferson began to attach importance to the creation of an American navy.

VIII

Such were the political views set forth by Jefferson in the serenity of his closet in his *Notes,* written on the request of the Marquis de Marbois for information of a different nature. The questions propounded by the Marquis called for the writing of a veritable encyclopedia of facts, and these were answered in minute detail. Here we have all that could have been said at the time on Virginia's mineral resources, gold, copper, coal, marble, lime, stone, along with descriptions of the mines and their locations; here are pages given over to the names of all the trees and plants of the Old Dominion, with both the Latin or botanical names and the native names, to the end that the foreigner might have 'precise information'; [16] and here, minutely and at great length, under the subject heads, is set forth all the outstanding events of Virginia history

[15] *Ibid.,* 182-83.
[16] *Ibid.,* 35.

from the time of the discovery to the hour that Jefferson's pen passed over the paper in his study.

Because of the frankness of his statement, it was inevitable that parts of the book would prove provocative. We have seen his controversy with de Buffon, and we shall see it continued a little later in Paris; we have noted the attacks of Luther Martin because of his introduction of the speech of Logan; but he was to be solemnly attacked later on from the pulpits of reactionary Federalist preachers as an enemy of Christianity because he had dared express some doubt as to the story of the universal flood. We can imagine his political enemies, in the bitter political struggle that culminated in Jefferson's election to the Presidency,[17] poring over the *Notes on Virginia* in search of material to be used against him. The Federalist politicians in the pulpit found it: Jefferson was an infidel! He was an enemy of Christianity! For he was not convinced that the rocks on the top of the Virginia mountains were proof of the universal flood in which Noah played his part!

A few days before the election of 1800, the Reverend Doctor John Mason, a fashionable political preacher in New York, would publish a pamphlet based on the *Notes* entitled, *A Voice of Warning to Christians on the Ensuing Election*. He would cite the skepticism of Jefferson regarding the universal flood, and triumphantly exclaim: 'Christians. It is thus that a man whom you are expected to elevate to the chief magistracy insults yourself and your Bible.' The reverend, if not revered, clergyman smote Jefferson hip and thigh on every subject and reached a climax of stupidity with the words: 'Send us, if Thou wilt, murrain upon our cattle, a famine upon our land, cleanness of teeth in our borders; send us pestilence to waste our cities; send us, if it pleases Thee, the sword to bathe itself in the blood of our sons, but spare us, Lord God Most Merciful, spare us that curse.'

Straining himself with his screaming, the blood gushed from the speaker's nose, and when his handkerchief was wet and red, he waved it as a bloody banner against the irreverent author of the *Notes*.

But God ignored the preacher's bloody appeal, and, after a century and a half, Jefferson's one book is still read, even by Christians,

[17] See author's *Jefferson and Hamilton*, 352-53.

and it remains a classic. He had set himself to the task of merely furnishing de Marbois with answers to his questions, but, in his enthusiasm, he had gone far afield, and set forth his views on politics, religion, science, education, and philosophy. Even so, he had no thought of appearing in the rôle of an author or of publishing for a general distribution. But he toyed with the idea of sending copies to his political friends and to the students of William and Mary. Three years after the completion of his task and while in Paris, he asked Madison to read the *Notes* and advise him as to the wisdom of following this impulse. Should he find nothing objectionable, Jefferson would send copies to the students. 'Otherwise, I shall only send over a few copies to particular friends in confidence, and burn all the rest,' he wrote. 'Do not view me as an author and attached to what he has written,' he added. 'I am neither. They were at first intended only for Marbois. When I had enlarged them I thought first of giving copies to three or four friends. I have since supposed they might set our young students into a useful train of thought, and in no event do I propose to admit them to go to the public at large.'[18]

We shall find later, in the chapters on his life in Paris, the circumstances which forced him to release the *Notes* for general circulation.

IX

While Jefferson, by no means idle as we have seen, was writing his *Notes,* he had not sunk into the oblivion and neglect that Doctor Eckenrode would have us believe in his hostile chapter in his book on *The Revolution in Virginia,* which he captions 'The Fall of Jefferson.' The very month of his retirement from the governorship, in disgrace, as the author would have us believe, he had been summoned by his countrymen to proceed to Europe as one of the plenipotentiaries in the negotiations of peace. He would have declined in any case because of his wife's delicate state of health, but nothing could have forced him to leave Virginia until he had faced his foes in the legislature, met the inane charges conceived by malice, and secured the complete vindication that he did. From June until

18 Ford, *Writings of Jefferson,* IV, 46.

December, when the legislature met, he may be said literally to have slept on his arms.

That the Jefferson, 'sulking in his tent' as his enemies would have it, was neither morose nor adverse to company is evident in the graphic picture drawn of him in those days at Monticello by the pen of a distinguished and cultivated Frenchman, the Marquis de Chastellux, in his valuable two-volume work on his travels in America.

The Marquis had long had a standing invitation to be the guest of Jefferson at Monticello, 'in the center of the mountains.' But when the courtly Frenchman appeared, he was momentarily chilled, as all strangers were, by his host's first cold, penetrating look. 'I found his appearance serious, nay even cold,' he wrote, 'but before I had been two hours with him, we were as intimate as if we had passed our whole lives together.' We may be sure the visitor enjoyed the Jefferson table, which was always good and abundant, and the wines of his cellar, which were always choice. But he was to remember most pleasantly the long walks on which his host took him over the grounds and into the mountains, the long enthusiastic discussions of books, with the latest of which, from Paris and London, the host was as familiar as the guest, and the fascinating conversations, 'always varied and interesting.'

The Marquis, who knew the best minds in France, found that these conversations with the author of the Declaration of Independence were 'always supported by the sweet satisfaction experienced by two persons, who, on communicating their sentiments and opinions, are invariably in unison, and who understand each other at the first hint.' He was to find his four-day sojourn passing 'like so many minutes.' The conversations ranged over a vast field, for no American of his time, including Franklin, was so versatile. They talked philosophy, discussed politics of America and Europe, and art. And the Marquis was astonished to find that 'no object had escaped Mr. Jefferson, and it seemed as if from his youth he had placed his mind, as he had his house, on an elevated situation from which he might contemplate the Universe.'

Because his guest was interested in raising deer, Jefferson took him over the grounds and told him how he fed them corn and showed him how they approached him trustfully to eat the corn grains from his hand. 'I followed him one evening down a deep valley,' the Marquis wrote, 'where they are accustomed to assemble toward the close of day, and saw them walk, run, and bound'; and Jefferson was delighted with the Marquis's observation that he had not seen their counterpart in Europe.

The evenings found the host and guest in the library about a bowl of punch, in the candlelight, deep in animated conversation about their favorite writers. One night the conversation turned to the poems of Ossian, after Mrs. Jefferson had retired. Both flamed, for they shared in the common enthusiasm of their day.

Whether these poems were the fragmentary remains of the legendary Celtic bard of the third century, famous in Irish song and tradition, or whether James Macpherson, the alleged discoverer of the ancient manuscript, wrote the poems himself, is not important. It was the poems, whoever the author, that appealed. They had been published in 1761, nineteen years before Jefferson and the Marquis sat by the punchbowl in the light of candles. And nine years before, we have evidence of Jefferson's partiality for the poems in a letter he wrote to Charles Macpherson. 'I understand you were related to the gentleman of your name, Mr. James Macpherson, to whom the world is so much indebted for the elegant collection, arrangement, and translation of Ossian's poems,' he wrote. 'These pieces have been, and will, I think, continue to be to me the source of daily and exalted pleasures. The tender and sublime emotions of the heart were never before so wrought up by the human mind. I am not ashamed to own that I think the rude bard of the North the greatest poet that ever existed.' The young enthusiast confessed that merely to read the poems in their original form, he was eager to master the Celtic language. Could he be sent a catalogue of all the books published in Celtic, together with a grammar and dictionary? And would it be possible to purchase some of the original manuscript of the Ossian poems? 'I would not regard expense,' he wrote. 'The glow of one warm thought is to me worth more than money.' [19] Written three and a half years before Jefferson wrote the Declaration of Independence and in the year after his marriage, the nine intervening years had in no sense chilled his enthusiasm.

The mention of Ossian had revealed that the Marquis shared

19 Washington, *Writings of Jefferson*, I, 195-96.

Jefferson's admiration and affection for the poems. 'It was like a spark of electricity which passed rapidly from one to the other,' wrote the Marquis. Each recalled and quoted his favorite passages, and then, in the boyish enthusiasm of the moment, Jefferson sprang up to seek the volume among his books. The book was found. And far into the night, drinking punch the while, and by the light of the flickering candles, the two turned the pages of their favorite poet, rereading the lines they loved most, many of which Jefferson had previously quoted from memory, and commented upon. This is a Jefferson little known to history — the Jefferson of literary enthusiasms, remote from politics.

When, at length, the Marquis took his departure, only the fact that Mrs. Jefferson was expecting a child prevented Jefferson from accompanying him eighty miles to the Natural Bridge. However, he did go with his guest sixteen miles upon his way, and a pleasurable interlude in Jefferson's life was over.

When, on his return to Paris, the Marquis wrote his travel book, *Voyages dans l'Amérique,* in two volumes, which was widely read, he could find no one in America on whom to lavish such generous praise as on the master of Monticello.

X

The Frenchman made but a reference to the amiability of Mrs. Jefferson, who was then in delicate health. Jefferson had long been concerned about her, and not least among the reasons that had impelled his retirement from Congress some years before had been his anxiety about her health. He was constantly being importuned to return to public life, or, as his petitioners put it, 'to the service of his country.' To all these appeals he had been adamant. It was assumed by some who did not understand the domestic circumstances that he was moved to obstinacy by his natural resentment of the disgraceful treatment accorded him, through the instigation of his enemies, at the close of his administration as Governor. Even his closest friends, not actually on the scene, were puzzled and alarmed.

Thus, one day, Jefferson sat reading, not without emotion, a letter from Monroe. Jefferson had been his mentor and his idol. Not only had the man of Monticello directed his reading of the law, but of history and literature in general. Writing Washington a little later, Monroe had said that he had 'gone through the course which, in the opinion of Mr. Jefferson, to whom I submitted the direction of my studies,' was wise.[20] When Monroe had planned a visit to Europe a little before, he had written Jefferson for letters and advice as to where to go, and what to see. At this time he was living 'a very sedentary life upon a small estate in King George's in course of which [he] had read all the books [Jefferson] mentioned on the subject of law.'[21]

Knowing, as Jefferson did, the complete devotion and confidence of his disciple, he was deeply moved by the letter he was reading from the younger man.

> It is publicly said here [wrote Monroe from Richmond] that the people of your county informed you that they had frequently elected you in times of less difficulty and danger than the present, to please you, but that now they had called you forth into public life to serve themselves. This is a language which has been often used in my presence and you will readily conceive that, as it furnishes those who argue on the fundamental maxims of republican government with ample field for declamation, the conclusion has always been you should not decline the service of your country. The present is generally conceived to be an important era which, of course, makes your attendance particularly necessary.[22]

The reference here was to Jefferson's declination of a summons to return to Congress.

That Jefferson immediately replied to his friend, explaining the domestic situation and the condition of Mrs. Jefferson, is evident in another letter from Monroe:

> I have been much distressed upon the subject of Mrs. Jefferson, and I have feared, as much from what you have suggested yourself as what I have heard from others, that the report of each succeeding day would inform me that she was no more. Indeed, this was awhile reported and believed, but I flatter myself that in this instance I shall experience that common fame, who when she has propagated reports unfavorable to myself and my friends I have rarely found it to be groundless, has failed, and that it may please heaven to restore our amiable friend to health and thereby to you

20 Hamilton, *Writings of Monroe,* I, 19.
21 *Ibid.,* I, 13.   22 *Ibid.,* I, 15-16.

a friend whose loss you would always lament, and for the children a parent which no change of circumstance could ever compensate for. . . . I shall forbear to trouble you with an answer to that part of your letter with respect to your retreat from public service.[23]

It was at this time and under these circumstances that Jefferson's other disciple and follower, James Madison, was complaining; but, unlike the more direct Monroe, not to Jefferson himself. Writing Edmund Randolph, he said:

Great as my partiality is for Mr. Jefferson, the mode in which he seems determined to revenge the wrong received from his country does not appear to me to be dictated either by philosophy or patriotism. It augurs, indeed, a keen sensibility and a strong consciousness of rectitude. But this sensibility ought to be as great toward the relentings as the misdoings of the Legislature, not to mention the injustice of visiting the faults of this body on their innocent constituents.[24]

The two letters throw a white light on the relative characters of the two writers. Monroe would have been incapable of writing the Madison letter to another man; he would, as he did, write to Jefferson himself.

Edmund Randolph had the courage, on hearing this from Madison, to write, like Monroe, to Jefferson himself: 'If you can justify this resolution [to refuse public service] to yourself, I am confident you cannot to the world.'[25]

XI

But the illness of Mrs. Jefferson was not a subterfuge. After the birth of her sixth child, she sank rapidly, and, in anguish of spirit, Jefferson sat by her side as she drifted away. He scarcely left her bedside, and his daughter, in later years, recalled his devotion in a letter which throws a human light on his reluctance to serve his country at some distant point while his wife was dying. This letter is necessary to a complete comprehension of his character:

As a nurse, no female ever had more tenderness or anxiety. He nursed my poor mother in turn with Aunt Carr and her own sister, sitting up with her and administering her medicine and drinks to

[23] *Ibid.*, I, 17-19.   [24] Hunt, *Writings of Madison,* I, 207-08.
[25] Conway, *Omitted Chapters of History,* 43.

the last. For the four months that she lingered he was never out of calling; when not at her bedside, he was writing in a small room which opened immediately at the head of her bed. A moment before the closing scene he was led from the room in a state of insensibility by his sister, Mrs. Carr, who, with great difficulty, got him into the library, where he fainted, and remained so long insensible that they feared he would never revive. The scene that followed I did not witness, but the violence of his emotion, when, almost by stealth, I entered his room by night, to this day I dare not describe to myself. He kept his room three weeks and I was never from his side. He walked almost incessantly, night and day, only lying down occasionally, when nature was completely exhausted, on a pallet that had been brought in during his long fainting fit. My aunts remained constantly with him for some weeks. When, at last, he left his room, he rode out, and from that time he was incessantly on horseback, rambling about the mountains in the least frequented roads, and just as often through the woods. In those melancholy rambles I was his constant companion — a solitary witness to many bursts of grief.[26]

It was not until two months after Mrs. Jefferson's death in September, 1782, that he turned sadly to his neglected correspondence. Writing of his neglect to the Marquis de Chastellux, he said that the latter's letter had found him 'a little emerging from the stupor of mind which had rendered me as dead to the world as she whose loss occasioned it.' Before that event he had rested his hopes on a life of retirement, devoted to his family and to literary and scientific pursuits. 'A single event wiped away all my plans and left me a blank which I had not the spirit to fill in.'[27]

No one with ordinary human and decent instincts can possibly misunderstand Jefferson's determination to remain by his dying wife until the end.

XII

Because of his wife's condition, Jefferson had not only declined the appointment to France immediately after leaving the gubernatorial office, but also his selection as a representative of Virginia in Congress. After recovering from the shock of his wife's death, there no longer were any obligations of humanity to hold him in

26 Randolph, *Domestic Life of Jefferson*, 62-63.   27 *Ibid.*, 68.

Monticello, which for a time had become the melancholy mausoleum of memories. Visiting Monticello about this time, Mazzei wrote that 'the memory of his saintly late wife saddened me, and the solitude rendered my sorrow even more profound.' [28]

Thus, when again he was chosen by Congress to join Franklin, John Adams, and Jay in the negotiations of peace in Paris, he accepted.

He set forth at once for Philadelphia. He was to carry with him additional instructions for the negotiators, details of the financial plans given him orally by Robert Morris, and papers intended to establish the right of the new nation to the fisheries, to the western country, and to the navigation of the Mississippi.

With British ships hovering along the coast, his special problem was that of finding a conveyance to France. He puzzled over various plans. He could go to Boston and embark there, but he dreaded the roads and the December weather, and he had no assurance that after the journey's end he would find a ship. Or he could remain in Baltimore, whence he had gone from Philadelphia, and await a possible opportunity there; or he could go to Hampton and seek a vessel there. None of these plans seemed promising. There was one other plan considered — that of chartering a vessel and asking a flag from the enemy. He doubted if Congress would care to make the request, or, if made, that it would be granted, but he knew there were abundant precedents. If captured on the high seas, however, his papers would be confiscated and he arrested, and probably, after the experience of Laurens, he would be consigned to the Tower in London.

Thus he passed a miserable interval of waiting. As time went on, he realized that the emergency of the negotiations could hardly be served by him after the long delay. When word reached him that peace was about to be made, he wrote Congress setting forth his view of the inutility of the journey, and Congress acquiesced.

Thus, having lost much time under the most uncomfortable circumstances, he turned homeward, but he had scarcely reached Monticello when again his people summoned him to their service in Congress. This time he accepted the call.

Soon thereafter he was on his way to his new duties.

[28] Mazzei, *Memoirs*, 282.

CHAPTER

XIII

IN THE DRIVER'S SEAT

I

WHEN MADISON, who had been so distressed by his friend's stubborn retirement from public life, heard that Jefferson had been elected to Congress at the head of the poll, he wrote Edmund Pendleton, 'I am exceedingly pleased to find Mr. Jefferson's name at the head of the new delegation,' and 'I hope it has been placed there with his knowledge and acquiescence.'[1]

We have seen, what Madison apparently could not understand, that the failure to entice Jefferson back into public service was due in large measure to the rapidly failing health of his wife. Now she was dead, and even the beloved Monticello was haunted with her memory. His had been a crowded and dramatic life since their voices rang out in song on the frosty air over the snow-capped mountain on the night of their honeymoon. And now he welcomed a pretext temporarily to abandon the scenes that tortured him with a realization of what he had lost. He was eager to escape from grief.

But he was not returned to Philadelphia, the scene of his previous congressional labors. The country was in a state of demoralization, and the Government was unable to meet the arrears of the soldiers' pay. This so aroused their ire that when these soldiers, without occupation and without a penny in their pockets, met members of Congress in the Philadelphia streets, they greeted them roughly with indecorous salutations. To escape the importunities, and, most of all, the imprecations, of these neglected and indignant

[1] Burnett, *Letters*, VII, 190.

313

warriors, Congress had moved to Trenton, and there was some possibility that it might again establish the seat of government in the village of Princeton.

Living at this time in this charming little town, dominated by its famous university, was Madison, who was concerned lest his mentor be unable to find suitable lodgings, since previously members of Congress when there had been unable to 'be decently provided for'; and others in subordinate positions had been utterly without accommodations. 'I shall lose no time looking out for quarters for you and entering into provisional engagements in your favor,' he wrote Jefferson.[2] But when Jefferson's conveyance rolled down the rough road from Monticello, there had been no indication of a change from Trenton.

Leaving Monticello on October 16, 1783, jolting over the rutty roads and occasionally mounting his horse and riding for greater comfort, he reached Trenton on November 3. He had taken three weeks on the journey. When he took his seat the following day, it was only to hear the announcement that Congress would leave Trenton for Annapolis, where it would convene on the twenty-sixth. There was nothing to do but to turn back as philosophically as possible over the crude highway he had just traversed.

He took advantage of the opportunity, however, to visit his daughter, Martha, whom he had placed in school in Philadelphia. He was, henceforth, to administer to his daughter's needs with all the tenderness and understanding of a mother. Thence he drove on to Annapolis, the picturesque capital of Maryland, in time for the opening of Congress. But, alas, he was to find that delegations from enough States had not yet arrived for the transaction of business under the Articles of the Confederation. He was to have two weeks of leisure to meditate on the significance of this dangerous indifference.

Meanwhile, Monroe, who looked upon Jefferson as his guide, philosopher, and friend, had reached Annapolis as a member of the Virginia delegation. They immediately arranged to take quarters together. A democrat in his policies, Jefferson was an aristocrat in his personal tastes and habits, and he recoiled from the congestion and familiarities of a tavern; and, having delicate tastes in food, a

[2] Hunt, *Writings of Madison,* II, 19.

boarding-house table presented a prospect of horrors. Thus the two
friends, master and disciple, took quarters that would assure some
privacy. We may be sure that it was Jefferson who insisted on the
engagement of Partout, a French chef. Since Monroe was then
unable to speak French and Partout could not speak English, it fell
to Jefferson to interpret his friend's instructions as to the cooking
of his eggs.[3]

They settled down and waited, wonderingly and as patiently as
possible, for the tardy arrival of the indifferent delegations, without
whom nothing could be undertaken. On December 5, Jefferson
wrote Marbois that 'we have yet but four States in Congress,' but
he hoped when all were assembled 'to dispatch the most urgent and
important business.' He thought the indifference was due to the
jealousies engendered by the idea, 'which has unaccountably taken
possession of the heads' of the people, that Congress was to be a
permanent body.[4] Indeed, the disorganization and demoralization
following the termination of the war were all too evident. So long
as the soldiers were fighting in the field, the interest in Congress
was sustained, but now that the struggle was over and the personal
danger had passed, that body had lost both interest and prestige.
Some of the States actually were urging less frequent meetings,
which threatened the gradual disintegration of even the Confederation. With the peace treaty ready for ratification and with a time
limit on such action set, the delegates waiting in Annapolis took
alarm. Urgent letters were dispatched to the Governors of the delinquent States. There was nothing to be done but wait.

II

Happily, the Annapolis of those days was not an unpleasant
place for loitering. It was not without its gaiety, its dances and
dinners, and it boasted a society that was both wealthy and cultured.
Jefferson's distaste for the prosy, shapeless frame houses without
architectural charm or dignity did not suffer here, where the old
Maryland aristocracy had put some pride and taste into the construction of substantial brick dwellings. On an elevation in the

[3] Hamilton, *Writings of Monroe*, I, 24.
[4] Letters to Marbois, *American Historical Review*, XII, 75-77.

center of the town, an impressive State House had been built a decade before, and its pillared portico and white dome, rising to a height of two hundred feet, dominated the scene. Close by was the stately home of Jefferson's friend of Philadelphia days, Charles Carroll of Carrollton. And Jefferson could regale himself with profit in the homes where men of character and culture took an intelligent interest in post-war problems of the new nation in the making.

And we may be sure that, during his six months in Annapolis, Jefferson availed himself of the pleasures of the theater and the races. 'By Authority,' the Annapolis Theater was announcing its opening with 'a tragedy called "A Roman Father"' within a few weeks after Congress convened,[5] and there were concerts that were sometimes cancelled or postponed because the stagecoach from Baltimore delayed the arrival of the artists. Thus, we find 'Mr. Brown making his apologies to the ladies and gentlemen' who had purchased tickets, promising 'a complete concert as soon as he can get the necessary performers,' to which those who had bought tickets would be admitted free.[6] But no disappointments met the followers of the races, for the Jockey Club was a going concern. Within a month after Jefferson's arrival 'the Jockey Club purse of sixty guineas' was run, 'free for any horse, mare, or gelding, belonging to a member of the club.' The purse was subscribed by the members, who met the day before at Mann's Tavern and paid their money down. That young Jefferson and Monroe witnessed the race there can be little doubt.

Then, too, the tardiness of Congress gave Jefferson time for correspondence with his daughter, Martha, who probably needed advice and encouragement in her unaccustomed surroundings in Philadelphia. He was writing Marbois of his appreciation of the Frenchman's services in providing her with a French tutor. 'I left with her a *Gil Blas* and a *Don Quixote*,' he wrote. He explained his interest in extending her education because of 'the chance that in marriage she will draw a blockhead.'[7]

His relations with his young daughters were not least among the remarkable features of the man. He was to plan and critically

[5] *Maryland Gazette,* February 19, 1783.   [6] *Ibid.,* January 16, 1784.
[7] Letters to Marbois, *American Historical Review,* XII, 75-77.

follow their studies, and to do their most intimate shopping throughout their girlhood, to advise on their tastes and habits, and even in the selection of their gowns and bonnets. Though he had paid Martha a visit after leaving Trenton, two days after he reached Annapolis found him at his desk writing her of his safe arrival and suggesting a division of her time. From nine to ten she was to practice music; from ten until one she was to practice dancing one day and drawing the next; from one until two she was to draw on the days she danced or write a letter; from two to four she was to read French, and from five until bedtime, English. 'I expect you to write me every post,' he wrote. 'Inform me what books you read, what tunes you learn, and enclose me your best copy of every lesson in drawing. . . . Keep my letters and read them at times that you may always have present in your mind those things which will endear you to me.'[8]

This letter probably exists today in the archives of some royal palace of England, for years later, when Victoria was a princess and requested an autograph of the author of the Declaration of Independence, the American Chargé d'Affaires made her a present of it.

A little later, still waiting for the delinquent members of Congress, Jefferson found time to reassure his daughter, who had been frightened by gossip interpreting an earthquake as a sign that the world was about to end. He wrote her, a bit impatiently:

I hope you will have sense enough to disregard these foolish predictions that the world is to be at an end soon. The Almighty has never made known to anybody at what time He created it; nor will He tell anybody when He will put an end to it, if He ever means to do it. As for preparations for that event, the best way is for you always to be prepared for it. The only way to do so is never to do or say a bad thing. If ever you are about to say anything amiss, or do anything wrong, consider beforehand that you will feel something within you which will tell you it is wrong, and ought not to be said or done. This is your conscience, and be sure and obey it. Our Maker has given us all this faithful internal monitor, and if you always obey it, you will always be prepared for the end of the world, or for a much more certain event, death.[9]

[8] Randolph, *Domestic Life of Jefferson,* 69-70.   [9] *Ibid.,* 70-71.

III

It was not until the thirteenth of December that the representation of enough States had arrived for Congress to begin its work, which was to be of the first importance during the six months that Jefferson was to serve. The body was smaller than during the Revolutionary days in Philadelphia, and many of the more imposing figures of those times had retired to other fields. John Adams was in Europe, Samuel Adams was in Boston among his stalwarts, Franklin was in Paris surrounded by adoring dowagers, Patrick Henry was in Richmond with George Wythe, whom Jefferson had placed upon the bench. John Dickinson, for the moment in eclipse because of his policy of appeasement, had retired to the rural pleasures of his country home, and Joseph Galloway, who had deserted his country in a crisis to espouse the cause of the enemy, was living in England in reduced circumstances.

But there were a few of the earlier Congress in Annapolis. Elbridge Gerry, who had been the host of the youthful Jefferson on his first visit to New York and who would be a faithful friend and follower all his life, was a patriot of sound ability. Roger Sherman, of Connecticut, and Robert Morris, of Pennsylvania, also responded to the roll-call. But the majority were younger men, like Monroe. In such an assembly, no one could approach Jefferson in national prestige or in stature as a statesman or in finesse and courage as a leader. He instantly was accorded pre-eminence by common consent, and his work during these six months was to leave a permanent imprint on the national life and enter into the making of American history.

IV

Within a week after the opening of Congress, the little capital was deeply stirred by the arrival of George Washington. A few days before, it was 'requested of the gentlemen who have served in the American army, now in town, on the arrival of his Excellency, General Washington, to appear with their union cockades, in compliment to his Excellency and our great and good ally, Louis XVI.' [10] The great Commander had finished his work at

[10] *Maryland Gazette,* December 4, 1783.

the head of the army and was ready to return his commission. He had previously inquired whether it was the wish of Congress for him to make a formal written tender or to appear personally in audience. Since he had accepted the commission in audience, it was agreed that the same procedure should be followed in giving it up.

With a view to making the ceremony in keeping with the solemnity of the occasion, a committee, under the chairmanship of Jefferson, was appointed to arrange the program. The procedure Jefferson thought appropriate to the occasion and the man was to be one of dignified simplicity. Washington was to make his appearance in the State House Hall at high noon on December 23, 1783, after everyone had been seated. In surrendering his commission, he was to speak briefly, and the President of the Congress was to make a brief and appropriate reply.

Long before noon on that historic day, members of Congress, federal and state officials, and the occupants of the fine old houses who could find the space, crowded into the little room. When he, who so valiantly and with such self-sacrifice had pledged his life and fortune to the cause of independence, entered the room, a tremor of emotion passed through the audience. All the memories of the trying days of the war flooded the minds of the spectators. He whose sword, whose patience, wisdom, and strategy had achieved the nation's independence was before them.

And, seated among them, inconspicuous and silent throughout, sat the man whose pen had phrased the Declaration that announced to the world the purpose and the reason of the struggle; and who had suffered abuse from the selfish and provincial because of his stout adherence to Washington's policy of manning and munitioning the armies beyond Virginia's borders. This silent man, modestly in the background, had planned the ceremony as he knew Washington would prefer it, and then he had stepped aside. But when, on the conclusion of Washington's touching and dignified speech of renunciation, Mifflin, the President, rose to reply, few there were who did not realize that, while the voice was that of Mifflin, the words were the words of Jefferson, the author. The phrasing was unmistakable.

Called upon by your country to defend its invaded rights, you accepted the sacred charge before it had formed alliances and while it was without funds, or a government to support you [read Mifflin]. You have conducted the great military contest with wisdom and fortitude, invariably regarding the rights of the civil power, through all the disasters and changes [unquestionably the words of Jefferson]. You have, by the love and confidence of your fellow citizens, enabled them to display their martial genius, and transmit their fame to posterity. You have persevered until these United States, aided by a magnanimous King and nation, have been enabled, under a just Providence, to close the war in freedom, safety, and independence. Having defended the standard of liberty in this new world; having taught a lesson useful to those who inflict, and to those who feel oppression, you return from the great theater of action with the blessings of your fellow citizens; but the glory of your virtues will not terminate with your military command — it will continue to animate remote ages. . . . We join you in commending the interest of our dearest country to the protection of Almighty God, beseeching Him to dispose the hearts and minds of the citizens to improve the opportunity afforded them of becoming a great, happy, and respected nation. And for you, we address to Him our earnest prayers that a life so beloved may be fostered with all His care; that your days may be happy, as they have been illustrious; and that He will finally give you that reward which this world will not give.

The ceremony was over. With deep emotion men crowded about to shake the hand of the Commander and filed slowly out into the street.

V

It was a day of emotion and festivity, and we may be sure that Jefferson sat down that day to a discussion with Washington of the multiplying public problems that were pressing. Jefferson had played his part. Could anything better illustrate his versatility, his industry, and capacity for concentration than the fact that on that very day he found time to write Martha, advising her on the importance of dress and neatness? It was probably in the evening that Jefferson was seated at his desk in his lodgings, with Monroe hovering in the background, writing:

I do not wish you to be gaily clothed at this time of life, but that your wear should be fine of its kind. But, above all things, and a all times, let your clothes be neat, white and properly put on. Do not fancy you must wear your clothes until the dirt is visible to the eye. You will be the last one who will be sensible of this. Some ladies think that they may, under the privilege of dishabille, be loose and negligent of their dress in the morning. But be you, from the moment you rise till you go to bed, as cleanly and properly dressed as at the hours of dinner or tea. A lady who has been seen as a sloven or slut in the morning will never efface the impression she has made with all the dress and pageantry she can afterwards involve herself in. Nothing is so disgusting to our sex as a want of cleanliness and delicacy in yours. I hope, therefore, the moment you rise from your bed, your first work will be to dress yourself in such style as you may be seen by any gentleman without his being able to discover a pin amiss, or any other circumstances of neatness wanting.[11]

Jefferson had supervised an historical ceremony, had conferred with Washington on public matters, and had written his young daughter on her clothing and person. It was a day.

VI

This, however, was not to be the last conference between Washington and Jefferson during the latter's six months in Annapolis. In 1783, the officers of the army formed a society, ambitiously called an Order, to which the principal officers, along with the French Ministers and officers who had served in the war, were eligible for membership. Perhaps because, like the Roman of old, most of them would soon retire to their farms, they called it the Order of the Cincinnati. The purely sentimental purpose of creating a society to preserve the friendly relations and the camp-fire comradery of the men who had commanded the Revolutionary soldiers would have met a cordial reception but for the fact that certain features aroused the distrust and hostility of thousands, who saw in it the seeds of an artificial aristocracy, opposed to democracy. The members were to wear, as their decoration, a golden eagle suspended by a ribbon of deep blue, edged with white, and Major l'Enfant had been sent to Paris to get the eagles.

[11] Randolph, *Domestic Life of Jefferson*, 71.

The provision which aroused the displeasure of the civilians and set the tongues of the unpaid private soldiers to wagging in the taverns and on the highways was that membership in the Order should be hereditary, descending to the eldest son, like the landed estates until Jefferson wiped out the law of primogeniture, thus perpetuating the organization. There was also a provision for honorary membership which presented some ominous political possibilities.

In hot pursuit of the announcement of the new Order came a pamphlet entitled *Considerations on the Order of the Cincinnati,* which was eagerly read and passed about among the thousands excluded from membership. It was the product of the pen of Aedanus Burke, a distinguished lawyer, jurist, and patriot of South Carolina. Born in Galway, Ireland, blessed with the Irish gift of eloquence in polemics, he bitterly attacked the organization as incompatible with the very spirit of the Revolution and in glaring contradiction to the spirit of democracy. Civilians, who believed that, in a good society, private soldiers, who had shivered in their rags at Valley Forge and tramped in bare feet the wintry muds of Jersey, should not have the doors of a patriotic order closed in their faces, found the Burke pamphlet much to their liking. Men like Jefferson, opposed to artificial distinctions that could be made to serve reactionary politics, found much in it to commend.

Soon the pamphlet had an astonishingly large circulation. In remote France it attracted the attention of Mirabeau, who translated it into French under his own name, and, from this edition, translations later were made into German.[12] Soon the Governor of South Carolina was denouncing the Cincinnati as aiming at the creation of an hereditary order irreconcilable with a democratic society, and the legislatures of Massachusetts, Pennsylvania, and Rhode Island passed resolutions of censure.

That these fears were not confined to demagogues and slighted private soldiers is evident in the correspondence of the time. Even John Jay, certainly conservative, was afraid the new Order 'will eventually divide us into two mighty factions.' He observed that, while permission was asked of the French King for French soldiers to affiliate, 'the compliment was not paid to our sovereign,' and that

---

[12] *Dictionary of American Biography,* III, 280.

Louis XVI had consented 'without having requested the opinion of congress on the subject.'[13] Samuel Adams wrote Gerry that he looked 'upon it as as rapid a stride toward an hereditary military nobility as ever was made in so short a time,' though his 'fears may be ill-grounded.'[14] And John Adams thought it 'an inroad upon our first principle, equality.' He thought it 'the deepest piece of cunning ever attempted . . . a sowing the seeds of all that European courts wish to grow up among us.' He had not written upon the subject because twenty years before, in an essay on the feudal law, he had expressed his sentiments.[15] The popular reaction was such that, in the spring of 1784, Edmund Randolph, writing Jefferson of an election in Virginia, said all soldiers running had been elected save one who was preparing to attend a convention of the Order.[16]

And, soon after reaching Annapolis, Jefferson was reading in the *Maryland Gazette* a description of the founding of the Order, its constitution in full, with a description of its coat of arms — a full page.[17] That he and Monroe discussed its possible implications there can be no doubt.

VII

As early as March, 1784, Washington knew of the great and increasing distrust of the Order, and in a letter to General Henry Knox on March 20, he urged a full attendance at the national meeting in Philadelphia in May, that it might 'obviate the prejudices which are already imbibed, and more than probably through ignorance, envy, and perhaps worse motives will increase and spread.'[18] On April 4, he wrote similarly to Jonathan Trumbull.[19]

Meanwhile, sitting on the veranda at peaceful Mount Vernon, reading the Burke indictment, Washington was considerably disturbed. When officers he trusted as soldiers and with whom he had been associated offered him membership, he had accepted with no remote thought of possible political implications or interpretations. The clamor aroused by Burke distressed him. After all, the

13 Austin, *Life of Gerry*, I, 421.   14 *Ibid.*, I, 425.   15 *Ibid.*, I, 427-28.
16 Conway, *Omitted Chapters of History*, 54.
17 *Maryland Gazette*, November 27, 1783.
18 Fitzpatrick, *Writings of Washington*, XXVII, 365.
19 *Ibid.*, XXVII, 386.

private in tattered uniform with a musket had been his comrade quite as much as the men with the sword. In his quandary, he turned for advice to Jefferson.

> The pamphlet [Burke's] has, I am told, had its effect [he wrote] People are alarmed, especially in the Eastern States; how justly and how contrary to the avowed principles of the Society, and the purity of their motives, I shall not declare, lest it should appear that I wished to bias your judgment rather than obtain an opinion which, if you please, might be accompanied with sentiments under the information here given, respecting the most eligible measure to be pursued by the Society at their next meeting. You may be assured, Sir, that to the good opinion alone which I entertain of your abilities and candor, this liberty is to be attributed.[20]

Washington could scarcely have been unmindful of Jefferson's opinion of all hereditary orders and of the privileges that usually find their way into them, since he had but recently put an end to primogeniture in Virginia. Jefferson replied with the candor that was invited. He had hoped that Washington, above all, should stand on ground separate from the Order, 'that the character that would be handed down to future ages as the head of our Revolution might, in no instance, be compromised by subordinate altercations.' He had thought of writing Washington, but had been deterred by the reflection that the General had abler advisers, though none could compete in judgment with Washington himself. But now that his candid opinion had been solicited, he would indicate the reasons most heard in opposition to the Society.

It was said, he wrote, that 'it is against the Confederation — against the letter of some of our Constitutions — against the spirit of them all'; since 'the foundation on which all of these are built is the natural equality of man, the denial of every pre-eminence than that annexed to legal office, and particularly a denial of the pre-eminence of birth.'

Then, too, the provision for taking in honorary members had dangerous possibilities, though these might be remote. Though improbable that many would accept such membership then, the time might come, with a change in dispositions, when the invita-

20 *Ibid.*, XXVII, 388.

tions would be flattering. Through a careful selection of men and talents, office, and wealth, a powerful political machine could be created that might easily affect the course of Government.

Even more dangerous, thought Jefferson, was the inclusion of foreign members who would be influenced by the wishes of foreign courts. Above all other objections, however, was this — 'experience has shown that the hereditary branches of foreign Governments are the patrons of privilege and prerogative, and not of the natural rights of the people whose oppressors they generally are.' And then, too, would it not be unfortunate if 'a distinction is kept up between the civil and military, which it is for the happiness of both to obliterate'?

But the greatest danger, he thought, might come through ambitious projects of the future, inimical to the liberties of the people, when unscrupulous men at the head of the Order might urge upon the members, 'under the habits of subordination,' policies hostile to the democratic principle. Was it not true that the moderation and virtue of a single character have probably prevented this Revolution from being closed, as most others have been, by a subversion of that liberty which it was intended to establish? But Washington was not immortal in a physical sense, and there could be no assurance that his successor at the head of the Order would not be led 'by false calculations into a less certain road to glory.'

Jefferson had replied with the perfect candor that always had been, and always would be, characteristic of his exchange of views with Washington. In the serene atmosphere of Mount Vernon, Washington had read the Burke pamphlet with uneasiness, and his mind could hardly have been put to rest in the reading of the candid letter of his friend of Monticello. He would think it over. There would be a meeting of the Order in Philadelphia in May, and he would stop over in Annapolis for a confidential conversation with Jefferson.

VIII

And so one evening in early May, it came to pass that Washington sat in Jefferson's room in earnest conversation on the Cincinnati. 'It was a little after candlelight when he arrived,' wrote Jefferson, 'and he sat with me until after midnight, conversing almost exclusively upon that subject.' Face to face in familiar intercourse, Jefferson frankly expressed his suspicions and fears, and the reasons for them. Washington spoke indulgently of the motives that probably inspired the conception of the Order; but that night, by the flickering light of the spluttering candles, he declared himself in complete accord with Jefferson's point of view.

Of course, said Jefferson, if the hereditary feature were removed, there could be no serious objections to the indulgence of the Order during the lifetime of the officers then living, 'who had actually served.' But Washington was convinced that night that no feature should be left that would be a ground of dissatisfaction and a line of separation between them and their country.

It was after midnight when Washington departed, thoroughly determined to use his influence at the Philadelphia meeting to effect a modification of the constitution or the dissolution of the Order.

A little later, on his return from Philadelphia, Washington again sat in Jefferson's room in Annapolis, relating his experiences at the meeting. He had done all within his power to persuade the officers to abandon the project, and the older officers had agreed. The opposition came from the younger ones. Conspicuous among these, Washington told Jefferson, was Colonel Smith, the son-in-law of John Adams. Even so, the meeting might have been the last but for the dramatic arrival from France, toward the close, of Major l'Enfant, later to be the architect of the city of Washington, with a lot of the gold eagles he had been sent to get. But more embarrassing, he brought letters of acceptance of membership from the French officers who had served in the Revolution; and more embarrassing still, an authorization from Louis XVI that these might wear the insignia of the Order. A dissolution now, or a rejection of the foreign members, would be difficult to explain to the French and might even be interpreted as an ungracious gesture toward the King.

Thus was a new problem presented, which changed the opinion of the older officers, and all that Washington undertook to do was to get what he thought was an agreement to the elimination of the hereditary feature and the abandonment of the plan for honorary memberships. Just before the meeting in Philadelphia, he had sent to the members his program which, it will be noted, was precisely along the lines of Jefferson's suggestions:

> Strike out every word, sentence, and clause which has a political tendency, without any substitution which can be construed into concealment or change of ground only; for this would, in my opinion, increase rather than allay suspicion.
>
> Admit no more honorary members into the society.[21]

This was before he had seen Jefferson, but after he had received his letter. It clearly appears, however, that Washington's desires were disregarded and that the State societies failed to act on the recommendations of the Philadelphia meeting. As late as August, 1785, he was complaining to Arthur St. Clair, that the State societies had not acted and reminding him that, but for the recommendations made, 'ere this we should have had the country in an uproar and a line of separation drawn between this society and their fellow citizens.'[22] And in December, 1785, nineteen months after the Philadelphia meeting, he was writing Alexander Hamilton:

> Sincerely do I wish that the several State Societies had, or would adopt, the alterations that were recommended. . . . I then thought, and have no cause to change my opinion, that if the Society of the Cincinnati mean to live in peace with the rest of their fellow Citizens they must subscribe to the alteration. . . . The fears of the people are not removed, they only sleep, and a very little matter will set them afloat.[23]

IX

But the Order flourished for a time, unpopular with the masses, more because of its possibilities than its actions. Judge Tucker, in 1836, fifty years after the conversation at Annapolis, found that it had then excited so little interest that 'its history is with difficulty traced.' At that time, he records, it was maintained 'in some of the States,' but in other States, 'after a lingering existence it had been suffered to a silent dissolution.' When the Order met in Virginia in 1822, it provided, in anticipation of its early demise, for the transfer of its funds to Washington College, and two years later the fifteen

[21] *Ibid.*, XXVII, 393.   [22] *Ibid.*, XXVIII, 239.   [23] *Ibid.*, XXVIII, 352.

thousand dollars in its treasury was turned over to the Treasurer of the State for the college.[24]

Even so, it appears that the hereditary provision still continues and that the eldest sons of the descendant are alone eligible to membership. Washington, who had thought he had a promise to eliminate this feature, had been mistaken. But the political influence of the Order is never felt, and the danger feared, of which the public was forewarned, passed long ago when Jefferson won his definitive victory for democracy in 1800.

This incident is important to our purpose as an illustration of Jefferson's vigilant guardianship of the democratic ideals, and his uncompromising hostility to the creation of any artificial aristocracy antipathetic to them. He had received too many blows from the privileged artificial aristocracy of the Old Dominion not to know what powerful and tenacious forces were at work to turn back the democratic tide. Very soon after his return from his mission to France, he was to be shocked by the monarchical, anti-democratic tone of the conversations of the more fashionable and snobbish drawing-rooms of New York and Philadelphia. And in his twelve years' struggle to make the Republic definitively democratic, he was to find abundant evidence of the determination of a brilliant and powerful group to convert the American Government into an oligarchy of privileged wealth.[25]

It was a realization of this disposition that gave vigor to his conversation with Washington, as these two greatest men of the Revolution sat that May night in Annapolis by the light of the flickering candles and discussed the problem of the Order of the Cincinnati.

He was militantly hostile to hereditary privileges.

He was bitterly opposed to the injection of an organized military domination or influence in the civil life of the nation or to setting the military above the civil.

He was passionately against the injection in any way of foreign influence in the American Government.

And it was his strategy in his historic fight for democracy invariably to meet the enemy on the frontier.

[24] Tucker, Life of Jefferson, I, 173.
[25] See author's Jefferson and Hamilton.

X

All this, while revealing a part of his activities in Annapolis, did not enter at all into his congressional work, which was of the first importance and significance. His pre-eminence in this Congress was conceded, for he loomed in reputation, past achievements, and ability conspicuously above his colleagues. Thus, when the peace treaty, ending the war of the Revolution with its concession of American independence, was signed in Paris and it was referred to a special committee, Jefferson was chairman entrusted with the duty of piloting it through to ratification.

It was he who submitted the report on the treaty, written by himself, on December 16, 1783. He recommended ratification and the appropriate legislation by the various States for the restitution of confiscated British property to their *bona-fide* owners. But he also sponsored a congressional resolution insisting upon the payment for slaves and other property taken by the British. And he pronounced any demand for interest on debts to British citizens which had accumulated during the war period 'highly inequitable and unjust.' [26] Four days later, he submitted his report on the letters from the American plenipotentiaries in Paris. He brushed aside the proposal of some members that all treaties with European nations should be negotiated in the United States, with the reminder that these nations, 'ancient and established as they are,' could hardly be expected to come as suppliants to a new nation.[27]

With the Articles of Confederation stipulating that treaties could not be ratified with delegates from less than nine States present, only seven were represented in Annapolis when the treaty was referred. Frantic appeals had been sent to the Governors of the absent States to hasten their delegations, with the warning that their absence imperiled the peace made possible after years of bloody struggle. And for weeks there was no response. Utterly incredible as it seems, this was but one of the proofs that, in the interval between the surrender of Cornwallis and the adoption of the Constitution some years later, the morale of the country was at its lowest. The marvel is that all that had been achieved by the heroic sacrifices of the war was not

[26] Woolery, *Relations of Thomas Jefferson to American Foreign Policy*, 5.
[27] *Ibid.*, 8.

then lightly thrown away. The indifference of the Governors receiving the appeals was almost flippant. After seven years of fighting and suffering for independence, it seemed that many were completely indifferent to a peace with victory.

The peace had been signed in Paris September 3, 1783; on December 23, the appeals to the Governors went forth; and three days later, Jefferson, with a meticulous regard for law and usage and the limitations set for the ratification, proposed that three vessels be chartered, stationed at different ports and held in readiness to sail immediately with the ratification to Europe. One of the vessels was to be stationed in New York, one at Annapolis, and the other at some unnamed eastern port. The motion was in the form of instructions to Robert Morris, the agent of the marine, and then a member of Congress.

Instantly, Lee, of Virginia, protested against the expense!

Millions of money and rivers of blood had been expended for seven years to win a victory, but not one penny was to be spent to consolidate it, when won.

And why the expense when seven States would be sufficient for a ratification, regardless of the Articles of Confederation specifically stipulating nine? demanded Lee. So many found this easy way out attractive that at length Read, of South Carolina, proposed immediate ratification.

Congress was plunged into an acrimonious debate of two days' duration, with the supporters of Read's motion urging that ratification was no more than a form, and that the act of signing the treaty definitively ended the war under the terms of the treaty.

Jefferson vigorously protested against such slovenly procedure, warmly supported by Monroe, Gerry, Howell, and Ellery. Under the modern practices of Europe, declared Jefferson, the ratification was considered the fact necessary to give validity to the treaty. Without that ratification, he contended, the treaty agreement would not be obligatory upon England. And did not the very commissions of the American signers reserve to Congress the right of ratification? And did not the treaty itself prescribe ratification? And did not the Confederation specifically deny the power to ratify without the presence of nine States? [28]

[28] *Autobiography,* 56.

But Read and his supporters were stubborn and unconvinced. He gave notice that he would press for a vote and demand the ayes and nays. To make the issue clear as light, Jefferson thereupon prepared a resolution enumerating pointedly his reasons for opposition. But in the meanwhile a canvass had revealed that Massachusetts alone would have supported the Read proposal, with Virginia and Rhode Island opposed, and with Delaware, Maryland, and North Carolina divided.

But Jefferson had an almost feminine sensitivity to atmosphere, and noting the disappointment and ill-temper of the defeated, this master in the art of conciliation now proposed a middle ground. He offered a resolution setting forth that the seven States present unanimously favored ratification, and, while divided as to the validity of ratification without the presence of nine States, the seven present ratified it so far as their powers permitted. This ratification was to be sent to the Ministers in Paris, with instructions not to use it unless circumstances made it necessary. They were to apply for an extension of the time limit, and, only in the event it was refused, should the doubtful ratification be submitted. Should the nine States appear and ratify in the meantime, it was not to be used at all.[29]

Even this precipitated another two days' debate. Always impatient of orators who missed no opportunity to discourse at length, Jefferson writhed in silent anguish of spirit. But after two days of gusty oratory, the resolution was adopted; and, since a vessel was sailing from Annapolis on the third day, Congress directed the President to write the plenipotentiaries in Paris accordingly.

But it was not until January 14, seven weeks after Congress convened and three weeks after the fight for ratification began, that Connecticut and South Carolina joined their sister States and the new ratification by nine States was sent to Paris.[30]

It is a startling commentary on the times that New York and Georgia had not thought it worth while to send their delegates in response to the frantic appeals. New York had held back for special instructions on the signing of the Declaration of Independence, and its vote was not recorded on the ratification of the peace treaty which brought the war to a successful termination.

[29] Ibid.   [30] Ibid.

Thus it came about that young Jefferson, who seven years before had written and reported the Declaration of Independence, wrote and reported the ratification of the peace treaty which crowned the Revolutionary struggle with success.

XI

It is astonishing to us today that the fate of the new nation hung on a slender thread between the surrender at Yorktown and the adoption of the Constitution which gave power and solidity to the Republic. The Government, such as it was, was in Congress, exercising both legislative and executive functions. During the long recesses there was no real executive authority at all.

Painfully impressed by the gravity of the situation should anything occur when Congress was not in session, Jefferson sought a remedy for the defect. The peace had laid a paralyzing hand on governmental activities. To have held Congress in permanent session would have aroused the ire of the State legislatures, already jealous of the federal body. The plan that Jefferson now proposed was the creation of a committee of the States, with one member for each, made possible by the ninth article of the Articles of Confederation, the committee to remain in session during the congressional recesses for the performance of executive functions. Since this plan was better than no provision at all, it was adopted.

Though the plan seemed promising enough on paper, it signally failed in operation after Jefferson had gone to Paris. The members quarreled among themselves. They divided into cliques and factions. Many, if not most, of the members deserted their posts in pique and returned to their homes, indifferent to whether or not the nation exercised executive authority.[31]

All these experiences entered into the molding of Jefferson's theories of stable government. He was forced to the very definite conclusion that duality in executive authority was impossible; and that a consolidated government with a central authority backed by a constitutional mandate, and this alone, would create a nation and preserve for the people the independence for which they had fought for seven years in the field.

[31] *Ibid.*, 54.

XII

With executive authority nebulous, it happened at this time that the States were threatened gravely in the management of the finances by the resignation from the Treasury of Robert Morris, 'the financier of the Revolution.' The finances of the country were in a bad way, and the retirement of Morris, who alone was familiar with all the intricacies of the office, threatened a state of chaos in the Treasury. A new man, however able, would find it confusing and difficult to find his way about. The work was a specialized work, with innumerable ramifications, and no new man could possibly master its secrets without time. In the meanwhile, there would be danger of confusion worse confounded.

When Morris resigned, a Grand Committee of Congress, with a representative from each State, was named, with Jefferson, as usual, at its head, to work out a new system. And again it was Jefferson who came forward with a plan.

Instead of one Treasurer, he proposed three Commissioners. He was not unmindful of the fact that here again he introduced duality in control, but for this he had a special reason. His primary thought was to guard against another interval during which an inexperienced man, unfamiliar with the work of the Treasury, would have to struggle in the dark. With three Commissioners, all familiar with the work, there would always be someone on hand to operate the machinery with intelligence, someone who would know his way about.

In later years, all this was changed by the introduction of the civil service, which guarantees that specialists of experience will always be on duty for the guidance of the head of the Treasury, however new. Indeed, the plan of Jefferson was based on the theory behind the civil service.

XIII

More interesting in the field of finance at this time was Jefferson's responsibility for another decision which has never been changed — he became the 'Father of the Dollar' as the money unit of the nation.

In the preceding congressional session much attention had been given to the subject of coinage and the money unit. Robert Morris with Gouverneur Morris as his assistant, had prepared an elaborate report. They had proposed as a money unit what they found to be the common measure in every State except South Carolina, without leaving the fraction of a penny. This, they had found, would be the four hundred and fortieth part of a dollar. Early in the Congress of which Jefferson was a member, the report with its recommendations was referred to a committee under his chairmanship.

Studying the report without prejudice, Jefferson was convinced of the soundness of the proposed extension of the decimal system to weights and measures, but the recommendation as to the money unit impressed him as fantastic and impractical. He thereupon proposed, as a substitute, the adoption of the Spanish dollar as the unit, with decimal divisions and subdivisions, and with the penny as the smallest coin. His objection to the Morris unit was its complexity, its divergence in use from the habits of the people, and the difficulties the average man or woman would meet in computation.

Having reached these conclusions he set them forth in an exhaustive report entitled 'Notes on the Establishment of a Money Unit and of a Coinage for the United States.' This, together with the report of the two Morrises, was then sent to all the members for their comparison and choice. In these notes he explained his objections to the recommendation of the financier with practical illustrations.

Thus, under the Morris plan a loaf of bread would cost one-twentieth of a dollar, or 72 units. A pound of butter, one-fifth of a dollar, or 288 units. A horse or cow of eighty dollars' value would cost 115,200 units. The public debt would amount to 115,200,000,000 units.

'Such a system,' he concluded, 'would be utterly unmanageable for the common purposes of society.'

Jefferson's colleagues on the committee accepted his view, but Morris, probably moved by a pride of authorship, and possibly by the conviction, so often to be heard expressed later by his political opponents, that Jefferson was a 'theorist,' 'impractical,' and 'ignorant of all things financial,' refused to accept the substitution. But the Congress did not hesitate between the Jefferson and the Morris plans, and, without embarrassment, it gave its approval to the former.

More than a century later, Francis Hirst, eminent English specialist on political economy and finance, was to declare that Jefferson's notes on his plan 'constitute an epoch in monetary history, ranking with Sir Isaac Newton's representation to the Lords of the Treasury in 1717, or with the Bullion Reports which led to the resumption of cash payments in England a few years after Waterloo'; and that 'Jefferson's easy mastery of a complex subject, his wisdom in adapting theory to the practical needs and habits of the people, and his skill in presenting the case to his fellow legislators must excite the admiration of experts and laymen alike.' [32]

It was natural that the two Morrises were thinking in terms of experts and bankers; Jefferson, in the terms of the average man. Just as we have seen him insisting on the simplification of the laws so that the average man would understand them, so he insisted on the simplification of the arithmetic of the coins.

'Everyone knows the facility of decimal arithmetic,' he wrote in his notes. The average man was 'used to be puzzled by adding the farthings, taking out the fours and carrying those on; adding the shillings, taking out the twenties and carrying them on; but when he came to pounds, where he had only tens to carry forward, it was easy and free from error.'

Such was the infinite variety of the labors of Jefferson during his last congressional career in Annapolis.

XIV

And now we come to one of the most dramatic, and rather disreputable, pages in the American history of those days.

It was during this session that history of lasting importance in the creation of the nation was written in the cession to the Union by Virginia of her Western lands. This empire comprised what were to become some of the greatest and richest States in the Union. And in the writing of the Ordinance of 1784, Jefferson again appears on a vital page of history.

Astonishing as it seems today, when Virginia made her more than generous proffer, it was met with a determined and un-

[32] Hirst, *Life of Jefferson*, 200.

scrupulous opposition. Even this early, the subordination of the good of the nation to the mercenary greed of small groups was in evidence.

By the action of the royal governor and his council, approved by the King, it was stipulated that no purchase of lands from the Indians would be valid without the approval of her legislature. In the face of this stipulation, numerous land companies, interested solely in speculative profits, made such purchases with a flippant contempt for the law. When the Indiana Company began selling lands, thus purchased, the Virginia Convention of 1776 issued a warning and appointed a commission to investigate and act.

This was met by the land companies with an appeal to Congress, setting forth the claim that this body had exclusive sovereignty over the territory before its cession by Virginia. The Virginia delegates had made a strong protest. But Congress, with lobbyists hanging on to its coat-tails with smirks and suggestive gestures, lacked the courage or the character to take a stand. On the contrary, it recommended that Virginia reconsider her act for opening a land office.

Speedily the answer came from the able and erudite George Mason, of Gunston Hall, in the form of a powerful remonstrance setting forth that, 'when Virginia acceded to the Articles of Confederation, her rights of sovereignty and jurisdiction within her own territory were reserved and secured to her, and cannot be infringed or altered without her consent.'

This brought a momentary pause, but the land companies had other weapons in their arsenal, not unknown in later years. Providentially a few members of Congress found themselves in possession of stock in these speculative companies through the payment of little or nothing. The Crédit Mobilier was anticipated by almost ninety years.

And then, too, at this time New York, Massachusetts, and Connecticut made a belated discovery that they owned parts of the Northwest Territory. With the chipper generosity of one who blithefully gives away the property of another, New York proposed to cede her claims to the Union. And then Maryland stepped in with the stout assertion that she never would join the Confederation until all the lands west of the frontiers were given to the federal alliance — all the lands, significantly enough, except that claimed and sold by the land companies. Maryland, for the moment, became the cupbearer of the speculators.

And now, with some congressmen caught by personal mercenary interest and with a corrupt lobby pushing its advantage, the land companies suavely proposed that Congress name arbitrators to resolve the controversy. The Virginians indignantly rejected this reflection on the dignity and sovereignty of the State.

By this time the activities of the land companies and their lobbyists had become a stench. It was known that certain members of Congress had been bought with shares. But never having had any other thought than of ceding her territory, Virginia proffered the cession as a matter of patriotism, provided Maryland entered the Confederation and abandoned her support of the speculators. When Maryland agreed, it seemed, for the moment, that all was well.

But now we come to the most incredible phase of all. When Virginia's offer reached Congress, its reception was cold, and the offer was referred to a committee of five members from States known to be in accord with the position of the crooked land companies. This committee had the temerity to summon Virginia to appear before it and defend her claims. She scornfully refused, point-blank. Instead, she demanded in her turn that Congress put an immediate end to the activities of this committee. The committee countered by refusing the cession on the ground that part belonged to Massachusetts, New York, and Connecticut. And to cap the climax and earn the bribe, it further recommended that the claims of the land companies be conceded. At least it had the decency to 'stay bought.'

Thoroughly aroused by this time by the all too evident corruption behind the maneuvering, the Virginians demanded that each member of Congress be called by name to declare upon his honor and his oath that he had not directly or indirectly become interested personally in the claims of the companies. This threw the guilty ones into confusion and demoralization, and those who had been most active in pressing the claims of the companies readily agreed to an indefinite postponement.

Such was the shady background of the fight of the land companies for private profit to the detriment of the public good when the cession again came up at Annapolis, where Jefferson was not only the acknowledged leader of Congress, but the head of the Virginia delegation.

XV

From the outside, Jefferson had followed the devious methods of the speculators with loathing and disgust. He now took a decided stand. In a letter to Governor Henry on March 1, 1784, he gave a chronological story of the proceedings in that Congress. He wrote that, upon the receipt of the instructions to the delegation from the legislature, the Virginians in Annapolis had agreed upon a form of deed. A copy of the proposed act of cession and a copy of the deed had been delivered, with the assurance that the deed would be executed whenever Congress 'should think proper to declare they would accept it.' This had been referred to a committee which had reported in favor of acceptance.

But Virginia's struggle to give away an empire was not yet over. Only eight States responded to the roll-call, and of these, New Jersey voted against the acceptance, while Pennsylvania and South Carolina were evenly divided. Thus again, nothing was done.

The comedy had now degenerated into such a ridiculous farce that Jefferson had decided that the Virginians should 'be still, having declared we were ready to execute,' and 'leave it to them to come forward and tell us they are ready to accept.' He advised that they 'meddle not at all,' and show 'perfect indifference.'

Meanwhile, with the arrival of the New Hampshire delegation, nine States had come to town, and it was proposed that the Virginians execute the deed and lay it on the table — where it might easily have remained indefinitely. 'We replied — no,' wrote Jefferson. 'If these lands are not offered for sale the ensuing spring, they will be taken from us all by adventurers. We will not, therefore, put it out of our power, by executing a deed, to sell them ourselves if Congress will not.'

Confronted by this firm stand of the Virginians under Jefferson's astute leadership, Rhode Island now proposed that Congress should accept. Very well, said a congressman from New Jersey — but with the stipulation that the acceptance would not be interpreted as a concession of Virginia's right.

'Unconditional, or nothing,' Jefferson replied.

Thus, for a moment, the matter was dropped and Congress turned to other business. Virginia was finding it very difficult to give away a mighty empire. But an hour later, Jefferson wrote, 'the dissenting Pennsylvanian asked and obtained leave to change from no to aye,' and Congress voted to accept. The deed was immediately executed.[33]

Nothing so fantastic is to be found in American history.

XVI

With the acceptance, a committee was named to draw up plans for a temporary government of the Territory, again under the chairmanship of Jefferson. His two colleagues on the committee were Samuel Chase, of Maryland, afterward an inveterate enemy of Jefferson, and one of the most vicious of the federal judges in the future days of the Sedition Law,[34] and David Howell, of Rhode Island. Of the two, we may be sure that Jefferson found Howell the more congenial. A graduate of Princeton College, a tutor, a professor of Natural Philosophy, and for a time acting President of Brown University, he was also a distinguished lawyer as well as jurist of the federal court.

The three men sat down to the discussion of the temporary government they would recommend, and inevitably they assigned the task of writing the Ordinance of 1784 to Jefferson, the foremost penman of the Revolution. In the State Department in Washington may be seen the draft in the handwriting of the author — the original draft. No task could have been more congenial to a constructive statesman than the opportunity of writing on a clean virgin slate. And this draft sheds more illumination on the political philosophy of Jefferson.

It provided for the early carving of the Territory into States, for the summoning of the people of each State for the establishment of a temporary government, and the adoption of a written constitution which would be open to revision by future legislatures. Each State

---

[33] The United States Supreme Court later sustained Virginia when sued by the Indiana Land Company.
[34] See author's *Jefferson and Hamilton*.

was to be divided into counties, and each county into townships. When the population of a State had reached twenty thousand, a constitutional convention was to be called for the establishment of a permanent government.

But there were Jeffersonian conditions to the establishment of either a temporary or permanent government. These conditions are enlightening:

First, 'they shall forever remain a part of the United States.'

Second, 'they shall be subject to the Government of the United States in Congress assembled and to the Articles of Confederation.'

Third, 'they shall be subject to pay a part of the national debt, contracted or to be contracted, to be apportioned on them by Congress according to the same rule and measure as in the case of the other States.'

Fourth, 'these governments shall be republican in form, and no one holding hereditary titles shall be admitted to citizenship.'

Fifth, 'after the year 1800 there shall be neither slavery nor involuntary servitude in any of the said States, otherwise than in punishment for crime.'

It was further provided that whenever any of these States had a population equal to that of the smallest existing State, it should be entitled to a delegate in Congress on equal footing with those of the other States. It could then be admitted to the Union by the vote of nine States, and, until admitted, would have a delegate in Congress with the privilege of debating without voting.

The one fantastic feature of the original draft of Jefferson was in the naming of the States to be created — Sylvania, Michigania, Assenisipia, Illinoia, Saratoga, Washington, and Polytotamia. But two of these, slightly changed, were to be adopted — Michigan and Illinois.

XVII

The proposed Jefferson Ordinance was called up for consideration in Congress on April 19, 1784. The opposition concentrated on two clauses, one inspired by understandable motives, the other by motives inexplicable.

The proposal to eliminate slavery in the new States after 1800 created much anxiety among the defenders of the slave system. These marshaled their forces to wipe this clause from the Ordinance. Spaight, of North Carolina, moved to strike it out. Read, of South Carolina, seconded the motion. The majority in Congress favored its retention.

The motion was put on whether the clause written by Jefferson should stand. The ayes and nays were called. The trend of public opinion and the sectional division were manifest in the result. Northern traders had profited by selling slaves to the South, but that was ended. Experience had shown that slavery would not be economically profitable in the bleaker North, while slaves could profitably be used in the South. There was no special nobility in the North and no special infamy in the South. And so all the Northern States — Massachusetts, New Hampshire, Rhode Island, Connecticut, New York, New Jersey, and Pennsylvania — voted to retain the Jefferson prohibition. Maryland, the home of Chase, one of the framing committee, and South Carolina voted unanimously to strike out. North Carolina was divided and lost her vote. And in the Virginia delegation there was also a division, and while but three of the delegates were present, two voted against Jefferson, to strike out. The vote of the Old Dominion was therefore recorded against the view of its most distinguished member who had penned the clause.

Some historians have found significance in the fact that an absentee, who naturally did not vote, was James Monroe, and there was a disposition among some contemporaries to assume that he remained away to escape the record. Since he shared lodgings with Jefferson, his most intimate friend in the Congress, the latter unquestionably knew the explanation of his absence. Monroe was prevented from attending the session by sickness. Had he been able to attend, Virginia by an equal division would have lost her vote.[35]

Thus, six States voted to end slavery in the Western lands after 1800, and but three voted against it. North Carolina lost her vote by a division, along with the States that were not then represented at all, and one State represented by but a single delegate. A majority of the States having failed to vote for the retention of the anti-slavery clause, it was consequently stricken out.

[35] Morgan, *Life of Monroe*, III.

But the significant fact remains that Jefferson had earnestly availed himself of another opportunity to strike a blow at slavery and had set a precedent for the anti-slavery clause included in the Northwest Ordinance of 1787.

Just why the clause refusing citizenship to any foreigners insisting on retaining the title of prince, duke, marquis, or count was objected to is not clear, but it, too, was eliminated.

Even so, the work of Jefferson has left a permanent imprint on the governments of Indiana, Ohio, Illinois, Michigan, and Wisconsin, and in none of them was slavery permitted long. There is a tradition that Jefferson wrote various people of his acquaintance in these new States urging the rejection of slavery in the constitutions to be adopted. The writer has often heard of a letter written to a former Virginian living in Covington, Indiana, but this cannot be verified, for the letter, if written, has disappeared along with the man who received it and his immediate descendants.[36]

XVIII

But Jefferson's work of lasting import was not yet finished in that Congress. Professor Woolery has written that 'in the years after 1783, the new State had to determine the basis for its commercial relations, protect its trade by treaties . . . in general to achieve a satisfactory position among the nations . . . a serious proposition to a government which was poorly adapted to overcome even the ordinary difficulties of domestic concerns.' And he concludes that 'for the solution Thomas Jefferson was largely responsible.'[37]

A nation was then in the making and with commercial reprisals against it from the country which had practically enforced a monopoly on its trade. Great Britain certainly could not have been interested in the success of the experiment in self-government or in the prosperity of the people. The welfare, nay the very existence, of the new nation dictated that commercial relations be established with other countries as rapidly as possible. When, in consequence, Congress decided to send diplomatic agents to Europe to negotiate

[36] Dr. William E. Dodd, the eminent historian, was convinced there had been such a letter.

[37] Woolery, *Relations of Jefferson to American Foreign Policy*, 8.

commercial treaties wherever desirable and possible, it turned once again to Jefferson for the preparation of the instructions. This, too, was almost a virgin field, but Jefferson had thought long and seriously upon the subject. He merely had to write the instructions out of the fullness of his reading and thinking. His instructions stipulated free admission of ships and merchandise into the ports of the two countries on paying the duties as the most favored nation.

They provided for more liberal terms for nations with territorial possessions in America.

They laid it down as mandatory that, in all treaties and in all cases growing out of them, the United States should be treated as one nation.

Private property and industry were to be protected by the contracting parties, and privateering was to be abolished.

Contraband articles no longer were to be liable to confiscation. They could be held on the payment of their value. And in the case of all other articles, not contraband, free ships were to make free goods.

Blockades were to be clearly defined, and the rights of neutrals were to be respected.

It was also stipulated that aliens should have the right to dispose of lands that had reached them by inheritance.

These proposed treaties were to be limited to ten years where possible, and were never to extend beyond fifteen. Attempts were to be made to negotiate such treaties with England, Hamburg, Saxony, Prussia, Denmark, Russia, Austria, Venice, Rome, Naples, Tuscany, Sardinia, Genoa, Spain, Portugal, the Porte, Algiers, Tripoli, Tunis, and Morocco. At this time treaties already existed with France, the Netherlands, and Sweden.

This report of Jefferson's placed the signposts of the foreign policy of the new nation, and with its adoption his work in Congress came to an end.

Having previously been offered the post in Paris, which had been declined for various reasons, it was natural that, in determining to send an additional negotiator to Europe to collaborate with Franklin and John Adams, the Congress should have turned to its foremost figure whose pen had written the instructions.

XIX

During his six months in Annapolis, Jefferson had been conceded a position of commanding leadership, and during these crowded months he had written more chapters into the history of the nation.

He had given the nation the dollar as its money unit.

He had wisely, though with difficulty, piloted the peace treaty through Congress without resorting to a degrading trick.

He had arranged the impressive and yet simple ceremonies incidental to the retirement of Washington from the command of the victorious army, and had expressed the nation's gratitude in the speech of the President.

He had drafted the Ordinance of 1784, which, with the Ordinance of 1787, first gave an organized society to the future States of Indiana, Ohio, Illinois, Michigan, and Wisconsin, that was in keeping with republican ideals. In the writing of the Ordinance, he had made another effort to strike down slavery.

He had prepared instructions to American plenipotentiaries for the negotiation of commercial treaties.

Looming high above all his colleagues, he had served on every important committee, had been chairman of most, and had written almost all the public papers of historical significance. With his leadership conceded, his popularity was unbounded. Few members of Congress through the entire period of the Revolution had made such personal contributions to the making of a nation.

Impatient of the fruitless garrulity of some of his colleagues whom he constantly compared with Washington and Franklin in deliberative bodies where they spoke but seldom, briefly, and always to the question, it is probable that without regret he passed now from what he thought was a cave of the winds. His life at Annapolis had been pleasant and his close association with Monroe had delighted him. The younger man had lived as a disciple at the master's feet, and the long, intimate conversations by candlelight had gone far toward molding the political character and career of James Monroe.

After Jefferson started on his journey, Monroe wrote him of his 'solitary situation.' He had supervised the sending of Jefferson's trunks by the packet to Baltimore, and had instructed the master of the packet to deliver them to Jefferson in person. And then, he added a bit wistfully, 'Partout and myself agree very well, only now and then we require the aid of an interpreter. I have had one or two comfortable solitary dinners upon little more than vegetables and coffee and cream.' [38]

Having so brilliantly served his country at home, Jefferson was now to continue his service in the most brilliant, if tragic, court in Europe, and to observe with fascination, at close hand, the emergence from the misery of the masses of another revolution aimed at the feudalism he detested. And in the Jefferson of the Paris days we shall have a different light upon his character as a man.

[38] Hamilton, *Writings of Monroe*, I, 24.

CHAPTER

XIV

JEFFERSON IN PARIS

1

J EFFERSON had gone directly from Annapolis to Philadelphia, where his eldest daughter was attending school, for he had determined to take her with him to Paris. The younger children, one too young to travel, a mere baby, were to be left in the care of Mrs. Eppes, a maternal aunt. Arranging to sail from Boston, he availed himself of the opportunity, long sought, to see something of New England, and he proceeded in leisurely fashion through the States of New Jersey, New York, Connecticut, Rhode Island, Massachusetts, and New Hampshire, acquainting himself as intimately as possible with the commercial possibilities of these regions with a view to their use in the negotiation of trade treaties. It was not then possible for a diplomat, setting forth on his mission, to sit down quietly in the grotesque structure that houses our State Department to the study of voluminous and minute information concerning such matters. Jefferson was pioneering.

The stout resistance of the Bostonians to the encroachments of the King preceding the Revolution had strongly prepossessed him in their favor, and while there he visited the scenes associated with the mighty struggle, now over. Inevitably, he found his way to the modest home of Samuel Adams, for whom he had admiration amounting to reverence. Just as it is a pity that no artist caught upon the canvas the picture of Washington and Jefferson seated in the light of candles at Annapolis, it is too bad that none transferred to canvas the picture of these two foremost fighting democrats and patriots in familiar converse in the Adams home. The visit was never to be forgotten by the aged warrior and his equally intrepid wife. Seventeen years later, when Adams was to write him a congratulatory letter on his election to the Presidency of the Republic, he was to add, as a postscript: 'My dear Mrs. Adams will not suffer me to close this letter till I let you know that she recollects the pleasure and entertainment you afforded us when you were about to embark for France.' [1]

No doubt they talked about the struggle, now happily ended, the days of the Committees of Correspondence, the fight in Philadelphia over independence, and the struggle ahead to make the Republic definitively democratic.

Jefferson found Gerry lingering in Philadelphia and assumed, as he wrote, that he was held there by 'the belles' of that town. He found Abigail Adams, whom he hoped to accompany to Europe, within thirty-six hours of sailing, but was unable to make his preparations in so short a time. And he stayed on 'employed by the hospitalities and civilities ... which [he] had experienced in the highest degree.' [2]

With his daughter, Jefferson embarked on the *Ceres*, under the command of Captain St. Barbe. Having learned that the owner of the vessel, Mr. Tracy, would sail on the ship, he wrote that he 'engaged [his] passage on her with the more pleasure since he was to go himself in her.' [3] There were but four other passengers, since the accommodations were so limited that but a small number of those applying for passage could be taken. It was a good, stout little vessel, and we may be sure the fare and service were beyond the ordinary, under the critical eyes of the owner. Martha Jefferson was to recall, years later, that the *Ceres* spread an abundant and excellent table. Happily, the sea was calm and the weather perfect. For three days the ship was becalmed on the Banks of Newfoundland, and the passengers, including Jefferson, regaled themselves by fishing for cod.

For nineteen days Jefferson was to walk the deck, go over his papers, and meditate upon his plans, and look after his daughter.

1 Wells, *Life of Samuel Adams*, III, 372.
2 To Gerry; Austin, *Life of Gerry*, I, 453.
3 *Ibid.*

He was to confess to a touch of seasickness, but, on the whole, he turned out to be a good sailor. Martha was less fortunate.

He had hoped, on approaching the coast of Europe, to transfer to a vessel that could put him down on the shores of France, but the weather on the coast was very thick and no other ship was encountered. On July 29, 1784, he disembarked at Portsmouth, where he was detained by a slight fever that had attacked Martha on the seventeenth day of the voyage. Whatever may have been his emotions on touching for the first time the soil of England, there is nothing on record to indicate them. By the time Martha was again fit to travel, the skies had cleared and he hired a small vessel to take him to Havre, where he arrived on the thirty-first.[4] Here he engaged a carriage to convey him to Paris. He was enchanted with the country through which he drove slowly to the capital, since he thought 'nothing can be more fertile, better cultivated, and more elegantly improved.' The harvest season was just beginning, and he found a farmer's pleasure in the animation of the fields.[5]

II

On reaching Paris, he first found accommodations at the Hôtel d'Orléans in the Rue des Petits Augustins. Here he was to remain until arrangements could be made for the house in the *cul-de-sac* Têtebout, which was near the boulevards, and for its furnishing. In the latter house he was to remain almost a year. He then leased the far more pretentious mansion and gardens of the Count de l'Avongeac, at the corner of the Champs Elysées and the Rue Neuve de Berri, where he was to live in perfect comfort throughout the remainder of his Parisian sojourn. It has been described as 'a very elegant one, even for Paris,' with 'an extensive garden, court, and outbuildings in the handsomest style.'[6] Mazzei described it as 'within gun shot of the stockade through which one must pass on the way to Versailles.'[7]

Here for four years Lafayette and the young French officers who had fought under Washington were to come and go constantly

---

[4] To Monroe, Ford, *Writings of Jefferson*, IV, 4.   [5] *Ibid.*
[6] Randolph, *Domestic Life of Jefferson*, 73-74.
[7] Mazzei, *Memoirs*, 291.

without ceremony, along with the French philosophers, writers, artists, politicians, and distinguished foreigners. Since there was abundant room and Jefferson was a widower, he invited Colonel Humphreys, who was assigned secretarial work of an official character, and Mr. Short, his private secretary, to share his home. Here they all lived in perfect concord, the younger men delighted with the luxury of the establishment and with the fruitful conversation of the philosopher, who was their chief. 'On my arrival I found that Governor Jefferson had been about a week in Paris,' Humphreys wrote a correspondent. 'He had taken lodgings and made provision for my accommodation. His politeness and generosity extended as far as to insist that I should live with him during our residence in Europe, adding, by way of inducement, that it would not be an augmentation to his expenses.'[8] This, it will be noted, was before he had taken the large mansion of the Count.

But, accustomed to the quiet and serenity of Monticello, Jefferson found it convenient, whenever he wished to work intensively on a public document or to meditate undisturbed by visitors, to have a 'hermitage' to which he could retire. At this time the Carthusian Monastery, situated on Mount Calvary, made a practice of renting rooms and taking in as many as forty boarders, who brought their servants with them. The paying guests breakfasted in their rooms and only assembled *en masse* for dinner in the evening. The utmost silence was enjoined, and voices were not expected to be heard outside the rooms. Whenever the roomers wished a breath of fresh air, they had the privilege of promenading the gardens.

Hither Jefferson was to repair at frequent intervals, and sometimes he remained as much as a week. He became a prime favorite of the monks, who often visited him in his home, and he was long to cherish an ivory broom, turned by one of the brothers, and presented to him by the Superior.

After Martha had been given an opportunity to familiarize herself with the scenes and shops of the city, she was placed in a convent school, though the father visited her frequently, and she was permitted to spend many weeks with him at his home.[9]

With his passion for system, Jefferson immediately organized his

8 Humphreys, *Life of David Humphreys*, I, 217.
9 Randolph, *Domestic Life of Jefferson*, 73-74.

life as nearly as possible in line with his habits at Monticello. In a
city feverishly given to frivolity and pleasure — as though forewarned of the tragic days ahead — he rose at six o'clock, when
fashionable society was just about retiring, and turned immediately
to his desk. Often he lingered at the breakfast table, charming his
two secretaries with his lighter conversation. The morning was set
aside exclusively for business. At one o'clock, he ordered his horse
saddled for a ride, or, more often, he fared forth for a long tramp
that soon made him familiar with almost every blade of grass in
the Bois de Boulogne, which he came to love. These solitary tramps
would take him often as much as seven miles into the country. He
found a tonic in the serenity of the countryside, the sight of peasants
bending in the fields, the sound of birds and of the wind rustling
through the branches of the trees, the smell of grass and flowers.[10]

Throughout his five years in Paris, Jefferson was to maintain an
establishment which in elegance compared favorably with the mis-
sions of most other countries, but almost immediately it was impressed upon him that he would suffer a personal loss in maintaining his country's dignity in a style to which it was not accustomed. He had no thought of making money on his mission, but
he could see no reason why the expenses incidental to and insep-
arable from it should not be defrayed by the Government he served.
Within a few months he was writing Monroe of his embarrassment:

> For the articles of household furniture, clothes, and a carriage,
> I have already paid 28,000 livres, and have still more to pay. For
> the greater part of this, I have been obliged to anticipate my salary,
> from which, however, I never shall be able to repay it. I find that,
> by a rigid economy, bordering on meanness, I can save perhaps 500
> livres a month, at least in the summer. The residue goes for ex-
> penses, so much of course and of necessity that I cannot avoid them
> without abandoning all respect to my public character. Yet I pray
> you to touch this spring, which I know to be a tender one with
> Congress, with the utmost delicacy.[11]

Monroe replied that he would 'with the utmost pleasure seek the
attainment . . . in a manner which will be most delicate and hon-

[10] Ibid.
[11] Bergh, Writings of Jefferson, V, 15-16.

orable to you.' Indeed, he thought, that all Ministers 'should have ive or six hundred pounds sterling more annually.'[12]

But nothing helpful was to come from it, and he was to continue his sacrifices to the end. It was all the more astonishing to Jefferson since Franklin had exacted that the Government should pay the rent of his house at Passy and that of Adams at The Hague had been met from the same quarter.[13] He was to continue throughout the remainder of his life to render the highest service to his country and to pay for the privilege at a sacrifice that was to leave him in straitened circumstances at the end.

Thus was he to live as Minister to France while laying the framework of the future commercial policy of the United States.

III

Meanwhile, Jefferson was engaged in his official duties. He had arrived in Paris to join two old friends, Franklin and Adams, for both of whom he had a sincere admiration. No one had a keener appreciation of the genius of the quaint philosopher or of the honest, robust patriotism of the Puritan. And both had admiration and affection for him. But the pioneer American diplomats in Paris had been in a state of turmoil previous to his arrival.

When the trio was composed of Franklin, Silas Deane, and Arthur Lee, there had been an atmosphere akin to that of a Donnybrook Fair. The inordinate vanity of Lee, the impetuous activities of Deane, and Franklin's consciousness of his superiority to both, while enjoying a personal popularity in France beyond the reach of either, resulted in conflicts, both open and disguised. When John Adams appeared, to take the place of Deane, it had been hoped that greater concord and unity would follow, but the vanity of the fighting Puritan was scarcely less distasteful to the philosopher than that of the Virginian with a peacock complex. The adulation pouring forth on Franklin, from the ladies of the court to the proletariat of the streets, made no favorable impression on Adams, who felt that the philosopher was too subservient to French influence. There had been difficulties from the start. And now Jefferson appeared as one of the trio.

[12] Hamilton, *Writings of Monroe*, I, 73.
[13] Bergh, *Writings of Jefferson*, V, 15-16.

Two men of mediocre talents had been succeeded by two men of genius, and one would have to search long to find in America three other men of such real greatness. Jefferson had looked with reverence on Franklin in the Continental Congress, where the philosopher of Philadelphia had humorously consoled him when he cringed under the criticism of the wording of the Declaration of Independence; and his gratitude to Adams for his vigorous support of the immortal document had given him the highest possible opinion, both of his ability in debate and of his militant patriotism. He liked both of his colleagues, and they liked him. And so delicate was his tact, so generous his nature, so modest his self-appraisement, that he was to maintain the closest friendship with both. If he knew the weaknesses of both, as he undoubtedly did, he pardoned everything to the limitations of human nature.

Immediately on reaching Paris and finding accommodations, Jefferson hastened to Passy, where Franklin was established in part of the Hôtel de Valentinois, generously put at his disposal without rent by M. Ray de Chaumont. He found the old philosopher serene and happy, despite the annoyances of his former colleagues and his occasional brushes with Adams. Jefferson's attitude was one of deference to his older colleagues and of complete confidence and admiration. When a French woman asked him if he was 'to take the place' of Franklin, he smiled deprecatingly, 'I am to succeed him; no one can take his place.' When, on observing women kissing the veteran Franklin, he asked if that was one of the emoluments of his office, the older man warned him that he was 'too young.' At this initial conference in Passy, it was agreed that Adams should be summoned immediately from The Hague for a working agreement on the general character of the commercial treaties to be sought.

In the simple ménage of Adams at Auteuil, Jefferson was to go and come without ceremony as one of the family, for the clever Abigail shared fully in her husband's fondness for the Virginian. The Puritan lady was unable to accord equal confidence to Franklin. She had been a bit shocked, at a scene during a dinner at Passy, by his seemingly familiar relations with the famous Madame Helvetius, whose manners she could not approve when, on entering the room, she had 'bawled out,' 'Mon Dieu, where is Franklin? Why did you not tell me there were ladies here?' Abigail was shocked to observe her 'chemise made of tiffany which she had on over a lutestring and which looked as much on a decay as her beauty,' her 'small straw hat with a dirty gauze half handkerchief round it.' And when she greeted Franklin 'with a double kiss on each cheek and another upon his forehead,' it was too much. And when, at table, she conducted most of the conversation, 'frequently locking her hand into the Doctor's' and 'throwing her arm carelessly upon the Doctor's neck,' and later threw herself upon a settee 'where she showed more than her feet,' the Puritan lady formed a very decided opinion of the French woman, 'although sixty years of age and a widow.' But she was even more astonished by 'the conduct of the good Doctor,' who had told her that in Madame Helvetius she would see 'a genuine French woman, free from affectation or stiffness of behavior and one of the best women in the world'; and concluded that she 'must take the Doctor's word for that,' but that she would have 'set her down as a very bad one.' [14] Now Jefferson also was to become a very good friend of the abandoned lady, but Abigail was sure that he would never give such countenance to such a hussy.

During the time that both Adams and Jefferson were in Paris, the latter was to make many visits to the house in Auteuil, and to enjoy his conversations with Abigail as much as with her less sprightly husband. 'Mr. Jefferson visits us in the friendly and social way,' she wrote. 'I shall really regret to leave Mr. Jefferson,' who, she recorded, 'is also a favorite of mine.' [15]

And the Adamses were treated as members of the family in the quarters of Jefferson. To Mrs. Adams we are indebted for one of the few descriptions of a social function at his home. She had found 'a pretty large company,' including Lafayette, Commodore Paul Jones, and the Chevalier de la Luzerne, and had been impressed by 'customs very curious here.' She noted that 'the gentlemen seldom or never sit down, but are standing or walking from one part of the room to the other with their swords on, and their *chapeau de bras,* which is a very small silk hat, always under the arms.' If they laid these aside while dining, they resumed them immediately afterward. She wondered 'how the fashion of standing crept in,' since she had 'suffered from it many times' — a complaint, not without

[14] Adams, *Letters of Abigail Adams,* 198.   [15] *Ibid.,* 77.

merit, often heard even to this day. She did not care for the *têtes-à-têtes* at table, and the low-voiced conversation between couples and groups afterward. Jefferson clearly had adopted the French customs when entertaining.[16]

Throughout his five years in France he was to maintain the most cordial relations with his colleagues of the Diplomatic Corps — which was to make him almost unique.

IV

The immediate mission with which the three American Commissioners were charged was the negotiation of commercial treaties with nineteen nations, enumerated in the last chapter, and the possible improvement of existing treaties with France, the Netherlands, and Sweden.[17]

Adams, responding to the summons, hurried back from The Hague, and the three men met at Franklin's house in Passy to formulate their plans and to prepare a model treaty to be submitted to each nation. They were agreed on the general character of the treaty outlined by Jefferson. Thus they made an early start, but it was not to prove an easy task. Jefferson proposed that they follow one of three plans, one providing that 'no duty shall be laid by either party on the productions of the other'; another, that 'each shall be permitted to equalize their duties to those laid by the other'; and the third, 'that each shall pay in the ports of the others such duties only as the most favored nations pay.'

But it was scarcely the period when high hopes of liberalizing trade in Europe could be entertained, because of the restrictions, monopolies, and tariffs, and Jefferson soon concluded that the best that could be expected would be treaties based on the most-favored-nation plan.[18] But, even so, he was to find little disposition to negotiate and hardly any interest in American trade.

Three weeks after the conference at Passy, the three Commissioners sat down in conference in the cabinet of Count Vergennes, the famous Foreign Minister of France. No one there but knew that, more than the King or court, Vergennes had been the architect of the Franco-American alliance, and though American ladies, who were royalists at heart, were to go into mourning for Louis XVI as the author of the alliance, Americans to this day have given little credit to the real sponsor of the plan.

From the cabinet of Vergennes, the American Commissioners hurried the next day to the Duke of Dorset, the British Minister, at his residence, to sound him as to the possibilities of a treaty with England. No one could have been found in England more sympathetic or realistic toward the new nation. In all the Diplomatic Corps accredited to France, Humphreys could find no one 'more civil to us than the Duke of Dorset, with whom [he] often dined, and who is the plainest and best bred Englishman [he] has seen in Paris.' [19] Jefferson's personal relations with him were more intimate than with any of his other colleagues, and the two London papers to which he subscribed were delivered from Dorset's diplomatic pouch. [20]

But he was soon to find that, however just and generous was Dorset, England not only had no desire for a commercial treaty with the United States, but that, through the propaganda of the press, she was conveying the impression that the new nation was in a state of anarchy as well as bankruptcy and that she was exerting all her ingenuity to discourage other nations from negotiating. 'We do not find it easy to make commercial arrangements in Europe,' he wrote General Horatio Gates. 'There is want of confidence in us.' [21] Adams, after his wont, was more bitter in expressing the same opinion in a letter to Gerry: 'I see so much enmity to the principles of our government, to the purity of our morals, the honest integrity and sincerity of our hearts; . . . I see so many proofs of their hatred; I see so many artifices practiced to debase everybody you send, or who comes to Europe.' [22]

After listening to the proposal of the three Commissioners, the Duke of Dorset had written to London for instructions, and these, on their arrival, left no doubt in Jefferson's mind that the British Government was entirely hostile. 'The letter from the Duke of

19 Humphreys, *Life of David Humphreys*, I, 328.
20 Jefferson to Adams, Bergh, *Writings of Jefferson*, V, 27.
21 Ford, *Writings of Jefferson*, IV, 25.
22 Austin, *Life of Gerry*, I, 382.

Dorset will, I dare say, surprise you all,' he wrote Monroe. 'It is folly above the highest that could be expected. I know from one who saw his instructions that he softened them much in his letter to us.'[23] Price had written Jefferson from England that 'there is, I fancy, no probability that Britain can be brought to consent to that reciprocity in trade which the U.S. expect,' and since the writer enjoyed a considerable intimacy with Pitt, Jefferson was convinced.[24] He conceded the right of England to stand aloof if she wished, though he marveled at the stupidity of it in the long view, but he bitterly resented the malicious propaganda of the British press, intended to discourage other nations from negotiating. He wrote to Monroe:

> The English papers so incessantly repeat their lies about the tumults, the anarchy, the bankruptcies and distresses of America, these ideas prevail pretty generally in Europe. At a large table where I dined the other day, a gentleman from Switzerland expressed his apprehensions for the fate of Doctor Franklin, as he had been informed that he would be received with stones by the people, who were generally dissatisfied with the Revolution and incensed against all those who had assisted in bringing it about. I told him his apprehensions were just and that the people of America would probably salute Doctor Franklin with the same stones they had thrown at the Marquis de Lafayette [25]

About this time he was writing Mrs. Adams in London that he noticed the London papers 'teem with every horror of which human nature is capable, assassinations, suicides, thefts, or robbery — the blackest slanders.' He hoped Adams would have enough philosophy to disregard such libels, but it would be impossible for him. In the bitterness of the moment his resentment flamed. 'I fancy it must be the quality of animal food eaten by the English nation which renders their character insusceptible of civilization,' he added. 'I suspect it is in their kitchen and not in their churches that their reformation must be worked and that missionaries of that description from hence [France] would avail more than those who would endeavor to tame them by precepts of religion and philosophy' — from which one gathers that he had not enjoyed his food at Portsmouth.[26]

[23] Ford, *Writings of Jefferson*, IV, 43-44.
[24] *Ibid.*   [25] *Ibid.*, IV, 87.   [26] *Ibid.*, IV, 100-01.

He was speedily to discover that the disintegrating process after the Revolution, with a certain disregard of monetary obligations, was shaking the confidence of Europe in both the integrity and future of the new nation. This, together with the doubt whether the treaties negotiated by Congress would be considered binding on all the States, convinced him early of the necessity of a strong federal union with the power, under a constitution, to enforce its decisions. When, at length, plans were being discussed in America for investing Congress with the power to regulate commerce, he observed a warming in Europe toward the States, even in England. He wrote Madison:

> It was not until these symptoms appeared in America that I have been able to discover the smallest token of respect toward the U.S. in any part of Europe. There was an enthusiasm toward us all over Europe at the moment of the peace. The torrent of lies published unremittingly in every day's London papers first made an impression and produced a coolness. The republication of these lies in most of the papers of Europe carried them home to the belief of every mind. They supposed everything in America anarchy, tumult, and civil war.[27]

Despite the difficulties, Prussia, Denmark, and Tuscany entered into negotiations, but such was the indifference of other nations it was not thought good policy to press them. Recalling the situation years later, Jefferson wrote: 'They seemed, in fact, to know little about us, but as rebels. They were ignorant of our commerce, which had been always monopolized by England, and of the exchange of articles it might offer advantageously to both parties. They were inclined, therefore, to stand aloof.'[28] Even Denmark and Tuscany became so cool in the negotiations that it was thought best to protract them until the powers of the Commissioners had expired, and then to await more propitious days to renew them.[29]

Only Prussia responded to the American approach. 'Old Frederick of Prussia met us cordially, and without hesitation, and appointed the Baron de Thulmeyer, his Minister at The Hague, to negotiate with us,' wrote Jefferson in his *Autobiography*.[30] The proposition submitted by the Americans was little changed by the King,

[27] Bergh, *Writings of Jefferson*, V, 108.
[28] *Autobiography*, 62-63.   [29] *Ibid*.   [30] *Ibid*.

and soon thereafter Jefferson sent Short to The Hague to sign the concluded treaty.

But at the moment this was not a reason for jubilation. Prussia was an inland nation with whom commercial relations were not thought highly desirable at best. The treaty agreed to by the Baron at The Hague contained two unusual stipulations which suggest the instructions written by Jefferson in Annapolis. Contraband was abolished in so far as it involved a loss of property to individuals, and the seizure of private property on land, simply because of enemy ownership and not because of the probability of hostile acts by the owners, was disavowed. In later years students of international relations have found this treaty 'symptomatic' in that it was 'idealistic and yet an idealism that the new world felt might be made practical'; and that in this document the negotiators had 'un-Europeanized its diplomacy' and 'placed the country in such a position among the nations as to make possible the preservation of an original liberalism and a unique influence on international obligations.' [31]

V

While the three Commissioners had full power to negotiate for a trade agreement with the Porte, Algiers, Tripoli, Tunis, and Morocco, Jefferson found himself face to face with the terroristic methods of their pirates and their domination of the Mediterranean. He loathed the thought of following the policy of other nations, including France, of humbly paying tribute for the privilege of sailing the sea. Within two months after he reached Paris, he was trying to learn how much the European nations were paying the Barbary pirates to purchase peace, but without success. 'They will not tell,' he wrote Monroe. He knew, however, that the sum paid was considerable and he thought it probable that as much as three hundred thousand dollars a year would be asked of the United States. Why not, he asked, offer them an equal treaty, and, should this be refused, 'why not go to war with them?' Since Spain, Portugal, Naples, France, and Venice were then practically at war with the pirates, the American ships could count on friendly ports. Was it not time to begin the building of a navy 'if we mean to carry on

[31] Woolery, *Relations of Jefferson to American Foreign Policy*, 19.

our commerce'? With Paul Jones and a half-dozen frigates he thought the infant nation could 'totally destroy their commerce.' He would not depend on bombardments, as did the Mediterranean states 'against the whole Barbary force brought to a point, but on constant cruising and cutting them to pieces by piecemeal.' [32]

This vigorous plan, deeply planted in Jefferson's mind, was never to be abandoned throughout his five years in Europe, but nothing was to come of it until years later, when, under his Presidency, the American Navy would take action against the pirates. It seemed incredible to him that all the nations paying tribute and suffering humiliations at the hands of the bandits of the waters could not unite and fight. He found them ashamed of their subjection, but partial to paying tribute. He found Adams unwilling to agree to the more direct and drastic action, though sympathizing entirely with Jefferson's point of view. Two years after Jefferson had proposed to fight and while he was still urging such action on his associate and friend, Adams was replying from London that he would like to see the pirates met by force, since it would 'raise the spirits of our people immediately, and we might gain the glory of finally breaking up these nests of banditti'; and that he favored the creation of a navy. But he thought such drastic action 'too rugged for our people to bear,' and he was sure the authorization of Congress could not be obtained. [33]

Jay was, in general, in complete accord with Jefferson, to whom he wrote that he hoped negotiations might be successful, since the American people preferred peace, but for his own part he would 'prefer war to tribute.' [34] And in his report to Congress, submitting the dispatches of Jefferson and Adams, he recommended that, since he had 'full confidence . . . in the integrity and discretion of those Ministers,' he was of opinion that 'it would be expedient to leave the terms of the proposed treaties to their prudence.' [35]

Thus it was that Jefferson, determined to test the nations as to cooperative naval action, personally submitted his plan for action to the Ministers in Paris of all the nations involved.

His plan provided for operations against the pirate states in con-

[32] Ford, *Writings of Jefferson*, IV, 4-13.
[33] Adams, *Works of John Adams*, VIII, 410.
[34] Johnson, *Correspondence of John Jay*, III, 178-79.   [35] *Ibid.*, III, 197.

cert; for the admission to the confederation of any other states in the future, 'reserving the right to prescribe the conditions of such accession'; for the reduction of the pirate states to a peaceable status 'without price'; for naval operations consisting of constant cruises on their coast with a naval force 'now to be agreed on.' It stipulated that the force agreed on should be furnished by the various nations in certain quotas now to be fixed; that in view of possible misunderstandings, due to the lack of harmony in officers, consideration should be given to a plan for having each nation contribute its quota in money, to 'be employed in fitting out and keeping on duty a single fleet of the forces agreed on'; that the management of the whole was to be lodged in the Ministers of all the nations accredited to Paris, forming a committee or council; that no offices should be created; that, in the event of war between any of the nations in the confederation, 'it shall not extend to the enterprise or interrupt it'; that after Algiers had been reduced to peace, the operations should continue against all the other pirate nations holding out for tribute; and that when this convention should be found in contravention to an existing treaty with the Barbary States, the treaty shall prevail and the withdrawal of the nation be sanctioned.

This plan was motivated partly by the suspicion that agents of Spain, England, France, and Holland were secretly thwarting all American efforts in Algiers.[36]

With his plan in hand, Jefferson made the rounds of the various legations. He found Portugal, Naples, the two Sicilies, Venice, Malta, Denmark, and Sweden favorable, but fearful lest the French interfere 'or secretly support the Barbary Powers.' They asked Jefferson to get an assurance from France covering this point.

Greatly encouraged, Jefferson hastened to Vergennes and mentioned the fear of the interference of the French.

'She would not dare do it,' said Vergennes.

This was enough to satisfy Jefferson, and he pressed the matter no further. When he hurried back to the Ministers with the reply of Vergennes, they expressed their complete satisfaction. Thus, all that was now required was consent from the United States for the formal presentation of the plan.

[36] Woolery, *Relations of Jefferson to American Foreign Policy*.

But it was not an easy matter to get prompt decision from Congress. Jay was to lament to Jefferson that he constantly experienced 'unseasonable delays and successive obstacles in obtaining the decision and sentiments of Congress, even on points which require dispatch.' [37] And Adams's fears were found well grounded. Because of the expense involved, the difficulty of the revenue under the existing system of the Confederation, and the possibility of failure, the project finally was abandoned.[38]

Thus, it would appear that among all the statesmen of the world, Jefferson first took the lead in a constructive way to end the piracy in the Mediterranean, which was to be acted against only when he became possessed of the powers of the Presidency.

VI

Soon after Jefferson reached Paris, Franklin, bowed down by age, the adulation and perhaps the kisses of Madame Helvetius, petitioned Congress for his release, that he might return to Philadelphia. There does not appear to have been the slightest doubt that Jefferson would succeed him as Minister to France. So certain was the event, because of his high standing in Congress, that Richard Henry Lee, who coveted the position for himself, vehemently pressed on Congress the special urgency and importance of the Spanish mission. Monroe had written Madison of Franklin's request and the certainty of Jefferson's appointment, since 'the opinion of all members seem to concur in the propriety of it.' [39] Lafayette and Marbois, who had inspired Jefferson's writing of the *Notes on Virginia,* and was to render great service to Jefferson in the negotiation of the purchase of Louisiana years later, had assured Monroe that it was the wish of France that Jefferson should follow in the wake of Franklin.[40] Monroe wrote Jefferson that he would almost certainly be appointed Minister, and probably would also be asked to negotiate with Spain on the navigation of the Mississippi.[41]

However, Lee continued his opposition by indirection in rather a bad temper, hotly resenting his colleagues' failure to be impressed

37 Johnson, *Correspondence of Jay*, III, 210.
38 *Autobiography*, 65-67.   39 Hamilton, *Writings of Monroe*, I, 51.
40 *Ibid.*, I, 56-60.   41 *Ibid.*, I, 52.

with the greater importance of the Spanish mission, until all hope was gone.[42]

Jefferson was chosen by Congress on March 10, 1785. He presented his credentials on May 14. In the court circle he had many friends, but he had never felt that the frivolous butterflies of fashion that fluttered about the court, contributing to its dissipation, had the slightest real friendship for the United States. He had no high opinion of the King, whom he found well intentioned but without ability or energy; and the Queen and the reactionaries that buzzed about her scarcely interested him at all. That he attended functions at Versailles there can be no doubt. But in his voluminous correspondence he did not think it worth while so much as to mention these occasions. Mazzei mentions a dinner which Jefferson attended, given by Marie Antoinette in honor of the newly arrived wife of the British Minister, and he must have conversed with the haughty lady, but he did not think it of sufficient interest to mention it.[43] But he differentiated sharply between the French people and the degenerate nobility that crowded like rabbits under the roof of Versailles. 'It is very much to our interest to keep the affections of this country, which is considerable,' he reported to John Jay. 'A court has no affections; but those of the people whom they govern influence their decisions, even in the most arbitrary governments.'[44]

On May 14, he appeared in the cabinet of Count Vergennes with his credentials, and three days later he drove to Versailles to present his letter of credence to Louis XVI. He was received in private audience. Adams would have given a microscopic account of the ceremony at the court, but Jefferson dismissed it with the words, 'went through the other ceremonies usual on such occasions.'[45] It is too bad that we have no painting of that audience with the King, two men occupying the opposite poles of thought, and that no Boswell was present to record the conversation. We may be sure that Jefferson's manner was as courtly as the most exacting courtier could have desired.

With Vergennes, the foremost Foreign Minister in Europe, with a long and brilliant record in diplomacy before he entered upon his long tenure in the Foreign Office, Jefferson was to have the best

---

[42] *Ibid.*, I, 56-60.   [43] Mazzei, *Memoirs,* 310.
[44] Bergh, *Writings of Jefferson,* V, 12.   [45] *Ibid.,* V, 8-10.

possible relations until that statesman's death. He had no illusions concerning the wily Minister. He understood perfectly that Vergennes, and not the King, as so many have been permitted to believe, had opened the way to the American alliance which rendered an immeasurable service to the colonies in the Revolution. But he also knew that it was not an interest in the welfare and freedom of the American people that had inspired him, but that he was motivated solely by a desire to cause the greatest possible embarrassment and inconvenience to the British. Jefferson knew him to be distinctly reactionary, worse than cynical toward democracy, and frankly skeptical about the future of the new nation. There were so many things about the Americans that annoyed him — the debts most of all, perhaps. But he was to play the rôle of friend, just as a consummate actor may realistically assume a rôle he does not feel, and play it without a flaw. Jefferson was to like him and admire him, and even to trust him when his word was given, and to find him helpful on many occasions.

Many years later, he was to write:

> The Count of Vergennes had a reputation with the diplomatic corps of being wary and slippery in his diplomatic intercourse; and so he might be with those whom he knew to be slippery and double-faced themselves. As he saw that I had no indirect views, practiced no subtleties, meddled in no intrigues, pursued no concealed objects, I found him as frank, as honorable, as easy of access to reason as any man with whom I have ever done business.[46]

Since no man ever lived, perhaps, more sensitive to atmosphere and with a keener intuition than Jefferson, we may suspect that his approach to Vergennes was not always without subtlety, but his methods were direct, his purpose open and avowed; and to Vergennes, accustomed to a diplomacy that reeked with hypocrisy and deceit, Jefferson must have seemed as a breath of fresh air from over a flowery meadow after a release from the atmosphere of a tannery. The two men got on well together.

The work of Jefferson now increased, but with no recognition of the fact from Congress, which gave no indication of the slightest disposition so much as to furnish him with a secretary. Franklin, though popularly thought to have been more simple than the Vir-

[46] *Autobiography*, 64-65.

ginian, invariably exacted whatever he thought himself entitled to
He had escaped house rent, which Congress left Jefferson to carry
and he had been supplied with a secretary. Three months after
Jefferson had presented his credentials, he had heard nothing. He
wrote Monroe:

> I have waited to see what was the pleasure of Congress as to the
> secretaryship of the office here, that is, to see whether they propose
> to appoint a secretary of legation, or leave me to appoint a private
> secretary. Colonel Humphreys's occupation in the dispatches and
> records of the matters which relate to the general commissions does
> not afford him leisure to aid me in my office, were I entitled to ask
> the aid. In the meantime, the lengthy papers which often accom-
> pany the communications between Ministers and myself and the
> other business of the office absolutely require a scribe. I shall,
> therefore, on Mr. Short's return from The Hague, appoint him my
> private secretary till Congress shall think proper to signify their
> pleasure. The salary allowed Mr. Franklin in the same office was
> one thousand dollars a year. I shall presume that Mr. Short may
> draw the same allowance.[47]

Thus Jefferson cut the Gordian knot, and Short continued as his
secretary. But with such clerical assistance as he was allowed, the
Minister was vastly overworked with his official communications
and his appallingly large personal correspondence.

Now that Jefferson has been more than a year in Paris, we may
pause, before continuing the narrative of his official activities, to take
note of his more personal life and his reactions to the Parisian scene.

VII

The first winter of his sojourn was not a little irksome. He was
confined to his home frequently by illness. 'A seasoning, as they
call it, is the lot of most strangers, and none, I believe, has experienced a more severe one than myself,' he wrote Monroe in the
spring of 1785. He ascribed his illness to the 'extremely damp'
weather, and to 'unwholesome water.' But with the reappearance
of the sun, his 'mighty physician,' he recovered both health and
spirits.[48]

[47] Ford, *Writings of Jefferson*, IV, 86.   [48] *Ibid.*, IV, 40.

Despite his illness, he was finding Paris fascinating, his mind eager for new impressions, his curiosity concerning French life insatiable. It was in keeping with his character that he had scarcely engaged quarters on his arrival before he was scouring the book-stalls, and writing Madison of his willingness to make any purchases desired. He found that books of prime importance 'are often to be met on stalls very cheap.' [49] Much interested in the reading of the two men who were to become his chief disciples and successors in the highest station, he was to write them constantly for five years about new books appearing from the press. 'Shall I send you so much of the Encyclopedia as is already published, or reserve it here until you come?' he wrote Monroe. 'It is about forty volumes, which probably is about half the work. Give yourself no uneasiness about the money. I may find it convenient to ask you to pay trifles occasionally for me in America,' he added tactfully.[50] Madison was writing him that 'all the purchases you have made for me are such as I should have made for myself with the same opportunities,' and enumerating many other books he would like.[51]

Along with Jefferson's interest in new books went an equally keen appetite for the news of the day. He followed the newspapers religiously and recommended them to others. 'I send you herewith the gazettes of Leyden and of France for the last two months, the latter because the best in this country, the former because the best in Europe,' he wrote Jay. The moment Adams reached his new post in London, he had a commission from his colleague of Paris. 'I ask the favor of you ... to choose two of the best London papers for me; one of each party,' he wrote. 'The Duke of Dorset has given me leave to have them put under his address and sent to the office from which his dispatches come.' [52] For Jefferson attached the greatest importance to the press as a mirror of public opinion, and he wished to follow equally the organs of the opposing parties.

But by no means did he confine his education to the library. He roamed the streets of Paris seeking historic scenes and beauty spots and visiting the shops. He was to insist on doing all the shopping for his daughters, since he found profit in his contacts and conversa-

49 *Ibid.*, IV, 3.   50 Bergh, *Writings of Jefferson*, V, 20.
51 Hunt, *Writings of Madison*, II, 133.
52 Bergh, *Writings of Jefferson*, V, 27.

tions with the tradesmen. Soon he was shopping for Abigail Adams. 'I immediately ordered the shoes you desired which will be ready tomorrow,' he wrote her. As a merchandise agent he was a rare correspondent:

> I have also procured you three plateaux de dessert with a silvered balustrade round them and four figures. With respect to the figures, I could only find three of those you named, matched in size. These were Minerva, Diana, and Apollo. I was obliged to add a fourth, unguided by your choice. They offered me a fine Venus; but I thought it out of taste to have two at table at the same time Paris and Helen were represented.   conceived it would be cruel to remove them from their peculiar shrine. . . . At length a fine Mars was offered, calm, bold, his falchion not drawn, but ready to be drawn. This will do, I think, for the table of the American Minister in London, where those it may concern may look and learn that, though wisdom is our guide and Song and Chase our supreme delight, yet we offer adoration to that titular god also who rocked the cradle of our birth, who has accepted our infant offerings and has shown himself the patron of our rights and the avenger of our wrongs. The group then was closed, and your party formed. Envy and malice never will be quiet. I hear it already whispered to you that in admitting Minerva to your table I have departed from the principles which made me reject Venus; in plain English, that I have paid a just respect to the daughter but failed to the mother. No, Madame, my respect to both is sincere. Wisdom, I know, is social. She seeks her fellows, but Beauty is jealous and illy bears the presence of a rival.[53]

Soon he would be buying a corset for Abigail's daughter and complaining that she had not sent her measurements. 'If they should be too small she will be so good as to lay them aside for a while,' he wrote. 'When the mountain refused to go to Mahomet, he went to the mountain.'

Thus, buying through him in Paris, Abigail received her full share of commissions to buy for him   London. He understood that 'the diaper and damask we used to import from England' could be had cheaper in London than in Paris. Would Abigail send him two sets of tablecloths and napkins for twenty covers each? [54]

In the meanderings of his shopping jaunts, he was constantly

[53] Ford, *Writings of Jefferson,* IV, 99-100.   [54] *Ibid.,* IV, 102.

intrigued by new inventions and mechanical devices and he was writing descriptions to his friends at home. To the former Secretary of the Continental Congress, he wrote in detail of a 'cylinder lamp lately invented here.' It gave light equal to that of six or eight candles, and, though olive oil was used, the consumption was light. Then 'they make shade candlesticks for studious men which are excellent for reading,' and cost but two guineas. And then, too, the new phosphoric matches — 'a beautiful discovery,' since 'the convenience of lighting a candle without getting out of bed, of sealing a letter without calling a servant, of kindling a fire without flint,' was worth while.[55]

In writing the President of Yale concerning some new publications, we find him turning enthusiastically to a mechanical device 'of moving a vessel on the water by a machine worked within the vessel.' Having heard of it, Jefferson had gone to see it. 'It is a screw with a very large thin worm, or rather it is a thin plate with its edge applied spirally round an axis,' and this, operating on the air, propels the vessel. 'The screw, I think, would be more effectual if placed beneath the surface of the water,' comments the diplomat.[56]

Liking the Parisians as he did, he playfully chided Abigail who had written glowingly of the superior equipages at The Hague:

> I consider your boasts of the splendor of your city and of its superb hackney coaches as a flout. I would not give the polite, self-denying, feeling, hospitable, and good-humored people of this country and their amiability in every point of view (though it must be confessed our streets are dirty and our fiacres rather indifferent) for ten such races of rich, proud, hectoring, swearing, squibbling, carnivorous animals as those among whom you are.

Indeed, he did 'love this people, with all [his] heart.'[57]

That he was not unmindful of the low state of morals at the time, and the consequent temptation to the young is constantly reflected in his correspondence. 'It is difficult for a young man to refuse it when beauty is begging in every street,' he wrote. But there were other reasons that prejudiced him against educating a young American in Europe. In England, he would 'learn drinking, horse-racing and dissipation,' become fascinated with the 'privileges

55 *Ibid.*, IV, 13-15. 56 Bergh, *Writings of Jefferson*, V, 35-37.
57 Ford, *Writings of Jefferson*, IV, 60-61.

of European aristocrats and monarchy,' and acquire 'a passion for
whores, destructive of his health.' ᴧ few years in Europe, he concluded, and the young man 'returns to his own country a stranger.' [58]

Even so, Jefferson was strongly attracted by the life in France.
'The roughness of the human mind is so thoroughly rubbed off with
them that it seems as if one might glide through the whole life
among them without a jostle,' he wrote Mrs. Trist. However, he
doubted if the abandonment of domestic bonds made permanently
for their happiness. 'Perhaps they may catch some moments of
transports above the level of the ordinary tranquil joys we experience, but they are separated by long intervals during which all
the passions are at sea without a rudder or a compass.' [59]

In a letter to Bellini, at the close of his first year in Paris, he sums
up his impressions:

> You are perhaps curious to know how this new scene has struck
> a savage from the mountains of America. Not advantageously, I
> assure you. I find the general fate of humanity here most de-
> plorable. The truth of Voltaire's observation offers itself per-
> petually, that every man here must be either the hammer or the
> anvil. . . . While the great mass of the people are thus suffering
> under physical and moral oppression, I have endeavored to examine
> more nearly the condition of the great, to appreciate the true value
> of the circumstances of their situation which dazzle the bulk of
> spectators, and especially compare it with that degree of happiness
> which is enjoyed in America by every class of people. Intrigues of
> love occupy the younger, and those of ambition the elder part of
> the great. Conjugal love, having no existence among them, do-
> mestic happiness, of which that is the basis, is utterly unknown.
> In lieu of this, are substituted pursuits which nourish and invigorate
> all our bad passions, and which offer only moments of ecstasy,
> amidst days and months of restlessness and torment. . . .

In science, he thought the masses 'two centuries behind ours,' and
though in literature 'half a dozen years before us,' he wondered if
there was not compensation in being placed 'out of reach of the
swarm of nonsensical publications which issue daily from a thous-
and presses and perish almost in issuing.'

But in polite manners he gave Frenchmen the palm, and hoped

[58] Bergh, *Writings of Jefferson*, V, 187.   [59] *Ibid.*, V, 80-81.

his countrymen would adopt 'so much of European politeness as to be ready to make all those little sacrifices of self, which really render European manners amiable, and relieve society of the disagreeable scenes to which rudeness often subjects it.' In France it seemed to him that one 'might pass a life without encountering a single rudeness.' He had 'never yet seen a man drunk in France, even among the lowest of the people.'

And he wanted words to describe his enjoyment of their sculpture, architecture, painting, music. 'I am almost ready to say,' he concluded, 'it is the only thing which, from my heart, I envy them.'[60]

VIII

Keenly interested in the advance of science and in the improvement of means of travel, he was fascinated by the plan of Monsieur Pilâtre de Rozier to cross the English Channel in a balloon. Locomotion by air was then in its early infancy. During the months that the aviators waited at Boulogne for favorable weather, the American awaited the event with zest. When, at length, in the summer of 1785, the attempt ended in tragedy, Jefferson wrote Monroe that this would 'probably damp the ardor with which aerial navigation has been pursued.' The balloon ascended, but, after proceeding about two leagues, a change in the wind brought it back to the French coast, and something happened to the balloon filled with inflammable gas when at a height of six thousand feet, and the aviator plunged to a pulp.

All scientific and mechanical experiments were to enter into all Jefferson's correspondence.[61]

It was that summer that Jefferson was both amused and amazed by the arrest of a French reviewer which occasioned much chatter in the drawing-rooms. Some years before, so the story was told, a chevalier was sent on a mission of state to some princess, though Jefferson, after hearing the recital fifty times, could never remember the name of the emissary or of the princess or the country involved. Failing in his mission, the emissary on his return consoled himself by writing a verse which escaped unscathed by authority; but some

[60] *Ibid.*, V, 153-54.   [61] Ford, *Writings of Jefferson*, IV, 60.

years later it was included in a collection of published songs. The reviewer for the *Journal de Paris* quoted the chevalier's song as a specimen of the contents of the book. Jefferson heard that he was 'seized in his bed that night and has never been heard of since,' and the paper was suppressed. 'Thus you see, Madame,' he wrote Abigail, 'the value of energy in Government; our feeble republic in such a case would probably have been wrapt in the flames of war and desolation for want of power lodged in a single hand to punish summarily those who write songs.' [62]

A little later, he sent Abigail a batch of news, apropos of the fate of the reviewer. The paper had resumed publication with the announcement that the reviewer had been discharged, and the assumption was that the offender was still languishing in the Bastille. With his strong convictions on the freedom of the press, Jefferson was prone to sneer. He wrote:

> I love energy in Government dearly. It is evident it has become necessary on this occasion and that a very daring spirit has lately appeared in this country, for notwithstanding the several examples lately made of suppressing the London papers, suppressing the *Leyden Gazette,* imprisoning Beaumarchais and imprisoning the redacteur of the *Journal,* the author of the *Mercure* of last week has had the presumption, speaking of the German papers, to say, 'car les journaux de ce pays-là ne sont pas forcés à s'en tenir à juger des hémistiches ou à annoncer des programes académiques.' Probably he is now suffering in jail the just punishment of his insolent sneer on this mild Government.[63]

Jefferson could not have dreamed when he wrote that a little later, when he would be leading the fight against the policies of his correspondent's husband, followers of his would be cast into jail for offenses of a similar nature.

IX

During his first summer in Paris, artistic duties were imposed upon him from home, in addition to his diplomatic obligations. The legislature of Virginia had authorized an act providing for the raising of a statue to Washington; and Patrick Henry, the Gov-

[62] *Ibid.*, IV, 61-63.   [63] *Ibid.*, IV, 68.

ernor, had committed to Jefferson the selection of the sculptor. He thought his task simple, since, as he wrote Henry, 'Mons. Houdon being unrivaled in Europe . . . and resorted to for the statues of most of the Sovereigns,' was clearly the man.

Thus, one day, accompanied by Franklin, Jefferson called at the studio of the artist, and they were easily persuaded that to make a statue without seeing the subject would be an impossibility. 'Statues are made every day from portraits,' wrote Jefferson, 'but if the person be living, they are always condemned by those who know him, for want of resemblance, and this furnishes a conclusive presumption that similar representations of the dead are equally unfaithful.'

But the Americans found Houdon so eager to associate his art with the figure of one he thought immortal that he had agreed to abandon for the time his statue of the King, close his studio, and journey to America. Jefferson thought, from his character, that he would not ask a considerable amount for the journey, probably two or three hundred guineas. Until the 'habit, attitude, and devices, etc.,' were determined, it would not be possible to make a contract. It is interesting to note that he and Franklin agreed that the figure should be of the exact measurements of Washington. He knew that statues were usually made larger because placed on an elevation, but Jefferson felt that there should be one figure of absolute accuracy from which others might afterward be made, and, if necessary, enlarged, to meet the requirements of the place in which it might be raised. 'The duty, as well as the glory, of this presentation, we think, belongs to Virginia,' he wrote. 'We are sensible that the eye, alone considered, will not be quite as well satisfied; but connecting the consideration that the whole, and every part of it, presents the true size of the life, we suppose the beholders will receive a greater pleasure of the whole.'

If an agreement could be reached, Houdon would leave in April, remain a month at Mount Vernon to prepare a bust of plaster. He would then return to Paris and devote two or three years to the marble creation.[64]

Six months later, Houdon was on his way, bearing a personal letter to Richard Henry Lee, in which Jefferson urged that every-

[64] *Ibid.*, IV, 26-28.

thing be done to facilitate the sculptor's work and favorably impress him on Congress as the proper person to be authorized by the nation to make an equestrian statue, since 'nothing but the expectation of this could have engaged him to undertake the voyage.' The pedestrian statue for Virginia would not have made it worth his while. It should be impressed on Congress that he was the greatest sculptor of his age, and that he would take the exact measurements of Washington, and that he had the facilities, house, furnace, and apparatus for the work.[65]

Meanwhile, Jefferson learned that the cost of the voyage and the expenses of the sojourn would be much more than he had originally written Henry. Nothing daunted, he wrote again to say that five thousand livres would be necessary; and, in the event of Houdon's death, en route, Virginia would 'pay his family ten thousand livres.' He confessed that the payment to the family was disagreeable to him, but Houdon 'has a father, mother and sisters who have no resources but in his labor; and he himself one of the best men in the world.' The State would be protected by getting insurance on the sculptor's life in London.

Thus it was that Jefferson, who selected the sculptor, determined to a large degree the character of the statue, made all the business arrangements with the artist, gave him money for the purchase of marble in Italy, advanced his own money for Houdon's expenses in France, and authorized Franklin, on his arrival in Philadelphia, to draw on him for other expenses. Houdon sailed with Franklin. This ends the first phase of the story of the Houdon statue which stands in Richmond today.[66]

X

In the midst of his official activities, never neglected, and running to and from the studio of Houdon, Jefferson in the intervals was bending over blueprints with a leading architect, working out plans for the new Capitol in Richmond and for a prison there. The Directors of Public Buildings in Virginia had asked him for plans. It was scarcely a reasonable request, since the plan for the Capitol was wanted in Richmond within six weeks of the arrival of the

[65] *Ibid.*, IV, 72-75.   [66] *Ibid.*, IV, 75-77.

letter, which left Jefferson but two, or at the utmost three, weeks for the work. But architecture was one of his loves and his heart was set on the architectural improvement of his country.

The moment he read the letter the model flashed on his mind. The Capitol would be patterned on the Maison Quarrée at Nismes, which he thought 'the best morsel of ancient architecture now standing'; and since it had 'obtained the approbation of fifteen or sixteen centuries,' it would be 'preferable to any design which might be newly contrived.' He was sure it would be 'superior in beauty to anything in America, and not inferior to anything in the world.' [67]

Happy in the prospect of the realization of his dream of beauty in the new Virginia Capitol, he engaged a leading architect. He and Jefferson, agreeing on their model, made rapid progress on the exterior, but more time and thought were necessary in so arranging the interior as to provide properly for the executive, legislative, and judicial departments of the Government to be housed therein. The pressure of official business prolonged this portion of the work, and, just as it was finished, Jefferson was horrified to hear that 'the first brick of the Capitol would be laid in a few days.' In hot resentment he wrote Madison, asking him to stop the work. He also made an appeal to Edmund Randolph. After all, he wrote, 'the loss will be only of the laying of the bricks already laid,' and the bricks themselves could be used again for the exterior walls. 'The loss is not to be weighed,' he wrote hotly, 'against the saving of money which will arise, against the comfort of laying out the public money for something honorable, the satisfaction of seeing an object and proof of national good taste, and the regret and mortification of erecting a monument of our barbarism which will be loaded with execrations as long as it shall endure.' The plans would be on their way within four weeks, or by the first of December. If the undertakers were 'afraid to undo what they have done,' he wrote, why not 'encourage them by a recommendation to the Assembly?' [68]

Meanwhile, when putting the finishing touches to his plans for the Capitol, Jefferson was feverishly working on plans for a model prison for Virginia, in which he worked out his ideas of humanity

[67] To Madison, Bergh, *Writings of Jefferson*, V, 110.
[68] To Madison, *ibid.*, V, 136-37.

and reform. The blueprints for both were on their way in January,[69] and while some changes were made in the Capitol plans, which Jefferson was to think had not been for the better, the historic old Capitol in Richmond remains a monument to his taste and a thing of beauty.

XI

Nor was this his only diversion in the artistic or intellectual sphere while he was dealing with tobacco and customs with Vergennes.

Finding the cost of printing his *Notes on Virginia* not prohibitive in France, he took the time to make a careful revision in the spring of 1785, and the book was printed for private distribution. After having had two hundred copies run off, he was assailed with doubts about sending them to any but his closest personal friends in America, and he appealed to the judgment of Madison, to whom one of the first two copies was addressed, the other copy going to Monroe. He had thought, as we have seen, to present copies to the young men of William and Mary, but he was fearful lest what he had said on slavery might lead to censure and do more harm than good.

But, unhappily as it turned out, he had presented copies to numerous men in Paris, and the *Notes* became so much a topic of conversation that a publisher, with a bad translation, was planning a pirated edition. Jefferson was to suffer no little annoyance and distress on this account, and in the end, in self-defense, he was forced to authorize a French edition with a carefully selected translator. The appearance of the book considerably enhanced his prestige among the intellectuals and accentuated interest in the land of liberty across the sea.

Intensely occupied as he was, the heart of Jefferson remained in his own country; and, unimpressed by the pomp and circumstance of public station, his mind turned constantly to home and friends. In his nostalgia, he was urging Madison and Monroe to visit him in Paris, promising 'a room, bed, and plate,' and sending estimates of the cost of the journey. And he was suggesting that Madison

[69] To Monroe, *ibid.*, V, 272.

establish a home near Monticello. Monroe had indicated a plan to do so, and so had Short. 'I shall believe that life still has some happiness in store for me,' he wrote. 'Agreeable society is the first essential in constituting happiness, and, of course, the value of our existence. . . . Looking back with fondness to the moment when I am again to be fixed in my own country, I view the prospect of this society as inestimable.' [70]

But almost a quarter of a century would intervene, with the exception of the three-year respite from 1794 to 1797, before he would again be the country gentleman of Monticello, and he had three crowded years in Europe yet before him.

And the labor of these years was just beginning, as we shall see.

[70] To Madison, *ibid.*, IV, 15-19.

CHAPTER

XV

FENCING WITH VERGENNES

I

FROM THE MOMENT he reached Paris, Jefferson had scanned the international horizon, observing with interest the gathering war clouds. For months it looked as though a European war over the navigation of the Scheldt was inevitable, everything depending on the Austrian Emperor. 'Those who expect peace have in view the Emperor's character which they represent as whimsical and eccentric and that he is easily affected in the Dog days,' he wrote Monroe.[1] The possible death of Catherine of Russia, whose health was precarious, might affect the plans of Vienna, but everything depended upon the 'ambition of a young man who has been taught to view his subjects as cattle.' Jefferson found the Dutch 'truly animated,' and ready to fight for their existence.[2]

While sympathizing with the prospective miseries of the people of Europe who might be used for cannon fodder, Jefferson was realistic enough to find a silver lining to the cloud for his own country. He thought England would probably try to evade involvement because of the lack of money, the danger of a rebellion in Ireland, and because 'the hatred of her people toward us has arisen to such a height as to prepare their minds for a recommencement of hostilities.'

But, assuming the Americans were not engaged again with England, Jefferson thought the European war would probably work to

[1] Ford, *Writings of Jefferson*, IV, 21.
[2] To General Gates, *ibid.*, IV, 24.

their advantage, by renewing 'that disposition to treat with us on liberal principles, a disposition which blazed out with enthusiasm at the conclusion of peace,' but had subsided as the result of the campaign of slander in the London press. But should war eventuate, he thought, the nations involved 'will be glad to endure our neutrality and a friendly disposition by a just treaty.' Thus, while hoping the people might be spared the miseries of war, if one should come Jefferson looked forward to getting any possible commercial advantage for his country.[3]

At the same time he was closely following the negotiations with the court of Spain regarding American rights to the navigation of the Mississippi. Sooner than most of his contemporaries, he understood the vital need; and, more persistent than most, he was to insist upon it doggedly. It was not until years later that he could find a satisfactory solution of this problem.[4] But word reaching him from Madrid indicated procrastination or indifference, or, at best, a proposition he found utterly impossible. 'I have a hint that they may agree to make New Orleans a free port for our vessels coming down the Mississippi, but without permission to us to export our produce thence,' he wrote Monroe in the autumn of 1784. Would Monroe feel the public pulse and ascertain whether this poor offer would be considered preferable to war? That Jefferson would prefer to fight is made quite clear.[5]

The diversification of his multitudinous duties is indicated in his observations on the imperative need of a postal treaty, of which no one had thought at home. He had encountered annoying difficulties in correspondence between America and France. 'If a letter is sent from South Carolina to France, it is deposited in New York until the French postage is paid,' he wrote Monroe. 'Every person, then, in France or America who expects a letter by post must keep an agent and a little bank in New York.' He thought they did these things better in Europe, where letters passed from one country to another without difficulty as a result of conventions between nations. 'Would it not be well for Congress to send us an instruction and power to form conventions?' asked the harassed diplomat.

[3] To Monroe, *ibid.*, IV, 4-13.
[4] See author's *Jefferson in Power.*
[5] *Ibid.*

II

And then, too, in his early period in Paris, Jefferson was intensely interested in a mysterious expedition being sent out by the French Government to the South Sea in command of Captain Peyrousse. It had been given out that the sole purpose was to improve the world's knowledge of the geography of that part of the world. Jefferson observed that men of eminence in different branches of science had been enlisted for the voyage, thus giving probability to the reasons officially set forth. But from conversations during the loading of the two vessels, Jefferson had become a bit skeptical as to the purely scientific purpose of the expedition. He wondered if the purpose was the colonization of the western coast of America or the establishment of factories for the fur trade. But what concerned him more was the possibility that France had not been 'weaned from the desire of possessing continental colonies in America.' Were that the purpose, Congress would be justified in prying into the game. He himself in that event would not be at all satisfied that the French would 'refuse one which should offer itself on the eastern side.'

Eager to learn all he could, his mind turned to Captain Paul Jones, who frequently had seen Jefferson in Paris and for whom he had a boundless admiration. This gallant sailor enveloped himself at times in mystery. One day Jefferson received a note from him requesting him to call at a certain hotel and to inquire, not for Jones, but for 'the gentleman just arrived,' since he had reasons for not wishing his presence known. It was at this meeting that Jefferson told him of a conversation with the Russian Ambassador, Simolin, in which it appeared that Catherine was eager to engage Jones for her navy in a war against the Turks. Jefferson had urged the sailor to enter her service, probably in the hope that this might lead to a trade treaty with the United States. But at this time the famous rover of the seas was in L'Orient, within a day's journey of Brest, where the Peyrousse expedition was being fitted out. Jefferson got into contact with him with the request that he go to Brest, in the event full information was not available in L'Orient, to inspect the equipment, and, as a sailor and practical man, give his opinion of the probable purpose of the expedition. He was instructed to conduct himself 'so as to excite no suspicion that we attended at all on

he expedition.' Jefferson knew his 'discretion could be relied on.'
The expenses would be 'trifling for satisfaction on this point,' and
Jefferson was sure he would be reimbursed for whatever outlay of
money might be required. All this was reported in a long letter
to John Jay, in charge of the Foreign Office of the Confederation.[6]

Thus the picturesque figure of Paul Jones, as secret agent of Jefferson, might have been seen tramping the waterfront at Brest,
mingling familiarly with the citizens and the members of the expedition in the rôle of a curious sailor on pleasure bent. He made his
report, which was not disturbing. But Jefferson's suspicions lingered, and months later he wrote Jay that the *Gazette* of France had
announced the arrival of the Peyrousse expedition in Brazil, and
that it 'would touch at Otaheite, and proceed to California and still
further northward.' Jefferson warned Jay that the *Gazette* 'gives out
such facts as the Court are willing the world to be possessed of,' and
that, in all probability, 'an establishment of some sort on the northern coast of America,' would eventuate.[7]

III

At this time there was a diplomat in Paris, representing the King
of Sweden, the Baron de Staël, who is known in history largely as
the complaisant husband of his wife. The marriage of the diplomat
with the free-and-easy daughter of Necker occurred two years after
Jefferson reached Paris, and while Madame de Staël is described
as a friend of Lafayette, she did not interest Jefferson enough for
him to mention her in his voluminous correspondence. Gouverneur
Morris thought her 'a woman of sense and somewhat masculine in
her character, but one who had very much the appearance of a
chambermaid.' Abigail Adams, in describing a dinner at the De
Staëls' before the marriage, when both Jefferson and Adams were
unable to attend because of illness, thought the Baron 'a well-made
genteel man, very polite and affable,' whose dinners would 'take
two years of an American Minister's salary to furnish the equipage
of plate.'[8] That the Baron was fairly competent as a diplomat may
be read in his dispatches on the Revolution, but that he was wholly

6 Bergh, *Writings of Jefferson,* V, 63-64.
7 *Ibid.,* V, 382.   8 Adams, *Letters of Abigail Adams,* 208.

incapable of coping with his madcap wife appears in the record. It may be assumed that the very sociable Baron had Jefferson at his table, but the American overlooked these occasions in his letters.

It was six months after the marriage that the Baron approached Jefferson with a query as to how the island of Saint Bartholomew, recently bought by his country, could best be made to serve trade between Sweden and the United States. Jefferson's reply reflects his disapproval of all artificial barriers of commerce. Assuming that the island was capable of furnishing few of its products to Sweden, he urged that it be made a free port. Then it could be used as an intermediary for such American goods as Sweden might require and for such Swedish products as the United States might want. As a free port, he thought, it would draw the tide of commerce then turning toward the Dutch and Danish islands. Then, too, American products could be deposited in the magazines of Saint Bartholomew, along with those of Sweden, and the exchange would be simple. Did the Baron object that 'this unrestrained license would give opportunity to subjects of other nations to carry on exchanges there, in which Sweden will not be interested?' To which Jefferson, enemy of artificial barriers, replied:

> What objections can Sweden have to other peoples meeting in one of her ports to carry on their commercial exchanges? On the contrary, would not every enlightened nation be glad if all the others would come to her as a common center for commercial operations? If all the merchants who make the exchanges of commerce in Amsterdam, London, Lisbon, Leghorn, etc., would go by common consent to Stockholm, would a wise Government obstruct such an assembly? If all the exchanges now made in the several parts of two continents of the islands of America . . . be transferred to Saint Bartholomew, would the island be rendered thereby less able to promote the commerce of the mother country?

He then enumerated the articles that might be exchanged between Sweden and America — Swedish iron particularly for American indigo, rice, and tobacco. Much of this exchange would be effected by the merchants in the ports of the two nations. But, he added, 'the surplus they cannot take at all unless Sweden will administer to them the means of paying for it.' This she could do by receiving at Saint Bartholomew whatever productions they would bring, such as flour, salt fish, and other things in the other ports of America. The Swedish merchants on the island would run into those ports and exchange their products for precious metals or commercial commodities; or the American merchant, performing these operations, could thus secure the money with which to buy the iron ready stored at Saint Bartholomew. Thus Jefferson played for a free port.[9]

These excursions beyond the limits of his duties as Minister to France illustrate how completely his activities ranged over the whole of Europe.

IV

However, his duties as Minister to a court verging on collapse were not neglected. But he was to be constantly embarrassed and harassed in his negotiations because of the slovenly nature of the Confederation. John Jay, who sympathized with his embarrassment, was utterly disgusted with 'the unreasonable delays . . . in obtaining the decisions and sentiments of Congress.' The failure of the States to meet their financial obligations promptly was maddening to their agents in the foreign field. Confidence in both the permanence and integrity of the young nation was early undermined all over Europe by the exaggerated, highly colored stories of weakness and depravity circulated through the English press. Recalling his chagrin in later life, Jefferson complained bitterly that 'some States contributed a little, some less and some nothing; and the last furnished at least an excuse for the first to do nothing else.'[10] He who could not bear to be personally in arrears in his financial obligations was literally tortured by streams of companies and individuals demanding money that was their due.

In early January, 1786, he was in despair over the prospect of having no money with which to pay the French officers whose payment the year before had created a favorable impression. The demands were pouring in upon him, and, with but twelve thousand livres on hand, the duns upon his desk amounted to forty-two thousand. The Treasury Board at home had made no provision.[11]

9 To De Staël, Ford, *Writings of Jefferson*, IV, 238-41.
10 *Autobiography*, 83.
11 To Adams, Bergh, *Writings of Jefferson*, V, 248.

And he could see but a feeble prospect of paying the debt to France — a debt of honor. It was in these days that the utter impotency and even the contemptible character of the Confederation was impressed upon him, and in indignation he wrote Monroe that 'there never will be money in the treasury till the Confederacy shows its teeth.' He thought 'the States must see the rod' and 'perhaps it must be felt by some of them.' The French officers who had fought with Washington, and who flocked in friendship to the house of Jefferson in Paris made him blush in humiliation. He found it embarrassing even to face Vergennes, who practiced the utmost toleration toward the Minister, knowing his feelings. One day, however, Jefferson cringed when the courtly count in conversation inquired 'if the condition of our finances was improving.' Jefferson was sure he was thinking of the arrears of the interest on the debt. He was forced to the lame explanation that 'the impost still found obstacles,' but that hopes were entertained from the sale of public land.[12] And from Jay he received but scant consolation. Jay wrote that 'a reluctance to taxes, an impatience of government, a rage for property and little regard to the means of acquiring it . . . seem to actuate the mass of those who are uneasy in their circumstances.' To these, he said, 'may be added the influence of ambitious adventurers and the speculations of the many characters who prefer private to public good, and of others who expect to gain more from wrecks made by tempests than from the produce of patient and honest industry.' And since 'the knaves and fools of this world are forever in alliance,' Jefferson should understand the difficulties of a wise administration.[13]

One gets the impression that Vergennes shared fully in the skepticism over the future of the United States, and that, while not unfriendly, his interest in the success of the young nation was not extravagant, now that his primary purpose in the alliance had been served.

This was the background of the long conversation of Jefferson and Vergennes covering the whole field of economic relations, in late December, 1785. Jefferson had attended several levees at the Foreign Minister's, but these invariably were crowded, the conferences

[12] To Jay, Bergh, *Writings of Jefferson*, V, 65.
[13] Johnson, *Correspondence of Jay*, III, 212.

rolonged, and, since precedence placed him toward the end, there
ever had been sufficient time for a real discussion. There had been
erfunctory discussions before, in which Jefferson had launched his
ght to bring about the abolishment of the tobacco monopoly. He
ad found that France consumed about twenty-four million pounds
year, and that in the selections of the Farmers General there was
n enormous loss in revenue to the Government. He had pressed
1e point vigorously that 'it is contrary to the spirit of trade and of
1e disposition of merchants to carry a commodity to any market
vhere but one person is allowed to buy it, and where, of course,
1at person fixes the price which the seller must receive or re-export
is commodity at the loss of his voyage thither.' He had argued
1at this resulted in the merchants carrying their produce to other
1arkets and taking in exchange the products of that country. He
ad shown that since the peace France had been forced to buy con-
iderable quantities of American tobacco in England and pay cash;
vhere, had it been sent to France, it would have been exchanged
or French products. Was it not true that the purchases made by
he Farmers General from America were paid in coin sent directly
o England? Did this not make an important part of the balance
upposed to be in favor of that nation against France? This ex-
•ortation of coin could be prevented were the operations left to the
"rench and American merchants instead of the Farmers General.

And, anticipating the question whether this would not mean a
oss of revenue to the King, he had replied: 'On the contrary, the
neasure I am proposing will increase his revenue, while it places
•oth the seller and the buyer on a better footing.' He had pressed
he point that, by eliminating the cost of the collection without the
oss of revenue, 'the consumer can buy cheaper by two or three
ivres per pound.' This reduction in price would spread the sale of
obacco to great numbers now unable to afford the luxury. The
King would get more revenue because of the greater consump-
ion.[14]

In time, as we shall see, this Jeffersonian crusade against the
"armers General monopoly was to make a favorable impression on
Vergennes.

[14] To Vergennes, Bergh, *Writings of Jefferson*, V, 68-76.

V

It was four months later that Jefferson journeyed to Versailles f
his special conference on commercial relations with the Ministe
When he was ushered into the presence of this famous statesman, I
was none too pleased to find Monsieur de Rayneval comfortab
ensconced. He was reputed to be 'one of the eyes of Vergenne
and in full possession of his confidence. But Jefferson thought hi
'more cunning than wise,' and his views 'neither great nor libera
He thought him a case-hardened bureaucrat, 'his heart susceptib
of little passions but not of good ones.' From his brother, Gérar
formerly in America and unfavorably received, he had unhapp
impressions of the new nation. Jefferson, in brief, found him a ma
of 'much duplicity,' and his presence in the department dealin
with American affairs most unfortunate.[15]

The conversation found Vergennes taking the offensive with th
complaint that American commerce had not found its way t
France, but continued to England, though no law compelled it.

True, said Jefferson, but that was due to the commercial relation
of the two nations. Merchants naturally take their wares to a mark
where they can make the most, and selling in England, they in
evitably bought there. Give the merchant an opportunity to sell a
a reasonable profit in France and he would not go to England t
buy.

Yes, agreed Vergennes, there could be no durable commerc
without an exchange of merchandise. When Vergennes agreed, Jef
ferson felt he had scored.

Furnished thus with an opening, Jefferson asked permission t
submit American products that might be sold in France. He cite
rice, which France bought from the Mediterranean.

Ah, said the Count, but the Egyptian rice is of a superior quality

And indigo, continued Jefferson, was produced in the French col
onies in sufficient quantity.

Yes, said the Count, and better than the American product.

And Jefferson hurried on — flour, fish, and provisions of all kind
were produced in abundance by the French. Thus, he concede

[15] To Madison, Ford, *Writings of Jefferson*, IV, 368.

rice, indigo, flour, fish, and other products had to be left out of consideration.

But, he went on, there were certain things France did not produce and could well buy from America. There, for example, were peltry and furs that could be furnished France to the amount of two million livres that would be spent with the French. This, he said, depended on the British giving up the posts, in accordance with the provisions of the peace treaty — a gentle hint to Vergennes. And then, Jefferson continued, America was experimenting to see if they could be transported to France. Vergennes gave assurance that France would take them if the experiment was favorable.

Turning then to whale oil, Jefferson said that the reduction in duty would enable America to sell profitably to France. In fact, a merchant named Barrett, known to Jefferson, had just arrived to settle at L'Orient for the purpose of selling the cargoes of whale oil and choosing the exchange. The first year, one-third would be taken in money and two-thirds in merchandise, since the fishermen needed money, but after the first year no money and only merchandise would be required. Jefferson observed that, while the reduction in duty was for one year only, it was to be assumed that it would be continued, else all the prospects would be lost.

Vergennes expressed satisfaction with the trade in oil, but failed to commit himself on the continuation of the reduction. Noting this omission, Jefferson did not think it necessary to remind him that 'we should claim its continuance under the treaty with the Hanseatic towns, which fixes this duty for them, and our own treaty which gives us the rights of the most favored nation.'

And then Jefferson launched on his favorite American product — tobacco. Again he reiterated the substance of his letter to Vergennes and the fact that, under the operation of the monopoly of the Farmers General, a vast amount of American money was spent in England that would be spent in France could American merchants sell their tobacco freely.

Yes, interjected Vergennes, but Jefferson must not forget that the King was receiving a revenue of twenty-eight million livres on this article and that there was a fear of tampering with the arrangement. Then, too, the revenue by way of farm was of very ancient date, and it would be hazardous to alter arrangements of long standing so intimately bound up with the fiscal system.

But, Jefferson replied, because of the ease of collection in the case of tobacco, this article could be withdrawn without in any way endangering the system. He assumed that the Government would confine the delivery to five or six ports where one collector would be sufficient.

Here, to Jefferson's amazement, Monsieur Rayneval broke in with an agreement as to the simplicity of the plan proposed by Jefferson and with the observation that propositions impractical at one time might become practical at another.

Which, said Jefferson, was precisely the reason he was pressing the matter now, when the question of the renewal of the contract was pending. And, turning to Vergennes, could not this particular article be separated or suspended until the Government could satisfy itself of the expediency of his proposal? But Vergennes thought no promise could be given.

Thus far, Jefferson had been swimming in smooth waters, but at this juncture Vergennes pushed him out into a rougher sea. He said bluntly that he had found in arrangements made with America no dependence could be put upon them. It was not a new complaint to Jefferson, since Vergennes had made it before one day at Fontainebleau when he had complained of the navigation acts of Massachusetts and New Hampshire. But a new complaint was now made in reference to the difficulties put in the way of the Chevalier de Mézières taking over, by inheritance, the Georgia lands of General Oglethorpe, whose heir he was.

The Minister was now in full swing. The administration of justice in America, he complained, was so slow that merchants thought the prospects desperate of collecting from American debtors. And more still — the commercial regulations of the States were disgusting to the merchants.

Finding these complaints new and serious, Jefferson passed them lightly for the moment, while calling attention to certain legal complications in the case of the lands of Oglethorpe.

Returning to his house, Jefferson prepared some observations covering all the new complaints. Vergennes had accepted as the law of the nation a sharp comment of Adams on the land case. Jefferson observed that the opinion of Adams not only did not count with the courts, but that his opinion would not be permitted to be read in the courts which would pass upon the rights of the Chevalier under the treaty, with a scrupulous regard for that instrument.

And tardiness of justice? Why, said Jefferson, in Virginia, where under the King it took eight years to get a judgment in the Supreme Court and from fifteen to twenty in the Court of Chancery because of the indolence of the judges, a judgment was now rendered in a year in the Supreme Court and within three years in the Court of Chancery. And — more to the point — for the protection of French commerce, a law was passed giving priority to the cases affecting the French merchants. And the case of the British merchants? That was on a different footing because no arrangements had been made by Britain to pay for the slaves she had carried off during the Revolution. And the Navigation Acts? Not one line in derogation of the treaty. And the complaint about the commercial regulations? No justification at all for that.

When, with this written reply, Jefferson went to Versailles, he was received, in the absence of Vergennes by Monsieur de Rayneval, who volunteered the opinion that the interest of the State dictated the removal of tobacco from the jurisdiction of the Farmers General. Indeed, he had strongly urged this on the Comptroller General, who had said that the contract with the Farmers General was so far advanced that the change of the single item would necessitate a complete revamping.

Yes, Jefferson said, but the right was reserved to the King to discontinue any article. Rayneval admitted it.[16]

VI

Jefferson was not through fighting, however. He had won over both Vergennes and Rayneval to his point that the elimination of the tobacco monopoly would be in the interest of France. But Robert Morris, the American, who was concerned with personal profit and not with the interests of either France or America, was resenting Jefferson's attack on the monopoly. Long after the event, Jefferson wrote Monroe of the personal animosity of 'a powerful person

16 Ford, *Writings of Jefferson*, IV, 117-30.

in Philadelphia who was profiting by that abuse.'[17] The fight of Jefferson, making an impression on the Ministry, had delayed the lease of the Farms six months, but in the end Morris got his contract for sixty thousand hogsheads of tobacco with the Farmers General, which shared his hostility toward Jefferson's crusade.[18] But a concession had been forced in the incorporation of a clause giving the King the power to discontinue the monopoly at any time.

It was at this juncture that Lafayette rushed to the support of Jefferson, whose friendship and affection he enjoyed. He proposed that Jefferson should meet two men who were familiar with the tobacco business. The meeting was held. These men, and Lafayette, urged that Jefferson propose to Vergennes the appointment of a committee to consider the case anew. Jefferson replied that it could scarcely comport with diplomatic propriety for him to suggest to the Minister a mode of procedure, but that he would press again for a more satisfactory arrangement. Lafayette thereupon agreed to urge the naming of a committee, and one was appointed which included him. All the facts and figures in Jefferson's possession were put at the disposition of the Marquis, who added to his knowledge by conversations with French experts.

Thus again Lafayette became the champion of America, giving battle to the two representatives of the Farmers General on the committee. After the new lease was made, the committee continued in action, primarily to show that the fight was not considered lost and also to give further enlightenment to the Government. But Jefferson had faint hopes of accomplishing anything so long as Calonne, a tool of the Farmers General, remained Minister of Finance. When, despairing of success, the committee urged certain palliatives intended to serve France, Jefferson lost interest.[19] 'I confess that I met them all with indifference, my object being a radical cure of the evils by discontinuing the Farm, and not a mere assuagement of it, which, rendering it more bearable, might lessen the necessity of removing it entirely,' he wrote Jay.[20]

The effect of the lease, which provided that the Farmers General

[17] Bergh, *Writings of Jefferson*, VI, 15-16.
[18] To James Ross, *ibid.*, V, 320.   [19] To Monroe, *ibid.*, V, 330.
[20] Ford, *Writings of Jefferson*, IV, 230-37.

should buy of but one mercantile house, and that the house of Morris, was to threaten other houses with ruin. Jefferson learned that merchants at L'Orient, both American and French, had been exchanging tobacco for French products, to the benefit of both countries, when the prohibition, in the interest of Morris, left them with sixty-four hundred hogsheads in L'Orient alone that they were thus prohibited to sell. This so enraged Jefferson's sense of justice that he carried the matter to Vergennes with the suggestion that common fairness dictated that the Farmers General be compelled to buy, to permit the merchants to 'wind up without loss the trans-action in which the new arrangement found them engaged.' [21] The great Minister instantly agreed to the compulsion.

This chapter closed with a note to Vergennes: 'I have been hon-ored by your Excellency's letter of yesterday enclosing a copy of the resolutions of the committee on the subject of tobacco . . . which will, I hope, by this measure be kept alive till more simple and per-manent arrangements become practical.' [22]

In the tenacity and stupidity with which France clung to old evils, such as those of the Farmers General, Jefferson was to find the explanation of her Revolution.

VII

Hearing from correspondents in Spain and Algiers that the United States might facilitate negotiations with the Barbary pirates, pro-vided she had a treaty with Turkey, Jefferson went to Versailles to consult Vergennes, who had served for some time in Constanti-nople. He wanted some idea of the cost of a mission. Vergennes assured him that it would be very expensive, since 'presents must be made to that court and everyone would be gaping after them.' Besides, said Vergennes, it would not procure a peace at Algiers one penny cheaper. He had found that, while the Barbary States ac-knowledged a sort of vassalage to Turkey, they remembered it only when they required something and forgot it when Turkey wished anything of them. No, said Vergennes, 'money is the sole agent at Algiers, except so far as fear can be induced also.'

Then, said Jefferson, returning to his mutton, why not have a

21 To Vergennes, Bergh, *Writings of Jefferson*, V, 301.
22 Bergh, *Writings of Jefferson*, V, 344.

constant cruise of frigates in the Mediterranean and even blockade Algiers? The Minister thought ten vessels would be needed. Jefferson thought it possible that, even in that event, England might give aid to the Algerians, but Vergennes thought it would create too much scandal.

Jefferson then introduced the subject of the trading posts being held by the British in violation of the peace treaty, and said they were not being held in retaliation for the debts to Englishmen, since the American merchants were quite willing to pay if given enough time. Vergennes was sure the posts were being held to divert the fur trade.

Cautiously feeling out the Minister on whether, in case the necessity for military action should arise in the case of the Western posts, France would be an active ally, as originally understood, Jefferson threw out the suggestion that England was not in a financial condition to wage war. When Vergennes, probably with a wry smile, replied that the United States was hardly in condition to wage war, Jefferson must have detected a sarcastic inflection in the tone. But, continued Jefferson, ignoring the thrust, the knowledge that France would support America in case of need would probably have a decisive effect on England. Vergennes replied vaguely that the United States could always count on the friendship of France.[23]

And, in truth, France was giving evidence of her friendly feeling. She had acted promptly, under the guidance of Vergennes, in the protection of the American merchants at L'Orient against the tobacco monopoly. She had agreed to the admission of American fish on the footing of the Hanseatic towns, which meant a reduction in duty. And she had made other commercial concessions she did not publicly announce. In a letter to the merchants engaged in the American trade, Jefferson had informed them, with the request that the information 'may not get into the public papers.'[24] And in a letter to Calonne, Minister of Finance, Jefferson had hailed these concessions as 'a new proof of his Majesty's friendship and of his willingness to multiply the ties of interest and intercourse between the two nations.'[25]

[23] To Jay, Ford, *Writings of Jefferson,* IV, 227.
[24] Bergh, *Writings of Jefferson,* V, 257-58.
[25] To Calonne, *ibid.,* V, 458.

But in a letter to Madison, Jefferson wrote that these concessions represented the negotiations of an entire year.[26]

VIII

And now Jefferson crossed the Channel to England.

He went to London on the urgent request of John Adams, the American Minister at that court. Adams had sent word by his son-in-law that the Minister from Tripoli, with whom negotiations might be begun, was in London, and that the Portuguese Minister there was ready to negotiate a commercial treaty.[27] No reference to possible negotiations with the English appears in the letter, but in his *Autobiography*, Jefferson says that Adams had 'thought he had discovered some symptoms of a better disposition toward us.' At any rate, negotiations with the English were to be undertaken.

Adams wrote Jay that he had requested the presence of Jefferson. 'Mr. Jefferson has long projected a visit to England, and this will be a good opportunity,' he wrote. 'No notice will be taken of it publicly in America, and his real errand will be concealed from the public here.'[28]

Jefferson immediately asked audience of Vergennes before his departure, and said he 'would be happy to be the bearer of any commands your Excellency may have for that place.'[29] He did not look forward with high hopes to negotiations with the English, since he had become convinced that their hostility to America had intensified since the peace. Two years before, he had written to Monroe that 'with the English, nothing will produce a treaty but an enforcement of the resolutions of Congress proposing that there shall be no trade where there is no treaty.'[30]

He drove to Calais and arrived in London six days later. From Adams and Abigail he received an enthusiastic welcome. Seven days later, at a levee, he was presented to his enemy, George III, and the Queen, and thought it 'impossible for anything to have been more ungracious than their notice of Mr. Adams and myself.' He saw

26 *Ibid.*, VI, 8.   27 To Jay, Ford, *Writings of Jefferson*, IV, 199.
28 Adams, *Works of John Adams*, VIII, 378.
29 Bergh, *Writings of Jefferson*, V, 286.
30 Ford, *Writings of Jefferson*, IV, 4-13.

at a glance that 'the ulcerations of mind in that quarter left nothing to be expected on the subject of my attendance.' And when, a few days later, he was received by the Marquis of Carmarthen, the Minister of Foreign Affairs, and noted the 'distance and disinclination which he betrayed in his conversation, the vagueness and evasions of his answers to us,' he was 'confirmed in the belief of their aversion to have anything to do with us.' Adams was not so despairing, but Jefferson could see no hope. And soon, even Adams was to be disillusioned when several requests for a conference with Carmarthen were refused, on some pretext or other.[31] The author of the *Summary View,* the Reply to Lord North, and the Declaration could hardly have expected a cordial greeting so soon after the humiliation of British arms; but he was soon to discover, to his chagrin, that men who had sympathized with the colonies in their struggle had turned cold toward the independent nation.

Soon he was to write Richard Henry Lee that the English 'feel we shall be glad of their commerce on their terms.' He had found no party in sympathy with America, 'in or out of power.' He had found even the Opposition concurring with the Ministers in this. In the Marquis of Lansdowne, and half a dozen others, he had found a spirit of friendship, but he could hardly consider Lansdowne as a party. And it was noticeable that even Lansdowne did not express in Parliament the cordial sentiments expressed in private conversation. Even though he were to enter the Ministry, he would have to bow to the King's will or leave, as he had done before. Hostility to America was the 'system' of the monarch. 'The object of the present Ministry is to buoy up the nation with flattering calculations of their present prosperity, and to make them believe that they are better without us than with us,' he wrote.

That courtesy to guests was not felt an obligation of gentility as to Americans was brought home to Jefferson at a private dinner where a General Clark, seated next him, declared that were America to petition to be taken back on their former footing, the petition would be generally rejected. 'He was serious in this and I think it was the sentiment of the company,' Jefferson wrote.[32] After several experiences of this sort, Jefferson wrote his friend, John Page: 'This nation hates us, their Ministers hate us, and their King more

[31] *Autobiography,* 63-64.   [32] Ford, *Writings of Jefferson,* IV, 206.

than all other men. They have the impudence to avow this, tho they acknowledge our trade important to them. But they think we cannot prevent our countrymen bringing it into their lap.'[33]

This general sentiment did not extend to Shelburne, the Marquis of Lansdowne, who warmly welcomed liberals to the generous hospitality of Lansdowne House, where Jefferson was received warmly. He found the Marquis most congenial and he liked him, but not without a realization that he had no influence on events. Even Pitt, with his free-trade ideas, of which he had given Ireland and France the benefit, held sternly aloof from America under the stupid frown of George III.

With the Government scarcely according scant courtesy to two famous Americans, one accredited to its court, the two diplomats were pounced upon angrily by English merchants, demanding the payment of the debts.

The occasion arose during the course of a conversation with a leading merchant who was astonished to find the attitude of the two Americans so reasonable. He was sufficiently impressed to request permission for a committee of the merchants, under the chairmanship of the head of the Association of British Merchants, to call for a conference. Jefferson and Adams expressed their pleasure.

The committee appeared. The diplomats set forth the grievances of the Americans because of the non-observance by England of the treaty of peace, including the refusal to give up the Western posts and the withdrawal of American property in violation of the agreement. The merchants complained, in their turn, of the obstructions of the legislatures in the collection of the debts. The diplomats reminded the merchants that they were authorized to treat of such matters with the British Government, which had refused to negotiate; and that the little circulating coin in the United States made impossible the immediate payment of the debts. The merchants admitted the impossibility of immediate payment and the propriety of official negotiations. They were willing to allow a reasonable time.

When the diplomats proposed a period of five years, with immediate judgments rendered, but with the payments spread, the merchants were astonished to find that they had been so willfully mis-

informed. The Americans then said that they were willing to acknowledge as the debt all the principal and interest before and after
the war. The merchants insisted that the interest accrued during the
war should be paid as well. The diplomats disagreed. The merchants could see the point made by the diplomats, but said it would
be a 'bitter pill.' Even so, the committee left in good humor, and
with the assurance from the chairman that he would immediately
communicate with the Minister of Foreign Affairs and that the
diplomats would hear from him. They never heard.[34]

In this connection it is interesting to note that Jefferson was not
personally in accord with popular sentiment in America on the payment of the English debts. Writing Monroe, he said that 'whether
England gives up the posts or not, these debts must be paid or our
character stained with infamy among all nations and all times.'[35]
The merchants would have been all the more astonished had they
known that Jefferson was of this opinion.

IX

One day, Jefferson and Adams sat down to a conference with the
Tripolitan Ambassador, Abdrahaman. The spokesman of the pirates
smiled ingratiatingly upon them as he smugly told them that Tripoli's price for peace was thirty thousand guineas. Tunis? Ah, yes,
he could speak for it. The price would be the same. Assuming that
Algiers and Morocco would demand an equal amount, the diplomats saw that the purchase of peace was quite beyond the capacity
of the United States. They prolonged the conversation solely for the
purpose of eliciting information, and dismissed the pirate from
their minds.[36]

More agreeable were the negotiations with the Chevalier Pinto,
of Portugal, but in the end, after a seeming success, they were to
turn out to be fruitless. The discussions ranged over a period of
six weeks. The general plan was that of the most favored nation.
Against all attempts to get concessions in Portugal's American possessions, Pinto held firmly. The only other item which was diffi-

[34] To Jay, Bergh, *Writings of Jefferson*, V, 298-301.
[35] Ford, *Writings of Jefferson*, IV, 222.
[36] To Carmichael, Bergh, *Writings of Jefferson*, V, 306.

:ult was the Americans' contention that American breadstuffs re-
:eived in Portugal should include flour as well as wheat. On this
he Americans were insistent. The Portuguese Ambassador was
frankly sympathetic, and finally signed the treaty with this stipulation, but with the warning, as Jefferson reported, that 'several
Nobles of great influence at their court were the owners of windmills in the neighborhood of Lisbon which depended much for
their profits on manufacturing our wheat, and that this stipulation
would endanger the whole treaty.' [37] And so it came to pass. For
months thereafter the correspondence between Jefferson and Adams
referred to the tardiness of the ratification in Lisbon.

The treaty never was ratified.

So terminated Jefferson's foray into the field of diplomacy in
England.

X

His general impression of England was expressed in a letter to
Page:

> I traversed that country much, and own both town and country
> fell short of my expectations. Comparing it with this [France], I
> found a much greater proportion of barrens, a soil in other parts
> not naturally so good as this, not better cultivated, but better
> manured, and therefore more productive. This proceeds from the
> practice of long leases there and short ones here. The laboring
> people here are poorer than in England. They pay about one-half
> their produce in rent; the English, in general about one-third. The
> gardening in that country is the article in which it surpasses all
> the earth. I mean their pleasure gardening. This, indeed, went far
> beyond my ideas. [38]

It would be interesting to know of his meanderings in London,
but his correspondence is singularly lacking regarding his impressions of that city. One must conclude that, aside from the King, the
Foreign Minister, and Lansdowne, who recognized in him a distinguished visitor, he saw no one of the public men who then gave
luster to public life. John Wilkes, who mentions having met him,
is the exception. [39] One would like to think that he had conversed

[37] *Autobiography*, 64.   [38] Bergh, *Writings of Jefferson*, V, 304.
[39] Wilkes, *Autobiography*.

with Burke, who had supported the position of the Americans and had revamped the *Summary View* for British eyes, and that he had enjoyed the eloquence of Fox about some cozy fireside and dined at Holland House in the brilliant company of liberals and lovers of liberty forever associated with the table of that most gracious gentleman of his time. He would have enjoyed the house so redolent of history, and in the spacious gardens would have found his spirit cleansed of the poison of prejudice which had come from his snubbing by the King. Was feeling then running so high that even the liberals dared not show an interest in the author of the Declaration of Independence? At any rate, Jefferson appears to have been so disgusted with the official snubs that he had turned with relish from the town to the country, and from the supercilious condescension of men to the solace and serenity of English gardens.

For eight days he drove with Adams through the always charming English countryside, the journey taking him to twenty-eight villages and towns, including Hampton Court, Reading, Stratford, Birmingham, Worcester, and Oxford. He went primarily to study the English gardens, taking with him Whately's standard book on gardening. 'I always walked over the gardens with his book in my hand,' he wrote, 'examined with attention the particular spots he described, and found them so justly characterized by him as to be easily recognized, and saw with wonder that his fine imagination had never been able to seduce him from the truth.' Among the more famous gardens he visited were those of Hampton Court, the Duke of Devonshire's at Chiswick, Lady Frances Pelham's huge garden of forty acres at Esher Place, that of Leasowes in Shropshire, Moor Park, and Blenheim. It is significant of Jefferson's jottings on his travels that, while he was an ardent admirer of Pope, the poet, when he visited his garden at Twickenham he confined his observations to the garden, merely describing the house and the obelisk to the poet's mother. At Stowe, the property of the Marquis of Buckingham, he was charmed with the garden, observing that the owner was the son of George Grenville, who had taken it from the famous diplomatist, Temple. At Stratford-on-Avon, he fell into no rhetorical rhapsodies over Shakespeare, and merely records 'seeing the house where Shakespeare was born.' Blenheim evoked no comment on Marlborough, and if Hampton Court summoned the ghost

of Wolsey, the robustious Henry, or the penitent tears of poor
Catherine Howard, he kept it to himself. Moor Park might well
have suggested Swift, whom he admired so much, but his love of
architecture here struggled alone with his love of gardens.

This dearth of descriptions, of poetizing and philosophizing, has
persuaded a French biographer that Jefferson had but little artistic
interest or appreciation, though there is a superabundance of evidence to the contrary. He who loved architecture and had a fine
historical imagination could see no reason for describing Hampton
Court or Blenheim, so often described before, or for indulging in
philosophical reflections on the history that had paraded through
their halls. On his travels we shall always find him writing down
only practical suggestions that might be useful to himself and
friends. He drove over England to study gardens; all else was chaff.

On returning to London, he sought in vain to make a farewell
call of courtesy on the Foreign Minister, who maintained his attitude of cold discourtesy, and then wrote a farewell note offering
his services for anything His Excellency might care to send to his
Ambassador in Paris. And he returned to France feeling he had
been roundly snubbed.

XI

He found Paris more cordial and entertaining. He was not disdainful of gossip and he retailed it to his friends. 'The marriage of
the Ambassador of Sweden and Miss Necker [Baroness de Staël]
you have heard of,' he wrote one. 'Houdon is about taking a wife
also.' [40] 'The Cardinal de Rohan and Cagliostro remain where they
did, in the Bastille, nor does the affair yet seem to draw toward a
conclusion,' he wrote another.[41]

Going in and out of his house this year, one might have seen
John Trumbull, the American painter whose great historic can-
vases adorn the rotunda of the Capitol in Washington today. He
was in Paris to have his 'Death of Montgomery' and his 'Bunker
Hill' engraved.[42] 'I persuaded him to stay and study here and then

40 To W. T. Franklin, Bergh, *Writings of Jefferson*, V, 313.
41 To Mr. Otto, *ibid.*, V, 317.
42 To Franklin, *ibid.*, V, 400.

proceed to Rome,' he wrote Humphreys.[43] It was during his London tribulations that Jefferson met the artist, who wrote his version of the relationship in Paris. 'He had a taste for the fine arts, and highly approved my intention of preparing myself for the accomplishment of a national work,' Trumbull wrote. 'He encouraged me to persevere in this pursuit, and kindly invited me to come to Paris, to see and study the fine work there and to make his house my home during my stay. I now availed myself of this invitation and went to his house . . . where I was most kindly received by him.' [44] It is interesting to know that the 'Signing of the Declaration of Independence' in the rotunda of the Capitol in Washington was begun under the roof of the author of that document. 'During my visit,' writes Trumbull, 'I began the composition of the "Declaration of Independence" with his information and advice.' [45]

The relations of host and guest were clearly agreeable. Trumbull went with Jefferson to dine with Madame Le Brun, the brilliant portrait painter, though strangely enough she is not mentioned in the Jefferson letters. Together they dined at Passy with the Abbés Chasse and Arnout, and though it was fast day, the painter was astonished with 'the luxury of the table in soups, fish and fruits, truly characteristic of the opulent clergy of the time.' [46] And they rose from the table of the clergy to visit Madame de Corny. When about this time the artists, Richard Cosway and his charming wife Maria, appeared in Paris, it was Trumbull who presented them to Jefferson, whom we shall find, a little later, romantically inclined toward the lady and in the meanderings of the group of artists over Paris, Jefferson invariably was along, with Maria as his particular companion.[47]

One Sunday in sizzling August, Jefferson went with Trumbull to witness the ceremony of the crowning of the rosière of Sarennes, a village near Saint-Cloud, four miles from Chaillot. Every year the most amiable, industrious, and virtuous poor girl of the parish was chosen to be received by all the villagers and strangers in a solemn ceremony in the little church. Jefferson that year was among the strangers. And after the ceremony, the diplomat and artist walked back to Paris over the Pont de Neuilly, 'a very beautiful stone

[43] Ibid., V, 401.   [44] Trumbull, Autobiography, 95-96.
[45] Ibid.   [46] Ibid., 116.   [47] Ibid., 118.

bridge over the Seine.'[48] It was some time later that one room in the house of Jefferson took on the appearance of a studio, and visitors might have seen the Minister posing for the artist in the painting of the portrait which is part of the company in the 'Signing of the Declaration.' It was there, too, that Trumbull painted the portrait of Major General Ross, a French officer, for the painting of the 'Surrender of Cornwallis.' 'I regard these as the best of my small portraits,' wrote Trumbull years later. 'They were painted from life in Mr. Jefferson's house.'[49]

XII

Thoroughly familiar with the work of the naturalist, Count de Buffon, as we have noted in his observations in his *Notes on Virginia,* Jefferson had several bones to pick with him. It was not until early in 1786 that the diplomat met him, and in their first conversation he was appalled by Buffon's ignorance of American elk and deer. 'He thought our deer never had horns more than a foot long,' he snorted, in a letter to a Virginia friend. Would not this friend 'take the trouble to procure for [him] the largest pair of buck horns you can, and a large skin of each color ... a red and a blue?' Would he not try to take these from a buck just killed, 'to leave all the bones in the head in the skin, with the horns on, to leave the bones in the legs with the skin on also, and the hoofs to it?' Then, by making 'only an incision all along the belly and neck to take the animal out, we could, by sewing that incision and stuffing the skin, present the true size and form of the animal,' and that 'would be a most precious present.'[50] And he hurried a similar request to another friend at home.[51] In this good-natured controversy with the French naturalist, Jefferson was to score a triumph that was to make the salons roar with laughter and to please him enormously.

He was finding much to compensate him for his homesickness. He was sending Patrick Henry an elaborate description of a new musket he had examined, since he had sought out the inventor and made experiments of his own with its operation.[52] He was writing

48 *Ibid.,* 101.   49 *Ibid.,* 151.
50 To A. V. Cary, Bergh, *Writings of Jefferson,* V, 244.
51 To Archibald Stuart, Ford, *Writings of Jefferson,* IV, 189.
52 *Ibid.,* IV, 136-37.

the Prévot des Marchands et Echevins de Paris, asking permission to present the municipality with a bust of Lafayette, done by Houdon.[53] Despite his multiplicity of occupations, when Monsieur de Meusnier was preparing an article entitled 'Economie, Politique et Diplomatique,' and submitted innumerable questions concerning the United States, Jefferson, wishing a correct picture presented in a publication he thought would go down 'to the late ages,' found time to prepare replies as minute and comprehensive as were his replies to Marbois when he wrote his *Notes on Virginia.* After the author had written his article, he submitted it to Jefferson for corrections. 'I read it, and was led by that into a still greater number of details by way of correcting what he had first written, which was, indeed, a mass of errors and misconceptions from beginning to end,' he wrote Adams. For this, he said, he had been paid for his trouble 'in the true coin of the country, most unmerciful compliments.'[54]

About the same time, Monsieur Soulé, writing his *Histoire des Troubles de l'Amérique et les Anglais,* sent proofsheets to Jefferson for correction. Again he turned author, in a letter of more than a thousand words, setting forth the written interpretation of Revolutionary events.[55] And when Jean Pierre Brissot de Warville, destined as a Girondist to the guillotine in the Terror, was writing his book on America, Jefferson made numerous corrections that were incorporated.[56]

This, too, was the year that Jefferson's Ordinance of Religious Freedom was finally passed in the Virginia legislature, and the author was beside himself with joy. 'Our act of religious freedom is extremely applauded,' he wrote Wythe. 'The ambassadors and ministers of the several nations of Europe resident at this court have asked me copies of it to send to their sovereigns, and it is inserted in full in several books now in the press; among others, the new Encyclopedia. I think it will produce considerable good even in these countries.'[57] He bubbled over with enthusiasm in a letter to Madison, boasting that it had been translated into French and Italian.[58]

Learning that Mirabeau, who was just emerging into the front

[53] Bergh, *Writings of Jefferson,* V, 429.
[54] Ford, *Writings of Jefferson,* IV, 296-97.   [55] *Ibid.,* IV, 300-11.
[56] *Ibid.,* IV, 281.   [57] *Ibid.,* IV, 267-68.   [58] *Ibid.,* IV, 334.

rank of pre-revolutionary statesmen, had not seen a copy, Jefferson sent him one, with the observation that 'the Count de Mirabeau will perhaps be able on some occasions to avail mankind of this example of emancipating human reason.' [59]

XIII

Most of this extra work was done during the hot summer in Paris, for Jefferson felt he could not afford the luxury of Fontainebleau. 'The Marquis [Lafayette] is gone into Auvergne for the summer,' he wrote Humphreys. 'The rest of the beau monde are also vanished for the season. We give and receive them, as you know, for the swallows.' [60] He would have liked to summer near the great palace of the monarchs and he did make occasional journeys thither. It was on one of these excursions that we get a glimpse of Jefferson's method of determining the state of a country, not by conversations with the powerful and high-placed, but with the ordinary folk.

As soon as I got clear of the town [he wrote Madison from Fontainebleau], I fell in with a poor woman walking at the same rate as myself and going the same course. Wishing to know the condition of the laboring poor, I entered into conversation with her, which I began by inquiries for the path which would lead to the mountain; and thence proceeded to inquiries into her vocation, condition and circumstances. She told me she was a day laborer at 8 sous or 4 d. sterling the day; that she had two children to maintain and pay rent of 30 livres for her home (which would consume the hire of 75 days), that often she could get no employment and of course was without bread. As we walked together near a mile and she had so far served as my guide, I gave on parting 24 sous. She burst into tears of gratitude which I could perceive were unfeigned, because she was unable to utter a word. She had probably never before received so great an aid. This little attendrissement, with the solitude of my walk, led me into a train of reflections on the unequal division of property which occasions the numberless instances of wretchedness which I have observed in this country and is to be observed all over Europe.[61]

59 *Ibid.*, IV, 283.   60 Bergh, *Writings of Jefferson,* V, 401.
61 Hunt, *Writings of Madison,* II, 246, note.

If he found himself 'alone' in the 'heat of Paris' that summer of 1786, he took his punishment in good humor and was able to write banteringly to Abigail Adams:

> It is an age since I had the honor of a letter from you, and an age and a half since I presumed to address one to you. I think my last was dated in the reign of King Amri, but under which of his successors you wrote I cannot recollect — Ocharias, Zoachair, Manahem, or some such hard name. At length it is resumed; I am honored with your favor of July 23 and am at this moment writing an answer to it. And first, we will dispatch business. The shoes you ordered will be ready this day and will accompany the present letter, but why send money for them? You know the balance of trade was always against me. You will observe by the enclosed account that it is I who am to export cash always, and the sum has been lessened by the bad bargains I have made for you and the good ones you have made for me. This is a gaining trade, and therefore I shall continue it, begging you will send no more money here. . . . You were right in conjecturing that both the gentlemen might forget to communicate to me the intelligence about Captain Stanhope. Mr. Adams's head was full of whale oil, and Colo. Smith's of German politics — but don't tell them this — so they left it to you to give me the news. I would rather receive it from you than from them. This proposition about the exchange of a son for my daughter puzzles me. I shall be very glad to have your son, but I cannot part with my daughter. Thus, you see, I have such a habit of gaining in trade with you that I always expect it. . . . Here, we have singing, dancing, laughter and merriment, no assassinations, no treasons, rebellions, nor other dark deeds. When our King goes out, they fall down and kiss the earth where he has trodden; and then they go on kissing one another, and this is the truest wisdom. They have as much happiness in a year as an Englishman in ten.[62]

Thus, buying shoes for Abigail, shopping for Martha, selecting a watch or a volume for Madison, and books for Monroe, he passed the hot season.

And every day he fared forth on a stroll of six or seven miles. On one of these walks with Maria Cosway, he stumbled and fell, fracturing his wrist. His companion did not realize he was hurt, for

[62] Ford, *Writings of Jefferson*, IV, 260-62.

unostentatiously holding his wrist, he continued the conversation, despite the excruciating pain. Nothing daunted, he practiced writing letters with his left hand, and his correspondence scarcely suffered. But the surgeon who attended him bungled the job, and for months Jefferson was to suffer torment. He had previously asked Congress for a short release for recreation, and now, hearing that the waters of Aix might be beneficial for his wrist, he also made plans for his journey into southern France, which was to take him as far as Milan in Italy. A few days before his accident, he had taken the elaborate mansion in the Champs Elysées, which was to be a useless burden for two months.

DIPLOMACY GRAVE AND GAY

I

BUT AFTER HE RETURNED to Paris, much water was to pass over the dam before Jefferson would fare forth on his southern journey. A man of impeccable personal integrity, with a high sense of monetary responsibility, he was suffering torment because unable to meet the obligations of his country in the payment of her debts. He found it especially painful to face the French officers who had fought with Washington and confess that he had not the means to pay the money due them. Since his home had become the rallying-point for many of these officers, he could not escape their reproving glances. When the Chevalier de Segond sent him a dunning letter, Jefferson replied that he felt 'with great sensibility the weight of these complaints, but it is neither in my province nor in my power to remedy them.' He explained that all money matters were with the Commissioners of the Treasury in New York and their bankers in Europe. He had written strongly to the Commissioners, who had assured him that they would provide the funds 'at the first moment it should be in their power.'[1]

Humiliated as a man, he was even more humiliated as an American, for he knew that, in the absence of adequate provisions for the payment of her debts, the prestige of his country was sinking lower every day. The idea that money might be borrowed from the Dutch for the payment of the French debt impressed him favorably, but he cringed at the thought of attempting the negotiations,

[1] Bergh, *Writings of Jefferson*, VI, 62.

and warmly urged Adams as the ideal bargainer.[2] 'For this I am the most unfit person living,' he wrote. 'I do not understand bargaining nor possess the dexterity requisite for the purpose,' and again he recommended Adams for the task.[3] 'More especially,' he wrote, 'is it necessary to get rid of the debt to the officers. Their connections at court are such as to excite very unfavorable feelings there against us, and some very hard things have been said. . . . The payment of the interest to the officers would have kept them quiet; but there are two years now due them.'[4]

Along with the ever-pressing problem of the debts, Jefferson's feelings were strongly enlisted in the war against Holland, inspired, as he thought, by England and supported by Prussia. When the dull Prussian monarch took warlike measures, the King of France declared that, in accordance with a pledge, he would oppose the Prussian aggression. Whereupon England notified France of the termination of the agreement as to giving notice of its naval armaments, and let it be known that she would oppose the French. Thus, a war between England and France seemed inevitable at the moment. That France was bound in honor to support the Dutch, there could be no doubt, and Jefferson had seen at The Hague the commitment in the handwriting of Vergennes. But Eden, the future Lord Auckland, hurried to Paris to assist the Duke of Dorset in the negotiations, and virtue was not militant at the then degenerate French court, though Marie Antoinette preferred war to dishonor. But, as Jefferson wrote Jay, 'the King goes for nothing. He hunts one half the day, is drunk the other, and signs whatever he is told.'[5]

In the end, France chose the way of dishonor. But in the meanwhile, Jefferson was concerned with the status of the United States in the event of a war between France and England. Convinced that great advantages would accrue were the States to maintain neutrality, he scarcely hoped that the English would permit it. 'Is it certain that Great Britain, by her searches, her seizures, and other measures for harassing us, will permit us to preserve our neutrality?' he asked Jay. If permitted, material benefits would come, though Jefferson doubted the effect of neutrality upon our morals or happiness.[6] He was to find that, having driven France into a dis-

[2] *Ibid.*, VI, 71.   [3] *Ibid.*, VI, 135.   [4] To Adams, *ibid.*, VI, 173.
[5] *Ibid.*, VI, 337-38.   [6] *Ibid.*, VI, 331.

honorable course, the English would attempt to force us also into a violation of our pledge. Eden, whom Jefferson thought tricky, called upon him to inquire the effect of the Franco-American treaty in the event of war and the intentions of the infant nation. Jefferson frankly said that the States were bound by treaty to receive the armed vessels of France with their prizes in American ports and to refuse admission to the prizes captured by her enemies. We had also guaranteed France her American possessions, and, should they be attacked, Jefferson was afraid we would be involved. 'Then there will be war!' shouted Eden, 'for they will most assuredly be attacked.' [7]

But with the surrender of the French at the expense of the Dutch, the war clouds were dissipated.

And there were other worries that preyed on Jefferson. A private letter to Jay, giving intimate details of Jefferson's conversations with Vergennes, had in some manner found its way in part into the public prints. Indignantly, he protested to Jay:

> It will tend to draw on the Count de Vergennes the formidable phalanx of the Farmers General; to prevent his committing himself to me in any conversation which he does not mean for the public papers; to inspire the same diffidence in all other Ministers with whom I might have to transact business; to defeat the little hope, if any exists, of getting rid of the Farm on the article of tobacco; and to damp the freedom of communication which the resolution of Congress of May 3, 1784, was intended to establish.[8]

With diplomatic letters regularly opened, read, and copied in all the countries of Europe, confidential correspondence could not be entrusted to the postoffice. Warning Jay against giving any but the most trusted people access to the letters of the American diplomats, Jefferson wrote that all the letters of Jay were regularly opened. 'Your letters which come by the packet, if put into the mail in New York or into the postoffice at Havre, wear proofs that they have been opened,' he wrote. 'The passengers to whom they are confided should be cautioned always to keep them in their own hands till they deliver them personally to Paris.' [9]

[7] *Autobiography*, 76; Ford, *Writings of Jefferson*, IV, 469.
[8] Bergh, *Writings of Jefferson*, VI, 42.
[9] Ford, *Writings of Jefferson*, IV, 465.

That Jay was equally chagrined is evident in his reply:

> It is greatly to be regretted that communications to Congress are not kept more private; a variety of reasons, which must be obvious to you, oppose it, and while the federal sovereignty remains just as it is, little secrecy can be expected. These circumstances must undoubtedly be a great restraint on those public and private characters from whom you would otherwise obtain useful hints and information. I, for my part, have long experienced the inconvenience of it, and in some instances very sensibly.[10]

Harassed and humiliated by importunate creditors, threatened with war, his most confidential letters given to the press, and his official correspondence opened at the postoffices, Jefferson was not unmindful of the fact that there was something electric in the atmosphere of Paris, denoting a change of a fundamental character. The old age was passing out; the new one, ushered in by the American Revolution, was knocking at the door. Politics was absorbing all conversation, even among the ladies. The cafés were becoming politically articulate. Jefferson was enormously interested as a spectator.

The passing of the old age was coincident with the passing of Vergennes, the greatest Foreign Minister in Europe, the strongest Minister of a feeble King. 'The Count de Vergennes has within these ten days had a very severe attack of what is deemed an unfixed gout,' Jefferson wrote Carrington. 'He has been well enough, however, to do business today. But anxieties for him are not yet quieted. He is a great and good Minister and an accident to him might endanger the peace of Europe.'[11] Jefferson had found him most agreeable, once his cynical amusement about popular governments was disregarded and the fact accepted that, while he might be useful to America, it would not be due to affection. Writing Madison ten days later that Vergennes was in danger, he drew a perfect thumbnail sketch of the statesman:

> He is a great Minister in European affairs, but has very imperfect ideas of our institutions, and no confidence in them. His devotion to the principle of pure despotism renders him unaffectionate to our Governments. But his fear of England makes him value us as a

10 Johnson, *Correspondence of Jay*, III, 243.
11 Ford, *Writings of Jefferson*, IV, 359.

makeweight. He is cool and reserved in political conversations, but free and familiar on other subjects, and a very attentive and agreeable person to do business with. It is impossible to have a clearer, better organized head; his age has chilled his heart.[12]

Thus, through January and early February in 1787, the great Minister, who had made such a decisive contribution to the achievement of American independence and who has been so utterly forgotten by the American people, appeared constantly in Jefferson's correspondence, as with real anxiety he watched the progress of his illness. By February, it was realized that he was 'seriously ill.' The doctors were puzzled. There was some hope, from the swelling of the foot, that it would turn out to be gout. And again Jefferson wrote, this time to Jay, that 'his loss at all times would have been great, but it would be immense during the critical poise of European affairs existing at this moment.' [13] Writing Jay again, a week later, he said he had delayed his letter in the hope of sending word of Vergennes' improvement, but, alas, he had not improved. On the contrary, he was growing weaker with the continuation of his illness.[14]

Within a week Vergennes was dead.

Jefferson saw Montmorin, his successor, and was 'pleased with his modesty, the simplicity of his manners, and his disposition toward us.' He promised himself 'a good deal of satisfaction in doing business with him.' He was to find him quite as friendly as his predecessor, but not nearly so able.[15] In the reorganization of the Ministry at this time, Jefferson was sure an improvement had been made. The re-entry of Malesherbes delighted him particularly. 'His knowledge, his integrity, render his value inappreciable, and the greater to me because while he had no views of office we had established together the most unreserved intimacy,' he wrote Madison. And Montmorin — 'his honesty proceeds from the heart as well as the head, and therefore may be more surely counted on.' [16]

A little later, Jefferson was sure that Montmorin and Baron de Breteuil were firmly in the saddle, but he thought the Archbishop of Toulouse, the confidant of the Queen, doomed to an early demise,

---

[12] *Ibid.*, IV, 366-67.   [13] Bergh, *Writings of Jefferson*, VI, 76.
[14] *Ibid.*, VI, 85.   [15] To Lafayette, *ibid.*, VI, 101.
[16] Ford, *Writings of Jefferson*, IV, 392-93.

and thought him possibly tolerated as an intended victim. 'His best actions are exciting against him a host of enemies, particularly the reduction of the pensions and reforms in other branches of economy,' Jefferson wrote Jay. And sooner or later, when the public learned of the betrayal of Holland, there would be a rumpus, and Toulouse would be the scapegoat. Indeed, he was to linger but a little while and gladly change his office for the red cap of a Cardinal.[17]

But the financial condition of France was desperate, the spirit of protest was spreading to the people, and Jefferson had little respect for the spendthrifts of the court and little confidence in any leadership from the Crown. 'The King loves business, economy, order and justice, and wishes sincerely the good of his people, but he is irascible, rude, very limited in his understanding, and religious bordering on bigotry,' Jefferson wrote Madison. He had no mistress and loved his queen, but since this made him subservient to her will, Jefferson doubted the advantage; for he found her 'capricious . . . devoted to pleasure and expense, and not remarkable for any other vices or virtues.' And, to make bad worse, the King was a glutton at the table and he had been drinking more heavily of late.[18]

It was after the death of Vergennes and the reorganization of the Ministry that in sheer desperation the King was driven to the summoning of the Assembly of Notables. Jefferson agreed with the average Frenchman that this event was 'the most important one that has taken place in their civil line during the present century.' He found that 'some promise great things, others nothing,' and he ventured no opinion.[19] But he was shocked and disturbed by the levity with which a great part of the people, especially in fashionable life, looked upon the event. He wrote in disgust to Abigail Adams:

> The most remarkable effect of this convention as yet is the number of puns and bon mots it has generated. I think, were they all collected, they would make a more voluminous work than the Encyclopedia. This, more than anything else I have seen, convinces me that this nation is incapable of any serious effort but under the word of command. The people at large view every object only as

17 *Ibid.*, IV, 462-65.   18 *Ibid.*, IV, 393.
19 To Carmichael, *ibid.*, IV, 358.

it may furnish puns and bon mots; and I pronounce that a good punster would disarm the whole nation were they ever so seriously disposed to revolt.[20]

But the common people did not figure in the salons, or in the fashionable society, or in the Assembly of Notables, and Jefferson soon was to find that these were not interested in puns, and within two years the Bastille would fall and no punster would undertake to disarm the people with a laugh.

No one, indeed, knew what the King had in mind in summoning the Notables for the first time in a hundred and sixty years. Many objects figured in the speculations of the gossips. 'This government practices secrecy so systematically that it never publishes its purpose or its proceedings, sooner, or more extensively than necessary,' Jefferson wrote Jay.[21] The fact that Lafayette was to figure in the Assembly gave Jefferson a keen personal interest, which crops out continually in his correspondence. He attended the opening session, made his farewell call on Montmorin, and at length started on his travels.

II

He wrote Adams, on the eve of his departure, that he had taken 'measures for the conveying to me on the road all letters, so that should anything extraordinary require it, I can at all times be recalled to Paris within a fortnight.'[22] He had his own well-defined ideas of travel, particularly for an American of that period. These he had set forth in a memorandum for Mr. Rutledge and Mr. Shippen. 'On arriving at a town,' he said, 'the first thing is to buy the plan of the town, and the book noting its curiosities. Walk round the ramparts when there are any, go to the top of a steeple to have a view of the town and its environs.' It would be wise, he thought, not to depend on professional guides to be overwhelmed with details, many imaginary. The national character, he warned, cannot be calculated from the people the traveler naturally sees most — the tavern keepers, valets de place, and postilions, since 'these are the hackneyed rascals of every country.' The American should give

20 *Ibid.*, IV, 370.   21 Bergh, *Writings of Jefferson,* VI, 45.
22 *Ibid.*, VI, 80.

his attention especially to agricultural life to determine what animals or plants might usefully be transported to the States; to mechanical arts, 'so far as they respect things necessary in America'; to manufacturing, superficially, since it was 'impossible that America should become a manufacturing country during the time of any man now living'; to pleasure gardens because America 'is the country of all others where the noblest gardens may be made without expense'; to architecture, since 'it is desirable to introduce taste into an art which shows so much'; to painting and statuary 'worth seeing but not studying,' since these were 'too expensive for the state of wealth among us.'

Naturally enough, he advised a careful study of politics in 'respect to internal affairs.' The purpose should be to determine their influence on the happiness of the people. 'Take every possible occasion for entering into the houses of the laborers, and especially at the moment of their repasts,' he urged. 'See what they eat, how they are clothed, whether they are obliged to work too hard; whether the Government or their landlord takes from them an unjust proportion of their labor; on what footing stands the property they call their own, their personal liberty, etc.' If possible, it would be well to see their courts, 'as you would see the Tower of London or menagerie of Versailles with their lions, tigers, hyenas, and other beasts of prey, standing in the same relation with their fellows.' Such an inspection, he thought, would convince the spectator that, 'under the most imposing exterior, they are the weakest and worst kind of mankind.' [23]

With these ideas of travel, Jefferson left Paris February 28, 1787, and drove up the Seine through Champagne and Burgundy; and then down the Rhone through the Beaujolais by Lyons, Avignon, Nismes, to Aix, where he was to linger long enough to try the effect of the waters on his wrist. Despite the necessity now of writing with his left hand, he could not but yield to the natural impulse to write his friends, even on his travels. In Nismes, he wrote the Countess de Tessé his impressions thus far on his journey:

> Here I am, Madame, gazing whole hours at the Maison Quarrée like a lover at his mistress. The stock weavers and silk spinners around it consider me a hypochondriac Englishman about to write

23 *Writings of Jefferson*, Definitive Edition, XVII, 290-93.

with a pistol the last chapter of his history. This is the second time I have been in love since I left Paris. The first was with Diana at the Château de Laye-Epinay in Beaujolais, a delicious morsel of sculpture by M. A. Slodtz. This, you will say, was in rule, to fall in love with female beauty; but with a house, it is out of precedent. No, Madame, it is not without precedent in my own history. While in Paris I was violently smitten with the Hôtel de Salm and used to go to the Tuileries almost daily to look at it. From Lyons to Nismes I have been nourished with the remains of Roman grandeur. . . . At Orange, too, I thought of you. I am sure you had seen with pleasure the sublime triumphant arch of Marius at the entrance to the city. I went then to the Arena. Would you believe, Madame, that in the eighteenth century in France, under the reign of Louis XVI, they are at this moment pulling down the circular wall of this superb remains to pave a road? . . . I thought of you again, and I was then in a great humour at the Pont du Gard, a sublime antiquity and well preserved. But most of all here, where Roman taste and magnificence excite ideas analogous to yours at every step, I could not longer oppose the inclination to avail myself of your permission to write to you. . . . Madame de Tott did me the same honor. But she, being only the descendant of some of those puny heroes who boiled their own kettles before the walls of Troy, I shall write to her from a Grecian rather than a Roman canton; when I shall find myself, for example, among the Phoenician relations at Marseilles.[24]

While trying the waters at Aix, he received a letter from Martha, who from her convent school had chided him on his journey as undertaken under the pretense of ministering to his wrist, when 'your voyage is rather for your pleasure than your health.' Jefferson read a girlish narrative of events not unmixed with juvenile worries. Martha had 'done a pretty handsome landscape with Pariseau — a little man playing on a violin — and begun another beautiful landscape.' But she 'went so slowly with my Tito [Livy], it being in such ancient Italian that I cannot read without my master, and very little with him even.' And did Jefferson really mean that she should dine at the abbess's table? The speech of the King and the Duke de Narbonne had been 'copied all over the convent.' And why had not Jefferson kept his word and written her? And

[24] Bergh, *Writings of Jefferson*, VI, 102-04.

'Titus Livius puts me out of my wits.' They were making history at the Assembly of the Notables, but she would not tell about it 'for fear of taking a trip to the Bastille.'

Not coddled in the least, Jefferson replied with parental severity: 'I do not like your saying that you are unable to read the ancient print of your Livy but with the aid of your master. We are always equal to what we undertake with resolution. A little degree of this will enable you to decipher your Livy. If you always lean on your master, you never will be able to proceed without him. It is part of the American character to consider nothing as desperate.' And of course he expected her to eat at the abbess's table. If he had not written, it was because he was constantly on the road. The journey had the possible restoration of his wrist as its purpose partly, but he also sought 'instruction, amusement and abstraction from business, of which I had too much in Paris.' [25]

At Toulon, Jefferson heard again from Martha, who would 'take up Livy if you desire it.' But 'there was a gentleman a few days ago who killed himself because he thought that his wife did not love him,' and the unsophisticated young girl of the convent must have astonished her father with the sage observation that 'if every husband in Paris was to do as much there would be nothing but widows left.' [26] Then, too, 'a coach and six, well shut up, was seen to go to the Bastille, and the Baron de Breteuil went two hours before to prepare an apartment. They supposed it to be Madame de Polignac and her sister.' And it all came about, wrote the little gossip, because the King asked d'Harcourt how much a year was necessary for the Dauphin, and when told two millions after looking over the accounts, the monarch was astonished and assumed that 'Madame de Polignac had pocketed the rest.' And then again that dreadful Tito Livy — 'it was in vain that I took courage; it serves to little good in the execution of a thing almost impossible.' [27]

Thus, throughout the three months' journey, the fencing match of father and daughter continued at intervals.

---

[25] Randolph, *Domestic Life of Jefferson*, 115-16; Ford, *Writings of Jefferson*, IV, 371-72.
[26] Randolph, *Domestic Life of Jefferson*, 118.
[27] *Ibid.*, 120-22.

III

From Nice, Jefferson wrote Lafayette, describing his methods and motives as a traveler. 'I am constantly roving about to see what I have never seen before and shall never see again. In the great cities, I go to see what travelers think alone worthy of being seen; but I make a job of it, and generally gulp it down in a day. On the other hand, I am never satiated with rambling through the fields and farms, examining the culture and cultivators, with a degree of curiosity which makes some take me to be a fool, and others to be much wiser than I am.' He had found among the people 'a less degree of physical misery than . . . expected,' since they were well clothed and had plenty to eat, 'not animal indeed but vegetable, which is as wholesome.' Perhaps they were overworked, and certainly the landlords insisted on too many hours' work a day.

Having taken Lafayette under his wing as a political protégé, he urged him to go about the country incognito to 'ferret out the people in their hovels as I have done, look into their kettles, eat their bread, loll on their beds under the pretense of resting yourself, but, in fact, to find out if they are soft.' That Jefferson had been acting on his own advice we may be sure. But Lafayette as a public man should do it, and then apply the knowledge gained 'to the softening of their beds, or the throwing of a morsel of meat into their kettle of vegetables.' [28]

It was from Marseilles that Jefferson wrote Jay of his plan to make a special study of rice on the journey. He wished to know if a different kind of machine was responsible for European rice reaching the market less broken than that from America. He had talked with numerous people who had been through the rice fields of Italy, but not one could intelligently describe the machine in use. Wishing to see for himself and hearing that this would be possible on entering Piedmont, he had later found that not a grain of 'Piedmont rice' was grown in Piedmont, and that he would have to go on to Lombardy. He went — only to find 'the machine the same as ours.' He concluded that the difference between American and Italian rice was in the species of grain, of which he had been told

[28] Bergh, *Writings of Jefferson*, VI, 106-09.

he Government of Turin 'is so sensitive that they prohibit the exportation of rough rice on pain of death.' [29]

Rice was to hold his attention throughout the whole of his journey on to Milan, but in every seaport town he touched, he interested himself in everything affecting American commerce. 'So far as carried in our own bottoms, I find it almost nothing and so it must probably remain till something can be done with the Algerians,' he wrote Jay.[30]

He was a husky traveler, as one had to be in the late eighteenth century in Europe, though he found the journey from Genoa to Aix 'fatiguing.' It meant two full days at sea, 'mortally sick,' and two more clambering over the cliffs of the Apennines, 'sometimes on foot, sometimes on a mule, according as the path was more or less difficult.' Nothing could have been more amusing to the spectator or more painful to the long-legged Jefferson than his travels astride a mule. Sometimes he traveled throughout the night without sleep.[31]

IV

From on board a boat on the canal of Languedoc, he wrote Martha more poetically than before:

I am at present sailing, as I have been for a week past, cloudless skies above, limpid waters below, and on each hand a row of nightingales in full chorus. This delightful bird has given me a rich treat before, at the fountain of Vaulus. After visiting the tomb of Laura at Avignon, I went to see this fountain — a noble one of itself, and rendered famous forever by the songs of Petrarch who lived near it. I arrived there somewhat fatigued, and sat down by the fountain to repose myself. It gushes, of the size of a river, from a secluded valley in the mountains, the ruins of Petrarch's château being perched on a rock two hundred feet perpendicular above. To add to the enchantment of the scene, every tree and bush was filled with nightingales in full song. I think you told me you had not noticed this bird. As you have trees in the gardens of the convent, there might be nightingales in them, and this is the season of their song.[32]

29 Ford, *Writings of Jefferson*, IV, 376-86.   30 *Ibid.*, IV, 376.
31 To Martha, *ibid.*, IV, 386.   32 *Ibid.*, IV, 388-89.

His love of the nightingale appears frequently in his travel notes 'The first nightingale I have heard this year is of today.' 'I have heard no nightingale since the last day of May.' 'I heard a nightingale today at Chanteloup.' The sounds of Nature pleased him 'The first frogs I have heard are of this day.' 'The first swallows I have seen are of today.' And the awakening of Nature in the spring delighted him: 'The wild gooseberry is in leaf.' 'The wild pear and sweet briar are in bud.' 'The almond is in bloom.'

But it was the study of rice that took him as far as Milan. 'Here [Nice] they tell me there are none [rice fields] nearer than Vercelli and Novarra, which is carrying me almost to Milan,' he wrote Short. 'However, I am embarked on the project and I shall go through with it.' [33]

The passage over the Alps for ninety miles to Coni was one requiring fortitude. He was forced to abandon his carriage at Nice, and it was necessary for him to drape his long legs over the sides of a short mule since the snow had not yet melted enough to permit the passage of vehicles.[34] But he had looked forward with some excitement to the hard journey as offering an opportunity to satisfy himself as to the passage taken by Hannibal in crossing the mountains. Carefully he had collected several books in which attempts had been made to identify the track of the man of Carthage, but he was to find that 'the descriptions given of his march are not sufficiently particular to enable us at this day even to guess at his track across the Alps.' [35]

In Lombardy he visited the rice fields and was shown every courtesy and attention by Count Del Vermi, to whom he was indebted for the best information he received there.[36] He studied commercial prospects at the ports of Marseilles, Bordeaux, Nantes, and L'Orient, talking with the merchants; and at Turin and Milan he became convinced of the possibility of selling American whale oil for their consumption. With their Governments he pressed the advantage to them of importing their American tobacco directly from the United States rather than indirectly from England.[37]

[33] Bergh, *Writings of Jefferson*, VI, 110.   [34] *Ibid.*
[35] To Wythe, Ford, *Writings of Jefferson*, IV, 443.
[36] Bergh, *Writings of Jefferson*, VI, 282.
[37] To Adams, Ford, *Writings of Jefferson*, IV, 396.

Bordeaux amused him, since he could see 'scarcely any beasts of draft not oxen.' Vergniaud, destined to be the brilliant leader of the party of the Gironde and the greatest orator in the approaching Revolution, was practicing law there, but he had not yet emerged, and Jefferson missed one of the most congenial men he could have met in France. In Nice he found 'a gay and dissipated society, a handsome city, good accommodations, and some commerce,' though he preferred Hyères, environed by 'delicious and extensive plains,' and with a 'society more contracted, and therefore more capable of esteem.' Marseilles impressed him favorably because of its 'extensive society, a good theater, freedom from military control, and the most animated commerce.' [38]

V

It was on this journey that Jefferson met, by appointment at Nismes, a young revolutionary conspirator from Brazil, Jose Joaquim da Maia. This youth was a student at the University of Montpellier, aglow with the liberal passions, and familiar with the part played by Jefferson in the American Revolution. Some months before, this stranger had asked for an interview with the promise of communicating something of importance, but because of frail health was unable to make the journey to Paris. Thus it was arranged that Jefferson should see him at Nismes. According to a tradition Jefferson and the youth talked as they rambled over the northern section of the historic town, and reaching the main gate of the Roman Circus they climbed the stone steps of the amphitheater to the second row of arcades where they continued their conversation. The young man's fervor and intelligence interested the diplomat, who, according to tradition, sympathized with his patriotic aspirations, but sought to moderate his expectations. Not long afterward the student died in France.

The story told by Jefferson is not inconsistent with the tradition. He informed Jay that the mysterious stranger was a native of Rio de Janeiro, then a city of thirty thousand. He told Jefferson the country was composed of Portuguese, native whites, black and mulatto slaves, and Indians, both civilized and savage. He said he

[38] To Short, Bergh, *Writings of Jefferson,* VI, 110.

had no hope of ever returning to his native country, and that the general sentiment of Brazil was in favor of a revolution, inspired by the success of the revolution in the United States. Only a leader was lacking, since no one cared to venture himself without the aid of some powerful nation; and they looked to America as the one most likely to give them honest support. They would need cannon, ammunition, ships, sailors, soldiers, and officers. If independence were attained, Brazil would want of the United States at all times shipping, corn, and salt fish, then bought from Portugal.

Reporting to Jay, Jefferson wrote:

> I took care to impress on him through the whole conversation that I had neither instructions nor authority to say a word to anybody on this subject, and that I could only give him my own ideas as a single individual; which were that we are not in a condition to meddle nationally in any war; that we wished particularly to cultivate the friendship of Portugal with whom we had an advantageous commerce. That yet, a successful revolution in Brazil would not be uninteresting to us.

It was not unnatural that South Americans, dreaming of independence, should turn hopefully for encouragement and aid to the nation that so recently had won its own. Just before leaving on his journey, Jefferson had been approached by a Mexican in Paris with a similar project. He, too, gave the impression that the mass of the Mexican people were eager to throw off the yoke of Spain, but, unlike the Brazilian, he did not make such specific requests. Jefferson wrote Jay that since this person was not only very intimate with the Spanish Ambassador in Paris, but was actually employed by Spain in the settlement of the boundaries of France and Spain in the Pyrenees, he had replied that a successful revolution in Mexico would have to await a greater enlightenment of the people, and that should Spain give the States advantageous commercial terms, it would be unlikely that the United States would be willing to abandon a present advantage for a possible remote one. The fencing diplomat thought this might be not only safely but advantageously conveyed to Madrid if his visitor was a secret agent. 'He had much the air of candor,' Jefferson wrote, 'but that can be borrowed; so I was not able to decide about him in my own mind.' [39]

[39] To Jay, Ford, *Writings of Jefferson*, IV, 376-86.

But Jefferson was returning to a Paris where actual revolution was making rapid progress.

VI

Throughout his journey Jefferson was keenly interested in commerce, agriculture, architecture, towns, and country, and it was typical of him that he pried into the lives of the workers, peasants, and artisans. He noted that in the neighborhood of Aix the laborers breakfasted on 'bread with an anchovy or an onion,' dined on 'soup and vegetables,' and for supper repeated the menu of the lunch. He inquired into the miserable wages paid the workers and made note of what they ate and the cost of the food. He was pleased when he found the peasants living on the farms instead of in villages where they were 'less happy and virtuous.' But nothing so distressed him as the treatment of women to which he frequently referred in his notes. 'The women here smite on the anvil and work with the maul and spade,' he wrote in disgust. When he found the locks on the canal of Languedoc operated by women, he thought 'the necessary operation much too laborious for them,' and he launched into an attack on the system:

> The encroachments by the men on the offices proper for the women is a great derangement of the order of things. Men are shoemakers, tailors, upholsterers, stay-makers, mantua-makers, cooks, housekeepers, house-cleaners, bed-makers; they coiffe the ladies and bring them to bed; the women, therefore, to live, are obliged to undertake the offices which they abandon. They become porters, carters, reapers, sailors, lock-keepers, smiters on the anvil, cultivators of the earth, etc. Can we wonder, if such of them as have a little beauty, prefer easier courses to get their livelihood, as long as that beauty lasts? Ladies who employ men in the offices which should be reserved for their sex — are they not bawds in effect? For every man whom they thus employ, some girl, whose place he has thus taken, is driven to whoredom.[40]

Thus it was a liberal who roamed over France and Italy that summer.

[40] Definitive Edition, *Writings of Jefferson*, XVII, 211-12.

VII

And now Jefferson was back in Paris.

The Assembly of Notables, confronted by a financial situation o
the greatest gravity, did little more than urge upon the King th
summoning of the States General, representing all elements of th
nation, for the first time since 1614, more than a hundred and sev
enty years before. The King was to hesitate for more than a ful
year before yielding to the demand.

In the meanwhile, Jefferson found the temper of the people ris
ing dangerously. While on his homeward journey he had hope
that some good might come from the minor reforms attempted b
the Notables. But he found, on reaching Paris, that the exposur
of the financial plight of the nation had frightened the people, with
the public credit affected, and 'such a spirit of discontent . . . as ha
never been seen.' The demand for the calling of the States Genera
rose to a scream, with the people speaking 'with a boldness unex
ampled.' The stubborn attitude of the spineless King he though
was doing harm.[41] To Washington he wrote that 'the discovery o
the abominable abuses of public money by the late Comptroller
General, some new expenses of the Court not of a piece with th
projects of reformation, and the imposition of new taxes, have, in
the course of a few weeks, raised a spirit of discontent in this nation
so great and general, as to threaten serious consequences.'[42] To
Adams he wrote that 'all tongues in Paris have been let loose and
never was a license of speaking against the government exercised
in London more freely or more universally.' Caricatures in papers
placards on the walls, bon mots indulged in by all ranks of people
had attracted his attention, and he had not heard of a single case
of punishment. He had seen mobs of many thousands surrounding
the *parlement* in Paris, applauding its favorites, taking the horses
from their carriages and drawing them home. He had seen the
thoroughly frightened Government multiplying the guards, order
ing regiments of soldiers into the neighborhood, patrolling the
streets. Clubs had been forbidden. The silly Count d'Artois had
been hissed and hooted, and the crowds, mistaking another woman
of the court for Madame de Polignac, had stopped her carriage

[41] To Monroe, Bergh, *Writings of Jefferson*, VI, 234.   [42] *Ibid.*, VI, 276.

The Queen, accompanied by Madame de Polignac, had been received with hisses at the theater in Versailles. And what was being done about it? 'The King, long in the habit of drowning his cares in wine, plunges deeper and deeper,' wrote Jefferson. 'The Queen cries but sins on.'[43]

That summer, Jefferson lingered as usual in Paris despite the heat. Again he was deserted by his French friends. 'The Duchess d'Enville is with some of her friends, the Duke and Duchess de la Rochefoucauld gone to the waters, the Countess d'Houdelot with Madame de la Britu,' he told a friend.[44]

But, aside from the political restlessness of the people, there were other changes in Paris that interested and consoled him in the heat. He wrote Humphreys that the 'wall of circumvallation round Paris and the palace by which we are to be let in and out are nearly completed; four hospitals are to be built instead of the old Hôtel-Dieu; one of the old bridges has all its houses demolished, and a second nearly so; a new bridge is begun at the Place Louis XIV.' And the Palais Royal had been 'gutted,' with much of the center of the garden dug out, and 'a subterranean circus begun, wherein will be equestrian exhibitions.' In society, 'the habit habillé is almost banished, and they begin to go even to great suppers in frock.' To which he added, slyly, 'the court and diplomatic corps, however, must always be excepted,' since 'they are too high to be reached by any improvement.'[45]

Jefferson still clung to the belief that out of the turmoil would come reforms without the uprooting of the monarchy, for he doubted if the people were ready for a republic. His friends were genuine reformers and not revolutionists.

VIII

And he had other things to occupy his mind. He still chafed under the propaganda, so general in Europe, depicting the United States as in a state of anarchy, with highway robbers infesting the roads. He wrote Monsieur Clavière:

> It is a happy truth for us, sir, that these evils do not exist, and never did exist in our part of America. That Sieur de Perponcher

[43] *Ibid.*, VI, 286.   [44] To Crèvecoeur, *ibid.*, VI, 253.   [45] *Ibid.*, VI, 278.

has suffered himself to be misled, probably by the English papers. I attended the bar of the Supreme Court of Virginia ten years as student and practitioner. There never was during that time a trial for robbery on the highroad, nor do I remember ever to have heard of one in that or any other of the States, except in the cities of New York and Philadelphia immediately after the departure of the British army.

To which he added, saltily: 'Some deserters from that army infested those cities for a while.' [46]

So sensitive had Jefferson become to this persistent slandering of his countrymen that he actually brought himself to the writing of a satirical letter to the editor of the *Journal de Paris* during the dog days of 1787:

When young, I was passionately fond of reading books of history and travels. Since the commencement of the late Revolution which separated us from Great Britain, our country has been thought worthy to employ the pens of historians and travelers. I cannot paint to you, Sir, the agonies which these have cost me, in obliging me to renounce those favorite branches of reading and in discovering to me at length that my whole life has been employed in nourishing my mind with fables and falsehoods. For thus I reason. If the histories of d'Auberteuil and of Longchamps, and the travels of the Abbé Robin can be published in the face of the world, can be read and believed by those who are contemporary with the events they pretend to relate, how may we expect that future ages shall be better informed? Would these rise from their graves to bear witness to the truth who would not while living lift their voices against falsehood? If contemporary histories are thus false, what will future compilations be?

Here Jefferson pointed out a lie about the Declaration of Independence which he was well able to contradict. 'With my regards and adieu to History, to Travels, to Mayer, and to you, sir.' [47]

Since we shall find that in later life, when he was engaged in bitter party struggles in his own country, that he shuddered at the thought of writing for the papers,[48] it is clear that he must have been greatly aroused to have written the editor of the *Journal de Paris.*

[46] Ford, *Writings of Jefferson,* IV, 402.
[47] *Ibid.,* IV, 439-43.   [48] See author's *Jefferson and Hamilton.*

IX

But the heat of the summer and his annoyances did not restrain him from pressing on Montmorin, the successor of the late lamented Vergennes, his pleas for more favorable trade arrangements. The new Minister had left an opening in writing Jefferson from Fontainebleau, asking certain information. He replied with some observations on the tax on American vessels entering the ports of France, and on potash and turpentine. This renewal of trade discussions impelled him to renew his protests and importunities regarding tobacco. He reminded the Minister that of the eighty million livres in raw material exported from the United States, tobacco alone represented thirty millions; and of this thirty millions only nine millions went directly to France. The Farmers General were still buying tobacco in England for cash, which did not find its way back to France. Were the tobacco all to be sent to France, then thirty millions in French products would be taken.

And, he added, if competition were permitted, better prices would result and France would get the benefit of that trade. Instead, the Farmers General had let the contract to a single person and thus rendered a disservice to the French nation. The letter was but a reiteration in large part of the long argument he had sent to Vergennes. But nothing was to come of it, for France was too much occupied with the incoming flood of revolution to be much interested any more.[49] But when, a little later, an arrêt appeared, prohibiting the importation of whale oil, the product of foreign fisheries, Jefferson sent a protest at once to Montmorin. He was sure, in view of the carefully considered agreement admitting American oil, made by the committee appointed to study how best to increase commerce between the United States and France, that the United States was not included in the arrêt. 'Commerce is slow in changing its channel,' he wrote. 'That between this country and the United States is as yet but beginning, and this beginning has received some checks. The arrêt in question would be a considerable one.'[50]

[49] Bergh, *Writings of Jefferson,* VI, 180-87.
[50] *Ibid.,* VI, 346.

X

Meanwhile, Jefferson was writhing under the necessity of bartering with the Algerian pirates for American prisoners taken by them and held for ransom. Unable to apply force, because his plan had not been accepted and would not be acted upon until years later during his Presidency, he was compelled to recommend an approach to the pirates through a religious order, the Order of Mathurins, which had acted for other Governments as intermediary with the pirates. He had heard of this order of begging priests, who undertook this work for a commission, and he made contact with the 'General' of the order, and then informed Adams. The latter opposed the plan on the technical ground that no Government redeemed prisoners except at the time of making peace, and that he and Jefferson had no right to establish a precedent. Since this would have meant a life imprisonment for some, Jefferson was not impressed, and he transmitted the plan to Jay, urging the utmost secrecy to keep the price down. He proposed that outwardly the Government assume an attitude of indifference. When the proposal was submitted to Congress, that body gracefully sidestepped and left everything to the judgment of Jefferson, while ordering the Treasury Board to furnish ways and means to meet the expense.

In writing the Board of the act of Congress, Jefferson informed it that for each of the twenty prisoners it would be necessary to pay five hundred dollars. Again he warned that in the public interest it would be highly desirable that the utmost secrecy be observed as to the principal in the transaction, since the discovery would mean an increase in the cost of the ransom.[51] The necessity of approaching the pirates as suppliants with money in hand, and of putting off the French and their officers demanding money due them, was gall and wormwood to Jefferson throughout the whole of his stay in France. The negotiations by the order of begging priests was doomed to failure. The pirates learned the identity of the principal behind the priests and the price per prisoner soared to twelve hundred dollars — beyond the capacity of the nation to pay. The queer acquiescence of Spain in the increase had not been helpful, and the

[51] *Ibid.*, VI, 303-04.

injection of private parties into negotiations with the pirates was disastrous.[52]

Jefferson envisioned a nation too big to beg for rights and too proud to evade its financial obligations. But his vision was broader and more far-reaching than that of many other Americans of his age. As early as 1787, before the adoption of the American Constitution, he was dreaming of the day when there would be a Panama Canal linking the two oceans. Writing Carmichael, in Spain, he expressed his interest:

> I have been told that the cutting through the isthmus of Panama, which the world has so often wished and supposed practical, has at times been thought of by the Government of Spain and that they once proceeded so far as to have a survey and examination made of the ground, but that the result was either impracticable or of too great difficulty. Probably the Count de Campomanes or Don Ulloa can give you information on this head. I should be exceedingly pleased to get as minute details as possible on it, and even copies of the survey reports, etc., if they could be obtained at a very moderate expense.[53]

Some months later, he was writing Carmichael again:

> With respect to the Isthmus of Panama, I am assured by Burgoyne, who would not choose to be named, however, that a survey was made, that a canal appeared very practical, and the idea was suppressed for political reasons altogether. He has seen and minutely examined the report.[54]

More than any other American of his time, Jefferson was conscious of America as a part of the world into which it had to fit itself with judgment based on a full knowledge of what was taking place in Europe. Constantly in his correspondence, we find him writing in detail and with perspicacity of the moves upon the checkerboard of European politics. But such was the isolationist passion of his countrymen at the time, and for more than a century afterward, that he wondered if his correspondents were really interested in his observations on the maneuverings of nations across the sea. He wrote Carmichael:

[52] Woolery, *Relations of Jefferson to American Foreign Policy.*
[53] Ford, *Writings of Jefferson,* IV, 473.   [54] *Ibid.,* V, 22.

I often doubt whether I should trouble Congress or my friends with these details of European politics. I know they do not excite that interest in America of which it is impossible to divest oneself here. I know, too, that it is a maxim with us, and I think it is a wise one, not to entangle ourselves with the affairs of Europe. Still, I think we should know them. The Turks have practiced the maxim of not meddling with the complicated wrangles of this continent. But they have unwisely chosen to be ignorant of them also, and it is this total ignorance of Europe, its combinations and its movements, which expose them to that annihilation possibly about taking place.[55]

It would not be until after the world upheaval in the war of 1914 that organizations would spring up over the United States devoted to the discussion of foreign affairs. Jefferson would have favored them in the earliest days of the Republic.

And so, too, it was the vision of Jefferson that pierced far beyond the Mississippi and realized the part it would play in the rounding-out of American destiny, long before other public men found that enormous, uncharted region of possible interest to the United States. One day John Ledyard, a rover of wild places, who had accompanied Captain Cook on his voyage of exploration in the Pacific, appeared in Paris. Jefferson immediately made contact with him. The adventurer had gone to Paris in the hope of interesting men of means in the organization of a company to engage in the fur trade of the western section of the American continent. In this venture he was to find scant encouragement, and with keen disappointment he abandoned the project. It was at this juncture that Jefferson saw and sought to interest him in a favorite project of his own — the exploration of the western country of which the American people were in complete ignorance.

It was Jefferson's plan that Ledyard should reach this region by going through St. Petersburg to Kamchatka, and proceeding thence, if possible, on some Russian vessel to Nootka Sound, whence he might find his way across the American continent from the west. Ledyard was a daring soul with a roaming disposition, and he readily fell in with the plan. Jefferson agreed to secure permission from Catherine the Great for him to pass through her territory.

[55] *Ibid.*, IV, 482.

The most influential Russian in Paris, with whom Jefferson had pleasant personal relations, was Baron Grimm, who was also the personal correspondent of Catherine. In his *Autobiography,* Jefferson says that she refused permission on the ground that the plan was chimerical. Undaunted by the rebuff, Ledyard determined, nevertheless, to proceed to St. Petersburg in the hope of persuading her. On reaching the Russian capital, he found that the Empress was in the Crimea. With the audacity of an adventurer he decided to take the permission for granted, and he had made his way as far as Kamchatka when he was caught, sent back to Poland, and released.

Jefferson had followed Ledyard's efforts with interest. The apprehension by Catherine's police put a period to the adventure. But the thought that so long had germinated in the mind of Jefferson was to persist, and years later during his Presidency, he was to organize, equip, and direct the famous expedition of Lewis and Clark.[56]

XI

It was at this time that an American of extraordinary brilliance and eloquence, with a wooden leg and no morals to speak of, appeared upon the scene in Paris, to become for months an almost constant caller at Jefferson's house and an informal guest times without number at his dinner-table. Gouverneur Morris, whose political ideas were the very antithesis of Jefferson's, was to become, next to Alexander Hamilton and possibly Fisher Ames, the most brilliant antagonist of Jefferson during the twelve years previous to the latter's election to the Presidency and during his administration up to the time Morris's constituency retired him to private life. But Jefferson never underestimated the talents of his foes and he always had a thorough appreciation of their capacities. Thus, during his Paris period, when he was approached for advice concerning the possible confiscation of an estate in the United States, he explained that only the Assembly of the State could give redress in New York. 'If he is unacquainted there,' he wrote, 'I would advise him to apply to Colo. Hamilton, who was aid to Gen-

[56] *Autobiography,* 68; author's *Jefferson in Power.*

eral Washington, and is now very eminent at the bar and much to be relied on.' Thus he paid tribute in a letter to David Hartley, who had approached him in behalf of a friend. Never was he to change his mind about the genius of his great rival.

But Morris was of a different type, resembling Hamilton only in his antipathy to democracy and in his cynical skepticism of republican institutions. He had gone to Paris as an agent of Robert Morris, and with views as to American relations with France not at all in accord with Jefferson's.[57] He was to succeed Jefferson as Minister to France, to align himself ardently with the reactionaries of the court party, and against the Revolution.

Despite their divergent views and Morris's publicly expressed dislike of Jefferson, the former had a brilliant man's appreciation of the extraordinary qualities of the man he disliked. But quite as great if not greater, was his appreciation of Jefferson's table, its wines and talk. During the Administration of Jefferson in Washington, while Morris was leading a bitter fight in the Senate against his policies, he never declined an invitation to dine with his enemy. Jefferson presented him to the Count de Montmorin, the Foreign Minister, and Morris wrote in his *Diary* that day that the Count 'is very civil, but the English of it seems to be that he had already more trouble than he desires with strangers.'[58]

Thence onward, until Jefferson left France, the Morris *Diary* reveals the innumerable contacts of the two men. When the Comte de Puisignieu, commander of a regiment of chasseurs, finding Morris's reactionary opinions more congenial than the more liberal principles of Jefferson, expressed to Morris the hope that he might displace the Virginian in the Legation in France, Morris wrote, no doubt sincerely: 'I assure him I have no desire to be in that place, even if it were vacant, much less now that it is well filled.'[59] When the reactionary soldier requested Morris to talk with the Minister of Commerce concerning trade with San Domingo, where he had a plantation, Morris properly replied: 'I would rather leave our affairs in the hands of our Minister and gave him my ideas.'[60]

[57] Ford, *Writings of Jefferson*, IV, 92. For Jefferson's relations with Morris and Hamilton see author's *Jefferson and Hamilton* and *Jefferson in Power*.
[58] Davenport, *Diary of Gouverneur Morris*, I, 5.
[59] *Ibid.*, I, 9.   [60] *Ibid.*, I, 14.

Even to mention the many times that Morris breakfasted and dined with Jefferson would be tiresome. Constantly he was dropping in upon the Minister for a discussion of current events. The two men, so different in character, went together to join in the procession of Longchamps on the last three days of Holy Week, when 'all the world and his wife,' as Morris phrased it, were going to the sacred concerts of the nuns in a Franciscan convent which was to be destroyed in the Revolution.[61] Together they had their profiles taken in the Rue Croix des Petits Champs.[62] One day Morris took Jefferson to La Muette 'to see the cotton machines.'[63] They walked and rode together in the Bois de Boulogne, and Jefferson took him to visit the bridge of Neuilly, which Morris had crossed four times without noticing its beauty until Jefferson called it to his attention.[64] When Jefferson requested him to sit to Houdon for the figure of Washington, he consented, thawed into acquiescence one cold day in June by the good blaze Jefferson had flaming in his fireplace.[65]

But Jefferson significantly refrained from introducing Morris to the Diplomatic Corps when the latter hinted a request, by explaining that 'they are not worth your acquaintance.'[66] This may have been his true feeling. Once, in conversation with Marmontel, he had remarked that he could not understand why the Ministers of foreign powers made a mystery of entirely trivial matters, to which Marmontel replied: 'That is true, they always padlock their lips, but if you take the padlock off, you'll see the trunk is empty.'[67]

On one occasion, Jefferson took Morris 'to the view of a house and garden which opens on the Champs Elysées and which are very beautiful,' though previously it had escaped Morris's attention.[68] As to Jefferson's personal popularity with his countrymen in Paris, Morris wrote that 'Mr. Jefferson lives well, keeps a good table and excellent wines which he distributes freely, and by his hospitality to his countrymen here possesses very much their good will.'[69] It is evident that he discussed everything with Jefferson, including American and French politics, wines, inventions, people, but if he took the Minister into his confidence concerning his love affairs, which occupied much of Morris's attention, there is no indication of it in

61 *Ibid.*, I, 34.   62 *Ibid.*, I, 50.   63 *Ibid.*   64 *Ibid.*, I, 83.
65 *Ibid.*, I, 108.   66 *Ibid.*, I, 135.   67 Mazzei, *Memoirs*, 292.
68 Davenport, *Diary of Gouverneur Morris*, I, 136.   69 *Ibid.*, I, 159.

the *Diary*. These would have been diverting, for had he not displaced Talleyrand as the lover of Madame de Flahaut, and was he not pursued by some of the finest ladies of the capital?

One looks in vain for any convincing evidence that Jefferson availed himself of fine ladies, or even of 'beauty begging in the streets,' but had he done so he would have been more reticent and discreet than his compatriot. That Jefferson was neither prude nor Puritan on such matters is clear enough in his tolerant acceptance of the exceedingly low moral standard of the Paris of the eve of the Revolution. He knew and liked women whose reputations were not untainted. When the Count de Moustier was sent as French Minister to America, and took along a woman relative, the charming Madame de Bréhan, Jefferson assured Madison that 'she is goodness itself,' and that 'the way to please her is to receive her as an acquaintance of a thousand years' standing.' And he wrote in a similar vein to Jay, especially recommending the lady to the patronage of Mrs. Jay. She accompanied the Count, wrote Jefferson, in the hope of improving her health and educating her boy, and, perhaps, because 'her husband is an officer and obliged by the times to remain with the army.' [70] But alas, the Americans had not the sophistication, the cultivation, or frankness of the Parisians; and since it was observed, when the Count and Madame traveled in New England, home of the Pilgrims' pride, that they occasionally occupied the same room at the hotels, there was a general snubbing of the lady, the Count lost his temper, and Jefferson sought to smooth his ruffled feathers in a long letter.[71]

For, after all, Jefferson was a good friend and correspondent of Madame. Now that the Revolution is approaching its height, we may pause to take note of his friendships in Paris, among men, but more especially with women.

[70] Ford, *Writings of Jefferson*, IV, 461. [71] *Ibid.*, V, 10-11.

SENTIMENTAL INTERLUDE

I

WHEN, in reply to a question from Monsieur Ségur, Gouverneur Morris said, a bit sadly we have no doubt, that there was no such thing as gallantry in America, the Frenchman, amazed and deeply sympathetic, was sure it could be 'introduced.' When asked about his own love affairs in Paris, Morris, lying like a gentleman, assured him there had been none, since he 'would not dare hazard offending a virtuous woman'; at which Ségur laughed heartily. No woman could be offended by such a thing, he said. It would 'frequently succeed,' he added sagely, but there 'was no harm done if it fails.'[1]

The Paris of the eve of the Revolution was hectically unhealthily gay, and the moral standard among the high-placed, socially, was notoriously low. The court itself was scarcely a seminary for young girls. Ladies of the bluest blood and the highest social rating flippantly flaunted their lovers and their husbands made no secret of their mistresses. The ease with which a man of intelligence and physical attraction could persuade acceptance as a lover has aroused a natural curiosity regarding the Parisian days of Jefferson, who had always appealed to women because of a benevolent manner, the charm of his conversation, and his physical attributes. The charming Duchess of Chartres, whose apartments in the old Palais Royal were not unknown to the American diplomat, habitually addressed him as 'Monsieur the Clever.'[2] Whatever may

---

[1] Davenport, *Diary of Gouverneur Morris*, I, 23.
[2] Russell, *John Paul Jones*, 174.

have occurred behind the scenes one cannot say, and Jefferson, unlike Morris, was not a man to write his amours down in a diary or to gossip about them in a letter. There is evidence enough that he was popular in the drawing-rooms, that he frequented some of the salons, that he numbered many women in Paris among his devoted friends, few of whom would have been offended by advances of an amatory nature; and yet there is but one case from which one might have a right to conclude a seriously sentimental attachment, as we shall see, but if there was any serious moral transgression on his part in the midst of the easy temptations, there is no evidence to reveal it.

It was a feverish, fast-moving city at this time. Morris thought the people he knew lived 'in a whirlwind which turns them around so fast that they can see nothing,' and were forced to pronounce their definite judgments 'from the first glance.' He found that the Parisians 'knew a wit by his snuffbox, a man of taste by his bow, and a statesman by the cut of his coat.'[3]

We have Jefferson's impressions of all this in a letter to Mrs. William Bingham, describing the life of the fashionable ladies in Paris:

> At eleven o'clock it is day, chez madame. Propped on bolsters and pillows, and her head scratched into a little order, the bulletins of the sick are read and the billets of the well. She writes to some of her acquaintances, and receives the visits of others. If the morning is not very thronged, she is able to get out and hobble round the cage of the Palais Royal, but she must hobble quickly, for the coiffeur's turn is come; and a tremendous turn it is. Happy if he does not make her arrive when dinner is half over! The torpitude of digestion a little passed, she flutters half an hour through the streets by way of paying visits, and then to the spectacles. These finished, another half hour is devoted to dodging in and out of the doors of her very sincere friends, and away to supper. After supper, cards; and after cards, bed; to rise at noon the next day and to tread like a mill horse the same trodden circle over again.[4]

Later, he wrote this charming and beautiful young woman in an effort to impress upon her the advantages of domestic life in

[3] Davenport, *Diary of Gouverneur Morris*, I, 45.
[4] Bergh, *Writings of Jefferson*, VI, 81-82.

America, to which she replied with spirit, since she had returned to Philadelphia with the disposition to introduce European customs into society. She was 'flattered by the honor of [his] letter from Paris,' and was 'very sensitive of [his] attentions.' But she would reply with equal candor, since he had brought out only the more frivolous side of Parisian life, and 'buried the good qualities in the shade.'

> The state of society in different countries requires corresponding manners and qualifications [she reminded him]. Those of the French women are by no means calculated for the meridian of America, neither are they adapted to render the sex so amiable or agreeable to the English acceptation of those words. But you must confess that they are more accomplished, and understand the intercourse of society better than in any other country. We are irresistibly pleased with them because they possess the happy art of making us pleased with ourselves. Their education is of a higher cast, and, by great cultivation, they procure a happy variety of genius, which forms their conversation to please either the fop or the philosopher.

And then, with a sly dig, she adds: 'I have the pleasure of knowing you too well to doubt of your subscribing to this opinion.'[5]

Since Jefferson liked to banter the ladies, we may be sure he enjoyed the rejoinder. His contacts with Mrs. Bingham, beginning when he met her in Paris, were to continue later when, as the hostess of the most elegant home in Philadelphia, she made it the center for the Federalists who were fighting Jefferson on the issue of democracy.[6] But there was a mutual admiration and liking which continued during the lady's life. She and her husband had spent some years in the court and aristocratic circles in London and Paris before settling down at home. Even the critical Abigail Adams admired her, describing her in 1784 as 'a very young lady, not more than twenty, very agreeable and very handsome; rather too much given to the foibles of the country for the mother of two children, which she already is.'[7] Jefferson was as impressionable as any man and the correspondence continued, and when he sent her what he

---

[5] Randolph, *Domestic Life of Jefferson*, 98-99.
[6] See author's *Jefferson and Hamilton.*
[7] Adams, *Letters of Abigail Adams*, 203.

knew she would appreciate most, the fashion journals of Paris, she wrote that he had 'furnished our ladies with many hints for the decoration of their persons, and I have informed them to whom they are indebted. . . . I shall hope . . . if you accompany another book of fashions with any new operas or comedies, you will infinitely oblige.' [8]

Jefferson's relations with Mrs. Bingham are cited to illustrate his unquestionable susceptibility to feminine charms.

His relations with Abigail Adams, for whom he shopped and even bought corsets, were those of a very sincere friend. He admired her forthright manner and her abundant common sense. Even in his letters to this staid Puritan lady, he introduced occasionally the note of the cavalier, more for her amusement than to make an impression. He enjoyed dropping in unceremoniously on the Adams house at Auteuil, and in chatting with the hostess, probably even more than with the host, whose conversation was apt to be a little disputatious and heavy.

It was inevitable that, among the first French women whom he met in Paris, was the Marquise de Lafayette. After Jefferson had gone to Paris, Lafayette, still in America, had written him:

> My home, dear sir, my family, and anything that is mine are entirely at your disposal, and I beg you will come and see Madame de Lafayette as you would act by your brother's wife. Her knowledge of the country may be of some use to Miss Jefferson whom she will be happy to attend in anything that may be agreeable to her. Indeed, my dear sir, I would be very angry with you, if either you or she did not consider my house as a second home. [9]

Throughout his sojourn in Paris, Jefferson fully availed himself of the proffered privilege, and frequently he dined with the Lafayettes, and they with him. Madame de Lafayette was so far from beautiful that she may be described as plain in appearance, but with a wholesome air. Her reputation, even in the Paris of that period, was not smirched by gossip, for she was known to love her husband and to be virtuous. Though her young blade was more affected by the light manner of the times and frequently was absent from his home, it does not appear that his lady was resentful or suspicious.

[8] Randolph, *Domestic Life of Jefferson*, 101.
[9] Chinard, *Letters of Lafayette and Jefferson*.

She spoke English with ease and was sprightly in manner, and, if occasion called, her tongue was sharp. That she affected the Parisian fashions may be assumed from the fact that at a dinner at the Adams house, Abigail thought that 'no lady in our country would go abroad so little dressed as the Marquise de Lafayette.' But even the disapproving Abigail did not doubt her chastity. Jefferson's relations with her were those prescribed by Lafayette himself — he treated her as though she were his brother's wife. There is nothing to indicate that he found her personal attractions worthy of notice. That she sympathized entirely with the views of both Jefferson and her husband is evident in her observation to Morris at a dinner party, that he injured 'the Cause, for that [his] sentiments are continually quoted against the good party.' Morris thereupon availed himself of the opportunity he never missed, then or later, to say that he was 'opposed to Democracy' because of his regard for liberty — whatever that might mean.[10]

Quite a different person was Lafayette's cousin, the Countess de Tessé, who, though at the time in the household of Marie Antoinette, was a pronounced revolutionist, an idolater of Voltaire. 'We dine with Madame de Tessé,' wrote Morris. 'Republican of the First Feather. The Countess, who is a very sensible woman, has formed her ideas of government in a manner, not suited, I think, to the situation, the circumstances, or the disposition of France, and there are many such.'[11] Indeed, few women in high social circles, even in those days, were more outspoken and combative, or more prone openly to refer to the court with cynicism and satire. She talked incessantly, and usually with a refreshing disregard of discretion, leading the more superficial to conclude her light and unworthy of serious attention. She had accepted the philosophers completely. She was liberal in her views, probably a deist, certainly a scoffer at the Bible, a revolutionist in spirit, with no reverence for the establishments of the old order. But Lafayette respected her judgment, and Jefferson liked nothing better than to listen to her chatter, finding in it grains of wisdom that delighted him. Very often he visited her at her place at Chaville, and Short, his secretary, once spent some time there. The fact that she loved trees, appreciated the choice things in architecture and painting, in statuary and

[10] Davenport, *Diary of Gouverneur Morris*, I, 121.   [11] *Ibid.*, I, 6.

music, made her congenial to Jefferson, and he saw her frequently. Very often he refers to her in his letters, and always with respect. There is nothing of record, beyond the fact that this aristocratic lady had the taste of a real Bohemian, to imply that she figured noticeably in the amours of the time.

Years later, when President, Jefferson wrote her that 'the friendship with which you honored me in Paris is among the circumstances which most contributed to my happiness there.' She had written him that she was planting trees and would appreciate some of the American variety, which Jefferson promised to send. 'When I left you at the close of 1790 [sic],' he wrote, 'I thought your situation in the best possible state; at the end of 1791 I saw that it was passed, and in the close of 1792 that all was desperate. After such a shipwreck it is fortunate, indeed, that you can resume the interest you take in planting trees.' [12] But the shipwreck had in no way altered the Countess's views, and when, after his retirement from the Presidency, she sent Jefferson the memoirs of the Margrave of Bayreuth, he wrote without fear of offending her: 'I am much indebted to you for this singular morsel of history which has given us a certain view of kings, queens, and princes, disrobed of their formalities. It is a peep into the state of the Egyptian god Apis. It would not be easy to find grosser manners, coarser vices, or more meanness in the poorest huts of our peasantry.' And had the Countess read the memoirs of Mrs. Clark of her 'darling prince'? 'Instead of the vulgarity and penury of the court of Berlin,' this presented 'the vulgarity and profusion of that of London, and the gross stupidity and profligacy of the latter, in lieu of the genius and misanthropism of the former.' He thought it might well be published as a supplement to Monsieur de Buffon, 'under the title of the Natural History of Kings and Princes, or as a separate work and called Medicine for Monarchists.' And had the Countess seen *The Intercepted Letters,* an English publication of great wit and humor which held these drones 'up as butts for the ridicule and contempt of mankind'? [13] Clearly Jefferson's fondness for the Countess grew out of similar views on democracy.

Again quite different was an older lady of whom Jefferson was very fond, the Duchess d'Enville, mother of the Duke de la Roche-

[12] Chinard, *Trois Amitiés,* 123.   [13] *Ibid.,* 136.

foucauld. Here certainly there was no sentimental attachment, for the lady was almost eighty years old. She appears to have been very much like the imperious dowager of caricature, a martinet among her followers and something of a bluestocking, but that Jefferson respected, admired, and liked her there can be no doubt. One of his last letters before leaving France was addressed to her, expressing his regret at his inability to pay her a farewell visit. 'It is a tribute I pay with cordiality to a character in which I saw but one error; it was that of treating me with a degree of favor I did not merit,' he wrote. 'Be assured that I shall ever retain a lively sense of all your goodness to me, which was a circumstance of principal happiness to me during my stay in Paris.' [14]

We are indebted to the letters of Abigail Adams for a description of this Parisian friend of Jefferson's as he must often have seen her:

> We found the old lady sitting in an easy chair. Around her, a circle of Academicians, and by her side, a young lady. Your uncle [Adams] presented us, and the old lady rose, and, as usual, gave us a salute. The Duchess is near eighty, very tall and lean. She was dressed in a silk chemise, with very large sleeves coming halfway down her arms, a large cape, a black velvet girdle around her waist, some very rich lace in her chemise, around her neck, and in her sleeves, but the lace was not sufficient to cover the upper part of her neck, which old Time had harrowed; she had no cap on, but a little black gause bonnet which did not reach her ears and tied under her chin; her venerable white hair in full view. . . . The old lady has all the vitality of a young one. She is the most learned woman in France; her house is the resort of all men of literature, with whom she converses on the most abstruse subjects. [15]

Here we have this friend of Jefferson's as he no doubt often saw her. Her mental agility, her vast scope of knowledge, were quite enough, with him, to compensate for her loss of youth. Morris would probably have found her tiresome, and not nearly so exciting as the lightheaded lady of uneasy virtue he so often saw in her quarters in the Louvre; to Jefferson she was fascinating because of her knowledge and of the men of intellectual distinction that flocked about her.

14 Ford, *Writings of Jefferson*, V, 154.
15 Adams, *Letters of Abigail Adams*, 250.

II

Because of his partiality for intellectual society, we know that Jefferson was seen in the famous salons of the period, which vibrated with the revolutionary and liberal philosophy of the times. As often as possible he found his way to the neighborhood of Auteuil to the home of the amusing Madame Helvetius to whom he had been presented by Franklin, with whom she was on flirting terms. Her celebrated husband had been one of the editors of the Encyclopedia, and about her gathered many of the most liberal and zealous reformers of the day and in her salon the most congenial and spirited conversation could be heard. Years later, Jefferson was to recall these visits in a letter to Cabanis, one of the group. 'Auteuil always appeared to me a delicious village,' he wrote, 'and Madame Helvetius's the most delicious spot in it. . . . In those days how sanguine we were, and how soon were the virtuous hopes of every good man blasted . . . and how many excellent friends have we lost.' [16] He was writing, during the tyranny of Napoleon, of the days when the most generous spirits of France were looking forward to the reforms in society that gave promise of a golden age. Unlike Abigail Adams, he was amused rather than shocked by Madame's free-and-easy manner with her dear friend, Franklin, who had once proposed to her, probably in jest. If Jefferson, too, noted a 'decay in her beauty,' which still indicated something of what it might have been before, and if she did persist in kissing her male guests on the cheek, and even though she was prone 'to throw herself upon a settee where she showed more than her feet,' it still amused rather than shocked him. It is impossible to imagine her draping her arms around his shoulders, holding his hand, or kissing him at all, for he was years younger than Franklin. He found the company with which she surrounded herself quite worth while. Perhaps the fact that she was sixty made a difference. [17]

Jefferson was also indebted to Franklin for his presentation to Madame d'Houdetôt on whom he was a frequent caller. She appears to have entertained a great admiration for him, not only because he was an American philosopher associated with the liberal

[16] Bergh, *Writings of Jefferson*, X, 404.
[17] Adams, *Letters of Abigail Adams*, 198.

spirit of the age, but quite as much, no doubt, because he had an even wider knowledge of American trees and plants than Franklin. She loved them, and Jefferson interested himself in getting seeds, bulbs, and even trees for her park of Sannois. In her drawing-room he often met Cabanis and the Abbé Morellet.

One gathers that he found his women friends in intellectual and Bohemian circles, and, aside from a few liberals like Madame de Tessé, he had few contacts with the women of the court circle. If, like Franklin, he ever found himself surrounded in the drawing-rooms of the palace of Versailles by adoring ladies, it is not of record and his correspondence indicates no such friendships.

Such were the more conspicuous of Jefferson's women friends in Paris with whom a sentimental attachment could hardly have existed. But there were others of whom this cannot so positively be said.

III

Biographers seem determined to find some mystery in his connection with Madame de Corny, wife of Ethis de Corny, a lawyer, much older than herself, living at Metz, who had accompanied Lafayette to America as commissary of war. He was a political economist of merit, a man of great industry devoted to his work, and a liberal, without being a rabid revolutionist. No doubt, Jefferson met Madame de Corny and her husband because of the latter's American connections. This couple lived at Rue Chaussée-d'Antin 17, and thither not only Jefferson but Morris found their way. There appears to be no doubt of her youth, beauty, and wit. It does not appear that Morris was so much a favorite with the lady as Jefferson, which may be counted in favor of her chastity or to Morris's reactionary views. But unquestionably she was a very intimate friend of Madame de Flahaut, whose reputation was suspected after she gave birth to a son of Talleyrand's, for years her lover. Nor is there any doubt that it was through her own solicitation and management that Madame de Flahaut was brought into contact with Morris through Madame de Corny, who could scarcely have had any doubt of the intentions of her friend. From which the evil-minded may conclude that she had acted in the rôle of a procuress.[18]

18 Davenport, *Diary of Gouverneur Morris*, I, 23.

But, considering the moral standards of the time and place, it would be unfair to assume that a woman of impeccable virtue would have been unfriendly with some known to be quite the opposite. Madame de Corny was far more intimate with another friend of Jefferson's, Angelica Church, sister of the wife of Alexander Hamilton, who was living at the time with her husband in London and made frequent visits to Paris. There is a tradition that Hamilton looked upon Angelica with something more than a brotherly feeling, though nothing to imply that his conduct toward her was other than proper. When Angelica's daughter was sent to Paris to school, she was under the protection of Madame de Corny, and Madame was occasionally a guest of the Churches in London. There is no doubt that she took it upon herself to play the part of friend and adviser to Jefferson's daughter, of whom she was very fond. It is reasonable to assume, from his character and inherited standards, that he never would have entrusted his daughter to the guidance of a woman who was his mistress. When Angelica's daughter, Kitty, appeared in Paris, it was at the house of the De Cornys that she stayed, until, after a consultation between Madame and the diplomat, Kitty was conducted to the convent to join Martha in her studies.

The home of Madame de Corny was beautifully and tastefully furnished, for we have the testimony of Morris that it was 'filled with beauty,' and similar testimony in a letter to her from Jefferson:

> I thank you, my dear Madame, for the charming glass you have sent me. The beauty of the form had struck me at your house, where all is beautiful, and I had meant to trouble your maître d'hôtel only with the commission you have been so friendly as to take on yourself. Coming, however, from you, it is doubly precious. It shall stand by my own plate every day and suggest the health I am to drink and for which I ever pray. I am sorry that at this moment it is not as good as could be wished. The bearer comes to ask you how you do today.[19]

Because she liked long walks and Jefferson was a famous pedestrian, the two fell into the habit of taking their strolls together, and these often took them into the wooded beauty of the Bois de Boulogne. Two commentators, drawing entirely upon their imag-

[19] Chinard, *Trois Amitiés,* 186.

ination, have taken it upon themselves to suggest that Madame probably had secretly resented Jefferson's failure to take advantage of his opportunities by playing the friend rather than lover under the trees of the Bois. But there is not a shred of evidence to support the assumption. On the contrary, it is well known that she adored her husband of whose work she was very proud. The letters from Jefferson to her that have come down to us might have been written by Abigail Adams, though they show that the friendship between them was on a familiar foundation. But the mutual devotion of husband and wife resulting in a competition between them as to which should yield to the other's preference was a source of amusement among their friends. These little contests became so heated that quarrels were narrowly avoided, and Jefferson, who often witnessed them, found them immensely diverting.

On returning from his London journey and finding her in London, he had written:

> On my return to Paris it was my first intention to go to the Rue Chaussée d'Antin No. 17, to inquire after my friends whom I had left there. I was told they were in England. And how do you like England, Madame? . . . I am in hopes that when the splendor of their shops, which is all that is worth seeing in London, shall have lost the charm of novelty, you will turn a wishful eye to the good people of Paris and find that you cannot be happy with any others. The Bois de Boulogne invites you earnestly to come and survey its beautiful verdure, to retire to its umbrage from the heats of the season. I was through it today, as I am every day. Every tree charged me with its invitation to you. Passing by La Muette, it wished you as a mistress. You want a country house, this is for sale; and in the Bois de Boulogne, which I have always insisted is the most worthy of your preference. Come, then, and buy it.[20]

There assuredly is nothing here that a man might not have written to his 'brother's wife.'

A little later he wrote her again, sending her, not a volume of amorous poetry, but — of all things — the *Memoir* of Calonne. He wrote:

> Do not injure yourself in hurrying its perusal. Only when you shall have read it at your leisure be so good as to send it back that

20 Randolph, *Domestic Life of Jefferson*, 128.

it may be returned to the Duke of Dorset. You will read it with pleasure. It has carried comfort to my heart because it must do the same to the King and the nation. Though it does not prove M. Calonne to be more innocent than his predecessors, it shows him not to have been the exaggerated scoundrel which the calculations and clamors of the public have supposed. . . . It shows him less wicked and France less badly governed than I had feared.

And then, referring no doubt to their long tramps together, he added:

How do you do this morning? I have feared you exerted and exposed yourself too much yesterday. . . . The sky is clearing and I shall away to my hermitage.[21]

Much of the speculation concerning the relations of Madame de Corny and Jefferson is based upon a letter of farewell written by him from Falmouth, as he was sailing back to the United States, saying he could not trust himself to say good-bye. But more convincing of a real affection are the letters written by her at the time. She had gone to Jefferson's house two hours after he had left and found Short distressed, 'and we both wept together at your absence. This you will call weakness, but although good-bye may be the saddest thing, I would have had a thousand things to say to you, and I wanted to receive a solemn promise that you would return to France.' And when later Jefferson wrote from America that he had accepted a post at home, she wrote again:

I was right in saying that I would not see you again. When I went to your house after your departure, extreme sadness was a very true presentiment. Well, be happy as you understand it in your way, very far from me. . . . It is then true that I shall never see you again. I can only love and regret my friends. My memory of you is certain, but yours — ah, how doubtful it is! I am going to foretell your future. You will marry again, yes, it is certain, and your wife will be happy, and you, also, I hope.[22]

The turmoils of the Revolution put an end to correspondence, but Jefferson was never to lose interest in her welfare. In 1793, Angelica Church wrote him that Madame de Corny was a widow with a very limited fortune and then retired to Rouen. Jefferson

[21] *Ibid.*, 133.　　[22] Chinard, *Trois Amitiés*, 153-54.

replied, expressing his sorrow and suggesting that he knew no country 'where the remains of a fortune could place her so much at her ease as here.' [23] Later, he suggested to Mrs. Church that she apply to Mrs. Monroe, then in Paris, for information. Thus he learned that she had been 'in extreme distress, her revenue being in rentes' and the money being worthless; and that she was 'living in hired lodgings furnished by herself, and everything about her as nice as you know she always had.' Though she visited the Monroes freely and familiarly, she would never dine when there was company nor remain if company came. At this time she thought seriously of going to America. [24]

Indeed, she had parted company with festivity. She wrote Jefferson that for fifteen years (1794 to 1809) she went to bed at nine, and for twenty years, from the beginning of the Revolution, she had not been to the theater and for fifteen years had not dined in town. 'All this is not for love of my health, but because I am far from the world which I have truly quitted.' [25] She painted a rather touching picture of her rented apartment. It was small and she loved flowers and fields, but she had only a little green plant in the window, and even this died 'because the cost of water in Paris' was too high for her purse.

In the second year of his Presidency, Jefferson wrote her of Mrs. Church and Kitty. Not only were they 'very distant,' but 'it happens that all their connections are of a party opposed to the present order of things, and Colo. Hamilton, who married Mrs. Church's sister, is the head of that party.' [26] It was that year that Jefferson sent her some tea, 'having understood that you were become a great tea drinker.' [27] Acknowledging it, she wrote, 'I think of you every morning and this habit is truly sweet to me.' [28] And four years later: 'Since your returns from China are so numerous, allow me to ask you for some tea. Tea is my constant déjeuner. It would be pleasant to owe it to you each day. Your good sense must not find this request familiar. I assure you it is only sentimental.' [29] Congratulating him on his re-election she added: 'I give a sigh for Monticello.'

Years went by in silence. It was 1817. And Jefferson was writing

[23] *Ibid.*, 160.   [24] *Ibid.*, 164.   [25] *Ibid.*, 232.   [26] *Ibid.*, 212.
[27] *Ibid.*, 221.   [28] *Ibid.*, 224.   [29] *Ibid.*, 216.

to Trumbull the painter. 'And Madame de Corny — what has become of her? Is she living or dead? Thus you see how your letter calls up recollections of our charming coterie in Paris.'[30]

Having found her address, he then wrote her, thirty years after their first meeting: 'Through what scenes, my dear friend, have we passed since those endeared to us by the society of Mrs. Church, Cosway, Trumbull, etc. What transitions from those of the tyrannies of Robespierre, of the Directories, of Bonaparte, and now of the Allies. These cannot have failed, by their sweeping afflictions, to have overshadowed even your life with gloom, if not with suffering, and when are these to end?'[31]

And so the curtain falls on a great friendship with a note of tragedy.

IV

A bit more puzzling was Jefferson's friendship with Madame de Bréhan, the sister-in-law of Count de Moustier, who went to America as the French Minister in the autumn of 1787, taking her along with her son. It is probable that it grew out of Jefferson's friendship with the Count. That he painted idealistic pictures of America for her delectation we may well believe, since she became interested in the new country, which she believed 'a country of pastoral simplicity, free from the vanities of the world.'[32] If Jefferson was not deceived, in his letters to Madison and Jay warmly recommending her to their hospitality and friendship, she was a very natural woman without affectations or a passion for fashion. She and the Count were not unknown to Jefferson's table, since we have her acceptance of an invitation, lamenting in advance her inability 'to speak English the whole time,' but expressing the hope that she may rapidly improve under his teaching. 'I will avail myself of your lessons, if you are so good as to give me any,' she wrote. Her letters lack the sprightly tone of his other correspondents and give the impression of a really good, conventional woman. The correspondence begins on the eve of her departure for America. Jefferson had written her not to be deceived as to American manners by 'the imitation of European manners which [she] would find in our towns. I beseech you to practice still your own, which will

[30] *Ibid.*, 170.   [31] *Ibid.*, 234.   [32] Chinard, *Trois Amitiés*, 14-15.

furnish them a model of what is perfect,' and should this seem singular, 'it will be by excellence,' and after a while she would see the effect of her example.[33] But Madame thought otherwise. 'You tell me, Sir, that I must keep my manners; it is better, I think, to take those of the country, and I will do so,' she replied.[34] On reaching New York, she found everyone interested in a new Constitution, and she wrote that 'if there were many Jeffersons and Madisons, everything, I believe, would be better.' She and the Count had 'often spoken of our dear Jefferson,' and she sent him the assurance of her 'tender friendship.'

But it appears that she, and especially the Count, were a little disappointed with their reception and with what they saw, and Jefferson wrote her a soothing letter. The 'new customs,' the 'perplexities of the language,' and her illness had probably made disagreeable things seem more so. But, 'patience, my dear friend, search in every object only what it contains of good; view, in those you see, patients to be cured of what is amiss by your example, encourage in them that simplicity which should be the armament of their country; in fine, follow the dispositions of your own benevolence and sweetness of temper, and you will be happy and make them so.'[35] He introduced her to Angelica Church, because it 'is an office of greatest pleasure to me . . . to bring good people together.' He envied the gift he was giving her, since he would like to 'take myself the very gift I make you.' He hoped Madame would load Angelica with civilities and was sure that 'both her character and yours will insure this.'[36]

But the Count was outraged by his neglect in the United States, and Jay wrote Jefferson that, while the diplomat had 'found the best disposition to make it agreeable to him,' he seemed to 'expect more particular and flattering marks of minute attention than we are inclined to pay to anybody.' Then, too, there is an intimation that Madame may have taken Jefferson's advice about practicing her 'own manners,' for Jay wrote further: 'Appearances, whether well or ill founded is not important, have created and diffused an opinion that an improper connection subsists between him and the Marchioness. You can easily conceive the influence of such an opinion on the minds and feelings of such people as ours.'

[33] *Ibid.*, 36. [34] *Ibid.*, 19. [35] *Ibid.*, 41–43. [36] *Ibid.*

Jay would not have written thus to any other person, but in the position Jefferson occupied, such information might 'have its uses.' [37] It seems that some snoopers in a New England town had made some observations that set the tongues a-wagging.

Just what was the effect of the revelation on Jefferson we do not know. He had warmly urged Madame on Mrs. Jay. And after his return to America it does not appear that he saw her much. When at length the couple departed for Berlin, where he went as Minister, Jefferson wrote his regrets because 'perverse arrangements of fortune, which seem to have made a point of disappointing all my wishes to be near you, and every occasion even of seeing you.' How unfortunate that Fate had sported with her sensibility by placing her in New York 'during the contests excited by our change of government.' [38]

Thus the curtain falls on a friendship which is vapory in its outlines. The Marchioness, who was in her thirties, found on returning to Europe some difficulty in readjusting herself to the manners of her own country.

V

We now reach the most sentimental attachment formed by Jefferson during his Parisian days. During the early days of the nineteenth century, the most brilliant English miniature painter of his time was Richard Cosway, born in 1742. His artistic genius is manifest in his work. At the age of twelve he went to London to study drawing. As a mere child he won the first prize given by the newly organized Society of Artists. When eighteen he began to exhibit his pictures to the Society, and among these was that of Shipley, his master, now the property of that organization. At nineteen he launched his career as a miniature painter, in which he was to attain high distinction and to paint many of the most celebrated men and famous beauties of his time. At twenty-two he was an associate of the Royal Academy, and the next year he was a Royal Academician. One of his earliest miniatures was one of Mrs. Fitzpatrick, the mistress of the Prince of Wales, who was so pleased that he became an ardent patron of the artist and contributed largely to

[37] *Ibid.*, 26.   [38] *Ibid.*, 57.

making him the most fashionable miniature painter in England. It is generally agreed that his most beautiful miniature was that of Madame du Barry, painted in 1791 when the mistress of Louis XV was living in Berkeley Square in London. Among his other English subjects was Mrs. Robinson, another too intimate friend of the Prince of Wales, who was wont to consult the artist on personal matters.

Brilliant and attractive as an artist, Cosway's foppishness and affectation made him less than pleasing as a man, and his vanity was immeasurable. His early success and his cultivation by the great and by the most charming women of the aristocracy appear to have turned his head completely, and he went through life under the delusion of grandeur. Many stories were told to illustrate his weakness. On one occasion he received the Prince of Wales at his studio at home, 'attired in a dove-colored suit, silver embroidered court dress, with sword, bag wig.' And when the Prince retired, the little man, for Cosway was physically unimpressive, accompanied him to his carriage, and in the presence of the crowd in the street retreated backward, with measured steps.[39] He lived in much splendor, for his were the ideas of royalty. His intimacy with the rakish Prince of Wales was so conspicuous as to occasion gossip, as we shall see.

VI

He was in his thirty-ninth year when, in January, 1781, he was married at St. George's Church in Hanover Square to Maria Hadfield, seventeen years his junior, who was not without a touch or more of genius.

She was born in Florence of English parentage. In an autobiographic letter her father appears to have been from Manchester and of a rich merchant and manufacturing family. Traveling in Italy and depressed by the lack of congenial accommodations for English travelers, he took first one large house and then two others, and fitted them in the English style. It was in one of these on the Arno that Maria was born. Though her parents were Protestants, they decided to rear her as a Catholic, and she was sent to a convent

[39] Williamson, *Richard Cosway*, 33.

school at the age of four, under the protection of the Grand Duke and Duchess of Tuscany. At eight she returned home, and, while she had several teachers, she was interested primarily in art. She studied some under Zofani, then living in Florence, and she haunted the Pitti Gallery, copying many of the richest paintings. Thence she was sent to study in Rome under the chaperonage of Mrs. Gore, the mother of Lady Cowper; and there she came to know intimately many of the first artists of the time. She had no regular instruction, but for a year and a half she tramped over Rome seeing everything beautiful in painting and sculpture, making sketches, copying. Of this Roman period, James Borthoote, R.A., has written, in a sketch: 'When she first came to Rome in 1778, aged eighteen, not unhandsome, endowed with considerable talent, and with a form extremely delicate, and a pleasing manner of the utmost simplicity; but, withal, ambitious, proud, and restless.' [40]

On her father's death, Maria, who from childhood had wished to be a nun, begged to return to her convent, but her mother would not consent; and so, with letters of introduction from Lady Rivers to many of the leaders of London fashion, she went to England. This decision was encouraged by Angelica Kauffmann, the miniature painter, who had often heard of Maria and of her promise. The mother took rooms first in Berkeley Square and then in Hanover Square, and soon after her arrival Maria was introduced into society by Angelica Kauffmann. Quite soon she had met most of the leading men and women of the realm. And despite the faint praise of the Royal Academicians, her charm and beauty brought her numerous admirers and suitors. Of these, the most persistent was Parsons, the composer, but Angelica Kauffmann dissuaded her from accepting him. A little later she met the successful little miniature painter, Cosway, whose suit was successful, though it does not appear that Maria ever really loved him, and that often she despised him. She herself once wrote, in an autobiographic letter, of her feelings for Cosway: 'At first,' she says, she 'feared him, then she worshipped him, later on admired him, gradually grew to like to be in his company, and finally loved him with her whole heart.' [41] But Maria was writing for the public, and the record scarcely bears out the adoration. Neither had grown old when the coldness of each

[40] *Ibid.*, 18.   [41] *Ibid.*, 20.

was such that they separated and never thereafter lived together. But this was some time after Jefferson knew her in Paris.

Soon after his marriage, Cosway, obsessed with grand ideas, took Schomberg House, a great palace built by the Duke of Schomberg, and there, after a short time, the painter and his wife launched themselves upon a career of entertainment. Maria began her evening concerts, those of Sunday evenings becoming extremely popular and fashionable. In her autobiographic letter, Maria numbers among her most intimate friends of this period, Lady Lyttleton, the Honorable Mrs. Damer, the Countess of Allesbury, Lady Cecilia Johnson, and the Marchioness of Townshend. These were always present at the concerts, and there, too, were Ministers of Government, picturesque figures like General Paoli, brilliant orators and wits like Erskine.[42] And always the rakish Prince of Wales was there. It was because of his intimacy with Cosway and h̶i̶s̶ attendance at Maria's parties that the gossips rolled their e̶y̶e̶s̶ led behind their fans, though there is no evidence that M̶ ̶ ̶ons with the Prince were other than the most regular. ̶ ̶ who attracted his eye, however, could escape the tongue̶ ̶

At the concerts, Maria, no mean musician, w̶ ̶ ̶f̶ performer, but the husband appears to have furnish̶ ̶ ̶er kind of entertainment, 'dressed up in the very extrem̶e̶ of fashion, he flitted through his gaily decorated rooms, ogling, flirting, and bowing, receiving his patrons with the air of a prince, flattering them to the top of his bent.' Pall Mall was packed with carriages and sedan chairs on these occasions, and Horace Walpole was often seen emerging from his chair at their door.[43]

Meanwhile, Maria continued painting, though her professionally jealous husband forbade her to paint for trade, or tried to prevent her doing so. The first of her pictures established her reputation, though she herself, in her autobiographic letter, ascribes their favorable reception 'to the novelty and my age . . . more than to real merit.' It was Maria's portrait of the famous Duchess of Devonshire, then at the height of her reign as queen of fashion, in the character of Cynthia from Spenser, which 'seemed to strike.'[44] Before Jefferson met her in France, she had exhibited several pictures at the Royal Academy, two in the year of her marriage, four

[42] *Ibid.*, 15.   [43] *Ibid.*, 33.   [44] *Ibid.*, 14.

the next year, and in 1783 and 1784, and five in 1786, one of these being the portrait of herself entitled 'Portrait of a Lady.'

VII

When, for Maria's health, the Cosways went to France, they traveled in style, taking their carriage and servants. Jefferson met her through an introduction by Trumbull and thereafter, says the American artist, 'Mr. Jefferson joined our party almost daily.' [45] Certainly Maria and her husband frequently were guests in the house on the Champs Elysées. Maria's character was probably beyond reproach, though gossip was to whisper at times that she was a mistress of the Prince of Wales, of Marchesi the singer, of Vincent Lunarda, secretary of the Neapolitan Ambassador, of J. L. Dusark the painter. It appears that she once traveled abroad with Marchesi under unconventional circumstances, but there is nothing of evidence to give color to the tales, many of them malicious.

At the time Jefferson met her she was very pretty, slender, and not more than twenty-six or -seven. She had great expressive soft blue eyes that smiled readily, and a great quantity of beautiful blond hair was her most noticeable feature. Her manner was kindly, simple, and intimate, and her expression amiable. Her interesting conversation sparkled with wit and glowed with humor.

During their Paris sojourn, Cosway, who had announced that he would take no commissions and rest, was persuaded, nevertheless, to paint miniatures of the Duchess of Devonshire, the Duchess d'Orléans and Madame de Polignac, the evil genius of Marie Antoinette. The Cosways met and became close friends of David the painter and Kosciusko the Polish supporter of the American Revolution, whose miniature was painted by Cosway while Maria sat beside the hero and talked so charmingly that he did not mind the sitting. Even Maria was permitted to practice her art, and in the Paris days she did some designs for Boydell's Shakespeare, and painted a few clever miniatures. But mostly she herself was painted, with artists begging for the privilege. Some of these pictures show a youngish woman of infinite charm. Even the cynical Gouverneur Morris, who saw her a little later in London, in her home 'filled

45 Trumbull, *Autobiography*, 118.

with princes and bohemians,' found her entrancing and was moved
to indite a verse to her:

> By Nature's various bounty blessed,
> Ah, why your wealth conceal?
> And why in cold indifference drest
> Her blessings not reveal?
>
> Vast treasures in a hoard confined
> No pleasure can impart,
> And so the Treasures of the Mind
> The Feelings of the Heart.
>
> Your conversation, like your coin,
> Is gold. But yet, 'tis strange
> How oft when Social Circles join
> You want a little change.

From which one gathers that Maria was merely polite with
Morris. She was much more than polite with Jefferson into whose
house in the Champs Elysées she ran in and out. Soon after he was
confined to his house with an injured wrist, she wrote:

> You don't always judge by appearance or it would be much to
> my disadvantage this day, without deserving it; it has been a day of
> contradictions. I meant to have seen you twice, and I have appeared
> a monster for not having sent to know how you were the whole
> day. I have been more uneasy than I can express. This morning
> my husband killed my project I had proposed to him, by burying
> himself among pictures and forgetting the hours. Though we were
> near your house, coming to see you, we were obliged to come back,
> the time being much past that we were to be at St. Cloud to dine
> with the Duchess of Kingston. Nothing was to hinder us from
> coming in the evening, but alas, my good intentions proved only
> a disturbance of your neighbors, and just late enough to break the
> rest of your servants and perhaps yourself. I came home with the
> disappointment of not having been able to make my apologies. . . .
> I hope you feel my distress instead of accusing me; the one I de-
> serve, the other not. We will come to see you tomorrow morning
> if nothing happens to prevent it. Oh, I wish you were well enough
> to come to us tomorrow to dinner, and stay the evening. I won't
> tell you what I shall have; temptations now are cruel for your situ-
> ation. I only mention my wishes. If the executing them should

be possible, your merit will be greater, as my satisfaction the more flattered. I would serve you and help you at dinner and divert your pain after with good music.[46]

One cannot but suspect that Jefferson found a way to appear at the dinner-table.

In a later letter, written on the eve of the Cosways' departure for London, there is an indication that Maria had enticed Jefferson into a tramp when his wrist was causing him pain:

> I am very sorry and blame myself for having been the cause of your pains in the wrist. Why should you go, and why was I not more friendly to you, and less so to myself by preventing you giving me the pleasure of your company? You repeatedly said it would do you no harm. I felt interested and did not insist. We shall go, I believe, this morning. Nothing seems ready, but Mr. Cosway seems more disposed than I have seen him all this time. I shall write to you from England; it is impossible to be wanting to a person who has been so excessively obliging. I don't attempt to make compliments — there can be none for you, but I beg you will think us sensible of your kindness and that it will be with exquisite pleasure I shall remember the charming days we have passed together, and shall long for next spring.
>
> You will make me very happy if you will send a line to the poste restante at Antwerp, that I may know you are well. Believe me, dear sir, your most obliged, affectionate servants.[47]

In writing the 'line to the poste restante,' Jefferson was to give us a remarkable letter of sentiment such as is found nowhere else in his correspondence, something never to be approached by anything he ever wrote to a woman thereafter. We have noted that he was not without sentiment in his youth, and since, if any lingered with him in later life after his return to America to become Secretary of State, it has not been disclosed, it would appear that this letter to Maria Cosway was a farewell flaming. It indicates other things as well. As a philosopher and politician, Jefferson seems cold as a steel engraving, but here we have unmistakable proof that he was not without susceptibility and sentiment where women were concerned.

That October day in 1786, when the Cosways took coach for the Channel, Jefferson accompanied them as far as Saint-Denis, where

[46] Randolph, *Domestic Life of Jefferson*, 80.   [47] *Ibid.*, 86.

he handed Maria into her carriage and saw her drive away. The letter is of such great length that only a portion can be given, but it will suffice to throw an unconventional light on Jefferson the man. Thousands of words in length, the fact that he was forced to struggle with his left hand is evidence enough that it was not written flippantly:

My dear Madame: Having performed the last sad office of handing you into your carriage at the pavillon de Saint-Denis, and seen the wheels get actually in motion, I turned on my heel and walked, more dead than alive, to the opposite door where my own was awaiting me. Mr. Danquierville was missing. He was sought for, found, and dragged down stairs. We were crammed into the carriage like recruits for the Bastille and not having soul enough to give orders to the coachman, he presumed Paris our destination and drove off. After a considerable interval, silence was broken with a 'Je suis vraiment affligé du départ de ces bons gens.' This was the signal for a mutual confession of distress. We began immediately to talk of Mr. and Mrs. Cosway, of their goodness, their talents, their amiability; and though we spoke of nothing else, we seemed hardly to have entered into the matter when the coachman announced the Rue Saint-Denis and that we were opposite Mr. Danquierville's. He insisted on descending there and traversing a short passage to his lodgings. I was carried home. Seated by my fireside, solitary and sad, the following dialogue took place between my Head and Heart.

HEAD — Well, friend, you seem to be in a pretty trim.

HEART — I am indeed the most wretched of all earthly beings. Overwhelmed with grief, every fiber of my frame distended beyond its natural powers to bear. I would willingly meet whatever catastrophe should leave me more to feel or to fear.

HEAD — These are the eternal consequences of your warmth and precipitation. This is one of the scrapes into which you are ever leading us. You confess your follies, indeed; but still you hug and cherish them; and no reformation can be hoped, where there is no repentance.

Here the HEART begged to be spared admonitions at the time, but the HEAD, observing that they accomplished nothing in times of triumph, continued:

HEAD — You will be pleased to remember that when our friend, Trumbull, used to be telling us of the merits and talents of these good people, I never ceased whispering to you that we had no occasion for new acquaintances; that the greater their merits and talents, the more dangerous their friendship to our tranquillity, because the regret at parting would be greater.

HEART — Accordingly, sir, this acquaintance was not the consequence of my doings. It was one of your projects that threw us in the way of it. It was you, remember, and not I, who desired the meeting at Legrand and Motino's. I never trouble myself with domes or arches. The Halle aux Bleds might have rotted down before I should have gone to see it. But you, forsooth, who are eternally getting us to sleep with your diagrams and crotchets must go and examine this wonderful piece of architecture. And when you had seen it, oh, it was the most superb thing on earth. What you had seen there was worth all you had yet seen in Paris. I thought so, too. But I meant it of the lady and gentleman to whom we had been presented; and not of the parcel of sticks and chips put together in pens. You, then, sir, not I, have been the cause of the present distress.

HEAD — It would have been better for you if my diagrams and crotchets had gotten you to sleep on that day, as you are pleased to say they invariably do. My visit to Legrand and Motino's had public utility for its object. A market is to be built in Richmond. What a commodious plan is that of Legrand and Motino's; especially if we put on it the noble dome of the Halle aux Bleds. . . . While I was occupied with these objects, you were dilating with your new acquaintances and contriving how to prevent a separation from them. Every hour of yours had an engagement that day. Yet all these were to be sacrificed that you might dine together. Lying messages were to be dispatched into every quarter of the city, with apologies for your breach of engagements. You particularly had the effrontery to send word to the Duchesse d'Enville that, on the moment we were setting out to dine with her, dispatches came to hand which required immediate attention. You wanted me to invent a more ingenious excuse; but I knew you were getting into a scrape and I would have nothing to do with it.

HEART — Oh, my dear friend, how you have revived me by recalling to my mind the transactions of that day. How well I remember them all and that, when I came home at night and looked back on the morning, it seemed to have been a month agone. Go on, then, like a mild comforter and paint to me the day we spent at St.-Germain. How beautiful was every object, the port de Reuilly, the hills along the Seine, the rainbows of the machine of Marly, the pavillon de Lucienne. Recollect, too, Madrid, Bagatelle, the King's garden, the Dessert. . . . And yet in the evening, when one took a retrospect of the day, what a mass of happiness had we traveled over. Retrace all these scenes to me, my good companion, and I will forgive the unkindness with which you are chiding me. The day we went to Saint-Germain was a little too warm, I think; was it not?

HEAD — Thou art the most incorrigible of all the beings that ever sinned! I reminded you of the follies of the first day, intending to deduce from these some useful lessons for you, but instead of listening to these, you kindle at the recollection, you retrace the whole series with a fondness which shows you want nothing but the opportunity to act it over again. I often told you during its course that you were imprudently engaging your affections under circumstances that must have cost you a great deal of pain; that the persons indeed were of greatest merit, possessing good sense, good humor, honest hearts, honest manners, and eminence in a lovely art; that the lady had, moreover, qualities and accomplishments belonging to her sex which might form a chapter apart for her; such as music, modesty, beauty, and that softness of disposition which is the ornament of hers and charm of ours, but that all these considerations would increase the pangs of separation; that their stay here was to be short; that you rake your whole system when you part from those you love, complaining that such a separation is worse than death, inasmuch as this ends our sufferings, whereas that only begins them; and that the separation would in this instance be all the more severe as you would probably never see them again.

HEART — But they told me they would come back again next year.

HEAD — But in the meantime, see what you suffer; and their return, too, depends on so many circumstances that if you had a grain of prudence you would not count upon it. Upon the whole, it is impossible and therefore you should abandon the idea of ever seeing them again.

HEART — May heaven abandon me if I do.

HEAD — Very well. Suppose then they come back. They are to stay two months and when these are expired, what is to follow? Perhaps you flatter yourself they may come to America.

HEART — I see nothing impossible in that supposition. Where

could they find such objects as in America for the exercise of their enchanting art? — especially the lady who paints landscapes so inimitably. She wants only subjects worthy of immortality to render her pencil immortal. The Falling Spring, the Cascade of Niagara, the Passage of the Potomac through the Blue Mountains, the Natural Bridge. It is worth a voyage across the Atlantic to see these objects; much more to paint and make them and thereby ourselves known to all ages. And our dear Monticello, where has Nature spread so rich a mantle under the eye? — mountains, forests, rocks, rivers. With what majesty do we there ride above the storms. How sublime to look down to the workhouse of Nature and see her clouds, hail, snow, rain, all fabricated at our feet; and the glorious sun when rising as if out of a distant water, just gilding the tops of the mountains and giving life to all nature.

HEAD — Well, let us put this possibility to trial then at another point. When you consider the character which is given of our country by the lying newspapers of London and their credulous copyers in other countries; when you reflect that all Europe is made to believe we are a lawless banditti in a state of absolute anarchy, cutting one another's throats and plundering without distinction, how can you expect that any reasonable creature would venture among us?

HEART — But you and I know all this is false; that there is not a country on earth where there is greater tranquillity, where the laws are milder, or better obeyed; where everyone is more attentive to his own business or meddles less with that of others; where strangers are better received, more hospitably treated and with a more sacred respect.

HEAD — Let us return, then, to our point. I wished to make you sensible how imprudent it is to place your affections without reserve on objects you must so soon lose and whose loss when it comes must cost you such severe pangs. Remember the last night. You knew your friends were to leave Paris today. This was enough to throw you into agonies. All night you tossed us from one side of the bed to the other. No sleep, no rest. The poor crippled wrist, too, never was left one moment in the same position, now up, now down, now here, now there; is it to be wondered at if its pains returned? The Surgeon then was to be called and to be rated as an ignoramus because he could not divine the cause of this extraordinary change. In fine, my friend, you must mend your manners.

HEART — But friendship is precious, not only in the shade but in the sunshine of life; and, thanks to a benevolent arrangement of things, the greater part of life is sunshine. I will recur for proof to the days we have lately passed. On these, indeed, the sun shone brightly. How gay did the face of Nature appear! Hills, valleys, châteaux, gardens, rivers, every object wore its loveliest hue. Whence did they borrow it? From the presence of our charming companion. They were pleasing because she seemed pleased. Alone, the scene would have been dull and insipid; the participation of it with her gave it relish.

And so the dialogue continues much longer, and then concludes:

And so I put an end to it by calling for my nightcap. Methinks I hear you wish to heaven I had called a little sooner and spared you the ennui of such a sermon. I did not interrupt him sooner because I was in a mood for hearing sermons. You, too, were the subject; and on such a thesis I never think the theme long; not even if I am to write it, and that slowly and awkwardly as now, with my left hand. But you may not be discouraged by a correspondence which begins so formidably. I will promise you on my honor that my future letters will be of reasonable length. I will even agree to express but half my esteem for you, for fear of cloying you with too full a dose. But on your part, no curtailing. If your letters are as long as the Bible, they will appear short to me. Only let them be brimful of affection. I shall read them with the dispositions with which Arlequin in 'Les deux billets,' spelt the words, 'je t'aime,' and wished that the whole alphabet had entered into their composition.

We have had incessant rains since your departure. These make me fear for your health, as well as that you had an uncomfortable journey. The same cause has prevented me from being able to give you any account of your friends here. The voyage to Fontainebleau will probably send the Count de Moustier and the Marquise de Bréhan to America. Danquierville promises to visit me, but has not done it as yet. De la Tude comes sometimes to take family soup with me, entertain me with anecdotes of his five and thirty years' imprisonment. How fertile is the mind of man which can make the Bastille and Dungeon of Vincennes yield interesting anecdotes. You know this was for making four verses on Mme. de Pompadour. As to myself, my health is good, except my wrist which mends slowly, and my mind which mends not at all, but broods constantly over your departure.[48]

It is a reasonable presumption that a man with a fractured wrist, writing at such amazing length with his left hand and with many political and diplomatic problems upon him, would not have taken the time or exhausted his energy writing a perfunctory note to a woman who had not made the most profound impression on his mind and heart. Here we catch occasional glimpses of his contacts with Maria Cosway, the meeting at Legrand and Motino's, the excursion to Saint-Germain, and the part played by Trumbull, whose historical paintings in the rotunda of the Capitol at Washington are immortal, in awakening Jefferson's interest in the English artist.

Before this unique letter was dispatched, however, Jefferson was reading a note from Maria, dated from Antwerp, which, from its bulk, promised a long letter. Along with the dialogue then went from Jefferson a note of gentle chiding:

> I prepared myself for a feast. I read two or three sentences; looked again at the signature to see if I had not mistaken it. It was visibly yours. Read a sentence or two more. Diable! Spelt your name distinctly. There was not a letter of it omitted. Began to read again. In fine, after reading a little and examining the signature, alternately half a dozen times, I found your name was to four lines only, instead of four pages. I thank you for the four lines, however, because they prove you think of me; a little, indeed, but better a little than none. To show you how much I think of you, I send you the enclosed letter of three sheets of paper, being a history of the evening I parted with you. But how expect you to read a letter of three mortal sheets of paper? I will tell you. Divide it into six doses of half a sheet each, and every day when the toilet begins, take a dose, that is to say read half a sheet. By this means it will have the only merit its length and dullness can aspire to, that of assisting your coiffeuse to procure you six good naps of sleep. I will even allow for twelve days to get through it, holding you rigorously to one condition only, that is, that at whatever hour you receive this, do not break the seal of the enclosed until the next toilet.[49]

---

[48] Ford, *Writings of Jefferson*, IV, 311.   [49] *Ibid.*, IV, 323.

It will be observed that the dialogue refers frequently to the 'delightful couple,' but one looks in vain for a single special reference to Cosway, and we may be sure the lady understood. It appears that after her return to London, Jefferson continued to write her, for in a long letter of her own a few months later, Maria complains that the last two letters from Jefferson had been much too brief, though she allowed for the reason. 'I must confess that the beginning of your correspondence has made me an enfant-gatée,' she wrote. 'I shall never learn to be reasonable in my expectations, and shall feel disappointed whenever your letters are not as long as the first one; thus you are the occasion for continual reproaching disposition in me. . . . I trust your friendship would wish to see me perfect, and mine to be so, but defects are, or are not, most conspicuous according to the feelings which we have for the objects which possess them.' And then: 'Are you to be painted in future ages, sitting solitary and sad on the beautiful Monticello, tormented with the shadow of a woman who will present you a deformed rod, broken and twisted, instead of the emblematical instrument belonging to the Muses, held by genius, inspired by wit . . . ?' And what did Jefferson think of the famous speech of Sheridan in the Hastings trial? Mr. Cosway had been with Hastings and had found him indifferent on the first day, but 'on the third day [of Sheridan's speech] he had been much affected and agitated.' She had been reading Jefferson's *Notes on Virginia.* How she would love to see 'those enchanted grottoes, those magnificent mountains, rivers, etc. Why am I not a man that I might set out immediately, satisfy my curiosity, and indulge my sight with wonders?' She was going to few parties, 'so excessively indolent I do not go out for months together.' She was painting some, and she had musical parties in the evenings and a few agreeable friends kept her company. But parties — no; 'nothing but crowded assemblies, uncomfortable heat, and not the least pleasure in meeting anybody.' The Opera in London was 'bad, the Zubendilli and Madame Mosa are the first singers.' But would not Jefferson tell her something about Madame de Polignac? 'They make a great deal about it here; we hardly hear anything else, and the stories are so different from one another that it is impossible to guess the real one.' She hoped to see Jefferson in the summer. 'If I shall be happy enough to come again in

the summer to Paris, I hope we shall pass many agreeable days,' she
wrote. But so many things might intervene. Her misgivings were
well founded. The Revolution was on the way.[50]

But at intervals the correspondence of Jefferson and Maria continued until both were old. Jefferson was in his last retirement at
Monticello, twelve years after he had left the White House, when
she wrote him of the death of her husband. 'I wish Monticello were
not so far away,' she wrote in 1821. 'I would pay you a visit were it
ever so much out of my way, but it is impossible. I long to hear
from you. The remembrance of a person I so highly esteem and
venerate affords me the happiest consolations, and your patriarchal
situation delights me — much as I expected from you. Notwithstanding your indifference for a world of which you make one of
the most distinguished ornaments and members, I wish you may
still enjoy many years and feel the happiness of a nation which produced such characters.' She was going to Paris, and she promised
Jefferson she would 'talk with Madame de Corny.'[51]

Two years later she wrote again, congratulating him on the
pleasure of planning the buildings of the University of Virginia,
and seeing them rise. 'I wish I could come and learn from you,'
she wrote. 'Were it the furtherest part of Europe, nothing would
prevent me, but that immense sea makes a great distance.' However, she hoped to hear from him as often as possible.[52]

When this letter was written, a great change had come into the
life of Maria. While she admired her husband's art, it seems certain
that she rather despised the affected fop, and in time they drifted
apart, living their separate lives. Under the encouragement of the
Archbishop of Toulouse, she founded a school for girls at Lodi,
Italy, to which she attached a religious order interested in female
education. Here she was to be reasonably happy, and, because of
the success of her venture, she was made a Baroness of the Empire
by the Emperor Francis I. Eleven years before she wrote the letter,
last quoted, to Jefferson, she had written him of her new career.
She herself thought it strange that she should have drifted into this
field. But after the tragic death of her daughter, she had found consolation in the training of girls. 'I am discharging the occupations

[50] Randolph, *Domestic Life of Jefferson,* 89-92.
[51] *Ibid.,* 374.   [52] *Ibid.,* 376.

of a nurse, happy in the self-gratification of doing my duty, with no other consolation,' she wrote. And then, showing how indelibly the memory of Jefferson's first letter was impressed upon her, she added: 'In your "Dialogue" your Head would tell you "that is enough"; your Heart perhaps will understand I might wish for more. God's will be done.' [53] Ten years later she wrote him: 'I am glad you approve my choice of Lodi. It is a pretty place and free from the bustle of the world which is becoming troublesome.' [54] To which she added: 'I saw Madame de Corny when in Paris. She is the same, only a little older' — only thirty-seven years older.

The last letter extant from Maria Cosway was written when she was sixty-five and Jefferson was eighty-one — thirty-nine years after the two had made the sentimental journey to Saint-Germain. It was written from Florence. Time had mellowed the unpleasant memories of her husband's affectations and foppishness and she found them not unpleasant in Florence, where many of his prints were in the art gallery. There she had placed a portrait of him. 'I have had my grand saloon painted with the representations of the four parts of the world, and the most distinguished objects of them,' she wrote. 'I am at a loss for America as I found very few small prints — however, Washington town is marked, and I have left a hill where I would place Monticello and the Seminary [University] if you favor me with some description that I might have them introduced.' [55]

With that, the curtain falls on a famous friendship that was not without sentiment, that must have gone beyond mere friendship. Two years later, Jefferson was dead. And twelve years after that, Maria died at her school in Lodi. She was buried in a vault under the chapel of the Church of Santa Maria delle Grazie, and there a monument has been erected to her memory.

That Maria Cosway was the nearest approach to a real sentimental attachment formed by Jefferson in Paris there can be little doubt.

VIII

Other women who entered into the pleasures of his Parisian life included Madame de Tott, a distinguished and popular painter of

[53] *Ibid.*, 372.   [54] *Ibid.*, 376.   [55] *Ibid.*

her time, whose art he appreciated and whose studio was not un
familiar to him, and Lucy Paradise, Countess Barziza. The latte
must have been a source of infinite amusement, since she has beer
described as 'an enfant terrible,' given to saying whatever came intc
her head; from which one gathers that she was a bit risquée. Tha
she was a chatterbox with a keen appetite for scandal must be
assumed from the assurances of her contemporaries and friends that
she had a keen relish for gossip and bowled down all pins in the
alley.

Her letters, written more than a century and a half ago to Jefferson, and which may be clearly read to this day, are a verification of
the general impression that women had confidence in his benevolence and discretion, and were prone to use him as a father confessor on their intimate troubles. Lucy was happily married to the
worthy Count Barziza, but her impecunious, penniless, and irresponsible parents who had reduced themselves to poverty had descended upon the Count as non-paying, unappreciative, and even
exacting guests, to the distress and mortification of the Countess.
Jefferson appears to have responded to her desperate appeals for
advice and assistance in the Count's effort to establish the father in
a more independent economic position, but the ailing parents do
not appear to have responded in a co-operative mood. 'On the part
of my marriage,' she wrote Jefferson a few months before the fall
of the Bastille, 'I have reason to thank the Almighty . . . on the part
of my parents I have reason to be overwhelmed. You, sir, are a just
man and I flatter myself that weighing your judgment, and giving
to all one's merits, you would continue your good offices and have us
in consideration for all the good that you can do us, being assured
that we shall be truly grateful.'

Nothing could more conclusively illustrate Jefferson's appeal to
women as a dependable friend and father confessor; for in the midst
of exacting occupations we here find him exerting himself as Lucy's
friend in an attempt to spare her humiliation and to prevent a possible wrecking of her marriage.[56]

That men also trusted him with their women is evident in an
incident involving John Paul Jones, the naval hero. The doughty

[56] MSS. Letters, Jefferson Coolidge Collection, Massachusetts Historical Society.

Captain appears to have been the lover of Aimée de Tellison, a natural daughter of Louis XV. 'I shall now tell you in confidence,' he wrote Jefferson in 1787, 'that she is the daughter of the late King and a lady of quality on whom his Majesty bestowed a large fortune.' [57] She is said to have been Jones's mistress and helper over a period of fourteen years. When he departed for Russia, he asked Jefferson to keep an eye on her and give her any assistance she might require. He readily agreed, but was rather nonplussed, on the lady's appearance, to find her a beautiful woman in her early twenties with flaming red hair. Later, Jones wrote Jefferson from Russia of his distress because the letters from the lady had not recently arrived. He was in great anxiety. Would not Jefferson ascertain her whereabouts and her situation and inform him at once? [58] With the Revolution on, we may imagine Jefferson turning momentarily from the marching mobs to scan the horizon of Paris in search of a flaming head of hair for the solacing of the soul of one of the naval heroes of the American Revolution.

[57] Russell, *John Paul Jones*, 182.
[58] *Ibid.*, 246.

CHAPTER

XVIII

DIPLOMACY AND REVOLUTION

I

THE MONTHS between the latter part of 1787 and the fall of the Bastille were crowded ones for Jefferson. The rapidly developing drama of the Revolution absorbed much of his attention throughout the entire period, without diverting him in the least from the performance of his diplomatic duties, which were becoming increasingly onerous and delicate. In this field this period was marked with some triumphs. Since there was no cleavage, in time, to separate the revolutionary events from the diplomatic activities and the more personal interests, we shall treat first his official actions and then his part in French politics, for the better clarification of the narrative.

In the late summer of 1787, his younger daughter, Polly, though her real name was Mary, arrived in Paris. Soon after reaching France, Jefferson had been shocked by the death of his youngest child, the baby left in Virginia with her aunt, and this determined him to send for Polly. Because of her tender age, he had a fear of her growing up without childhood memories of her father and sister. She even then had become so attached to her aunt that she could not bear the thought of leaving her. And when Jefferson sought to reconcile her to the proposed change, with the promise that in Paris she should be 'taught to play on the harpsichord, to draw, to dance, to read and talk French,' she replied: 'I don't want to go to France; I want to stay with Aunt Eppes.'[1] And when

[1] Randolph, *Domestic Life of Jefferson*, 106.

Jefferson wrote her how much he wished to see her, she replied: 'I should be very happy to see you, but I cannot go to France, and I hope you and sister are well.'[2] When at length she was persuaded and she embarked on the sea, Jefferson was in an agony of apprehension. 'I endeavor not to think of her till I know she is landed,' he wrote.[3] But on the voyage she was zealously served by Captain Ramsey, and when the time for landing came, she had become so attached to him that she literally had to be torn from her protector. During the three weeks she remained in London, Abigail Adams treated her with the tenderness of a mother and to her she became so attached that it was with difficulty she could be persuaded to leave her.[4] Several days of pleading were necessary to win her consent to the trip across the Channel, and Abigail never was to forget it.

On Polly's arrival in Paris, Martha was withdrawn from her convent for a week to be with her and to conduct her on visits to it until she became familiar with it. Soon she was established there with her sister. Jefferson thought the school 'altogether the best in France.' When, on Polly's arrival, it was found she had no recollection of her father or of Martha, he was more than ever certain of his wisdom in summoning her to Paris.[5] Jefferson's character cannot be understood without an understanding of his relations with his two daughters, to whom he was a congenial companion as well as father.

Jefferson had carried to France a familiarity with the work of the Count de Buffon, the celebrated French naturalist, some of whose conclusions concerning animals in America he had vigorously challenged in his *Notes on Virginia*. The Count was one of the few men he sought in Paris during the first months he was in the country. Jefferson took advantage of the time to prepare his case against him. As we have seen, he had written Virginians to send him the skins, horns, etc., of animals in dispute, with which to confute the naturalist. Long before their arrival, however, he had met Buffon and their disagreements were well known in Paris

[2] *Ibid.*
[3] *Ibid.*, 107.
[4] Jefferson to Mrs. Bolling, Ford, *Writings of Jefferson*, IV, 411.
[5] *Ibid.*

drawing-rooms. At length the bones, skins, and horns arrived, and Jefferson hurried them to the Count.

> I am happy to be able to present you at this moment the bones and skin of a Moose, the horns of the Caribou, the elk, the deer ... the spiked-horned bucks and Roebucks of America. They all came from New Hampshire and Massachusetts. The skin of the moose was dressed with the hair on, but a great deal of it has come off. ... The horns of the elk are remarkably small. I have certainly seen some of them which would weigh six times as much. This is the animal which we call elk ... and of which I have given some description in the *Notes on Virginia* of which I had the honor of presenting you a copy. ... I wish these spoils, sir, may have the merit of adding anything new to the treasures of Nature which have so fortunately come under your observation and of which she seems to have given you the key.[6]

Thus, Jefferson won his debate with the naturalist by the evidence of the horns, bones, skins of the animals in dispute, and the salons of Paris laughed heartily over the discomfiture of Buffon.

It was at this time that Jefferson was pressing Adams in London to permit Brown, the English artist, to paint his portrait, as he previously had painted one of Jefferson. 'Trumbull does not paint of the size of life and could not be asked to hazard himself to it,' he wrote Adams's son-in-law. The Brown portrait of Jefferson has mysteriously disappeared, though a copy may be seen to this day in the Adams house at Quincy. It was this portrait that was used in Appleton's *Cyclopaedia of American Biography*.[7]

II

This was a period of diplomatic activity. During the American Revolution, three prizes, captured at sea from the British by Commodore Paul Jones and taken into the port of Bergen in distress, had been restored to the British on the order of the King of Denmark. As early as December, 1789, Franklin had made demand for compensation, and ten thousand pounds was suggested to him as an indemnity by the Danish Minister in Paris. But with the departure of both the Minister and Franklin, the correspondence had been

[6] *Ibid.*, IV, 457.   [7] *Ibid.*, V, 2-3.

abandoned. Jefferson now revived it in a letter to Count Bernstorff, Minister of Foreign Affairs in Copenhagen, in which he sharply said that the 'United States continues to be sensibly affected by this delivery of their prizes to Great Britain, and the more so as no part of their conduct had forfeited their claim to those rights of hospitality which civilized nations extend to each other.' He announced that he was sending Paul Jones to Copenhagen as a special agent 'to attend the pleasure of his Majesty.' [8] Even in the days of the disintegrating Confederation, Jefferson was speaking boldly to the nations of Europe.

Nor did he use terms less bold in speaking to France. During the American Revolution a demand had been made on Franklin by the house of Schweighauser and Dobree at Nantes, and by Puehilberg of L'Orient, for money which had been refused for perfectly sound reasons. When, later, America purchased certain military stores in France, which had been deposited at Nantes for embarkation, the claimants had seized them by judicial process and had held them for many months. Jefferson now made demand on Montmorin for the unconditional release of American property. 'Unwilling to trouble your Excellency whenever it can be avoided,' he wrote, 'I proposed to the parties to have the question decided by arbitrators to be chosen by us jointly. They have refused it, as you will see by the answers to my letters, copies of both of which I have the honor to enclose to you.' He submitted that 'it is well settled in practice that the property of one sovereign is not permitted to be seized within the dominion of another; and that this practice is founded not only on mutual respect but on mutual utility.' He reminded Montmorin that the seizure of these stores by an ally, at a time when the Americans were in desperate need of them, was a matter of some gravity. The claimants had even gone so far as to make a merit of their failure to seize an American ship. 'Certainly the principles which permit the seizure of arms would admit that of a whole fleet, and would often furnish an enemy the easiest means of defeating an expedition,' he added. He was, therefore, 'under the necessity of asking an order from you for the immediate delivery of the stores and other property of the United States at Nantes.' [9]

[8] *Ibid.*, IV, 414.   [9] Bergh, *Writings of Jefferson*, VII, 141-42.

At the same time he wrote more sharply to de Rayneval, who had been 'the eye of Vergennes,' and still retained his post, and enclosed a copy to Montmorin: 'I shall hope an acknowledgment in respect to us of the principle which holds as to other nations: that our public property here cannot be seized by the territorial judge.' And then he pointed out the interest of France in the controversy. 'It is the more interesting to us, as we shall be more and longer exposed than other nations, to draw arms and military stores from Europe. Our preference of this country has occasioned us to draw them from hence alone, since the peace; and the friendship we have constantly experienced from the Government will, we doubt not, on this and every other occasion, insure to us the protection of what we purchase.'[10]

Within a month, Jefferson was able to report to Jay that he had been promised the delivery of the stores, but that certain formalities to be observed would mean a slight delay. The proceeding would be for the King to call the case before himself when the order to deliver the stores would be given.[11]

At a time when Jefferson was being constantly dunned on American debts, it required some temerity for him to make his demands with dignity.

About this time, too, an arrêt had been issued prohibiting the importation of whale oil when Jefferson thought an agreement had been reached permitting the sale in France of oil from the United States. He instantly wrote Montmorin that he assumed this did not apply to America. 'The importance of the subject to one of the principal members of our Union induces me to attend with great anxiety a reassurance from your Excellency that no change has taken place in his Majesty's views on this subject; and that his disposition to multiply, rather than diminish, the combinations of interests between the two peoples continues unaltered.'[12]

It appears that the reason for the arrêt was that the British had glutted the market, and that in the original arrêt the United States had been excepted. Writing Jay, Jefferson said that, 'without my having warning or suspicion,' this exception had been struck out, as he suspected by the Count de la Puzerne, the Minister of Marine. In numerous conferences with Montmorin and other Ministers,

[10] *Ibid.*, VII, 154-55.   [11] *Ibid.*, VII, 170.   [12] *Ibid.*, VII, 156.

Jefferson found them prepossessed 'by the partial information of their Dunkirk fishermen.' This led Jefferson to a fuller expression of his views than might otherwise have been thought necessary. His purpose was to disgust Necker, as an economist, with their new fisheries 'by letting him foresee their expense.' Finally, at a full meeting, when Lafayette, who was supporting Jefferson, was present, it was agreed to except the United States from the arrêt. 'But,' warned Jefferson, 'they will require rigorous assurance that the oils coming under our name are really of our fisheries,' since 'they fear we shall cover the introduction of the English oils from Halifax.' [13]

III

Meanwhile, despite the lordly tones he assumed in dealing with Montmorin, Jefferson was more than ever alarmed over the financial status of the new nation. He was being constantly besieged at his home with creditors of his country. He was greatly disturbed by references to the American debts in the debates of the Assembly of Notables, who, while moderating their tone, disclosed, nevertheless, a growing impatience. He himself was particularly apprehensive over the inability to pay the French officers. 'Their wants, the nature of their services, their access to high characters and connection with them, bespeak the reason for this,' he wrote Jay.[14] It had long been evident to Jefferson that until the Confederation was replaced by a more stable government, with power nationally to levy and collect taxes, the credit and honor of the country would remain in peril.

In February, 1788, another crisis was at hand, and Adams, who had dealt exclusively with the loans, was on the verge of his departure for America. The responsibility of dealing alone with all such matters was passed on to Jefferson, who wrote that he had 'no powers, no instructions, no means, and no familiarity with the subject.' [15] At this time the bankers and agents in Amsterdam, Wilhelm and Jan Willincks and Jacob Van Staphorsts, wrote Adams that they had received a letter from Jefferson informing them of the need of fifty-one thousand florins to meet the obligations coming

[13] *Ibid.*, VII, 192-93.   [14] *Ibid.*, VI, 248.   [15] *Ibid.*

due. 'He presses us in the most energetic style to furnish the money, informing us he had wrote your Excellency,' said the agents. They were, therefore, waiting to hear from Adams. They regretted they had been approached so late as to make impossible communication with the Board of Treasury, and, without authorization from that quarter, they would have to assume 'unnecessary responsibility.' The funds in their possession would suffice to pay interest soon falling due and leave just enough surplus to take care of the personal needs of Jefferson and Adams. Thus, an advance of fifty-one thousand florins would have to come from their own pocket. They thought it improbable that the bonds of the last loan of the United States would sell, since there were so many loans open with long-established countries noted for punctuality in payments.[16]

On the receipt of this letter, Adams wrote Jefferson that America was about to be the victim of a 'plot.' He utterly disbelieved the story that the new bonds would not sell. The fact was that these bankers and agents had been buying up large quantities of American paper, which they planned to have acknowledged and paid in Europe. Of course, wrote Adams, neither he nor Jefferson could ever agree to that. These certificates and the interest were to be paid in America at the Treasury, and if a precedent otherwise could be created, the effect would be 'horrid.' 'If the brokers, undertakers, and money-lenders will take such advantage of us, it is high time we have done with them, pay what is due as fast as we can, but never contract another farthing of debt with them,' wrote the enraged Puritan. If he were not on the verge of departing, he would go to Amsterdam and open a new loan before he would submit. And Adams closed on a dolorous note:

> My dear friend, farewell. I pity you. In your situation, dunned and teased as you will be, all your philosophy will be wanting to support you. But be not discouraged. I have been constantly vexed with such terrible complaints, and frightened with such long faces, these ten years. Depend upon it, the Amsterdamers love money too well to execute their threats. They expect to get too much by American credit to destroy it.[17]

Jefferson replied that he had been eagerly awaiting a letter from Adams, and that the letters containing the proposition to the Board

---

[16] Adams, *Works of John Adams*, VIII, 469-70.   [17] *Ibid.*, VIII, 473-75.

of Treasury could not possibly be answered in time.[18] But he was distressed by the possibilities. The failure to meet the obligation, concerning which he had written the bankers in Amsterdam, would 'destroy the credit of the United States and all future prospects of obtaining money there.'[19] Knowing there was not a moment to lose, he wrote Adams, who was then in The Hague:

> Our affairs at Amsterdam press on my mind like a mountain. I have no information to go on but that of Willincks and Van Staphorsts, and, according to that, something seems necessary to be done. I am so anxious to confer with you on the subject, and to see you and them together, and get some effectual arrangement made in time, that I determined to meet you at The Hague. I will set out the moment some repairs are made to my carriage; it is promised me at three o'clock tomorrow; and probably they will make it that night and I may not get off till Tuesday morning. In that case I shall be at The Hague on Friday night. . . . I am sensible how irksome this must be to you in the moment of your departure. But it is a great interest of the United States which is at stake, and I am sure you will sacrifice to that your feelings and your interest.[20]

It was a thoroughly worried and harassed diplomat who fared forth on the road to Amsterdam on the mission, as he believed, of saving the credit and prestige of the United States. He passed through Louvres, Senlis, Roye, Pont Saint-Maxence, Bois le Duc, Gournai, Péronne, Cambrai, Bouchain, Valenciennes, Mons, Bruxelles, Malines, Antwerp, Moerdijk, and Rotterdam, and reached The Hague in less than three days of constant driving. There he found Adams waiting.

They agreed that there was some danger in acting without authority of Congress, but that the gravity of the situation called upon them to risk themselves to save the credit of the country. Neither doubted that, on the establishment of the new Government, satisfactory arrangements would be made, but that there would be an inevitable delay in getting the money from taxes into the Treasury. Consequently, they agreed that in any new loan provision should be made for the years 1788, 1789, and 1790, to maintain the credit

[18] *Ibid.*, VIII, 475. [19] *Autobiography*, 83-84.
[20] Bergh, *Writings of Jefferson*, VI, 434.

and dignity of the nation in the interval. They would borrow a million florins.

Having agreed on the means, the two men set forth by way of Leyden and reached Amsterdam.[21] The two staunch patriots of the Revolution were riding forth on a mission as necessary and patriotic as any that had been undertaken from the hour that independence was declared in 1776. On reaching Amsterdam, Jefferson wrote Jay that he had gone there 'to have the benefit of [Adams's] interference in a department which had been his peculiarly, from the beginning.'[22] The two agreed that to ask a million florins to cover the waiting period would create a better impression as to the resources of the nation than to borrow more frequently in driblets. They had no difficulty making the loan.

That achieved, Adams left, and Jefferson remained on for ten days to attend to all the details. Thus, after his humiliating experiences in Paris, Jefferson found some relief from the constant embarrassment, born of the slovenly operations of the Confederation. 'I had the satisfaction to reflect,' he wrote, 'that, by this journey, our credit was secured, the new government was placed at ease for two years to come, and that, as well as myself, relieved from the torment of incessant duns, whose just complaints could not be silenced by any means within our power.'[23]

IV

He then availed himself of the opportunity of seeing something of Germany. Hurriedly, he visited Utrecht, Düsseldorf, Cologne, Bonn, Coblenz, Frankfort, Worms, Mannheim, Heidelberg, and less important towns. His interests were not dissimilar to those manifested in his journey through southern France and into Italy. That he was in search of utilitarian knowledge is evident in his notations on Amsterdam, where he made drawings of 'windows opening so that they admit air and not rain,' and where he saw 'a manner of fixing a flagstaff on the mast of a vessel,' 'a machine for drawing light empty boats over a dam,' windmills and their construction, 'a bridge across a canal formed by two scows,' a 'lantern

---

[21] *Autobiography*, 83-84.   [22] Bergh, *Writings of Jefferson*, VI, 438.
[23] *Autobiography*, 85.

over the street doors which gives light equally into the antechamber and the street,' 'a bridge on a canal turning on a swivel,' and a Dutch wheelbarrow of which he made a sketch.

While traveling through the country, he notes the state of cultivation, the care of the fields, the grain grown, the state of the people. After passing the border, he is impressed by 'the transition from ease and opulence to extreme poverty,' observing that the soil and climate were the same and 'the governments alone differ.' He notes that 'the villages . . . seem to be falling down,' that there was 'an overproportion of women.' But, true to his nature, he does not fail to notice that 'the gooseberry is beginning to leaf.' He describes the villages and the comparative lack of merchandise in the stores. At Duisburg he was anxious to locate the encampment of Varus, 'in which he and his legions fell by the arms of Arminius,' but since no one spoke English, French, Italian, or Latin, he could make no inquiries. At Düsseldorf he visited the art gallery, finding the rooms of Vanderwerff particularly interesting; and he passes at once from art to the Westphalian hog, 'of which the celebrated ham is made,' 'finding the animal tall, gaunt, and with heavy lop ears.' Cologne commerce interested him; the predominance of the poor there depressed him and the intolerant restrictions on Protestant merchants amazed him. Again he visited the vineyards and observed the making of the Moselle wines. Just as he had found Catholic intolerance in Cologne, he found Protestant intolerance in Frankfort, which confirmed his poor opinion of religious intolerance anywhere and of any kind. He found Hanau depressing, 'the drum and fife all that is heard,' and the streets clean as a German floor 'because nobody passes them.' He visits the seat of the landgrave near Hanau and makes sketches of the architecture of an old ruined castle.

Always the operations of government intrigue him, and he notices that 'the little tyrants roundabout, having disarmed the people and made it very criminal to kill game, one knows when he quits the territory of Frankfort by the quantity of game which is seen.' Again he is shocked by the heavy manual work of the women — 'they dig the earth, plough, saw, cut and split wood.' The château on the hill at Heidelberg seems to him 'the most noble ruin I have ever seen,' but he thinks little of the château of the Margrave of Baden, and thinks the great amount of money spent to have done 'more harm than good,' with the straight alleys cut through the oak forest. In Hesse, he is horrified because the roads 'have been strung with beggars.'

When he crosses the border into France, he notes again that 'the women . . . as in Germany do all kinds of work,' and this disgusts him. 'While one considers them as useful and rational companions, one cannot forget that they are also objects of our pleasure; nor can they ever forget it,' he writes. 'While employed in dirt and drudgery, some tag of a ribbon, some ring, or bit of bracelet, earbob or necklace . . . will show that the desire of pleasing is never suspended in them.' And again he ascribes the plight of women to bad government. 'Here is so heavy a military establishment that the civil part of the population is reduced to women only,' he explains. 'But this is a barbarous perversion of the natural destination of the two sexes. Women are formed by nature for attentions and not hard labor. A woman never forgets one of the numerous train of little offices which belong to her. A man forgets often.'

There is nothing in his notes to indicate that he made this journey other than as an ordinary tourist. If he met public functionaries, he makes no mention of them. But he found an unexpected pleasure, when, in passing through a town in Hesse where the roads were 'strung with beggars,' he found his old friend of the prison camp, Baron de Geismer, who frequently had enjoyed the hospitality of Monticello, stationed there in command of a regiment of Hessian soldiers. He had often told his fellow officers of the kindness of Jefferson to the prisoners and the American was given a warm-hearted and enthusiastic welcome. It was probably the most thoroughly human encounter of his German journey.

V

He was now back in the comfortable quarters in the Champs Elysées. Awaiting him on his desk were instructions to negotiate a consular convention to displace that made by Franklin, who had agreed to certain provisions wholly inconsistent with the laws of several of the American States. Jefferson himself had thought these provisions 'offensive to a free State.' But when he called on Mont-morin, he found the Minister loath to make the concessions asked.

Reluctantly, he agreed to a redrafting of the convention, which Jefferson found 'not such as [he] would have wished, but such as could be obtained with good humor and friendship.' [24]

One of the changes withdrew from consuls the privileges of the law of nations and subjected them to the laws of the land; another denied them the right of sanctuary in their homes; another deprived them of coercive powers over passengers from ships, confining these powers to action against deserters from the crew. In his negotiations Jefferson had dealt mostly with Monsieur de Rayneval, 'and in justice to him,' he wrote Jay, 'I must say I could not have desired more reasonable and friendly dispositions.' [25]

One of Jefferson's last duties was one that caused him some personal embarrassment, growing out of his friendship for the French Minister to the United States, Count de Moustier and his companion, the Marquise de Bréhan. The Count had made himself most offensive to the American Government by the insulting tone he had assumed in his discussions of the debts. This undoubtedly was his revenge on the long tongue of gossip which had made free with his relations to the Marquise, but since the Government had in no way discriminated against him on that account, his arrogance was pointless. The matter was so delicate, particularly as the Minister's offense was in pressing for the payment of the debts, that Jefferson had recourse to Lafayette, who saw Montmorin for him. It was agreed that any notes on the debts thereafter should be prepared in Paris, with only the Minister's name added in America. Montmorin was quite agreeable to this suggestion, but the recall of the Minister was a different and more difficult matter. There was no other mission vacant at the moment, or he could have been shifted. But Montmorin recalled an ambiguous sentence in one of Moustier's letters, written while squirming under the pin-pricks of the Mother Grundys, which could be interpreted into a request for a leave of absence. Splendid! The request would be granted. And Paris would neglect to send him back.[26] Ultimately he went to Berlin, taking the Marquise with him.

[24] *Autobiography*, 85.
[25] Bergh, *Writings of Jefferson*, VII, 165-66.
[26] *Ibid.*, VII, 279-80.

VI

Meanwhile, the French Revolution was advancing by forced marches. Jefferson was to watch it with fascination and a keen intelligence. He was surprised to note how the fermentation had increased during his brief absence in Holland. He was to conclude that had the premier, Toulouse, soon to be made a Cardinal, immediately or speedily put into execution the reforms agreed upon by the Notables, there would have been a moderation of the tension. But Toulouse acted slowly, one by one, and with long intervals between, which gave the public time to formulate new demands and to pick flaws with the new laws.

But Jefferson was tolerant of the dissatisfaction of the people. He wrote in his *Autobiography*:

> Nor should we wonder at this pressure when we consider the monstrous abuses under which the people were ground to powder; when we pass in review the weight of their taxes and the inequality of their distribution; the oppressions of the tithes, the tailles, the corvées, the gabelles, the farms and the barriers; the shackles on commerce of the monopolies; on industry by guilds and corporations; on the freedom of conscience, of thought, and of speech; on the freedom of the press by the censor; and of the person by Lettres de Cachet; the cruelty of the criminal code generally; the atrocities of the Rack; the venality of the Judges and their partialities to the rich; the monopoly of military honors by the Noblesse; the enormous expenses of the Queen, the Princes, and the Court; the prodigalities of pensions; and the riches, indolence, luxury, and immorality of the Clergy. Surely under such a mass of misrule and oppression, a people might justly press for a thorough reformation and might even dismount their rough-shod riders, and leave them to walk on their own legs.[27]

He felt that the atmosphere in Paris indicated an inevitable upheaval. Even Gouverneur Morris was shocked at the 'utter prostration in morals,' the 'degree of depravity.' He wrote that 'a hundred anecdotes and a thousand examples are required to show the extreme rottenness of every member' of society. He saw that 'there are men and women who are greatly and eminently virtuous . . .

[27] *Autobiography*, VIII, 506.

but they stand forward from a background deeply and darkly shaded.' [28]

But Morris managed to play his part in this depravity of society, and, with notable zest about this time, he shared the company of his mistress, Madame de Flahaut, living at the Louvre with her former lover, Talleyrand; and as the roué and libertine of the clergy read the 'Protest of the Nobles and Clergy of Brittany,' Morris, tired of politics even in a boudoir, fell asleep in his chair; [29] and when about this time Morris gave a dinner and the guests, including the host, got drunk, he wandered about afterward in the Palais Royal until 'picked up' and returned to his home at midnight, 'the object of [his] own contempt and aversion.' [30]

The Paris of 1789 buzzed and hummed with politics, the shrill voices of the women rising above those of the men. 'We are in need of something to make us laugh,' wrote Jefferson to Mrs. Bingham, 'for the topics of the times are sad and eventful. The gay and thoughtless Paris is now become a furnace of politics. All the world is now politically mad. Men, women, and children talk nothing else and you know that naturally they talk much, loud and warm. Society is spoiled by it, at least for those, who, like myself, are but lookers on.' [31]

And Jefferson could find nothing in the Ministers to offer promise. Toulouse had fallen short of expectations, based on his brilliancy in society. Montmorin, whom he liked, he thought 'weak,' 'indolent, and inattentive.' The new Ministers, Villedeuil and Lambert, had 'no will of their own.' [32] And Jefferson was doubtful about the people, whom he did not think 'ripe for the blessings to which they are entitled.' Indeed, he doubted if they would 'accept of a habeas corpus law if offered them by the King.' [33]

But the people were aroused and on the march, to the horror of the Court Party, and of not a few philosophers of the salons, who had not taken their own talk seriously. In April, 1788, ten thousand soldiers were ordered into the neighborhood of Paris, with the French and Swiss Guards inside the barrier. Morris thought that, should a revolution come, it promised to be 'warm work.' He found

---

[28] Davenport, *Diary of Gouverneur Morris*, I, 61.
[29] *Ibid.*, I, 55. [30] *Ibid.*, I, 44. [31] Ford, *Writings of Jefferson*, V, 9.
[32] To Madison, *ibid.*, V, 43-48. [33] *Ibid.*, V, 53-54.

the Ministers contributing to the chaos by having no idea what they were doing. But no one missed an opportunity to laugh. Lafayette told Morris that the constituents of the Duc de Coigny, mentioned as one of the Queen's lovers by the gossips, had instructed him to move that the Queen should not, in case of accident, be Regent; and that Lafayette, hated by both the King and Queen, was opposed to the motion.[34]

But it was not all laughter. More than a year before the attack on the Bastille, bread riots had broken out in the workers' section of Saint Antoine, but even this ended with a laugh, when Baron de Besenval ordered two pieces of cannon with the Swiss Guards; and because the people turned and ran as preparations were being made to fire, it was generally agreed among the aristocracy that the Baron was a great general. 'As the women say so, it would be folly to controvert the opinion,' wrote Morris.[35]

But Jefferson felt a personal interest when the Court Party turned on his friend and protégé, Lafayette, because of his insistence on a constitution and his liberal principles, and 'disgraced' him by depriving him of a function to which he had been assigned. There was some momentary whispering about the Bastille, but Jefferson discounted this and thought his 'disgrace' would work to his ultimate advantage and 'recommend him favorably to the nation.'[36] He was sure the action taken was merely to save appearances for his enemies, and that nothing serious was intended, since those responsible for his 'disgrace' were 'constantly conferring and communicating with him.' He was now numbered among the foremost of the patriots.[37]

It was soon thereafter that Lafayette was trying his hand on the hustings as a candidate for the States General from Auvergne, with the influence of the Princes and the Queen exerted to defeat him and with his own order prejudiced against him. Even the cynical Morris records at the time that he 'played the orator with as much éclat as ever he played the soldier, and is at this moment as much envied and hated as his heart could wish.' To which he added: 'He is also much beloved by the nation.'[38] At any rate, he was triumphantly

[34] Davenport, *Diary of Gouverneur Morris,* I, 43.
[35] *Ibid.,* I, 64.
[36] To Madison, Ford, *Writings of Jefferson,* V, 43.
[37] *Ibid.,* V, 64.
[38] Davenport, *Diary of Gouverneur Morris,* I, 61.

elected, and Jefferson's interest in the forthcoming meeting of the States General was accentuated.

VII

There has been so much slovenliness and slop, inspired by partisan malice, concerning Jefferson and the French Revolution and his alleged association and affiliation 'with the Jacobins' that, on the eve of the first meeting of the States General, we may advantageously pause to make a survey of the little group of political friends who played their part in the early days of the great upheaval. It may be said at once that there was no Jacobin Club when Jefferson departed for America. There is a half-substantiated story that, before the Revolution, a green, slender young lawyer from the provinces, named Robespierre, took or sent Jefferson a copy of a speech he had made on some literary subject before a literary club of his home town. If so, it made so little impression on Jefferson that no mention of the incident is to be found in his voluminous correspondence. Of course he had not heard of Marat. During Jefferson's stay in Paris, Danton was a young lawyer without clients, frequenting the cafés that knew not Jefferson at all, and it is highly improbable that Jefferson ever heard the name of the revolutionary orator before he rose to power, long after Jefferson was at the head of Washington's Cabinet.

Of Mirabeau he had heard, as had everyone else in Paris, as a brilliant man who had written much and who posed as a liberal. That Jefferson had some respect for his influence and talents we may assume from the fact that he sent the orator a copy of his Ordinance of Religious Freedom, in the hope that he might spread its gospel. But there is nothing of record to show that Jefferson and Mirabeau ever met. Or that he ever met Talleyrand, who was then a friend of the orator.

Who, then, were the 'Jacobins' with whom Jefferson associated?

Among those who played a part in the dawning days of the Revolution, Jefferson's most conspicuous associate was Lafayette, whom the American took under his wing and coached. The French patriot's intimate association with the American Revolution had converted him into a republican of liberal principles which warred, naturally, with the system then existing in France. Constantly, Jefferson was writing Washington, Madison, and Monroe of this association, of his hopes and fears for his young protégé. But Lafayette was not one of the butchers of the French Terror.

Another of Jefferson's friends was Barnave, who was one of the most brilliant, eloquent, and generally distinguished members of the States General, in the early stages rivaling Mirabeau as an orator of that body. Since he was born in Grenoble, of a distinguished family, the apologists of Marie Antoinette, who have pictured him as a crude underling in the presence of the Queen, when he was one of the three members of the Convention that brought the royal family back from their flight, seem more malicious than convincing. He was in every sense a gentleman, studious, and at the same time social, passionate, and yet thoughtful, handsome in person and graceful in manner. At the age of twenty-two he had won distinction in the local *parlement* with the discourse on the division of political powers. Elected to the States General as a member of the Third Estate, he immediately was conceded rank among the foremost. It was he who prepared the first address to the King, and he supported Sieyès in his demand for the merging of the three orders into one body. A passionate lover of liberty, he still hoped, with Jefferson, that this might be secured under the monarchy. He engaged in a famous debate with Mirabeau on the right of the King to make peace or war. In the crowded carriage with the King and Marie Antoinette on their return from their flight, he made an impression on the latter as a man of principle and ability; and such were his humanitarian impulses that her sad plight converted him into a friend and adviser. He was an infinitely greater gentleman than most of the dandies of the court. He spoke powerfully in maintaining the inviolability of the King's person, and, suspected by the extremists, he was denounced and he died by the guillotine. He was not of the anarchists or terrorists.

Still another of Jefferson's associates was Count Alexandre Lameth, who was not yet thirty when accustomed to visit Jefferson frequently and consult with him. He was elected to the States General as a representative of the nobles and was one of the triumvirate which, in the beginning, controlled forty votes and threw them to the leftists. It was he who made the notable report to the lawmakers on the organization of the army; and he who denounced

Mirabeau when convinced of his treachery. After the return of the monarchs from their flight, he became reconciled to the court, and, when accused of treason, he fled the country and was imprisoned by the Austrians. After his release he remained in exile until the time of the Consulate. Later, he served both the Empire and the Restoration, and his memory is embalmed in his excellent two-volume history of the Constituent Assembly.

There was no blood on his hands and no loot in his pocket.

Another of Jefferson's associates was Adrien Duport, a Parisian, a distinguished lawyer, an influential advocate in the *parlement* of Paris — a judiciary body, not to be confused with the lawmaking body of representative governments — who led the fight against Calonne and Brienne. He, too, was elected as a representative of the nobles. He was a brilliant orator and an erudite jurist and played a prominent part in the organization of the judiciary of France. He had often heard Jefferson in conversation expound the wisdom of the jury system, and Duport championed it in France, though unable to have it extended to civil cases. It was he who, along with Barnave and Lameth, for   umvirate which dominated the States General   After the flight of the King, he sought to defe   er of the commission that questioned the King, he sought   use him; and when the Jacobins brought their accusation of treason, he opposed them. Arrested during the turmoils of August, 1792, he escaped, through the help of Danton, and took refuge in Switzerland, where he died in exile.

He had no complicity in the horrors of the Revolution.

Still another of Jefferson's associates was Jean Joseph Mounier, also a great lawyer and a distinguished jurist. Elected as a repre-sentative of the Third Estate, he supported the popular side, insist-ing on the merging of the three orders. He was conspicuous in the creation of the new constitution. He demanded the return of Necker after his dismissal. For a time he was president of the Con-stituent Assembly. But when the pendulum of the Revolution began to swing to the extreme left, he retired from the Assembly; and when he became a suspect, he fled to Switzerland, where he re-mained until 1801. Later he became a Councilor of State under Napoleon.

To these may be added the famous Abbé Sieyès, who, though not so intimately associated with Jefferson, was often a caller at the house on the Champs Elysées, where he talked political philosophy with his host and sometimes of the state of France. His ability was greatly in excess of his character. A brilliant man, he was cold, calculating, and, where his personal safety was involved, cautious to the point of cowardice. A reformer in the beginning, when the extremists seized control of the Revolution he deftly stepped into the shadows to emerge later in the days of Napoleon, and to reply to the question as to what he did during the reign of Robespierre with two words — 'I lived.'

These were Jefferson's 'bloody Jacobin friends' — men of unusual mental powers, of social grace, of moderate views; liberals and lovers of liberty, all of whom were quite willing to maintain the monarchy after the liberalization of the system and the granting of liberal reforms. Of the six, Lafayette, who was a republican, was probably the most extreme.

Doubting as he did the preparation of the French of those days for republican institutions, Jefferson hoped for constitutional reforms in the monarchy.

VIII

In May, 1788, Jefferson was forewarning Jay of the serious trouble inherent in the quarrel of the King and the Notables. He foresaw plans for 'some act of high-handed authority,' since an extra number of printers were at work in the Government plant, with soldiers guarding their occupation from publicity. The commanders of the provinces had been ordered to be at their posts on a certain day. The *parlement* of Paris, to forestall any attempt to silence it, issued a declaration of rights.[39]

Three weeks later, Jefferson wrote Jay of the realization of his expectations. The very night he wrote the letter just quoted, guards seized two members of the *parlement* in their houses. Making their escape, they took refuge in the *parlement* house where all the members assembled. A battalion of guards entered the house and again seized the two members, who were sent to prison, one to Lyons,

[39] To Jay, Bergh, *Writings of Jefferson*, VII, 5.

the other, 'the most obnoxious,' to an island in the Mediterranean.[40]

Jefferson doubted if there was any head or body in the nation capable of standing up against two hundred thousand soldiers, and while some doubted the loyalty of the army, he suspected that, having been drilled to strict obedience, they could be counted upon against the people.[41]

But four days later, when he again wrote Jay, he was more optimistic about the gains made by the popular movement. The Government had been forced to admit its inability to impose a new tax, and the calling of the States General was now inevitable. This promised a restoration of representative government after more than two and a half centuries. Jefferson thought that 'the King's dispositions are solidly good'; that he was 'capable of great sacrifices,' and that he would go along with the States General. He, therefore, hoped that the needed reforms could come without convulsions. There had been gross exaggerations in the English press. A few minor riots? Yes, but 'as yet not a single life has been lost.' The arrest of the deputies of Bretagne had brought no insurrection, but Lafayette, who had signed a petition for their release, had been 'disgraced' by being removed from his command in the South. But, thought Jefferson, 'this dishonors them at court ... but it will probably honor him in the eyes of the nation.'[42]

But the distress of the Government intensified, excitement increased, and Marie Antoinette agreed to the dismissal of her favorite, the Archbishop Toulouse, and the summoning of Necker to power. Jefferson curiously watched the people amusing themselves with trying and burning the Archbishop in effigy and rejoicing on the appointment of Necker. When the commanding officer of the city guards sought in vain to end the demonstrations, he ordered a bayonet charge and some were killed and wounded. The crowd retaliated the next day when they attacked the guards at various points, killed two or three of them, and burned ten or twelve guard houses. Then martial law restored order. So Jefferson reported to Jay.[43]

But even Nature was turning against the monarchy. In August, the country was swept by a hailstorm, and Jefferson, doubting the

40 *Ibid.*, VII, 15. 41 *Ibid.*, VII, 19.
42 *Ibid.*, VII, 186-88. 43 *Ibid.*, VII, 132-33.

press reports that some of the hailstones weighed ten pounds, was assured later by the Duke de la Rochefoucauld that he had seen some of that size. Liberal contributions were made for the relief of the sufferers, but Jefferson observed in a letter to de Crèvecoeur that this would be 'like a drop of water from the finger of Lazarus,' since 'there is no remedy . . . but to bring the people to a state of ease, so as not to be ruined by the loss of a single crop.' He feared that 'this hail may be considered as the coup de grâce to an expiring victim.'[44]

Then quickly followed the most bitterly cold winter in the memory of men. Jefferson wrote Jay that the cold was so severe that military operations had been stopped in Europe, and that in France the cold was without parallel, increasing the distress of the Government. 'They had before to struggle with a want of money and want of bread for the people, and now the want of fuel and the want of employment.'[45] He foretold an inevitable scarcity of corn and flour and a probable appeal for both to the United States.[46] He was appalled by the magnitude of the tragedy, with all outdoor work suspended and laborers left without food or fuel, with great fires burning at the cross-streets and the poor gathered about them to save themselves from freezing.[47] But equally was Jefferson delighted with the upsurging of the benevolence of the nation, which 'went beyond [his] expectation.'[48]

It was at this juncture that Montmorin summoned Jefferson to Versailles to inform him that, over and above the market price, a premium would be given on what was sent from America. Jefferson urged his countrymen to send as much and as rapidly as possible, and during March, April, and May there poured into French ports from the United States twenty-one thousand barrels of flour.[49]

Meanwhile, Jefferson was keenly observing the progress of the Revolution, convinced that the nobility and clergy, long exempt from taxation, would never consent to it without force. 'They then remain to be squeezed,' he wrote Doctor Price in London, 'and no agent is powerful enough for this but the people.'[50] He pinned his

44 *Ibid.*, VII, 115.   45 *Ibid.*, VII, 259.
46 *Ibid.*, VII, 235-36.   47 *Autobiography*, 89.
48 To Count de Moustier, Bergh, *Writings of Jefferson*, VII, 306
49 *Autobiography*, 89.
50 Bergh, *Writings of Jefferson*, VII, 256-57.

hope on the States General, though he foresaw 'great difficulty in preventing twelve hundred people from becoming a mob.'[51]

The Paris of that spring, just before the fall of the Bastille, was beautifying itself nevertheless, as he wrote Madame de Bréhan. The winter had been dreadful, with dinners and suppers suppressed and the money saved given to charity, and for two months heavily loaded carriages thundered over the thick ice on the Seine. The opera, which had cost one hundred thousand crowns in the last year, had been sacrificed to economy. The new wall about the city was an eyesore, but Jefferson found compensation in 'the fine Boulevards within and without the walls,' affording 'beautiful drives around the city of between fifteen and twenty miles.' Of art, he had nothing to report. 'I do not feel an interest in any pencil but that of David,' he wrote.[52]

It was that March that saw France seething with the excitement of electioneering. 'All the world here is electioneering,' Jefferson wrote Count de Moustier. 'Paris is deserted, at least as to that description of persons who think they may be chosen themselves or aid the choice of their friends.' Mirabeau had already been elected by the Third Estate, after his order had declared him not a noble.[53] Elections were something novel in France, and every village was aflame with enthusiasm, the elections converted into festivals and carnivals and everyone inspired by a religious exaltation.

IX

With the colorful, terribly significant opening of the States General, we are concerned only with Jefferson's contact with the event. It is improbable that Jefferson saw the procession, since he was with the Diplomatic Corps in their places when it entered the building. Morris, who did, was so shocked by the lack of a single cheer for Marie Antoinette that he tried to persuade the people about him to applaud, but without success. He thought, with evident approval, that 'she looks with contempt upon the scene,' though he learned later from Madame de Chastellux that the Queen was infuriated

---

51 To Carmichael, Ford, *Writings of Jefferson*, V, 73-74.
52 *Ibid.*, V, 78-80.
53 Bergh, *Writings of Jefferson*, VII, 305-06.

and the King hurt.[54] Jefferson, more interested in the scenes within the hall, wrote Carmichael that 'the King's speech was exactly what it should have been, and very well delivered.' But not a word of the Chancellor's speech could be heard 'by anybody,' and Necker's was as good as any discourse filled with figures could be, though Jefferson was surprised that he had not touched more on the great constitutional reforms 'which his Rapport au roy had prepared us to expect.'[55] Many years later, Jefferson was to recall his disappointment because Necker had 'tripped too lightly over the constitutional reforms which were expected.'[56]

For days before the meeting, conversation was feverish with speculation as to whether the three orders, the Third Estate, the Nobles, and the Clergy, would vote separately as orders or all together as separate individuals. The King himself had favored giving the Third Estate as many seats as the two others combined, but from the nobles and the clergy there was a stubborn opposition. Because of the liberality of the nobles in and near Paris, long affected by the liberal tone of the salons and drawing-rooms, it had been expected that the representatives of the nobility would be found in a conciliatory and liberal mood. Jefferson reported to Jay, however, that 'the great mass of the deputies of that order who come from the country show that the habits of tyranny over the people are deeply rooted in them.' He found they would consent to equal taxation, 'but five-sixths of that chamber are thought to be decidedly in favor of voting by orders.' More astonishing, thought Jefferson, was the fact that, where it had been assumed that the elections would sweep in the higher ecclesiastics, five-sixths of the representatives of that order elected were of the lower clergy, the parish priests. 'These are the sons of peasants,' reported Jefferson, 'who have done all the drudgery of the service for ten, twenty, and thirty guineas a year, and whose oppressions and penury, contrasted with the pride and luxury of the high clergy, have rendered them perfectly disposed to humble the latter.' At any rate, he thought, high hopes were pinned on the clergy. The Third Estate stood firmly for voting by persons.[57]

[54] Davenport, *Diary of Gouverneur Morris*, I, 67.
[55] Bergh, *Writings of Jefferson*, VII, 277.
[56] *Autobiography*, 90.   [57] Bergh, *Writings of Jefferson*, VII, 343-44.

It was with manifest anxiety and apprehension that, from his watch-tower, Jefferson followed this contest, the result of which was to give direction and impulse to the Revolution. He was deeply concerned over the position of Lafayette, and he wrote him a long letter, rich in the wisdom of a consummate politician. He thought the nobles would go wrong, and he said, 'I am uneasy for you' — because Lafayette had been elected as a representative of the nobles. 'Your principles are decidedly of the tiers état, and your instructions against them,' he wrote. To vote with one sometimes and with the other at other times would give the appearance of trimming and 'lose you both.' In the end, Lafayette would 'go over to the tiers état, because it will be impossible for you to live in a constant sacrifice of your own sentiments to the prejudice of the Noblesse.' But were he to be irresolute too long and then go over to the tiers état, he would 'be received coldly and without confidence.' And then Jefferson bore down:

> It appears to me to be the moment to take at once that honest and manly stand with them which your own principles dictate. This will win their hearts forever, be approved by the world which marks and honors you as a man of the people, and will be an eternal consolation to yourself. [Of course the noblesse, and especially the noblesse of Auvergne] will always prefer men who will do their dirty work for them [but] you are not made for that.

Continuing his argument, Jefferson pressed down hard:

> Suppose a schism should take place. The priests and nobles will secede, the nation will remain in place, and, with the King, will do its own business. If violence should be attempted, where would you be? You cannot then take sides with the people in opposition to your own vote, that very vote which would have helped to procure the schism. Still less can you array yourself against the people. That is impossible. Your instructions are, indeed, a difficulty. But to state this at its worst, it is only a single difficulty, which a single effort surmounts. . . . Your instructions can never embarrass you a second time, whereas an acquiescence under them will produce greater difficulties every day and without end.

And then, realizing that he had written as would a leader instructing a follower, Jefferson closed on an apologetic note:

> Forgive me, my dear, if my anxiety for you makes me talk of
> things I know nothing about. You must not consider this as advice.
> Believe it merely as the expression of my uneasiness and the effusion
> of that sincere friendship, with which, I am, dear sir, etc.[58]

A few days before Jefferson wrote thus to Lafayette, a serious riot
had been precipitated under the pretense, as Jefferson wrote, that a
paper manufacturer had proposed a reduction of fifteen sous a day
in the wages of his workers. He reported to Jay that the mob had
rifled the manufacturer's house, destroyed everything in his shops,
and had been stopped only when troops opened fire and killed
scores of the rioters. Jefferson's sympathy was not with the mob.
'They were the most abandoned banditti in Paris, and never was a
riot more unprovoked and unpitied,' he wrote Jay.[59] He probably
was right in saying that neither this nor other riots had any pro-
fessed connection with the political situation; what he did not
realize was that this banditti would ultimately, for a time, sway
the destinies of France.

Most fascinating to Jefferson was the bitter struggle of the three
orders. He discussed it with friends about the dinner-table, and
thought about it as he tramped the wooded paths of the Bois. His
sympathy was entirely with the Third Estate, which he described,
in a letter to Tom Paine, as 'immovable, not only firm, but a little
disdainful.' He said were he in authority, he would invite the two
other orders to join them; that a majority of the clergy would, a
minority of the nobles; and should the King refuse to do business
and adhere to the nobles, 'the common chamber will declare all
taxes at an end.'[60] He was persuaded that most of the clergy
would finally join the commons, and that public opinion favored
the voting by persons. 'This is the opinion à la mode at present,
and mode has acted a wonderful part in the present instance,'
he wrote Humphreys. 'All the handsome young women . . .
are for the tiers état, and that is an army more powerful in France
than the two hundred thousand men of the King.'[61]

Every day during the struggle Jefferson drove to Versailles. From
the gallery set aside for the diplomats he looked down upon the

58 Ford, *Writings of Jefferson*, V, 91.
59 Bergh, *Writings of Jefferson*, VII, 341.
60 *Ibid.*, VII, 362.   61 Ford, *Writings of Jefferson*, V, 86.

drama. Lafayette was in and out of the house on the Champs Elysées soliciting advice day by day. He had asked Jefferson if there was any precedent in England for the Parliament buying bread and supervising its distribution. Jefferson knew of no precedent and no precedent there for the desperate need of food. He supposed that in England the Parliament would merely appropriate the money and 'petition the King to employ it for the best, since that would be the business of the executive.' Fearing he would be unable to see Lafayette at Versailles personally to reply, he put his answer in a letter and himself left it at his friend's door.[62]

X

Meanwhile, with conditions growing worse and with Necker doing little, Jefferson was forming an opinion of that stilted Minister which history generally has adopted as its own. He found him lacking, not only in skill, but in courage. He wrote Jay:

Eloquence in a high degree, knowledge in matters of account and order, are distinguishing traits of his character. Ambition is his first passion, virtue his second. He has not discovered that sublime truth, that a bold, unequivocal virtue is the best handmaiden, even to ambition, and would carry him further in the end than the temporizing, wavering policy he pursues. His judgment is not of the first order, scarcely even of the second; his resolution frail; and upon the whole it is rare to meet an instance of a person so much below the reputation he has obtained.[63]

All the while, Jefferson was following with a sharp eye the intrigues of the Court Party, under the Queen and the two Princes. They had proposed that the King should go to Marly and there declare for the nobles. Necker and Montmorin interfered. They and Saint-Priest, thought Jefferson, were the only men about the King favoring the commons.[64] His faith in the clergy going over to the commons weakened when he heard that 'the bishops and archbishops have been very successful by bribes and intrigues in detaching the curés from the commons, to whom they were at first attached, to a man.'[65] However, he found all the talents of the

62 Bergh, *Writings of Jefferson*, VII, 374.
63 *Ibid.*, VII, 375-82.   64 *Ibid.*   65 *Ibid.*, VII, 388.

nation in the commons — 'firm and bold, yet moderate.' A few hot-
heads, yes; 'but those of most influence are cool, temperate, and
sagacious.' The nobles he thought 'absolutely out of their senses,'
the clergy were 'waiting to profit by every incident to secure themselves and have no other object in view.' [66]

The climax came at Marly in the Council of the King. Necker
submitted a declaration criticizing all sides, but ultimately siding
with the commons. Unknown to the men at the Council, the clergy
at that moment had voted to join the commons. No one was more
distressed by the action of the clergy than the American aristocrat,
Morris, who wrote that day in his *Diary* that this was 'fatal to the
Noblesse . . . unless the Royal authority is interposed to save the
nobles.' Morris was primarily interested in serving the nobles; just
as Jefferson was primarily concerned with the cause of the
commons.[67]

It was at this juncture that the court made the fatal blunder of
locking the commons out of their meeting-place. They adjourned
to the tennis court, joined by the greater part of the clergy, and
defiantly announced that they would not disband until their work
was finished. The weak King, isolated at Marly, was ignorant of
what had occurred, and the Court Party deceived him as to the
situation. The latter called another meeting, when d'Artois, the
flippant fop, light-headed as a feather, viciously attacked Necker,
who shriveled before the blast. When the Council went with
d'Artois, Necker resigned. 'No, sir,' shouted that stupid Prince,
'you must be kept as a hostage' — or so Jefferson was told that day.

Thoroughly absorbed by the drama, Jefferson hurried back and
forth between Paris and Versailles. He was there in the days when
the King appeared before the States General, passing in an ominous
silence between the lines of soldiers, and ordered the members to
follow him and resume their deliberations on the morrow. The
nobles and a small number of the clergy obeyed; the commons and
a majority of the clergy remained. When ordered out, Mirabeau
thundered his immortal challenge. Crowds gathered in the streets,
cheering Necker. In Paris a run on the bank began. The carriage
of the Archbishop of Paris was attacked with mud and stones until

[66] To Madison, *ibid.*, VII, 388.
[67] Davenport, *Diary of Gouverneur Morris*, I, 119.

he agreed to join the commons. The next day, forty-eight of the nobles joined the Third Estate. But to Jefferson's distress, Lafayette, embarrassed by his instructions, was not among them. He wrote his constituents asking for a change in his instructions or the acceptance of his resignation.

Writing Jay of the scenes, Jefferson described the streets in Versailles as 'embarrassed with soldiers,' with a hundred on horseback in front of the hall of the States General and guarding the doors. The two thousand spectators, who regularly had looked on from the galleries, were excluded. The commons demanded the removal of the soldiers with the threat otherwise to move elsewhere. Thoroughly alarmed, the King now asked the nobles and the clergy to join the commons. The fight was over. The King had lost. The people were sovereign — though few realized what that would come to mean.[68]

XI

Meanwhile, Jefferson was seeing men of diverse views. Morris was calling almost daily for tea and conversation, and finding his host not forming 'just estimates of character but rather assigning too many to the rank of fools.'[69] On June 3, 1789, he took a liberal nobleman, Baron de Montbellet, to call on Jefferson, at the Baron's request, and Morris was disgusted with the liberal talk he heard. Ah, these 'literary people,' sighed Morris, 'imagining everything must go for the better in proportion as it recedes from the present establishment.' The Baron leaves. Morris takes Jefferson to call on Monsieur Le Vieillard, and returns home, as Jefferson strides off for one of his brisk walks in the Bois.[70] What Morris did not know was that, on the morning of his call, Jefferson had written a proposed Charter of Rights to be presented to the King.

The turbulence, the increasing temperature of the people, the uncertainty as to the disposition of the army, had awakened his fears. During these days he was being constantly consulted by leading members of the States General — by men like Barnave, Lameth,

[68] To Jay, Bergh, *Writings of Jefferson*, VII, 390-96; VII, 400.
[69] Davenport, *Diary of Gouverneur Morris*, I, 100.
[70] *Ibid.*, I, 104.

Lafayette, Saint-Etienne, whom, he wrote later, '. . . were disposed to my acquaintance and had some confidence in me.' In these unofficial personal conferences, he now urged 'most strenuously an immediate compromise, to secure what the Government was now ready to yield and trust to future occasions for what might still be wanting.' He was thoroughly convinced that the King at that moment was prepared to grant freedom of person by habeas corpus, freedom of conscience, freedom of the press, trial by jury, a representative legislature with annual meetings and the origination of laws, and the exclusive right of taxation and appropriation, with the responsibility of Ministers.[71]

The evening before Morris's visit, Jefferson had put his ideas into concrete form. That same day he sent this to Saint-Etienne, with a letter proposing that the King, in a séance royal, 'should come forward with a charter of rights in his hand to be signed by himself and every member of the three orders.' Should the King consent, Jefferson assured Saint-Etienne that the patriots would 'carry back to [their] constituents more good than ever was offered before, without violence.' Thus, too, 'time would be gained,' the 'public mind would continue to ripen.' But, added Jefferson apologetically, 'what excuse can I offer for this presumption? I have none but an immeasurable love for your nation and a painful anxiety lest Despotism, after an unaccepted offer to bind its own hands, shall seize you again with a tenfold fury.'

This, then, is Jefferson's actual contribution to the patriots of the French Revolution — his proposed Charter of Rights:

1. The States General shall assemble, uncalled, on the third day of November annually, and shall remain together so long as they shall see cause. They shall regulate their own elections and proceedings, and, until they shall ordain otherwise, their elections shall be in the forms observed in the present year, and shall be triennial.

2. The States General alone shall levy the money on the nation and shall appropriate it.

3. Laws shall be made by the States General only, with the consent of the King.

4. No person shall be restrained of his liberty but by regular process from a court of justice, authorized by a general law (except

71 *Autobiography*, 93-94.

that a noble may be imprisoned by order of a court of justice, on a prayer of twelve of his nearest relations). On complaint of an unlawful imprisonment, to any judge whatever, he shall have the prisoner brought immediately before him if his imprisonment is unlawful. The officer in whose custody the prisoner is shall obey the orders of the judge; and both judge and officer shall be responsible, civilly and criminally, for a failure of duty therein.

5. The military shall be subordinate to the civil authority.

6. Printers shall be liable for legal prosecution for printing and publishing false facts, injurious to the party prosecuting; but they shall be under no other restraint.

7. All pecuniary privileges and exemptions enjoyed by any description of persons is abolished.

8. All debts already contracted by the King are hereby made the debts of the nation; and the faith thereof is pledged to their payment in due time.

9. Eighty million of livres are now granted to the King to be raised by loan, and reimbursed by the nation; and the taxes heretofore paid shall continue to be paid to the end of the present year, and no longer.

10. The States General shall now separate and meet again on the first of November next.

Done on behalf of the whole nation, by the King, and their representatives in the States General at Versailles, this — day of June, 1789.[72]

Here, then, was Jefferson's plan, recommended to his friends in the States General, which, in his opinion, would have wrought a peaceable revolution without disturbing the monarchy. It made no provision for the separation of Church and State, none for the abolition of tithes, none for a redistribution of property. Other reforms he would have left to evolutionary processes.

But unhappily the King was not to appear with this charter in his hand. That he might gracefully have acquiesced is seen in the fact that Necker's Report to the King had conceded almost every point in Jefferson's charter. 'But his mind was weakness itself,' wrote Jefferson years later, 'his constitution timid, his judgment null, and without sufficient firmness even to stand by the faith of his word. His queen, too, haughty and bearing no contradiction, had an abso-

72 Ford, *Writings of Jefferson*, V, 99, 101.

lute ascendancy over him; and around her were rallied the King's incredibly stupid brothers and the aristocratic part of his Ministry.' [73]

He was to conclude long afterward that, 'had there been no Queen, there would have been no revolution.'

XII

Keenly conscious of the impropriety of his interference in the internal politics of the country to which he was accredited, he had done no more than express his views to personal friends who called upon him. One day he found himself embarrassed. He had received a note from Lafayette saying he would bring a company of six or eight friends to dine with Jefferson on the morrow. This was not unusual. The next day Lafayette appeared with Duport, Barnave, Alexandre Lameth, and four others, all patriots in the States General, and representing different points of view. After the cloth was removed and the wine set on the table, Lafayette introduced the object of the conference. This was Jefferson's first intimation that it was a conference that had assembled under his roof. The discussions began at four and continued for six hours. Throughout, Jefferson was a silent spectator, greatly impressed by the lofty tone, the eloquence, and brilliance of the conversation.

Much humiliated, he thought it best to call on Montmorin and tell him the truth. That Minister replied that he knew about the conference in detail, but, 'so far from taking umbrage at the use made of [Jefferson's] house, he earnestly wished that [he] would habitually assist at such a conference, being sure that [he] would be useful in moderating the warmer spirits and promoting a wholesome and practical reformation only.' Jefferson was to conclude that this conference was previously known and approved by Montmorin, who was in the confidence and in communication with the patriots.

Thus came in the fateful July of 1789.

XIII

In the first days of the month, Jefferson found himself unpleasantly involved in Mirabeau's fight against Necker. On the floor of the

[73] *Autobiography*, 88.

States General, the great orator had declared that Jefferson had made an offer to Necker of American corn and flour, which had been refused. On learning of this, Jefferson wrote Lafayette, denying the statement, and explaining that he had merely told the Minister that he would inform his countrymen of Necker's message that corn and flour from America would find a market in France. 'I must beg leave to avail myself of your friendship and of your position to have a communication of these facts made to the honorable Assembly of the Nation, of which you are a member.'[74]

Lafayette went immediately to Mirabeau with Jefferson's letter. The orator gave assurance that he would make the correction himself. Jefferson then sent a note to Necker, enclosing a copy of his letter to Lafayette and informing him of Mirabeau's agreement to retract the charge.[75] True to his word, Mirabeau rose in his place, admitted that he had been in error, and read Jefferson's letter, which seemed handsomely fair to the American. He had been unwilling that Mirabeau should use him in an attack on Necker; but when the friends of Necker began to scatter 'scandalous versions' of Jefferson's letter, he wrote Lafayette that he was quite as unwilling to be used to the injury of Mirabeau.[76] He was convinced that Mirabeau had acted in good faith. When Lafayette showed him Jefferson's letter, the orator took from his desk a newspaper from which he had drawn his conclusion and then found he had misread it.[77] Thus, there is nothing to indicate personal relations between Jefferson and the orator of the Revolution, but it is clear that each respected the genius of the other and that there was a mutual regard.

At the time of this incident, the black reactionaries of the Queen's party had closed in upon the King who had peremptorily dismissed Necker from his post and from the country. The Minister had received a curt note at the breakfast-table and had hurriedly left for Switzerland. The people did not misinterpret the meaning of the dismissal, and the sections began to roar their protest. The town was in commotion. 'The little hunchback, Abbé Bertrand,' having sallied forth in a fiacre, was so frightened by the crowds in the Rue Saint-Honoré that Morris conducted him to his home and then

[74] Bergh, *Writings of Jefferson,* VII, 400.
[75] *Ibid.,* VII, 401.   [76] *Ibid.,* VII, 404.   [77] To Jay, *ibid.,* VII, 411.

started to the house of Jefferson. Suddenly Morris observed that carriages and pedestrians going in his direction had turned sharply and were going back. Then he saw 'a body of cavalry with their sabers drawn,' approaching at half speed. In the Place de la Concorde he noticed a crowd picking up stones, and when the cavalry returned, Morris drew up 'to see the fray.' Officers were knocked from their horses and shots were fired without damage. Morris now hurried to the Champs Elysées to Jefferson's house to find some Swiss guards posted with cannon. He finally was permitted to enter the house. It was from Morris that Jefferson heard of the incident, and he was told by Jefferson the details of Necker's dismissal.[78]

The next day the turmoil in the town had so increased that Morris's coachman refused to drive out. The people were seeking arms wherever they could find them. Morris turns pedestrian, swallows his pride, decorates his cap with a green bow in honor of the Third Estate. He hears that the court at Versailles is treating the disturbance lightly, but the Assembly had demanded the return of Necker.[79]

Then dawned the Fourteenth of July.

XIV

Again Morris's coachman refuses to go out, but he finally relents. While driving toward the Temple, the carriage is stopped twice and searched for arms. That evening Morris hears the epic story of the fall of the Bastille.[80]

And that day Jefferson had placed the right interpretation on the dismissal of the Minister. The King clearly had surrendered to the blackest of the reactionaries — 'the principals among whom had been noted all their lives for the Turkish despotism of their characters.'[81] He was to write Jay a vivid dramatic report on the tumult that followed.[82]

In search of the gossip of the town, he went that day to call on his friend, Madame de Corny. The magistrates had sent her husband to the Hôtel des Invalides to ask arms. He went, and, when re-

---

[78] Davenport, *Diary of Gouverneur Morris,* I, 144.
[79] *Ibid.,* I, 146.   [80] *Ibid.,* I, 148.
[81] To Jay, Bergh, *Writings of Jefferson,* VII, 409.   [82] *Ibid.*

fused, he advised the mob to retire and set the example. The mob remained and took the arms. Jefferson thought it remarkable that the Invalides offered no resistance, and that 'five thousand foreign troops encamped within four hundred yards never stirred.'[83] De Corny was then sent to ask arms at the Bastille — and the result is familiar history.

It was while Jefferson was in the beautiful house of Madame de Corny, conversing with his hostess, that her husband returned, and it was from his lips that Jefferson heard of the fall of the Bastille.[84] With the beheading of the Governor of the Bastille, the Court Party lost its bravado. D'Artois, most insolent of the aristocratic reactionaries, hastened now to the King to beg him to grant the States General everything it asked. That night d'Artois, Madame de Polignac, Count de Vaudreuil, the Prince of Condé, the Duke of Bourbon, and the Abbé de Vermond, confessor of the Queen, and all the party of Marie Antoinette fled the country. The great exodus had begun.[85]

Meanwhile, accompanied by Short, Jefferson fared forth daily into the street, exploring all parts of the town, to learn with certainty what was going on, since he had found that nothing, not seen, could be believed.[86]

The rest is history, known to all: the surrender of the King; the humiliating recall of Necker; the acclaim that greeted his return; the monarch's tragic visit to Paris to do obeisance to the mob; the restoration of Montmorin.

Jefferson drove at once to Versailles to satisfy himself of what had passed there. He found the wildest stories circulating within the shadow of the palace. He was told that three thousand had been killed in Paris. He concluded that, while in the mob there were criminals, bandits, and assassins, these were exceptions, and that the greater part had acted from patriotic motives. 'Bags of money offered on various occasions through fear or guilt have been uniformly refused by the mobs,' he reported to Jay. Atheism had not yet appeared. 'The churches are now occupied in singing "De profundis" and "Requiems" for the repose of the souls of the brave and valiant citizens who have sealed with their blood the liberty of the nation,' he added.[87]

83 *Ibid.*   84 *Autobiography,* 98.   85 *Ibid.*   86 *Ibid.*
87 Bergh, *Writings of Jefferson,* VII, 409-28.

Even so, he was not unmindful of the rising flood of crime. When, on the eve of the fall of the Bastille, his house was robbed three times, he wrote Montmorin asking for a guard and the better policing of that section of the city.[88] The mind of the professional criminal invariably finds opportunity in popular political uprisings, no matter how justified these may be. After assuming that tranquillity had been restored, Jefferson was forced to report to Jay the taking and beheading of Foulon, one of the most hated of the functionaries. 'Indeed it is hard to say,' he wrote, 'at what distance of time the presence of one of these Ministers, or of any of the most obnoxious of the fugitive courtiers, will not rekindle the same bloodthirsty spirit.' He hoped it was 'extinguished as to everybody else, and [that] yesterday's example may teach them to keep out of the way.'[89]

More of this he was to see and his interest was not to abate, but he was at this time following with intense interest events in the United States, as we shall see.

[88] *Ibid.*, VII, 402.
[89] *Ibid.*, VII, 428-29.

AMERICA CALLS HIM HOME

I

DURING THE REMAINDER of his tenure in Paris, Jefferson's interest in the fascinating drama of French politics never lagged, but nothing more of a sensational nature developed. The people continued in a state of unrest, the masses more and more imposed their will, and, with many of the Court Party in ignominious flight, it was more and more apparent that the monarchy was in dire danger of extinction. All this Jefferson followed with fascination. Liberal leaders continued to cross his threshold, and Lafayette appeared frequently with news and for advice. But the real preoccupation of Jefferson at this time was with political developments at home.

Throughout his five years in France he had maintained intimate contact with all that was happening in the United States, and interesting as he found the unfolding drama of the French Revolution, his mind was never remote from the building of a nation in the United States. The very performance of his diplomatic functions, reinforced by his conversations with Europeans in the drawing-rooms, had impressed upon him from the beginning, as we have seen, the imperative need for a complete reorganization of the American Government, making for a national authority in the matters of taxation, commerce, and foreign affairs. No one had a keener realization of the inefficiency of the Continental Congress even at its best, and he had seen it deteriorate at the close of the war, until, as has been seen, it was almost impossible to get a representation in Congress sufficient for the ratification of the treaty of peace. In Paris, when struggling with the collectors who pressed upon and harassed him with their duns, it was painfully clear to him that, without a government of sufficient authority to impose and collect taxes for national needs in all the States, all that had been achieved in the Revolution would be lost. All this stands out like a pillar of fire in his correspondence with his American friends. The dependence of American diplomats in foreign capitals on the free-and-easy methods of the Continental Congress had disgusted him.

When Madison wrote him that the Virginia Assembly had taken a stand in favor of the centralization, in the nation, of control in all matters pertaining to foreign affairs, he was encouraged. 'The politics of Europe render it indispensably necessary that, with respect to everything external, we be one nation only, firmly hooped together,' he wrote his disciple.[1] The supervision and direction of foreign affairs by the Congress distressed him. He had been but a few months in Paris when he wrote bitterly to Monroe of the difficulties of the American diplomats. He had heard from Monroe, and in a letter from Jay to Franklin, enough to convince him that Congress had 'done something in regard to England and Spain,' but he had no idea what it was. No word had come. He supposed Congress had some idea about dealing with the Barbary pirates, but it was carefully concealing it from the men it had sent to Europe to deal with such matters.[2]

Thus constantly he was urging on his followers the necessity for a real union. Referring to Virginia's stand for turning the regulation of commerce over to a federal head, he wrote that 'if it could be seen in Europe that all our States could be brought to concur in what the Virginia Assembly has done, it would produce a total revolution in their opinion of us and respect for us.'[3]

Thus, he was in complete sympathy with the meeting at Annapolis which paved the way to a Constitutional Convention. And when he learned that the States had agreed to such a convention, he wrote that he was 'happy to find that the States have come so

[1] Ford, *Writings of Jefferson,* IV, 192.
[2] To Monroe, *ibid.,* IV, 43-44.
[3] *Ibid.,* IV, 192.

generally into the scheme of a federal convention, from which I am sure we shall see wise propositions.'

Evidently he did not at this time foresee the extent of the change in the governmental structure to be proposed. 'I confess,' he wrote Edward Carrington of Virginia, 'I do not go so far in the reforms thought necessary by some of my correspondents in America, but if the convention should adopt such propositions, I shall suppose them necessary.' And to this he added: 'My general plan would be to make the States one as to everything connected with foreign nations and several as to everything purely domestic.' He thought the Confederation had been discredited by the assumption, so generally held, that it had no power 'to enforce anything, e.g., contributions of money.' But he thought the weakness lay, not in the lack of the power, but in the failure to use it. 'It was not necessary to give them the power expressly,' he wrote. 'They have it by the law of nature. When two parties make a compact there results to each power of compelling the other to execute it.' And in any reorganization of the governmental structure, he favored the separation of the executive and legislative powers 'as the Judiciary already are in some degree.' [4]

While the agitation in favor of a Constitutional Convention was rippling the placid currents of American life, Jefferson received mere driblets of news from home, and it was during this period that he was grappling with the problem of how to save American honor and credit through a meeting of its financial obligations in Europe.

When the Convention was a certainty, and Madison's part in it was assured, Jefferson wrote his disciple again, urging the division of governmental powers into executive, legislative, and judicial. He had seen the stupidity of the attempt to place executive authority in the hands of Congress. But he was clearly annoyed by the suggestion that had reached him of giving the Federal Congress the power to veto the legislation of the various States. 'I do not like it,' he wrote Madison. 'It fails in an essential character: that the hole and the patch should be commensurate. But this proposes to mend a small hole by covering the entire garment.' And why? 'Not more than one out of a hundred State acts concerns the confederacy. This proposition, then, in order to give them one degree

[4] Ibid., IV, 423.

of power, which they ought to have, gives them ninety-nine more, which they ought not to have, on the presumption that they will not exercise the ninety-nine.' Would it not be better, he asked, to provide an appeal from the State judiciary to the federal court? True, it might be said that this federal court would encroach on the jurisdiction of the State courts. 'It may,' he wrote. 'But there will be a power, to wit, Congress, to watch and restrain them. But place the same authority in Congress itself, and there will be no power above them to perform the same office.' [5]

Throughout this period it does not appear that Jefferson played a part more conspicuous than that of a correspondent exchanging views with a friend. Just before he set forth on his journey into Southern France, he had received a copy of John Adams's pretentious work, *Defence of the American Constitution,* and had written his friends that he would read it on the journey. However, he was delayed in setting out, so he was able to read it before leaving Paris and he found one thing he deemed objectionable. With the preliminary flattery he knew would be pleasing, he passed on, in his letter to Adams, to his criticism: 'There is one opinion in it, however, which I would ask you to reconsider, because it appears to me to be entirely inaccurate, and not likely to do good — "Congress is not a legislative assembly." I doubt if they are at all a diplomatic assembly' — as Adams had suggested. This criticism was handsomely sandwiched in between the preliminary praise and the announcement at the end that Jefferson was arranging for a translation of the Adams book to prevent it from falling into the hands of an incompetent.[6]

II

One November day in 1787, a bulky letter from Madison was placed on Jefferson's study table. It contained the full draft of the Constitution as it came from the Convention. Eagerly the eyes of the recipient passed over the document, and the feelings of the reader were mixed. Washington had presided over the Convention. Madison, a disciple, had been its most useful member. Jefferson

[5] Bergh, *Writings of Jefferson,* VII, 131-33.
[6] Adams, *Works of John Adams,* VIII, 432-33.

had implicit confidence in both. But he had scarcely expected a change so sweeping, though this was not the reason for his perturbation. He looked carefully through the document for things he thought essential for the protection of the rights and liberties of the citizen, and failing to find them, he instantly took fire. He does not appear to have found fault with the creation of a strong government, but more important to him was the protection of a free people. He had written the preamble of the Declaration of Independence. It had embodied the fundamentals of a democracy of free men, and he found nothing in the Constitution in keeping with it. He had not written the preamble as an exercise in rhetoric. He meant it. He would fight for it. And here was a challenge. Instantly he took up the gage of battle, and in letters to Washington, Madison, and Monroe and many others in other States, he made his criticism clarion-clear. That he was disgusted and humiliated by this omission by the members of the Constitutional Convention is not surprising. He had just proposed a charter of rights to be offered by the King of France to the people as embodying the American idea of the rights of free men, and the American people were denied even a Bill of Rights.

Acknowledging another copy from either Adams or his son-in-law, William S. Smith, he had written the latter that 'there are good articles in it and very bad,' and that he 'did not know which predominate.' This was his first impression when smarting under the discovery that no provision had been made for the protection of a free society. From the little he then knew, he clearly felt that too much emphasis had been laid on the creation of a strong government and too little on the safeguarding of the rights of free men. He was sure the Convention had been unduly impressed by the Shays Rebellion in Massachusetts, and feared that it was 'setting up a kite to keep the hen yard in order.'[7]

In a letter to Carmichael in Madrid, he went into more detail, referring to the powerful attacks being made upon the proposed Constitution. He marshaled the objections he had heard and marched them in procession. Thus, 'in proposing to melt all down to one government, they had fenced the people with no declaration of rights; they have not renounced the power of keeping a standing

[7] Ford, *Writings of Jefferson*, IV, 466-67.

army; they have not secured the liberty of the press; they have reserved the power of abolishing trial by jury in civil cases.'

Even so, he noted that the Constitution had been received with great enthusiasm. 'In the Eastern States the printers will print nothing against it, unless the writer subscribes his name,' he wrote. He thought there would be a division in New York, with Clinton opposing; that the factions in Pennsylvania would renew their feuds; that Jersey would accept; that Delaware would follow Pennsylvania. In Virginia there would be a fight, with Mason, Henry, and Harrison against it, and the Lees and Washington for it, though 'it is not in his [Washington's] character to exert himself much in the case.' He thought, as it came to pass, that 'Madison would be the main pillar, but though an immensely powerful one, it is questionable whether he can bear the weight of such a host.' He thought it possible that when sentiment was known, Congress might insist on a new Convention to eliminate the objectionable parts and to make needed additions.[8]

But it was to his own disciple, Madison, that he unburdened himself:

I like the organization of the government into legislative, judiciary, and executive.

I like the power given the legislature to levy taxes, and for that reason, solely, I approve of the greater House being chosen by the people directly.

I am captivated by the compromise of the opposite claims of the great and little States, of the latter to equal, and the former to proportionate, influence.

I am pleased, too, with the substitution of the method of voting by persons, instead of that of voting by States; and I like the negative given to the Executive, conjointly with a third of either House; though I should have liked it better had the judiciary been associated for that purpose, or invested separately with a similar power.

I will tell you now what I do not like:

First the omission of a Bill of Rights, providing clearly, and without the aid of sophism, for freedom of religion, freedom of the press, protection against standing armies, restriction of monopolies, the eternal and unremitting force of the habeas corpus, and trials

8 Bergh, *Writings of Jefferson*, VI, 380.

by juries in all matters of fact triable by the laws of the land, and not by the laws of nations.

And then, sharply, this:

> Let me add that a Bill of Rights is what the people are entitled to, against every government on earth, general or particular, and what no just government should refuse or rest on inference.

Such was his first reaction. He suggested the possibility of a revision or of a new Convention.[9]

To Washington, who had presided over the Convention, he wrote: 'There are two things, however, which I dislike strongly. (1) The want of a declaration of rights. (2) The perpetual re-eligibility of the President.' [10]

III

But some months later, after he had meditated upon the document, he wrote Carrington that it had 'gained' on him. He had seen at the beginning that 'the great mass and groundwork was good.' He had found objections to a number of features, but 'reflection and discussion have cleared off most of these.' But one objection remained — there was no Bill of Rights. Therefore, certain amendments were necessary for the preservation of the rights and liberties of the people, and his first wish had been that nine States, enough to launch the new Government, would ratify, and that the others would hold off until the amendments were written into the fundamental law. The most important would be the incorporation of a Bill of Rights.

Assuming that Washington would be the first President, he added: 'The natural progress of things is for liberty to yield and government to gain ground. As yet, our spirits are free. Our jealousy is only put to sleep by the unlimited confidence we all repose in the person to whom we all look as our President. After him, inferior characters may perhaps succeed and awaken us to the danger which his merit had led us into.'

And then he added: 'For the present, however, the general adoption is to be prayed for.' [11]

9 *Ibid.*, VI, 385-89.   10 Ford, *Writings of Jefferson*, V, 8.
11 *Ibid.*, V, 192.

When Washington was unanimously chosen President, Jefferson said no more about an amendment against re-eligibility. Writing Francis Hopkinson in March, 1789, he said he had found himself differing from the majority of his countrymen on this feature, since but three out of eleven States had desired an amendment. 'And, indeed,' he added, 'since the thing is established, I would wish it not to be altered during the lifetime of our great leader, whose executive talents are superior to those . . . of any man in the world, and who alone, by the authority of his name and the confidence reposed in his perfect integrity, is fully qualified to put the new government so under way as to secure it against the efforts of opposition.' [12]

As time went on, Jefferson's fear of a monarchy, resulting from the re-eligibility of the President, subsided and died out entirely; and when, years later, he could have had a third term, he based his declination, not on a principle, but on his health and declining powers.

IV

But he continued with ever-increasing fervor and determination his demand for the incorporation of a Bill of Rights. As we have seen, he felt, even under the dynasty of the Bourbons, the liberties of the people would have been safeguarded by a Charter of Rights, and he was shocked to find that an American Constitutional Convention had rejected the idea. Then, one day, he read, in a letter from Madison, a long extenuation for the failure to incorporate a Bill of Rights. This dismayed him. 'I have never thought the omission a material defect,' wrote Madison, 'nor been anxious to supply it even by subsequent amendment.' He was not particularly opposed, and would favor an amendment of the sort, since it 'could not be of disservice.' But a Bill of Rights would be disregarded by a triumphant majority in control of Government, and this was inevitable. And then, too, the determination of what should be included in a Bill of Rights would introduce many controversial subjects.[13] He might have added that the matter had been discussed in the Convention and that numerous delegates, including Alexander Hamilton,

[12] Ibid., V, 77-78.   [13] Hunt, Writings of James Madison, V, 269-75.

had taken the position that a Bill of Rights was not necessary, and that Madison himself doubted the propriety of injecting it into the fundamental law.

Thoroughly aroused, and a little disgusted, Jefferson wrote with unaccustomed sharpness to a disciple:

> I cannot refrain from making short answers to the objections your letter states to have been raised.
>
> (1) That the rights in question are reserved by the manner in which the federal powers are granted.
>
> Answer: The constitutive act may certainly be so formed as to need no declaration of rights. The act itself has the force of a declaration as far as it goes; and if it goes to all material points, nothing more is wanting. In a draft of a Constitution which I had once thought of proposing in Virginia, and printed afterwards, I endeavored to reach all the great objects of public liberty and did not mean to add a declaration of rights. Probably the object was imperfectly executed; but the deficiencies would have been supplied by others in the course of discussion. But in a constitutive act, which leaves some precious articles unnoticed and raises implications against others, a declaration of rights becomes necessary by way of supplement. This is the case of our federal constitution.
>
> (2) A positive declaration of essential rights could not be obtained in the requisite latitude.
>
> Answer: Half a loaf is better than no loaf. If we cannot secure all our rights, let us secure what we can.
>
> (3) The limited powers of the federal government and jealousy of subordinate governments afford a security which exists in no other instance.
>
> Answer: The first number of this seems resolvable into the first objections before stated. The jealousy of the subordinate governments is a precious reliance. But observe that those governments are only agents. They must have principles furnished them whereon to found their opposition. The declaration of rights will be the text by which they will try all the acts of the federal government. In this way it is necessary for the federal government also; as by the same texts they may try the opposition of the subordinate governments.
>
> (4) Experience proves the inefficiency of a bill of rights.
>
> Answer: True. But though it is not absolutely efficacious under all circumstances, it is of great potency always, and rarely ineffica-

cious. A brace the more will often keep up the building which would have fallen with that brace the less. There is a remarkable difference in the inconveniencies which attend a Declaration of Rights, and those that attend the want of it. The inconveniences of the Declaration are that it may cramp government in its useful exertions. But the evils of this are short-lived, trivial, and reparable. The inconveniences of a want of a Declaration are permanent, afflicting, and irreparable. They are in constant progression from bad to worse. The executive in our government is not the sole, it is scarcely the principal, object of my jealousy. The tyranny of the legislatures is the more formidable dread at present, and will be for long years. That of the executive will come in its turn, but it will be at a remote period.[14]

This unique debate on paper between Jefferson the master and Madison the disciple is usually passed over by biographers and historians without a notice, and yet it is one of the most decisive documents on events of paramount importance.

Incidentally, it throws an unaccustomed light on Madison, who later was to introduce the Bill of Rights into Congress as amendments.

V

Throughout the months when the Constitution was under discussion, preliminary to the State Conventions called to pass on its ratification, Jefferson was writing letters to public men throughout the United States, all urging the imperative necessity of a Bill of Rights. That he urged on many the plan of having nine States ratify, and the others refuse until a Bill of Rights had been incorporated, we have ample evidence. That a supposed letter, which existed in tradition only, had an effect on the Convention in North Carolina is believed by many in that State. There is a tradition that, at a noon recess after a morning session during which the ratificationists apparently had won, Willie Jones, an ardent follower of Jefferson, sat with a number of delegates whittling on a stick after lunch and passed around a letter from Jefferson to him, suggesting the plan of withholding the ratification until the amendments were pledged. However that may be, we know that, after the action of Massachusetts

[14] Ford, *Writings of Jefferson*, V, 80-83.

in permanently instructing her delegates in Congress to an unremitting demand for the amendments, Jefferson abandoned his original idea and advised the adoption of the Massachusetts plan.

He followed the fight in America from afar, well served by his correspondents. When Madison sent him various numbers of *The Federalist* as they appeared, he read them with admiration and approval. Madison had confided to him that the papers were the joint product of himself, Hamilton, and Jay, but that the latter had written little. Jefferson replied that he had been previously informed as to the authorship, and that in reading the papers he had been satisfied 'there was nothing in it by one of these hands [Jay] and not a great deal by a second [Hamilton]'— which in the latter case was an erroneous idea. For while conceding Hamilton high rank at the bar and recommending him to a prospective client as a man 'to be relied on,' Jefferson was, as yet, unfamiliar with his political genius. And then, too, he was partial to Madison. 'It does the highest honor to the third,' he wrote Madison, 'as being in my opinion the best commentary on the principles of government which ever was written.' To which he added: 'I confess it has rectified me in several points. As to the Bill of Rights, however, I still think it should be added.' [15]

He followed with the keenest interest the State Conventions, weeks afterward to be sure, but as closely as communications then permitted. The position of Massachusetts completely changed his course of action. 'The conduct of Massachusetts has been noble,' he wrote Carmichael. 'She accepted the Constitution, but voted that it should stand as a perpetual instruction to her delegates to endeavor to obtain such and such reformations. I am now convinced that the plan of Massachusetts is the best — that is, to accept and to amend afterwards. If the States which were to decide after her should all do the same, it is impossible but they must obtain the essential amendments.' [16]

VI

He was most concerned, however, about the Convention in Virginia. There the hottest of fights was in prospect, involving on op-

[15] *Ibid.*, V, 53.   [16] Bergh, *Writings of Jefferson*, VII, 29.

posing sides two of his foremost disciples, Monroe and Madison. While both these men were followers and beneficiaries of Jefferson, the former, more than the latter, was in complete accord with Jefferson's instinctive thinking. He would not have found it necessary to argue with Monroe over a Bill of Rights.

Never, perhaps, in any assembly were abler men pitted against one another. There was Madison, leading the fight for ratification, assisted by Lee, John Marshall, Pendleton, Nicholas, and Wythe, the latter favoring ratification with amendments afterward. Opposing these were Patrick Henry, George Mason, Grayson, and Monroe.

Madison wrote Jefferson that Mason, of Gunston Hall, was making mountains out of molehills, like Jefferson, insisting on a Bill of Rights. Monroe's opposition in the Convention was based largely on the objections of Jefferson. It was inevitable that in the course of the debate, Jefferson should have been dragged into the controversy. The quiet man in the house on the Champs Elysées had written his early views to a correspondent who had put the letter at the disposition of Patrick Henry. This consummate strategist was too clever in a fight not to avail himself of every weapon within reach. The great orator introduced the letter into the debate.

The letter had been written to A. Donald in February, 1788, before the action of the Massachusetts Convention had weaned Jefferson away from his original plan of having nine States ratify and the others refuse until the amendments demanded had been pledged.

Referring to the letter and the attempt of a ratificationist to interpret it as favoring ratification by the Virginia Convention, Henry sneered at the interpretation. 'The honorable gentleman has endeavored to explain the opinion of Mr. Jefferson, our common friend, into an advice to adopt this new Government,' he said with a smile.[17]

Aroused as an advocate if not also as a friend, Madison took the floor.

> The honorable member, in order to influence our decision, has mentioned the opinion of a citizen who is an ornament to this State. When the name of this distinguished character was introduced, I was much surprised. I believe that were that gentleman upon the floor he would be for the adoption of this constitution.

[17] Elliot, *Debates on Ratification*, III, 300.

I wish his name had never been mentioned. I wish everything spoken here, relative to his opinion, may be suppressed if our debates should be published. I know that the delicacy of his feelings will be wounded when he will see in print, what has, and may be said, concerning him on this occasion. I am in some measure acquainted with his sentiments on the subject. It is not right for me to unfold what he has informed me. But I will venture to assert that the clause now discussed is not objected to by Mr. Jefferson. He approves of it because it enables the Government to carry on its operations.

And then, carefully selecting from Jefferson's letters to him, he went on:

He admires several parts of it which have been reprobated with vehemence in this house. He is captivated by equality of suffrage in the senate, which the honorable gentleman [Mr. Henry] calls the rotten part of the Constitution. But whatever be the opinion of the illustrious citizen, considerations of personal delicacy should dissuade him from introducing them here.[18]

Probably Monroe was not so sure that it would be an injustice to mention Jefferson's insistence on a Bill of Rights. But more important for our purpose is the disclosure that Jefferson's status in Virginia was so lofty and imposing that, instead of dismissing the letter lightly, it entered into the debate with discussions 'as to the construction of the contents of such a letter.' Madison wrote Jefferson that he was 'happy to find the great attention and universal respect with which the opinion was treated, as well as the great regard and high estimation in which the author of it was held.' He realized that Jefferson must have found it 'painful to have thus been made a party in this transaction.'[19]

In the end, the ratificationists prevailed. The debate in point of ability had been well balanced; the controversialists, being men of great erudition for the most part and innate dignity, had carefully refrained from personalities or expressions that might rankle; and the victory was accepted by the victors without a provocative exultation and by the defeated in good temper.[20]

That Jefferson's influence, across three thousand miles of sea, was

18 *Ibid.*, III, 312-13.   19 Hunt, *Writings of James Madison*, I, 184-88.
20 *Ibid.*

distinctly felt in the deliberations of the conventions and in the formation of public sentiment is thoroughly established in all the correspondence of the time. His stout insistence on a Bill of Rights finally convinced Madison of its need, and it was he who eventually, in the first days of the First Congress, offered the ten amendments which form the most sacred and immortal part of the Constitution.

VII

Jefferson never had the slightest doubt that Washington would be made the Chief Magistrate, but he was curious as to the probable identity of the Vice-President. He confessed to a very strong partiality for Franklin, and in August, 1788, he wrote that 'the age of Doctor Franklin and the doubt whether he would accept it are the only circumstances that admit but that he would be the man.' With Franklin eliminated, he counted among the possibilities John Adams, Hancock, Jay, Madison, and Rutledge in the order named. It clearly did not occur to him that he might well have been among those considered.[21] Madison had written him that, since Washington was from the South, the Vice-President should come from the North, and while he was reconciled to the choice of Adams, he had some misgivings.[22]

Even before news of Washington's election had reached him, Jefferson wrote his friend of Mount Vernon:

Though we have not heard of the actual opening of the new Congress, consequently have not official information of your election as President of the United States, yet as there never could be a doubt entertained of it, permit me to express here my felicitations, not to yourself, but to my country. Nobody who has tried both public and private life can doubt that you were much happier on the banks of the Potomac than you will be in New York. But there was nobody so well qualified as yourself to put our new machine into a regular course of action, nobody the authority of whose name could have so effectually crushed opposition at home and prolonged respect abroad. I am sensible of the immensity of the sacrifice on your part. Your measure of fame was full to the brim;

---

21 To Carmichael, Bergh, *Writings of Jefferson,* VII, 125.
22 Hunt, *Writings of James Madison* V. 333-38.

and therefore you have nothing to gain. But there are cases wherein there is a duty to risk all against nothing, and I believe this was exactly the case. We may presume, too, according to every rule of probability that, after doing a great deal of good, you will be found to have lost nothing but private repose.[23]

VIII

And the man in Paris — had he any thought of preferment in the new Government? There is not the slightest indication, but much to be found to the contrary. Madison had written him to ask if he would be willing to accept an appointment. The reply was frank and unequivocal: 'You know the circumstances which led me from retirement, step by step, and from one nomination to another up to the present,' he wrote. 'My object is a return to the same retirement. Whenever, therefore, I quit the present, it will not be to engage in any other office, and most especially any one that would require a constant residence from home.'[24] There can be no doubt of the complete sincerity of this declaration.

Though doomed to many years of exile from his beloved Monticello and from his familiar friends, Jefferson suffered from both. When an old friend, not distinguished in public life, wrote him in Paris, Jefferson replied with more feeling than usually creeps into his correspondence:

> Your letter has kindled all the fond recollections much dearer to me than anything I have ever known. There are minds which can be pleased with honors and preferments; but I see nothing in them but envy and enmity. It is only necessary to possess them to know how little they contribute to happiness, or rather how hostile they are to it. No attachments soothe the mind so much as those contracted in early life; nor do I recollect any societies which have given me more pleasure than these which you have partaken with me.

And then he added:

> I would rather be shut up in a very modest cottage, with my books, my family, and a few old friends, dining on simple bacon,

23 Ford, *Writings of Jefferson*, V, 93-95.   24 *Ibid.*, V, 114-15.

and letting the world roll by as it liked, than to occupy the most splendid post which any human power can give.[25]

Despite his voluminous correspondence in Paris, he suffered acutely from the lack of 'homey' letters. Madison, Monroe, Jay, Adams — most of his correspondents wrote him about politics and international affairs. Even his two most intimate friends had but little gift for gossipy letters about neighbors. Time and again he appealed to them for news of humble neighbors. That is the reason he so much enjoyed the letters of Abigail Adams. That he really was homesick is quite clear. He almost pleaded with Archibald Stuart for 'homey' letters. Did his correspondent think that simple news of simple people and happenings of the neighborhood were unworthy of notice? 'A very mistaken opinion,' wrote Jefferson, 'as anyone may observe by recollecting that, when he has been long absent from his neighborhood, the small news of that is more pleasing and occupies his first attention, either when he meets with a person from thence or returns thither himself. I shall hope, therefore, that the letters in which you may be so good as to give me the minute occurrences of the neighborhood of Monticello may yet come to hand.'[26]

IX

Meanwhile, he followed with interest, and not without an occasional smile, the early proceedings of the new Congress. He was immensely diverted by the solemn debate as to what the President should be called, and particularly by the flamboyant proposal of his friend, John Adams. 'The President's title as proposed by the Senate was the most superlatively ridiculous thing I ever heard of,' he wrote Madison. 'Adams had proposed "Most Highness." It is a proof the more of the justice of the character given by Doctor Franklin of my friend. Always an honest one, often a great one, but sometimes absolutely mad. I wish he could have been here during the late scenes; if he could then have had one fibre of aristocracy left in his frame, he would have been a proper subject for Bedlam.'[27]

[25] Bergh, *Writings of Jefferson*, VI, 427.
[26] Ford, *Writings of Jefferson*, IV, 187.   [27] *Ibid.*, V, 104.

He had applied for leave after five years' absence. He had written Madison of his desire to spend the summer at home, but Madison had been compelled to report his regret that this plan had been 'defeated.' He had discussed the desired leave with Jay, who 'explained that the impossibility of giving effect to [Jefferson's] wishes, since no Congress having been formed under the old Confederation since the receipt of his letter.' Madison thought 'the most that can be done will be to obtain from the new authority, as early as possible, some act which may leave the matter to your own discretion.' Perhaps it would be just as convenient to return in the fall as in the spring. From which one concludes that Madison had no appreciation of Jefferson's love for growing things.[28]

Jefferson had written Jay that he had left America with the thought that his mission would take two years, and so hurriedly that he had not had the opportunity to arrange about his affairs. Then, too, he wished to take his daughters back to their own country. He had allowed three months for the voyage home and back, and wished two months at home, five in all.[29] Later, he wrote in the same vein to Washington.[30]

An incident connected with Martha, the elder daughter, may easily have convinced him that his daughter would be better at home among her own people. She had been a prime favorite with the nuns at the convent, for whom she had naturally formed a deep affection. Jefferson, who made frequent visits to her at the convent, was thoroughly appreciative of all the nuns had done for her, and the nuns, in turn, had a high regard for Jefferson and often visited his house. They had made his daughter happy.

But one day he was astonished on receiving a letter from Martha expressing a disposition to enter the convent and devote her life to religious duties. Though Jefferson was not a Catholic, his breadth of view justifies the conclusion that his opposition was not on the ground of faith. He was always to insist that a man's or a woman's relations with religion was a matter for their conscience. But Martha was very young, too young, he considered, to have carefully thought out her project. Instead of replying by letter, Jefferson

---

[28] Hunt, *Writings of James Madison*, V, 333-38.
[29] To Jay, Bergh, *Writings of Jefferson*, VII, 194.
[30] Ford, *Writings of Jefferson*, VII, 59.

drove to the convent two days later and had a long interview with
the Abbess. The latter, greatly admired and respected by Jefferson,
was a woman of worldly wisdom, and we may be sure that it was
agreed between them that a young girl's impulse was not to be
trusted without a trial. At any rate, Martha was taken to the house
on the Champs Elysées, where she came into contact with society
and her desire to become a nun was soon forgotten. Through the
life of both father and daughter, there persisted a sense of gratitude
for the nuns who had mothered the orphaned girls and made them
happy in Paris.

X

After the fall of the Bastille, the murder of the corrupt Foulon,
and the stabbing to death in the streets of his notoriously loathsome
son-in-law, Berthier, the Revolution for a very short while marked
time. True, stories percolated into Paris that in various parts of the
country the châteaux of the nobility were burning. Many of Jefferson's friends were scattered during the heat of August, and Morris,
who was accustomed to drop in unceremoniously, had gone to London bearing a letter of introduction to Maria Cosway from Jefferson, to be delighted with the winsome lady. No longer was there
any doubt that power had passed from the King to the Assembly,
and, unknown of course to Jefferson, there were whisperings in the
court of a possible flight of the royal family. Everything now depended on the moderation of the Assembly. Madame de Polignac
had fled, and Marie Antoinette, writing her in her safe retreat, informed her that a new governess had been found for the children.
Jefferson was busy with his plans for his departure as soon as
authorization should reach him. In and out of his house darted
Lafayette, now in fine feather, high in the confidence of the revolutionists, and Jefferson advised him and secretly feared for him.
He drove about the city for the air, made excursions now and then
to Versailles, took long walks in the Bois, and spent hours at his
desk writing letters.

We may be sure that he meditated much on the changing scene
at home under the new Government created by the Constitution.
With his usual long, long view, he was already interesting himself

in the location of the new national capital. Even then his mind was fixed on the site ultimately chosen through his bargain with Hamilton.[31] Four years before, he had written Monroe expressing the hope that Congress would remain in New York for some time to come. Later, 'when a sufficient number of States come in,' he thought, 'they will remove [the capital] to Georgetown.' In the meanwhile, he was sure 'it is to our interest that it shall remain where it is, and give no new pretensions to any other place.'[32] But, as it was to turn out, it would not be necessary to await the entrance of western States, and Jefferson would play a major part in fixing the capital in what is now the City of Washington.

And he was already thinking in terms of American politics, though parties did not enter into his calculations. So firmly was he convinced of the national necessity of a federal union that when he learned that a majority of the members of the new Congress were federalists, he wrote jubilantly about it to William Short. Naming the principal figures, he added: 'All of these are federalists, except those of Virginia; so that a majority of the federalists are secured in the Senate and expected in the House of Representatives.' He looked with grave misgivings on the anti-federalists in his own State, where they had a large majority in the legislature. He feared the effect of the influence of Patrick Henry, the foe of ratification, as too 'omnipotent.' He did not like the defeat of Madison for the Senate through Henry's influence. Nor did he love Henry for his philippic against Madison during the latter's absence in Philadelphia, when he could not reply; and he feared that through his gerrymandering activities Henry might even exclude Madison from the House where he wished most to go.[33]

In the sense that he favored a strong federal union, Jefferson was such a federalist as Madison, but he could not have realized at this time and at this distance from the scene that men who also had favored a federal union, but who held political ideas and ideals hostile to his own, would seize upon the name 'Federalist,' for the political party they would create. Almost all the federalists whose election to Congress he had found encouraging would very soon

31 See author's *Jefferson and Hamilton*.
32 Ford, *Writings of Jefferson*, IV, 52.
33 *Ibid.*, V, 70-71.

be arrayed against all the fundamental principles that Jefferson stood for, and against the democracy which he favored.

But he was soon to learn the truth, when Francis Hopkinson wrote him that he had heard Jefferson was an 'anti-federalist.' Jefferson's reply was frank enough:

> My opinion was never worthy enough of notice to merit citing; but since you ask it I will tell you. I am not a Federalist, because I never submitted the whole system of my opinions to the creed of any party of men whatever, in religion, in philosophy, in politics, or in anything else where I was capable of thinking for myself. Such an addiction is the last degradation of a free and moral agent. If I could not go to heaven but in a party, I wouldn't go there at all. There, I protest to that I am not of the party of the Federalists.

But having in mind the discrimination between federalism and the Federalist political party, he added:

> But I am much further from that of any anti-federalist. I approved from the first moment of the great mass of what is the new Constitution, the consolidation of the government, the organization into Executive, Legislative, and Judiciary, the subdivision of the legislature, the happy compromise of interests between the great and little States. . . . What I disapproved from the first moment was the want of a Bill of Rights to guard liberty against the legislature as well as the executive branch of the government; that is to say, to secure freedom of religion, freedom of the press, freedom from monopolies, freedom from unlawful imprisonment, freedom from a permanent military, and a trial by jury in all cases determinable by the laws of the land.[34]

Later, the Federalists were to clamor about the infamy of parties — except their own — calling them 'factions,' after Jefferson had organized and become the head of a political party; but the fact remains that the Federalists formed the first party and that of Jefferson became necessary in combating its anti-democratic views.

That Jefferson, as he prepared for his voyage home, had not the most remote notion of playing a conspicuous part in political and party warfare is clear enough in his ardent wish to return to his post in Paris on the expiration of his leave. A brilliant English writer, in his life of Talleyrand, draws heavily on his imagination

[34] *Ibid.*, V, 77-78.

and an utter ignorance of the character of Jefferson to imply that he left France because it was 'safer.' A very casual search for the truth would have discovered abundant proof that he had no other thought or desire than to return to Paris.[35] In fact he hated fights and quarrels. He hated the fierce light that beats on party leaders. 'My great wish,' he wrote Hopkinson, 'is to go in strict but silent performance of my duty; to avoid attracting notice and to keep my name out of newspapers, because I find the pain of a little censure, even when it is unfounded, more acute than the pleasure of much praise. The attaching circumstance of my present office is that I can do its duties, unseen by those for whom they are done.'[36]

XI

Leave having been granted, Jefferson was now busy with his preparations. The French patriots continued to pour into his house. The moment Morris returned from England, he again became a constant visitor. The instant he recovered from the illness of fatigue, he called on Jefferson to invite him to a Sunday dinner with Madame de Corny.[37] The next day he called on Jefferson again, to find that the famous Marquis de Condorcet, described by him in his Diary as 'encyclopedist, progressive, revolutionary,' had preceded him; and after a while the Duc de la Rochefoucauld appeared, fresh from the Assembly, followed closely by Lafayette. The four men sat down to dinner. Morris asked Lafayette if his troops would obey him. The Marquis replied with a smile that they would not 'mount guard when it rains,' but he thought they would 'follow him into action.' He was gravely concerned over the scarcity of bread. There was a discussion of a new book on commerce in grain, and then much discussion of the crisis in France. Morris was not pleased with the political complexion of the company.[38]

A few days later, Jefferson drove to Versailles to take formal leave of Necker and to inquire what he could do in America toward furnishing provisions for France, but Necker was ill and could not be seen. Jefferson wrote him later, suggesting the purchase of salted

35 Duff Cooper, Talleyrand.
36 Ford, Writings of Jefferson, V, 78.
37 Davenport, Diary of Gouverneur Morris, I, 220.   38 Ibid., I, 221.

beef, which could be bought at a cheap price and might reduce the demand for bread.[39] He called on Montmorin to press the idea upon him.

On returning to Paris, he found Morris waiting at his house. He appears to have been ignorant of the arrangements Jefferson and Adams had made in Holland to save the credit of the nation and he urged that Jefferson go to Amsterdam to see what could be done. When he received no encouragement from the silent host, he concluded that 'his main objection in the present juncture lies in a journey which would postpone his return to America.'[40] From which one gathers that the friend and agent of the tobacco monopoly did not enjoy the intimate confidence of Jefferson.

Meanwhile, he had engaged a ship to take him to Cowes, but at Havre he was detained for ten days by the weather, and at Cowes the inclemency of the weather held him for ten days more. En route, he wrote the old Duchess d'Enville a farewell note reiterating his appreciation of her unvarying kindness to him, and to Madame de Corny he indicted the short letter — excusing his failure to take leave of her, since he could not trust himself to say farewell — which was to be a treasure-trove to many biographers.

In the company of his daughters he made the most of his detention at Cowes, visiting various parts of the island, and particularly Carisbrooke Castle, which interested him as the place where Charles I was confined. It was not until October 23, 1789, that his ship sailed in the company of more than thirty other vessels that had been detained by contrary winds. William Pitt had graciously given orders that his baggage was not to be searched.

The first five or six days were bad sailing because of the fog, but on the sixth day the sun came out. Jefferson did not relish the stiff breeze which confined him to his cabin, but he was going home. Soon he would have the solace of his beloved hilltop, the company of old familiar friends, the gossip of the neighborhood, and then he would return to Paris. He would follow the developing drama of the Revolution, take his long walks in the Bois again with Madame de Corny, and have his long talks again with the generous spirits of France who stood for liberty without license.

[39] Bergh, *Writings of Jefferson*, VIII, 478.
[40] Davenport, *Diary of Gouverneur Morris*, I, 227.

But he was never to see France again.

Soon after he reached home he was writing to Madame de Corny:

> I had the happiness, my dear friend, to arrive in Virginia after a voyage of twenty-six days only, of the finest autumn weather. . . . On my arrival I found my name announced in the papers as Secretary of State. I made light of it, supposing I had only to say 'no,' and there would be an end of it. It turned out, however, otherwise. For though I was left free to return to France, if I insisted on it, yet I found it better in the end to sacrifice my own inclinations to those of others.[41]

XII

Thus closed a most vital phase of Jefferson's career, the revolutionary phase, having to do with the making of the American nation. No one, including Washington, had played a more brilliant part.

He had been foremost in a small group of militant patriots who had wrested the control in Virginia from the more conservative appeasers, whose policy spelled defeat.

In his *Summary View* he had written the most effective, most thoroughly reasoned, the most vigorous, presentation of the colony's position, which had made such an impression in England that Edmund Burke had played a part in its publication there.

He had written the Declaration of Independence with a preamble which foreshadowed the spirit of the new nation to be built.

He had laid the foundations for a real democracy in the reforms he had wrought in Virginia.

In his Ordinance of Religious Freedom he had laid the cornerstone of that religious freedom and toleration which was to become one of the most civilized contributions of the new nation to humanity.

As Governor he had supported the military policy and strategy of Washington, and had taken the abuse of men less loyal to the great Commander and less prone to think of the revolutionary struggle as national.

He had made a liberal contribution to the new Americanism in

41 Randolph, *Domestic Life of Jefferson*, 177.

the writing of the Ordinance of 1784. And in the direct influence of that Ordinance on the Northwest Ordinance of 1787.

He had taken his stand with moderation, common sense, and toleration for the ultimate elimination of slavery.

He had, with more farseeing vision than his contemporaries, envisioned the westward sweep of the nation to the Pacific Ocean, and, before anyone else, had urged and planned the blazing of the trail of trade across the western wilderness.

He had stoutly insisted on the new nation's freedom of navigation on the Mississippi, and had interested himself in the digging of the Panama Canal to join the oceans.

In France he had played a brilliant part in the laying of the foundation of the international policy of the new nation and set for the future the highest standard of dignified diplomacy; and, at a personal risk, at a critical moment and without authorization, had saved the credit and honor of his country.

He had vigorously demanded and notably contributed to the forcing into the Constitution of the Bill of Rights — the noblest part of the fundamental law which perpetually preserves the liberty of the citizen.

Had his career ended when he sailed from France, he would be numbered as one of the four immortals among the founders of the American Republic.

XIII

He had hoped to return to France to serve another three years and then to retire to the shades of Monticello, there to live in philosophic meditation among his friends. Monroe had bought land within the shadow of Monticello where he planned to live close to his idol. Madison would be in a neighboring county within easy reach. Jefferson could ask no more congenial company. Out under the trees they could sit in the long afternoons, remote from turmoil and bitterness, and discuss the events of the day objectively.

But Fate had put a period to the earlier phase of his career. Never again would he be in Paris to exchange views with the philosophers and politicians, to rummage in the bookstalls and frequent the salons, or walk beside the Seine at Saint-Germain with

Maria Cosway, or stroll with Madame de Corny under the fragrant foliage of the Bois. The French companions of his dinner-table he would not see again, for some would pass to exile and some would ride the tumbril to the guillotine — none but Lafayette, who, in old age, would meet him, trembling with time, upon the lawn at Monticello for a last embrace. Nor would he find solace for the lost pleasures of Paris in the realization of his dream of a serene retirement at Monticello. How he had longed for that!

He returned to America to find an organized and brilliantly led fight against democracy, and for twelve years he would battle unceasingly amidst bitterness until the people positively determined that the new Republic would be definitively democratic.[42]

42 For this see author's *Jefferson and Hamilton.*

THE END

Maria Cosway, or stroll with Madame de Corny under the fragrant foliage of the Bois. The French companions of his dinner-table he would not see again for some would pass to exile and some would ride the tumbril to the guillotine — none but Lafayette, who in old age, would meet him, trembling with time, upon the lawn at Monticello for a last embrace. Nor would he find solace for the lost pleasures of Paris in the realization of his dream of a serene retirement at Monticello. How he had longed for that!

He returned to America to find an organized and brilliantly led fight against democracy, and for twelve years he would battle increasingly amidst bitterness until the people positively determined that the new Republic would be definitively democratic.[14]

[14] For this see author's Jefferson and Hamilton.

THE END

BOOKS, PAMPHLETS, NEWSPAPERS, MAGAZINES, AND MANUSCRIPTS, CITED OR CONSULTED

BOOKS

ADAMS, ABIGAIL. *See* Charles Francis Adams.

ADAMS, CHARLES FRANCIS (editor).
  Letters of Abigail Adams. Boston, 1848.
  Works of John Adams, Volume VIII. Boston, 1853.
  Letters of John Adams to His Wife. Boston, 1841.

ADAMS, JOHN. *See* Charles Francis Adams.

ADAMS, SAMUEL. *See* William V. Wells.

Anonymous. Williamsburg in Virginia. Richmond, 1935.

ALBION, ROBERT G. (editor). *Journal of Philip Vickers Fithian, 1775-76.* Princeton, 1934.

AUSTIN, JAMES T. *Life of Elbridge Gerry,* two volumes. Boston, 1828.

BALLAGH, J. C. (editor). *Letters of Richard Henry Lee,* two volumes. New York, 1911.

BECKER, CARL. *The Declaration of Independence: A Study in the History of Political Ideas.* New York, 1942.

BEMIS, SAMUEL FLAGG. *John Jay,* Volume I, *The American Secretaries of State and Their Diplomacy.* New York, 1927.

BERGH, ALBERT E. (editor). *Writings of Thomas Jefferson,* Volumes V, VI, VII.

Biographical Directory of the American Congress. Washington, 1928.

BOYD, JULIAN P. *The Drafting of the Declaration of Independence.* Library of Congress Publication. Washington, 1943.

BURNETT, EDMUND C. (editor). *Letters of Members of the Continental Congress,* eight volumes. Washington, 1921.

BURK, JOHN. *History of Virginia,* three volumes. Richmond, 1804.

BOWERS, CLAUDE G.
  Jefferson and Hamilton. Boston, 1925.
  Jefferson in Power. Boston, 1936.

CHASTELLUX, MARQUIS DE. *Voyages dans l'Amérique,* two volumes. Paris, 1786.

CHINARD, GILBERT.
  Thomas Jefferson: Apostle of Americanism. Boston, 1929.
  (Editor). *Trois Amitiés Françaises de Jefferson.* Paris, 1927.
  Letters of Lafayette and Jefferson. Baltimore, 1929.
  The Commonplace Book of Thomas Jefferson. Baltimore, 1926.
  Lafayette in Virginia. Baltimore, 1928.

CONWAY, MONCURE D. *Omitted Chapters of History Disclosed in the Life and Papers of Edmund Randolph.* New York, 1926.

COSWAY, RICHARD. *See* George C. Williamson.

COSWAY, MARIA. *See* George C. Williamson.

CREWE, LORD. *Lord Rosebery,* two volumes. New York and London, 1931.

DAVENPORT, BEATRICE CAREY (editor). *Diary of the French Revolution of Gouverneur Morris,* two volumes. Boston, 1939.

DEANE, SILAS. *Correspondence of Silas Deane,* Collections of Connecticut Historical Society, Volume II. Hartford, 1870.

DICKINSON, JOHN. *See* Charles J. Stillé.

Dictionary of American Biography. Edited by Allan Johnson and Dumas Malone. New York, 1930-34.

DODSON, LEONIDAS (editor). *Journal of Philip Vickers Fithian.* Princeton, 1934.

DONALDSON, THOMAS. *The House in Which Thomas Jefferson Wrote the Declaration of Independence.* Philadelphia, 1897.

ECKENRODE, H. J.
    Separation of Church and State in Virginia. Richmond, 1910.
    The Revolution in Virginia. Boston, 1916.

ELLIOT, JONATHAN (editor). *Debates of the State Conventions on the Ratification of the Federal Constitution,* Volume III. Washington, 1936.

FITHIAN, PHILIP VICKERS. *See* Robert G. Albion and Leonidas Dodson.

FITZPATRICK, JOHN C. (editor). *Writings of George Washington from the Original Manuscript,* Volumes XXV, XXVI, XXVII, and XXVIII. Washington, 1931-1944.

FOLEY, JOHN P. *The Jeffersonian Cyclopedia.* Washington, 1900.

FORD, PAUL LEICESTER (editor). *Writings of Thomas Jefferson,* Volumes II, IV, and V. New York, 1893.

GERRY, ELBRIDGE. *See* James T. Austin.

GILMAN, DANIEL C. *James Monroe.* Boston, 1895.

GIRARDIN, LOUIS HUE. *History of Virginia.* Petersburg, 1816.

GRAYDON, ALEXANDER. *Memoirs of His Own Time.* Philadelphia, 1846.

GRIGSBY, HUGH BLAIR. *The Virginia Convention of 1776.* Richmond, 1855.

HAMILTON, ALEXANDER. *See* Allan McLane Hamilton.

HAMILTON, ALLAN McLANE. *The Intimate Life of Alexander Hamilton.* New York, 1911.

HAMILTON, S. M. (editor). *The Writings of James Monroe,* Volume I. New York, 1898.

HAZELTON, JOHN H. *The Declaration of Independence: Its History.* New York, 1908.

HENDRICK, BURTON J. *The Lees of Virginia.* Boston, 1935.

HENRY, PATRICK. *See* William Wirt and William Wirt Henry.

HENRY, WILLIAM WIRT. *Life, Correspondence and Speeches of Patrick Henry,* three volumes. New York, 1891.

HILLDRUP, ROBERT L. *Life and Times of Edmund Pendleton.* Chapel Hill, 1939.

HIRST, FRANCIS W. *Life and Letters of Thomas Jefferson.* New York, 1926.

HONEYWELL, ROY J. *The Educational Work of Thomas Jefferson.* Cambridge, 1931.

HUMPHREYS, DAVID. *See* Frank L. Humphreys.

HUMPHREYS, FRANK L. *Life of David Humphreys,* two volumes. New York, 1917.

HUNT, GAILLARD (editor). *Writings of James Madison,* Volumes I and II. New York, 1901.

JAY, JOHN. *See* Henry P. Johnson and Samuel Flagg Bemis.

JEFFERSON, THOMAS. *See* A. E. Bergh, C. G. Bowers, G. Chinard, T. Donaldson, P. L. Ford, F. W. Hirst, R. J. Honeywell, F. Kimball, M. Kimball, W. A. Lambeth, W. H. Pedans, H. S. Randall, S. N. Randolph, G. Tucker, H. A. Washington, Thomas E. Watson, Paul Wilstach, William Kirk Woolery.

JOHNSON, HENRY P. (editor). *Correspondence and Public Papers of John Jay,* Volumes I and III. New York, 1891.

JONES, JOHN PAUL. *See* Philip Russell.

KIMBALL, FISKE. *Thomas Jefferson, Architect.* Boston, 1916.

KIMBALL, MARIE. *Jefferson: The Road to Glory.* New York, 1943.

LAFAYETTE, MARQUIS DE. *See* Gilbert Chinard.

LAMBETH, WILLIAM A. (co-author). *Thomas Jefferson as an Architect and Landscape Gardener.* Boston, 1913.

LEE, RICHARD HENRY. *See* R. H. Lee and Burton J. Hendrick.

LEE, R. H. *Memoir of the Life of Richard Henry Lee,* two volumes. Philadelphia, 1825.

LEWIS, WILLIAM DRAPER (editor). *Great American Lawyers,* Volume I. Philadelphia, 1907.

MADISON, JAMES. *See* William C. Rives and Gaillard Hunt.

MASON, GEORGE. *See* Kate Rowland and Robert C. Mason.

MASON, ROBERT C. *George Mason of Virginia.* New York, 1919.

MAZZEI, PHILIP. *Memoirs of the Life of the Florentine, Philip Mazzei.* New York, 1942.

MONROE, JAMES. *See* George Morgan, S. M. Hamilton, and D. C. Gilman.

MORGAN, GEORGE. *Life of James Monroe*. Boston, 1921.

MORRIS, GOUVERNEUR. *See* Beatrice Carey Davenport and Theodore Roosevelt.

OBERHOLTZER, E. P. *Robert Morris, Patriot and Financier*. New York, 1903.

PEDANS, WILLIAM H. *Some Aspects of Jefferson's Bibliography*. Lexington, 1941.

PELLEW, GEORGE. *John Jay*. Boston, 1899.

PENDLETON, EDMUND. *See* Robert L. Hilldrup.

RANDALL, HENRY S. *The Life of Thomas Jefferson*, three volumes. Philadelphia, 1871.

RANDOLPH, EDMUND. *See* M. D. Conway.

RANDOLPH, SARAH N. *Domestic Life of Thomas Jefferson*. New York, 1871.

REED, JOSEPH R. *See* William B. Reed.

REED, WILLIAM B. *The Life and Correspondence of Joseph Reed*, two volumes. Philadelphia, 1847.

REPPLIER, AGNES. *Philadelphia, the Place and the People*, two volumes. Philadelphia, 1898.

RIEDESEL, MADAME. *Letters and Memoirs*. New York, 1827.

RIVES, WILLIAM C. *History of the Life and Times of James Madison*, three volumes. Boston, 1869.

ROOSEVELT, THEODORE. *Gouverneur Morris*. Boston, 1899.

ROSEBERY, LORD. *See* Lord Crewe.

ROWLAND, KATE MASON. *Life of George Mason*, two volumes. New York, 1892.

RUSSELL, PHILIP. *John Paul Jones*. New York, 1927.

SCHARF, THOMAS J. *History of Philadelphia*, three volumes. Philadelphia, 1884.

SCHOEPF, JOHANN DAVID. *Travels in the Confederation*, two volumes. Philadelphia, 1911.

SMYTHE, J. F. D. *A Tour in the United States*, two volumes. London, 1784.

STILLÉ, CHARLES J. *Life and Times of John Dickinson*. Philadelphia, 1891.

TRUMBULL, JOHN. *Autobiography, Reminiscences and Letters of John Trumbull*. New York, 1841.

TUCKER, GEORGE. *Life of Thomas Jefferson*, two volumes. Philadelphia, 1837.

TYLER, LYON G.
Williamsburg, The Old Colonial Capital. Richmond, 1907.
Letters and Times of the Tylers, two volumes. Richmond, 1884.
George Wythe. (Volume I, Great American Lawyers. Philadelphia, 1907.)

VAN DOREN, CARL. Benjamin Franklin. New York, 1938.

VAN TYNE, CLAUDE H. The Loyalists of the American Revolution. New York, 1929.

WALSH, CORREA MOYLAN. The Political Science of John Adams. New York, 1915.

WASHINGTON, GEORGE. See John C. Fitzpatrick.

WASHINGTON, H. A. (editor). Writings of Thomas Jefferson, Volume I. 1853-54.

WATSON, JOHN F. Annals of Philadelphia and Pennsylvania in Ye Olden Times, two volumes. Philadelphia, 1857.

WATSON, THOMAS E. Life and Times of Thomas Jefferson. New York, 1903.

WELLS, WILLIAM V. Life and Speeches of Samuel Adams, three volumes. Boston, 1865.

WERTENBAKER, THOMAS J.
Patrician and Plebeian in Virginia. Charlottesville, 1910.
The Planters of Colonial Virginia. Princeton, 1922.

WILLIAMSON, GEORGE C. Richard Cosway. London, 1905.

WILSTACH, PAUL. Jefferson and Monticello. New York, 1938.

WIRT, WILLIAM. Sketches of the Life and Character of Patrick Henry. Philadelphia, 1818.

WOOLERY, WILLIAM KIRK. The Relations of Thomas Jefferson to American Foreign Policy (Johns Hopkins Studies in Historical and Political Science). Baltimore, 1927.

WYTHE, GEORGE. See Lyon G. Tyler.

PAMPHLETS

JEFFERSON, THOMAS. A Summary View of the Rights of British America. Philadelphia, 1774.

PRICE, RICHARD. Observations on the Nature of Civil Liberty, the Principles of Government, and the Justice and Policy of the War with America. London, eighth edition, 1776.

NEWSPAPERS

Annapolis.
Maryland Gazette.

Boston.
  Draper's Massachusetts Gazette.
  Independent Chronicle.
  New England Chronicle.
Philadelphia.
  Dunlap's Pennsylvania Packet and Advertiser.
  Pennsylvania Evening Post.
  Pennsylvania Gazette.
Williamsburg.
  Virginia Gazette.

Magazines

American Historical Review.
Virginia Magazine of History and Biography.

Manuscripts

Jefferson Coolidge Collection, Massachusetts Historical Society, Boston.
Jefferson MSS. Congressional Library.
Jefferson MSS. Department of State, Washington.
Edmund Randolph's MS. History. Richmond.

Official Government Publications

Secret Journals of the Congress of the Confederation, five volumes, issued by Department of State, Washington, 1820.
Journal of the Virginia House of Delegates.

Index

INDEX

P